Supercritical Fluid Extraction

Principles and Practice

Supercritical Fluid Extraction

Principles and Practice

Mark A. McHugh
Department of Chemical Engineering
The Johns Hopkins University

Val J. Krukonis
Phasex Corporation

BUTTERWORTHS
Boston   London   Durban   Singapore   Sydney   Toronto   Wellington

Library of Congress Cataloging-in-Publication Data

McHugh, Mark A.
  Supercritical fluid extraction.

  Bibliography: p.
  Includes index.
  1. Extraction (Chemistry) 2. High Pressure (Technology)
I. Krukonis, Val J. II. Title.
TP156.E8M39 1986   660.2′84248   85–31346
ISBN 0–409–90015–X

Butterworth Publishers
80 Montvale Avenue
Stoneham, MA 02180

10 9 8 7 6 5 4 3 2

Printed in the United States of America

To *Tom* and *Beth* who allowed MAMc the time to write this book and especially to *Barbara* who nurtured it to its completion.

To *Mary, Margo, Mona,* and *Greg* who provided VJK with continuing encouragement during the writing of this book.

Contents

Preface

During the past ten years the principles and practice of supercritical fluid (SCF) solvent technology have experienced rapid advances. Supercritical fluids have been applied to areas as diverse as polymer fractionation, lemon oil concentration, monomer purification, and spice extraction.

Although the breadth of application covers a wide spectrum, the underlying thermodynamic principles in operation in a supercritical fluid solvent process are similar, if not identical, to those in operation in more familiar separations processes. Numerous research papers and symposium compendia on many aspects of SCF technology have been published, but at the time of the writing of this book, there was no text which unified the thermodynamic principles, extraction process operation, and applications research of supercritical fluids. This book is designed to explain the wealth of information available about supercritical fluids to enable the reader to evaluate the potential of the technology for his particular needs.

This book represents the efforts of more than just the authors. Acknowledgment is due to graduate students Tom Yogan, Rimas Victora, Jim Mladenik, Marc Malone, Evan Bauman, Nicole Remily, Irene Liau, Jeff Igel, Ron Occhiogrosso, Andy Seckner, and Alan McClellan who have worked with one of the authors (MAMc) in pursuit of advanced degrees in Chemical Engineering. Their hard work and perseverence have made his experimental program a reality. We also acknowledge the substantial help of Dr. Bala Subramaniam in the writing of Chapter 11, and the generosity of the industrial concerns that allowed substantial analytical data to be used in the writing of Chapter 9.

Supercritical Fluid Extraction

Principles and Practice

1

Introduction

Within the past decade numerous industrial and academic research and development laboratories have investigated the underlying fundamentals and process applications of supercritical fluid solvents, that is, gases or liquids above their critical points (McHugh, n.d.; Paulaitis et al., 1983a; Paulaitis and McHugh, 1981). When a supercritical fluid (SCF) is used as an extractive solvent, it is possible to separate a multicomponent mixture by capitalizing on both the differences in component volatilities (i.e., the salient feature of distillation) and the differences in the specific interactions between the mixture components and the SCF solvent (i.e., the salient feature of liquid extraction). The application of SCF solvents is based on the experimental observation that many gases exhibit enhanced solvating power when compressed to conditions above the critical point. Scientists and engineers have been aware of this experimental fact for more than one hundred years, but it is only in the past decade or so that supercritical fluid solvents have been the focus of active research and development programs. Symposia dealing exclusively with supercritical fluids, a large number of review papers (Schneider, Stahl, and Wilke, 1980; Paul and Wise, 1971; Irani and Funk, 1977; Gangoli and Thodos, 1977; Williams, 1981; Brunner and Peter, 1981; Paulaitis et al., 1983a, 1983b; McHugh, 1986; Johnston, 1984; Randall, 1982; Booth and Bidwell, 1949; Rowlinson and Richardson, 1958; Ellis, 1971; Valteris, 1966), and the recent development of short courses or tutorials on SCFs (McHugh, Krukonis, and Davidson, 1985; McHugh and Krukonis, 1984; Mansoori et al., 1985) all attest to the magnitude of interest in this new technology.

The motivation for the development of SCF solvent technology as a viable separations technique is a result of:

1. a sharp increase in the cost of energy, which has increased the cost of traditional, energy-intensive separation techniques, such as distillation;
2. increased governmental scrutiny and regulation of common industrial solvents, such as chlorinated hydrocarbons, which has made nontoxic, environmentally acceptable supercritical fluid solvents such as CO_2 very attractive as alternative industrial solvents;

3. more stringent pollution-control legislation, which has caused industry to consider alternative means of waste treatment; and
4. increased performance demands on materials, which traditional processing techniques cannot meet.

A great deal of information about SCF technology can be obtained from several recently published review papers and symposium books. These papers and books are listed in table 1.1. A large portion of the information available from these sources is included in this book.

To capitalize fully on the unique solvent characteristics of supercritical fluids it is necessary to understand the phase behavior of pure SCF solvents and of SCF-solute mixtures. Let us first consider the pure SCF solvent. The

Table 1.1   Review Literature on SCF Technology

Title	Reference	Comments
"Extraction with supercritical fluids"	McHugh, 1986	Review paper
Ber. Bunsenges. Phys. Chem., Vol. 88, 1984		Papers presented at a symposium held in Königstein, W. Germany
Journal of Fluid Phase Equilibria, Vol. 10, 1983		Papers presented at a symposium held in England
"Chemical Engineering at Supercritical Fluid Conditions"	Paulaitis, Penninger, Gray, and Davidson, 1983b	Papers presented at the 1981 AIChE Meeting in New Orleans; theory, data, and applications
"Supercritical fluid extraction"	Paulaitis, Krukonis, Kurnik, and Reid, 1983a	Review paper on theory and application; a large data tabulation is included
"The present status of dense (supercritical) gas extraction and dense gas chromatography: impetus for DGC/MS development"	Randall, 1982	Review paper emphasizing SCF chromatography and including a large data tabulation
"Supercritical fluids"	Johnston, 1984	A chapter in the *Encyclopedia of chemical technology*
"Zum stand der Extraktion mit Komprimierten Gasen"	Brunner and Peter, 1981	Review paper
"Extraction with supercritical gases"	Williams, 1981	Review paper

(Table 1.1   continued)

Title	Reference	Comments
"Extraction with supercritical gases"	Schneider, Stahl, and Wilke, 1980	Papers presented at a 1978 symposium held in Essen, W. Germany; includes examples of extraction with CO_2
"Separations using supercritical gases"	Irani and Funk, 1977	Literature review; comparison of distillation and SCF extraction
"The Principles of Gas Extraction"	Paul and Wise, 1971	Introduction to basic concepts of SCF technology; review of SCF chromatography
"Vapor phase extraction process"	Ellis, 1971	Review paper with an emphasis on early applications
"The solubility of materials in compressed hydrocarbon gases"	Valteris, 1966	Early review paper

critical region for a pure component is shown by the crosshatched area in the pressure-temperature (*P-T*) diagram in figure 1.1. Table 1.2 lists the critical temperatures and pressures for a number of gases and liquids. A cursory inspection of this table reveals the following trends:

1.   most hydrocarbons have a critical pressure (P_c) close to 50 atm;
2.   the critical temperatures (T_c) for the light hydrocarbons, such as ethylene and ethane, are around room temperature; cyclic aliphatics and aromatics have higher critical temperatures;
3.   carbon dioxide has a mild critical temperature and a slightly elevated critical pressure; and
4.   the last two compounds have high critical temperatures or pressures, which is a result of polarity and hydrogen bonding.

   The authors of virtually all the previously mentioned review papers suggest that, to a first approximation, the solvent power of a supercritical fluid can be related to the solvent density in the critical region. This statement can be rationalized by considering the density behavior of a pure component, which is shown schematically in figure 1.2. For a reduced temperature (T_R) range of 0.9 to 1.2 and at reduced pressures (P_R) greater than 1.0, the reduced density (ρ_R) of the solvent can change from a value of about 0.1, a gaslike density, to about 2.5, a liquidlike density. As the reduced densities become liquidlike, the

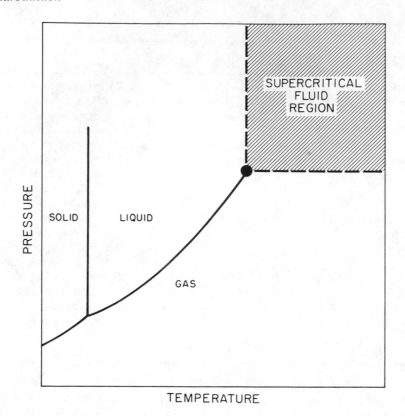

Figure 1.1   Pressure-temperature diagram for a pure component.

Table 1.2   Critical Conditions for Various Supercritical Solvents

Solvents	Critical Temperature (°C)	Critical Pressure (atm)
Carbon dioxide	31.1	72.8
Ethane	32.3	48.2
Ethylene	9.3	49.7
Propane	96.7	41.9
Propylene	91.9	45.6
Cyclohexane	280.3	40.2
Isopropanol	235.2	47.0
Benzene	289.0	48.3
Toluene	318.6	40.6
p-Xylene	343.1	34.7
Chlorotrifluoromethane	28.9	38.7
Trichlorofluoromethane	198.1	43.5
Ammonia	132.5	111.3
Water	374.2	217.6

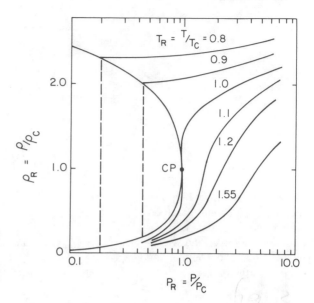

Figure 1.2 Variation of the reduced density (ρ_R) of a pure component in the vicinity of its critical point.

supercritical fluid begins to act as a liquid solvent. Note, however, that as the reduced temperature is increased to a value of 1.55, the supercritical fluid becomes more expanded. Therefore, if liquidlike densities are to be reached, the reduced pressure must be increased to values as high as 10.0. When operating in the critical region both pressure and temperature can now be used to regulate the density and, therefore, the solvent power of a supercritical fluid.

The unique feature of a supercritical fluid is that it displays a wide spectrum of solvent characteristics. As an example of the ability to "fine-tune" the solvent power of an SCF, consider the solubility behavior shown in figure 1.3 for the solid naphthalene ($T_m = 80.2°C$)–supercritical ethylene ($T_c = 9.3°C$, $P_c = 49.8$ atm) system near the critical point of pure ethylene (Diepen and Scheffer, 1953; Tsekhanskaya, Iomtev, and Mushkina, 1964). At a temperature of 12°C ($T_R = 1.01$), the solubility of solid naphthalene in supercritical ethylene increases quite dramatically as the pressure is increased to 50 atm and higher. At pressures below 50 atm, naphthalene solubility is extremely low, as would be expected for the solubility of a solid in a gas. At pressures much greater than about 90 atm, the solubility of naphthalene in ethylene reaches a limiting value of about 1.5 mole-%. The solubility behavior along this isotherm can be interpreted by considering the reduced-density isotherm at 1.0, shown in figure 1.2. Note that the 12°C isotherm has the same characteristic shape as the reduced-density isotherm at 1.0. From this example, one can readily see why the solvent behavior of an SCF is related (to a first approximation) to the solvent density behavior in the critical region.

To obtain an appreciation of the enhanced solvent power of supercritical ethylene, let us compare the experimentally observed naphthalene solubility

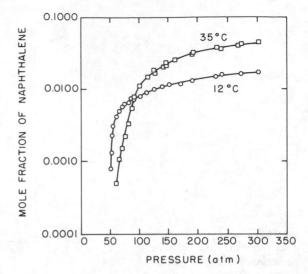

Figure 1.3 Solubility behavior of solid naphthalene in super-critical ethylene (data of Tsekhanskaya, Iomtev, and Mushkina, 1962, and Diepen and Scheffer, 1948b).

(y) at 100 atm and 12°C with the solubility that is calculated when the super-critical fluid phase is assumed to act like an ideal gas. In this instance we use the following expression:

$$y_2 = \left[\frac{P_2^{sub}}{P} \right] \exp \left[\int_{P_2^{sub}}^{P} \frac{v_2^s}{RT} \, dP \right], \tag{1.1}$$

where the subscript 2 represents naphthalene, P_2^{sub} represents the sublimation pressure of solid naphthalene, and v_2^s represents the molar volume of solid naphthalene (Prausnitz, 1969). At 12°C and 100 atm the sublimation pressure is equal to 0.0000303 atm (Diepen and Scheffer, 1953). For pressures up to about 1,000 atm, it can be assumed that v_2^s is a constant equal to 111.9 cc/g-mol (Vaidya and Kennedy, 1971). At 100 atm and 12°C, we find

$$\frac{y_2 \text{ (observed)}}{y_2 \text{ (calculated)}} = 16,156. \tag{1.2}$$

This simple calculation, although not rigorous, does indicate the large increase in solvent capacity of supercritical ethylene relative to the capacity of ethylene considered as an ideal gas at 100 atm. The large increase in solvent power of ethylene cannot be attributed to a hydrostatic pressure effect since the pressure effect is explicitly accounted for in the exponential term in equation 1.1. Instead, the large difference in experimental and calculated naphthalene solubility at high pressures is associated with the nonideal behavior of ethylene as it is compressed to liquidlike densities in its critical region.

Considering now the 35° ($T_R = 1.09$) isotherm in figure 1.3, we see that the solubility behavior is not as sensitive to pressure in the region near 50 atm as it was for the 12°C isotherm. However, at pressures greater than 100 atm, where ethylene exhibits liquidlike densities, the 35°C isotherm reaches a higher limiting solubility value (about 5 mole-%).

At pressures greater than about 150 atm ($P_R = 3$) the difference in the density of supercritical ethylene at 12°C ($T_R = 1.01$) and at 35°C ($T_R = 1.09$) is not very large (see figure 1.2). Therefore, the higher naphthalene solubilities at 35°C and elevated pressures can only be explained by the increase in the sublimation pressure of naphthalene on heating from 12°C to 35°C. These solubility data highlight the two competing factors, SCF density and solid sublimation pressure, that affect the solubility of solids in supercritical fluids. (Because solid polymers have virtually no sublimation pressure, they represent a distinctly different class of SCF solubility behavior as compared with the solubility behavior of crystalline solids in SCFs. SCF-solid polymer systems are considered in a later chapter in this book.)

As further verification of the fluid density versus sublimation pressure effect, consider the change in naphthalene solubility in supercritical ethylene when the temperature is increased from 12°C to 35°C at a constant pressure of about 50 atm. As figure 1.3 shows, naphthalene solubility drops by more than an order of magnitude for this 23° change in temperature. This sharp decrease in solubility upon heating the mixture isobarically near the critical point of ethylene is attributed to the large decrease in ethylene density. The density behavior is shown schematically in figure 1.2, where the reduced density is seen to decrease sharply when the reduced temperature is isobarically changed from 1.0 to 1.2 near a reduced pressure of 1.0. Again, the shapes of the 1.0 and 1.2 reduced-density isotherms are similar to the 12° and 35°C naphthalene solubility isotherms.

This SCF-solid solubility behavior may be used as a model system whose principles can be applied to many practical SCF separation problems, such as the extraction of (almost solid) oleoresins, the color and taste ingredients from spices and red peppers (Stahl et al., 1980); the separation of solid aromatic isomers (Krukonis and Kurnik, 1985); and the removal of lower-molecular-weight constituents from coal at elevated temperatures using an SCF with a high critical temperature, such as toluene (Williams, 1981).

Of course, there are many other examples of industrial separations in which the components to be separated are liquids and not solids. The SCF solvent can be appreciably soluble in the liquid mixture, whereas it was previously assumed that the SCF solvent did not dissolve in the crystalline solid. (It is noted again that another distinct subset of solid-SCF behavior occurs with amorphous solid polymers that can sorb large amounts of SCF solvent [Liau and McHugh, 1985].) The mutual solubility of SCFs and liquids does complicate the phase diagrams, but these diagrams are no more complicated than the ones used to describe conventional liquid-liquid extraction processes (McCabe and Smith, 1976).

In contrast to a liquid-liquid extraction process, where the solvent in the extract phase is separated by distillation, an SCF-liquid extraction process has

Figure 1.4   Phase behavior of the ethanol–water–supercritical ethane system at 40.0°C (McHugh, Mallett, and Kohn, 1983). The open triangles represent the 50-atm isobar and the open circles represent the 80-atm isobar.

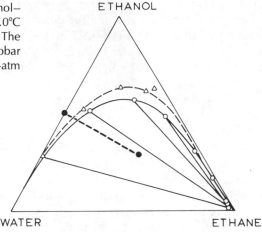

the advantage that the solvent can be recovered by decreasing the system pressure (Elgin and Weinstock, 1959). As an example of a single-stage SCF-liquid extraction process, let us consider the separation of ethanol from water using supercritical fluids. A variety of SCF solvents such as carbon dioxide, ethane, and ethylene have been tested for recovering ethanol from water. For example, figure 1.4 shows the phase behavior for the ethanol-water-ethane system (McHugh, Mallett, and Kohn, 1983). One possible procedure for extracting ethanol from a 50:50 mixture of ethanol and water using supercritical ethane is depicted by the dashed line in figure 1.4. The 50:50 mixture, incidentally, is not one of industrial importance, but it is a convenient example for explaining the general behavior of ternary systems. Enough supercritical ethane is introduced into the system at a constant temperature and pressure until the overall ethanol-water-ethane composition coincides with a value well within the two-phase liquid-fluid region of the diagram (e.g., at coordinates of 30:30:40 ethanol:water:ethane). If a tie-line were drawn at this point a liquid phase of 40 mole–% ethanol, 40 mole–% water, and 20 mole–% ethane exists in equilibrium with a fluid phase of 4 mole–% ethanol, 1 mole–% water, and 95 mole–% ethane. The selectivity of supercritical ethane for ethanol relative to water as defined by

$$\text{selectivity} = \frac{[(x_1)_F]/[(x_1)_L]}{[(x_2)_F]/[(x_2)_L]} \tag{1.3}$$

where x denotes composition, subscripts 1 and 2 denote ethanol and water, respectively, and subscripts F and L denote the fluid and liquid phases, is approximately 2.5. The loading or amount of ethanol in the fluid phase is only 4 mole–%; therefore, large amounts of ethane are needed to recover the ethanol from the feed solution. This example indicates that the values for both the loading and the selectivity of ethanol in the supercritical fluid phase must be considered when designing an SCF extraction process. Numerous examples of SCF-liquid separations are described in a later chapter of this book.

In addition to its unique solubility characteristics, an SCF solvent possesses certain other physicochemical properties that add to its attractiveness as a solvent. For example, even though it possesses a liquidlike density over much of the range of industrial interest, it exhibits gaslike transport properties of diffusivity and viscosity (Schneider, 1978). Additionally, the zero surface tension of supercritical fluids allows facile penetration into microporous materials.

Figure 1.5 shows the self-diffusivity of carbon dioxide over a wide pressure-temperature range and, for comparative purposes, the range of diffusivities for solutes in organic liquids (averaging, as is well known, about 10^{-5} cm²/sec) is also provided (Paulaitis et al., 1983a). The self-diffusion coefficient for carbon

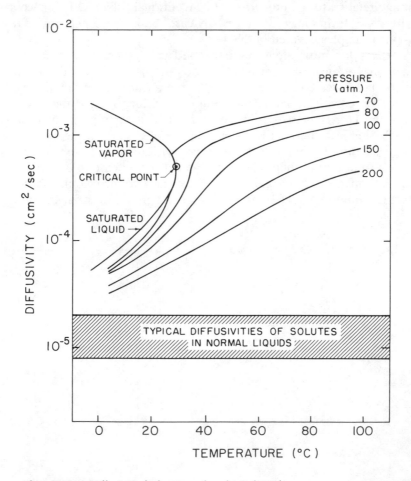

Figure 1.5 Diffusivity behavior of carbon dioxide.

dioxide (which is approximately the same as the diffusion coefficient of a similarly sized molecule diffusing through carbon dioxide) is about 1–2 orders of magnitude higher than the diffusivity of solutes in liquids.

The viscosity of carbon dioxide is shown in figure 1.6. Although the viscosity is seen to change rapidly in the critical region (as was the case with diffusivity, shown in figure 1.5), even at the high pressure levels of 300–400 atm it is only about 0.09 centipoise (cps), an order of magnitude below typical viscosities of liquid organic solvents (deFillipi et al., 1980).

The properties of gaslike diffusivity and viscosity, zero surface tension, and liquidlike density combined with the pressure-dependent solvent power of a supercritical fluid have provided the impetus for applying SCF technology to a gamut of separations problems experienced in many segments of industry. Although the combination of properties of an SCF solvent does indeed make it a potentially attractive solvent, on occasion these properties may offer no advantage relative to the properties of conventional solvents. It is necessary to evaluate SCF technology on a case-by-case basis, as is illustrated by the numerous examples covered in this book.

Perhaps the most often misinterpreted properties of supercritical fluids are their mass-transfer properties. For example, it is often claimed that SCF extraction processes do not experience the mass-transfer limitations of a liquid extraction process. This statement is quite often incorrect. If the rate-limiting step (or the largest mass-transfer resistance) of a separations process is the actual transfer of a material from the surface of a solid to the extract phase, then a gaslike diffusivity will certainly enhance diffusion in an extraction carried out with a supercritical fluid relative to the extraction carried out with a liquid solvent. If, on the other hand, the extraction is from a liquid phase into a supercritical fluid phase, as is probably a more typical industrial situation, then

Figure 1.6 Viscosity behavior of carbon dioxide.

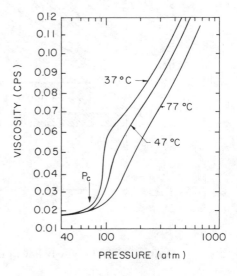

the resistance to diffusion in the liquid phase will probably be the rate-determining step. In this situation the gaslike diffusion characteristics of the SCF solvent will not have an enhancing effect on the overall mass-transfer rate. Similarly, if the extraction is occurring from within a nonporous particle, such as a polymer, where internal solid-phase diffusion will probably govern the overall rate of mass transfer, the external-phase diffusion (of a gas, a liquid, or an SCF) will have little or no effect on the rate of mass transfer. An exception will occur, however, if the SCF phase alters the internal characteristics of the polymer, which, in fact, can occur with certain SCF-polymer systems, as discussed in chapters 9 and 12.

As noted at the beginning of this chapter, the possibilities of processing with supercritical fluid solvents have captured the imagination of a large number of research and development groups. Because they embody the right combination of solvent and physicochemical properties, supercritical fluid solvents appear to be a panacea for many separations problems found in the chemical process industries. But how many SCF extraction processes have been commercialized? Why aren't there scores of SCF processes now in operation?

These questions are addressed and some answers are developed as we progress through the chapters of this book. The practical as well as fundamental principles governing SCF processing are considered in some detail in later chapters. These principles have fascinated chemists and chemical engineers for more than a century. The history of these unique solvents is detailed in chapter 2. The reader will, in fact, find that a substantial amount of information was known about supercritical fluids as far back as the early 1800s.

2

Historical Perspective

The ability of a supercritical fluid to dissolve low-vapor-pressure solid materials was first reported by Hannay and Hogarth at a meeting of the Royal Society of London in 1879 (Hannay and Hogarth, 1879, 1880). Hannay and Hogarth described their experiments, carried out in small-diameter glass tubes, in which they observed that changes in pressure caused several inorganic salts (e.g., cobalt chloride, potassium iodide, and potassium bromide) to dissolve in or precipitate from ethanol at a temperature above the critical temperature of ethanol (T_c = 234°C). They found that increasing the pressure on the system caused the solutes to dissolve and that decreasing the pressure caused the dissolved materials to nucleate and precipitate "as a snow."

A brief description of the apparatus used by late-nineteenth-century scientists measuring critical phenomena and SCF solubility is presented to highlight the experimental techniques, care, and precision of these studies. Shown in figure 2.1a is a schematic diagram of the glass view cell, pressure generator, and pressure-measuring device used by Hannay and Hogarth. The liquid or solid phase is first placed inside a small-bore glass tube, which is then bent and inserted into the pressure-generator system. The tee bar seen at the right in figure 2.1a is a screw-feed plunger that is fitted and sealed against leakage inside a small-bore glass tube filled with mercury. The vertical tube seen in the figure is an air manometer used for pressure measurement. As the plunger is advanced, it compresses both the air column in the air manometer and the contents in the glass tube. From the observed volume decrease of air and the accepted volumetric properties of air, the pressure in the system is calculated. The temperature of the material in the bent tube is adjusted by the bath shown in figure 2.1b.

Other types of early experimental designs described in the literature attest to the creativity of Hannay and Hogarth's predecessors and contemporaries working with high pressures. For example, Baron Cagniard de la Tour discovered the critical point of a substance in 1822. In fact, for many years the critical point was referred to as the "Cagniard de la Tour" point. In his earliest experiments Cagniard de la Tour (1822) used a piece of rifled cannon for his high-pressure investigations. He sealed a liquid and a flint ball in the cannon barrel, heated the barrel, and rocked it while listening for changes in the sound

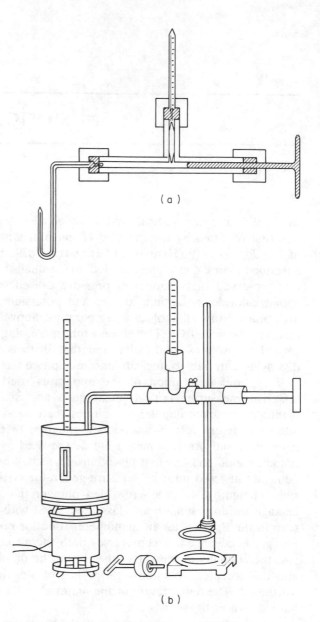

Figure 2.1 Schematic diagram of the experimental apparatus used by Hannay and Hogarth to obtain solid solubilities in supercritical fluids. The glass tubing shown in the left of figure (a) is first connected to an air manometer and is then immersed in the constant-temperature bath as shown in (b).

of the rolling ball or for changes in the sound made when the barrel was tapped. Discontinuities in the sound (noted, incidentally, while the baron held his ear to the sealed end of the cannon) led him to describe the point we today know as the critical point. He later carried out experiments in glass tubes so that he could visually observe critical phenomenon.

Supercritical carbon dioxide attracted much attention in the latter half of the nineteenth century. Dr. Thomas Andrews, vice-president of Queen's College, Belfast, carried out an extensive investigation in the mid-1800s on the phase behavior of carbon dioxide. In his now quite famous Bakerian Lecture delivered to the Royal Society in 1869 he described his experimental apparatus (which was modified slightly by Hannay and Hogarth) and his observations of the critical properties of CO_2 (Andrews, 1875–76). In his lecture he related that

> On partially liquifying carbonic acid by pressure alone, and gradually raising at the same time the temperature to 88°Fahr., the surface of demarcation between the liquid and gas became fainter, lost its curvature, and at last disappeared. The space was then occupied by a homogeneous fluid, which exhibited, when the pressure was suddenly diminished or the temperature slightly lowered, a peculiar appearance or flickering striae throughout its entire mass. At temperatures above 88° (F) no apparent liquifaction of carbonic acid, or separation into two distinct forms of matter, could be effected, even when a pressure of 300 or 400 atmospheres was applied.

The values that Dr. Andrews reported for the critical point of carbon dioxide, 30.92°C and 73.0 atm, are in close agreement to presently accepted values, 31.1°C and 72.8 atm.

In 1879 Amagat described a method for compressing gases to 400 atm using mercury columns extending to the bottom of a mine shaft (Amagat, 1879). And in 1891, two years after the construction of the Eiffel Tower, Cailletet generated high pressures with a mercury column reaching to the top of the tower (Cailletet, 1891). These high-pressure experiments were not without their problems, however, as many reports of ruptured steel tubes (of quarter-inch inside and two-inch outside diameter) are recorded in the literature during this period.

There was substantial controversy about the initial finding of the pressure dependence of solubility in a supercritical fluid after it was first reported at the October 1879 Royal Society meeting. One month after hearing the paper of Hannay and Hogarth, Professor William Ramsay of the Chemistry Department, University College, Bristol, reported to the Royal Society that he had carried out the experiments described by Hannay and Hogarth and concluded from these reproductions that "the gentlemen have observed nothing unusual, but merely the ordinary phenomenon of solubility of a solid in a hot liquid" (Ramsay, 1880).

In later presentations to the Royal Society, Hannay responded to Ramsay's charge, asking "permission to point out some errors into which Prof. Ramsay had fallen." In addition to pointing out those errors, Hannay discussed still other experiments that later substantiated the pressure-dependent dissolving power of a supercritical fluid as a new phenomenon (Hannay, 1880).

As might be concluded from this debate, the literature provides some interesting reading. Professor Ramsay, who questioned the results of Hannay and Hogarth, went on to write scores of papers on critical-point phenomena, thermodynamics, and vapor-liquid equilibria, but he was wrong about his "hot liquid" conclusion. It must be remembered that the exchanges at the Royal Society meetings cited above occurred when critical-point phenomena were still incompletely understood or accepted. During this period such luminaries as van der Waals were explaining the volumetric behavior of real gases, and Amagat, Joule, Thomson, Cailletet, Clausius, and Dewar were engaged in other experimental and theoretical investigations of critical phenomena.

Although Hannay and Hogarth first studied the solubility of inorganic salts in supercritical ethanol, the pressure-dependent dissolving power of an SCF is not limited to inorganic salt solutes. It is a general phenomenon exhibited by all supercritical solvent–solute pairs (as long as the solute is not infinitely miscible with the solvent). After the first report by Hannay and Hogarth, a number of other authors reported solubility phenomena with a variety of SCF solvents and organic solid and liquid solutes. SCF solvents included carbon dioxide, nitrous oxide, and the light hydrocarbons; and solutes covered the gamut of organic compounds, namely, aliphatics, aromatics, halogenated hydrocarbons, heteromolecules, triglycerides, and the like.

Although emphasis in this book is given to solubility phenomena at supercritical conditions, a number of early studies were reported in the literature that focused on the phase behavior and solvent characteristics of near-critical, liquid carbon dioxide. The earliest published work on liquid CO_2 as a solvent is that of Gore (1861). Gore found naphthalene and camphor to be soluble in liquid CO_2, but he concludes that liquid CO_2 is "a very feeble solvent of substances in general." He made this general conclusion after having tested only a small number of organic compounds, some of which just happened to exhibit very low solubility. As we shall see later in this chapter, liquid carbon dioxide is a very good solvent for many classes of compounds.

In 1896 Villard published a review of supercritical fluid solubility phenomena (Villard, 1896). He described the ability of methane, ethylene, carbon dioxide, and nitrous oxide to dissolve a number of liquids and solid hydrocarbons such as carbon disulfide, camphor, stearic acid, and paraffin wax. He reported on a (then) strange phenomenon, that as solid camphor is subjected to ethylene at increasing pressure it is liquefied and then it "vaporizes" (i.e., it dissolves in the ethylene at higher pressures). This is, perhaps, the first reported observation of the interaction of a high-pressure gas with a solid hydrocarbon resulting in the lowering of the normal melting point of the pure solid. (The melting-point depression and the topic of solid solubilities in supercritical fluids is discussed at length in chapter 3, where the work of Diepen, Scheffer, and coworkers is described.) Villard published other papers on high-pressure phenomena and he is perhaps better known for his experimental work on gas hydrates (Villard, 1888).

Several years after Villard's paper, E. H. Büchner reviewed the literature and also made significant additions to the experimental data base of high-pressure SCF-solute mixtures (Büchner, 1906). He carried out his studies over a wide temperature range, and he used observations of cloud points, freezing points, and the number of phases present for his solubility determinations.

Although his work was primarily of a qualitative nature, the concept of a cloud point and a freezing- (or melting-) point depression of a solid can be extended to yield quantitative solubility information. The experimental techniques used to determine the melting-point depression of a solid are covered in chapter 4.

Within the past ten years a large number of authors have cited the solubility behavior of the naphthalene-ethylene system as the impetus for their own SCF studies. It is instructive to trace the origins of naphthalene-SCF phase-behavior studies because this system has, in fact, been very extensively studied and the features of the phase behavior are evident in many other solute-SCF systems. Büchner was the first to investigate the solubility behavior of naphthalene in carbon dioxide. A few years later, Prins explored the solubility of naphthalene in both supercritical ethane and carbon dioxide (Prins, 1915). Prins determined three-phase border curves and critical end points for naphthalene in both gases. Researchers of the late 1800s and early 1900s met and overcame many obstacles in carrying out their studies. Today if one desires to measure the solubility of naphthalene in ethane, for example, the acquisition of materials would be quite easy. Calling the appropriate manufacturers and suppliers of chemicals and gases and placing the orders is all that is required, but it is of historical value to relate how Prins "acquired" his ethane. As he stated in his paper

> The ethane was prepared by electrolyzing sodium acetate. The anode gas was purified by bromine water and a strong solution of potassium hydroxide dried over soda lime and condensed in a receiver with liquid air. Subsequently it was again dried over phosphorous pentoxide and separated from the more volatile part by fractionating by the use of liquid air. The disappearance of the discharge in a Geisler tube attached to the apparatus served as criterion on purity.

All this just to get the ethane for his supercritical fluid solubility studies.

Investigations of naphthalene solubility in supercritical fluids slowed until the late 1940s when Professor Scheffer and co-workers of Delft University began to publish extensively on ethylene-naphthalene phase behavior. In 1948, a study of the solubility and phase behavior of naphthalene dissolved in supercritical ethylene was reported (Diepen and Scheffer, 1948b). This now-classic paper was followed by several other high-pressure phase-behavior papers by the two authors and their co-workers (van Gunst, Scheffer, and Diepen, 1953a, 1953b; van Welie and Diepen, 1963, 1961a–e; van Hest and Diepen, 1963; Swelheim, de Swaan Arons, and Diepen, 1965; Koningsveld, Diepen, and Chermin, 1966; Koningsveld, Kleintjens, and Diepen, 1984; Koningsveld and Diepen, 1983; de Swaan Arons and Diepen, 1963; de Loss, Poot, and Diepen, 1983). These publications provided the impetus for other groups to examine the characteristics of naphthalene solubility in a variety of supercritical fluid solvents.

In the early 1960s, the solubility of naphthalene in a variety of other gases was studied. Tsekhanskaya, Iomtev, and Mushkina (1962, 1964) from the Soviet Union measured naphthalene solubilities in ethylene and in carbon dioxide. Other naphthalene-SCF investigators included the following: King and Robertson (1962), who studied the solubility of naphthalene in supercritical hydrogen, helium, and argon; Najour and King (1966), who studied the solubility of naphthalene in supercritical methane, ethylene, and carbon dioxide; McHugh and Paulaitis (1980), who studied the solubility of naphthalene in supercritical carbon dioxide; Kurnik, Holla, and Reid (1981), who also studied the solubility of naphthalene in supercritical carbon dioxide; Schmitt and Reid (1984), who studied the solubility of naphthalene in supercritical ethane, trifluoromethane, and chlorotrifluoromethane; and, most recently, Krukonis, McHugh, and Seckner (1984), who studied the solubility and phase behavior of naphthalene using, as the solvent, supercritical xenon. As might reasonably be concluded from this long list of references, naphthalene solubility has been tested quite thoroughly, and a large amount of data exists on its behavior over a wide range of pressures, temperatures, and compositions.

Scores of other researchers have investigated solubility phenomena with supercritical fluid solvents, and much of this work will be cited in subsequent chapters of this book. However, the work of one man, A. W. Francis, far surpasses the work of his contemporaries when one considers the breadth of mixtures that he studied. In a single 1954 paper, A. W. Francis presented an extensive, quantitative study on the solvent properties of liquid CO_2 with hundreds of compounds (Francis, 1954). Francis, primarily interested in the phase behavior of ternary systems containing liquid CO_2, collected data for 464 ternary phase diagrams and determined the solubilities of 261 compounds in near-critical, liquid CO_2. He included many classes of organic compounds, e.g., aliphatics, aromatics, heterocyclics, and compounds with a large variety of functional groups. From his tables of data it is possible to formulate general rules on the solubility behavior of compounds in carbon dioxide. As an example of the breadth of his solubility studies, table 2.1 lists about fifty compounds and their solubilities in CO_2 studied by Francis.

Although Francis studied solubility behavior in liquid carbon dioxide (at approximately 25°C, 950 psia), his results are very general. For example, a compound that is soluble in liquid carbon dioxide will also be soluble in supercritical carbon dioxide. Thus, the data can be used to assess the potential of supercritical fluid extraction for many separations before any experimental work need be carried out. The importance of Francis's contribution cannot be overemphasized.

Since naphthalene-SCF mixtures have been so widely studied, it is instructive to consider the solubility behavior of just one of these systems, the naphthalene-CO_2 system, to highlight the solvent properties of a supercritical fluid solvent. In chapter 1 the effects of pressure and temperature on the solubility of naphthalene in ethylene were described. The solubility behavior is quite similar in carbon dioxide, or in trifluoromethane, or even in xenon, although there are differences among the systems in the absolute solubility levels of naphthalene that are achieved.

Figure 2.2 assembles data on the solubility of naphthalene in supercritical

Table 2.1 Solubilities of Selected Compounds in Liquid Carbon Dioxide at 25°C

	Weight Percent		Weight Percent
Esters		*Amines and Heterocyclics*	
Benzyl benzoate	10	Aniline	3
Butyl oxalate	M[a]	o-Chloroaniline	5
Butyl phthalate	8	m-Chloroaniline	1
Butyl stearate	3	N,N-Diethylaniline	17
Ethyl acetate	M	N,N-Dimethylaniline	M
Ethyl acetoacetate	M	Diphenylamine	1
Ethyl benzoate	M	N-Ethylaniline	13
Ethyl chloroformate	M	N-Methylaniline	20
Ethyl maleate	M	α-Naphthylamine	1
Ethyl oxalate	M	2,5-Dimethyl-pyrrole	5
Ethyl phthalate	10	Pyridine	M
Methyl salicylate	M	o-Toluidine	7
Phenyl phthalate	1	m-Toluidine	15
Phenyl salicylate	9	p-Toluidine	7
Alcohols		*Phenols*	
t-Amyl alcohol	M	o-Chlorophenol	M
Benzyl alcohol	8	p-Chlorophenol	8
Cinnamyl alcohol	5	o-Cresol	2
Cyclohexanol	4	m-Cresol	4
1-Decyl alcohol	1	p-Cresol	2
Methyl alcohol	M	2,4-Dichlorophenol	14
Ethyl alcohol	M	p-Ethylphenol	1
2-Ethylhexanol	17	o-Nitrophenol	M
Furfuryl alcohol	4	Phenol (MP 41°C)	3
Heptyl alcohol	6	β-Methoxyethanol	M
Hexyl alcohol	11	Phenylethanol	3
Carboxylic Acids		*Nitriles and Amides*	
Acetic acid	M	Acetonitrile	M
Caproic acid	M	Acrylonitrile	M
Caprylic acid	M	Phenylacetonitrile	13
Formic acid	M	Succinonitrile	2
Isocaproic acid	M	Tolunitriles (mixed)	M
Lactic acid	0.5	Acetamide	1
Lauric acid	1	N,N-Diethylacetamide	M
Oleic acid	2	N,N-Dimethylacetamide	M
		Formamide	0.5

[a]M = miscible.

carbon dioxide from the large number of previously mentioned naphthalene studies. The data in this figure are plotted in slightly different format, i.e., as solubility isobars. This method of displaying data removes the crossing of the

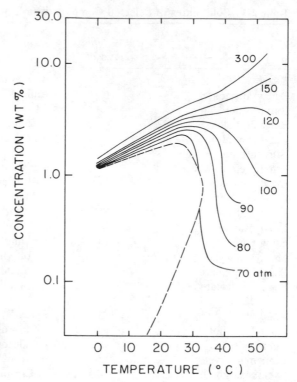

Figure 2.2 Solubility of solid naphthalene in supercritical carbon dioxide (data assembled by Modell et al., 1979).

curves seen in figure 1.2. Depending upon the pressure level, the temperature is seen to affect naphthalene solubility quite differently. For example, at 300 atm an increase in the temperature increases the solubility of naphthalene in carbon dioxide, whereas at a low pressure of 80 or 90 atm an increase in temperature decreases naphthalene's solubility.

The silica-water system shown in figure 2.3 is an example of another system that exhibits the general solubility behavior shown in figure 2.2. The critical properties of water are quite different from those of carbon dioxide and the solubility levels on the respective graphs are 1–2 orders of magnitude apart. However, a comparison of the two figures shows that the characteristic shapes of the solubility curves are similar. At a high pressure level, 1,750 atm in this case, increasing temperature causes the solubility of silica to increase, whereas at the "low" pressure of 400 atm the solubility falls with increasing temperature.

Some background to the study of the solubility of silica in supercritical water is rather interesting and is presented here to illustrate that the phenomena first studied in the laboratory in 1879 have some far-reaching influences in industry. During the production of high-pressure steam, silica that is present in the water is dissolved. The silica, incidentally, enters the (almost) closed-

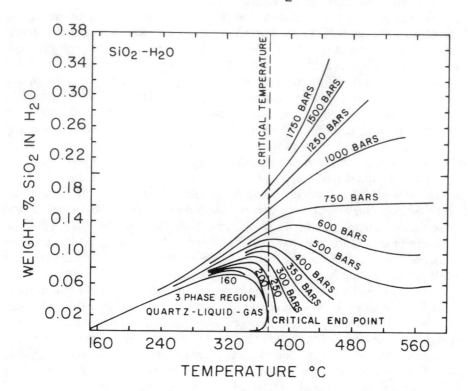

Figure 2.3 Solubility behavior of solid silica in supercritical water (Kennedy, 1950).

loop steam side partly through makeup-water and mostly from condensor water leakage (and as is known silica is ubiquitously distributed in all ground water). The silica dissolved in the supercritical steam is transported as dissolved species to the turbines. During the pressure decrease as the steam travels through the turbine, the silica deposits on the turbine blades, eventually resulting in a shutdown for cleaning. The presence of the silica in the turbines was not fully understood until the solubility and phase equilibria of the silica-water system were studied, however.

Besides silica-water, many other solid systems, such as phenanthrene, benzoic acid, phenol, and biphenyl, exhibit the same characteristic behavior as shown in figure 2.3 (Van Leer and Paulaitis, 1980; McHugh and Paulaitis, 1980; Kurnik, Holla, and Reid, 1981; Johnston, Ziger, and Eckert, 1982; Johnston and Eckert, 1981).

It is by now quite clear to the reader that the phenomenon of enhanced solubility in supercritical fluids has been known for more than a century. We ended Chapter 1 with the question: Why are there not scores of supercritical fluid extraction processes in operation today?

It is important to remember that during the first three quarters of the 20th century energy was cheap. Therefore, there was no motivation for developing energy–efficient processes. We shall see in chapter 8 that the preoccupation with energy conservation and efficiency virtually became a national obsession. This drive for energy efficiency was a major impetus for many research and development programs in the mid to late 1970's. As noted in chapters 7 and 9, however, there were a few high–pressure processes that were developed in the late 1930s and early 1940s, not because they were necessarily more energy efficient than competing processes, but because there was no other way to produce the desired product (e.g., low density polyethylene).

It is also important to realize that the development of a high-pressure process depends on an understanding of the phase behavior of the system and that phase behavior at high pressures can be quite perplexing. A cursory review of the thermodynamic textbooks used in the 1940s through the 1960s will show that very little attention is paid to the phase behavior of mixtures at high pressures. Information on the high pressure phase behavior of mixtures has developed quite rapidly within the past two decades or so.

In the following chapters we shall progress to a discussion of high-pressure phase behavior and to an examination of applications research that has been described in the literature. The phase behavior of SCF-solute systems exhibits enough peculiarities that the timetable of a research and development program stands the chance of being lengthened because of seemingly unexplainable data. The engineer must be aware of the phase behavior that is exhibited by SCF-solute mixtures so that he can take advantage of this behavior in novel ways in the development of supercritical fluid processes. The high-pressure phase behavior of SCF-solute systems is considered in some detail in chapter 3.

3

Phase Diagrams for Supercritical Fluid–Solute Mixtures

The development of new applications for SCF solvent technology often hinges on our ability to interpret the experimental information obtained in a laboratory or pilot-plant study. That is to say that our ideas for applying this new technology are often limited by our ability to understand the phase behavior of mixtures in the critical region. Interpreting as well as extrapolating high-pressure phase-behavior data can be a formidable task, since high-pressure phase behavior near critical points can be complex even for simple binary mixtures in which the components are chemically similar but have different molecular sizes, such as methane-n-hexane (Hicks and Young, 1975). For a given practical application of SCF solvent technology, it is highly likely that not only will the mixture components differ in molecular size, but they will also differ in molecular shape, structure, or polarity. The individual components of the mixture may even be ill defined (e.g., petroleum residuum). When the mixture components are so chemically diverse, or when the mixture has numerous components, the resultant phase behavior can be quite complex.

To minimize the complexity of the phase diagrams applicable to multi-component mixtures, let us first describe the limiting case of a phase diagram of a binary mixture consisting of a single SCF solvent and a single solute (Streett, 1983). An understanding of the phase behavior of this limiting case provides a basis for understanding and generalizing the phase-equilibrium principles that are operative during the SCF solvent extraction of mixtures.

Complex phase diagrams can be interpreted and clarified in a relatively straightforward manner using the phase rule. As described by Streett, the phase rule imposes certain geometrical constraints on the construction of phase diagrams for mixtures (Streett, 1983). The phase rule is given by the simple relation:

$$F = c + 2 - p, \tag{3.1}$$

23

where F is the number of independent variables, c is the number of components, and p is the number of phases. Shown in table 3.1 are the geometrical constraints imposed by the phase rule for phase-diagram representations of multiphase-multicomponent equilibria. These geometrical constraints simplify the representation of multiphase regions in the phase diagram.

During an SCF solvent extraction process, the most important regions in pressure-temperature-composition (P-T-x) space are those of two-phase liquid-vapor (LV), solid-vapor (SV), or liquid-liquid (LL) equilibria, three-phase liquid-liquid-vapor (LLV), solid-liquid-vapor (SLV) or solid-solid-vapor (SSV) equilibria, and sometimes four-phase liquid-liquid-solid-vapor (LLSV) or liquid-solid-solid-vapor equilibria (LSSV). When these regions of multiple phases are projected onto a two-dimensional pressure-temperature (P-T) diagram, their geometrical representations are simplified because pressure and temperature are field variables (Streett, 1983)—that is, variables that are the same in each of the equilibrium phases. Pressure, temperature, and chemical potential are field variables, whereas molar volume is not. For instance, two surfaces representing equilibrium between two phases in P-T-x space project as a single surface in P-T space; three lines representing three equilibrium phases in P-T-x space project as a single line in P-T space, and four points representing four equilibrium phases in P-T-x space project as a single point in P-T space. Therefore, complex phase behavior can be more readily interpreted when a P-T diagram (i.e., a field-variable diagram) is used.

Although nature provides us with countless numbers of possible binary phase diagrams, Scott and van Konynenburg show that these diagrams can be reduced to five basic types (Scott, 1972; Scott and van Konynenburg, 1970). Scott and van Konynenburg demonstrate that virtually all the experimentally observed binary phase diagrams can be qualitatively described using the van der Waals equation of state. (Street [1983] describes a sixth classification not predicted by the van der Waals equation; however, that type of phase diagram is much less common and it is not described here.) The phase-diagram classification scheme is simplified by using a two-dimensional projection of critical mixture curves and three-phase lines from three-dimensional P-T-x diagrams.

Table 3.1 Summary of the Geometrical Features of Phase Diagrams for One- and Two-Component Systems

Number of Equilibrium Phases			
One-Component System	*Two-Component System*	*Degrees of Freedom*	*Geometrical Features*
3	4	0	Points
2	3	1	Lines
1	2	2	Surfaces
*	1	3	Volumes

Source: Streett (1983).

The five classes of possible fluid-phase diagrams that are described in this chapter are shown in figure 3.1. In these diagrams the occurrence of solid phases at low (cryogenic) temperatures is omitted. The formation of solid phases as well as multiple liquid phases at cryogenic temperatures is discussed

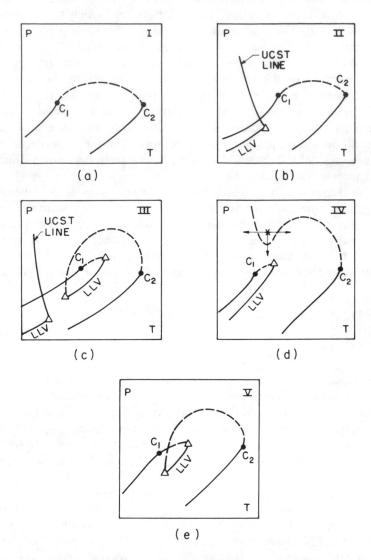

Figure 3.1 Five classes of possible binary phase diagrams as determined from the van der Waals equation of state. Points C_1 and C_2 represent the critical points of components 1 and 2, respectively. The dashed curve in these figures represents the critical mixture curve for the binary mixture. The open triangles represent critical end points.

in detail elsewhere (Luks and Kohn, 1984; Rowlinson and Swinton, 1982) and is not presented here because cryogenic process operations are not germane to SCF processing.

Before describing the five classes of possible phase diagrams exhibited by SCF-solute systems, we will first define some abbreviations that appear in the discussion of these diagrams. These definitions, which are shown in table 3.2, are used to describe points in *P-T-x* space where two phases merge or coalesce into a single phase (Rowlinson and Swinton, 1982). Sometimes this merging takes place in the presence of a third phase, which acts as an "uninterested observer" of the phase transition. For instance, the lower critical-solution temperature (LCST) defines the temperature at which two liquid phases become critically identical in the presence of a noncritical gas phase. Unfortunately, the designation LCST is also used for a liquid + liquid → liquid transition when a gas phase is not present. These definitions are a matter of bookkeeping; table 3.2 should be used to decipher the abbreviations found in this chapter of the book.

Quite frequently three-dimensional *P-T-x* diagrams can be overwhelming at first glance, especially for some of the more complex systems. Since it is very common to determine *P-x* diagrams experimentally, the *P-T-x* diagrams will be constructed by compiling a number of isothermal *P-x* diagrams onto one *P-T-x* diagram. Constructing the *P-T-x* diagram should remove the confusion associated with the two-dimensional *P-T* projection of the *P-T-x* diagram.

PHASE DIAGRAMS FOR BINARY MIXTURES

Type I

Shown previously in figure 3.1a is the simplest possible binary phase diagram for a type-I system. The distinguishing trait of type-I phase behavior is that the critical-mixture curve runs continuously from the critical point of the heavier component to the critical point of the lighter component. Type-I systems are usually composed of components that are of similar chemical type or that have critical properties of comparable magnitude (Rowlinson and Swinton, 1982). Constituents from a particular homologous series, such as the normal paraffins, usually deviate from type-I phase behavior only when the size difference between the constituents exceeds a certain value. In addition to the type of critical-mixture curve shown in figure 3.1a, it is also possible to have critical-mixture curves that have azeotropes, that exhibit a pressure minimum with increasing temperature, and that are linear between the critical points of the components (Schneider, 1970).

Type-I phase behavior is probably most familiar to chemical engineers, since the description of this phase behavior can be found in most undergraduate thermodynamic textbooks. For example, shown in figure 3.2 are *P-x* diagrams of two binary mixtures exhibiting type-I phase behavior obtained from the literature (Li, Dillard, and Robinson, 1981; Ng and Robinson, 1978).

Table 3.2 Definitions of Phase Transitions Occuring at High Pressures

Abbreviation	Transition	Description
LCST	lower critical-solution temperature	(a) Temperature at which two liquids critically merge to form a single liquid phase as the system temperature is lowered. (b) Temperature at which transition as described in (a) occurs in the presence of a noncritical gas phase.
UCST	upper critical-solution temperature	Temperature at which two liquids critically merge to form a single liquid phase as the system temperature is raised; the UCST is a lower temperature than the LCST.
UCEP	upper critical end point	(a) For solid–supercritical fluid systems the UCEP is the point at which the higher-temperature branch of the solid-liquid-gas line intersects the critical-mixture curve; at the UCEP a liquid and gas phase critically merge to form a single fluid phase in the presence of a noncritical solid phase. (b) For liquid–supercritical fluid systems the UCEP occurs at the intersection of the UCST curve and a three-phase liquid-liquid-vapor curve; at the UCEP a liquid and vapor phase critically merge to form a single liquid phase in the presence of another noncritical liquid phase as the temperature is increased.
LCEP	lower critical end point	For solid–supercritical fluid systems the LCEP occurs at the intersection of the low-temperature branch of the solid-liquid-gas line and the critical-mixture curve; at the LCEP a liquid and gas phase critically merge to form a single fluid phase in the presence of a noncritical solid phase.

Now let us progress to a discussion of the general three-dimensional P-T-x behavior for type-I binary mixtures, as shown in figure 3.3. The P-T-x diagram can be constructed by compiling a number of isothermal P-x plots, as shown in figures 3.3c and 3.3d. Throughout this chapter x denotes the com-

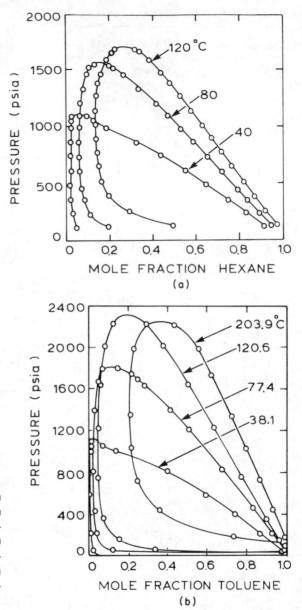

Figure 3.2 Pressure-composition (*P-x*) behavior of the (a) carbon dioxide–*n*-hexane system (Li, Dillard, and Robinson, 1981) and (b) the carbon dioxide–toluene system (Ng and Robinson, 1978). Both systems exhibit type-I phase behavior.

position of the heavy component. Shown in figure 3.3c is a *P-x* plot at temperature T_1, a temperature which is below the critical temperature of both of the components. In this figure is the familiar vapor-liquid envelope that intersects the pressure axis at two locations: the vapor pressure of pure component 1 $[P_1^{vap}(T_1)]$ and the vapor pressure of the other pure component $[P_2^{vap}(T_1)]$. At a fixed overall composition (denoted by x^* in this figure) there first exists a single vapor phase at low pressures. As the pressure is isothermally increased,

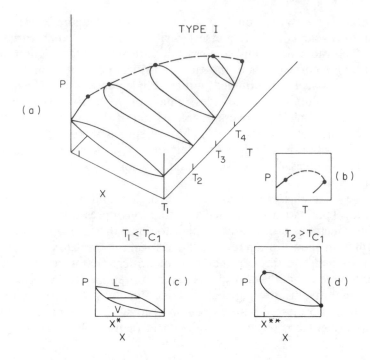

Figure 3.3 *P-T-x* (a), *P-T* (b), and *P-x* (c and d) diagrams for a type-I binary mixture.

the two-phase vapor-liquid envelope is intersected and a dew or liquid phase now appears. The locus of points that separates the two-phase vapor-liquid region from the one-phase vapor region is called the "dew-point curve." The concentration of the equilibrium vapor and liquid phases within the two-phase boundary of the vapor-liquid envelope is determined by a horizontal tie line similar to the one depicted in this figure.

As the pressure is further increased, the amount of mixture in the liquid phase increases while the amount of mixture in the vapor phase shrinks until only a small bubble of vapor remains. If the pressure is still further increased, the bubble of vapor disappears as the vapor-liquid envelope is finally crossed and now a single liquid phase exists. The locus of points that separates the two-phase vapor-liquid region from the one-phase liquid region is called the "bubble-point curve." This vapor-liquid envelope is also shown in the three-dimensional *P-T-x* diagram in figure 3.3a.

If we now determine the *P-x* diagram at temperature T_2, we observe the behavior shown in figure 3.3d. The vapor-liquid envelope in figure 3.3d is similar to that described in figure 3.3c; however, the envelope intersects the pressure axis only at $P_2^{vap}(T_2)$. Since T_2 is greater than T_{C1}, the critical temperature of component 1, the left-hand side of the vapor-liquid envelope does not touch the pressure axis, because the vapor-liquid equilibrium line for component 1 is never crossed at this temperature. If an experiment is performed at an overall composition equal to x^{**} (as shown in figure 3.3d), then the vapor-liquid envelope is first intersected along the dew-point curve at low pressures. The vapor-liquid envelope is again intersected at its highest pressure. This intersection corresponds to the mixture critical point at T_2 and x^{**}. If the P-x diagram is visually determined, critical opalescence—that is, the appearance of bright colors such as oranges, blues, or yellows—is observed at the mixture critical point. If the overall composition of the mixture is to the right of x^{**}, a bubble point is observed if the pressure is increased; if the overall mixture composition is slightly to the left of x^{**}, a dew point is observed if the pressure is increased. This vapor-liquid envelope at T_2 is also shown in the P-T-x diagram in figure 3.3a.

As P-x diagrams are determined at higher and higher temperatures, mixture critical points are determined as a function of pressure and composition. If these P-x diagrams are then assembled to form the three-dimensional P-T-x representation shown in figure 3.3a, the critical-mixture curve is obtained by drawing a dashed line through the locus of critical-mixture points. It should now be self-evident that the critical-mixture curve represents the locus of critical points for mixtures of differing composition. Finally, if the three-dimensional P-T-x diagram is projected onto a two-dimensional P-T diagram, a continuous critical-mixture curve is observed, as shown in figure 3.3b.

Type II

Type-II phase behavior is shown in figure 3.1b. The phase diagram for this type of system exhibits certain similarities to that of the previously described type-I system. In this case the critical-mixture curve is again a continuous curve running between the critical points of the two pure components. Now, however, there is a region in the P-T diagram that has three phases in equilibrium (i.e., a liquid-liquid-vapor region). A liquid-liquid-vapor line ending at an upper critical end point (UCEP) is now evident at temperatures lower than the critical temperature of either component. A three-dimensional P-T-x representation of the three-phase liquid-liquid-vapor (LLV) region ending at a UCEP is shown in figure 3.4. Notice that the three lines representing the LLV region project as a single line on a P-T diagram. As explained above, this is a consequence of using two field variables, pressure and temperature, to represent the phase behavior (Streett, 1983). At conditions between the two critical points, type-II mixtures exhibit the same features as type-I mixtures. The carbon dioxide–n-octane system is an example of a binary mixture exhibiting this type of phase behavior.

Type III

Type-III phase behavior is shown in figure 3.1c. The distinguishing trait of type-III phase behavior is the occurrence of an LLV region located very close

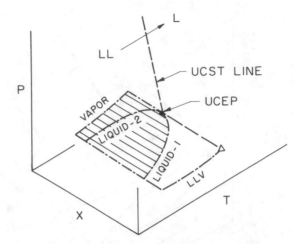

Figure 3.4 *P-T-x* diagram for the three-phase liquid-liquid-vapor region of a binary mixture.

to the critical point of the more volatile component. The branch of the critical-mixture curve starting at the critical point of the component with the higher critical temperature intersects the LLV line at the lower critical-solution temperature (LCST). The other branch of the critical-mixture curve, which starts at the critical point of the other component, intersects the LLV line at a UCEP. At temperatures below the LCST, a region of LLV behavior appears similar to that found for type-II phase behavior.

When the critical properties of the mixture components differ substantially, type-III phase behavior is usually observed. For example, with binary methane-hydrocarbon mixtures LLV behavior near the critical point of methane occurs when the ratio of carbon atoms between methane and the second component exceeds 6.0. For binary ethane-hydrocarbon mixtures the ratio of carbon atoms between ethane and the second component must exceed 9.5 for the same effect to occur. And for binary propane-hydrocarbon mixtures the ratio of carbon atoms between propane and the second component must exceed 13.5 for LLV behavior to occur (Rowlinson and Swinton, 1982).

The *P-T-x* diagram for type-III phase behavior is shown in figure 3.5. The lower-temperature portion of this diagram is omitted since, for all practical purposes, the *P-T* region of interest for SCF technology is located between the critical points of the pure components.

In the *P-T-x* diagram of figure 3.5a we see the previously described simple vapor-liquid *P-x* behavior at T_1, a temperature well below T_{C1}. If the temperature is raised slightly to T_2, the *P-x* diagram in figure 3.5c takes on the characteristic shape of a system on the verge of liquid immiscibility (i.e., the single liquid phase of the vapor-liquid envelope is on the verge of splitting into two liquids to form a three-phase LLV mixture). Shown in figure 3.5c is a tie line, which is drawn precisely at the horizontal inflection in the bubble-point curve of the vapor-liquid envelope. If the temperature is increased just slightly, two liquids will appear along with the vapor phase. The horizontal inflection

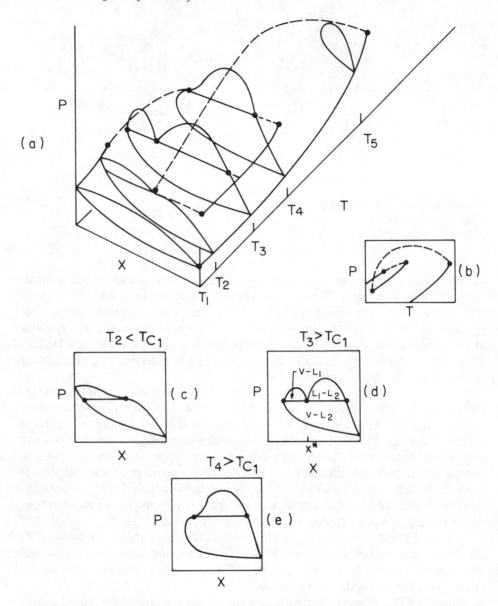

Figure 3.5   *P-T-x* (a), *P-T* (b), and *P-x* (c, d, and e) diagrams for a type-III binary mixture. The low-temperature portion of this diagram is omitted. T_{c_I} is the critical temperature of the more volatile component.

in the bubble-point curve represents the location of the LCST. Therefore, one branch of the critical-mixture curve intersects the LLV line precisely at this point, as shown in figure 3.5a.

The *P-x* diagram at temperature T_3 is shown in figure 3.5d. At low pressures a single vapor phase exists. When, at a higher pressure, the dew-point curve of the vapor-liquid envelope is intersected, an equilibrium liquid and a vapor phase are formed. As the pressure is increased further, the three-phase LLV line is intersected, as indicated by the horizontal tie line shown in this diagram. There now exists a single vapor phase and two liquid phases. If the pressure is increased further and if the overall mixture composition is less than x^*, we observe a vapor-liquid envelope very similar to those shown in figure 3.3. A liquid-vapor critical point is observed at a pressure corresponding to the very top of this vapor-liquid envelope. However, if the overall mixture composition is greater than x^*, we observe a liquid-liquid envelope, which is very similar to the vapor-liquid envelope observed for concentrations less than x^*. For this liquid-liquid envelope a liquid-liquid criticality is observed at a pressure corresponding to the very top of the liquid-liquid envelope. At this temperature, then, two critical points are observed, depending on the overall composition of the mixture. In fact, the vapor-liquid and the liquid-liquid critical points both exhibit virtually the same physical characteristics, such as critical opalescence. The P-x diagram of figure 3.5d is also shown in the P-T-x diagram of figure 3.5a. Todd and Elgin (1955) found several examples of type-III mixtures in their early phase-behavior studies with supercritical eth-ylene. Shown in figure 3.6 are P-x diagrams for the ethylene-n-propanol and the ethylene-o-dichlorobenzene systems determined by Todd and Elgin.

If a P-x diagram is constructed at a temperature corresponding to T_4, the phase behavior shown in figure 3.5e is observed. In this instance, the vapor-liquid envelope that exists at low-mixture compositions at pressures above the three-phase pressure shrinks to a horizontal inflection point on the P-x diagram. The tie line shown in figure 3.5e is precisely located at the inflection point of the curve. At T_4, then, only two phases exist over the entire pressure range. Notice that when this P-x diagram is added to the P-T-x diagram in Figure 3.5a the branch of the critical-mixture curve that starts at the critical point of the more volatile component terminates at the inflection point.

At temperatures above T_4 the critical mixture curve is intersected only once. Also, the three-phase LLV line is no longer intersected and, therefore, the simple P-x loops as described for a type-I system are now observed. One such simple P-x loop is shown in Figure 3.5a at temperature T_5. The two branches of the critical-mixture curve are now clearly evident in figure 3.5. The tie lines representing the compositions of the three equilibrium phases in the LLV region project as a single line on the temperature face of the P-T-x diagram. A two-dimensional P-T projection of the P-T-x is shown in Figure 3.5b.

Type IV

Type-IV phase behavior is shown in the P-T diagram of figure 3.1d. Notice that in this case the critical-mixture curve has two branches. However, the branch of the critical-mixture curve that starts at the critical point of the less

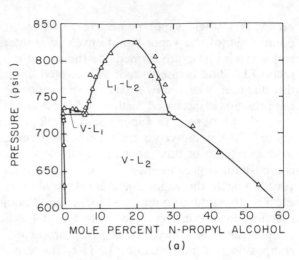

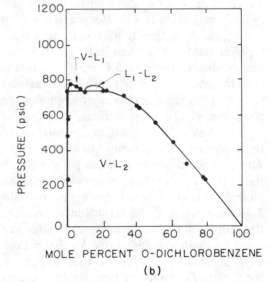

Figure 3.6 Two examples of type-III mixtures found by Todd and Elgin (1955). Both the ethylene-*n*-propanol (a) and the ethylene-*o*-dichlorobenzene (b) systems were obtained at 14.5°C.

volatile component no longer intersects a region of LLV behavior, as it did for type-III phase behavior. The lower-temperature branch of the critical mixture curve is similar to that described for type-III phase behavior.

Type-IV phase behavior in three-dimensional P-T-x space is shown in figure 3.7. Shown in figure 3.7c is the P-x diagram at T_1. At low pressures only a single vapor phase exists. At a higher pressure the dew-point curve is intersected and a liquid and vapor phase now exists. As the pressure is increased further the three-phase LLV line is intersected. If the pressure is increased still further and if the overall mixture composition is less than x^* we observe

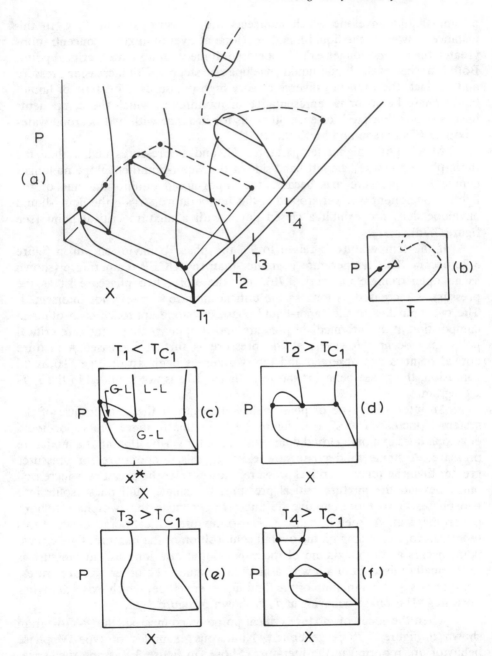

Figure 3.7   *P-T-x* (a), *P-T* (b), and *P-x* (c–f) diagrams for a type-IV binary mixture. In these diagrams G, which denotes a gas, is used interchangeably with V which denotes a vapor. T_{c_1} is the critical temperature of the volatile component.

a vapor-liquid envelope which intersects the pressure axis at P_1^{vap}. In this instance, however, the liquid-liquid envelope at overall mixture concentrations greater than x^* no longer exhibits a closed dome with a mixture critical point. Both branches of the liquid-liquid envelope rise steeply with increasing pressure and, in fact, the branches diverge at very high pressures. This type of liquid-liquid phase behavior is representative of mixtures in which the components have a strong "dislike" for each other, as for instance with hydrocarbon-water mixtures (Culberson and McKetta, 1951).

At a slightly higher temperature, T_2, and at pressures higher than the three-phase pressure, the left-hand side of the vapor-liquid envelope no longer contacts the pressure axis because the vapor-liquid equilibrium line of the lighter component is never crossed at this temperature. Again the liquid-liquid envelope does not exhibit a closed dome with a mixture critical point (see figure 3.7d).

If the temperature is raised to T_3, the phase behavior shown in figure 3.7e occurs. This temperature is greater than the UCEP temperature (shown as an open triangle in figure 3.7b) and, therefore, two phases exist as the pressure is increased as long as the critical-mixture curve is not intersected. The two branches of the vapor-liquid phase envelope approach each other in composition at an intermediate pressure and it appears that a mixture critical point may occur. However, as the pressure is further increased a mixture critical point is not observed and the two curves begin to diverge. To avoid confusion, the phase behavior shown in figure 3.7e is not included in the *P-T-x* diagram.

An interesting type of phase behavior occurs if the temperature of the system is increased to T_4 (see figure 3.7f). In this instance the vapor-liquid envelope does exhibit a closed dome with a mixture critical point at a moderate pressure. A single fluid phase now exists at this temperature for pressures greater than the mixture critical pressure. However, if the pressure is increased much beyond the mixture critical pressure, the single fluid phase splits into two phases. Two representative tie lines are shown in the two-phase regions of this diagram. As seen in figure 3.7f, two mixture critical points occur at this temperature, depending on the overall composition of the mixture. One critical point occurs at the maximum of the vapor-liquid envelope as the pressure is isothermally raised from a low to a moderate value. The other mixture critical point occurs at the minimum of the fluid-liquid envelope, which exists at higher pressures. The phase behavior at T_4 is shown in figure 3.7a.

When the locus of mixture critical points is connected, the *P-T* diagram shown in figure 3.7b is generated. Numerous examples of type-IV phase behavior are reported in the literature. Shown in figure 3.8 is one such case, the carbon dioxide–squalane system (Liphard and Schneider, 1975). Finally we note that the branch of the mixture critical curve that starts at the critical point of the less volatile component can actually have many shapes, as shown in figure 3.9.

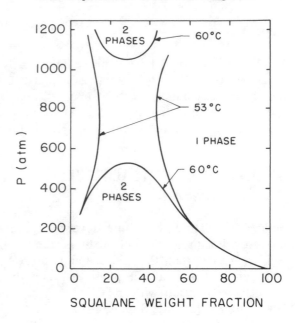

Figure 3.8 *P-x* behavior for the carbon dioxide–squalane system (Liphard and Schneider, 1975). At 53°C the two phases do not merge into a single fluid phase regardless of the pressure level, whereas at 60°C the two phases first merge into a single fluid phase at approximately 500 atm but then split into two phases as the pressure is further increased above about 1,050 atm. These two isotherms are similar to isotherms T_3 and T_4 shown in figures 3.7e and 3.7f.

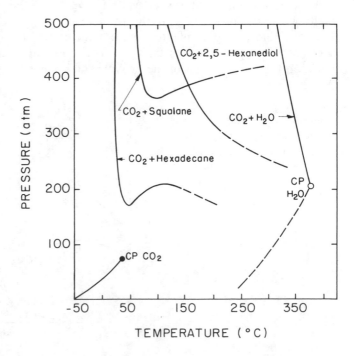

Figure 3.9 Examples of the various types of critical-mixture curves that can occur for a type-IV system (Schneider, 1970). For purposes of clarity the vapor-pressure curves for squalane, hexadecane, and the 2,5-hexanediol are not shown in this figure.

Type V

As shown in figure 3.1e, this phase behavior is very similar to the previously described type-III system. In type-V phase behavior, however, there is no region of liquid immiscibility at temperatures below the LCST. Examples of systems exhibiting this type of behavior include the ethane-ethanol system (McHugh, Mallett, and Kohn, 1983; Kuenen and Robson, 1899).

SOLID–SUPERCRITICAL FLUID PHASE DIAGRAMS

Solid-SCF mixtures constitute a very large and important subset of binary mixtures. For these types of mixtures, the normal melting temperature of the solid is greater than the critical temperature of the SCF. It is instructive to consider the two solid-SCF phase diagrams that depict those cases in which a solid is in equilibrium with an SCF to very high pressures (Diepen and Scheffer, 1948a; McHugh, 1981; Streett, 1976).

　　In the following descriptions of solid-supercritical fluid phase diagrams the designations vapor (V) and gas (G) are used interchangeably. Shown in figure 3.10 is the simplest *P-T* diagram of a solid-SCF system. Curves *CD* and *MH* are the pure-component vapor-pressure curves of the light (SCF) and heavy (solid) component, respectively. Curve *MN* is the pure heavy-component melting curve, and curve *EM* the pure heavy-component sublimation curve. Points *D* and *H* represent pure-component critical points. The distinguishing trait for this type system is that the critical-mixture curve runs continuously between the critical point of the heavier component to the critical point of the

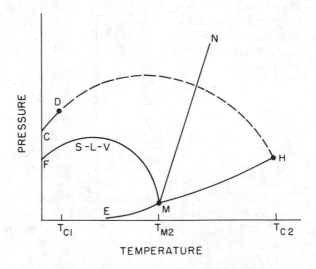

Figure 3.10　*P-T* diagram for a heavy solid–supercritical fluid system. In this instance the SLV curve is a continuous curve.

lighter component. Also, a continuous three-phase solid-liquid-vapor (SLV) line is observed. This SLV line begins at the normal melting point of the heavy component, bends back toward lower temperatures as the pressure is increased, and finally ends at a temperature usually well below the critical temperature of the lighter component. As shown in this diagram, increasing hydrostatic pressure normally increases the melting point of the pure solid. However, when the solid is compressed in the presence of an SCF, the melting point of the solid usually decreases with increasing pressure. The reason for this melting-point (or freezing-point) depression is analogous to the reason water freezes below its normal freezing point when salt is added to the water. As the pressure increases, more and more gas dissolves in the heavy liquid phase. Therefore, the temperature needed to freeze the heavy solid decreases substantially (de Swaan Arons and Diepen, 1963). This depression of the solid melting point is manifested as an SLV line as shown in figure 3.10.

Shown in figure 3.11a is the *P-T-x* diagram for this type of solid-SCF system. The phase behavior depicted in figure 3.11c is observed if a *P-x* diagram is experimentally determined at T_1, a temperature below the critical temperature of the lighter component T_{C1}. At low pressures solid-vapor equilibria are observed until the three-phase SLV line is intersected. At this pressure there exists three equilibrium phases, a pure solid, a liquid, and a gas.

If the overall mixture composition is less than that of the liquid phase, then a vapor-liquid envelope is observed as the pressure is further increased. The vapor-liquid envelope eventually intersects the pressure axis at the vapor pressure of pure component 1, since T_1 is less than the critical temperature of component 1. If the overall mixture composition is greater than that of the liquid phase, then liquid-solid equilibria exist as the pressure is increased above the three-phase pressure. The isothermal *P-x* phase behavior at T_1 is also shown in figure 3.11a.

If the temperature is increased to T_2, a temperature greater than the critical temperature of component 1, the phase behavior shown in figure 3.11d is observed. In this instance, note that the left-hand side of the vapor-liquid envelope no longer contacts the pressure axis and that a vapor-liquid mixture critical point occurs at the highest pressure of the vapor-liquid envelope. The vapor-liquid envelope is also much larger at T_2 than at T_1, because of the higher operating temperature. Again, there is liquid-solid phase equilibria at pressures above the SLV-line pressure for mixtures rich in the heavy component. Notice, also, that the concentration of heavy component in the liquid phase has increased substantially as a result of the higher operating temperature. This *P-x* phase behavior is also included in the three-dimensional diagram of figure 3.11a (Rowlinson and Richardson, 1958).

If an operating point is chosen that is much greater than the normal melting point of the heavy component, then the much simpler phase behavior depicted in figure 3.11e occurs. In this case the straightforward vapor-liquid envelope is observed with a mixture critical point at the highest pressure of the envelope. Figure 3.11b is obtained if the constant pressure tie-lines rep-

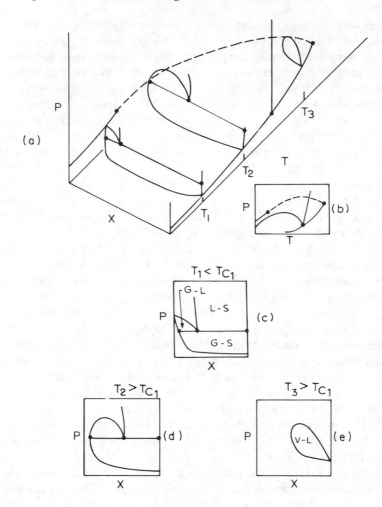

Figure 3.11   *P-T-x* (a), *P-T* (b), and *P-x* (c–e) diagrams for the heavy solid–supercritical fluid system depicted in figure 3.10. T_{c_1} is the critical temperature of the more volatile component.

resenting three phase SLV equilibrium in figure 3.11a are projected onto the temperature face of the *P-T-x* diagram along with the projections of the critical-mixture curve and the pure-component equilibrium curves.

Numerous examples of this type of solid-SCF phase behavior are reported in the literature. Normally this type of phase behavior occurs for mixtures whose components are chemically similar. Shown in figure 3.12 is one example of such a solid-SCF system (Donnelly and Katz, 1954).

The previously described solid-SCF phase behavior represents the simpler of two possible types. In the case of the other type of solid-SCF phase behavior, the SLV line is no longer a continuous curve and the critical-mixture curve is

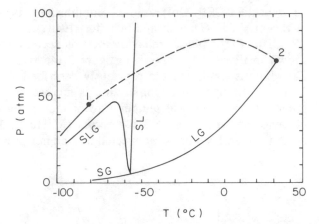

Figure 3.12 *P-T* diagram for the methane–carbon dioxide system (Donnelly and Katz, 1954). Component 1 represents methane and component 2 represents carbon dioxide.

also no longer continuous. This second type of solid-SCF phase behavior, which is shown in figure 3.13, usually occurs when the solid and the SCF differ considerably in molecular size, shape, or polarity. In fact, the ethylene-naphthalene system briefly described in chapter 1 falls into this category of phase behavior. In descriptive terms, this type of solid-SCF phase behavior occurs for systems in which the two components of the system do not "like" each other nearly as much as they do in the previously described solid-SCF system. In this second type of system the light gas is not very soluble in the heavy liquid, even at high pressures. Therefore, the melting-point depression of the heavy solid is not extremely large. The branch of the three-phase SLV line starting at the normal melting point of the heavy solid does not bend toward lower temperatures with increasing pressure, but instead it rises steeply with increasing pressure and it intersects the critical-mixture curve at a UCEP. The other, lower-temperature branch of the SLV line intersects the critical-mixture

Figure 3.13 *P-T* diagram for a mixture consisting of a heavy nonvolatile solid and a light supercritical fluid solvent whose critical temperature is less than the melting point of the solid. Note that the SLV curve is no longer continuous.

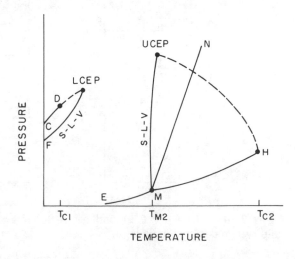

curve at the LCEP. Only solid-gas equilibria exists between these two branches of the SLV line (Diepen and Scheffer, 1948a).

The *P-T-x* phase behavior for this second type of solid-SCF system is shown in figure 3.14. Shown in figure 3.14a is a *P-x* diagram at temperature T_1, which is similar to the previously described *P-x* diagram shown in figure 3.11c. If the operating temperature is increased to a temperature T_2 slightly greater than the critical temperature of the lighter component T_{CI}, the phase behavior shown in figure 3.14c occurs (McHugh, 1981). At this higher temperature the SLV line is intersected at a higher pressure. Notice, also, that the

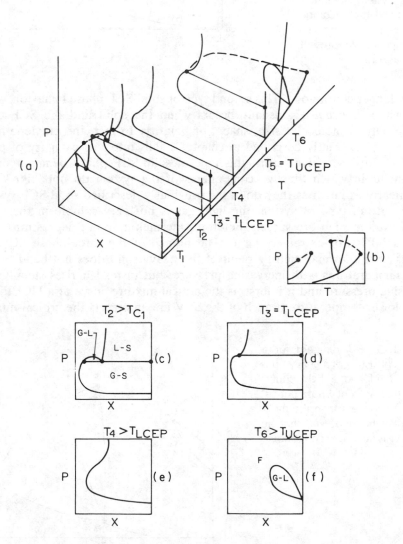

Figure 3.14   *P-T-x* (a), *P-T* (b), and *P-x* (c–f) diagrams for the binary solid–supercritical fluid system depicted in figure 3.13.

vapor-liquid envelope has shrunk considerably and that the pressure of the vapor-liquid mixture critical point is only slightly greater than the three-phase pressure. This *P-x* diagram is incorporated in the *P-T-x* diagram of figure 3.14a.

If the operating temperature is now increased to T_3, the phase behavior shown in figure 3.14d occurs. At T_3 the mixture critical-point pressure of the vapor-liquid envelope occurs precisely at the same pressure at which the three-phase SLV line is intersected. Hence, a vapor-liquid mixture critical point is observed in the presence of excess solid. This vapor-liquid, mixture critical point in the presence of excess solid is the lower critical end point (LCEP) (Diepen and Scheffer, 1948a). If the temperature is increased slightly above the LCEP temperature, only solid-SCF phase behavior is observed at all pressures, since the three-phase (SLV) line ends at the LCEP.

A schematic representation of solid-SCF phase behavior is shown in figure 3.14e. The curve shown in this figure represents the solubility of the heavy solid in the SCF phase. By operating at a temperature in close proximity to the LCEP temperature, the solid solubility curve shows an inflection (i.e., a solubility enhancement) at pressures close to the LCEP pressure. At any vapor-liquid critical point the vapor (or dew point) curve must exhibit a zero slope on a *P-x* diagram (i.e., $(dP/dx)_T = 0$ [Rowlinson and Swinton, 1982]). Therefore, at the LCEP the solubility of the heavy component in the vapor (or gas) phase increases very rapidly. If the temperature is increased slightly above T_{LCEP} a vapor-liquid envelope no longer exists as shown in figure 3.14e. The solid solubility isotherm is influenced by the vapor-liquid critical behavior at the LCEP and it also tries to exhibit a zero slope in *P-x* space (i.e., it also tries to exhibit a large solubility enhancement). Referring to figure 1.3 in chapter 1, we can now explain the sudden increase in the solubility of naphthalene in supercritical ethylene at approximately 50 atm and 12°C. This solubility increase is a result of being very close to the LCEP for this system, which is 10.7°C and 51.2 atm (Diepen and Scheffer, 1948a). As shown in table 3.3, the LCEP usually occurs very close to the critical point of the pure SCF for most of the solid-SCF systems reported in the literature, and even though there is a large solubility enhancement the amount of solid in the SCF phase at the LCEP is quite low.

If the temperature is increased the solubility of heavy solid will increase as shown previously in figure 1.3. One cannot, however, indefinitely raise the system temperature to increase the solubility of the solid in the SCF phase, because the other branch of the SLV line appears at a higher temperature. The other branch of the SLV line begins at the normal melting temperature of the heavy solid and ends at the intersection of the critical-mixture curve with the SLV line at the upper critical end point (UCEP). At the UCEP, a vapor-liquid mixture critical point occurs in the presence of excess solid, similar to the phase behavior observed at the LCEP. At temperatures slightly below the UCEP temperature, a large solid-solubility enhancement is observed in the vicinity of the UCEP pressure as a result of the vapor-liquid mixture critical-point behavior. As shown in table 3.3, the solubility of a heavy solid in the

Table 3.3 Experimentally Observed LCEPs and UCEPs for Binary Mixtures

System Component 1 + Component 2	Component 1 T_c °C	Component 1 P_c atm	LCEP T °C	LCEP P atm	UCEP T °C	UCEP P atm	UCEP mole-%
ethylene + naphthalene[a,c]	9.2	49.7	10.7	51.2	52.1	174.2	16.8
ethylene + biphenyl[a,f]			11.2	51.0	41.6	225.5	*
ethylene + anthracene[e]			9.4	50.5	*	*	*
ethylene + octacosane[a,f]			9.5	49.9	43.0	206.4	*
ethylene + hexaethylbenzene[e]			11.6	52.2	*	*	*
ethylene + hexamethylbenzene[e]			9.8	50.4	*	*	*
ethylene + stilbene[e]			9.5	50.2	*	*	*
ethylene + dinitrobenzene[e]			9.3	50.0	*	*	*
ethylene + hexachloroethane[e]			12.4	52.7	*	*	*
ethylene + 1,3,5-trichlorobenzene[f]			13.1	52.7	*	*	*
ethylene + p-chlorobromobenzene[f]			13.4	53.1	*	*	*
ethylene + p-chloroiodobenzene[f]			12.0	51.9	*	*	*
ethylene + p-dibromobenzene[f]			10.6	50.7	*	*	*
ethylene + hexatriacontane[f]			9.6	49.9	*	*	*
ethylene + benzophenone[f]			9.9	50.2	*	*	*
methane + naphthalene[c]	−82.6	45.4	*	*	87.3	1303.0	18.5

ethane + naphthalene[a,d]	32.2	48.2	36.8	51.5	56.5	122.5	19.8
ethane + biphenyl[a]			*	*	48.7	196.5	*
ethane + octacosane[a]			*	*	38.9	86.4	*
CO_2 + naphthalene[a]	31.0	72.8	*	*	60.1	252.7	~16.0
CO_2 + biphenyl[a]			*	*	55.1	469.0	~17.0
CO_2 + octacosane[a,b]			32.2	72.6	*	*	*

[a]McHugh and Yogan (1984).
[b]McHugh, Seckner, and Krukonis (1984).
[c]van Hest and Diepen (1963).
[d]van Welie and Diepen (1963).
[e]van Gunst, Scheffer, and Diepen (1953a).
[f]Diepen and Scheffer (1948a).
*No data available

SCF phase can be very large near the UCEP (van Welie and Diepen, 1961c; van Hest and Diepen, 1963; McHugh and Paulaitis, 1980). A *P-x* isotherm precisely at T_{UCEP} is shown in figure 3.14a. Notice that this isotherm looks similar to that in figure 3.14d. At temperatures greater than the melting temperature of the heavy solid, the now familiar vapor-liquid envelope is observed, as shown in figure 3.14f at T_6. Figure 3.14b is obtained if the constant pressure tie-lines representing three phase SLV equilibrium in figure 3.14a are projected onto the temperature face of the *P-T-x* diagram along with the projections of the critical mixture curves and the pure component equilibrium curves.

As noted by McHugh and Paulaitis, very different high-pressure phase behavior can occur for solid-SCF mixtures that are superficially quite similar (McHugh, 1981; McHugh, Seckner, and Krukonis, 1984; McHugh, 1986; Paulaitis, McHugh, and Chai, 1983). For instance, let us compare the solid-solubility behavior for the naphthalene-ethylene system (Diepen and Scheffer, 1953) with that of the biphenyl–carbon dioxide system (McHugh, 1981; McHugh and Yogan, 1984). Both naphthalene and biphenyl are heavy, nonvolatile solids with melting temperatures well above room temperature, 80.2° and 69.5°C, respectively. And both ethylene and carbon dioxide are light gases at ambient conditions with relatively mild critical conditions, 9.3°C and 49.7 atm and 31.1°C and 72.8 atm, respectively. Hence, one might expect the characteristic shapes of the solid-solubility isotherms of these two systems to be quite similar.

Shown in figure 3.15a are three solubility isotherms for the naphthalene-ethylene system. Notice that the 50°C isotherm exhibits a large solubility enhancement, which is sensitive to small changes in pressure around 175 atm. Notice also that for an isobar of approximately 200 atm the increase in the solubility of naphthalene in ethylene from 45° to 50°C is substantially greater than that from 25° to 45°C. The sensitivity of the solubility to small changes in pressure as well as temperature near 175 atm and 50°C is a consequence of being extremely close to the naphthalene-ethylene UCEP, 52.1°C and 175 atm (Diepen and Scheffer, 1948a, 1948b, 1953). Also, the loading of naphthalene in supercritical ethylene can be quite substantial near the UCEP (i.e., 15 mol-% naphthalene corresponds to approximately 45 wt-% naphthalene in supercritical ethylene).

Now compare the solubility behavior of the previously described naphthalene-ethylene system with that exhibited by the biphenyl–carbon dioxide system shown in figure 3.16a. For example, the 55°C isotherm has certain characteristics that are similar to the 50°C isotherm of the naphthalene-ethylene system shown in figure 3.15a. The 55°C isotherm exhibits a large solubility enhancement that is sensitive to small changes in pressure near 460 atm. The isobaric solubility behavior of the biphenyl–carbon dioxide system near 450 atm is similar to that of the naphthalene-ethylene system near 200 atm. The increase in the solubility of biphenyl in supercritical carbon dioxide from 50° to 55°C is substantially greater than the increase from 36° to 50°C. The sensitivity of the solubility to small changes in pressure as well as tem-

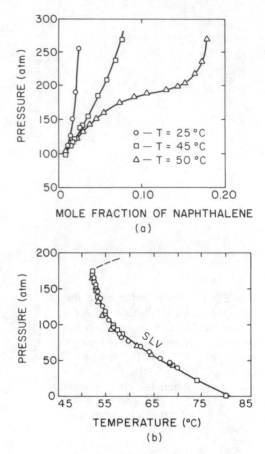

Figure 3.15 Phase behavior of the naphthalene-ethylene system: (a) the solubility of naphthalene in supercritical ethylene at temperatures of 25°C, 45°C, and 50°C (Diepen and Scheffer, 1948a, 1948b); (b) the *P-T* projection of the naphthalene-ethylene three-phase SLV line ending at the mixture UCEP (van Gunst, Scheffer, and Diepen, 1953a, 1953b).

perature near 460 atm and 55°C is a consequence of being extremely close to the biphenyl–carbon dioxide UCEP, 55.1°C and 469.0 atm (McHugh, 1981; McHugh and Yogan, 1984; McHugh and Paulaitis, 1980). Also, as with the naphthalene-ethylene system, the loading of biphenyl in supercritical carbon dioxide is very high near the mixture UCEP (i.e., 15 mol-% biphenyl is equivalent to approximately 32.8 wt-% biphenyl in supercritical carbon dioxide).

The similarity in *P-x* behavior near the UCEP for naphthalene-ethylene and biphenyl–carbon dioxide suggests that the location of the UCEP can be estimated solely from solubility data. Hence, it is possible to assume (incorrectly) that the solubility data of both the naphthalene-ethylene and the biphenyl–carbon dioxide systems represent solid solubilities in a supercritical fluid solvent. Notice, however, that the *P-x* behavior for these systems is very different at pressures greater than their respective UCEP pressures. At 55°C and at pressures greater than 460 atm, the solubility of biphenyl in supercritical carbon dioxide decreases dramatically for a small increase in pressure; at 50°C and at pressures greater than 174 atm, the solubility of naphthalene in super-

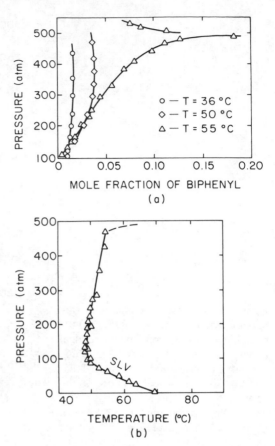

Figure 3.16 Phase behavior of the biphenyl–carbon dioxide system: (a) the solubility of biphenyl in supercritical carbon dioxide at temperatures of 36°C, 50°C, and 55°C (McHugh, n.d.); (b) the *P-T* projection of the biphenyl–carbon dioxide three-phase SLV line ending at the mixture UCEP (McHugh and Yogan, 1984).

critical ethylene increases for a small increase in pressure until at higher pressures the solubility eventually reaches a limiting value.

Obviously these two systems are not entirely identical. How can we explain these experimental observations?

The differences in the solubility behavior of the naphthalene-ethylene and biphenyl–carbon dioxide systems near their mixture UCEPs can be readily explained by considering the *P-T* trace of the three-phase SLV line for each system. Shown in figure 3.15b is the *P-T* trace of the SLV line along with the *P-x* isotherms for the naphthalene-ethylene system. Shown in figure 3.16b are the similar diagrams for the biphenyl–carbon dioxide system. Note that the biphenyl–carbon dioxide SLV line exhibits a temperature minimum with increasing pressure, whereas the naphthalene-ethylene SLV line does not exhibit such a minimum. The different shapes of the SLV lines is a consequence of the amount of "like" or "dislike" that the components of the mixture have for each other. The reason for the differences in the solubility behavior for these two systems near their UCEPs is directly related to the mutual solubility (i.e., "like" or "dislike") of the mixture components.

The naphthalene-ethylene solubility behavior can be explained by examining the *P-T* and *P-x* diagrams shown in figure 3.17. Shown schematically in figure 3.17b is the solubility behavior of naphthalene in supercritical ethylene at a temperature greater than the UCEP temperature. Solid-gas equilibria exist at low pressures until the three-phase SLV line is intersected. The equilibrium vapor, liquid, and solid phases are depicted as points on the horizontal tie line at pressure P_d. As the pressure is further increased a vapor-liquid envelope is observed for overall mixture concentrations less than x_L. A critical-mixture point is observed for this vapor-liquid envelope, as described earlier. If the

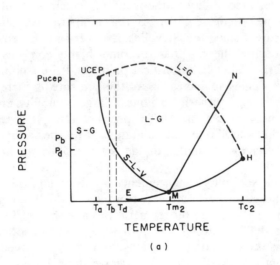

(a)

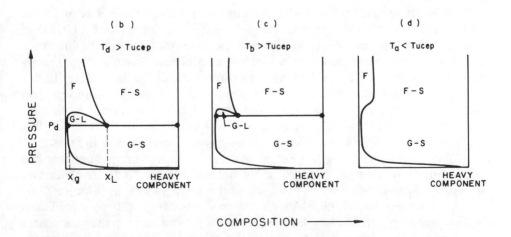

Figure 3.17 Schematic *P-T* (a) and *P-x* (b–d) diagrams for the naphthalene-ethylene system (McHugh, 1981).

overall mixture composition is greater than x_L, then solid-gas equilibria are observed as the pressure is increased above P_d.

Shown in figure 3.17c is a solubility isotherm at a temperature, T_b, that is less than the previous temperature, T_d, but still higher than the UCEP temperature. The solubility behavior at T_b is similar to that in figure 3.17b. However, at T_b the three-phase SLV line is intersected at a higher pressure, which is closer to the UCEP pressure. Hence, the vapor-liquid envelope has diminished in size. Also, the solid-gas equilibrium curve is shifted toward higher solvent concentrations. As a result, the solid-gas curve is now much closer to the vapor branch of the vapor-liquid envelope.

Now consider a solubility isotherm at T_a, which is slightly less than the UCEP temperature (figure 3.17d). At this temperature solid-gas equilibria exist at all pressures, since the SLV line is never intersected. As the UCEP pressure is approached the gas phase becomes highly compressible because of the influence of the vapor-liquid critical point, and the solubility of the solid in the gas phase begins to increase. As the pressure is increased above the UCEP pressure the T_a isotherm exhibits a large solubility enhancement. At pressures much higher than the UCEP pressure the gas is less compressible and, therefore, the solubility of the solid quickly reaches a limiting value. This solid-solubility behavior is similar to that of the 50°C naphthalene-ethylene isotherm.

Less dramatic solubility enhancements are observed for isotherms at lower temperatures, those further removed from the UCEP temperature. Solid-solubility isotherms at these lower temperatures are observed to have the same characteristics as the 25° and 45°C naphthalene-ethylene isotherms (see figure 3.15a). Hence, as the operating conditions are further removed in temperature and pressure from the UCEP, the less sensitive the solid-solubility isotherm is to changes in pressure or temperature.

Now let us use *P-T* and *P-x* diagrams to examine the behavior of the biphenyl–carbon dioxide system. The solubility behavior near the UCEP of the biphenyl–carbon dioxide system differs from that of the naphthalene-ethylene system because of the temperature minimum exhibited by the biphenyl–carbon dioxide SLV line, as shown schematically in figure 3.18. In this instance we will first consider a solubility isotherm at a temperature less than the UCEP temperature and then proceed to higher-temperature isotherms. The solubility isotherms at temperatures below the minimum in the SLV line are of little interest in this case because solid-gas equilibria exist at all pressures.

Shown in figure 3.19a is a *P-x* isotherm at a temperature greater than the temperature minimum of the SLV line but still less than the UCEP temperature. A variety of phase behaviors is exhibited at this temperature, as is indicated by the two intersections of the SLV line. At low pressures solid-gas equilibrium is maintained until the system reaches pressure P_a. The three equilibrium phases are depicted by a horizontal tie line in this diagram. Depending on the concentration of the overall mixture, either liquid-gas, solid-liquid, or a single liquid phase exists as the pressure is increased. With increasing pressure the

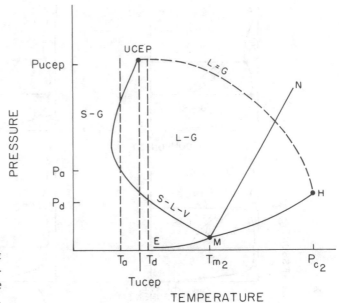

Figure 3.18 Schematic *P-T* diagram for the biphenyl–carbon dioxide system (McHugh, 1981).

solid-liquid equilibrium curve bends back toward compositions richer in the light component. Eventually it merges with the liquid branch of the liquid-gas loop, where the three-phase line is again intersected at a higher pressure. At this point the liquid and gas phases are closer in composition than they are at the point represented by the intersection of the three-phase line at the lower pressure. As the pressure is increased above the three-phase pressure, solid-fluid equilibrium is maintained. At these high pressures the fluid phase, which is now less compressible, quickly attains a limiting solubility value.

Shown as a solid line in figure 3.19b is the portion of the solubility isotherm that is obtained if only the SCF phase is sampled while solubilities are determined and if the phases at equilibrium are not visually detected. (Techniques for visually determining high-pressure phase behavior are described in chapter 4.) The solid line starting at pressures greater than the critical pressure of the light component represents the solubility of the heavy component in the SCF phase at a temperature greater than the temperature minimum of the three-phase line but still less than the UCEP temperature. The dashed lines show all possible phase behaviors, as described in figure 3.19a. It is evident from this figure that a vast majority of phase-behavior information is missed when only the solubility of the heavy component in the SCF phase is determined. Also, it is self-evident that the solubility of the heavy component in the SCF phase represents liquid solubilities at low to moderate pressures and solid solubilities at elevated pressures. Referring back to figure 3.16, it should also now be obvious that the 50°C biphenyl–carbon dioxide isotherm represents the solubility of liquid biphenyl in carbon dioxide for

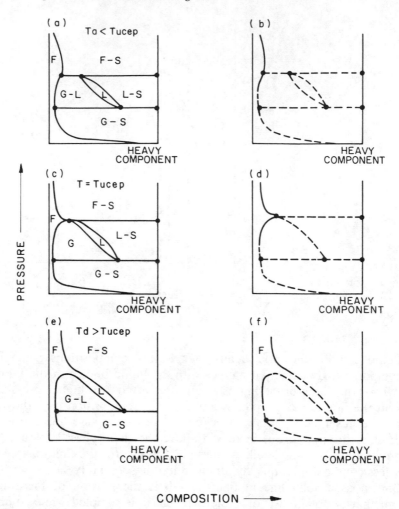

Figure 3.19   Schematic *P*-*x* diagrams for the carbon dioxide–biphenyl system (McHugh, 1981).

pressures up to approximately 300 atm and of solid biphenyl for pressures greater than 300 atm.

Now consider the case depicted in figure 3.19c, which shows an isotherm precisely at the UCEP temperature (see figure 3.18). At the UCEP pressure the solid-liquid equilibrium curve must intersect the liquid-gas loop precisely at the binary liquid-gas critical point. Therefore, it approaches a negative horizontal inflection at the UCEP pressure. Notice that in this case the vapor-liquid envelope has not shrunk to a point, as it did for the naphthalene-ethylene case at its UCEP. Shown in figure 3.19d as a solid curve is the solubility isotherm obtained if only the solubility in the SCF phase is determined. This solid curve has the characteristics of the 55°C biphenyl–carbon dioxide isotherm as shown in figure 3.16. Hence, the 55°C isotherm represents liquid biphenyl solubilities at pressures below about 450 atm and solid biphenyl solubilities at pressures above 450 atm.

For the naphthalene-ethylene and biphenyl–carbon dioxide systems the effect of the binary liquid-gas critical point is rapidly diminished as the pressure is increased above the UCEP pressure. For the naphthalene-ethylene system, where the UCEP pressure is not extremely high, the solid-fluid equilibrium curve quickly attains a limiting solubility at pressures greater than the UCEP pressure. However, for the biphenyl–carbon dioxide system, where the UCEP pressure is more than twice that of the naphthalene-ethylene system, the solid-fluid equilibrium curve decreases sharply to lower heavy-component concentrations as the pressure is increased above the UCEP pressure. This solubility behavior is a consequence of a free-volume effect resulting from the large disparity in size between biphenyl and carbon dioxide (Rance and Cussler, 1974; von Tapavicza and Prausnitz, 1976). At very high pressures, increasing the pressure further reduces the free volume between carbon dioxide molecules available to the biphenyl molecules and hence reduces the solubility of biphenyl.

Shown in figure 3.19e is the solubility behavior at a temperature well above the UCEP temperature (see figure 3.18). As seen in this diagram, a variety of phase behaviors can exist at high pressures. Also note that now the liquid-solid equilibrium curve does not reintersect the liquid-gas envelope at high pressures, since the SLV line is not reintersected at high pressures.

A number of solid-SCF systems have been reported in which a temperature minimum exists in the three-phase SLV line (van Hest and Diepen, 1963; McHugh and Yogan, 1984). Some examples are shown in figure 3.20. It is very important to be aware that a high-melting solid can melt at relatively mild temperatures when in contact with a supercritical fluid at high pressures. For instance, King and co-workers describe a spectroscopic technique for obtaining solid-solubility data at high pressures; the solubility data were subsequently used to calculate the second cross-virial coefficient for the solid-SCF mixture (King and Robertson, 1962; Najour and King, 1966). However, their thermodynamic analysis of the data is wrong in some cases. They did not recognize that the heavy solid had, in fact, melted at certain experimental temperatures and pressures. If only solubility data are obtained it may not be possible to discern whether the solid had melted on the basis of the shape of the solubility isotherm. For example, by inspection of the 50°C biphenyl–carbon dioxide isotherm in figure 3.16, it is virtually impossible to determine whether the solubility data at this temperature represent solid-SCF or liquid-SCF equilibria.

Another pitfall awaits the experimentalist who is unaware of the melting behavior of a heavy solid under the influence of an SCF. It is possible that the liquid phase that is formed when the solid melts can be less dense than the SCF phase. If this density inversion occurs, the heavy liquid phase would be pushed out of the extractor by the SCF-rich phase in a flow-type experiment. Such a density inversion is observed by McHugh and co-workers for the carbon

Figure 3.20 Examples of binary solid–supercritical fluid systems with a temperature minimum in the SLV line: (a) carbon dioxide–solid systems (McHugh and Yogan, 1984);   (b) methane-naphthalene system (van Hest and Diepen, 1963).

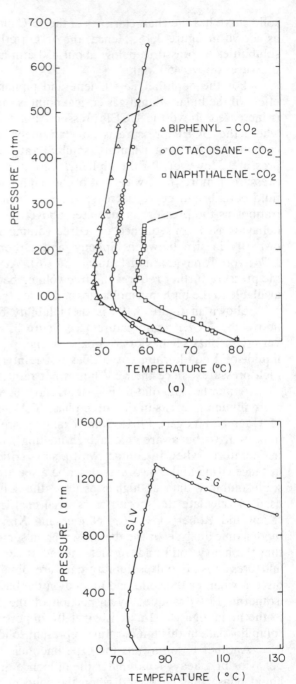

(a)

(b)

dioxide–octacosane system (McHugh and Yogan, 1984). At 52°C and at pressures above about 260 atm, the carbon dioxide–rich "gas" phase becomes more dense than the octacosane-rich liquid phase. The *P-T* and *P-x* diagrams for this system are shown in figure 3.21. McHugh, Seckner, and Krukonis (1984)

Figure 3.21 Phase behavior of the carbon dioxide–octacosane system (McHugh, Seckner, and Yogan, 1984): (a) *P-T* trace of the SLV lines; (b) *P-x* diagram. The pressure limitation of the equipment was reached before the UCEP was obtained.

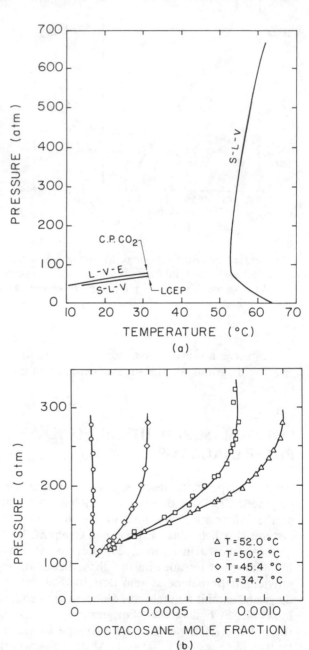

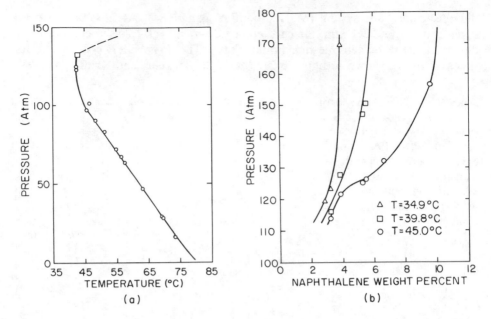

Figure 3.22 Phase behavior of the xenon-naphthalene system (Krukonis, McHugh, and Seckner, 1984): (a) *P-T* trace of the SLV line starting at the normal melting point; (b) *P-x* diagram. The open square in (a) represents an estimate for the location of the UCEP.

also observe a density inversion for the xenon-naphthalene system. The *P-T* and *P-x* diagrams for the supercritical xenon-naphthalene system are shown in figure 3.22.

POLYMER–SUPERCRITICAL FLUID PHASE DIAGRAMS

Another important subset of phase diagrams for binary mixtures is the set of polymer-SCF phase diagrams. Ehrlich and co-workers have published the bulk of the information available in the literature on high-pressure polymer-SCF systems (Ehrlich, 1965; Ehrlich and Graham, 1960; Ehrlich and Kurpen, 1963).

As shown in figure 3.23, polymer-SCF systems having a solidification boundary that intrudes on the phase behavior are schematically similar to the ethylene-naphthalene system described above. However, polymer-SCF phase diagrams exhibit a number of different characteristics as compared with smaller molecule–SCF diagrams. For instance, notice that the pressures needed for the polymer-SCF vapor-liquid envelope to exhibit a mixture critical point can be well in excess of 1,200 atm. Also, the concentration of polymer in the SCF-

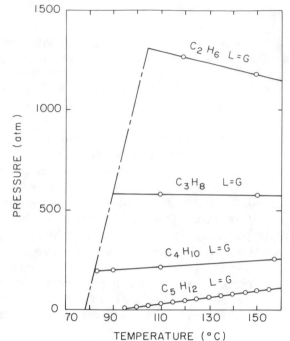

Figure 3.23 Phase behavior of several polyethylene–supercritical fluid mixtures (Ehrlich and Kurpen, 1963). The broken line is a representation of the SLV line. The L = G lines represent the system's critical-mixture curve. The molecular weight of the polyethylene is 250,000.

rich phase even at these elevated pressures is usually quite low, on the order of a few weight percent.

It should also be noted that the SLV line observed for the naphthalene-ethylene system is more appropriately termed a "crystallization boundary" for a polymer-SCF system. Because of the large size of polymer molecules and the distribution of the polymer's molecular weight, the crystalline solid polymer does not melt and solidify at precisely the same temperature. Also, the melting-point depression of the solid polymer is much less than that exhibited by other low-molecular-weight solids, since the solubility of the SCF in the polymer liquid is quite low. Unlike other crystalline solids, such as naphthalene, solid polymers that are only partially crystalline can sorb a considerable amount of solvent and, as a result, can undergo morphological changes (i.e., swelling as well as internal structure rearrangement). The sorption of the solvent occurs in the amorphous regions of the polymer.

Both the molecular weight and the molecular-weight distribution of the polymer have a dramatic effect on polymer-solvent phase behavior. Research shows that a polydisperse molecular-weight distribution shifts the mixture's vapor-liquid critical point for various polyethylene-ethylene mixtures from the maximum of the pressure-composition curve to a point on the curve at much higher concentrations of polymer (de Loos, Poot, and Diepen, 1983). This shift in the critical-mixture composition causes problems when the phase behavior is modeled. Also, not surprisingly, an increase in the average molecular weight of the polymer increases the pressure needed for the vapor-liquid envelope to exhibit a mixture critical point.

The phase behavior for a pseudobinary polymer-solvent mixture, in which a solid polymer phase is not observed, follows type-III classification (Freeman and Rowlinson, 1960; Allen and Baker, 1965; Baker, Clemson, and Allen, 1966; Zeman et al., 1972; Zeman and Patterson, 1972; Siow, Delmas, and Patterson, 1972; McHugh and Guckes, 1985; McClellan, Bauman, and Mc-Hugh, 1985; McClellan and McHugh, 1986. This type of polymer-solvent phase behavior forms the basis for a separation process for recovering polymer from its solvent (to be described in detail in chapters 6 and 10) and for the deasphalting of petroleum liquids (described in chapter 7).

As shown in figure 3.24, the only topological difference between a polymer-solvent phase diagram and the previously described phase diagram for a type-III mixture is that the LLV line in a polymer-solvent system projects onto the vapor-liquid equilibrium curve for the pure solvent. If the polymer's molecular-weight distribution is quite large, the LLV line becomes an area. Hence, the LLV line shown in figure 3.24 represents the highest pressure at which three phases exist for a highly polydisperse system.

The nomenclature used to describe polymer-solvent phase diagrams differs slightly from that used for type-III binary mixtures. For a polymer-solvent system the branch of the critical-mixture curve very close to the critical point of the solvent is now called the "lower critical-solution temperature (LCST) curve." The intersection of the LCST curve with the LLV line that was formerly designated the LCST is now called the "lower critical end point (LCEP)." Numerous examples of polymer-solvent phase diagrams are available in the literature. Some of these systems are described in detail in chapers 6 and 10.

Figure 3.24   Phase behavior of a polymer–organic solvent mixture (McClellan, Bauman, and Mc-Hugh, 1985). The inset in this diagram shows the full phase diagram; the area outlined by the dashed line is expanded to show more detail near the critical point of the solvent.

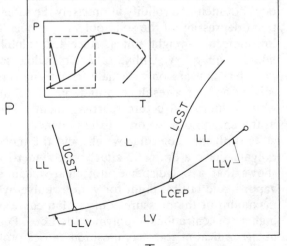

PHASE DIAGRAMS FOR TERNARY MIXTURES

In the 1950s Francis compiled what is probably the single largest collection of ternary phase diagrams for mixtures with carbon dioxide at 25°C and its saturation pressure (Francis, 1954). Although Francis did not extend his phase-behavior studies into the critical region of carbon dioxide, his work does provide a basis for obtaining a qualitative estimate of the ability of supercritical carbon dioxide to separate a wide variety of binary mixtures. Recently, Dandge, Heller, and Wilson (1985) reformulated Francis's work in a manner which describes the effect of functional groups on the solubility behavior of carbon dioxide–solute systems. More will be said about the factors affecting the phase behavior of SCF-solute mixtures in a later chapter.

Unfortunately, the number of ternary phase diagrams reported in the literature for mixtures in which one of the components is a supercritical fluid is much more scarce than are low-pressure ternary phase diagrams. However, a compilation of supercritical ethylene–water–organic solvent phase diagrams can be found in the work of Elgin and co-workers (Elgin and Weinstock, 1959; Weinstock, 1952). Elgin and co-workers also report on the phase behavior of a large number of binary SCF–organic solvent mixtures with the objective of extrapolating binary phase behavior to ternary systems at conditions very near the critical point of the SCF (Chappelear, 1960; Close, 1951; Todd, 1952). It is instructive to consider the phase-behavior classification scheme for ternary systems consisting of an organic solvent (S), water (H_2O), and ethylene (C_2H_4), as these basic phase-diagram constructions are similar for other SCF-solvent mixtures. They group the ternary phase diagrams into three classes based on the appearance of LLV regions which occur for the ternary mixture.

Type I

Ternary phase behavior of type I is shown in figure 3.25. The three diagrams in this figure represent mixtures at a fixed temperature slightly higher than the critical temperature of ethylene. The distinguishing feature of type-I ternary phase behavior is the absence of LLV immiscibility regions within the ternary diagram. The phase behavior for this system at atmospheric pressure is shown in figure 3.25a. At this pressure water is miscible in all proportions with the organic solvent, while ethylene is virtually insoluble in water and only slightly soluble in the organic solvent. The solubility curve has a slight curvature to it, reflecting the solubility of ethylene in the solvent. The tie line shown in this diagram indicates that the gas phase is virtually pure ethylene at this temperature and pressure. Strictly speaking there should be a very small single phase vapor region very near 100% C_2H_4 in figures 3.25a and b. However, since the temperature is so low the vapor pressures of the organic solvent and the water

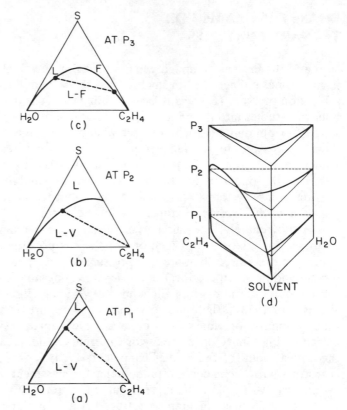

Figure 3.25 Phase diagrams of a type-I ternary mixture (Weinstock, 1952).

are extremely low and, therefore, the vapor phases in figures 3.25a and b are virtually pure C_2H_4 and the single vapor region is extremely small.

In figure 3.25b the pressure of the system has been increased to a point slightly below the critical pressure of ethylene. At this pressure ethylene still remains virtually insoluble in water, although now its solubility in the organic solvent has increased markedly. Hence, the gas-solubility curve begins to bend more toward the ethylene apex. As shown by a typical tie line in this figure, the vapor-phase composition remains essentially pure ethylene since, at this temperature, the vapor pressures of the water and the pure organic solvent are extremely low.

In figure 3.25c the pressure has now been increased to a value greater than the critical pressure for the ethylene–organic solvent binary mixture. Ethylene is now miscible in all proportions with the organic solvent, and the solubility curve no longer intersects the ethylene-solvent binary axis of the ternary diagram. However, even at this elevated pressure, ethylene still remains virtually insoluble in water. This is not a surprising result for water-hydrocarbon mixtures (Culberson and McKetta, 1951). As shown in figure 3.25c, the gas-solubility curve intersects the ethylene-water binary axis in two locations. The

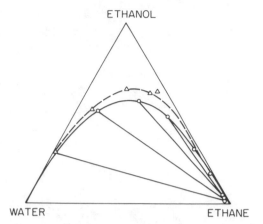

Figure 3.26 Phase behavior of the ternary ethanol–water–supercritical ethane system at a temperature of 50°C and pressures of 50 atm (represented by triangles) and 80 atm (represented by circles) (McHugh, Mallett, and Kohn, 1983).

tie lines for this system now indicate that a liquid phase, which is mostly water and organic solvent, is in equilibrium with a fluid phase, which is mainly ethylene and organic solvent. Therefore, the organic solvent, which is miscible with water at low pressures, is now selectively extracted from the water–organic solvent mixture with supercritical ethylene. An example of this type of SCF extraction process is suggested by the phase behavior shown in figure 3.26 for the ethanol–water–supercritical ethane system (McHugh, Mallett, and Kohn, 1983). Notice that there exist, at most, only two phases in this phase diagram. This type of phase behavior is also observed for the ethanol–water–carbon dioxide system (Paulaitis et al., 1981), the ethanol–water–ethylene system (Paulaitis, Gilbert, and Nash, 1981), and the isopropanol–water–carbon dioxide system (Kuk and Montagna, 1983). Elgin and Weinstock (1959) also present a number of organic solvent–water–ethylene systems that exhibit type-I ternary phase behavior.

To construct an isothermal pressure-composition phase diagram, one uses a solid prism, as shown in figure 3.25d (Elgin and Weinstock, 1959; Treybal, 1968). The three faces of the prism represent the isothermal pressure-composition behavior for the binary mixtures comprising the ternary mixture.

Type II

Type-II phase behavior is depicted in the isothermal ternary phase diagrams shown in figure 3.27. The distinguishing feature of type-II ternary phase behavior is that a liquid-phase miscibility gap appears within the pressure-composition prism but does not extend to the ethylene–organic solvent face of the prism. The phase behavior at atmospheric pressure, shown in figure 3.27a, is identical to that previously described for type-I ternary phase behavior shown in figure 3.25a. If the pressure is increased to P_2, a pressure below the critical pressure of ethylene, a miscibility gap appears for water–organic solvent–

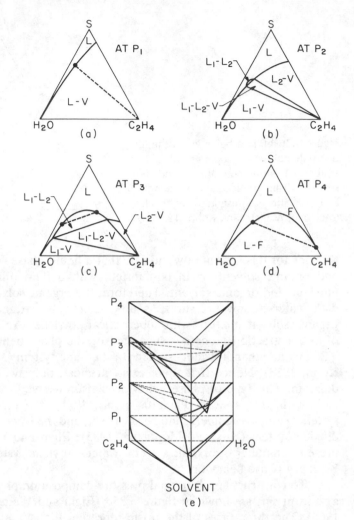

Figure 3.27 Phase behavior of a type-II ternary mixture (Weinstock, 1952).

ethylene compositions, thus creating both liquid-liquid (LL) and liquid-liquid-vapor (LLV) regions in the phase diagram (see figure 3.27b). Notice that the tie lines in the LL region are somewhat parallel to the water–organic solvent axis. When the tie lines are parallel to the water-solvent binary axis the selectivity, as defined in equation 1.3, can approach values much greater than 1.0, thus indicating that a very good separation of organic solvent from water is realized at this condition. Again, strictly speaking there should be a very small single phase vapor near 100% C_2H_4.

In the LLV region of the phase diagram the composition of the three equilibrium phases is invariant. Therefore, within the LLV region of the phase diagram the composition of the three phases remains fixed, although the amount of each phase will vary. The composition of each of the three phases is defined

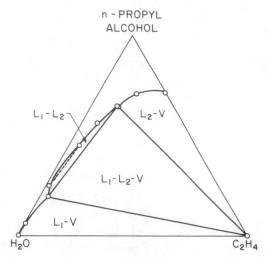

Figure 3.28 Phase behavior of a ternary *n*-propanol–water–ethylene system at a temperature of 15°C and a pressure of 750 psia (Weinstock, 1952).

by the location of the three corners of the LLV region within the ternary diagram.

As the pressure is increased further (see figure 3.27c), the LL and LLV regions expand considerably. As these regions expand the selectivity values also increase and, therefore, the separation of organic solvent from water improves. Notice, however, that the loading of organic solvent in the organic solvent–rich phase decreases slightly.

If the pressure is further increased above the critical pressure for the ethylene–organic solvent binary mixture, as shown in figure 3.27d, the miscibility gap disappears and the phase behavior becomes identical to that described for a type-I ternary system at the same pressure. At this pressure there exist, at most, only two phases. An example of type-II ternary phase behavior is shown in figure 3.28 for the *n*-propanol–water–ethylene system (Weinstock, 1952). Numerous other type-II ternary systems are reported in the literature (Elgin and Weinstock, 1959; Paulaitis, Gilbert, and Nash, 1981; Paulaitis, Kander, and DiAndreth, 1984; Kuk and Montagna, 1983).

Type III

The distinguishing feature of type-III ternary phase behavior is that the miscibility gap of the three-component system intersects the water–organic solvent binary axis of the pressure-composition diagram. This large miscibility gap is a consequence of either the chemical nature of the solvent or the low temperature of the system (Weinstock, 1952).

At atmospheric pressure the water–organic solvent binary system already shows LL immiscibility (see figure 3.29a). Hence, there is a very large LLV region in this diagram. As the pressure is increased (see figure 3.29b), the

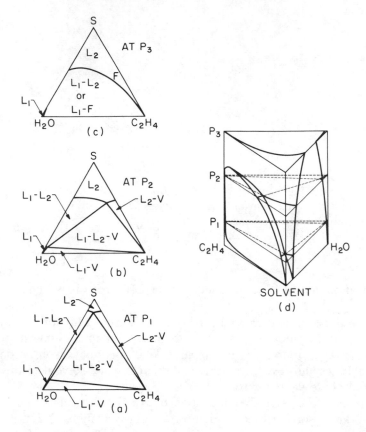

Figure 3.29   Phase behavior of a type-III ternary mixture (Weinstock, 1952).

water–organic solvent LL region expands. As the pressure is increased to a value greater than the critical pressure for the organic solvent–ethylene binary mixture, a single liquid-fluid solubility curve exists. In figure 3.29c the liquid-fluid solubility curve intersects the water–organic solvent axis in two locations, indicating that even at an elevated pressure a miscibility region still exists in the water–organic solvent binary system.

For type-III ternary systems the LL region increases with increasing ethylene content (see figure 3.29b). Although the organic solvent is only slightly miscible with water at low pressures and in the absence of ethylene, it is now possible to use supercritical ethylene to separate even more water from the solvent.

The methyl ethyl ketone (MEK)–water–ethylene system exhibits type-III ternary phase behavior, as shown in figure 3.30. Elgin and Weinstock (1959) use this phase behavior as a basis for a proposed single-stage process for dehydrating MEK-water mixtures using supercritical ethylene.

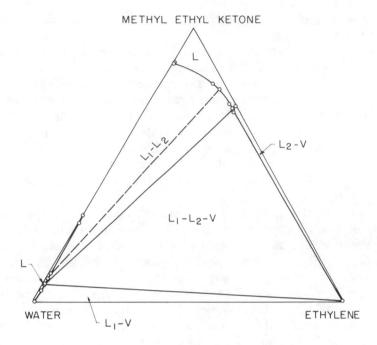

Figure 3.30 Phase behavior of the ternary methyl ethyl ketone–water–ethylene system at 15.0°C and 715 psia (Weinstock, 1952).

Although the classification of ternary phase behavior is described here at a fixed temperature, it is important to remember that a single ternary system can exhibit all three types of phase behaviors as the temperature of the system changes. Because of the previously described classification of binary-mixture phase behavior, one might assume that a ternary mixture that exhibits type-I ternary phase behavior at temperatures above the critical temperature of the SCF solvent may revert to type-II ternary phase behavior as the system temperature is isobarically decreased to values near the critical temperature of the SCF solvent. Kohn, Luks, and co-workers have compiled an extensive body of information on the binary and ternary phase behavior for mixtures consisting of normal hydrocarbons ranging from C_1 through C_{36} with Co_2, N_2, and various alcohols (Kohn, 1967; Kohn et al., 1980; Kohn, Merrill, and Luks, 1983; Tiffin et al., 1978a, 1978b; Merrill, 1983; Merrill, Luks, and Kohn, 1983; Fall, Fall, and Luks, 1985; Fall and Luks, 1984; Hottovy, Kohn, and Luks, 1981, 1982; Huie, Luks, and Kohn, 1973; Yang, Luks, and Kohn, 1976; Zarah, Luks, and Kohn, 1974; Rodrigues, McCaffrey, and Kohn, 1968; Rodrigues and Kohn, 1967; Wagner, McCaffrey, and Kohn, 1968; Kim et al., 1967). Although most of their work is performed at cryogenic temperatures and, thus, has application in the liquefied natural gas industry, the phase behavior observed for these systems is entirely analogous to the phase behavior of the previously described binary and ternary mixtures at much higher temperatures near the critical point of one of the components.

Kohn and co-workers also report on the phase behavior of ternary systems consisting of ethane (C_2) with *n*-hexadecane (C_{16}) + *n*-eicosane (C_{20}) (Wagner, McCaffrey, and Kohn, 1968) and with *n*-nonadecane (C_{19}) + *n*-eicosane (C_{20}) (Kim et al., 1967). Both ternary mixtures exhibit liquid-liquid-vapor (LLV) behavior in the vicinity of the critical point of ethane. For these systems it is possible to use supercritical ethane to separate C_{16} from C_{20} and to a lesser degree to separate C_{19} from C_{20} along the LLV curve. That is, the selectivity for the two liquid phases along the LLV curve, on an ethane-free basis, is approximately 1.3 for the C_2-C_{16}-C_{20} system, as compared with approximately 1.1 for the C_2-C_{19}-C_{20} system.

The amount of experimental information available for ternary mixtures consisting of a single supercritical solvent and two nonvolatile solids is very limited. The *P-T* diagram for such a system was described in detail in 1953 (van Gunst, Scheffer, and Diepen, 1953b), in a work that was an extension of research done by Smits in the early 1900s (Smits, 1903). An example of the *P-T* behavior for solid$_1$-solid$_2$-SCF systems is shown in figure 3.31. The solubility data for the ethylene-naphthalene-hexachloroethane system was reported by van Gunst in his Ph.D. dissertation (van Gunst, 1950). For solid$_1$-solid$_2$-SCF systems it is possible to have a liquid-gas criticality occur in the presence of both solids at a "double critical end point." The solubility of both solids in the SCF-rich phase increases substantially because of the liquid-gas critical point, as explained previously for solid-SCF mixtures.

Recently, Kurnik and Reid (1982) described the solubility behavior for a

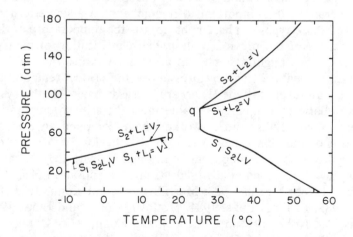

Figure 3.31   *P-T* behavior of a ternary mixture consisting of naphthalene, hexachloroethane, and supercritical ethylene (van Gunst, Scheffer, and Diepen, 1953b). The S$_1$S$_2$LV, S$_2$ + L$_1$ = V, and S$_1$ + L$_1$ = V lines superpose on one another. The S$_2$ + L$_1$ = V and S$_1$ + L$_1$ = V lines represent critical-mixture curves that occur when a solid phase is present.

number of binary solid mixtures consisting of combinations of phenanthrene, naphthalene, benzoic acid, and 2,3- (and 2,6-) dimethylnaphthalene extracted with supercritical carbon dioxide and ethylene. They found that for a binary solid mixture, the presence of one of the solid components solubilized in the SCF-rich phase enhances the solubility of the other solid component in the SCF-rich phase. They suggest that, in this instance, the first solid component acts as an "entrainer" or a so-called cosolvent that enhances the solvent power of the pure SCF. For example, they show that the presence of naphthalene can enhance the solubility of phenanthrene by 200% to 300%. Although the solubility enhancements reported by Kurnik and Reid are very high, the absolute amount of the second component solubilized in the SCF-rich phase is still quite low. This behavior might be anticipated because the solubility of the entrainer solid is quite high (e.g., about 10 wt-%), which substantially changes the solvent power of this solvent mixture relative to that of the pure SCF solvent. Conversely, the solubility of the entrainer solid is not materially enhanced by the small amount of the second component in the SCF-rich phase.

In a recently completed study, Schmitt (1984) verifies the entrainer behavior reported by Kurnik and Reid. Schmitt and Reid (1984) have recently published the results of Schmitt's dissertation showing that very small amounts of an entrainer in the SCF-rich phase has very little effect on the solubility of a second component in that phase. This observation is consistent with the work of Kohn and Luks for ternary mixtures at cryogenic temperatures. The data of Kurnik and Reid have been corroborated for the naphthalene–phenanthrene–carbon dioxide system (Gopal et al., 1983).

Just a few years ago, some thirty years after their classic work on the phase behavior of solid$_1$-solid$_2$-SCF systems, Koningsveld and Diepen described in detail the phase diagrams for systems consisting of two nonvolatile solids and a single SCF solvent (Koningsveld and Diepen, 1983; Koningsveld, Kleintjens, and Diepen, 1984). In this instance the ternary diagrams describe the solubility behavior that can be expected in various regions in P-T space. Because of the complex phase behavior for this type of ternary system, no general guidelines are given for determining the selectivity of the SCF solvent for a given solid in a binary solid mixture.

Very few high-pressure ternary phase diagrams are available for polymer–organic solvent–SCF solvent mixtures. In one study the high-pressure phase behavior of the butanone-acetone-polystyrene system is investigated (Wolf, Breitenbach, and Senftl, 1970). LCST and UCST phenomena are determined for various ratios of butanone to acetone. This type of information defines the pressures and temperatures needed to split a polymer–organic solvent–SCF solvent mixture from a single phase to two phases, thus separating the polymer from the solvent. This type of phase behavior is considered by McHugh and co-workers in some detail (McHugh and Guckes, 1985; McClellan, Bauman, and McHugh, 1985; McClellan and McHugh, 1985). The principles underlying such a polymer-solvent phase split are similar to those used in the propane deasphalting of petroleum mixtures, which are described in detail in chapters 6 and 7.

4

Experimental Techniques in High-Pressure Studies

As described in the previous chapter, a wide variety of phase behavior can occur for mixtures at high pressures. It is important to be cognizant of the types of phase behavior that are possible for the particular mixture being investigated. It should also now be obvious that it is extremely important to pinpoint the P-T location of phase-border curves, such as LLV and SLV curves, while doing solubility studies. The experimental techniques for measuring the solubility of a heavy liquid in a supercritical fluid (SCF) and a heavy solid in an SCF are described in this chapter. These techniques are either *dynamic,* in the case where the solute is continually swept with the SCF, or *static,* in the case where both the solute and solvent are loaded into some type of cell. Static techniques are used to determine both the location of phase-border curves in P-T space and the solubility of a heavy solute in an SCF. Dynamic or flow techniques are normally used for determining solute solubilities in an SCF and also for stripping and fractionating studies.

The advantages and limitations of dynamic and static techniques are presented in this chapter. Suffice it to say that since poor experimental techniques can impede the progress of an SCF project, it is worth spending time in designing an experimental system in which the maximum amount of information can be obtained with the minimum amount of time and effort.

DYNAMIC METHODS FOR MEASURING SOLUBILITIES IN SUPERCRITICAL FLUIDS

A flow apparatus representative of the type used to determine the solubility of a heavy liquid or solid in an SCF is shown in figure 4.1. The description of the apparatus and procedures for this system is taken from Van Leer and Paulaitis (1980). Although other flow methods are described in the literature, Van Leer's technique embodies all the main features of a typical flow method for obtaining solubility information (Kurnik, Holla, and Reid, 1981; Krukonis and Kurnik, 1985; Simnick et al., 1977; Johnston and Eckert, 1981; Prausnitz

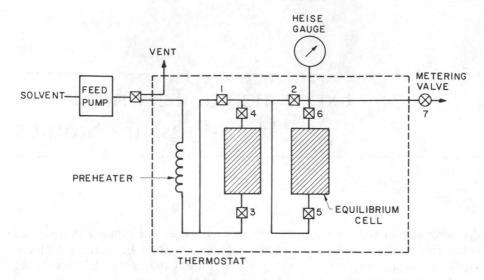

Figure 4.1   Schematic diagram of a dynamic flow apparatus used to obtain liquid or solid solubilities in a supercritical fluid (Van Leer and Paulaitis, 1980).

and Benson, 1959). In the discussion of this method it is assumed that super-critical carbon dioxide is being investigated, but the experimental techniques are clearly applicable to any SCF.

Liquid carbon dioxide at ambient temperatures is charged to the system with a high-pressure pump and compressed to the desired operating pressure. The pump used in this step can be a high-pressure liquid chromatographic pump or perhaps a small diaphragm compressor. The high-pressure pump is used to deliver continuously CO_2 at flow rates slow enough to insure that equilibrium is obtained between the heavy solute and the CO_2 as it flows through the system. Typical equilibrium-type flow rates are 60–500 cm³/min of CO_2 as determined at 1 atm and 0°C.

The CO_2 flows through a section of tubing within the constant-temperature bath to insure that it reaches the bath temperature before it contacts the heavy solute. After reaching thermal equilibrium, the CO_2 is fed to the high-pressure equilibrium columns, which are packed with the heavy solute. The CO_2 flows slowly through the columns and becomes saturated with the heavy solute prior to exiting the second column. Entrainment of the heavy solute in the CO_2-rich phase is prevented by glass wool plugs inserted at the exit of each packed column.

After the saturated CO_2-rich phase exits the second cell, it is expanded to atmospheric pressure across a heated metering valve and the heavy component falls out of solution and is collected in a cold trap. The temperature of the cold trap is dictated by the vapor (or sublimation) pressure of the heavy solute. In order to avoid clogging, the metering valve is maintained at a high temperature so as to eliminate any dry-ice formation during the expansion of the CO_2 and to vaporize the heavy solute. Since the pressure of the system is determined by the pumping rate of the CO_2 and by the regulation of the metering valve, it is important to minimize the clogging of the valve in order to maintain a constant flow rate and pressure. The amount of heavy solute collected in the cold trap for a given amount of time is determined gravimetrically and the corresponding volume of CO_2 is measured with a wet-test or dry-test meter. The instantaneous flow rate of the expanded CO_2 is measured with a simple rotameter or bubble-flow meter.

The equilibrium pressure of the system is measured at the exit of the second column with a Bourdon-tube Heise pressure gauge. Fluctuations in the system pressure due to the high-pressure pump are usually less than ± 25 psi over a wide pressure range. The temperature of the system, which is measured with any of several suitable devices, can usually be maintained easily within 0.1°C.

The advantages of this type of flow system are:

- off-the-shelf equipment is used;
- a straightforward sampling procedure is used;
- reasonably large amounts of solubility data can usually be obtained rapidly and reproducibly; and
- equilibrium, stripping, or fractionation data can be obtained.

However, the disadvantages of this type of flow system are:

- a heavy solid or liquid can clog the metering valve and cause solute holdup, which leads to errors in measuring solubilities;
- with a liquid solute, entrainment of the liquid in the SCF-rich phase is possible at high SCF flow rates;
- undetected phase changes can occur in the columns (e.g., transitions such as solid $\rightarrow$ liquid and liquid$_1$ $\rightarrow$ liquid$_1$ + liquid$_2$);
- high pressures can cause the density of the SCF-rich phase to become greater than the density of the solute-rich liquid phase, which results in the SCF-rich phase's pushing the liquid phase out of the columns thus leading to erroneous solubility information;
- because only the lighter phase is sampled, there is no way of knowing the solubility of the SCF in the liquid phase; and
- equilibrium experiments with multicomponent mixtures must be carefully designed to avoid completely depleting one or more of the components during the experiment.

Even with its disadvantages, a flow technique is still widely used. It is possible to overcome each disadvantage by modifying the apparatus. The simplest and most straightforward modification of this flow apparatus is to add a sampling valve to the system to obtain a sample of the SCF-rich phase before the SCF-rich phase flows through the heated metering valve. In this manner, holdup problems are avoided and it is possible to determine the molar volume of the SCF-rich phase. This sampling technique is shown in figure 4.2a and is described below (McHugh and Paulaitis, 1980).

The contents of the sample loop are analyzed in the following manner (see figure 4.2b). When the loop is switched out of the system, the sample expands into the transfer lines between valves A and B (the total volume of the sample loop and transfer lines is approximately 0.5 ml). As a result of this expansion into the transfer lines, some of the heavy component precipitates in

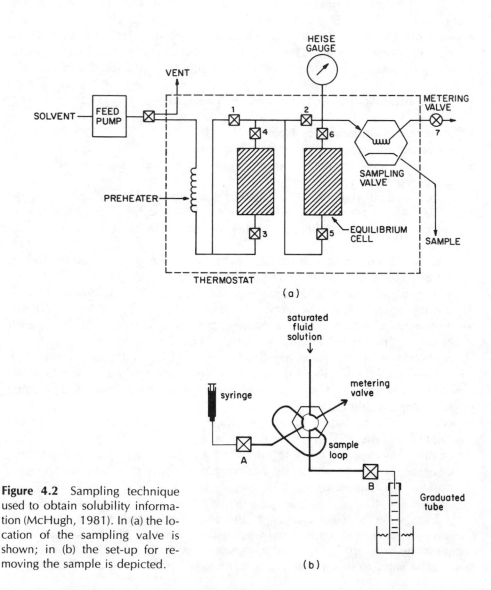

Figure 4.2 Sampling technique used to obtain solubility information (McHugh, 1981). In (a) the location of the sampling valve is shown; in (b) the set-up for removing the sample is depicted.

the lines. The amount of CO_2 in the sample loop can be ascertained by slowly opening valve B to vent the CO_2 into a graduated tube (e.g., a 100-ml class-A burette with the bottom removed) filled with CO_2-saturated water at a known temperature. As the CO_2 is expanded to atmospheric pressure, its solvent power drops significantly and the solid or liquid solute quickly drops out of solution. As the CO_2 is being vented, care must be exercised to avoid entrainment of the heavy solute in the CO_2 gas phase. The volume of CO_2 vented from the sample loop is determined by the volume of the water displaced corrected for the vapor pressure of water and the volume of CO_2 remaining in the sample loop. The heavy component that has precipitated in the sample loop and transfer lines can be removed by replacing the graduated tube in figure 4.2b with a volumetric flask and flushing a large amount of a suitable liquid organic solvent through the system at valve A. The amount of heavy component in the solvent solution is determined by gas or liquid chromatography.

Although this sample-loop technique offers a solution to the metering-valve problem, it is still possible to have phase transitions occurring in the columns without the experimenter's knowledge. Chang and Morrell (1985) overcome this problem by installing a high-pressure glass gauge packed with the heavy solute in parallel with their packed columns. By this expedient, they can observe any phase transitions that may occur during an experiment. Alternatively, the solute-SCF phase-border curves can be determined prior to the solubility studies. A method for determining the *P-T* trace of phase-border curves is described later in this chapter. McHugh and co-workers recommend performing static, constant-composition experiments in which phase-border curves and solubility measurements can be determined simultaneously (McHugh, Seckner, and Yogan, 1984).

STATIC METHODS FOR MEASURING SOLUBILITIES IN SUPERCRITICAL FLUIDS

A representative static apparatus is shown in figure 4.3. The description of the apparatus and procedures is taken from McHugh, Seckner, and Yogan (1984). The main component of this system is a high-pressure, variable-volume view cell similar to the view cell described by Li, Dillard, and Robinson (1981) and Jacoby and Rzasa (1952). This cell allows for visual determination of the phases present at equilibrium. Carbon dioxide is charged at ambient temperature to a high-pressure pump or a gas/liquid compressor, where it is compressed and delivered to a holding tank located in a forced-convection air bath. The temperature of the air surrounding the view cell, maintained constant to within $\pm 0.1°C$, is measured with an accuracy of $\pm 0.10°C$ with a platinum resistance element.

With valves 1 and 2 closed (see figure 4.3), the pressure of the gas is measured with a Bourdon-tube Heise gauge having a range of 0–10,000 psig

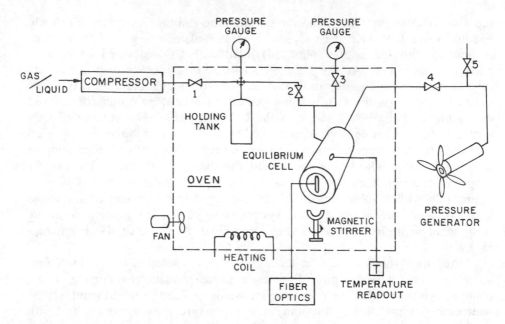

Figure 4.3 Schematic diagram of a constant-composition view-cell apparatus used to obtain solid and liquid solubilities in a supercritical fluid (McHugh, Seckner, and Yogan, 1984).

and an accuracy of ± 10 psi so as to determine when the gas attains thermal equilibrium with the bath air. This normally takes approximately 30 minutes. The amount of gas in the holding tank is determined from the gas density, which is obtained from a suitable equation and the volume of the holding tank. The gas is then transferred to the view cell, which has been previously charged with a known amount of heavy solute. The amount of gas transferred is determined by a mass balance based on the density of the gas remaining in the holding tank and the transfer lines and on the volume of the tank and lines.

The variable-volume, high-pressure view cell used by McHugh, Seckner, and Yogan (1984) is designed to operate to a pressure of 10,000 psig and a temperature of 260°C. The view cell is maintained at a constant temperature normally within ± 0.1°C as determined by a platinum resistance element located on the outside skin of the cell. The cell contents, illuminated by a 0.25-inch-diameter fiber-light pipe, are viewed through a 0.5-inch-thick by 1.5-inch-diameter quartz window that is secured by a cell end cap, which has a 0.25-inch by 0.75-inch view slit. The cell contents are mixed by a magnetic stirring bar activated by a magnet located below the cell. The contents of the cell can be compressed to the desired operating pressure by a movable piston fitted with Teflon O-rings and driven by a low-vapor-pressure silicone oil, which is pressurized by a syringe-type pressure generator. With this apparatus the pressure of the solute-CO_2 mixture is adjusted isothermally at a fixed overall composition by varying the mixture volume.

The solubility of a solid in supercritical CO_2 is determined in the following manner (McHugh, Seckner, and Yogan, 1984). The pressure of the solid-CO_2 mixture is isothermally increased until all the solid is solubilized in the CO_2. At this point a clear, single fluid phase is present in the view cell. The mixture is now slowly decompressed until solid precipitates from solution and at this point two phases exist in the view cell. Hence, the actual solubility point is in the pressure interval between this two-phase state and the previous single fluid-phase state. The solid can be alternately solubilized and precipitated a number of times in an effort to decrease the pressure interval from two phases to one phase to within approximately ±1.0% of the absolute pressure. The solid solubility in this pressure interval is known from the amounts of CO_2 and solid loaded into the view cell.

If a liquid solute is being studied, the vapor-liquid phase transition is determined in a similar manner (Occhiogrosso, 1985). The piston is slowly adjusted to lower the system pressure into the two-phase region. This decompression step is performed very slowly. If the pressure of the system is within 25 psi of the phase-split pressure, the rate of decompression is usually maintained at approximately 0.5 psi/sec. As for the case of the solid solute, the actual phase transition for the liquid solute is in the pressure interval between this two-phase state and the previous single, fluid-phase state. The entire procedure is then performed several times in an effort to decrease the pressure interval from two phases to one phase to within ±5 psi. The system temperature is now raised and the entire procedure is repeated to obtain more VLE information without having to reload the cell. In this manner, without sampling, an isopleth (constant composition at various temperatures and pressures) is obtained.

Between the one-phase and two-phase region a bubble point, a dew point, or a mixture critical point is visually observed. A bubble point is defined as the condition at which a small vapor bubble appears in the cell as the pressure is lowered. The liquid concentration is determined from the amount of material loaded in the cell, exclusive of the negligible amount of material contained in the vapor bubble. A dew point is defined as the condition at which a small amount of dew, or fog, forms in the cell as the pressure is lowered. When determining the concentration of the vapor phase at the dew point, the negligible amount of material in the dew is ignored. The mixture critical point is defined to be the pressure and temperature at which critical opalescence is observed for a slight change in either pressure or temperature. Also, at the mixture critical point a slight change in temperature or pressure causes a dramatic change in the amount of SCF phase or liquid phase present in the view cell. As an example of the dramatic change that occurs, the phases present in the cell change from a single SCF phase to about 50 volume-percent liquid phase and 50 volume-percent vapor phase when the pressure is adjusted by only 5 psi or the temperature is adjusted by 0.10°C.

The advantages of a variable-volume view-cell apparatus are:

- the equilibrium phases are determined visually;
- the phase transitions are also determined visually, and phase inversions are easily detected;
- the solubilities of solids and liquids in binary mixtures are obtained without sampling;
- heavy solids, liquids, or polymers can be studied;
- minimum amounts of heavy components or SCFs are used in an experiment;
- the pressure of the mixture can be continuously adjusted at a fixed composition and temperature; and
- with multicomponent mixtures, the equilibrium phases can be sampled.

The disadvantages of this type of system are:

- "SCF stripping" data are not as easily obtained;
- the windows can fail at high pressures. (Window failures can be minimized by the use of slightly thicker windows than are necessary.)

METHODS FOR DETERMINING
PHASE-BORDER CURVES

As noted in chapter 5, it is possible to predict qualitatively, and in some cases semiquantitatively, solid-solubility data by first measuring the system's P-T trace of three-phase SLV line. This is a relatively straightforward experiment since there is no sampling involved. The previously described high-pressure view cell can be used to determine phase-border curves. The advantage with this apparatus is that with it a wide variety of phase-border curves can be easily determined (e.g., SLV, LLV, and critical-mixture curves) (Krukonis, McHugh, and Seckner, 1984). However, an even simpler technique is available for determination of the P-T trace of a three-phase SLV phase-border curve. In this instance a constant-volume view cell (i.e., a Jerguson gauge) is used as the high-pressure view cell. The description of this apparatus (see figure 4.4) and procedures is taken from McHugh and Yogan (1984).

The supercritical fluid of interest is charged at ambient temperature to a suitable gas/liquid compressor, where it is compressed and delivered to a high-pressure equilibrium view cell. The constant-volume high-pressure view cell is immersed in a water bath, which is controlled at a constant temperature to within ±0.1°C by a platinum resistance element calibrated on the 1968 IPTS scale. The pressure of the system is measured with a Bourdon-tube Heise gauge with a range of 0–10,000 psig and an accuracy of ±10psi. The cell contents are mixed when the cell is rocked approximately 180 degrees, causing a small stirring bar previously inserted into the cell to move through the cell contents.

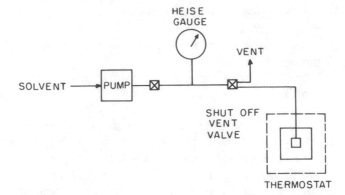

Figure 4.4 Schematic diagram of an experimental apparatus used to obtain the pressure-temperature trace of the three-phase SLV line.

The *P-T* trace of the three-phase solid-liquid-gas line is determined by the following procedure. The view cell, loaded with a heavy solid, is pressurized to approximately 50 psig with CO_2 and then purged to remove any residual air from the system. After three or four purgings, the system is brought to the desired operating pressure and maintained there for approximately 30 minutes to ensure thermal equilibrium. Starting with a solid-fluid condition in the cell, the temperature is then raised until the solid begins to melt. This temperature is maintained with periodic stirring for 10–20 minutes to determine if complete melting occurs. The procedure is repeated until complete melting occurs and a liquid-fluid condition exists in the cell. At that point, the three-phase temperature is in the interval between this liquid-fluid state and the previous solid-fluid state. The solid is alternately solidified and melted a number of times so as to decrease the temperature interval between solid-fluid and liquid-fluid phases to within 0.1°C.

As described in chapter 3, one branch of the SLV line ends at the LCEP and the other branch ends at the UCEP. The UCEP for these systems is defined to be the pressure and temperature at which critical opalescence is observed for a very slight change in either pressure or temperature. Also, at the UCEP a small change in temperature or pressure causes a dramatic change in the amount of supercritical fluid phase, liquid phase, or solid phase present in the view cell. For example, in certain instances adjusting the temperature approximately 0.1°C can change the phases present in the cell in only a few seconds from a single supercritical fluid phase to about 50 volume-% liquid phase and 50 volume-% supercritical fluid phase. The same critical phenomena are observed at the LCEP.

The advantages of this type of static system are:

- it consists of a simple experimental design and procedures;
- off-the-shelf equipment is used;
- the solubility map for a given SCF-solid system can be qualitatively estimated by fitting the SLV data to an equation of state (see chapter 5).

The disadvantages with this equipment are:

- the composition of the equilibrium phases along the SLV line is not determined;
- the pressure of the system is controlled by the amount of SCF introduced to the cell.

The experimental techniques described in this chapter have been successfully used to determine high-pressure SCF-solute phase behavior. Regardless of the techniques that are used, it is important for the experimentalist to perform the experiments with a great deal of care, since a wide variety of phase behavior can occur at high pressures. However, it is possible to reduce the amount of experimental work on SCF-solute systems by modeling the resultant phase behavior and thus extending the phase-behavior information with calculated phase diagrams. The equations used to model high-pressure phase behavior are developed in chapter 5.

5

Thermodynamic Modeling of Supercritical Fluid–Solute Phase Behavior

The experiments that are done to obtain high-pressure phase-equilibrium data can be difficult and costly to perform. Hence, it is extremely useful to have a thermodynamic model or correlation scheme to extend and complement the experimentally obtained data for SCF-solute systems at high pressures. A calculation scheme that pinpoints the regions in *P-T* space in which LLV behavior appears is an extremely useful tool for guiding further experimentation. There are, however, two major problems associated with developing a reliable mathematical model of SCF-solute phase behavior. The first problem is associated with our lack of understanding of the dense fluid state. Simple cubic equations of state (EOSs) do not represent liquid-phase properties to a high degree of accuracy. Also, cubic EOSs do only a fair job representing the critical compressibility of most hydrocarbons. The second problem to overcome in developing a mathematical model of SCF-solute phase behavior resides in the description of the interaction of molecules that significantly differ in molecular size, shape, or polarity. The formulations that describe how the properties of a mixture are to be averaged for use in the EOS are strictly empirical. Although the difficulties in using an EOS have not been fully resolved, certain EOS models are available that describe high-pressure phase behavior in a qualitative (Scott and van Konynenburg, 1970) if not semiquantitative manner (Paulaitis et al., 1983a). It is worth considering these models in some detail since their implementation can reduce the amount of experimental work that is needed to understand a particular SCF-solute system.

Any mathematical model used to calculate the phase behavior of an SCF-solute system must satisfy the following thermodynamic relationships for two equilibrium phases, one designated by a prime (′) and the other by a double prime (″):

$$f_i' = f_i'' \qquad i = 1, 2, 3 \ldots m \qquad (5.1)$$

where f_i is the fugacity of component i. As shown in the schematic P-T-x diagrams in chapter 3, numerous types of phase equilibria are possible with SCF-solute systems. These phase equilibria include liquid-vapor (LV), liquid-liquid-vapor (LLV), solid-vapor (SV), and solid-liquid-vapor (SLV) equilibria. Each type of phase equilibrium will be considered here. (The vapor phase is also used to designate the supercritical fluid phase.)

LIQUID-VAPOR PHASE BEHAVIOR

Various modeling procedures have been proposed in the literature to predict the phase behavior of liquid-vapor (LV) systems at high pressures. The most computationally straightforward and thermodynamically consistent method for calculating high-pressure phase behavior is to choose an EOS to model the equilibrium liquid and (SCF) vapor phases. The fugacity equation (5.1) of component i becomes, at T and P,

$$f_i^V (T,P,y_i) = f_i^L (T,P,x_i) \tag{5.2}$$

where f_i^L is the fugacity of component i in the liquid phase, f_i^V is the fugacity of component i in the vapor phase, x_i is the mole fraction of component i in the liquid phase, y_i is the mole fraction of component i in the vapor or SCF phase. The fugacity in each phase can be written as

$$f_i^L (T,P,x_i) = x_i \phi_i^L P \tag{5.3}$$

$$f_i^V (T,P,y_i) = y_i \phi_i^V P \tag{5.4}$$

where ϕ_i^L is the fugacity coefficient of i in the liquid phase, P is the system pressure, T is the system temperature, and ϕ_i^V is the fugacity coefficient of i in the vapor phase. Fugacity coefficients are calculated from the following exact thermodynamic relationship (Prausnitz, 1969):

$$\ln \phi_i = \frac{1}{RT} \int_V^\infty \left[\left(\frac{\partial P}{\partial n_i} \right)_{T, V, n_j \neq n_i} - \frac{RT}{V} \right] dV - \ln Z, \tag{5.5}$$

where R is the gas constant, V is the total system volume, n_i and n_j are the mole numbers of components i and j, respectively, and Z is the compressibility factor. A single equation of state is used in equation (5.5) to calculate both fugacity coefficients. The most commonly used cubic EOSs are the Peng-Robinson (Peng and Robinson, 1976) equation and the Soave-Redlich-Kwong (Soave, 1972) equation. Let us just consider the Peng-Robinson equation of state:

$$P = \frac{RT}{v - b} - \frac{a(T)}{v(v + b) + b(v - b)}, \tag{5.6}$$

where v is the molar volume, a accounts for interactions between the species in the mixture, and b accounts for size differences between the species of the mixture. For the pure components,

$$b = 0.07780 \left(\frac{RT_c}{P_c}\right) \tag{5.7}$$

$$a(T) = a(T_c)\alpha(T_R, \omega) \tag{5.8}$$

$$a(T_c) = 0.45724 \left(\frac{R^2 T_c^2}{P_c}\right) \tag{5.9}$$

$$\alpha^{1/2}(\omega) = 1 + m(1 - T_R^{1/2}) \tag{5.10}$$

and

$$m = 0.37464 + 1.54226\omega - 0.26992\omega^2, \tag{5.11}$$

where T_c is the critical temperature, P_c is the critical pressure, T_R is the reduced temperature $(T_R = T/T_c)$, and ω is the acentric factor for component i.
For mixtures, the following mixing rule can be used for "a":

$$a = \sum_i^N \sum_j^N x_i x_j a_{ij} \tag{5.12}$$

and

$$a_{ij} = (1 - \delta_{ij}) \sqrt{a_i a_j}, \tag{5.13}$$

where δ_{ij} is an adjustable interaction parameter obtained by regressing experimental equilibrium data. This parameter accounts for specific binary interactions between components i and j in the mixture.
For b the mixing rule is

$$b = \sum_i^N \sum_j^N x_i x_j b_{ij} \tag{5.14}$$

and

$$b_{ij} = (1 - \eta_{ij}) \left(\frac{b_i + b_j}{2}\right), \tag{5.15}$$

where η_{ij} is an adjustable size parameter determined, along with δ_{ij}, by fitting the equation of state to experimental equilibrium data.

Neither δ_{ij} nor η_{ij} is expected to be a function of temperature, pressure, or composition. Normally, both are expected to have an absolute value much less than 1.0. The parameter δ_{ij} usually never gets larger than about 0.150. It can also be negative, although a negative value usually indicates that specific chemical interactions, such as hydrogen bonding, are present in the mixture. It is questionable whether an EOS approach should be used in a hydrogen-bonded system, because a cubic EOS accounts only for dispersion forces between the mixture components and not for chemical forces. Although η_{ij} can be both positive and negative, it is less apparent how to interpret a negative value for η_{ij}. More work is needed on regressing experimental data to develop trends in η_{ij}.

Peng and Robinson (1976) usually set η_{ij} equal to zero, which reduces equation 5.14 to

$$b = \sum_{i}^{N} x_i \, b_i. \tag{5.16}$$

Deiters and Schneider (1976), however, recommend using both parameters when calculating high-pressure phase behavior with the Redlich-Kwong equation. They calculate P-x diagrams for binary mixtures for pressures up to the mixture critical pressure. They also calculate the critical-mixture curves for a number of binary mixtures. Their modeling studies are conducted at pressures as high as 3,000 atm. Both adjustable parameters, δ_{ij} and η_{ij}, are used because the components in the binary mixtures that they modeled differ considerably in structure, size, and polarity. The results from their studies indicate that a cubic equation of state with two fitted parameters per binary pair in the mixture will successfully model high-pressure fluid-phase equilibrium data in the mixture critical region. Similar results are expected when the PR EOS is used with two adjustable parameters per binary pair.

When the Peng-Robinson EOS is incorporated into the expression for the fugacity coefficient of the components (equation 5.5) using mixing rules given by equations (5.12) and (5.14), the following closed-form expression for the fugacity coefficient is obtained:

$$\ln \phi_i = \frac{(bN)'}{b}\,[Z-1] - \ln[Z-B]$$

$$- \left[\frac{A}{2.828B}\right]\left[\left(\frac{2\sum_{j}^{N} x_j\, a_{ij}}{a}\right) - \frac{(bN)'}{b}\right]\left[\ln \frac{Z + 2.414B}{Z - 0.414B}\right], \tag{5.17}$$

where

$$A = \frac{aP}{R^2 T^2} \qquad (5.17a)$$

$$B = \frac{bP}{RT} \qquad (5.17b)$$

$$Z = \frac{Pv}{RT} \qquad (5.17c)$$

and

$$(bN)' = 2 \sum_{k}^{N} x_k\, b_{ik} - \sum_{j}^{N} x_j^2\, b_{jj} - 2 \sum_{j=1}^{N-1} \sum_{i=j+1}^{N} x_i\, x_{i-j}\, b_{ij}. \qquad (5.17d)$$

Equation 5.17 is used to find fugacity coefficients for components in both the liquid and vapor phase.

If η_{ij} is set equal to zero in equation 5.14, the closed-form expression for ϕ_i reduces to the simpler expression suggested by Peng and Robinson (1976). Hence, equation (5.17) offers the flexibility of using two parameters to fit phase-equilibrium data.

LIQUID-LIQUID-VAPOR PHASE BEHAVIOR

The following fundamental relationships must be satisfied for each component i in a mixture when three phases are in equilibrium:

$$f_i^{L_1} = f_i^{V} \qquad (5.18)$$

$$f_i^{L_2} = f_i^{V}, \qquad (5.19)$$

where superscript L_1 represents one liquid phase and superscript L_2 represents the other liquid phase. In other words, the fugacity of a component in one phase must be equal to that component's fugacity in each of the other two phases. We can also write the expressions for the component fugacities as

$$f_i^{L_1} = x_i^{L_1}\, \phi_i^{L_1}\, P \qquad (5.20)$$

$$f_i^{L_2} = x_i^{L_2}\, \phi_i^{L_2}\, P \qquad (5.21)$$

$$f_i^{V} = y_i\, \phi_i^{V}\, P. \qquad (5.22)$$

The fugacity coefficients are calculated with equation (5.17). The expressions for the equation of state and the mixing rules are given in equations (5.6) through (5.15). The computer programs used to calculate LV and LLV equilibria are given in appendix B.

Let us consider a straightforward example of using an EOS to generate a model of the phase behavior for a ternary mixture consisting of methane-ethane-octane (Igel, 1985). In particular, we are interested in predicting the occurrence of an LLV region at $-67°C$ and 54 atm. Let us use only one adjustable parameter, δ_{ij}, for each of the binary mixtures comprising the ternary mixture—that is, for methane-ethane, methane-octane, and ethane-octane. The physical properties for these three components are given in table 5.1. Our problem reduces to the following steps:

1. fit available experimental *P-x* data for each of the binary mixtures to determine the δ_{ij} for each binary pair;
2. using the best-fit parameters δ_{ij}, calculate the ternary phase diagram for the ternary mixture; and
3. compare the calculated phase diagram with the experimentally obtained diagram and adjust the δ_{ij} for each binary pair to obtain a better fit of the experimental data.

Shown in figure 5.1 is a comparison of calculated and experimental *P-x* isotherms for the methane-ethane system. A good fit of the experimental data is obtained with a value of 0.02 for δ_{ij} and zero for η_{ij}. Note that the temperature of the system described in figure 5.1 is much higher than $-67°C$.

Shown in figure 5.2 is a comparison of calculated and experimental *P-x* isotherms for the ethane-octane system. A good fit of these experimental data is obtained with η_{ij} equal to zero and δ_{ij} equal to 0.017. Again, the temperature of the system described here is much higher than $-67°C$.

Finally, the available *P-x* data for the methane-octane system, as shown in figure 5.3, is fit with δ_{ij} equal to 0.01 and η_{ij} equal to zero.

Using the values obtained from fitting binary *P-x* data, the ternary phase diagram for the methane-ethane-octane system at $-67.0°C$ and 54 atm can now be calculated. The results of these calculations are shown in figure 5.4. An LLV region is, in fact, predicted for this system; however, two regions are

Table 5.1 Physical Properties of Methane, Ethane, and *n*-Octane

	Methane	*Ethane*	n-*Octane*
Molecular formula	CH_4	CH_3CH_3	$CH_3(CH_2)_6CH_3$
Molecular weight	16.04	30.07	114.23
Critical temperature (°K)	190.6	305.4	568.8
Critical pressure (atm)	45.4	48.2	24.5
Acentric factor (ω)	0.007	0.091	0.394

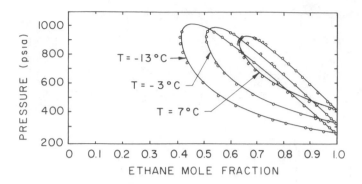

Figure 5.1 A comparison of calculated (lines) and experimental (circles) data for the methane–ethane binary system. For these calculations δ_{ij} is 0.02 (Igel, 1985).

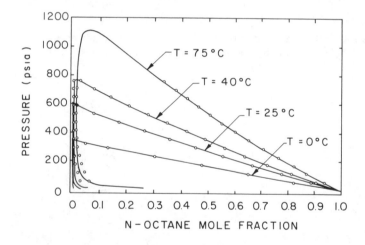

Figure 5.2 A comparison of calculated (lines) and experimental (circles) data for the ethane–n-octane binary system. For these calculations δ_{ij} is 0.017 (Igel, 1985).

missing from the phase diagram. If only data for binary pairs with one adjustable parameter per binary pair are used, the PR EOS correctly predicts the occurrence of an LLV region at $-67.0°C$ and 54.0 atm. However, the concentrations of the three equilibrium phases are not quantitatively modeled. Nevertheless, even when no experiments on the ternary system are performed, the model can be used to pinpoint regions in P-T space where multiple phases could exist. Finally, if the parameters δ_{ij} are adjusted slightly, better agreement between calculated and experimental data is obtained and the two missing LL

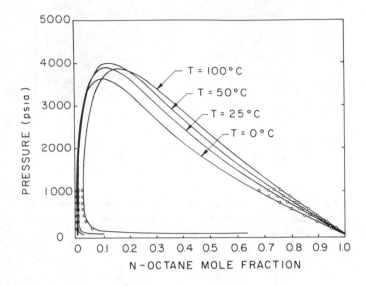

Figure 5.3   A comparison of calculated (lines) and experimental (circles) data for the methane–*n*-octane binary system. For these calculations δ_{ij} is 0.01 (Igel, 1985).

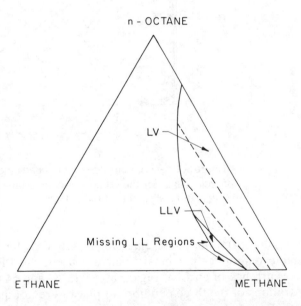

Figure 5.4   A comparison of calculated and experimental data at −67°C and 54.1 atm for the methane–ethane–*n*-octane system using interaction parameters obtained from the best fit of data for binary pairs. The dashed lines are tie lines (Igel, 1985).

regions can now be calculated (see figure 5.5). Having to change the δ_{ij}'s to get a better fit of the ternary data suggests that δ_{ij} is a function of temperature. This result is consistent with the results found by numerous other researchers.

Before proceeding to solid-SCF systems, we will demonstrate use of the

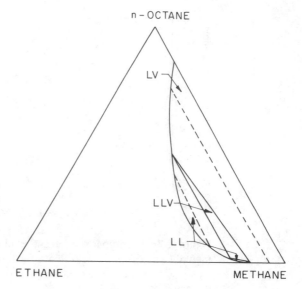

Figure 5.5 A comparison of calculated and experimental data at −67°C and 54.1 atm for the methane–ethane–*n*-octane system using adjusted interaction parameters. The dashed lines in the figure are tie lines (Igel, 1985).

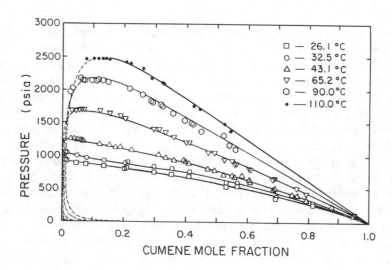

Figure 5.6 A comparison of calculated (lines) and experimental (symbols) data for the isopropyl benzene–CO₂ system. For these calculations δ_{ij} is 0.066 and η_{ij} is −0.044 (Occhiogrosso, 1985).

Peng-Robinson EOS with nonzero values for both δ_{ij} and η_{ij}. In this instance, let us consider the work of McHugh and co-workers, who studied the isopropyl benzene–CO₂ system (Occhiogrosso, 1985; Occhiogrosso, Igel, and McHugh, 1986).

Shown in figure 5.6 is a comparison of experimental and calculated P-x

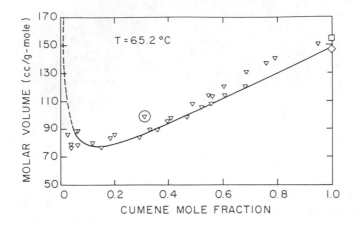

Figure 5.7 A comparison of calculated (lines) and experimental (symbols) volumetric data for the isopropyl benzene–CO_2 system. For these calculations δ_{ij} is 0.066 and η_{ij} is -0.044 (Occhiogrosso, 1985).

diagrams for the isopropyl benzene (also known as "cumene")–CO_2 system. In this instance, the isotherms span a temperature range between 26.1°C and 110.0°C. This system exhibits type-I phase behavior as described in chapter 3. Notice that in this instance, δ_{ij}, equal to 0.066, and η_{ij}, equal to -0.040, are constant over this wide range of temperatures. Although not mentioned earlier, the PR EOS does predict the mixture molar volume of the equilibrium vapor and liquid phases. An example of the fit of volume-composition data for the isopropyl benzene–CO_2 system is shown in figure 5.7. Finally, using the values of δ_{ij} and η_{ij} found from regressing P-x data, we can calculate the P-T diagram for this system. The results of this calculation are shown in figure 5.8.

From this example, it is evident that the PR EOS with two fitted parameters can be used along with a few good data points to generate a good representation of the phase behavior over wide ranges of temperature and pressure. It is not hard to imagine how this combined calculation-experimental approach can save a fair amount of time and experimental anguish. Some data are needed, however, to fit the parameters in the equations of state. Similar results using two parameters are shown in figure 5.9 for the toluene-CO_2 and the m-xylene–CO_2 systems. With a judicious guess for δ_{ij} and η_{ij} it seems reasonable to expect that a good representation of other aromatic-CO_2 systems, such as the styrene-CO_2, can be obtained from calculations alone.

SOLID–SUPERCRITICAL FLUID PHASE BEHAVIOR

For solid–SCF solvent equilibria, the fugacity of component i in the SCF solvent phase can be calculated in the previously described manner—that is,

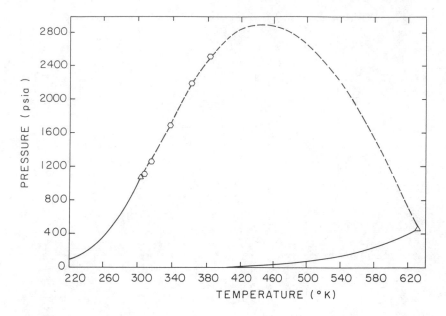

Figure 5.8 A comparison of the calculated (lines) and experimental (symbols) pressure-temperature trace of the critical-mixture curve for the isopropyl benzene–CO_2 system (Occhiogrosso, 1985).

$$f_i^{SCF} = y_i \phi_i^{SCF} P \quad i = 1, 2, 3 \ldots m. \tag{5.4}$$

Because the solid phase is normally considered a pure solid, the fugacity of component i as a pure solid phase (denoted by the OS superscript) is

$$f_i^{OS} = P_i^{sub}(T) \, \phi_i^{sub}(T, \, P_i^{sub}) \, \exp\left[\int_{P_i^{sub}}^{P} \left(\frac{v_i^{OS}}{RT} \right) dP \right], \tag{5.23}$$

where $P_i^{sub}(T)$ is the sublimation pressure of the pure solid at the system temperature, v_i^{OS} is the molar volume of the pure solid, $\phi_i^{sub}(T, P_i^{sub})$ is the fugacity coefficient at T and P_i^{sub}, and the exponential term is the Poynting correction for the fugacity of the pure solid. Therefore, combining equations 5.4 and 5.23, the solubility of a heavy nonvolatile solid in the supercritical fluid solvent phase now becomes

$$y_i = \frac{P_i^{sub}(T) \, \phi_i^{sub}(T) \, \exp\left[\int_{P_i^{sub}}^{P} \left(\frac{v_i^{OS}}{RT} \right) dP \right]}{\phi_i^{SCF} P} \tag{5.24}$$

Kurnik, Holla, and Reid (1981) show that the Peng-Robinson equation with a single adjustable mixture parameter (δ_{ij}) adequately represents solid-

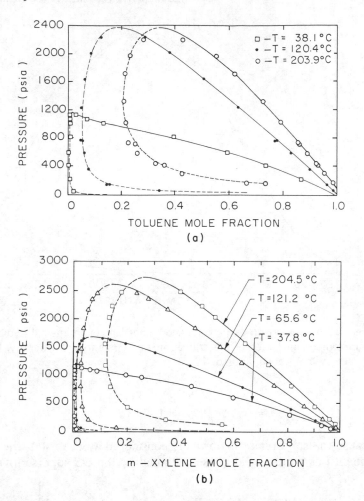

Figure 5.9   A comparison of calculated (lines) and experimental (symbols) data for the (a) toluene-CO_2 and the (b) m-xylene–CO_2 systems. For these calculations δ_{ij} is 0.066 and η_{ij} is -0.044 (Occhiogrosso, 1985).

solubility behavior. However, they made the interaction parameter a weak function of temperature so that it would fit their data. Examples of solid-solubility calculations are shown in figure 5.10.

To account for the large disparity in size between a heavy nonvolatile solid and a light SCF solvent, Chai (1981; Paulaitis, McHugh, and Chai, 1983) and others (Deiters and Schneider, 1976) incorporate a second adjustable parameter into the equation of state. Johnston and Eckert (1981; Johnston, Ziger, and Eckert, 1982) forego the PR EOS and use an augmented van der Waals equation of state to predict solid solubilities in SCF solvents. They

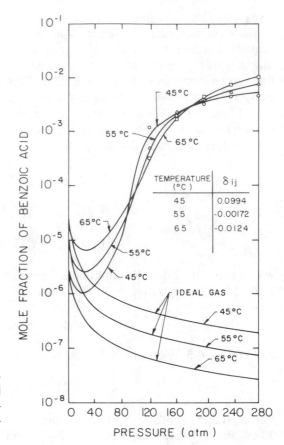

Figure 5.10 A comparison of calculated (lines) and experimental (symbols) data for the benzoic acid–CO_2 system at three different temperatures (Kurnik, 1981).

combine the Carnahan-Starling equation for the repulsive contribution to the pressure with the attractive term of the van der Waals equation. Their approach is reasonably successful, especially for extremely nonvolatile solids for which sublimation pressures or critical-property information has not been reported.

Kurnik and Reid (1982) also use the Peng-Robinson EOS to correlate their data on the solubility of two pure solids in an SCF solvent. Their results are very sensitive to the value of the binary $solid_1$-$solid_2$ interaction parameter they use. Gopal and co-workers (1983) find similar results, and they also show that the calculated solid solubilities are dependent on whether the mixture consists of two pure solids or whether the solids have melted and formed a single mixed-solid phase.

As described in some detail in chapter 3, it is extremely important to determine the location of the SLV border curves for solid-SCF systems. Normally, one branch of the SLV line is very close to the vapor-pressure curve of the pure light component (see figure 3.21). The other branch of the SLV curve is near the melting temperature of the heavy solid. McHugh, Seckner, and

Krukonis (1984) suggest that the amount of experimentation on solid-SCF systems (in this case the xenon-naphthalene system) can be reduced by first visually determining the *P-T* trace of the branch of the three-phase SLV line that begins at the normal melting temperature of the heavy solid. This SLV line can be modeled with the PR EOS and fair estimates of the solid solubilities can then be calculated without any more experiments being required.

First, the SLV line is visually determined as described in chapter 4. The parameters needed in the PR EOS to model the SLV line are determined by solving equations 5.25 through 5.29.

$$f_2^V(T,P,y_2) = f_2^L(T,P,x_2) \qquad (5.25)$$

$$f_2^{OS}(T,P) = f_2^V(T,P,y_2) \qquad (5.26)$$

$$f_1^L(T,P,x_1) = f_1^V(T,P,y_1), \qquad (5.27)$$

where subscript 2 denotes naphthalene and subscript 1 denotes xenon. Equation 5.26 reduces to equation 5.24. Equation 5.27 reduces to

$$x_1\phi_1^L = y_1\phi_1^V \qquad (5.28)$$

and equation 5.25 becomes

$$x_2\phi_2^L = y_2\phi_2^V \qquad (5.29)$$

For crystalline solids such as naphthalene v_2^{os} is virtually incompressible up to 1,000 atm (Vaidya and Kennedy, 1971) and the integral in equation 5.24 is easily solved.

The computer program used to fit the SLV line with the PR EOS is also given in appendix B.

The fit of the xenon-naphthalene SLV line is shown in figure 5.11. The fit of the data is reasonably good with δ_{ij} equal to 0.030 and η_{ij} equal to zero. Although the fit of the data is not very good near the UCEP for this system, the general trends in the data are well modeled.

As mentioned previously, the PR EOS does a fairly good job in representing the mixture molar volume of the vapor and liquid phases. As shown in figure 5.12, this equation also predicts the solid-liquid and liquid-supercritical fluid phase inversions that are experimentally observed along the SLV line.

Solid-SCF solubility calculations are compared with the experimental data in figure 5.13. Although the data are not quantitatively modeled, the order of magnitude of the solid solubilities is well represented. Had the model been better at representing the SLV line near the UCEP, it probably would have more quantitatively modeled the solid-supercritical fluid phase behavior.

This example illustrates the advantages of using a cubic EOS for reducing the amount of experimental information needed to estimate solid solubilities

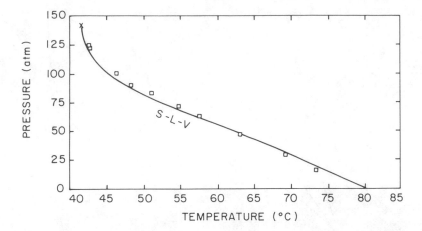

Figure 5.11   A comparison of the calculated (line) and experimental (symbols) SLV line for the xenon-naphthalene system (McHugh, 1984).

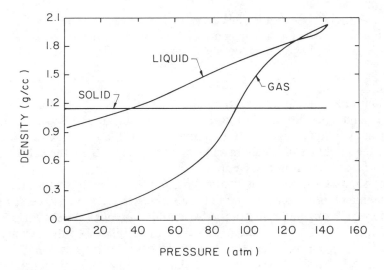

Figure 5.12   Calculated density inversions for the xenon-naphthalene system at conditions along the SLV line (McHugh, 1984).

in an SCF. As described in chapter 4, the visual determination of the *P-T* trace of the SLV line is a relatively straightforward experiment.

At the high pressures and liquidlike densities encountered in an SCF solvent extraction process, the distinction between gas and liquid phases becomes less clear. It is, therefore, also possible to model the SCF solvent phase as an expanded liquid rather than as a compressed gas (Paulaitis et al., 1982;

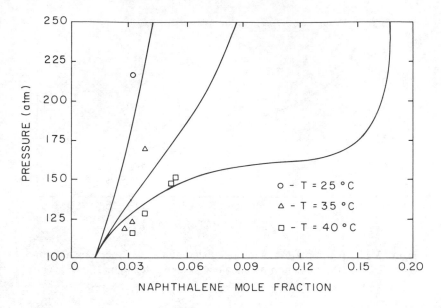

Figure 5.13   A comparision of calculated (lines) and experimental (symbols) solid-solubility data for the xenon-naphthalene system using parameters fit to the *P-T* trace of the SLV line (McHugh, 1984).

Balder and Prausnitz, 1966). Mackay and Paulaitis (1979) use this approach to calculate solid solubilities. They state that although an activity-coefficient parameter and an equation-of-state parameter are needed, it may be possible to estimate the solubility of a solid in an SCF solvent phase from the solid solubility in the corresponding liquid solvent.

For solid-SCF systems it is also possible to correlate experimental data by examining plots of concentration of the solid in the SCF phase versus density of the pure SCF or the density of the SCF-solute mixture. As shown in chapter 1, the solubility of a heavy solid in an SCF can be related to the density of the pure SCF. An example of a composition-density plot is shown in figure 5.14 for the naphthalene-CO_2 system. Note that the curves in this plot are linear and parallel to each other. Schmitt uses concentration-density plots to correlate solid-solubility data for a large number of organic compounds. These types of plots can also be used for interpolating the experimental data. It should be noted, however, that there are limitations to using composition-density plots. These types of plots are good only for solid-SCF systems. The resultant linear curves on these plots are a consequence of the high degree of correlation between the compressibility of the SCF and the solubility of the solid in the SCF. Therefore, the isothermal solubility curves deviate from linearity as the SCF approaches a highly compressed constant density, at which point the solid solubility reaches a limiting value. The solubility curves will also deviate from

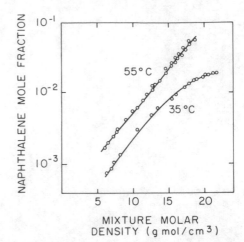

Figure 5.14   Solid naphthalene–supercritical CO_2 solubility data plotted as a function of mixture density (Paulaitis et al., 1984).

linearity as the UCEP for the solid-SCF mixture is approached. This deviation from linearity near the system UCEP is clearly shown in the work of Schmitt and Reid (1984) for the naphthalene-ethylene system. Finally, the solubility curves will deviate from linearity if there are specific solute-solvent interactions, such as acid-base interactions or hydrogen bonding (Schmitt, 1984).

6

Process Operations

As is by now evident to the reader, the phenomenon of solubility in supercritical fluids is not new. Since 1879 (or 1861, if we include the high-pressure, near-critical liquid carbon dioxide studies of Gore), solubility, phase, and spectroscopic studies have been performed on a large number of solute-SCF mixtures. These investigations, which received resurgent interest with the work of Diepen, Scheffer, and co-workers in the late 1940s and early 1950s, were made for their inherent scientific and technical interest and value.

In 1955 Todd and Elgin reported on the phase behavior of a number of liquid and solid solutes in supercritical ethylene. Aromatics, substituted aromatics, aldehydes, short- and long-chain alcohols, acids, and paraffins were studied. Examples of the various types of high-pressure phase equilibria described in chapter 3 were found in this work. Todd and Elgin extrapolated their high-pressure phase-equilibrium data to the design of a new process for separating mixtures. It is perhaps appropriate that a description of the concept of supercritical fluid extraction appeared in the first issue of the *AIChE Journal*. To wit,

> Besides the theoretical interest in the unusual phase behavior encountered in these systems, the principles involved can be applied in operations wherein the nonideality is intentionally created. The magnitude of solubility of a compound of low volatility in a gas above its critical temperature . . . is sufficient to consider the gas as an extracting medium, that is fluid-liquid or fluid-solid extraction analogous to liquid-liquid extraction and leaching. In this case the solute is removed and the solvent recovered by partial decompression. . . . Thus compression of a gas over a mixture of compounds could selectively dissolve one compound, permitting it to be removed from the mixture. Partial decompression of the fluid elsewhere would drop out the dissolved compound, and the gas could be reused for further extraction. (Todd and Elgin, 1955)

In the period between 1970 and the present, the technical and trade literature has reported many "new" and "novel" applications of supercritical fluid extraction, but as we shall see in appendix A, where many supercritical fluid extraction patents are reviewed, the process principles were applied as long as fifty years ago.

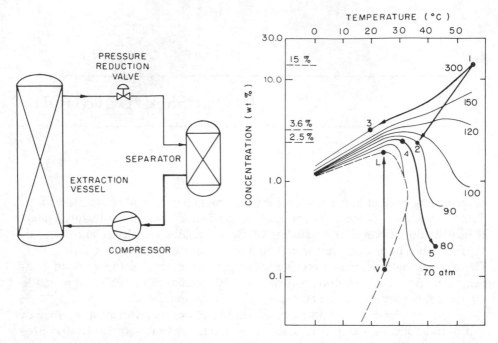

Figure 6.1   Schematic diagram of a supercritical fluid extraction process; solubility data for naphthalene in CO_2 is illustrated.

A schematic diagram of the supercritical fluid extraction process described by Todd and Elgin is shown in figure 6.1. Four major pieces of equipment are shown, namely, an extraction vessel, a pressure-reduction valve, a separator, and a compressor. (For simplicity and ease of discussion, ancillary equipment, such as gauges, controls, facilities for storing gas, etc., is not shown in the figure.)

To illustrate the operation of the process, let us assume that the extractor has been filled with a 50/50 mixture of naphthalene and powdered chalk (powdered chalk does not dissolve in carbon dioxide). Incidentally, the filling of the vessel with the solid mixture, although "an engineering detail" for this discussion, is not necessarily an easy task and is, furthermore, not without substantial capital and operating costs in the overall separation process. The mixture is probably not continuously "pumpable" into the extraction vessel during high-pressure operation; it instead will probably be charged in a batch mode through quick-acting gate valves or through some other motor-activated opening. Because the filling and extraction operations are done in a batch mode, it might be desirable to have two or three extraction vessels in parallel. The extension of the concepts discussed in this section is easily extrapolated to a multivessel system with different solid substances and SCF solvents.

Once the naphthalene-chalk dust mixture is charged to the vessel, carbon dioxide is compressed and heated to the desired operating conditions. When the pressure reaches the desired operating level, the pressure-reduction valve is actuated and CO_2 flow commences. Let us assume that the extraction conditions are 300 atm and 55°C. As carbon dioxide flows through the vessel, naphthalene dissolves in the stream of CO_2 to a concentration level of 15 wt-% (see point 1 in figure 6.1). The loaded CO_2 phase leaving the extractor is expanded to 90 atm through the pressure-reduction valve. When the pressure is lowered, naphthalene precipitates from solution (see point 2 in figure 6.1). If we assume an isenthalpic (i.e., constant-enthalpy) expansion of the carbon dioxide–rich stream, a concomitant 19°C drop in temperature occurs (as calculated from thermodynamic data for pure carbon dioxide) and, thus, the expansion path on the naphthalene solubility diagram is shown as an oblique line.

At 90 atm and 36°C the equilibrium solubility of naphthalene in CO_2 is only 2.5 wt-%. The precipitated naphthalene is collected in the separator and the carbon dioxide stream is recompressed to the initial extraction conditions of 55°C and 300 atm and is recycled to the extractor.

It is informative to follow the process cycle on a carbon dioxide Mollier diagram for the purpose of determining the energy requirements of this SCF process relative to some other process, such as the vaporization of the naphthalene at its boiling point (218°C). An enlarged view of the pertinent section of the temperature-entropy diagram of carbon dioxide is given in figure 6.2. The arrows on this figure trace the path of CO_2 in the process cycle. As previously described, the extraction step occurs at 55°C and 300 atm. The CO_2-

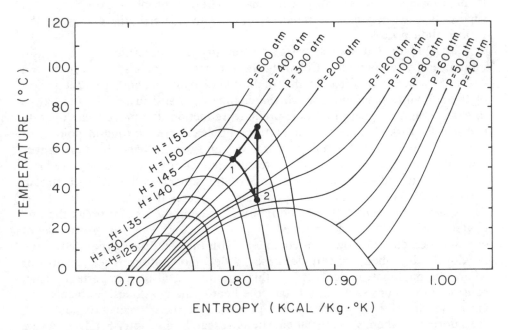

Figure 6.2 Temperature-entropy diagram for pure carbon dioxide.

naphthalene solution leaving the extractor is isenthalpically expanded across the pressure-reduction valve to 90 atm. During the expansion step, the temperature of the CO_2 solution falls about 19°C (if we ignore the heat effects associated with the formation of solid naphthalene). The stream of carbon dioxide leaving the separator is now at 36°C and 90 atm. As this stream is isentropically compressed to 300 atm, its temperature rises to 72°C. The energy required to compress CO_2 to 300 atm, 7 kcal/kg (12.6 Btu/lb) of CO_2, can be read directly from the Mollier diagram. In completing the process cycle the CO_2 stream is isobarically cooled to 55°C, the initial extraction temperature. No attempt is made to integrate the heat-exchange steps in this process. Since the expansion of CO_2 results in a solubility decrease from 15 wt-% to 2.5 wt-%, it is readily calculated that it is necessary to recycle about 6.7 pounds of CO_2 to extract one pound of naphthalene.

The energy required to extract naphthalene is compared to the energy needed to vaporize naphthalene from the chalk dust mixture. The electrical energy required to compress 6.7 lbs of CO_2 in the recycle stream (at 12.6 Btu/lb CO_2) is 84.4 Btu, i.e., that is the electrical energy input to the process to extract one pound of naphthalene. The equivalent thermal energy of this step is 222 Btu assuming 38% Carnot efficiency. The vaporization process requires energy input for latent and sensible heat. The heat of vaporization is 84 Btu/lb naphthalene, and in order to raise the bed temperature from ambient to 218°C (the boiling point of naphthalene) a sensible heat input of 350 Btu/lb naphthalene is required. Thus the total thermal energy requirement is 434 Btu/lb naphthalene. We see that with this separation problem extraction with supercritical carbon dioxide requires only about one half the energy of the vaporization process.

In chapter 3 it was shown that solubility in supercritical fluids is also influenced by temperature. Changing the temperature of a system can have a dramatic or moderate effect on the solubility behavior, depending on the region of the solubility diagram in which the change occurs. Thus, as an alternative to extraction and separation using pressure reduction, the process can operate isobarically with changes in temperature. For example, starting at point 1 of figure 6.1, the stream leaving the extractor can flow through a heat exchanger (which is not shown) instead of a pressure-reduction valve and be cooled to 20°C, as indicated by the arrow on the 300-atm isobar. As the CO_2-rich stream is cooled, the concentration of naphthalene decreases from 15 wt-% to 3.6 wt-%, as shown by point 3. The carbon dioxide leaving the separator can then be heated back to 55°C and recycled to the extractor. This isobaric mode of operation employs a blower, as compared with the compressor required in the previously described pressure-decrease mode of operation. The question of where the naphthalene "collects" in this operation is also an important design consideration. For example, if it coats the heat-exchanger tubes, problems may ensue. (Some of these practical areas, previously termed "engineering details," are addressed when we cover applications research in chapter 8.) The recycle ratio, as calculated from the solubility data shown in figure 6.1, for this mode of operation is about 7.5 pounds of CO_2 per pound of naphthalene.

Temperature variations can be used advantageously in another region of the solubility diagram, the "low"-pressure region or retrograde-condensation region where increasing temperature causes a decrease in solubility. Specifically, for the case of the naphthalene–chalk dust separation, the process can operate isobarically between points 4 and 5 in figure 6.1. Extraction occurs at 80 atm and 32°C. Raising the temperature of the loaded CO_2 stream by only 8°C causes the solubility to drop by more than an order of magnitude. The carbon dioxide leaving the separator is cooled back to 32°C and recycled to the extractor.

A fourth alternative for carrying out the naphthalene extraction utilizes the dissolving capacity of near-critical liquid carbon dioxide. This operating mode is illustrated in figure 6.1 by the LV tie line. Liquid carbon dioxide is employed to dissolve and extract the naphthalene from the mixture, and the solution leaving the extractor is heated to vaporize the carbon dioxide and recover the naphthalene. The carbon dioxide is then condensed and recycled to the extractor.

In summary, there exist four modes of operating the supercritical extraction of solid substances. The specific mode employed in any instance is a function of many factors, for example, the sensitivity of the material(s) to temperature and the ease of condensation or nucleation. Many facets and parameters must be considered and evaluated before one selects a process and operating conditions. Supercritical fluid extraction is no exception to this rule.

Enough groundwork on the "generic" nature of solubility behavior in SCF solvents has been developed in the previous chapters of this book for the reader to extrapolate from the idealized situation of separating a mixture of naphthalene and chalk dust to other, more practical systems. For example, other systems may include the extraction of oleoresins from spices where the desired product is the extract, or the extraction of monomers and oligomers from polymers where the desired product is the purified polymer, or the separation of a mixture of chemicals where both streams are valuable products.

There exists an alternative operating scheme for utilizing the properties of supercritical fluids in the separation of liquid mixtures. A supercritical fluid can separate certain pairs of miscible liquids without "extracting" them. Elgin and Weinstock (1959) discuss the separation of water-organic mixtures where supercritical ethylene is used to "salt out" the water. The ternary phase behavior exhibited by certain water–organic–supercritical fluid mixtures was discussed in detail in chapter 3. The "SCF salting out" concept is not applicable only for water-organic solutions, however. If the supercritical fluid is highly soluble in, or miscible with, one of the liquids and is insoluble or scarcely soluble in the other, a liquid-liquid phase split can occur when the liquid solution is contacted with the supercritical fluid. The next section of this chapter describes the features of phase-splitting phenomena for polymer–organic solvent–supercritical fluid solvent mixtures. Although the phase behavior of polymer mixtures is explicitly described, it should be evident from the information presented in chapter 3 that the same phase-behavior principles apply to oligomer species having molecular weights well below 1,000.

Polymer-solvent mixtures can be separated and the polymer recovered from solution at the lower critical-solution temperature (LCST)—that is, the temperature at which the miscible polymer-solvent mixture separates into a polymer-rich phase and a solvent-rich phase. LCST phenomena can be related to the chemical nature of the components of the mixture, the molecular weight of the components, especially the polymer, and the critical temperature and critical pressure of the solvent (Allen and Baker, 1965). As the single-phase polymer solution is isobarically heated to conditions near the critical point of the solvent, the polymer and solvent thermally expand at different rates (which means that their free volumes change at different rates [Patterson, 1969]). The thermal expansion of the solvent is much greater than that of the polymer. Near its critical point, the solvent has expanded so much that it no longer is able to solubilize the polymer. Hence, the polymer falls out of solution. If the molecular weight of the polymer is on the order of ten thousand, a polymer-solvent LCST can occur within about 20°C–30°C of the solvent's critical temperature. If the molecular weight of the polymer is closer to one million, then the LCST phase separation can occur at a temperature as low as 120°C below the critical temperature of the solvent.

In general, saturated cyclic hydrocarbons, such as cyclohexane or methyl cyclopentane, tend to be good polymer solvents. These types of solvents have very high critical temperatures and therefore it is often necessary to raise the temperature of the system to well over 200°C to obtain an LCST phase split. At these high temperatures it may be possible to degrade the polymer thermally. Polymer degradation can be avoided at high LCSTs by adding stabilizers to the polymer solution (Anolick and Slocum, 1973; Anolick and Goffinet, 1971; Caywood, 1970).

Recently, Irani, Cosewith, and Kasegrande (1982) patented a process for lowering the LCST of a polymer-solvent mixture by adding an SCF solvent to the mixture. The effect of an SCF additive on the polymer-solution phase behavior is shown in figure 6.3. Note that the UCST line has been omitted from figure 6.3. Addition of between 5 and 15 wt-% supercritical propylene to a poly (ethylene-co-propylene)–hexane mixture shifts the phase-border curves for this system to lower temperatures. The polymer-rich phase that is recovered is highly concentrated in polymer, approximately 40 wt-%. Conventional solvent-stripping techniques, such as steam stripping, can then be used to recover the polymer from this polymer-rich phase. In this process the amount of residual polymer remaining in the solvent-rich phase at the LCST is reduced by about a factor of three (in some instances from about 0.22 wt-% polymer to about 0.08 wt-%).

A diagram for a proposed process for a polymer-solvent-SCF additive process is shown in figure 6.4 (Irani, Cosewith, and Kasegrande, 1982). Sub-

Figure 6.3 Schematic representation of the effect of an SCF solvent on the phase behavior of
polymer–organic solvent mixtures: (a) *P-T* projection of various
phase-boundary curves for a polymer–organic solvent mixture with
an SCF solvent added to the system; (b) same as (a) but without the
SCF solvent (McHugh, n.d.).

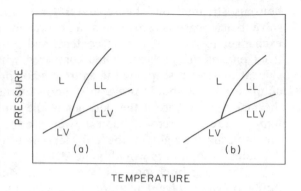

Figure 6.4 Diagram of a proposed process for recovering polymer from solution by adding
an SCF solvent to the mixture (McHugh, 1986).

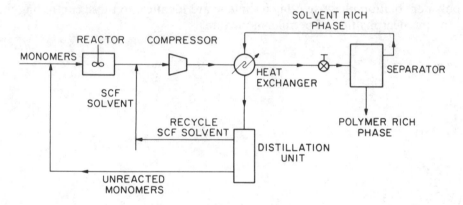

critical propylene (T_c = 91.9°C, P_c = 45.6 atm) is added to the reactor product
stream prior to the compressor. Although other SCF additives will also shift
the LCST to lower temperatures (McHugh and Guckes, 1985), propylene is
already present in the product stream and therefore does not represent an
added component to the system. The entire mixture is compressed to the
desired operating pressure and then heated to much higher temperatures. The
mixture, now a single liquid phase, is throttled to lower pressures. As the
pressure is reduced, the LCST curve is intersected and a polymer-rich liquid
phase and a solvent-rich liquid phase are formed. If the pressure is further
reduced, three phases (LLV) will form in the separator. Irani, Cosewith, and
Kasegrande suggest that a better solvent-polymer split is obtained when the
system is operating in the LLV region of the phase diagram, as compared with
the LL region. Also, a lower operating pressure can be used, and the small
amount of vapor formed in the LLV region can be vented to maintain a
constant operating pressure. The denser polymer-rich phase is recovered as a

bottoms stream from the separator for further processing. The less dense solvent-rich phase is recovered as an overhead stream, integrated with the heat exchanger to recover its heat content, and purified and recycled back to the front end of the process. When compared with recovering the polymer and solvent by stream stripping the entire reactor product stream, this SCF-solvent additive process should prove less energy-intensive. There should also be less thermal degradation of the polymer at the more moderate process-operating temperature. Therefore, control over product quality (i.e., distribution of the molecular weight of the polymer) should be easier, and less polymer-degradation inhibitors would be needed.

Described in chapter 9 is the work of McHugh and co-workers on separating polymer-solvent mixtures by adding an SCF additive to the mixture. Also, as is noted in the following chapter, the underlying fundamentals of this polymer-solution phase-splitting technique are identical to those controlling the propane deasphalting of petroleum mixtures.

7

Early Industrial Applications

Before progressing to a discussion of recent supercritical fluid process and applications development, we shall first describe other very early processes that employed "unusual" solvents.

PROPANE DEASPHALTING

Half a century ago Wilson, Keith, and Haylett (1936) devised a process for phase-equilibrium separations that became the basis of the propane deasphalting process still in use today for refining lube oils. Although the process is not, strictly speaking, a supercritical fluid extraction process (because the initial extraction step is not carried out at supercritical conditions), propane deasphalting does make use of the change in the solvent power of a liquid in the vicinity of its critical point. It is also an example of a process using near-critical property changes to improve energy and phase-separation efficiency. Since the solvent characteristics of propane can be changed dramatically in various regimes of pressure-temperature phase space, this single solvent can be used selectively to separate a lube-oil feedstock into paraffin wax, asphalt, heavy ends, naphthenes, color bodies, and the desired product, a purified light oil.

Let us briefly consider the propane lube-oil refining process as shown in the schematic diagram in figure 7.1. In the asphalt settler saturated, liquid propane at approximately 50°C dissolves all the constituents of a lube-oil feedstock except for the asphalt. Because the propane–lube oil mixture possesses a low viscosity, the asphalt fraction is readily separated from the mixture and, hence, easily recovered. The refrigerant properties of liquid propane are exploited so that the waxes are precipitated from the mixture by reducing pressure, which, by evaporating a small portion of the solution, causes the temperature of the mixture to decrease to approximately 4°C. (The dewaxing section of the process is not shown in the figure.) Heating the remaining propane-oil mixture to temperatures near 100°C decreases the solvent power of liquid propane, resulting in the sequential precipitation of the resins, the heavy ends, and the naphthenic constituents, thus leaving only the lightest paraffins in solution. Figure 7.1 shows only the asphalt and resin-removing sections of the process.

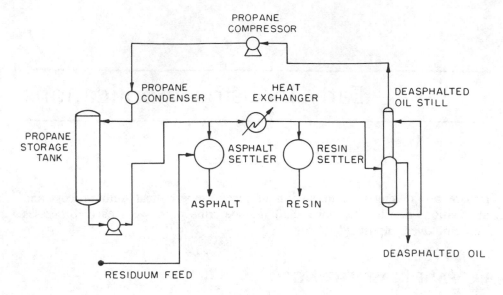

Figure 7.1 Schematic diagram of the propane–lube oil refining process (Wilson, Keith, and Haylett, 1936).

Before explaining the thermodynamic framework of the propane-deas-phalting process, we present several paragraphs from the 1936 paper by Wilson, Keith, and Haylett to highlight what was known fifty years ago about near-critical and supercritical fluid processing.

Although there are numerous ways of removing these impurities, the oil industry within the past few years has focused its attention upon the use of selective solvents. Selective solvents quickly made progress in the fields of separating the naphthenic from the paraffinic constituents of lubricating oils which otherwise required the use of large quantities of sulfuric acid with the attendant acid sludge nuisance. Some solvents were found which were able to remove both naphthenic and asphaltic constituents, but, since the resulting extract was a mixture of asphalt and naphthenic hydrocarbons, it required further refining and separation to make marketable by-products and hence was not very promising. . . . After the oil refiner had learned of the efficiency and cheapness of selective solvents, he was anxious to find solvents (or antisolvents) which would remove not only one or two impurities, but all of the undesirable constituents of lubricating oils, preferably one at a time in order that the by-products might be recovered in useful form. In an effort to discover such a universal solvent, chemists have searched Bielstein and other sources without finding any single chemical whose solvent properties are such that it will selectively remove all these impurities, although several of the improved solvents for the removal of naphthenic compounds have been studied as a result of this search.

Unfortunately, during most of this search for solvents, the refiner neglected to look at his own raw materials. In every refinery and in every crude field, millions of tons of propane gas are available, which, by simple compression and liquefaction, can be converted into a solvent with the unique property (under proper conditions of temperature and pressure) of tending to separate every one of the undesirable constituents. Further, assuming recovery facilities are available, propane is the cheapest liquid per gallon available in the refinery with the exception of water; it is nontoxic, noncorrosive, and extremely stable.

If we consider the diverse chemical and physical characteristics of the five undesirable constituents listed, it would seem almost inconceivable to anyone familiar with the theory of fractional solution that any one solvent could possibly throw all of these different compounds out of solution. As a matter of fact, propane cannot be expected to, and does not, separate them all at the same temperature and pressure. It owes its versatility as a precipitant to the fact that its properties change rapidly over the particular temperature range between $-44°$ and $+215°F$. Over this range it possesses the properties of a series of solvents, any one of which can be obtained by raising or lowering the temperature or changing the pressure or combining those two operations.

Incidentally, its viscosity and surface tension decrease to nearly negligible values as the critical temperature is approached. Over this range propane changes from a typical liquid to a fluid possessing substantially the properties of gas. As the 220°F isotherm indicates, gaseous propane at a pressure of 1000 pounds per square inch is much more dense . . . than liquid propane at 212°F and its saturation pressure. (Authors' Note: Wilson et al. were a few degrees off on the critical temperature of propane. However, this does not detract from the importance of their work.) Also, as the liquid approaches its critical temperature, it becomes highly compressible.

At temperatures near the critical, increasing the pressure (which increases density) . . . increases the solubility of oil in propane. The dissolving power of propane appears to be roughly proportional to the density of the propane, and even compressed propane gas at 220°F and 1000 pounds per square inch pressure dissolves substantially more oil than does liquid propane at 600 pounds and 204°F. Thus the solvent properties of propane can be strikingly changed by changes in either temperature or pressure or both; and in the magnitude of the resulting change it is probably unique among liquids.

As a result of these unique properties propane is today being commercially employed in numerous large installations for the separation of all five of the undesirable constituents of lubricating oils. That this development should have taken place in the short period of three years is a remarkable tribute both to the versatility of propane and the progressiveness of the petroleum refiner.

As is evident in these paragraphs, the authors clearly are excited about the possibilities of processing with a single solvent that has the properties of many solvents. In order to explain the events that are occurring at various points in the propane–lube oil refining process, we shall first examine schematic pressure-temperature (*P-T*) and ternary phase diagrams.

Shown in figure 7.2 is a *P-T* representation of the phase behavior of a propane–distillate oil mixture (Wilson, Keith, and Haylett, 1936). Notice that this phase diagram is similar to the polymer-solvent diagram described in chapters 3 and 6. As shown in figure 7.2, the single-phase propane-oil mixture

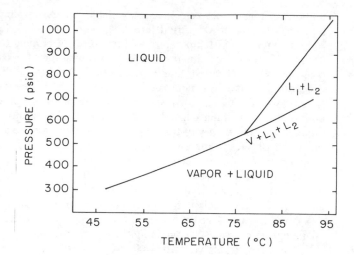

Figure 7.2 *P-T* representation of the phase behavior of the propane–lube oil mixture (Wilson, Keith, and Haylett, 1936).

splits into two liquid phases when the temperature is increased such that the LL curve is crossed. This is the type of phase separation that occurs when the resins, heavy ends, and naphthenic constituents are separated from the lube-oil mixture with increasing temperature. At the intersection of the LL curve with the LLV curve two liquid phases become critically identical in the presence of the vapor phase. Technically, this intersection is called the "lower critical-solution temperature"; however, using polymer-separation terminology, this intersection is renamed the "lower critical end point" (LCEP) and the LL curve is called the "LCST curve."

Although it is not shown on this diagram, the single-phase lube-oil mixture also splits into two phases when the temperature is decreased and the UCST curve is crossed at very cold temperatures. This phenomenon is used to separate the wax from the oil.

For the oil-propane mixture the LCEP occurs within about 22°C of the critical temperature of propane and within about 70 psia of propane's critical pressure. Because the oil distillate consists of high-molecular-weight components, the reason for the occurrence of the LCEP is analogous to the reason the LCEP for polymer-solvent systems occurs near the critical point of the solvent. As the single-phase mixture is heated to conditions near the critical point of propane, the mixture components thermally expand at different rates (Patterson, 1968). The thermal expansion of the propane is much greater than that of the heavy components in the oil distillate. Near its critical point, propane has expanded to the point where it no longer is able to solubilize the highest-molecular-weight fraction in the oil distillate (i.e., the heavy ends). Hence, the heavy ends of the oil precipitate from solution. The degree of separation of the heavy ends can be illustrated by a ternary diagram for an asphalt-oil-propane mixture. Of course, the asphalt and the oil are not single components and, as such, the ternary diagrams are only a qualitative representation of the actual phase behavior.

Shown in figure 7.3 are three schematic ternary diagrams representing the phase behavior of asphalt-oil-propane mixtures at three temperatures (Wilson, Keith, and Haylett, 1936). The principles governing the phase behavior shown in these diagrams are exactly the same as those described for the ternary systems presented in chapter 3. At 37.8°C propane is entirely miscible with the oil, the oil is entirely miscible with the asphalt, but the propane is only partially miscible with the asphalt and, therefore, the asphalt falls out of solution. This represents the first step of the lube-oil refining process. The phase behavior depicted in this diagram indicates that only oil distillates with high concentrations of asphalt are separated by propane at this temperature.

If the temperature is increased to 60°C the two-phase region of the diagram expands considerably. Since this temperature is much closer to the critical temperature of propane, liquid propane is in a much more expanded state than at 38°C. Notice that the critical point on this diagram has moved toward greater propane-oil concentrations. If enough propane is added to a

Figure 7.3 Ternary phase behavior of the asphalt-oil-propane mixture at three different temperatures (Wilson, Keith, and Haylett, 1936).

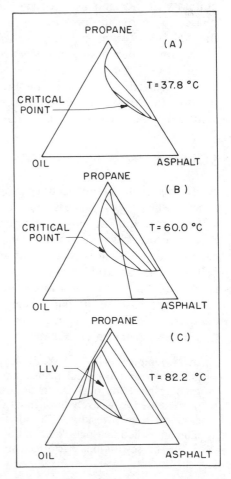

75% asphalt and 25% oil mixture such that the two-phase region of the diagram is entered, we see that further increasing the amount of propane increases the amount of the light propane-rich phase while improving the degree of separation of the original asphalt-oil mixture. In this case, increased amounts of propane added to the asphalt-oil mixture decreases the solvent power of the oil for the asphalt.

If the temperature is now increased to 82.2°C, the oil-propane binary mixture develops an LV region on the oil-propane axis of the ternary phase diagram and an LLV region appears in the interior of the ternary phase diagram. The three-phase behavior in this ternary diagram is similar to that of type-II ternary phase behavior described in chapter 3. The LLV behavior occurs since we are in close proximity of the critical point of propane. The degree of separation appears to have improved at this temperature for asphalt-oil feed mixtures which are at least about 60% asphalt.

Wilson, Keith, and Haylett conclude that (1) higher operating temperatures reduce the solubility of the asphalt in the propane-rich phase; (2) increased amounts of propane also reduce the amount of asphalt in the propane-rich phase; (3) increasing pressure in the LL region of the *P-T* diagram increases the solubility of asphalt in the propane-rich phase (see figure 7.2); and (4) compressed propane gas dissolves more oil than does liquid propane at slightly lower temperatures and pressures. Their work certainly promotes the use of near-critical (and, by implication, supercritical) fluids. It is quite impressive that this fundamental work was done and the process commercialized some fifty years before the current awareness of the unique properties of SCFs.

SOLEXOL PROCESS

A few years after the concept of propane deasphalting was developed a similar process, the Solexol process, was developed for the purification and separation of vegetable and fish oils (Dickinson and Meyers, 1952). The purpose of the Solexol process was to concentrate the polyunsaturated triglycerides (the so-called drying oils) in vegetable oils and to extract the vitamin-A "values" from fish oils. The Solexol process, which also uses propane as a selective solvent, is described in two publications (Dickinson and Meyers, 1952; Passino, 1949). As for the case of propane–lube oil refining, we present for purposes of comparison with contemporary developments of SCF extraction some descriptive phrases from an early paper.

> In November, 1946, M. W. Kellogg Company, engineers and contractors of petroleum and chemical plants, announced to industry a solvent process for treating glyceride oils. Given the name "Solexol," it was a development of a process used extensively throughout the world to fractionate lubricating oils from crude petroleum residues. The solvent used in the process is ordinary propane, familiar as liquified petroleum gas or "bottled gas."
>
> The separations performed in Solexol pilot plants, some of which were

described in an article by H. J. Passino, are in many instances, little short of amazing, not only of themselves but in the infinite variety of things which have been done with a single solvent and in a single tower. However, in the almost five years since the announcement there has been a scarcity of information on the extent to which sound commercial operations have borne out the promise for plant explorations.

At this writing there are five commercial Solexol plants in regular service, and a sixth is under construction. Furthermore two of the Solexol units are supplemented by a continuous fractional crystallization (or winterizing) process, not heretofore announced, which goes by the name of "Propane Destearnizing." As the name suggests, it also employs versatile propane as solvent. (Dickinson and Meyers, 1952)

Dickinson and Meyers go on to describe triglyceride refining plants, some of which operate at throughputs as high as 200,000 pounds per day. In the same vein of excitement as exhibited by the authors who wrote about propane deasphalting, the authors of the Solexol paper describe the properties of near-critical and supercritical propane and the ability to extend these properties to the development and, more importantly, to the commercialization of a propane-refining process.

A schematic diagram of the Solexol processing of fish oils is shown in figure 7.4. The fish oils are fed to a train of countercurrent extractors where column-to-column variations in temperature as well as temperature variations within each specific column can affect the solvent power of propane in a manner similar to that seen with propane deasphalting.

Fish-oil triglycerides are complex compounds consisting of various saturated and unsaturated fatty acids on a glycerol backbone. However, staging the temperature within an extraction column and supplying a recycle stream allows the separation of the fish-oil triglycerides by virtue of the variable dissolving power of near-critical propane and by virtue of the lower propane solubility of unsaturated triglycerides relative to the propane solubility of saturated triglycerides. At room temperature propane dissolves all the triglycerides. Heating liquid propane decreases its solvent power, as seen for the propane deasphalting process. Within what is termed the "paracritical region" (the region where the dissolving power can be influenced strongly by pressure and temperature) it is possible to choose operating conditions such that progressive temperature changes near the critical temperature of propane can result in the successive precipitation of various fish-oil fractions. With multiple-extraction towers it is possible to separate color bodies, "insolubles," oil fractions with low and high unsaturation levels, and a vitamin-A concentrate with a 10–20-fold increase in vitamin potency relative to the crude fish-oil feed. It is possible to tailor operating conditions so as to concentrate the unsaturated triglycerides from seed and fish oils for use as drying oils in the paint and varnish industry.

The underlying thermodynamic principles for this process are identical to

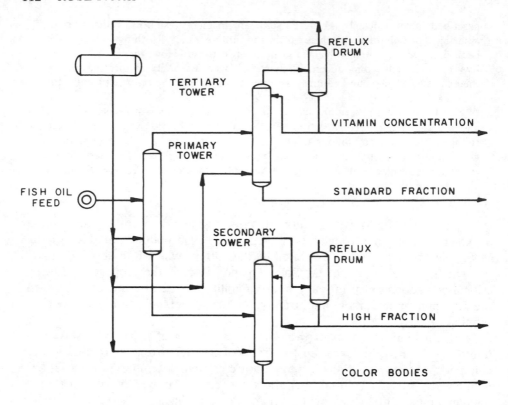

Figure 7.4 A schematic diagram of the Solexol process for separating fish oils (Dickinson and Meyers, 1952).

those exhibited for the propane deasphalting process. This process is yet another example of the use of the unique solvent characteristics of near-critical and supercritical fluids developed some forty years ago.

ROSE PROCESS

Following chronological order and progressing to developments in the 1970s, we come to another process, Kerr McGee's Residuum Oil Supercritical Extraction (ROSE) process, which we will compare with the previous two processes (Gearhart and Garwin, 1976). The ROSE process is also not, strictly speaking, a supercritical fluid extraction process. For example, the primary extraction step of the ROSE process is not carried out at supercritical conditions, but instead at liquid conditions. Nevertheless, the process does take clever advantage of the variable solvent power of a near-critical liquid at various stages of the extraction/separation process. The process derives its supercritical acronym from the operation of the last stage of the process. The thermody-

namics and phase-equilibrium principles used in the ROSE process are analogous to those of the propane deasphalting process and as such are not repeated
here.

A schematic diagram of the ROSE process is shown in figure 7.5. The
first stage of the ROSE process consists of mixing residuum with compressed
liquid butane or pentane and precipitating the undesired asphaltene fraction.
This step is similar in sequencing to the previously described propane-deas-
phalting process. The reason butane is used, incidentally, is that it has a higher
solvent power for the heavy hydrocarbons. This fact is explicitly stated by
Wilson, Keith, and Haylett (1936) in their publication. Hence, for the higher
molecular weight resid, butane is an effective solvent in dissolving the desired
high-molecular-weight components and precipitating the asphaltenes. (It is "too
effective" in the lube-oil refining process because the molecular weights of all
the components, desired and undesired, are much lower, with the result that
the components cannot be differentiated finely enough by butane.)

If an intermediate resin fraction is desired, another separator and stripper
system would be installed right after the asphaltene separator in figure 7.5. To
recover a resin fraction the overhead solution from the asphaltene separator,
which now consists of butane, resins, and light oils, is heated to near the
critical temperature of butane. At this elevated, near-critical temperature the
solvent power of compressed liquid butane decreases and the resins precipitate
from solution. The overhead stream from this separator consists of light oils
dissolved in near-critical liquid butane.

The butane-oil solution from the resin separator (or from the AR separator as shown in figure 7.5) is heated to a temperature "slightly above" the
critical temperature of pure butane. At this condition the solvent power of the
now supercritical butane decreases and the light oils are precipitated from
solution. This final separation step is best explained with reference to the
naphthalene–carbon dioxide diagram shown previously as part of figure 6.1
and reproduced here as figure 7.6. The light-oil precipitation step of the ROSE
process is designated schematically as the path $D \rightarrow P$ in figure 7.6. The
idealized path from D (a near-critical liquid) to P (a "near supercritical," low-
density fluid) results in a tenfold decrease in dissolving power of supercritical
carbon dioxide. In an analogous decrease in the solvent power of supercritical
butane, the separation of the desired oil from solution occurs with just a small
input of heat in the last step of the ROSE process.

The ROSE process is an optimally engineered process that operates in
the vicinity of the critical point of the solvent. The ROSE process, the propane
deasphalting process, and the Solexol process all apply thermodynamic fundamentals and high-pressure phase-equilibria principles to the design of energy-
efficient processes. Binary and ternary equilibrium data along with the properties of near-critical and supercritical fluids first obtained in the laboratory
were extended to the development of a separation process, which in the case
of propane deasphalting has still not been replaced. It is no exaggeration to
suggest that, had early workers merely put lube-oil feed stock into a vessel

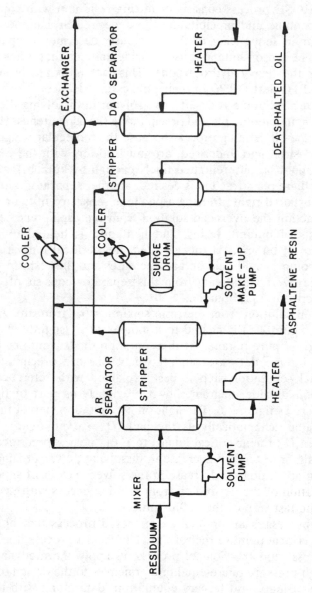

Figure 7.5 A schematic diagram of the ROSE process for separating residuum using a supercritical fluid solvent (Anon., 1981).

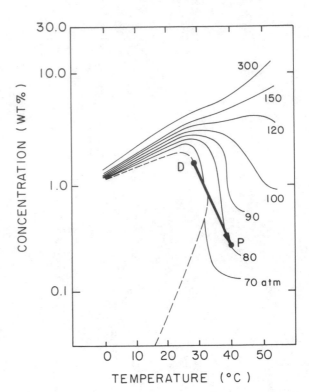

Figure 7.6 Solubility behavior of naphthalene in supercritical CO_2. Line from *D* to *P* represents path to separate dissolved oils in ROSE process.

and mixed it with a high-pressure gas (as one often hears being done today for "quick and dirty" supercritical fluid extraction tests), the separation processes described in this chapter would not have been developed. Suffice it to say that the work reported by the original investigators of these three separation processes indicates that the authors are cognizant of the high-pressure phase-equilibrium principles in operation in their respective processes. Using sound engineering principles, these authors were able to develop unique separation processes.

Numerous other SCF applications are currently being pursued in industrial research and development laboratories in the United States. As yet none of these applications has enjoyed the success of the three previously described processes. (In West Germany two commercial plants employing supercritical carbon dioxide are in operation, one in Bremenhaven for decaffeinating coffee, and the other in Münchsmünster for extracting hops.) In chapters 8–10 we shall describe the state of the art in research of supercritical fluids.

Authors' Note: Since the first printing of this book Pfizer Corporation announced the operation of a manufacturing facility, located in Sydney, Nebraska, for extracting hops with carbon dioxide. This announcement was made at the Bulk Pharmaceutical Manufacturers' Association meeting in Newport, RI in May, 1987. Foster Wheeler (USA) is currently engineering and constructing a multimillion dollar installation for a food manufacturing company. Foster Wheeler is also engineering a similar facility for another industry.

8

Supercritical Fluid Process Development Studies: 1976–1981

As described in chapter 1, the factors that motivated the use of supercritical fluid solvents in developing separation processes were that the cost of energy was increasing quite rapidly in the 1970s, industrial solvents were under increased scrutiny by the government, the public was exhibiting an increased awareness about pollution control, and specialized materials were facing increasing performance demands.

The energy shortage in the early and late 1970s was largely responsible for the resurgent interest in supercritical fluid extraction in the United States and was the motivation for a great effort in research and development (R&D), initiated both in industry and in academia. A large number of researchers investigated SCF extraction for separating organics from water, as a process which could displace the more traditional method of distillation. In many instances it is theoretically possible that separation of organic mixtures by supercritical fluid processing will require less energy than is required by distillation or evaporation. For these two processes compression energy for the recycled solvent and the heat of vaporization for the organics must be compared.

Reducing energy costs became a national obsession in the 1970s. For example, membrane separation processes, such as ultrafiltration and reverse osmosis, have proliferated because of energy considerations. Concentration or separation of a liquid stream requires less energy in membrane technologies because the compression energy necessary to overcome osmotic forces is much less than the evaporation energy needed to separate a liquid from its dissolved salts. Similarly, as we saw in chapter 6, supercritical fluid extraction can be less energy-intensive than evaporation, but as we have stated it must be evaluated on a case-by-case basis.

By the late 1970s evidence had accumulated on the potential hazards of certain extraction solvents, especially chlorinated hydrocarbons. Increased scrutiny of "traditional" industrial solvents is responsible for spawning another

117

large body of R&D programs on SCF processes. Increased consumer awareness of potential chemical hazards coupled with the uncertainty of future governmental regulatory action motivated an examination of supercritical fluids as extraction solvents for foods, beverages, and spices.

During the 1970s the public became aware of the concept of zero-discharge. The challenge of zero-waste discharge, although not strictly legislated, has resulted in an examination of a variety of cleanup and destruction processes for treating liquid and solid waste materials. Also, increased attention has been given to improving traditional pollution-control processes, such as incineration and adsorption. SCF technology found favor with those concerned with the waste problem, and several new SCF processes for accomplishing a variety of cleanup tasks were developed. These SCF processes are described in subsequent sections of this and the following chapters.

In the 1970s, manufacturers found increased performance demands being placed on various materials, such as chemicals, polymers, and pharmaceuticals. They found that many of the conventional processing technologies could not satisfy the new requirements. SCF processing is being evaluated in an attempt to find the solution to these problems. SCF extraction is being tested for the removal of residual solvents and monomers from high-molecular-weight polymers; for the purification of heat-labile intermediate chemicals and monomers, such as soft-lens and dental monomers; for the fractionation of sensitive specialty polymers; and for many other purposes illustrated in subsequent sections of this book.

Numerous examples of SCF research are examined in this book. Some of the work described in this chapter has only recently been presented at national meetings; some of our own, as yet unpublished research is included to illustrate the breadth of application of SCF technology.

ACTIVATED-CARBON REGENERATION

The forerunner of all the recent applications of SCF technology reported in the United States is the SCF regeneration of activated carbon first described at an American Chemical Society meeting in 1978 (Modell, de Fillipi, and Krukonis, 1978). The phenomena in operation during adsorption of organics from wastewater and the "desorption" of organics from the activated carbon using supercritical carbon dioxide are similar to those active in other supercritical fluid extraction processes. Therefore, it is informative to examine this process in some detail in this section.

The advantages of SCF regeneration are reduced energy requirements and lower carbon loss as compared with the thermal regeneration process currently in operation. It is suggested that, because many organic compounds can be dissolved by supercritical fluid solvents, the organic materials adsorbed onto activated carbon during the cleanup of a wastewater stream can be desorbed by supercritical carbon dioxide at conditions that are less severe than the 1,000°C temperature level of an industrial regeneration furnace.

For small-scale processes, which use activated carbon at a rate of a few thousand pounds per day, the desorbers can also serve as fixed-bed adsorption vessels. Hence, *in situ* carbon regeneration can be carried out when the carbon bed is "spent," that is, fully loaded with adsorbed organics. For much larger activated-carbon-usage processes and for systems requiring many large adsorption vessels, such as those at municipal waste-treatment facilities, the spent carbon can be removed from the adsorbers and transferred to the desorbers for regeneration. The transfer of the spent activated carbon from adsorbers to the thermal regeneration furnace is currently standard industrial practice. The spent carbon is transferred by water slurry pumps, sequenced valves, and motor-activated closures. Here we discuss the large activated-carbon-usage process.

Shown in figure 8.1 is a schematic diagram of a system for regenerating activated carbon using supercritical carbon dioxide. Initially, the desorption vessel shown in figure 8.1 is filled with spent carbon. Since current activated-carbon regeneration technology uses slurry pumping to transfer spent carbon to the thermal regeneration furnace, the slurry method is utilized in the schematic design of the SCF regeneration system. After the desorber vessel is filled with spent activated carbon, the water is allowed to drain from the vessel and the vessel is pressurized with carbon dioxide to the desired operating conditions. Flow of supercritical carbon dioxide through the vessel commences when the pressure-reduction valve is actuated. The adsorbed organics are dissolved by the CO_2 flowing through the carbon bed. The organic-laden stream of carbon dioxide leaving the vessel is then expanded to a lower pressure in order to precipitate the organics and collect them in the separator vessel shown in the figure. The solute-free carbon dioxide leaving the separator is recompressed and recycled to the desorber vessel, and the process is continued until the activated carbon has been stripped of its adsorbed organics.

At the end of the regeneration step, the CO_2 flow is stopped, the vessel is opened to allow the CO_2 to depressurize, and the activated carbon is removed via slurry pumps. The vessel is then refilled with spent activated carbon, the water drained, and the desorption process repeated. Incidentally, the CO_2 that is left in the vessel at the end of the regeneration cycle is lost in this procedure. Although the cost of carbon dioxide is rather low, about 5–10 cents per pound depending upon the volume used, its consumption should be considered in evaluating the viability of a process, especially if the cost of the material being extracted is low. The CO_2 that is lost represents an economic penalty for this process, but part or all of it can be recovered with the installation of an additional CO_2 surge tank system.

The economic viability of any process, not just of a supercritical fluid extraction process, requires that equipment utilization be efficient because off-line time is a capital investment penalty. In the present activated-carbon

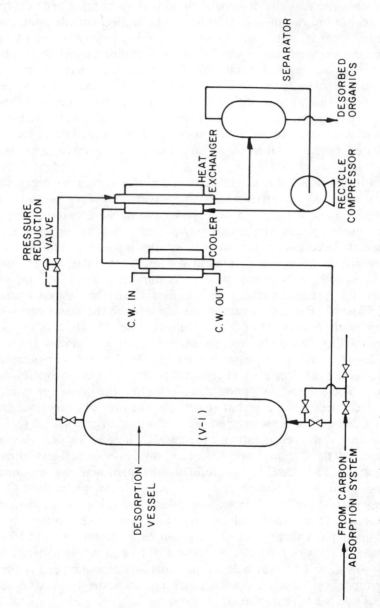

Figure 8.1 Schematic diagram of an apparatus used for regenerating activated carbon with a supercritical fluid solvent.

regeneration case, the batch-mode filling and emptying portions of the process requires a finite amount of time that may be a significant portion of the total processing sequence.

Let us now consider the operation of the regeneration process using a second desorber vessel, which can increase equipment utilization. The added vessel provides the capability of minimizing or eliminating the filling and emptying downtime. In the two-vessel operation shown schematically in figure 8.2, while the regeneration process is being carried out in the first vessel, the second vessel is filled with spent activated carbon and the water is drained from the vessel. At the end of the regeneration step (in vessel 1), the CO_2 flow is stopped, the vessels are allowed to communicate so that one-half the CO_2 is transferred to the second vessel. The CO_2 remaining in the first vessel is allowed to vent to the atmosphere, and in this two-vessel operation part of the CO_2 is saved. The regeneration is started when CO_2 flow to the second vessel is commenced; the first vessel is emptied and filled while the regeneration of activated carbon in the second vessel is occurring. Thus, part of the CO_2 is recovered and about one-half the downtime is eliminated by the addition of the second vessel to the process layout.

Whether the previously described process is economically optimized depends, of course, on many factors. Whether to recover the CO_2, how much to recover, how much downtime can be endured, and similar considerations are a strong function of the amount of activated carbon to be processed, the operating conditions, the cost of the activated carbon, the cost of the equipment, and similar items. For the case of activated-carbon regeneration, recovery of CO_2 should probably be considered, and the additional capital expense of the second vessel may be justified.

This activated-carbon regeneration study (de Fillipi et al., 1980) was directed to an evaluation of the regeneration of activated carbon used in the cleaning of wastewaters that emanate from pesticide manufacturing plants. A wide range of pesticides as well as various types of activated carbon were investigated. A large matrix of temperatures and pressures was first examined in order to determine the solubility characteristics of the pesticides before carrying out the more involved adsorption/desorption tests. Illustrative results of this study, which is described in detail in a report prepared by Arthur D. Little, Inc., for the United States Environmental Protection Agency (de Fillipi et al., 1980), are presented in the following paragraphs.

Figure 8.3 shows the molecular structure of six pesticides that were tested and their solubility levels in supercritical carbon dioxide at one set of test conditions, 4,000 psia and 100°C. Also included in this figure is the solubility of phenol, which was studied because it is a raw material in the production of some of the pesticides and thus might be found in pesticide plant wastewaters. The solubility of these compounds varies over a one hundredfold concentration range, but as is noted subsequently the regenerability of activated carbon is not necessarily related solely to the solubility level. Specifically, a high solubility

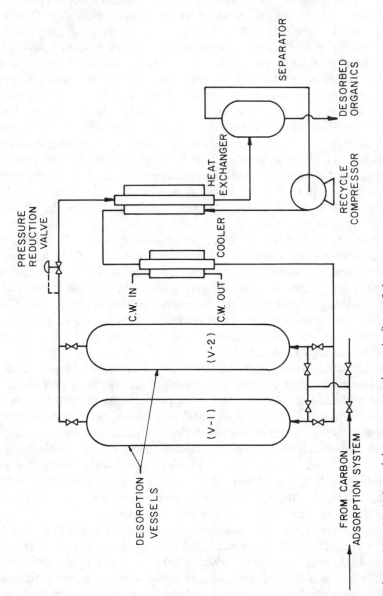

Figure 8.2 Variation of the apparatus shown in figure 8.1.

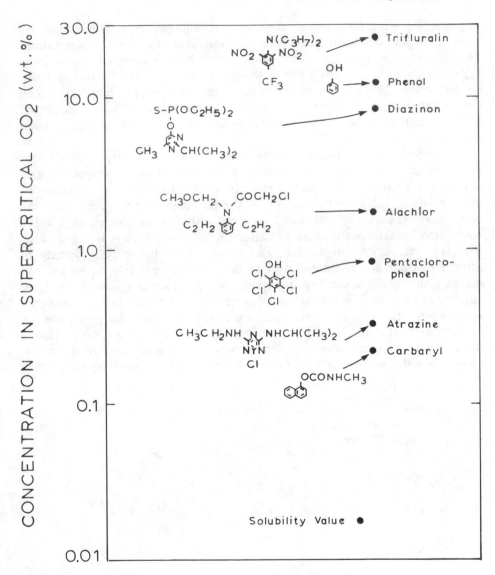

Figure 8.3 Molecular structure and supercritical carbon dioxide solubility of six pesticides at 100°C and 4,000 psia.

in supercritical CO_2 does not ensure that adsorbed pesticide will be removed from the activated carbon.

For the purpose of evaluating the efficacy of using supercritical carbon dioxide to regenerate spent activated carbon, a series of adsorption and desorption experiments are performed and the capacity and capacity recovery of the activated carbon are measured. A fixed bed of activated carbon is exposed to a synthetic wastewater stream containing a single pesticide. The wastewater in most cases is synthesized at a concentration level of about 80% saturation. The effluent water from the carbon adsorption column is analyzed on-line using UV-spectrophotometry. With this technique, a "breakthrough" curve is determined. When the pesticide in the column effluent stream reaches the feed concentration, the water flow is stopped, the water is drained from the column, and supercritical carbon dioxide, typically at 4,000 psia and 100°C, is passed through the carbon bed.

Synthetic alachlor solutions were studied most thoroughly since alachlor exhibited the best regeneration behavior. A series of alachlor-adsorption curves is shown in figure 8.4. The area above the adsorption curve is a measure of the capacity of the activated carbon for the pesticide. Curve 1 represents the adsorption breakthrough measured on fresh activated carbon, curve 2 is the adsorption breakthrough, measured after the activated carbon is regenerated with supercritical carbon dioxide, and so on. The "first-cycle" capacity of activated carbon for alachlor is greater than subsequent-cycle capacities, but curves 2 through 7 essentially superpose, which indicates that a steady-state adsorption capacity is achieved with supercritical carbon dioxide regeneration. Incidentally, the reasons for the decrease in capacity after the first cycle are not discussed in detail here, but probably are the same as those reported by workers who have examined liquid organic solvent regeneration of spent carbon. It is well known that the heat of adsorption of a compound varies with

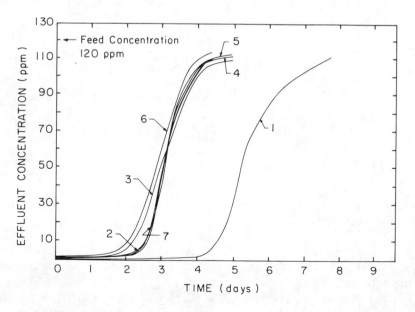

Figure 8.4   Adsorption breakthrough curves of alachlor on activated carbon; numbers on the curves indicate the number of the cycle.

the loading of that compound on the activated carbon. At low loadings the heat of adsorption is very high (approaching chemisorption strength) while at higher loadings the heat of adsorption decreases in strength. The heat of adsorption is equated to the high sorption forces between the very active carbon sites and the organic compound. The most active sites are used first and as they become titrated the adsorption forces decrease to levels that are typical of physical adsorption strengths. Thus, it might be concluded that "some" sites of activated carbon are easier to regenerate than others. The ability to achieve a constant but lower adsorption capacity, as shown in curves 2 through 7, probably is a manifestation of such relative forces representing the ability of supercritical CO_2 to remove the less strongly held molecules. The first regeneration cycle probably removes only the molecules held by weaker physical adsorption. Thus, there is a drop in the capacity of the carbon bed and subsequent adsorptions and regenerations probably operate only on the available low-energy sites.

As mentioned previously, alachlor is one pesticide that is easily removed from the activated carbon. Some of the other pesticides are not as readily removed by treatment with supercritical carbon dioxide. The compounds diazinon, pentachlorophenol, and carbaryl exhibit extremely strong adsorption strengths, which renders the activated carbon unregenerable. Hence, the adsorptive capacity of the carbon falls to almost zero after two or three cycles. Although the specific interactions between the activated carbon and the pesticide that lead to the decline in carbon capacity are not reported, the differences in the solubility level of the neat pesticides in carbon dioxide are not the only explanation. Figure 8.3 shows that the solubility of diazanon is five times that of alachlor, yet diazanon-spent carbon cannot be regenerated. For example, figure 8.5 shows three adsorption curves with diazinon, and a comparison of the area above the curves shows that the capacity of the activated carbon has fallen to 10% after two adsorption-desorption cycles. Although the primary function of this study was to screen a number of pesticides and not to investigate sorption phenomena, it is probably accurate to assign the inability of supercritical carbon dioxide to remove these compounds from activated carbon to strong sorption forces or possibly to surface chemical reactions.

Some desorption tests will next be described in some detail because they have relevance to other solid and liquid SCF extraction studies currently in progress at other industrial and academic laboratories. The results of the desorption tests explain some of the phenomena that are reported in other process studies, and the results also point out some limitations of those processes. Figure 8.6 shows a typical desorption profile; in this case the alachlor concentration in the carbon dioxide leaving the activated carbon column is illustrated. The concentration scale represents the average concentration of alachlor in the CO_2 and the length of the line segment marks the volume of CO_2 passed through the bed in a given interval over which the concentration is measured gravimetrically. Recall that neat alachlor solubility at these con-

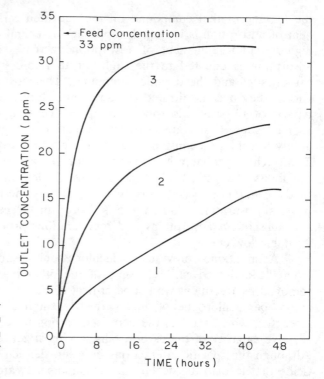

Figure 8.5 Adsorption breakthrough curves of diazinon on activated carbon; numbers on the curves indicate the number of the cycle.

ditions is 10 wt-%, as shown in figure 8.3, but note that the concentrations in figure 8.6 are much lower. Mass-transfer limitations, either from the surface of the activated carbon or through the pellet pores, are one explanation for the decrease in alachlor concentration measured during desorption. A test of this hypothesis is to carry out the carbon regeneration at different volumetric flow rates, linear velocities, carbon-particle sizes, and so on. The results of such studies are shown in figure 8.7. The regeneration curves from these tests superpose, indicating that SCF regeneration is essentially independent of the parameters tested. The conclusion from these tests is that simple mass-transfer limitations are not the controlling factors in the SCF regeneration process.

Another explanation for the shape of the regeneration curves is found in the existence of an adsorption equilibrium in the supercritical carbon dioxide–alachlor–activated carbon system, which is similar to the adsorption equilibria that have been measured for water–organic–activated carbon systems. It is found that the analogue of the adsorption isotherm in water systems represents the controlling mechanism for the desorption process. Adsorption equilibria for the more common water–organic–activated carbon systems are usually given as Langmuir and/or Freundlich isotherms, which correlate the loading of the organic on the activated carbon with the concentration of the organic in the water phase. The shape and slope of these isotherms are found to be related to the adsorptive strength of the organic on the carbon. When the

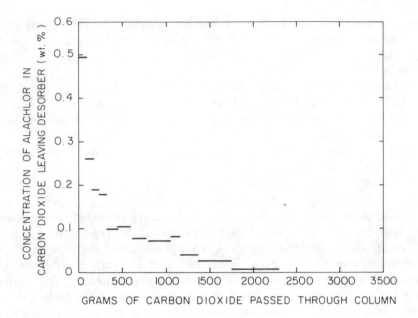

Figure 8.6 Desorption profile of alachlor from activated carbon using supercritical carbon dioxide.

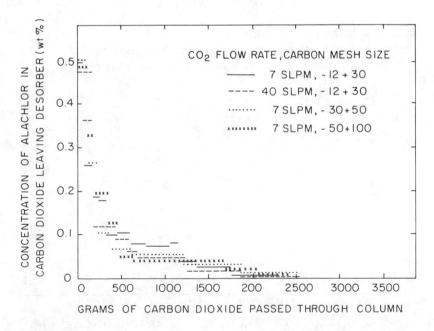

Figure 8.7 Comparison of effects of mass-transfer limitations in the desorption of alachlor from activated carbon using supercritical carbon dioxide; tests with several flow rates and carbon mesh size. (Standard liters per minute [SLPM])

isotherms are fit to a Langmuir or Freundlich model, the parameters of the model can be determined. These same models should be applicable for the case of carbon dioxide, and from the values of the fitted parameters, the data given in figure 8.7 can be explained.

An equilibrium between the pesticide in the supercritical carbon dioxide phase and the pesticide in the solid phase has been measured. Data for the supercritical carbon dioxide–alachlor–activated carbon system are correlated as a Freundlich isotherm, as shown in figure 8.8 (Krukonis, 1977). It is surprising that even at very low concentrations of alachlor, two orders of magnitude below the solubility level shown in figure 8.3, the equilibrium loading on activated carbon is as high as 0.2 g/g. The magnitude of the loading lends credence to the assumption that adsorption-equilibrium limitations are responsible for the shape of the desorption curve and that the solubility in supercritical carbon dioxide does not represent the limiting step of the regeneration process.

The model and mathematics for the case of adsorbent regeneration, which is governed by equilibrium effects, is covered in many texts. The discussion by Sherwood, Pigford, and Wilke (1975) is especially complete. The material balance between the concentration of dissolved material in the carbon dioxide and the concentration "in" the solid activated carbon during the course of the desorption is given by the relation

$$\epsilon(\partial c/\partial t) + p(\partial q/\partial t) + \epsilon v(\partial c/\partial x) = 0, \tag{8.1}$$

where ϵ is the bed void volume,
  c is the concentration of species in the carbon dioxide,
  p is the bulk density of activated carbon (approximately 0.8),

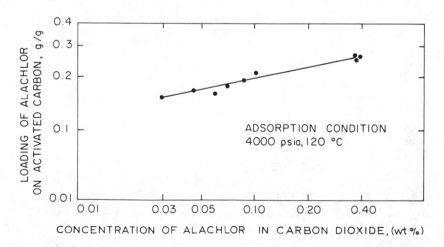

Figure 8.8 Data for the supercritical carbon dioxide–alachlor–activated carbon system fit to a Freundlich isotherm.

q is the concentration of species in the activated carbon, and
v is the linear velocity of carbon dioxide through the bed.

If the relation between c and q is known either analytically, for example as a Langmuir isotherm $q = f(c)$, or graphically as in figure 8.8, equation 8.1 can be solved to give concentration profiles in the carbon dioxide and in the bed as a function of time. This relation is referred to as the "local-equilibrium-theory model."

With the data in figure 8.8 and the assumption of local equilibrium, one can calculate as a function of time the concentration profile of alachlor in the effluent carbon dioxide and the concentration profile of alachlor in the bed of activated carbon. Figure 8.9 shows the calculated profile superposed on the measured regeneration curves given in figure 8.7. The agreement of the measured and calculated profiles is seen to be quite good in both shape and magnitude, which strongly suggests that the local-equilibrium theory correctly explains the measured desorption profile (Modell, et al., 1979).

The existence of the adsorption equilibrium in the carbon dioxide–alachlor–activated carbon system is a fundamental limitation of the supercritical carbon dioxide regeneration process. For example, one of the ramifications of local equilibrium is the requirement that one or two orders of magnitude more carbon dioxide be passed through the bed to regenerate the activated carbon than is predicted from neat alachlor–carbon dioxide solubility data. The findings of this study transcend the topic of activated carbon regeneration and have

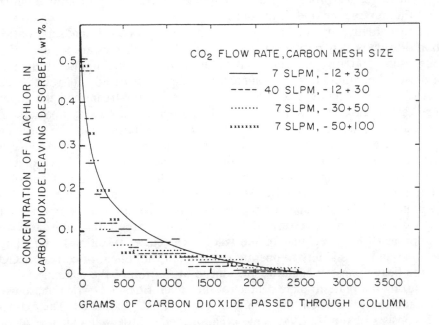

Figure 8.9 Comparison of calculated and experimental desorption data.

implications in other seemingly unrelated SCF extractions. In particular, SCF coffee decaffeination is an example of another system that exhibits an equilibrium isotherm remarkably similar in appearance to the alachlor-SCF isotherm shown in figure 8.8. Therefore, understanding the SCF activated-carbon regeneration process provides a basis for interpreting other SCF processes. We shall discuss the decaffeination of coffee later in chapter 10.

SEPARATION OF ORGANIC-WATER SOLUTIONS

Ethanol-Water

The energy shortages of the 1970s were an impetus for evaluating the use of supercritical fluids for separating organics from water. A process receiving substantial governmental and industrial funding is the supercritical carbon dioxide separation of ethanol from water (Paulaitis, Gilbert, and Nash, 1981; Moses, Goklen, and de Filippi, 1982; Jonas, 1981; Kuk and Montagna, 1983). A primary goal of the work is to break the ethanol-water azeotrope of 95.5 wt-% ethanol. However, if the azeotrope cannot be broken, then a parallel goal is the demonstration of a less energy-intensive process using supercritical fluid extraction in tandem with "normal" azeotropic distillation. In much the same manner that, for example, reverse osmosis and evaporation can be combined to reduce processing costs, it might be possible to combine supercritical fluid extraction and distillation.

Conceptually, the ethanol-water separation process using supercritical carbon dioxide is a chemical engineer's dream. It is not necessary to feed solids through slurry pumps and sequenced solenoid valves. A simplified schematic diagram of the continuous and countercurrent process of ethanol-water separation is shown in figure 8.10. The ethanol-water feed stream and the supercritical carbon dioxide recycle stream can be pumped continuously to a column, the product stream can be drawn off from a separator, and the raffinate (depleted in ethanol) can be discharged from the column through a valve as shown in the figure. (The internals of the extractor may be sieve trays or various packing arrangements.) The feed flows down the column from plate to plate through downcomers against the upward flow of carbon dioxide. There is an upper limit on the operating pressure if the process is to be operated as described since at high pressures the density of the carbon dioxide–rich phase can approach or exceed that of the water-rich phase, resulting in no phase separation and an inability to operate the column (although, of course, if CO_2 were the heavy phase it could be introduced at the top of the column).

During the plate-to-plate contact of the supercritical CO_2–rich phase with the ethanol-water solution, the ethanol is preferentially extracted. The extract, which consists of mostly CO_2, some ethanol, and a little water, leaves at the top of the column. As shown in figure 8.10 the CO_2-rich solution is expanded

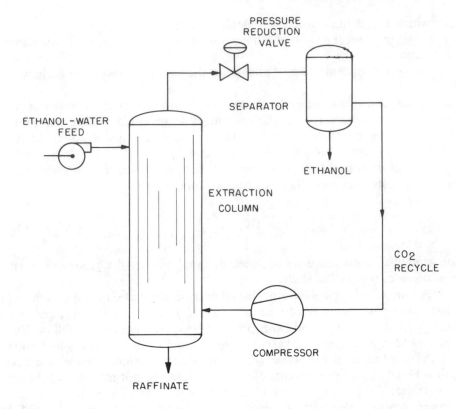

Figure 8.10 Schematic diagram of a supercritical fluid solvent process for extracting ethanol from water.

across a pressure-reduction valve, reducing the solvent power of the carbon dioxide and causing the ethanol to precipitate in the separator. The carbon dioxide is then recompressed and recycled to the extractor.

Let us consider the equations that describe the equilibrium extraction of a material from one phase to another. In practice equilibrium concentrations in two-phase systems are described in terms of a distribution coefficient (sometimes called a "partition coefficient"), which relates the equilibrium concentrations of a species in each of the two phases. Physical chemistry texts usually define the distribution coefficient for a ternary system in terms of a ratio of ratios; for example, the ethanol distribution coefficient in the carbon dioxide–ethanol–water system is given as

$$\text{DC} = \frac{\left(\dfrac{y_e}{1 - y_e}\right)}{\left(\dfrac{x_e}{1 - x_e}\right)} \tag{8.2}$$

where DC is the distribution coefficient,

y_e is the concentration of ethanol dissolved in the carbon dioxide phase, and

x_e is the concentration of ethanol in the water phase at equilibrium.

Although x_e and y_e may be given in any consistent units, such as mole fraction, weight percent, or grams/liter, the units must be specified so that distribution coefficients can be compared on a dimensionally consistent basis. All DC values in this chapter are given in weight units.

For small concentrations of ethanol, say, less than 10 wt-% in either phase, the distribution coefficient relation simplifies to

$$DC = \frac{y_e}{x_e}. \tag{8.3}$$

This simplified equation is more generally employed by the groups discussing ethanol-water separation studies.

A number of groups have published data on the carbon dioxide–ethanol–water system over a range of ethanol concentrations, temperatures, and pressures (Paulaitis, Gilbert, and Nash, 1981; Moses, Goklen, and de Fillipi, 1982; Kuk and Montagna, 1983). These data are plotted in figure 8.11, which shows that the conditions of extraction (i.e., whether the carbon dioxide is a near-critical liquid or a high-pressure supercritical fluid) do not materially influence the extractability (i.e., the distribution coefficient is not affected to a significant degree). A straight line fits the entire collection of data shown in figure 8.11 to within about ±30%. The distribution coefficient, which is the slope of the line in this figure, is about 0.09 (weight basis). The selectivity of carbon dioxide for ethanol from an ethanol-water mixture is quite high. At an ethanol-in-water concentration of 10 wt-%, the concentration of ethanol in the carbon dioxide–rich phase is 0.9 wt-%. Other measurements show the accompanying water concentration is about 0.1 wt-% at 25°C. From these values the selectivity is calculated as 81.

For the case of a constant distribution coefficient, Treybal (1968) shows that the theoretical minimum solvent-to-feed ratio necessary to extract all of a component from a feed stream is equal to the inverse of the distribution coefficient. Recall, however, that the theoretical minimum value of the solvent-to-feed ratio requires an infinitely tall column. In actual practice a greater solvent-to-feed ratio, typically 1.3 to 1.5 times minimum, is employed. Some elementary but informative graphical design procedures are presented here to illustrate the relationship between the distribution coefficient and the operation of the supercritical fluid extraction process for separating ethanol-water.

Let us assume that the concentration of the feed ethanol is 10 wt-% (that level can be readily produced by fermentation processes). For simplicity, let us assume furthermore that the recycled carbon dioxide contains no ethanol and that the desired recovery of alcohol is 95%. Figure 8.12 reproduces the

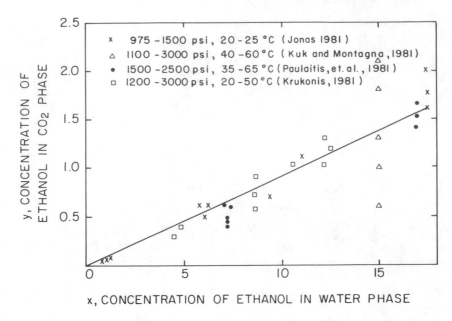

Figure 8.11 Experimental results of several studies of the ethanol–water–carbon dioxide system.

equilibrium line shown previously in figure 8.11. In this case, the minimum solvent-to-feed (S/F) ratio is shown in figure 8.12 by the so-called operating line, which is the dashed line drawn between the abscissa at 0.5 wt-% ethanol in water (remember that we specified that the recovery of ethanol from the feed is 95%) and the equilibrium line at 10 wt-% ethanol (the feed concentration). The minimum S/F ratio is 10.5 for this case. This S/F ratio is the equivalent of 105 lbs of CO_2/lb of ethanol in the feed stream; this is a rather high solvent requirement. Since the operating line "touches" the equilibrium line, an infinitely tall column is required. We shall use an operating line with a solvent-to-feed ratio 1.3 times the minimum (see figure 8.12).

A mathematical solution of the number of extraction stages required to recover 95% of the ethanol via supercritical carbon dioxide is obtained by a graphical procedure called "stepping off plates." Slightly more than seven (7.3) equilibrium trays are needed for this separation using the graphical construction, as is shown in figure 8.12. In the placement of the operating line and determination of the number of equilibrium stages in figure 8.12, it is assumed that the entering (recycled) carbon dioxide contains no ethanol; in a real case the entering carbon dioxide will contain some ethanol. In some situations, the presence of a small amount of recycled product has a great impact on the operation, cost, and efficiency of the process. For example, in the case of a very low distribution coefficient, such as that for the ethanol-water separation, the presence of recycled product increases the difficulty of obtaining a high recovery of ethanol, as we shall discuss.

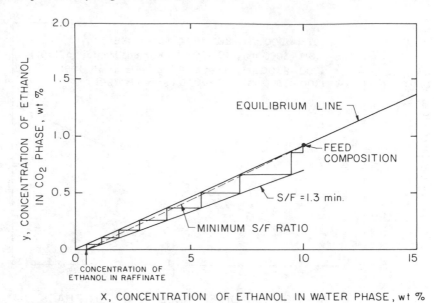

Figure 8.12   Equilibrium and operating lines for the ethanol–water–carbon dioxide system; in this instance there is no ethanol in the recycled carbon dioxide.

For the ethanol-water separation, the requirement of thorough removal of ethanol from the recycled carbon dioxide represents a technical challenge that increases the complexity and cost of the process relative to the simplified diagram shown in figure 8.10. The reasons for the increased complexity are explained below. Figure 8.13 illustrates the ethanol extraction process in the instance where the recycled carbon dioxide has an ethanol concentration of 0.1 wt-%. At the raffinate section of the extractor the ethanol concentration in the water-rich phase is now dictated by considerations of equilibrium and by the value of the distribution coefficient. The limitation attributed to equilibrium is indicated by the operating line in figure 8.13, which has an inverse slope of 13.7 (the same slope as the operating line in figure 8.12) and which touches the equilibrium line at coordinates of $x = 1.1$, $y = 0.1$. As shown by the simple construction in figure 8.13, the presence of a small amount of ethanol in the recycled carbon dioxide stream places an upper limit on the amount of ethanol that can be recovered from the feed stream. The ethanol concentration in the raffinate cannot be lowered to below 1.1 wt-%; thus, for the case of 0.1 wt-% ethanol in the recycle stream, the maximum recovery of ethanol (even with an infinitely tall column) is only 89%.

There are trade-offs to be considered in optimizing recovery costs. When designing a process, the design engineer must make some concessions on the percent recovery of ethanol versus the capital and operating costs of the

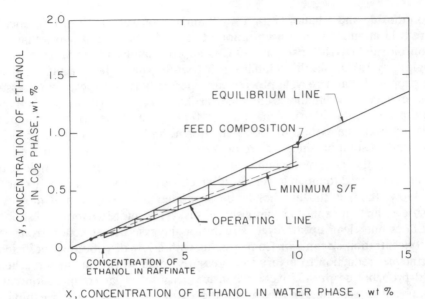

Figure 8.13 Equilibrium and operating lines for the ethanol–water–carbon dioxide system; in this instance there is 0.1 wt-% ethanol in the recycled carbon dioxide.

proposed process. One "real" operating line is drawn on figure 8.13 (for this example the minimum operating line is shifted so that the number of equilibrium trays is again 7.3). The raffinate stream in this case leaves the column with 1.4 wt-% ethanol, achieving a total ethanol recovery of 86%. An economically optimum design depends on many factors, such as the cost of making ethanol by fermentation; the local pollution-control legislation, which may place limits on ethanol discharge; and, of course, the cost of competing separation technologies. The process described in figure 8.13 is presented pedagogically, as an explanation of the extraction-column operation, and it is not to be construed as an example of analysis of an economic-parameter trade-off or sensitivity.

As yet we have not described recycle cleanup and product recovery, but we have assumed that the concentration of ethanol in the recycle is 0.1 wt-%. How did we get it there? Some researchers who present data for ternary phase equilibria for the carbon dioxide–ethanol–water system suggest that decreasing the operating pressure or raising the temperature, or both, can result in the precipitation of ethanol from the supercritical carbon dioxide phase and that with recompression the carbon dioxide can then be recycled. These statements are incorrect because they are based on an extrapolation of data from the two-phase liquid-vapor region of the ternary phase diagram without regard to the type of phase behavior that exists for a pseudobinary mixture consisting of carbon dioxide and ethanol (with a small amount of water). With reference to Figure 8.11 at an ethanol concentration of 15 wt-% the solubility of ethanol in carbon dioxide at 1,100 psia and 40°C is approximately 0.5 wt-% (the lowest triangle). At 3,000 psia the solubility is 2.1 wt-% (the highest triangle). It has been proposed that a recycle process can operate between these two pressure levels; extraction of ethanol from water at 3,000 psia and recovery of ethanol from the carbon dioxide-rich phase at 1,100 psia. All of the ethanol cannot be recovered from the carbon-dioxide rich stream, and in fact a large percentage will remain in solution since we are operating very close to the mixture critical point. Thus, the process as depicted in Figure 8.10 cannot work unless the pressure is reduced to much lower levels which may not be economically viable.

How, then, is the ethanol to be separated from the carbon dioxide if pressure reduction cannot accomplish the task? The more general question is, How does one clean up a recycle stream for the case of extraction from very low-concentration streams or from systems with a low distribution coefficient? In principle, reduction to a very low pressure would work, but such a scheme would probably be prohibitively expensive because of gas-compression costs. An alternative scheme for recovering the extracted ethanol and cleaning up the recycle stream is described in U.S. patent #4,349,415 (de Fillipi and Vivian, 1982). In this method, a high-pressure distillation column is utilized to distill the carbon dioxide from the condensed carbon dioxide–ethanol mixture. A schematic diagram of the full extraction and carbon-dioxide-cleanup process is shown in figure 8.14. Ethanol is extracted at about 20°C, and 800 psia with liquid carbon dioxide, and the carbon dioxide–ethanol extract stream leaving the top of the extractor is expanded slightly to about 700 psia to form a liquid phase and a vapor phase. The two-phase stream is fed to a short distillation

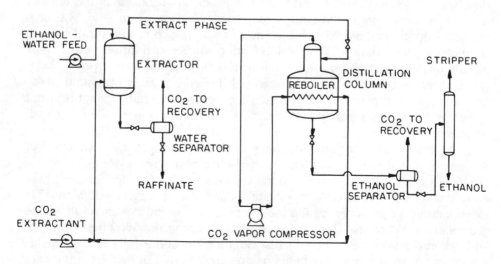

Figure 8.14 Schematic diagram of a process using supercritical carbon dioxide for extracting ethanol from water combined with distillation for carbon dioxide cleanup.

tower in which carbon dioxide vapor essentially free of ethanol is separated from the carbon dioxide–ethanol phase. The carbon dioxide vapor leaving the tower overhead is compressed to about 900 psia. The carbon dioxide stream, which is heated slightly because of the compression work that has been added by the vapor recompressor, is discharged from the compressor to the tube side of the heat exchanger of the distillation reboiler. Transfer of sensible and latent heat occurs from the condensing carbon dioxide inside the reboiler tubes to the boiling ethanol–carbon dioxide solution. The cooled liquid carbon dioxide is then pumped to the bottom of the extractor to complete the cycle and to continue the extraction process.

The low distribution coefficients, the attendant requirement of recycling carbon dioxide containing very little ethanol in order to achieve a high recovery of ethanol from the feed stream, and the inability to achieve the separation of ethanol from the extract stream by pressure letdown required the development of this SCF extraction–distillation process. The diagram shown in figure 8.14 pictorially summarizes that an "old" distillation technique can be combined with "new" supercritical carbon extraction to solve the separation problem; supercritical CO_2 can extract the ethanol from the feed stream, distillation can separate and regenerate the solvent for recycle, and vapor compression can achieve energy efficiency.

Other Alcohol-Water Systems

The phase-splitting techniques first described by Elgin and Weinstock (1959) for recovering methyl ethyl ketone from water using supercritical ethylene can also be used to separate alcohol-water mixtures. Let us consider recovering *n*-propanol from water using supercritical carbon dioxide (Kuk and Montagna, 1983). Supercritical carbon dioxide can be used in two different ways to split *n*-propanol–water mixtures in the range of approximately 20 wt-% to 75 wt-% *n*-propanol. The recovery of *n*-propanol from water can be accomplished in a system operating either in the two-phase liquid-liquid (LL) region or in the three-phase liquid-liquid-vapor (LLV) region of the ternary *n*-propanol–water–CO_2 phase diagram shown in figure 8.15. If it is assumed that the process operates in the LLV region of the diagram, then there are no degrees of freedom for this system (see table 3.1), because the temperature is fixed at 40°C and the pressure is fixed at 1,500 psia. Therefore, the composition of the three equilibrium phases is defined by the corners of the triangular LLV region within the ternary phase diagram. Although the relative amounts of the three equilibrium phases will depend on the overall mixture composition within this region, the compositions of the three phases always remain fixed at approximately 18 wt-% *n*-propanol–72 wt-% water–10 wt-% CO_2, 45 wt-% *n*-propanol–20 wt-% water–35 wt-% CO_2, and 12 wt-% *n*-propanol–1 wt-% water–87 wt-% CO_2. Thus, in a single-stage extractor, the *n*-propanol can be recovered

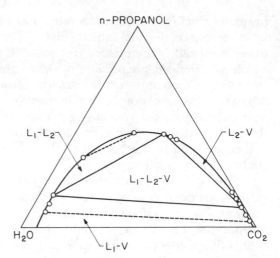

Figure 8.15 Ternary phase diagram for the *n*-propanol–water–carbon dioxide system at 40°C and 103 atm (Kuk and Montagna, 1983).

by removing either the CO_2-rich phase (the phase in which the ratio of *n*-propanol to water is 12 to 1) or by removing the middle *n*-propanol–rich phase (the phase in which the ratio of *n*-propanol to water is 2.25 to 1). The costs of the particular process will dictate whether it is more economical to recover *n*-propanol from the middle liquid phase, which has a high loading of *n*-propanol but a low selectivity of *n*-propanol to water, or the CO_2-rich phase, which has less alcohol but a much higher alcohol-to-water ratio.

The *n*-propanol–water–CO_2 system is another example of a system that exhibits LLV equilibria at conditions near the critical temperature and pressure of CO_2. This type of phase behavior is described in detail in chapter 3. A large number of other organic solvent–water–SCF solvent systems can be found in the work of Elgin and co-workers.

The extraction of alcohol from water using supercritical fluids has also been described in some detail by Paulaitis and co-workers (Kander and Paulaitis, 1984; Diandreth and Paulaitis, 1984; Paulaitis, Kander, and Diandreth, 1984; Paulaitis, Gilbert, and Nash, 1981). These researchers show that when a separation process operates in the vicinity of the mixture critical point (i.e., the plait point for a ternary system), large changes in alcohol selectivity and loading in the supercritical fluid phase can occur for relatively small changes in temperature or pressure. Such changes are apparent in the two sets of isopropanol-water-CO_2 diagrams shown in figures 8.16 and 8.17. It has been suggested in the works cited that the two factors controlling the selectivity and loading for alcohol-water mixtures are the compressibility of the SCF solvent and the differences in the liquid-phase nonidealities exhibited by the binary alcohol-SCF and alcohol-water mixtures (e.g., the degree of hydrogen bonding present in these mixtures). These two factors, SCF compressibility and mixture nonidealities, determine whether the alcohol-water-SCF mixture will split into an LLV mixture. Full advantage should be taken in alcohol-water-SCF sepa-

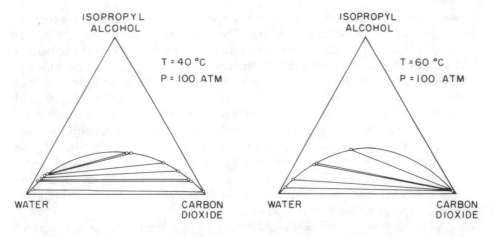

Figure 8.16 Effect of temperature on the selectivity and loading of isopropanol in supercritical carbon dioxide (Paulaitis, Kander, and Diandreth, 1984).

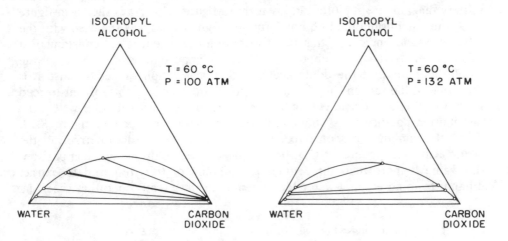

Figure 8.17 Effect of pressure on the selectivity and loading of isopropanol in supercritical carbon dioxide (Paulaitis, Kander, and Diandreth, 1984).

ration processes of the multiphase behavior that occurs for these systems and that greatly affects the selectivity and loading of the SCF solvent.

Acetic Acid–Water

The potential for achieving a lower-energy process also motivated a substantial effort to examine supercritical fluid extraction for separating acetic acid from water. The work falls into two subcategories: separation of fermentation-derived acetic acid and separation of acetic acid–water solutions that are formed during production of cellulose acetate. The recovery of acetic acid from fermentation broths is similar to the previously described problem of recovering ethanol from fermentation broths. In the cellulose acetate production process, cellulose reacts with glacial acetic acid and acetic anhydride to form cellulose triacetate. Water is then added to the cellulose triacetate–glacial acetic acid solution, which results in the removal of a fraction of the acetate moieties from the cellulose backbone. Water also causes the precipitation of cellulose acetate and, of course, dilutes the acetic acid. The cellulose acetate is filtered, the acetic acid–water solution is separated by distillation, and the glacial acetic acid is recycled to the cellulose acetate reactor. The distillation step is a huge energy consumer and, thus, alternate technologies are continually being evaluated for separating the two compounds.

As we shall see, acetic acid is quite difficult to extract with carbon dioxide; moreover, this fact was known thirty years ago when Francis studied the carbon dioxide–water–acetic acid system (Francis, 1954). A ternary equilibrium diagram of this system is shown in figure 8.18 and the tie-line data from the ternary diagram are replotted in *x-y* form in figure 8.19. As is shown in figure 8.19, the equilibrium data do not form a straight line as was the case with the ethanol system, indicating that the distribution coefficient is not constant. But this fact in itself is not important. What is important is the slope of the equilibrium curve at the dilute acetic acid concentration range, because it is the slope of the tangent line in this region that determines the solvent-to-feed ratio. Over an acetic acid concentration range of 0 wt-% to about 5 wt-%, the distribution coefficient is about 0.03 (weight basis), as seen in figure 8.19. Thus, the minimum carbon dioxide–to–feed ratio required to extract all the acetic acid is 33 pounds of CO_2 per pound of feed solution. For comparison, this value is more than three times the amount of CO_2 required to extract ethanol from an ethanol-water feed stream. In the "real" operating case, the

Figure 8.18 Ternary phase behavior of the acetic acid–water–carbon dioxide system (Francis, 1954).

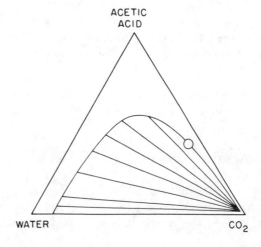

ACETIC ACID

WATER CO_2

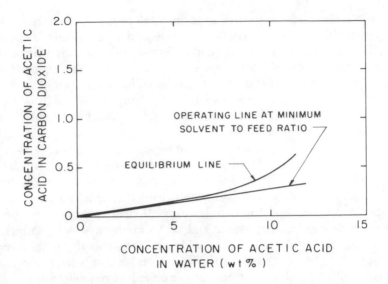

Figure 8.19 Plot of the equilibrium and operating lines for the acetic acid–water–carbon dioxide system.

solvent-to-feed ratio as determined by 1.3 times the minimum is, of course, almost 40 pounds of CO_2 per pound of feed solution, which is considered to be prohibitively high.

As if the low distribution coefficient does not present enough of an obstacle, extraction of acetic acid from fermentation broths is made still more unattractive by the high pH of the solutions. For the bioprocesses being evaluated, acetic acid will be produced in a solution with a pH of about 6.0. The pK of acetic acid is 4.8 and thus, at a pH of 6.0, virtually all the acetic acid produced in solution exists as an acetate ion. Current extraction/recovery schemes entail acidification (with HCl for example) to convert the acetate ion to free acetic acid. Then the free acid can be extracted with an organic solvent. If carbon dioxide is used as the extractant HCl is not required; carbonic acid from the CO_2-water equilibrium will neutralize part, but not all, of the acetate ion as can be determined from a material and charge balance of species in solution.

A recent patent covering the concept of extraction of organic acids from high-pH solutions provides data from which the extraction efficiency of this concept can be analyzed (Shimshick, 1981). Example 6 from the patent is reproduced.

Carbon dioxide at 2400 ±200 psig . . . and 50° ±2°C. was used to extract acetic acid from an aqueous Clostridium thermoaceticum fermentation broth containing about 0.23 M sodium acetate and 0.03 M acetic acid, pH 5.7. About 1% of the acetic acid/sodium acetate in the fermentation broth was recovered as acetic acid in bomb 32, trap 33 and trap 34.

From the data and from the experimental procedure described in the patent the overall distribution coefficient based on total acetate is calculated as 0.004. This is an extremely small number, which, of course, is a consequence of the small amount of free acid available in solution at the high pH of the solution. Other authors (Yates, 1981; Busche, Shimshick, and Yates, 1982) address the problem of incomplete extraction of organic acids from high pH solutions using carbon dioxide. The authors suggest that the raffinate from the extractor can be recycled to the fermentor.

In the past few years, many other organic-water separations have been screened in feasibility tests. Some have received substantial research and development effort because they require large consumptions of energy for separation by distillation. A partial list of the organics includes dioxane, acetone, formamide, *N, N*-dimethyl formamide, and ethylene glycol. Most of these compounds hydrogen-bond to water and to themselves, which inhibits facile extraction with carbon dioxide. Formamide and ethylene glycol are two compounds that readily hydrogen-bond to themselves and to water. Therefore, it is especially difficult to extract these compounds from water with carbon dioxide. For instance, formamide exhibits an extremely poor distribution coefficient of 0.001. From a distribution coefficient that low it can be concluded that it is virtually impossible to extract formamide from water. As a matter of interest, the selectivity of carbon dioxide for formamide is less than 1.0, that is, carbon dioxide extracts water preferentially from formamide-water solutions (Krukonis, 1981b).

The examples presented in this section highlight many facets of the development of SCF processes and applications that need to be addressed, understood, and solved before scale-up is considered. The same procedure, of course, is necessary for any kind of separation process. Because supercritical fluid extraction has the potential to reduce energy costs does not necessarily mean that it will be a less-expensive process overall. Frequently, capital and other operating costs can more than offset decreased energy costs. Subsequent chapters discuss developments in the application of supercritical fluid solvents to the solution of technically and economically difficult separation problems in which the improved performance of the supercritical fluid processed materials can support the processing cost.

9

Polymer and Monomer Processing

Relatively little has been reported in the literature regarding the use of super-critical fluids to process polymers on an industrial scale. The polymer studies reported to date can be categorized into five general groups: high-pressure polyethylene polymerization/fractionation; extraction of low-molecular-weight oligomers from polymers; supercritical fluid chromatography analysis of poly-styrene; polymer fractionation; and polymer–organic solvent phase separation. Each of these areas is discussed in this chapter. (The polyethylene polymeri-zation is also discussed in chapter 11, where the effects of negative partial molal volumes on reaction-rate kinetics are presented.)

HIGH-PRESSURE POLYETHYLENE POLYMERIZATION

The high-pressure polyethylene process is described in the literature (Shreve and Brink, 1977; Anon., 1981). Figure 9.1 is a diagram of the now forty-year-old process redrawn from the *Kirk-Othmer Encyclopedia of Science and Tech-nology*. It is noteworthy to point out here that this process was under devel-opment at the Imperial Chemical Industries laboratories in the late 1930s; and as is seen from a rapid scan of the operating conditions in the reactor section shown in figure 9.1, pressure levels of 40,000 psia(!) are required. Either a well-stirred autoclave or a tubular reactor is used to carry out the polymeri-zation. Ethylene is compressed to 40,000 psia and a free-radical initiator, such as trace amounts of oxygen or a peroxide, is injected into the stream to promote the polymerization. The polyethylene polymer that is formed remains dissolved in the supercritical-ethylene phase at the operating temperature of 250°C. The heat of reaction is removed either by through-wall heat transfer when the tubular reactor is used or by regulating the rate of addition of initiator when the autoclave reactor is used.

Downstream of the reactor the polyethylene-ethylene solution is expanded to a lower pressure, typically to about 5,000 psia. Because the solvent power

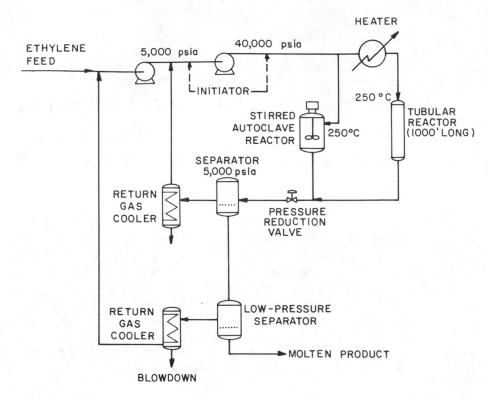

Figure 9.1 Schematic diagram of the high-pressure polyethylene process, in which either a stirred autoclave or a tubular reactor is used.

of supercritical ethylene is lowered during the pressure reduction, the polyethylene formed in the reactor nucleates, precipitates from solution, and is collected in the separator. The low-pressure ethylene is recompressed and recycled to the reactor. Interestingly, in this process ethylene is both the reactant and the solvent for the product.

There are some other facets to the operation of this process that are worth noting, since they illustrate the SCF phenomena that are in operation and that can be understood with the aid of the naphthalene-solubility diagram. Recall that it was stated a number of times in chapter 6 that many SCF-solute systems exhibit generic solubility behavior (see figure 6.1). The same generic solubility isobars (but, again, not the absolute solubility values) describe the solubility behavior of polyethylene in supercritical ethylene. Although the concentration profiles for the polyethylene-ethylene system are not presented here, the slope of the 40,000-psia solubility isobar is positive with temperature; that is, concentration increases with increasing temperature. (A concentration-pressure-temperature diagram for the polyethylene-ethylene binary is given in chapter 11.) In the preceding discussion of the operation of the tubular-reactor polymerization scheme, it was stated that the heat of reaction is removed by through-wall heat transfer. What is the situation in the vicinity of the wall? If the high-pressure (300 atm) naphthalene isobar is an accurate model of high-pressure polyethylene solubility, from it we can predict that polyethylene will precipitate in the boundary layer near the (cold) wall. If the precipitation of polyethylene does occur near the wall and if it is not appropriately removed, the buildup of the polymer on the wall and the attendant decrease in heat transfer can lead to the runaway reaction that is occasionally encountered in high-pressure polyethylene plants.

The removal of precipitated polyethylene from the wall is an interesting operation. About once every 2–3 seconds the expansion valve is opened more fully than required for the expansion/precipitation function, which results in a rapid decrease in pressure in the reactor of as much as 5,000 or 10,000 psia. The concomitant rapid increase in the velocity of the gas phase in the tubular reactor shears the walls and strips off the deposited polyethylene.

This description of the operation of the polymerization process, the polyethylene-precipitation step, and the accentuated expansion, which maintains a clean wall and a high heat-transfer coefficient, are presented here not only to illustrate the interesting SCF solubility behavior but also to supply some information on the commercial reality of high-pressure processing in an extreme case. Quite often the sentiment is expressed that high-pressure phase equilibria studies are interesting academically, and the SCF applications development effort might work at the laboratory level, but extension to industrial levels is considered skeptically. Response to the skepticism is best provided by relating that polyethylene has been produced in plants operating at 200,000,000–300,000,000 pounds per year at pressures of 40,000 psia and temperatures of 200–300°C with pressure-expansion ratios of 10 across small orifices and, moreover, with valves cycling every few seconds. These plants operate continuously for months at a time and, furthermore, have been in operation since the early 1950s. SCF extraction applications that will operate at the much more modest conditions of "only" 5,000 psia present no new design and operating problems.

Polymer fractionation is described in the patent literature dating to the 1940s. United States patents 2,388,160 (Krase, 1945) and 2,396,791 (Krase and Lawrence, 1946), both assigned to E. I. du Pont; 2,457,238 (Hunter and Richards, 1945), to Imperial Chemical Industries; and 3,294,772 (Cottle, 1966), to Phillips Petroleum, describe fractionation results primarily with polyethylene. The ability to achieve separation by molecular weight was reported and the following excerpt from the ICI patent describes a high-pressure polyethylene fractionation process.

> The process involves the lowering of the reaction pressure under constant temperature by a series of stages and collecting the products which precipitate at each stage. It is possible to obtain high molecular weight products from ethylene that vary in physical characteristics from hard horny solids to waxy semisolids with a large group of intermediate products.

The Imperical Chemical Industries patent also discusses processing of polystyrene and polyisobutylene. However, these polymers are extracted of their low-molecular-weight oligomers rather than fractionated.

OLIGOMER EXTRACTION FROM POLYMERS

There are a number of studies in the literature that describe the use of supercritical fluids to extract cyclic and low-molecular-weight oligomers from polymers. United States patent 4,306,058 (Copelin, 1981), assigned to E. I. du Pont, describes the removal of cyclic oligomers from polyoxyalkylene. For instance, bubbling supercritical propylene at conditions of 100°C and 80 atm through the polymer is effective in reducing the cyclic content in the polymer from 8 wt-% to 2 wt-%. These cyclic oligomers which are saturated entities are considered impurities since they are not incorporated in the polyurethane that is formed when the polyoxyalkylene is subsequently reacted. For strict accuracy, the results described in the patent represent not the fractionation of a polymer but instead the extraction of low-molecular-weight oligomers from polymers in a wider range of molecular weights. Nevertheless, the examples given in this patent do point out the ability of supercritical fluids to purify a polymer, which would be quite difficult to purify by distillation or by liquid organic-solvent extraction.

Another reference on the supercritical extraction of low-molecular-weight oligomers from polymers describes the upgrading of a silicone polymer, designated OV-17, used as a gas-chromatography stationary phase (Barry, Ferioli, and Hubball, 1983). The material tested, a polyphenylmethylsiloxane, is a very viscous polymer containing macrocyclic and low molecular weight linear oligomers that interfere with the performance of the material when it is used as a chromatographic substrate in a wide-temperature-scan, temperature-programmed analysis. The low-molecular-weight oligomers bleed from the chromatographic column during the analysis. It is reported that supercritical carbon dioxide at conditions of about 140 atm and 35°C is found to extract 30% of the original polymer, and the residual heavier-molecular-weight portion yielded much improved characteristics in the chromatography application. The specific extraction test described in the paper is not strictly a fractionation into a number of narrow cuts, as suggested by the title of the paper, but the results given in the paper show that polyphenylmethylsiloxane polymers can be dissolved by supercritical carbon dioxide at quite modest pressures. Other work has been carried out on both extraction and fractionation of OV-17, and quite different results were obtained (Krukonis, 1982b). The fractionation results are given later in this chapter (in the section on silicone oils and polymers), but, in summary here, the results show that carbon dioxide at 40 to 100°C and at pressure levels as high as 6,500 psia cannot dissolve the phenylmethylsiloxane polymer and that less than 5% of the material can be extracted at this pressure level.

SUPERCRITICAL FLUID CHROMATOGRAPHY ANALYSIS OF POLYSTYRENE

The third category of supercritical fluid–polymer activity reported in the literature describes the use of SCF chromatography to separate oligomers. The classic paper in this field is by Jentoft and Gouw (1969), who reported their work on the supercritical fluid chromatographic separation of a "monodisperse" polystyrene. (Jentoft and Gouw use the quotation marks because, as they report later in the article, the polystyrene sample that they tested contains a large number of oligomers.) The particular material that is tested is a highly purified calibration standard used for determining gel permeation chromatography elution profiles. The authors show that the "monodisperse" standard can be separated into at least seventeen separate oligomers. In this instance the SCF mobile phase of the chromatograph is *n*-pentane containing 5 wt-% methyl alcohol. Figure 9.2 shows the resolution achieved with the SCF chromatograph. In a later paper, Jentoft and Gouw (1970) present the data verifying the molecular-weight fractionation that they achieved.

Figure 9.2 Chromatogram of a polystyrene sample fractionated in a process using a supercritical fluid chromatograph (redrawn from Jentoft and Gouw, 1969). The sample has a nominal molecular weight of 600.

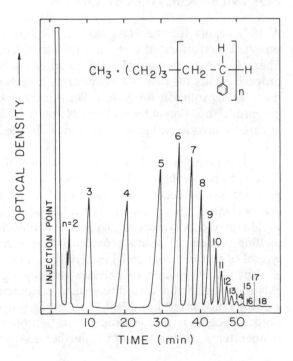

It should be noted that the resolution of the polystyrene oligomers shown in figure 9.2 is influenced more by the interactions of the small amount of methanol in the mobile phase with the stationary phase of the chromatographic column than by the pressure-dependent dissolving capabilities of a supercritical fluid. Supercritical pentane is such a good solvent for polystyrene that without 5 wt-% methanol the polystyrene would quickly elute from the column unfractionated. After the Jentoft and Gouw paper appeared, many other authors published on the use of supercritical fluid chromatography to fractionate low-molecular-weight oligomers of polystyrene (Klesper and Hartmann, 1977) and polyethylene glycol and polyvinyl chloride (Giddings, Myers, and King, 1969).

Fractionation of a polymer into its separate oligomers as reported by Jentoft and Gouw is an impressive achievement for supercritical fluid solvents. However, in general it is achieved only in conjunction with chromatography with materials processed at micro- to milligram levels. Supercritical fluid chromatography is not covered in this book in any detail; but the polymer-resolution studies are given for their relevance in this section. Enough literature exists on supercritical fluid chromatography, dating from the first paper by Klesper and co-workers in 1964 to the present, to fill a comprehensive volume on that subject alone. It is noteworthy to point out that in March 1985 fifteen papers on supercritical fluid chromatography were presented at the Pittsburgh Conference in New Orleans.

POLYMER FRACTIONATION

A 1977 report for the National Science Foundation describes an interesting program, performed at Georgia Institute of Technology, for spinning polymer fibers from a supercritical fluid solution (Bangert et al., 1977). This novel process entails dissolving a polymer in a high-pressure fluid and "extruding" the gaseous solution through a die. Polymers studied in the program include polypropylene, polybutene-1, and Nylon-6. The solubilities of these materials in carbon dioxide and in *n*-butane, given in the report, are reproduced in table 9.1.

The Georgia Tech workers show that the polymers dissolve in carbon dioxide to high solubility levels at modest pressures. As noted in chapter 3 the pressure levels needed to dissolve a polymer are directly related to the molecular weight of the polymer. No information on the comparative molecular weight of the polymers is given in the report. However, from the data on melting (softening) points provided it is inferred that the molecular weight is typical of that of commercial material. Polymer solubility in supercritical fluids is also directly related to polymer tacticity (Krukonis, 1981e). The polypropylene tested in the solubility studies is isotactic, as is also inferred from the melting range listed in table 9.1; a melting range around 170°C is typical of an isotactic polymer. In comparison, atactic (amorphous) polypropylene melts at temperatures as low as 80°C. Furthermore, atactic polypropylene is quite

Table 9.1 Solubility of Polymers

Polymer	Gas	Pressure	Temperature	Solubility (wt-%)	Polymer Melting Range (°C)
Polypropylene	CO_2	450–850 atm	163–208°C	6–38	162–176
Nylon-6	CO_2	400–510 atm	233–241°C	13–16	212–225
Polybutene-1	CO_2	300–900 atm	131–150°C	6–38	~126
Polybutene-1	n-butane	120–170 atm	167–190°C	5–21	~126
Polypropylene	n-butane	130–190 atm	166–186°C	5–20	162–176

soluble in carbon dioxide at low pressure and temperature levels. Solubility at 100°C and 250 atm is 10–20 wt-%, depending upon the grade of atactic polypropylene, and for comparison, the solubility of isotactic polypropylene in carbon dioxide at these conditions is virtually nil (Krukonis, 1981e).

An interesting statement is made in the NSF report about the relative solubilities of the three polymers in carbon dioxide (Bangert et al., 1977). For example, it is found at 400 atm pressure that the solubility of Nylon-6 is about twice that of the other two polymers. Notice in table 9.1 that the temperature tested to dissolve Nylon-6 is 50 to 100°C higher than that for polypropylene and polybutene-1. The substantially higher temperature of 240°C might be expected to lower the solvent power of CO_2 relative to that at 130–150°C level tested for polybutene-1. However, in spite of the higher temperature nylon dissolves to a higher concentration. From this finding the researchers suggest that "carbon dioxide with no dipoles but with strong quadrapoles . . . may be a good solvent for relatively polar hydrogen bonded and, perhaps, other dipole bonded polymers." Although a higher temperature is needed to dissolve Nylon-6, the density of CO_2 is still 0.44 g/cc to 0.52 g/cc at 400 to 500 atm. We believe that higher temperatures are needed to soften the polymer and to impart enough thermal motion to the molecules to weaken the nylon-nylon interactions, which allows more facile solvation by carbon dioxide. The report goes on to describe the spinning studies that are the major thrust of the program, and it is reported that fibers with diameters ranging up to 25 microns can be spun from polypropylene dissolved in supercritical propylene.

From the information presented heretofore it can be concluded that the solvent characteristics of supercritical fluids are especially attractive in the processing of high-molecular-weight oils and polymers. The research studies described subsequently cover other broad categories of oil and polymer fractionation, monomer purification, and residual-monomer extraction. Most of the materials that are discussed are refractory in their inability to be handled by conventional processing to achieve the specific product performance desired, and the results that are described point out that supercritical fluid processing of oils and polymers can be a viable concept in treating such materials.

Silicone oils, perfluoroalkyl polyethers, polycarbosilanes, and polyhalo-carbons are specialty materials usually requiring high purity and narrow molecular-weight ranges for use as lubricants, hydraulic fluids, and surfactants. Many of these materials are currently processed by molecular distillation to achieve the requisite qualities. However, molecular distillation is limited in its separation capabilities when, for example, the vapor pressure of the oil is less than 10^{-3} mm, the oil is heat-sensitive, or the impurities present in the feed material exhibit the same vapor pressure as the desired fractions.

Supercritical fluid fractionation of a synthetic oil or polymer is carried out in a multiple, sequential-pressure reduction system, which is an extension of the operation philosophy previously described in chapter 6. A schematic diagram of a continuous fractionation system employing a supercritical fluid to separate the homologous-series members of a synthetic polymer is shown in figure 9.3 (Krukonis, 1983a). Four extraction/separation vessels are (arbitrarily) shown in this figure. During operation of the fractionation process an oil is pumped in at the top of the primary contractor and the supercritical fluid enters at the bottom. Although the density of the supercritical extractant is typically lower than that of the oil, the column could as easily operate "upside down"; that is, if the density of the supercritical extractant were higher than that of the feed oil the inlet positions of the respective streams shown in figure 9.3 would be reversed. The extract phase leaving the vessel contains the dissolved oil. The solubility level is consistent with the solubility characteristics and operating parameters in the vessel. (In the figure, a "heavy" fraction

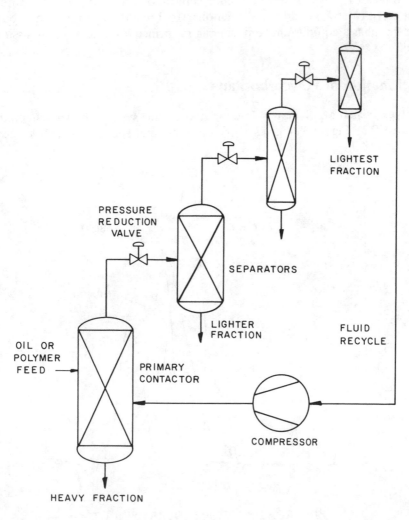

Figure 9.3 Schematic diagram of an apparatus using a supercritical fluid solvent to fractionate a polymer.

leaving the primary contactor vessel is indicated. If the extraction conditions are changed, the entire feed could just as easily be dissolved.) The solution of oil and SCF extractant is expanded to some lower pressure, which causes the highest-molecular-weight oligomers in the solution to precipitate. The remaining stream is further stagewise reduced in pressure through the expansion valves to fractionate the oil. After expansion to the lowest pressure, the almost solute-free gas is recompressed and recycled. The number of fractions that are obtained is consistent with the number of pressure-reduction stages, and the molecular-weight range of each fraction is related to the ratio of pressure reduction per stage. In the remainder of this chapter we present a large number of examples of polymer and monomer separations to point out the potential of supercritical fractionation. We emphasize breadth of application, but we integrate phase equilibrium and chemistry principles into the discussion of results.

Fractionation of Polycarbosilane

A polycarbosilane polymer is fractionated in the system shown schematically in figure 9.3. Figure 9.4 gives a pictorial comparison of the gel-permeation

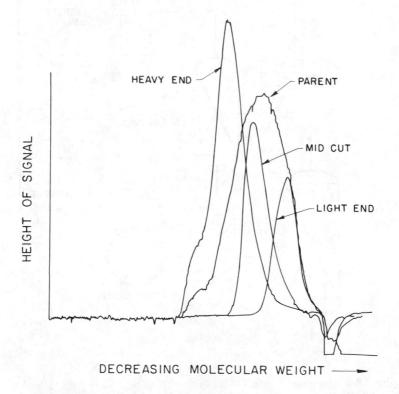

Figure 9.4 Gel-permeation chromatogram (GPC) of a polycarbosilane fractionated with supercritical ethylene.

chromatograms (GPCs) of a polycarbosilane with a nominal molecular weight of 7,000 and the three fractions obtained using supercritical ethylene as the fractionating solvent. The operating conditions are at 100°C and over a pressure range of 2,800–7,500 psia. This particular polymer is a developmental material being examined for use in producing silicon carbide shapes used in high-temperature applications, such as turbine blades or vanes for advanced aircraft engines. Ceramics such as silicon carbide and silicone nitride are being evaluated as materials for extending combustion temperatures in engines to higher levels, thus achieving higher energy-conversion efficiency. The ceramic parts are currently produced by hot-pressing or sintering powders at a very high temperature, typically 2,500°C. The production process is quite expensive and the sintering process requires the use of SiC or Si_3N_4 powder of high purity, which is also quite expensive. Polycarbosilane polymers can be molded to shape and converted to silicon carbide at about 1200°C and thus represent the potential for developing a lower-cost process for making ceramics parts, especially for forming complex shapes.

Polycarbosilane is also of interest for its use in spinning fibers that can be converted into silicon carbide reinforcements. A midcut of intermediate molecular weight is desired for one application. An inspection of the peak widths of the respective fractions in figure 9.4 shows that a substantial narrowing of the molecular-weight range in each fraction has been achieved and that high- and low-molecular-weight oligomers can be excluded from the desired fraction.

Fractionation of Silicone Oils and Polymers

Other studies reported in the literature concern the fractionation of a high-molecular-weight silicone oil, a poly(dimethyl)siloxane (Krukonis, 1983c). The material is being tested for an electronics application, but migration of low-molecular-weight species hinders the performance of the polymer. Figure 9.5 is a GPC of the parent oil from which it can be seen that the oil contains some non-Gaussian low-molecular-weight species. The polymer was extracted with supercritical carbon dioxide at 80°C over an ascending pressure range from 1,800 psia to 6,500 psia. Six relatively arbitrary fractions are separated from the parent charge. The molecular-weight analysis of the parent and of the fractions is given in table 9.2. The fractions are not of equal size and the percent contributions of each fraction is listed in the third column of the table.

As a pictorial comparison of the peak widths of these fractions, figure 9.6 superposes the GPCs of fraction 1 and fraction 6 onto the GPC of the parent. As can be seen from inspection of figure 9.6, fraction 1 contains only the low-molecular-weight cyclics and linears. The degree of fractionation depicted in this figure is an excellent example of the "adjustable" dissolving and extracting power of a supercritical fluid. Notice also that the GPC of the high-molecular-weight fraction shown in figure 9.6 and the corresponding data in table 9.2 show that a silicone polymer with a molecular weight of 100,000 can be dissolved by supercritical carbon dioxide at 6,500 psia.

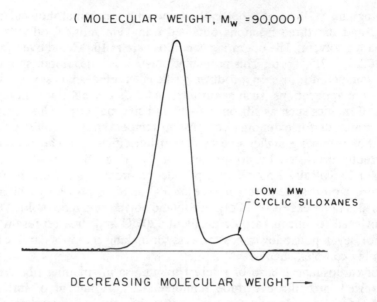

(MOLECULAR WEIGHT, M_W = 90,000)

LOW MW
CYCLIC SILOXANES

DECREASING MOLECULAR WEIGHT ⟶

Figure 9.5 Gel-permeation chromatogram of a poly-(dimethyl)siloxane polymer.

Table 9.2 Molecular-Weight Distribution in Parent Poly(dimethyl)siloxane and in Fractions Separated by Supercritical Fluid Processing

Fraction	Number Average Molecular Weight	Weight Average Molecular Weight	Wt-% of Parent
Parent	42,500	90,000	100
1	428	789	4.0
2	3,310	11,500	5.1
3	27,100	53,200	27.7
4	43,000	57,500	27.9
5	58,900	91,500	28.3
6	112,600	149,900	7.0

The behavior of poly(phenylmethyl)siloxane is quite different from poly(dimethyl)siloxane. The replacement of one of the methyl groups on the silicon with a phenyl group lowers the solubility dramatically. The molecular-weight of the parent polymer is given in table 9.3. The average molecular weight of the parent is about 2,100, and the polymer of this molecular weight does not dissolve to any reasonable extent in carbon dioxide. For example, in stripping tests at the extraction pressures as high as 6,500 psia and over a temperature range of 40–100°C, only 4 wt-% of the polymer is found to be extracted (Krukonis, 1982c). These results are not in agreement with the results

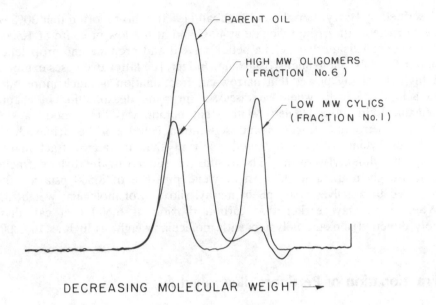

Figure 9.6 Gel-permeation chromatogram of the parent poly-(dimethyl)siloxane polymer with fractions 1 and 6 obtained by fractionating the polymer with a supercritical fluid solvent.

Table 9.3 Molecular-Weight Distribution in Parent Poly(phenylmethyl)siloxane and in Fractions Separated by Supercritical Fluid Processing

Fraction	Number Average Molecular Weight	Weight Average Molecular Weight	Wt-% of Parent
Parent	2,130[a]	2,610	100
1	1,510	1,587	4.5
2	1,530	1,628	3.1
3	1,534	1,637	12.3
4	1,730	1,839	17.7
5	1,810	2,134	25.8
6	2,660	2,825	9.3
7	3,420	3,780	25.0
8	5,300	6,500	2.3

[a]The poly(phenylmethyl)siloxane used for gas-chromatography substrates derives from a molecular distillation of commercial poly(phenylmethyl)siloxane and hence contains little low-molecular-weight material. The typical commercial material has a distribution of number average molecular weight 1,380–weight average molecular weight 2,260.

described by Barry, Ferioli, and Hubball (1983), who reported that 30% could be extracted with carbon dioxide at 40°C and at the low pressure of 1,500 psi.

Supercritical ethylene is a better solvent and propane and propylene still better for poly(phenylmethyl)siloxane. In fact, the latter two gases exhibit such a high dissolving power that narrow-cut fractionation is much more difficult to achieve. Recall, when we discussed propane deasphalting in chapter 7 Wilson, Keith, and Haylett related that butane was "too good" a solvent for the petroleum fractions and separation could not be achieved. Similarly propylene is such a "good" solvent that it cannot fractionate the poly(phenylmethyl)siloxane. The results of supercritical ethylene fractionation are given in table 9.3. An ethylene pressure of 8,500 psia at 80°C is required to dissolve a poly(phenylmethyl)siloxane of molecular weight 5,000. Whereas we saw earlier that carbon dioxide at 6,500 psia can dissolve poly(dimethyl)siloxane polymers with molecular weight as high as 100,000.

Fractionation of Perfluoroalkylpolyether

Krukonis (1983c) reports on the fractionation of a perfluoroalkylpolyether, which is an example of a polymer with a chemical makeup different from that of the siloxanes and carbosilanes. The perfluoroalkylpolyether has the structure

$$\left[CF(CF_3)CF_2O \right]_n C_2F_5$$

This oil exhibits an extremely low vapor pressure and is resistant to attack by corrosive or oxidizing materials. Thus, it is used as a diaphragm fluid in severe-service pumping such as compressing fluorine, oxygen, uranium hexafluoride, and similar refractory gases. Its viscosity and lubrication properties coupled with its very low vapor pressure have also motivated its use as a computer disc lubricant and as a seal fluid for computer disc drives. Its low vapor pressure precludes "bleeding" into the disc cavity in the drive applications. In its applications as a computer disc lubricant it provides a long-lasting barrier between the magnetic head and the ferric oxide particles on the surface of the computer disc.

The fluoroether dissolves in a number of gases, e.g., carbon dioxide, ethylene, ethane, etc. Carbon dioxide was selected for the tests described below. The fluoroether was fractionated with supercritical carbon dioxide at 80°C over a pressure range from 1,200 psia to 4,000 psia. Five equal fractions were obtained and were analyzed for their viscosity characteristics. The results of the viscosity analysis are shown in figure 9.7. Published data on the fluoroether oil gives the molecular weight of the commercial oil as about 7,000 (Anon., duPont Tech. Bull., G–6). The viscosity of the parent oil at room temperature is seen to be about 2,000 cps, whereas the viscosities of the five

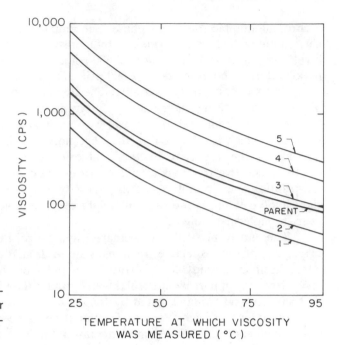

Figure 9.7 Viscosity behavior of a perfluoroether fractionated with a supercritical carbon dioxide.

fractions at room temperature range from 800 cps to 9,000 cps. If an eight-tenths-power relationship between viscosity and molecular weight is assumed, the average molecular weights of the fractions range from about 3,400 to 23,000.

Interestingly, information in the brochure on fluoroether technical products states that the fluoroether oil is not soluble in hexane. The solvent properties of carbon dioxide are often compared to those of hexane (Hyatt, 1984). For example, to a good first approximation, one can generally assess the ability of supercritical carbon dioxide to dissolve a compound by examining the solubility of the compound in hexane. A quite high percentage of compounds that exhibit hexane solubility dissolve also in carbon dioxide. However, in the case of the fluoroether the behavior of hexane and carbon dioxide are completely different. The reasons for this discrepancy are not understood.

Fractionation of Polystyrene

Earlier in this section, several references are discussed on the supercritical fluid chromatography fractionation of a polystyrene standard of molecular weight 600. The same polystyrene standard is used by Krukonis (1983b) to investigate the ability of supercritical fluids to fractionate polystyrene without the use of a chromatographic stationary phase. Sequential stripping of the polystyrene is carried out with carbon dioxide at a temperature of 100°C and at seven pressure levels ranging from 1,500 psia to 7,600 psia. In this case, all of the polymer is dissolved by carbon dioxide at 7,600 psia. The resulting fractions are analyzed by gel-permeation chromatography. The degree of polymerization (DP) of the oligomers comprising the original polystyrene standard ranges from about 2 to 9. The results from the supercritical carbon dioxide fractionation are given in table 9.4, which lists the DP of the oligomers and the concentrations of each oligomer in the respective fraction. Table 9.5 gives the molecular-weight data for the respective fractions calculated from the compositions (degree of poly-merization) given in table 9.4. Polydispersity, values for which are given in the right-hand column, is the ratio of weight average molecular weight to number average molecular weight.

The narrowing of the molecular-weight range, i.e., the decrease in poly-dispersity, of the respective fractions is quite dramatic. The polystyrene stan-dard, itself an already low-polydispersity polymer, has been separated into seven fractions of narrow molecular weight and still lower polydispersity. Recall that supercritical pentane tested by Jentoft and Gouw is "too good" a solvent for polystyrene: it achieved no fractionation. However, the addition of 5 wt-% methanol to the pentane increased the interaction of the dissolved polymer with the chromatographic stationary phase which resulted in a relative elution of oligomers.

Jentoft and Gouw's (1969, 1970) work on supercritical fluid chromatog-raphy was done at the microgram level; the work whose results are given in tables 9.4 and 9.5 was done at the multigram level and is easily extrapolatable to the level of hundreds or thousands of kilos. Although the requirement for thousands of kilos of narrow-molecular-weight polystyrene has not been re-ported, other polymers described earlier or to be described subsequently in this chapter can reach or surpass that level if they are successfully developed by the respective research groups studying them.

Fractionation of Chlorotrifluoroethylene

One other oligomer of still different chemistry, chlorotrifluoroethylene, is examined by Krukonis (1982a). These results have not yet been reported in the literature, and they are given here as another example of the general separation capabilities of supercritical fluids for use in polymers. The only requirement in achieving fractionation of a polymer with a supercritical fluid solvent is, of course, that the polymer be soluble in a supercritical fluid. Carbon dioxide and the light hydrocarbons, such as ethylene, ethane, propylene, and propane, are quite wide-ranging in their dissolving characteristics for polymers, and the highest critical temperature in the group, 96.7°C for propane, is well below the decomposition temperature of most polymers.

Table 9.4   Analysis of Polystyrene of Molecular Weight 600 and Fractions Obtained with Supercritical Carbon Dioxide

	Composition (%) of Degrees of Polymerization								
Fraction	*1*	*2*	*3*	*4*	*5*	*6*	*7*	*8*	*9*
Parent	0.7	5.4	12.3	15.8	16.6	15.7	12.7	20.7	*
1	5.7	45.0	33.4	11.4	3.6	–	–	–	–
2	2.6	21.5	35.6	23.5	11.2	5.7	–	–	–
3	–	6.0	18.3	26.7	23.8	15.7	9.5	–	–
4	–	3.3	8.7	14.1	18.9	19.7	35.2	–	–
5	–	1.3	2.7	5.3	10.1	13.8	18.0	48.8	–
6	–	–	–	–	10.2	13.0	17.7	19.1	40.0
7	–	–	–	–	–	19.3	17.0	20.4	41.8

*This oligomer was not resolved in the parent polymer.

Table 9.5   Molecular Weights of Polystyrene Standard and Fractions

Fraction	Number Average Molecular Weight	Weight Average Molecular Weight	Polydispersity
Parent	552	634	1.15
1	305	330	1.08
2	370	408	1.10
3	489	530	1.08
4	590	647	1.10
5	736	792	1.08
6	827	854	1.03
7	857	875	1.02

Chlorotrifluoroethylene (CTFE) polymer oils are being evaluated as flotation fluids for inertial guidance devices in space applications. These fluids operate in extremely high-*g* rotational environments, where polymers containing a range of oligomers can actually be fractionated by sedimentation brought about by the high centrifugal forces. The sedimentation interferes with the operation and performance of the guidance system. Substantial effort is being directed to the synthesis of oils and polymers of appropriate density and composition and to the fractionation of the CTFE oil into narrow-polydispersity fractions (or into actual monodisperse oligomers) using molecular distillation or prep scale liquid chromatography. In general, molecular distillation and prep scale liquid chromatography are expensive separations processes, and supercritical fluid extraction or fractionation can be viable as an alternative, especially if a superior product can be obtained.

Figure 9.8 is a gas chromatography–mass spectroscopy (GC-MS) analysis of the CTFE parent which contains four primary peaks corresponding to degrees of polymerization of 6, 7, 8, and 9, respectively. The relative amounts of each of the oligomers in the parent oil are given in table 9.6. As figure 9.8 and the data in table 9.6 show, the oil is composed of primarily 7-mer and 8-mer oligomers.

CTFE dissolves in a number of gases, e.g., carbon dioxide, ethylene, and the chlorofluorocarbons. In this instance, ethylene is arbitrarily chosen. The polymer is easily fractionated by supercritical ethylene at a temperature level of 90°C and a pressure range from 1,800 psia to 4,800 psia. Although eight fractions are obtained (see table 9.6), these fractions do not represent the results of an optimized SCF fractionation study. Instead, the results are presented for the purpose of indicating the breadth of application of supercritical fluid fractionation.

The composition data in table 9.6 show that substantial changes in the ratios of mers is achieved in any one fraction relative to the parent. For example, in fractions 3 and 6 the predominant oligomer represents about 90% of the fraction. To give a pictorial comparison of the composition of those two

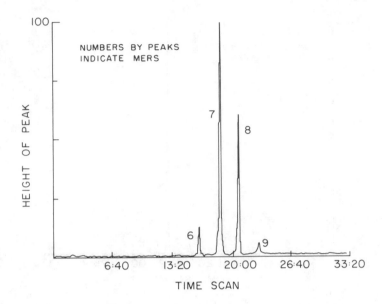

Figure 9.8 GC-MS chromatogram of a chlorotrifluoroethylene polymer.

Table 9.6 Composition of Fractions Chlorotrifluoroethylene Polymer Obtained by Supercritical Ethylene Processing

| Fraction | Oligomer Composition (Wt-%) | | | | Wt-% of Parent |
	6-mer	7-mer	8-mer	9-mer	
Parent	4.5	49.5	39.5	6.5	100.0
1	51.1	37.6	12.3	–	5.8
2	24.4	73.5	2.0	–	8.6
3	7.6	86.4	6.0	–	20.2
4	1.8	75.3	22.9	–	15.2
5	0.7	38.7	58.1	2.5	22.8
6	–	5.7	94.2	0.1	15.6
7	–	0.6	66.4	33.0	10.5
8	–	3.0	55.5	41.5	1.3

fractions relative to that of the parent material, we give the GC-MS traces of the two fractions, fractions 3 and 6, in figures 9.9 and 9.10, respectively. As can be seen from a comparison of the figures and the data in table 9.6, supercritical ethylene is a reasonably effective fractionation solvent. Again, no effort is made to optimize this SCF fractionation.

Krukonis (1982a) also finds that in some cases supercritical fluid fractionation can concentrate polymer species that escape detection during "con-

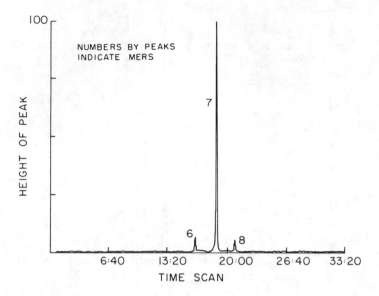

Figure 9.9   GC-MS chromatogram of fraction 3 of the chlorotri-fluoroethylene polymer fractionated with supercritical ethylene.

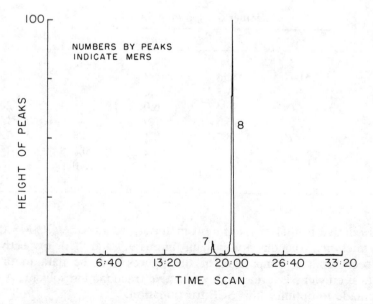

Figure 9.10   GC-MS chromatogram of fraction 6 of the chlorotri-fluoroethylene polymer fractionated with supercritical ethylene.

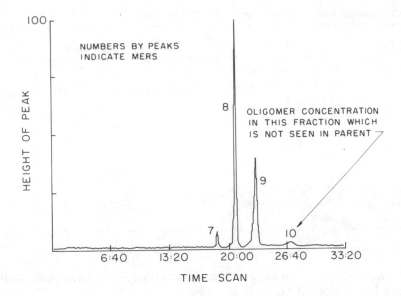

Figure 9.11 GC-MS chromatogram of fraction 8 of the chlorotrifluo-roethylene polymer fractionated with supercritical ethylene.

ventional" analysis of the parent polymer. Consider, for example, figure 9.11, which is the GC-MS trace of fraction 8, whose composition was given in table 9.6. Although the integrator calculated the 7-, 8-, and 9-mer concentrations of this fraction to total to 100%, a trace of a higher mer (identified by mass spectroscopy to be a 10-mer) is now evident and is identified in figure 9.11. The presence of the additional peak in figure 9.11 is indicative of the ability of supercritical fluid solvents to concentrate and, hence, identify minute quantities of compounds that are present in a mixture.

Fractionation of Liquid Crystal and Photoresist Polymers

A recent report of the results of a program completed under National Science Foundation funding describes the supercritical fluid fractionation of a number of liquid-crystal and photoresist polymers (Krukonis, 1984b). Table 9.7 gives the structures of several polymers tested. Results with three of these polymers are presented in order to illustrate the extent of separation that can be achieved by supercritical fluid fractionation.

The functionally terminated polysiloxanes are currently under evaluation as precursors of liquid-crystal polymers. Fundamental studies on the effects of molecular structure, molecular weight, and polydispersity on polymer characteristics and performance are being carried out at a number of laboratories,

Table 9.7   Structure of Polymers Tested for Fractionation

Type of Polymer	Name	Structure
Liquid crystal	Several functionally terminated poly(dimethyl)-siloxanes, e.g.	$.H_2N-(CH_2)_3 - \begin{bmatrix} CH_3 \\ Si-O \\ CH_3 \end{bmatrix}_x - \begin{bmatrix} \bigcirc \\ Si-O \\ \bigcirc \end{bmatrix}_y - \begin{matrix} CH_3 \\ Si-(CH_2)_3\,NH_2 \\ CH_3 \end{matrix}$
Photoresist	Polysilastyrene	$(CH_3)_3\,Si - \begin{bmatrix} \bigcirc \\ Si \\ CH_3 \end{bmatrix}_x - \begin{bmatrix} CH_3 \\ Si \\ CH_3 \end{bmatrix}_y - Si(CH_3)_3$
Polymeric surfactant	Carboxylic acid–terminated perfluoralkyl-polyether	$HOOC - \begin{bmatrix} CF(CF_3)CF_2O \end{bmatrix}_n C_2F_5$

e.g., by McGrath and Wilkes and co-workers at Virginia Polytechnic Institute and State University (McGrath et al., 1982).

Like other poly(dimethyl)siloxanes this polymer dissolves in a number of gases. Table 9.8 gives the average molecular weight of the parent carboxypropl-terminated poly(dimethyl)siloxane and the seven fractions derived from the parent by fractionation using supercritical carbon dioxide. The molecular-weight analysis is carried out by end-group titration. Fraction 1 contains no titratable functionality and is designated "cyclics" (octamethyl cyclotetrasiloxane). As is seen from the data in the table, the nominal 6,000-molecular-weight polymer is fractionated into cuts with molecular weight as high as 13,000.

A pictorial presentation of the fractionation is given in figure 9.12, which compares the GPCs of each supercritical-fluid-separated fraction with that of the parent polymer. The narrowing of the molecular-weight range in the fraction and the progression of average molecular weights is ascertained from the GPCs assembled below the chromatogram of the parent polymer.

Table 9.8   Fractionation of Carboxypropyl-Terminated Poly(dimethyl)siloxane of Nominal Molecular Weight 6,000 with Supercritical Carbon Dioxide

Fraction	% of Parent	Number Average Molecular Weight	Weight Average Molecular Weight	Polydispersity
Parent	100	6,400	13,310	2.08
1	4.5		Cyclics	
2	5.0	1,580	2,000	1.27
3	20.7	3,300	4,690	1.42
4	22.2	5,700	7,350	1.29
5	11.6	7,350	9,480	1.28
6	24.2	10,300	13,080	1.27
7	9.0	12,850	16,320	1.27

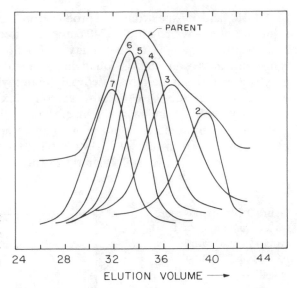

Figure 9.12 GPC of the parent carboxypropyl-terminated poly-(dimethyl)siloxane and the fractions obtained by fractionation with supercritical carbon dioxide.

Some additional chemical and instrumental analyses are carried out on some of the fractions. Fraction 1, which was shown by end-group titration to contain no carboxylic groups, is concluded to be composed of cyclic siloxanes. Additional corroboration of the conclusion is found in the Fourier Transform-infrared (FT-IR) spectrum of this fraction as given in figure 9.13. Very little carboxylic signature at a wavelength of about 1,740/cm is evident in figure 9.13, verifying the titration result that showed no carboxylic functionality present in the fraction. A sample of another fraction, fraction 7, is also analyzed

Figure 9.13 (FT-IR) spectra of fraction 1 of the carboxypropyl-terminated poly(dimethyl)-siloxane.

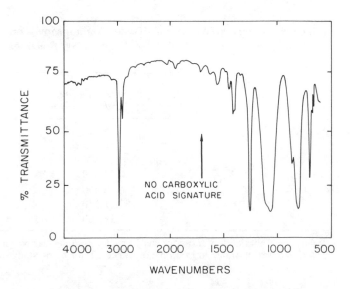

by FT-IR, and its spectrum is reproduced in figure 9.14. The carboxylic-acid signature at a wavelength of 1,740/cm is accented with an arrow.

Another example of the ability to fractionate a wide molecular-weight range into narrower cuts is found in the results obtained with supercritical ethylene and an amine-terminated poly(dimethyl)siloxane. Supercritical ethylene is used in this case because carbon dioxide reacts with primary and secondary aliphatic amines. A temperature of 70°C and a pressure range of 1,400–4,000 psia is effective in achieving an acceptable fractionation, the result of which is shown in table 9.9. As the results again show, cyclics are concentrated, and the average molecular weight progresses monotonically from very

Figure 9.14   FT-IR spectra of fraction 7 of the carboxypropyl-terminated poly(dimethyl)-siloxane.

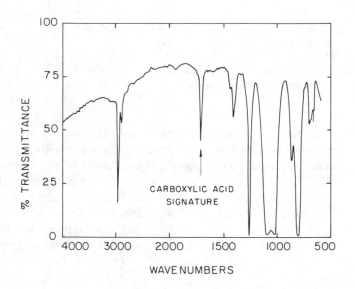

Table 9.9   Molecular-Weight Analysis of Aminopropyl-Terminated Poly(dimethyl)siloxane of Molecular Weight 6,000 Fractionated with Supercritical Ethylene

Fraction	Number Average Molecular Weight[a]	Wt-% of Parent
Parent	5,910	100
1	cyclics	4.4
2	2,820	7.7
3	5,030	15.8
4	8,250	29.6
5	11,530	16.3
6	13,000[b]	26.2

[a]Values were obtained by titration; weight-averaged molecular weights were not ascertainable.
[b]Fraction 6 was insoluble in isopropanol and could not be titrated; value is estimated.

low to very high as the pressure is increased. The GPCs of the parent polymer and the SCF fractions are similar in appearance to those shown in figure 9.11 and are not reproduced here.

As the next step in the evaluation of supercritical fluid fractionation of the polysiloxane polymers, narrow-molecular-weight fractions are currently being converted into liquid-crystal copolymers for the purpose of determining the properties that derive from the fractionation of the parent materials.

Another class of polymers receiving increasing attention is the polysilanes, i.e., polymers with an Si-Si backbone. Because Si-Si bonds are sensitive to incident photons and because the sensitivity to a particular wavelength can be altered and controlled by the nature of the pendant group on the Si and by the molecular weight, these polymers are being examined as photoresists in the processing of semiconductor wafers. The synthesis reactions forming polysilanes produce a wide range of molecular weights, as was the case with polysiloxanes. This wide molecular-weight range reduces the effectiveness of the polymer because of the variable sensitivity to light energy brought about by the molecular-weight spread.

Structures of some of the polysilane polymers reported in the NSF study (Krukonis, 1984b) are shown in table 9.7; a cyclohexyl substituted polysilane is selected for further discussion here. Figure 9.15 is a GPC of the material as synthesized. Three primary molecular-weight groupings of 500,000, 50,000, and 10,000 molecular weight comprise the polymer and are designated in the figure. The desired material is the fraction of 500,000 molecular weight. Notice, however, that the 10,000-molecular-weight fraction shown in figure 9.15 is more than 50% of the total polymer.

This silane polymer is found to be virtually insoluble in carbon dioxide at pressure and temperature levels up to 8,000 psia and 120°C, respectively. Additionally, it is difficult to solubilize in supercritical ethylene and ethane at the same conditions. Supercritical propane proves a better solvent in this case,

Figure 9.15 GPC of a synthesized cyclohexyl-substituted polysilane polymer.

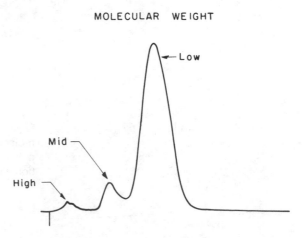

and an extraction of the low-molecular-weight oligomers is accomplished at conditions of 7,000 psia and 120°C.

A GPC of the extract is shown in figure 9.16. Three GPCs are reproduced in the figure because the extract is sequentially collected in three steps and a slight progression to higher molecular weights is seen. Figure 9.17 is the GPC of the desired polymer. The low-molecular-weight material has been completely extracted. At the operating conditions of 7,000 psia the fraction of molecular weight 50,000 did not dissolve; this result is to be compared with the results given in table 9.2, which shows that poly(dimethyl)siloxane of 100,000 molecular weight can be dissolved in carbon dioxide. Except for the studies on polyethylene-ethylene equilibria and the work on supercritical fluid chromatography of polystyrene, little work has been reported on the fractionation of polymer systems with any supercritical fluids. It is no surprise, however, that polysiloxane and polysilane polymers exhibit differences in solubility behavior in supercritical fluids; they behave differently with normal liquid solvents.

Krukonis (1982b) has found that supercritical fluid processing is also effective for fractionating a variety of other silicone oils and gums, such as diphenylsiloxanes and fluoro-substituted oils, and reactive silicones with hydroxy, alkoxy, amine, carboxylic, and methacryloxy functionalities. These oils are used for chromatographic stationary phases, lubricants, and other specialty purposes. The ability to use an SCF to process materials at near room temperatures is an attractive option for fractionating heat-labile materials, for example, with methacryloxy functionalities. The high temperature associated with conventional molecular distillation can result in some degradation or, in fact, polymerization as the oil is being purified.

Figure 9.16   GPCs of the fractions of the low-molecular-weight cyclohexyl-substituted polysilane polymer fractionated with supercritical propane. (A, B, & C are sequential fractions.)

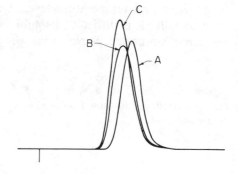

MOLECULAR   WEIGHT

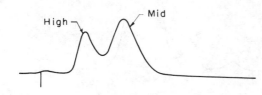

Figure 9.17   GPC of the mid- and high-molecular-weight cyclohexyl-substituted polysilane polymer remaining after fractionation with supercritical propane.

Fractionation of Polyisobutylene Surfactant

One final example of SCF fractionation of polymers is given in this section to show the breadth of this technology. The polymer tested in a study by Krukonis (1983c) is a polyisobutylene–succinic anhydride copolymer surfactant used in engine lubricants. The surface-active ends of the polymer complex to inorganic and carbon particles, preventing their interference with the lubrication of sliding metal parts. This polymer is also an excellent surfactant for stabilizing suspensions containing high levels of 100-A particles of magnetite in a hydrocarbon carrier used for seals in computer disc drives. The polymer exhibits a wide molecular-weight range and the wide range of chain length introduces adverse effects on the viscosity of the suspension. Because of the presence of long chains in the polymer, the hydrodynamic radius of the suspended particles (and surfactant) is quite large, causing interaction among the suspended particles at relatively low concentrations of solids. The interaction results in a higher-than-desired viscosity. The polymeric surfactant has not been successfully fractionated by solvent-antisolvent methods. Supercritical fluid fractionation is successfully applied to obtain a mid-cut of molecular weight of this polyisobutylene polymer.

The polymer surfactant is fractionated with supercritical ethylene at 120°C and a decreasing pressure range of 4,600 psia to 900 psia. For the purpose of determining the degree of fractionation achievable, eleven separate fractions were obtained in the feasibility test. Table 9.10 gives the results of GPC analysis of the molecular weight of the parent polymer and of the fractions. As the table shows, the nominal 4,000-molecular-weight surfactant is separated into fractions whose molecular weights range from 1,000 to 10,000. In this specific application the removal of the low-molecular-weight and the high-molecular-

Table 9.10 Molecular-Weight Analysis of Polyisobutylene-Succinic Anhydride Copolymer Fractions

Fraction	Molecular Weight	wt-% of parent
Parent	4,000	100
1	480	15.9
2	480	9.7
3	530	2.9
4	1,500	7.6
5	2,000	7.6
6	3,000	11.3
7	5,500	26.4
8	7,100	5.3
9	8,000	5.1
10	9,000	5.1
11	9,000	3.3

weight species produces a more efficient surfactant (on a weight basis) and concurrently allows a higher solid loading to be achieved without adverse effects on viscosity.

POLYMER–ORGANIC SOLVENT PHASE SEPARATION

The final type of SCF-polymer separation technique to be discussed in this section is that used to separate polymer solutions. Shown in figure 9.18 is a schematic representation of polymer-solution phase behavior. Note that a miscible polymer solution located at a temperature and pressure in the single-liquid-phase region of the *P-T* diagram in figure 9.18 can be split into a polymer-rich phase and a solvent-rich phase either by isobarically lowering the temperature until the UCST curve is intersected or by isobarically increasing the temperature until the LCST curve is intersected. For many polymer solutions the UCST curve is not observed, since the polymer solution freezes before the liquid mixture splits into two phases. By contrast, most polymer-solvent mixtures "go the route of an LCST" (Flory, 1984) if they are heated to a high temperature.

As noted in chapter 6, the LCST is a function of the chemical nature of the solvent, the polymer's molecular weight, and the critical properties of the solvent. For example, a ratio of the LCST (measured at the vapor pressure of the mixture) to the solvent's critical temperature as low as 0.73 is found for the polyisobutylene–*n*-pentane system (Bardin and Patterson, 1969), whereas the temperature ratio for the polyisobutylene-cyclooctane system is 0.98. Cyclooctane is a better solvent for polyisobutylene than n-pentane and, therefore,

Figure 9.18 Schematic representation of the *P-T* behavior of a polymer–organic solvent mixture. The insert in this diagram shows the full phase diagram while the hatched area is expanded to show more detail near the critical point of the solvent (McClellan, Bauman, and McHugh, 1984).

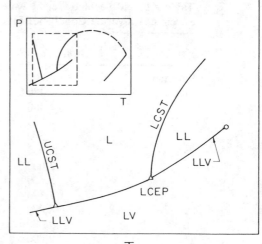

the polyisobutylene stays in solution at lower temperatures. Also, the higher the molecular weight of the polymer, the lower the LCST.

The phase behavior for numerous polymer-solvent mixtures has been discussed in the literature (Freeman and Rowlinson, 1960; Baker et al., 1966; Zeman and Patterson, 1972; Zeman et al., 1972; Allen and Baker, 1965; Saeki et al., 1974; Cowie and McEwen, 1974). In all of these studies the LCST behavior of the polymer solution is measured at the vapor pressure of the mixture. As described in some detail in chapter 6, using an LCST phase split to recover polymer from solution offers certain advantages as compared with other conventional separation techniques, such as steam stripping. However, it is still necessary to heat the polymer solution to temperatures near the solvent's critical temperature. For good polymer solvents such as cyclohexane (T_c = 280.3°C), the critical temperature can be high enough to cause thermal degradation of the polymer.

As described in chapter 6, Irani, Cosewith, and Kasegrande (1982) are able to shift the LCST curve to lower temperatures by adding a near-critical or supercritical fluid to the polymer solution. Recently, McHugh and co-workers have extended the SCF-additive work of Irani (McHugh and Guckes, 1985; McClellan and McHugh, 1985; McClellan, Bauman, and McHugh, 1985). They find that an increased amount of SCF additive significantly shifts the LCST curve of the polymer solution to lower temperatures, as shown for the poly(ethylene-co-propylene)–hexane–ethylene system in figure 9.19. In fact, if enough SCF additive is added, the LCST curve is shifted to sufficiently low temperatures and the UCST curve is also simultaneously shifted to sufficiently

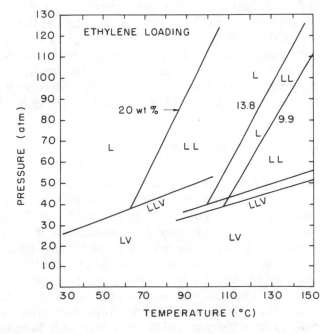

Figure 9.19 *P-T* behavior of the poly(ethylene-co-propylene)–hexane–ethylene system (McHugh and Guckes, 1985).

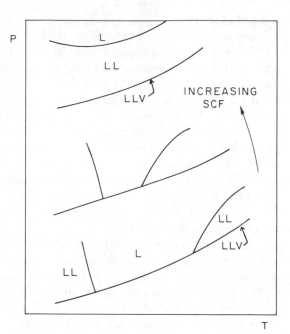

Figure 9.20 Schematic representation of the effect of an SCF additive on the *P-T* behavior of a polymer solution (McClellan, Bauman, & McHugh, 1984).

high temperatures that these curves merge to form a single curve. This type of polymer–solvent–SCF additive behavior is shown schematically in figure 9.20 and is demonstrated for the poly(ethylene-co-propylene)-hexane-ethylene system in figure 9.21. Similar polymer-solution phase behavior is observed for polystyrene-toluene-SCF mixtures (McClellan, Bauman, and McHugh, 1984). When the LCST and UCST curves merge, a wide range of temperatures and pressures can be used for separating polymer from solution. A polymer of different molecular weight and molecular-weight distribution is expected for the polymer solubilized in the solvent-rich phase in the LL region of the phase diagram as compared with the polymer in the polymer-rich phase.

MONOMER PURIFICATION

Reactive monomers, which are used in applications that require high purity but which are difficult to process by distillation because of their sensitivity to temperature, can potentially be purified by SCF processing techniques (Krukonis, 1982c). Supercritical fluid purification of three monomers that are converted to diverse products is discussed in this subsection.

Next-generation soft contact lenses, dental polymers, surface coatings, and similar materials are produced from compounds of varying structure and reactive functionality. For example, currently in development are new soft lenses that will be manufactured from monomers that have been synthesized with dimethylsiloxane backbones. The dimethylsiloxane backbone is terminated

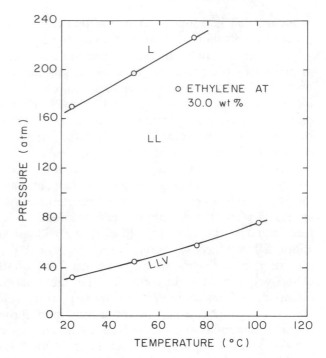

Figure 9.21 Effect of increased amounts of ethylene on the poly(ethylene-co-propylene)–hexane system (McHugh and Guckes, 1985).

with a methacryloxy funcationality that supplies the site for polymerization. The siloxane provides lens "softness." Occasionally the functionality is formed on both ends of the monomer resulting in undesired properties. The compound BisGMA, is a monomer that is polymerized to form hard dental structures. In the monomer synthesis process impurities are coproduced that interfere with the polymerization. Finally, diacetone acrylamide used in a copolymerization process is another specialty monomer that is occasionally contaminated with difficult-to-remove impurities. These three monomers are quite reactive at modest temperature and cannot be purified by distillation. The three examples that are presented here derive from as yet unpublished research (Krukonis, 1982c).

One soft-lens monomer currently in early development is being synthesized in batches of about 1–10 kilograms. The resulting product is usually found to be contaminated with about 5 wt-% difunctional material coproduced in the monomer synthesis scheme. In the subsequent soft-lens manufacturing process, the monomer is polymerized across the vinyl groups at a temperature of about 80°C, but cross-linking can occur if two methacryloxy groups are situated on the monomer which obviously is detrimental to "softness." The monomer cannot be purified by distillation because at a temperature of 80°C there is very little difference in the vapor pressures of the desired monomer and the impurity, which makes them virtually unseparable even if high-vacuum distillation is used. Additionally, a higher distillation temperature cannot be used because the monomer will prematurely polymerize. This type of separation problem, that is, a reactive material that cannot be purified by conventional processing, is tailor-made for SCF extraction.

Before describing the SCF extraction tests, let us attempt to determine a priori whether supercritical fluid extraction can be used for this separation problem. We have seen in previous sections of this chapter that siloxanes with molecular weights as high as 100,000 will dissolve in supercritical carbon dioxide. We have also mentioned the work of Francis (1954; see chapter 2), who measured the solubilities of a large number of high-molecular-weight carboxylic acids and found them quite soluble in near-critical liquid CO_2. Francis also showed that the esterification of an acid, polyacid, or polyhydroxyl compound confers a higher solubility to the compound in carbon dioxide. Thus, the methacrylic-ester moiety on the short dimethylsiloxane chain should not adversely affect the dimethylsiloxane solubility in an SCF solvent; it may, in fact, enhance the solubility. Finally, we will assume that incorporating an additional methacryloxy group on a fairly small siloxane oligomer will affect the solubility behavior of the substance. All of these considerations taken collectively lead us to the conclusion that the monofunctional monomer should be separable from the difunctional impurity using supercritical fluid extraction.

Figure 9.22 is a high-performance liquid chromatogram (HPLC) of the solution containing the synthesized monomer, associated raw materials, and the difunctional impurity. As seen in the figure, HPLC does not completely resolve the monofunctional and difunctional materials in the solution. The signature of the difunctional impurity is visible as the shoulder on the major peak in the solution. Incidentally, the other peaks to the left of the major peak represent unreacted raw materials, which, as seen in the figure, can be resolved from the monofunctional monomer in the HPLC analysis. These unreacted raw materials are also quite readily removed from solution by conventional processing techniques. Thus, the major problem in the development of the new lens monomer is the separation of the difunctional impurity.

The monofunctional and difunctional compounds can be separated with supercritical carbon dioxide at 2,400 psia and 60°C. Although the difference in vapor pressure between the two compounds is not great enough to allow facile separation by distillation, supercritical carbon dioxide is able to separate these compounds, which differ by only one methacryloxy group. Figures 9.23a and 9.23b are HPLCs of the two fractions obtained from the extraction. The same scale that is used for the HPLC of the parent solution is drawn on both fractions. As is seen in these figures, the major peaks in the supercritical fluid–processed fractions have eluted at different times.

As related at the start of this section, dental materials are increasingly being subjected to the demand of improved performance. Monomers and resins that can be photopolymerized at room temperature to form extremely hard cross-linked structures have been developed, and increasingly sensitive initiators (activated by incident photons) have created the need for purer monomers.

BisGMA resin is an advanced restorative material currently in use, but it suffers from certain drawbacks. (The chemical name of BisGMA is 2,2-*bis*(*p*-2′-hydroxy-3′-methacryloxypropoxy)-phenylene-propane.) The impurities pres-

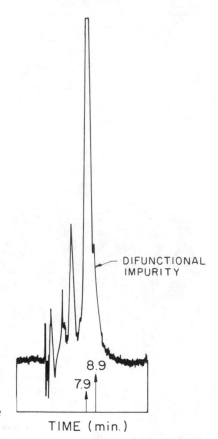

Figure 9.22 HPLC chromatogram of the silicone lens monomer and difunctional impurity.

ent in the resin can limit its shelf life and can also interfere with the polymerization reaction to form impervious enamellike structures. These impurities exhibit very low vapor pressures and cannot readily be removed by conventional distillation techniques. As described for the soft-lens monomer case, heating the mixture of BisGMA results in the premature polymerization of the resin. The ease of polymerization of BisGMA, although advantageous for its end use, can limit its ability to be purified.

BisGMA is synthesized commercially in a two-step process. The first step reacts Bisphenol A and epichlorohydrin to form diglycidyl ether of Bisphenol A (DGEBA). The second step reacts DGEBA and methacrylic acid to form BisGMA. Excess epichlorohydrin is used in the first reaction step to ensure the complete solubilization of Bisphenol A and to ensure a good yield. The excess epichlorohydrin, however, is difficult to remove. During the second step of the process the epichlorohydrin causes the conversion of some methacrylic acid to 1-chloro-isopropanol methacrylate, which also is virtually impossible to remove by conventional distillation or vacuum stripping. The chloromethacrylate impurity adversely affects the behavior of BisGMA in the end-use polymerization reaction as explained below.

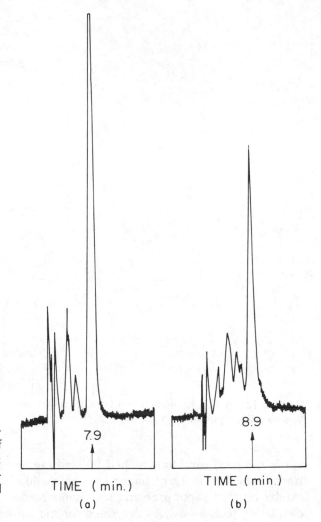

Figure 9.23   Two HPLC chromatograms of the fractions of the silicone lens monomer: (a) purified monomer (no difunctional impurity present) and (b) concentrated impurity.

The BisGMA monomer is polymerized by either of two free-radical mechanisms: a thermally induced peroxide initiation or a photo-induced α,β-diketone initiation. Many of the initiator formulations are proprietary to their respective manufacturers, but a typical peroxide initiator is benzoyl peroxide, which forms free radicals when the temperature is raised. The α,β-diketone initiator responds to incident light energy to form free radicals.

In the peroxide formulation initiation, the organochlorine impurities that are present in commercial BisGMA accelerate the decomposition of the peroxides, a process that forms free radicals and reduces the stability and shelf life of the resin. In the α,β-diketone formulation, the organochlorine impurities complex with other additives in the formulation that are present to enhance free-radical formation. The presence of the impurities thus reduces the photoefficiency and negates the advantages of simple photo-initiated diketone curing.

The problems with the chlorinized impurities notwithstanding, BisGMA is the superior dental material available today. If the impurity-induced limitations could be eliminated or reduced, the use of BisGMA could proliferate into other applications, such as prosthetic bones, in which the advantages of the high tensile and compressive strength of the cross-linked polymer can be coupled to the ease and efficiency of polymerizing the purified monomer into the desired forms.

BisGMA, then, is another material that exhibits the potential for supercritical fluid upgrading. It is quite reactive (in fact, its reactivity near ambient temperature is one of its attractive properties); it cannot be purified readily by conventional processing; and as improvements in the initiators continue, it is being faced with a greater performance demand. Figure 9.24 is an HPLC of a commercial BisGMA sample. The major peak in this figure is the product, BisGMA. Two of the other peaks are the 1-chloro-isopropanol methacrylate, which is the predominant impurity, and diglycidyl ether of Bisphenol A (which, although it is an "impurity," does not interfere with either the thermal or photolytic initiation of BisGMA).

An initial test, using carbon dioxide, was made at arbitrarily selected extraction conditions of 1,800 psia. The temperature level is kept at 45°C in order to reduce the tendency for the BisGMA to polymerize during extraction. The choice of parameters, although arbitrarily chosen for this first BisGMA test, derives from consideration of previous results on the extraction of low-molecular-weight cyclic siloxanes from a high-viscosity silicone oil. Very frequently, the solubilities of homologous mers decreases with increasing molecular weight; analogously, the relative extraction or selectivity is greatest at the lowest solubility levels (at the lower-pressure isobars as previously seen in

Figure 9.24 HPLC chromatogram of commercially available BisGMA: (1) 1-chloro-isopropanol methacrylate; (2) BisGMA; and (3) diglycidyl ether of Bisphenol-A.

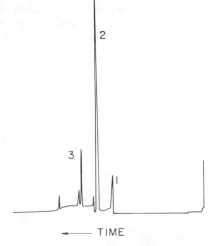

TIME

figure 2.2). The 1-chloro compound is of lower molecular weight than the BisGMA, and it is thus reasoned that the former compound might mimic the behavior of a cyclosiloxane present in admixture with higher-molecular-weight linear siloxanes. Although such simplistic reasoning is usually correct with polymers and homologous-series oils, it can break down when comparing compounds of very differing functionalities or molecular weights. For example, a compound with two ester groups might be more soluble than the same parent compound containing one ester and one hydroxy end. Even though the hydroxy compound has a lower molecular weight, hydrogen bonding can decrease the solubility relative to the di-ester.

The SCF-extracted residual material is analyzed by HPLC, and the chromatogram of the purified material is shown in figure 9.25. As can readily be ascertained from a comparison of figures 9.24 and 9.25, the concentration of the impurities and the concentrations of many of the unidentified components have decreased almost by a factor of 5. Hence, SCF extraction works quite well in this instance.

The last monomer to be discussed in this section is a solid, diacetone acrylamide, which is currently used in a specialty copolymerization process. This monomer is also quite heat-labile. Figure 9.26 is the HPLC signature of this monomer. The chromatogram shows the presence of another peak, designated "impurity," and in the particular sample analyzed it is present at about 100 ppm. The impurity has been identified as a condensation product formed occasionally and unpredictably during the monomer-synthesis reaction. When it is found to be present, the impurity-containing batch cannot be used, because the impurity interferes in subsequent polymerization reactions. The monomer cannot be separated from the impurity by conventional processing and the batch is used in applications not requiring the extremely high purity demanded

Figure 9.25 HPLC chromatogram of the purified fraction obtained by extracting BisGMA with supercritical carbon dioxide: (1) 1-chloro-isopropanol methacrylate; (2) BisGMA; and (3) diglycidyl ether of Bisphenol-A.

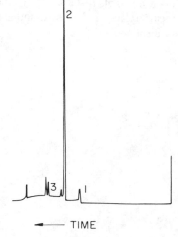

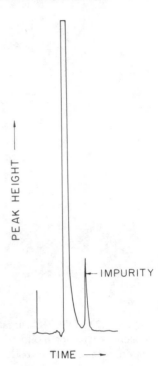

PEAK HEIGHT ——————→

←—IMPURITY

TIME ——→

Figure 9.26   HPLC chromatogram of the monomer diacetone acrylamide.

in copolymerization. Both the impurity and the monomer are quite soluble in traditional liquid solvents and neither crystallization nor antisolvent methods are effective in causing a separation of the two. Distillation is also not effective because the monomer tends to degrade (or polymerize) at quite low temperatures. Thus, again, supercritical fluid extraction is a potential solution for this problem, because, on the basis solely of homologous-series size considerations, the monomer and the much larger condensation product should exhibit differing solubilities.

However, supercritical fluid extraction is not a panacea for all problems, and again it must be evaluated on a case-by-case basis. Supercritical carbon dioxide at 40°C is quite effective in separating the monomer from its condensation impurity (Krukonis, 1981d). A temperature of 40°C is chosen to carry out the extraction because diacetone acrylamide becomes increasingly reactive as the temperature is raised higher. Figure 9.27 shows the HPLC of the purified monomer obtained by supercritical carbon dioxide extraction. As the chromatogram shows, the impurity is not present. For completeness, figure 9.28 is included to show the impurity-containing fraction and it is seen that the impurity has been concentrated manyfold. The separation of the impurity from the desired monomer is not "perfect," as seen by the presence of a monomer peak in figure 9.28, but isolating the impurity is not important. More importantly, the yield of purified monomer is quite high at 90%.

Figure 9.27   HPLC chromatogram of the purified di-acetone acrylamide monomer obtained by treatment with supercritical carbon dioxide.

Figure 9.28   HPLC chromatogram of the impurity-containing fraction removed from the diacetone acrylamide monomer.

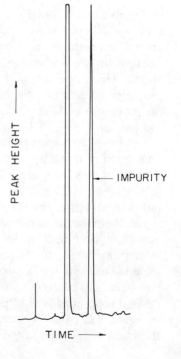

10

Processing Pharmaceuticals, Natural Products, Specialty Chemicals, and Waste Streams

A large body of experimental data has been accumulated on the solubility and extractability of natural products, such as steroids, alkaloids, anticancer agents, oils from seeds, and caffeine from coffee beans, in various SCF solvents such as CO_2, ethane, ethylene, and N_2O. Carbon dioxide is probably the most widely investigated SCF solvent since its critical temperature ($T_c = 31.1°C$) makes it an ideal solvent for extracting materials that are thermally labile. Also, CO_2 is nontoxic, nonflammable, environmentally acceptable, and inexpensive.

To determine the solubility characteristics of compounds in SCFs Stahl and co-workers (Stahl and Quirin, 1983; Stahl et al., 1980) have developed a microextraction apparatus that they directly couple with thin-layer chromatography. They find that a number of variables control the solubility of natural products in supercritical CO_2. They corroborate some of the trends detailed in the preceding pages. For instance, they report that:

1. fractionation of liquids or solids is possible if the constituents of the mixture exhibit large differences in vapor pressure, mass, and polarity;
2. low-molecular-weight hydrocarbons and lipophilic organic compounds, such as esters, ethers, and lactones, are easily extractable;
3. hydroxyl and carboxyl substituent groups on the mixture constituents reduce the solubility of the substance in the SCF and therefore make the extraction extremely difficult; and
4. sugars and amino acids are not extracted by supercritical CO_2.

In one study Stahl and Quirin (1983) determined the solubility level of tetracyclic steroids that differed in structure but all of which had virtually the same vapor pressure at the operating temperature of the system using supercritical CO_2. The carboxyl groups on the steroids, such as bile acids, rendered the steroids virtually insoluble in supercritical CO_2, whereas carbonyl groups had very little effect on the solubility of similar steroids. The differences in the molecular weights and melting points of the steroids had no direct influence on the solubility behavior. Numerous other SCF extraction studies have been performed by Stahl and co-workers. Their work, along with the work of Francis and others, forms a large data base that should be referred to when one is considering whether a compound is soluble in CO_2.

In this section the SCF processing of two natural products, coffee and edible oils, is described and other previously unpublished data are presented.

COFFEE DECAFFEINATION

Coffee decaffeination with carbon dioxide has been the object of a large amount of effort in research and development at the Max Planck Institute for Coal Research in Germany and at other academic and industrial laboratories in Europe and the United States. As an indication of the intensity of effort applied to this process, the reader is referred to a review article that listed the United States patents on decaffeination granted as of the end of 1981 (Paulaitis et al., 1983a). Several earlier patents had been inadvertently omitted from that list, and a corrected tabulation is given in table 10.1. Research activity on super-critical fluid extraction of stimulants from coffee, tea, and cocoa has continued, as is indicated by the number of United States patents granted since that review article was published, some of which are listed in table 10.2.

Each patent has somewhat different features and claims, but it is of value to select one patent for more detailed discussion to highlight certain technical facets of the process. It is also pertinent to explain first the (often misunderstood) effect of water on the extractability of caffeine by "selective" supercritical carbon dioxide. As is reported in a number of references, dry carbon dioxide cannot extract caffeine from dry coffee, either green or roasted, but it is reported that moist carbon dioxide can. The inability of dry carbon dioxide to extract caffeine from coffee should not be misconstrued to mean that dry carbon dioxide cannot dissolve neat caffeine. This same moist-versus-dry effect is experienced if, for example, methylene chloride is used to extract caffeine from coffee. Dry methylene chloride cannot decaffeinate dry coffee, but if the coffee is moistened it can be decaffeinated. It is thought that the caffeine is chemically bound in a chlorogenic acid structure present in the coffee bean. Thus, water somehow acts as a chemical agent freeing caffeine from its bound form in the coffee matrix, in both the carbon dioxide and methylene chloride processes.

The topic of selectivity (or, more accurately, the lack of selectivity) of carbon dioxide is further clarified by a comparison of the extraction results with roasted and green coffee. Moist carbon dioxide extracts the caffeine from green coffee beans. Very little else present in green coffee dissolves in carbon

Table 10.1 United States Patents on Coffee Decaffeination (1981 and Earlier)

Date	Patent Number	Title	Assignee
Apr. 23, 1974	3,806,619	Process for recovering caffeine	Studiengesellschaft Kohle, mbH
Oct. 22, 1974	3,843,824	Method for the production of caffeine-free coffee extract	HAG Aktiengesellschaft
Apr. 22, 1975	3,879,569	Process for the decaffeination of raw coffee	HAG Aktiengesellschaft
Sept. 18, 1979	4,168,324	Process for extracting stimulants from coffee	HAG Aktiengesellschaft
Jan. 20, 1981	4,246,291	Decaffeination of aqueous extracts	General Foods Corporation
Jan. 27, 1981	4,247,570	Process for the decaffeination of coffee	Studiengesellschaft Kohle, mbH
Feb. 17, 1981	4,251,559	Decaffeination process	Société d'Assistance Technique pour Produits Nestlé S.A.
Mar. 10, 1981	4,255,461	Preparation of a decaffeinated roasted coffee blend	General Foods Corporation
Mar. 10, 1981	4,255,458	Method for the selective extraction of caffeine from vegetable materials	HAG Aktiengesellschaft
Apr. 7, 1981	4,260,639	Process for the decaffeination of coffee	Studiengesellschaft Kohle, mbH
Jun. 30, 1981	4,276,315	Method for decaffeinating coffee	General Foods Corporation

Table 10.2 United States Patents on Coffee Decaffeination (1982 and Later)

Date	Patent Number	Title	Assignee
Mar. 30, 1982	4,322,445	Process for decaffeinating coffee	S. Peter and G. Brunner
May 4, 1982	4,328,255	Method of extraction of coffee containing aroma constituents from roasted coffee	Studiengesellschaft Kohle, mbH
Jun. 4, 1982	4,341,804	Decaffeination of aqueous roasted coffee extract	General Foods Corporation
Aug. 17, 1982	4,344,974	Process for decaffeinizing raw coffee	Kaffee-Veredelungs-Werk Koffeinfrei Kaffee GmbH & Co
Sept. 7, 1982	4,348,422	Process for the direct decaffeination of aqueous coffee extract solutions	Studiengesellschaft Kohle, mbH
Dec. 21, 1982	4,364,965	Process for extracting caffeine from solutions thereof in carbon dioxide under high pressure	D. E. J. International Research Company B.V.
Oct. 25, 1983	4,411,923	Process for the extraction of caffeine super-critical solutions	HAG Aktiengesellschaft
Sept. 18, 1984	4,472,442	Decaffeination process	General Foods Corporation

dioxide. Coffee aroma oils also dissolve in carbon dioxide but they are not present in green coffee beans; they are generated during the roasting process. If moist carbon dioxide is used to extract roasted coffee beans, the aroma oils are extracted along with the caffeine. Thus, moist carbon dioxide should not be considered selective for extracting caffeine in green coffee any more than it should be considered selective for extracting naphthalene from (insoluble) chalk dust. The supercritical carbon dioxide extraction of coffee is a sound and clever process. The plant in West Germany operates at a processing level of 60,000,000 pounds per year. Moreover, it is the first example of a supercritical fluid process that has reached the commercial processing level and whose primary step is, indeed, supercritical extraction.

Let us proceed to some of the technical facets of the decaffeination process. Figure 10.1 is a graph of the solubility of neat caffeine in carbon dioxide (Krukonis, 1981a). Note for purposes of subsequent discussion that the solubility of caffeine is about 0.2 wt-% at conditions of 60°C and 300 atm. The caffeine content of most coffees is about 1 wt-%. If, during the extraction process, the caffeine in coffee dissolves to the solubility limit during extraction at, say, 60°C and 300 atm, the amount of carbon dioxide required to decaffeinate coffee is easily calculated. It is 5.0 pounds per pound of coffee.

The data from one example of an early coffee-decaffeination patent are summarized to highlight the specifics of the process (Roselius, Vitzthum, and Hubert, 1974). Four hundred grams of rough-ground de-oiled roast coffee is

Figure 10.1 Solubility of neat caffeine in supercritical carbon dioxide.

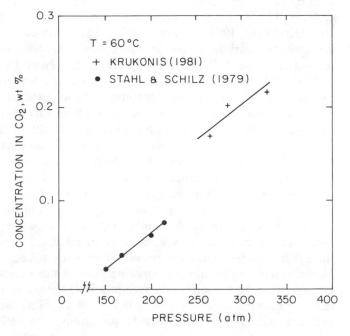

T = 60°C

+ KRUKONIS (1981)

● STAHL & SCHILZ (1979)

CONCENTRATION IN CO_2, wt %

PRESSURE (atm)

wetted with 200 milliliters of water and is treated with supercritical CO_2 with an apparatus similar to the one previously described for regenerating activated carbon. Sixty kilograms of carbon dioxide at 300 atm and 45°C are circulated through a bed packed with the coffee for approximately 5 hours. Two hundred milliliters of water and 4.2 grams of caffeine contaminated with some residual oil are separated in a collector vessel when the pressure is reduced to 60 atm and the temperature is decreased to 22°C. The percent caffeine in the roast coffee is reduced from an initial value of 1.25 wt-% to a final value of 0.06 wt-%. Note that 150 pounds of carbon dioxide per pound of coffee is passed through the bed to reduce the caffeine content by 95%. (Recall in chapter 8 that we calculated a solvent requirement of 105 pounds of CO_2 per pound of ethanol in the feed stream. Approximately the same solvent requirement is needed for coffee decaffeination. However, coffee sells for more than ethanol does and, therefore, the economics in these two cases will be different.) As is indicated subsequently, this large excess of carbon dioxide is not related solely to mass-transfer limitations. If, for example, the coffee is ground to a different mesh size or if several flow-rate levels are tested during decaffeination, the total carbon dioxide requirement is not markedly changed. These experimental findings are similar to those found for activated-carbon regeneration discussed in some detail in chapter 8.

A large excess of carbon dioxide is required because caffeine does not dissolve to its (neat) solubility limit during the extraction of coffee beans. Instead, the concentration achieved in the carbon dioxide phase is governed by an equilibrium interaction that is present in the carbon dioxide–caffeine–coffee system (or, more precisely, the carbon dioxide–water–caffeine–coffee system). The measured equilibrium isotherm for the system is given in figure 10.2 (Krukonis, 1981a). Note that it is similar in appearance to the isotherm for activated carbon shown in figure 8.8. The phenomenon active in these respective systems is probably different, however. In the case of activated carbon, high adsorption-strength forces lower the activity of an organic on the carbon, thus limiting the concentration of the pesticide in the carbon dioxide phase. For the coffee case it is speculated here that chemical binding between caffeine and the coffee substrate (which again is influenced by moisture) lowers the activity of caffeine so that it also does not dissolve to its neat solubility level. In both systems an amount of carbon dioxide in excess of that calculated from solubility considerations is needed to remove the soluble compound as a result of the interactions with the solid phase.

In this instance the separation of caffeine from the carbon dioxide phase leaving the extractor is also more complicated than using a simple pressure reduction. Recall that for the recovery of ethanol from the CO_2-rich phase in the ethanol-water extraction process a pressure-reduction step does not satisfactorily reduce the ethanol concentration in the recycled CO_2 unless a very large pressure reduction is taken. Similarly in the coffee decaffeination process, because caffeine dissolves to well below its solubility limit, an extremely large pressure reduction is necessary to precipitate the caffeine from the carbon dioxide phase. The ternary equilibrium isotherm for caffeine shown in figure 10.2 indicates that the carbon dioxide recycled to the coffee bed must be essentially free of caffeine. For example, if carbon dioxide is recycled with a caffeine concentration as little as 0.002 wt-%, we see from the data in figure 10.2 that the caffeine content of the coffee cannot be reduced to below 0.16 wt-% (which equates to a caffeine removal of only 84% for a coffee containing 1.0 wt-% caffeine).

As was asked earlier for the ethanol–water extraction process, how is the carbon dioxide cleaned up for recycle in the decaffeination process if pressure reduction cannot accomplish the task? Two options, stripping with water or adsorption onto activated carbon, are described in the patent literature. A brief summary of these processes is presented here.

Distribution coefficients for the ternary system carbon dioxide–caffeine–water have been measured (Krukonis, 1981c). At conditions of about 80°C and 4,500 psia, the distribution coefficient is about 0.03–0.04 (weight basis). Although the distribution coefficient is rather small for extracting caffeine from coffee solution with carbon dioxide, it is excellent for the reverse process of removing caffeine from carbon dioxide with a water wash. Two United States patents discuss in more detail the water washing of recycled carbon dioxide (Prasad, Gottesman, and Scarella, 1981; Zosel, 1982).

The other cleanup method utilizes the adsorptive properties of activated carbon to remove caffeine from the carbon dioxide before recycle (Zosel, 1981). An adsorption isotherm of the carbon dioxide–caffeine–activated carbon system, which is shown in figure 10.3, indicates that it is possible to adsorb the caffeine in the carbon dioxide–rich stream onto activated carbon (Krukonis, 1983a). It is interesting to note that in this industrial application an activated carbon bed is used to remove a component from a supercritical carbon dioxide–

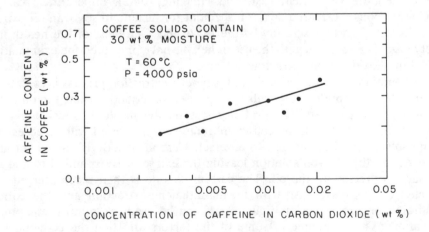

Figure 10.2 Equilibrium isotherm for the caffeine–coffee–carbon dioxide system.

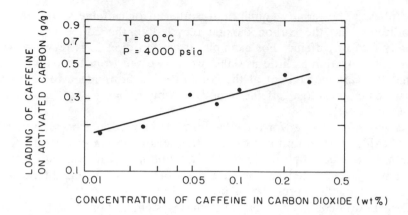

Figure 10.3   Adsorption isotherm for the caffeine–carbon dioxide–activated carbon system.

rich stream rather than having the activated carbon being regenerated by the supercritical carbon dioxide. It is, perhaps, no surprise, then, that spent activated carbon is difficult to regenerate with carbon dioxide, as was discussed in chapter 8.

EDIBLE-OILS EXTRACTION

The process-development work being carried out at the United States Department of Agriculture's (USDA) Northern Regional Research Center on the extraction of vegetable oils with supercritical fluid solvents has been reported in the literature (Friedrich, List, and Heaking, 1982). Supercritical carbon dioxide is being considered as a replacement for hexane in soybean-oil extraction. As stated earlier, scrutiny by the FDA and awareness of the health and safety hazards associated with the use of hexane have prompted the examination of carbon dioxide as an extracting solvent.

Operation of a supercritical fluid–soybean extraction process is essentially identical to the naphthalene–chalk dust process described earlier; the oil is the SCF-soluble species, and the protein substrate the insoluble species. Flaked soybean (flaked to break the cell membrane walls so the oil will be accessible to the solvent) is first charged to a vessel. Carbon dioxide is passed through the bed, and the CO_2-oil solution leaving the extractor is expanded to a lower pressure to precipitate the oil. The carbon dioxide is then recompressed and recycled to the vessel. As with the naphthalene-extraction and the coffee-decaffeination processes, multiple vessels can be used to optimize equipment utilization. As an example of some of the factors affecting the economics of the SCF–soybean oil process, the potential of continuous feeding and removal of soybean solids is being explored. One group of investigators considers the development of the continuous feeding of soybean solids as an important factor for demonstrating economic viability for the supercritical carbon dioxide extraction of soybeans. A typical soybean extraction plant using hexane operates at a level of 2,000 tons per day; the operating philosophy and economics will certainly be different from, for example, those of a hops extraction plant operating at 2 tons per day. Also to be considered in the viability analysis is the cost of the products: soybean oil sells for $.25 per pound while hop extract sells for $30.00 per pound.

Data on the extraction and oil composition of soybean oil have been described in a number of journals (see, for example, Friedrich and Pryde, 1984), but some not yet widely known information is given here. A number of United States and European researchers have reported triglyceride solubility data (Christianson et al., 1984; List, Friedrich, and Pominski, 1984; Snyder, Friedrich, and Christianson, 1984; Stahl et al., 1980; Stahl et al., 1984). Until a few years ago 9,000 psia was the maximum pressure level tested in soybean extraction or triglyceride solubility determinations. In 1982, Friedrich of the USDA extended the test pressures to 1,000 atm and found some quite interesting results. A copy of the solubility data reproduced from United States patent 4,466,923 (Friedrich, 1984) is given in figure 10.4. At conditions of 70°C and 800 atm, carbon dioxide and soybean triglycerides become miscible, and

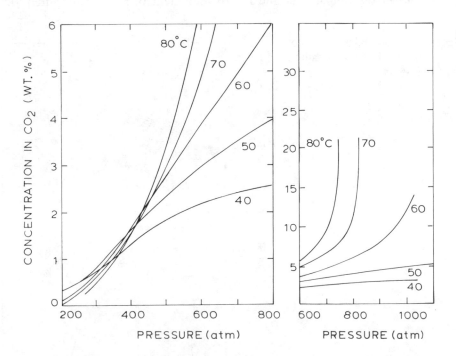

Figure 10.4 Solubility behavior of soybean triglicerides in supercritical carbon dioxide (Friedrich, 1984).

this finding is the basis of a patented extraction process that operates in a relatively narrow range at high pressure. As the solubility data show, the separation of much of the oil from a 800 atm carbon dioxide-oil stream can be carried out by dropping the pressure by only 150 or 200 atm at 70°C. Incidentally, the triglyceride data shown in figure 10.4 exhibit the same retrograde behavior as the solids-solubility data shown in chapter 1. That is, the solubility isotherms cross at low pressure, although "low" in this case is about 275 atm. The triglyceride data are replotted as solubility isobars in figure 10.5. Interestingly, the curves are quite similar in shape to the naphthalene–carbon dioxide and silica-water data shown in chapter 2.

Carbon dioxide has been tested with other materials, such as corn and wheat germ, sunflower and safflower seeds, and peanuts. To a very good first approximation, the solubility of all vegetable triglyercides is identical, and all these seeds can be extracted completely if the cells are macerated to make the oil accessible.

Some work on the supercritical carbon dioxide concentration of active-fatty-acid fractions of fish oils has also been reported recently (Krukonis, 1984c). Evidence has accumulated that suggests that certain polyunsaturated fatty acids comprising fish-oil triglycerides have a therapeutic effect on the cardiovascular system. Increasing attention is being directed to clinical studies of fish oils in the human diet and the development of new refining methods

Figure 10.5 Solubility isobars of the soybean triglyceride–carbon dioxide system.

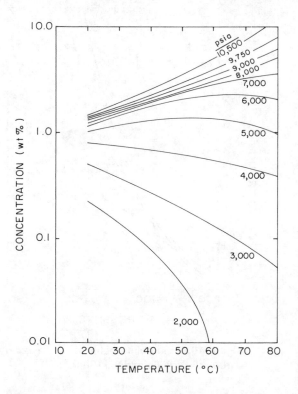

for purifying and concentrating the active components, such as eicosapentaenoic acid (EPA). The active components possess a high degree of unsaturation and conventional processing by high-vacuum and molecular distillation can cause degradative reactions at the high-temperature levels required to separate the fish oils from free fatty acids, protein residues, and polychlorinated biphenyls.

Because the active-fatty-acid moieties are in relatively low concentration in fish oils, because they are dispersed on the triglyceride chains with other fatty acids, and because there are many fatty acids with identical carbon number but with varying saturation, it is difficult to concentrate the 20:5 component (a fatty acid having 20 carbons and 5 double bonds) by distillation or by supercritical fluid extraction. If, however, the triglycerides are first transesterified to methyl (or ethyl) esters, the EPA fraction can be concentrated using supercritical carbon dioxide fractionation. Table 10.3 tabulates the concentrations of the individual fatty acids in four SCF fractions relative to the parent compound. It is seen that the components having 20 carbons can be increased twofold. A recent paper describes the addition of a reflux stage to the process and reports that in a two-pass processing sequence the 20:5 component fatty acid concentration can be increased to 60 wt-% concentration in a selected fraction (Eisenbach, 1984).

Several trade journals describe development work on a supercritical carbon dioxide process for extracting oils from potato chips and other snack foods, an extension of seed- and fish-oils extraction (Hannigan, 1981; Wolkomer, 1984). The motivation for the work lies in increasing consumer awareness of the caloric content of foods and beverages. "Light" beers, wines, and soft drinks are currently very popular, along with "light" peanuts and "light" Pringles brand potato chips. Figure 10.6 shows a schematic diagram of a proposed potato chip de-oiling process. It is reported that potato chips containing about 40–45 wt-% oil can be extracted of about one-half their oils while retaining the original flavor and texture. Furthermore, the oils can be reused in subsequent frying operations.

Table 10.3 Composition of Feed and SCF Fractions (Methyl Esters of Anchovy Oil)

| | *Component* | | | | | |
Fraction	14:0[a]	16:0	18:1	20:5	22:6	Wt-% of Parent
Parent (%)	8.8	21.3	13.0	15.4	10.1	100
1	21.0	32.8	12.9	5.1	1.7	14.6
2	10.9	29.9	17.4	6.1	1.9	35.8
3	3.5	14.3	14.6	22.4	11.7	30.5
4	2.5	6.1	3.4	29.5	45.8	19.1

[a]14:0 designates the methyl ester composed of a fatty acid having 14 carbons and no unsaturation, i.e., myristic acid; 18:1 designates a fatty acid having 18 carbons and 1 double bond, i.e., oleic acid; etc.

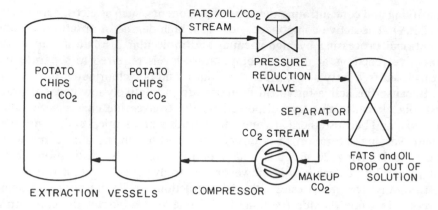

Figure 10.6   Schematic diagram of the process for de-oiling potato chips with supercritical carbon dioxide.

Recently, a supercritical carbon dioxide process has been proposed to concentrate certain aromatic constituents in lemon oils, specifically the oxygenated components from limonene (Robey and Sunder, 1984). Although the components can be concentrated by either steam distillation or liquid-liquid extraction, these processes suffer from certain drawbacks, such as product degradation, low yields, or the requirement of subsequent removal of solvent. The supercritical carbon dioxide process being developed operates at 60°C, thus precluding degradation of the sensitive essential oils. The extraction and separation steps operate between the pressure levels of 1,500 psia and 800 psia, respectively. The results to date show that a tenfold concentration of aromatics can be achieved in a single extraction stage, and from the single-stage data the results are extrapolated to a continuous multistage extractor with computer models predicting a twentyfold concentration at 99% yield. At a ten- or twentyfold concentration of aromatics the supercritical fluid process is competitive with the traditional processes, and, in fact, the flavor of the essential oil may be superior. This beneficial factor has not yet been included in the economic comparison.

EXTRACTION OF CHEMOTHERAPEUTIC AGENTS

As we have suggested throughout this chapter, the properties of carbon dioxide are especially attractive for extracting compounds from biological materials. This section describes some work carried out on the extraction of antineoplastic agents from plant materials (Krukonis, Branfman, and Broome, 1979). The plant materials tested, which are listed in table 10.4, are confirmed by the National Cancer Institute (NCI) to contain active species. As an example of the complexity of the active species, figure 10.7 shows the structure of may-

Table 10.4 Plant Materials Containing Potential
Antineoplastic Agents Tested for Supercritical Carbon
Dioxide Extractability

NCI Designation	Plant Material (Specific Name, Variety, Origin)
B628201	*Maytenus senegalensis* Celastraceae Tanzania
B628259	*Maytenus putterlickoiades* Celastraceae Kenya
B628318	*Maytenus rothiana* Celastraceae India
B634635	*Gypsophilia paniculata* Caryophyllaceae Michigan
B638786	*Citharexylum caudatum* Verbenaceae Panama
B805592	*Maquire calophylla* Moraceae Peru
B806512	*Rollinia papillionela* Annonaceae Peru

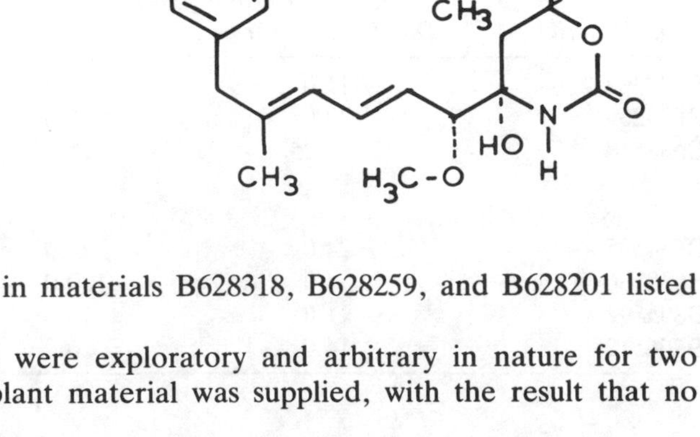

Figure 10.7 Structure of maytansine, which is found in plant materials.

tansine, which is present in materials B628318, B628259, and B628201 listed in table 10.4.

The extraction tests were exploratory and arbitrary in nature for two reasons: relatively little plant material was supplied, with the result that no "optimization" studies could be carried out; and pure material was unavailable for solubility testing. Hence, not only were optimization studies impossible but also the extraction conditions were selected from experience with other complex organic compounds.

Extraction of the plant materials was performed in a flow apparatus similar to the one discussed previously in chapter 4. The current National Cancer Institute protocol for extracting new plant materials consists of Soxhlet extraction with 95% ethanol. (For comparison purposes a Soxhlet extraction was also done for this study.) Carbon dioxide conditions of 275 atm and 35°C were chosen to achieve a high density at a temperature reasonably close to ambient temperature. About 20 grams of plant material were used for each extraction. The material was contacted with 200 standard liters of carbon dioxide in a flow extractor, and the extract that was collected when the carbon dioxide was expanded to ambient pressure was tested in a bioassay test.

For the bioassay or cytotoxicity tests the extract (from both the super-critical extraction and 95% ethanol extraction procedures) is dissolved to various concentration levels in 95% ethanol, and the bioactivity is tested *in vitro* with the 9KB leukemia cell. Samples of cells are treated with various concentration levels of the extract and are then incubated. Cell-growth inhibition is determined from protein measurements, which can be correlated to the number of cells. The ED_{50} value, expressed in mg/l, is defined as the extract concentration at which 50% of the cell growth is inhibited. Obviously, the lower the value, the more cytotoxic the extract.

The results of the cytotoxicity assay are shown in table 10.5. As was stated earlier, no optimization of the supercritical fluid extraction was carried out with respect to pressure, temperature, total amount of gas, etc. However, the data in table 10.5 show that all the supercritical fluid extracts yielded positive cytotoxicity results. In fact, for one of the plant materials, B638786,

Table 10.5   Cytotoxicity of Extracts Tested in 9KB Assay

| | ED_{50} Values (mg extract/l C_2H_5OH) | | |
Plant Material	Supercritical Carbon Dioxide Extraction	Ambient-Temperature Ethanol Extraction	Other Extractions
B638302	11.0	3.7	
B628259	30.0	11.0	
B638318	0.25	0.11	(1) 0.19; (2) 0.03 (sequential collection of extract)
B634635	24.0	43.0	
B638786	4.0	>100.0	
B805592	21.0	16.0	2.3 (ethylene)
B806512	14.0	6.2	0.057 (liquid CO_2)

the supercritical fluid extract was substantially more active (i.e., it had a much lower ED_{50}) than the standard ethanol extract.

The individual components in the supercritical fluid extracts from the plant materials were not identified, but from visual inspection it was concluded that the extracts probably contained a large percentage of glyceride components in admixture with the active species. It is known that triglycerides and fatty acids exhibit high solubility characteristics relative to more complex species such as alkaloids. For example, many glycerides, fatty acids, and esters exhibit solubility levels in the 1–10 wt-% range. Thus, based upon two such different solubility levels, a stripping or fractionation scheme could result in the separation of about 90 or more percent of the inactive components in the plant materials. During passage of the first 10% of the supercritical fluid through the material, most of the normal vegetable matter present in the plant might be dissolved and be collected separately. The remaining extract would thus be enhanced in the active species. The sequential collection test was carried out on sample B628318, and the results of the 9KB bioassay are given in the right-hand column of table 10.5. The data show that the second fraction (which by visual inspection contained little triglyceride component) exhibited a higher activity than the first fraction, thus lending credence to the simple fractionation concept.

Two other extraction tests were carried out, one using supercritical ethylene and the other using liquid carbon dioxide. Plant material B805592 was extracted with 200 standard liters of ethylene at 4,000 psia and 20°C. The bioassay results of the extract show the ethylene extract to be more active than the supercritical carbon dioxide extract. Plant material B806512 was extracted with 200 standard liters of liquid carbon dioxide at 275 atm and 20°C. The cytotoxicity results ($ED_{50} = 0.057$ mg/l) show that the extract was more active than the extract obtained from supercritical carbon dioxide ($ED_{50} = 14$ mg/l). It is not known whether the extracting fluids were more specific for the active component or if the differences are related to statistical spread of the combined extraction and bioassay tests. The results show that carbon dioxide and ethylene can dissolve quite complex organic compounds.

ISOMER SEPARATIONS

A number of aromatic isomers serve as raw materials for a wide variety of chemical, pharmaceutical, and polymer products. Some isomers are difficult to obtain in pure form and frequently the purification of the isomers involves separating an ortho-para pair. For the purpose of evaluating the potential of employing supercritical solvents in separating aromatic isomers, the solubilities of one family of isomers, *o-, m-,* and *p*-hydroxybenzoic acids, were measured in supercritical carbon dioxide. This family was chosen as one example for laboratory study because it is representative of a group of isomers that have practical applications. The hydroxybenzoic acids are frequently desired in

relatively pure ortho and para forms for subsequent conversion to other compounds, and they most commonly must be separated from each other in a
mixture not usually containing the meta isomer. The isomers can be separated
by crystallization promoted by lowering the pH of a high-pH solution containing
both salts. The pK for the para acid is typically higher than that of the ortho
acid, resulting in a preferential precipitation of the para acid form. A relatively
pure para-isomer fraction can usually be prepared by such a process, but the
remaining salt form of the ortho isomer in solution is usually contaminated
with some unprecipitated para isomer, which is also present as dissolved salt.

The solubility curves of the hydroxybenzoic acid isomers in carbon dioxide
are shown in figure 10.8 (Krukonis and Kurnik, 1985). The isomer that melts
most readily, *o*-hydroxybenzoic acid, exhibits the highest solubility in carbon
dioxide, and its solubility is almost two orders of magnitude higher than the
solubilities of the meta and para isomers.

The relation between solubility and isomer melting point is not surprising
nor unexpected. The same type of solid-solubility behavior is found with liquid
organic solvents. The reasons for the inverse relationship between the solubility
of aromatic isomers in liquid organic solvents and their melting points has been
discussed elsewhere (Morrison and Boyd, 1983). In families of disubstituted
benzenes the para isomer usually melts considerably higher than the other two
isomers because of its symmetry and thus it is more easily accommodated into
a crystal lattice. Since dissolution of a crystal, like melting, involves overcoming

Figure 10.8 Solubility isotherms for
hydroxybenzoic acid isomers in supercritical carbon dioxide (Krukonis
and Kurnik, 1985).

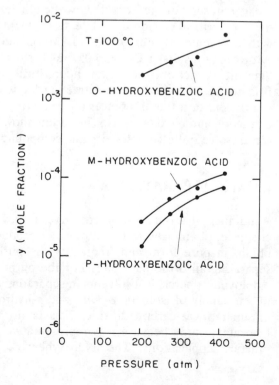

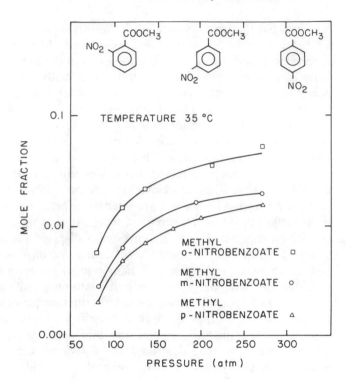

Figure 10.9 Solubility of methyl nitrobenzoate isomers in supercritical carbon dioxide (Chang and Morrell, 1985).

intermolecular forces, a lower solubility of the para isomer in a given solvent is expected. Supercritical carbon dioxide, then, acts in a manner quite similar to organic liquid solvents in its dissolving characteristics for ortho and para isomers. It exhibits, however, the additional feature of a pressure-dependent dissolving power at constant temperature, as shown by the data in figure 10.8.

The solubilities of another family of isomers, methyl nitrobenzoate isomers, have been measured in supercritical carbon dioxide at 35°C (Chang and Morrell, 1985). The methyl *o*-nitrobenzoate isomer is a liquid at ambient conditions, whereas the other two isomers are solids at both ambient and extraction conditions. For the methyl nitrobenzoates, the ortho isomer has the highest solubility, followed by the meta isomer, and then by the para isomers, as seen in figure 10.9. Solubilities of several other isomers in supercritical carbon dioxide have been reported by Stahl and co-workers, whose qualitative results are consistent with the observation that the closer the functional groups of an isomer, the higher the solubility of the isomer in supercritical carbon dioxide (Stahl et al., 1978). The positional relation usually determines the stacking pattern in the crystal lattice and thus influences the melting point.

TREATMENT OF WASTE STREAMS

The industrial research efforts on coffee decaffeination, spice extraction, and flavors concentration are, to a great extent, shrouded by the cloak of proprietary security, but the investigations of the use of supercritical fluids to treat various waste streams is reasonably well publicized. Most familiar, perhaps, is the supercritical wastewater detoxification process developed by Modar, Inc., which is potentially attractive for detoxifying especially refractory chemicals such as polychlorinated biphenyls, dioxin, and other toxic materials (Anon., 1982; Modell, 1982). In the Modar process, the toxic chemicals are homogenously reacted with oxygen in supercritical water, which is the solvent for the organics and for the oxygen. The main feature of the process is a chemical reaction, rather than an extraction, and it is discussed in more detail in chapter 11.

A waste process directed to the cleanup of drilling fluids is being developed by Critical Fluid Systems, Inc. (Anon., 1982). Oil-based drilling fluids (commonly termed "muds") are used to lubricate and cool drill bits and to flush drill cuttings to the surface during the drilling of an oil well. The muds and oil-contaminated cuttings represent a disposal problem, especially for offshore platform drilling operations. Because of increasing environmental concerns, nations are instituting increasingly strict pollution control measures which preclude the dumping of hydrocarbon-containing drilling muds and cuttings off shore. A supercritical carbon dioxide extraction process is in development to remove the oil so that the oil-free cuttings can be dumped off shore. The drilling mud, a mixture of solid and oily material, would be processed in a system similar to that described for activated-carbon regeneration, i.e., a multiple-vessel, batch-continuous operation. In this case, as in all the other development studies discussed, the economics of the supercritical fluid process depends upon many factors. For example, the drilling mud and cuttings can alternatively be barged to shore for on-land disposal, and these costs must be compared with the capital and operating costs of the on-platform supercritical carbon dioxide processing of the cuttings. The economics of the process are being evaluated at present.

Another process, the supercritical fluid extraction of oil from mill scale, has been described in trade journals and at a national technical society meeting (de Fillipi, 1983). Mill scale, i.e., small particle–size iron and iron oxide, is formed during rolling operations at steel mills, where oil-lubricated rollers shape and form red-hot steel ingots. Concern about oil leaching in landfills is placing severe limitations on dumping of such oil-contaminated material. A supercritical fluid extraction process is being evaluated under Environmental Protection Agency funding (de Fillipi and Chung, 1985).

11

Chemical Reactions in
Supercritical Fluids

One very interesting and, as yet, not fully investigated area of supercritical fluid extraction technology is the use of a supercritical solvent as a reaction medium in which the solvent either actively participates in the reaction or functions solely as the solvent medium for the reactants, catalysts, and products. With an SCF medium it may be possible to increase the selectivity of a reaction while maintaining high conversions, to dissolve reactants and catalyst in a single fluid phase and carry out the reaction homogeneously, and to capitalize on the solvent characteristics of the supercritical fluid to separate the product species from the reactants, catalyst, and unwanted by-products. Reaction rates may also be enhanced while the process is operating in the mixture critical region as a result of the potentially favorable effect of applied hydrostatic pressure. They also may be enhanced because the highly negative partial molar volumes of the product species, which can occur with dilute reaction mixtures operating near the critical point of the pure SCF solvent.

To take full advantage of an SCF reaction medium it is necessary to be cognizant of the phase behavior exhibited by the reaction mixture at high pressures. For instance, it has been shown that some of the kinetic studies reported in the literature on the high-pressure polymerization of ethylene are of little value, since the reaction-rate data were analyzed according to the assumption that the reaction was operated homogeneously when in fact two phases were present (Ehrlich and Mortimer, 1970). It should be evident after one has read chapter 3 that various types of phase behavior are possible with SCF reaction mixtures. Careful experimentation is therefore necessary when performing high-pressure reaction studies.

An example of investigating the phase behavior of a system before doing reaction studies is given in a patent describing a hydrocarbon isomerization process (Leder, Kramer, and Solomon, 1976). In this instance, the reacting mixture, consisting of a hydrocarbon feed, such as n-hexane, a metal halide catalyst, a hydrogen-halide solvent, such as HCl, and hydrogen, exhibits type-I phase behavior. A schematic P-T diagram for this mixture is shown in figure 11.1. Kramer and Leder recommend operating the reaction at P-T conditions

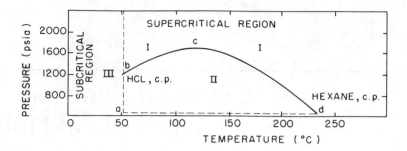

Figure 11.1 Schematic *P-T* diagram of the reacting mixture in the hy-drocarbon-isomerization process proposed by Leder, Kramer, and Solomon (1976).

within region II bounded by the points *abcd* shown in figure 11.1. Even though this is not strictly a supercritical fluid reaction, since it is run in the near-critical liquid region, it does provide an example of a case in which the researchers first determine the critical-mixture behavior of the reactants (see figure 11.2) and then proceed with the reaction studies in a well-defined region of the phase diagram.

As a reaction proceeds the resultant product species, if it contains a different functional group as compared with the reactant, may induce the reactant-product-SCF mixture to split into multiple phases near the critical point of the SCF. The work of Francis (1954), Dandge, Heller, and Wilson

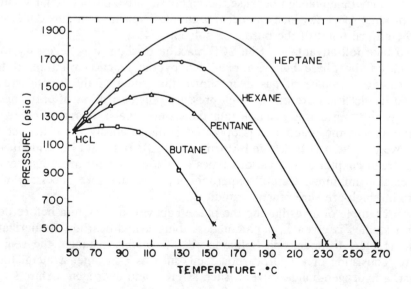

Figure 11.2 Critical-mixture behavior for various hydrocarbon-HCl mixtures (Leder, Kramer, and Solomon, 1976).

(1985), and Stahl and co-workers (Stahl and Quirin, 1983; Stahl et al., 1980) should be consulted for information on the types of functional groups that affect the miscibility behavior of solute-SCF mixtures. Since it was shown in chapter 3 that binary mixtures tend to exhibit multiphase LLV behavior as the differences in the molecular weights of the mixture components increase (Rowlinson and Swinton, 1982), it is reasonable to assume that a reacting mixture would also exhibit multiple phases if the product species were quite large relative to the SCF solvent.

It may be possible to design novel reaction/separation schemes using the information given in chapter 3 on the five basic types of phase behavior that can occur for binary mixtures at high pressures. For instance, type-IV phase behavior suggests a number of interesting reaction/separation scenarios. If one assumed that the reactant-product-SCF mixture exhibited type-IV behavior, it would be possible to run the reaction homogeneously at the temperature and pressure indicated by the asterisk in figure 11.3. Product recovery could be facilitated by splitting the reaction mixture into two phases when the critical-mixture curve is crossed, by either isothermally reducing the pressure or by isobarically increasing or decreasing the temperature. The reaction mixture could thus be cycled between a single-phase reaction step and a two-phase recovery step.

As mentioned previously, it may be possible to precipitate the product from the reaction mixture as the reaction proceeds. In this manner, unwanted side-reactions may be avoided if the product species is immediately removed from the reacting system as it precipitates from solution. Alexander and Paulaitis (1984) describe such a reaction/separation scenario for the Diels-Alder reaction of isoprene with maleic anhydride in supercritical CO_2. They find that the product precipitates as a solid from the reaction mixture as the reaction proceeds. In this case, the reaction is run at fairly low concentrations of reactants in supercritical CO_2 near the critical point of pure CO_2.

As also mentioned earlier, reaction rates may be improved if the reaction is run in the mixture critical region. A rate enhancement can potentially occur as a result of applied hydrostatic pressure and as a result of the unusual partial molar volume behavior of a heavy solute solubilized in a supercritical solvent. Numerous authors have used transition-state analysis (Laidler, 1965; Eckert,

Figure 11.3 *P-T* diagram for a type-IV binary mixture.

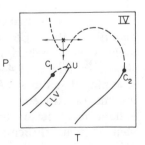

1972; Ehrlich, 1971) to explain the rate enhancement that can occur at high pressures. For a bimolecular reaction, a chemical equilibrium is assumed to exist between the reactants A and B and the transition state $M^{\pm}$:

$$A + B \rightleftarrows M^{\pm} \rightarrow \text{Products.} \qquad (11.1)$$

The variation of the reaction-rate constant k with pressure is given by

$$\left(\frac{\partial \ln k}{\partial P}\right)_T = -\frac{\Delta V^{\pm}}{RT}, \qquad (11.2)$$

where $\Delta V^{\pm}$, the volume of activation, is the difference in the partial molar volumes of the activated complex and the reactants and is given by

$$\Delta V^{\pm} = \overline{V}_M - \overline{V}_A - \overline{V}_B. \qquad (11.3)$$

As shown in equation 11.2, a reaction with a positive activation volume is hindered by pressure, while one with a negative activation volume is enhanced by pressure. (As noted by Eckert (1972), equation 11.2 is applicable only if the reaction rate is expressed in terms of mole fractions not concentrations. Otherwise a second term is needed which accounts for the compressibility of the reaction mixture.)

Let us consider the application of transition-state analysis to interpret the work of Ehrlich and co-workers on the reaction behavior of ethylene polymerization in supercritical ethylene (Ehrlich, 1971). Ehrlich presents experimental data on the polymerization of ethylene at 130°C and 30,000 psia. At these conditions supercritical ethylene can solubilize approximately 5 wt-% to 10 wt-% high-molecular-weight polyethylene, which is produced during the reaction. Normally, the conversions are kept to less than 10%, and, therefore, from independent phase-behavior studies (Ehrlich, 1965), it is concluded that the reacting supercritical ethylene-polyethylene mixture is near a mixture critical point. Ehrlich argues that the partial molar volume of $M^{\pm}$, which has volumetric properties similar to the product polymer, can have a very large negative value in supercritical ethylene. It is well known that very large, negative partial molar volumes can exist for mixtures in which the solute is in dilute concentrations and the solvent is very close to its critical conditions or the mixture is close to the mixture critical point (Eckert et al., 1983; Chappelear and Elgin, 1961; Ehrlich and Wu, 1973). For example, consider the partial-molar-volume behavior of vinyl chloride solubilized in supercritical ethylene, shown in figure 11.4 (Ehrlich and Fariss, 1969). Using equation 11.2 and assuming that the absolute value of $\overline{V}_M$ is much greater than the partial molar volume of ethylene, one would conclude that there should be a large rate enhancement occurring near the mixture critical point of the ethylene-polyethylene system. Ehrlich uses transition-state analysis to explain the large pressure effect on the polymerization rate as the pressure is dropped toward the mixture

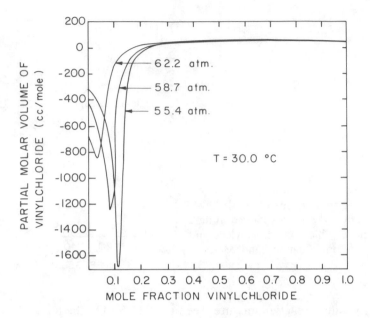

Figure 11.4 Calculated partial-molar-volume behavior of vinyl chloride solubilized in supercritical ethylene (Ehrlich and Fariss, 1969).

critical value, the small pressure effect on the polymerization rate when crystalline polymer is formed and falls out of solution, and the very high anomalous activation energy for polymerization at a temperature of 100°–130°C (the so-called critical polymerization boundary). However, in more recent work Ehrlich and co-workers find that the anomalous activation energy for ethylene polymerization in supercritical ethylene may be attributed to the presence of dissolved oxygen, which can be both a free-radical inhibitor in the subcritical liquid-gas region and a free-radical initiator in the supercritical region (Takahashi and Ehrlich, 1982; Ehrlich and Pittilo, 1960). Without the presence of dissolved oxygen in the system, the polymerization rates are very slow. Hence, the rate enhancements suggested by transition-state analysis are quite small in this instance.

Simmons and Mason (1972) employ transition-state analysis with an equation of state (EOS) (i.e., Redlich-Kwong and the virial equation) in an attempt to derive an expression for the pressure dependence of the dimerization-rate constant of chlorotrifluoroethylene (T_c = 105.7°C, P_c = 40.1 atm). They attempt to predict the volumetric properties of the reactants by fitting experimental rate data. They can obtain the thermodynamic properties, such as the fugacity coefficient and partial molar volume, of the activated complex. The predicted fugacity coefficient of the activated complex exhibits the same trends as that of a normal molecular species. Also, quite interestingly, the partial molar volume of the activated complex, $\overline{V}_M$, decreases sharply near the critical

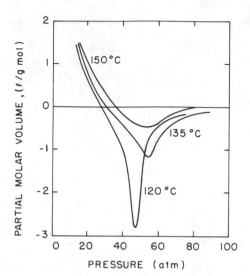

Figure 11.5 Partial-molar-volume behavior of the activated complex formed in the dimerization of chlorotrifluoroethylene in its critical region (Simmons and Mason, 1972).

point of the dilute reaction mixture (see figure 11.5). On the basis of transition-state analysis one might expect enhanced reaction rates at conditions very near the critical point of the pure chlorotrifluoroethylene. However, the observed rate enhancement is only 30% for pressures up to 100 atm. Unfortunately, the Redlich-Kwong EOS does not correlate the experimental data within 30%. Hence, more rate data are needed at higher pressures to better ascertain the pressure enhancement and to provide a more stringent test of the EOS.

For all practical purposes the large rate enhancements that occur as a result of large solute partial molar volumes are limited to the dilute-concentration region as shown in figure 11.4 and implied in figure 11.5. Although an enhancement of the reaction rate can occur as a result of hydrostatic pressure alone, excessively high pressures (i.e., greater than 1,000 atm) are needed for pressure to have any appreciable effect (Eckert, 1972).

HIGH-TEMPERATURE REACTIONS

It may be possible to use an SCF reaction medium to lower the operating temperature of pyrolysis reactions. The carbon formation that occurs at the high temperatures normally encountered in pyrolysis reactions can therefore be minimized. Improved yields, selectivities, and product separation have been attained in an SCF reaction medium, as compared with conventional pyrolysis methods.

Köll and Metzger (1978) report on the use of supercritical acetone as the reaction medium for the thermal degradation of cellulose and chitnin. Since the pyrolysis of these polysaccharides occurs at such high temperatures, it is necessary to remove the primary products from the reaction zone as soon as they are formed to avoid degradation of the products into coke. The high operating temperature also adversely affects both yield and product distribution. It is possible to reduce the carbon formation by carrying out the pyrolysis under vacuum, but the reaction rate is also reduced because of the poor heat transfer to the reactants.

As an alternative pyrolysis technique, Köll and Metzger react the cellulose in the presence of supercritical acetone (T_c = 235.7°C, P_c = 47.0 atm), using a flow reactor. The reactor, operated isobarically at 250 atm, is temperature programmed from 150°C to 290°C. At SCF conditions, 98% extraction of the initial cellulose is achieved. The yield of glucosan, which is 38.8%, compares favorably with the 28.1% yield obtained with vacuum pyrolysis. Interestingly, the cellulose residue has the same crystallinity as the starting cellulose even after 50% degradation. Thus, the use of supercritical acetone as a reaction medium in the thermal degradation of cellulose results in an appreciable amount of extraction, less carbon formation, and better yield at temperatures lower than those used for conventional pyrolysis.

While doing their cellulose and chitnin studies Köll and Metzger found condensation products of acetone (such as diacetone alcohol and mesityl oxide) that were apparently formed by a thermally induced aldol condensation (Köll and Metzger, 1978). This is an interesting finding since pyrolysis reactions are expected to dominate at these high temperatures. Metzger and co-workers (1983) initiated a program to investigate systematically thermal intermolecular reactions at high temperatures (~500°C) and high pressures (~500 atm) using a flow reactor with residence times of 1–10 minutes. It is assumed that at such high temperatures and pressures the reacting mixture is a single supercritical fluid. The researchers find that alkanes are added to alkenes (e.g., *n*-alkenes, acrylonitrile, methyl acrylate, methyl vinyl ketone), to 1,3-dienes (e.g., 1,3-cyclohexadiene), and to alkynes (acetylene). Thus, functional groups are added to hydrocarbons at supercritical conditions. The reactant mixture typically consists of an alkane-to-alkene feed in the ratio of 20:100. For example, when cyclohexane (T_c = 280.3°C, P_c = 40.4 atm) is the representative alkane and methyl acrylate (T_c = 263°C, P_c = 42 atm) is the representative alkene, the yield at 500°C (based on methyl acrylate) increases significantly with pressure up to 100 atm and thereafter remains essentially constant. The increase in yield is explained by the increase of density of the reacting mixture with pressure. At higher densities the intermolecular reaction proceeds at a much higher rate.

Other reactions studied by these authors include the thermal dimerization of methyl acrylate and the reaction of benzene with certain alkynes in a Diels-Alder reaction. Supercritical extraction in coal processing may also be classified under this scheme. However, this subject is reviewed adequately elsewhere (Williams, 1981) and, hence, is not included in this chapter.

HETEROGENEOUS CATALYSIS

For certain heterogeneous catalytic reactions the catalyst activity can be renewed by adjusting the pressure and temperature so that the reacting medium is in the supercritical state. The activity of the catalyst can be periodically regenerated by treatment with an SCF solvent or, in fact, the reaction can be run at supercritical conditions, thus maintaining high levels of catalytic activity for longer periods of time.

Tiltscher, Wolf, and Schelchshorn (1984) describe the influence of an SCF reaction medium on the activity of a heterogeneous catalyst used in a high-pressure differential-recycle reactor to study the catalytic isomerization of 1-hexene (T_c = 231°C, P_c = 30.7 atm) on σ-AL_2O_3 with 2-chlorohexane as a cocatalyst. In this isomerization reaction they produce 1-hexene, cis-2-hexene, trans-2-hexene, and trans-3-hexene. The authors demonstrate how an SCF reaction medium can be used to reactivate a catalyst that has been poisoned by three different methods.

If the isomerization reaction is carried out in the gaseous phase (T = 250°C, P = 14.8 atm), the resulting conversion-versus-time curve is characteristic of a curve in which a deactivation process occurs in parallel with the reaction (figure 11.6). The deactivation of the catalyst is a result of the unwanted low-volatile oligomeric compounds (C_{12}–C_{30}) that accumulate on the catalyst surface and eventually cause coking. If the reaction mixture is isothermally compressed to 493.3 atm, the oligomers are stripped from the catalyst surface. Although the phase behavior of the reactant-product system is not reported by Tiltscher and co-workers, it seems safe to assume the following: (1) the isomerization products are so similar to 1-hexene that the critical temperature and critical pressure of the reactant-product(s) mixture is very close to that of pure 1-hexene; and (2) the small amount of chlorohexane present in the system does not significantly affect the pressures and temperatures needed to obtain a single, fluid-phase mixture. Therefore, a pressure of 493.3 atm is more than sufficient to ensure that the reaction mixture plus the stripped oligomers is indeed a single fluid phase. If an elevated operating pressure is maintained at this high pressure level, a twofold increase in the overall isomerization rate and about a 30% increase in the cis-/trans-2-hexene ratio is observed (Tiltscher, Wolf, and Schelchshorn, 1984). At SCF conditions the catalyst activity is maintained at precoking levels even after twelve hours

Figure 11.6 Effect of unwanted oligomeric by-products formed during the catalytic isomerization of 1-hexene (Tiltscher, Wolf, and Schelchshorn, 1981).

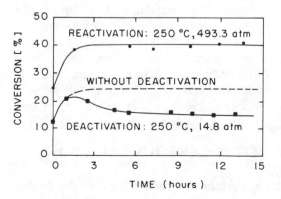

of reaction time, as noted from the upper curve of figure 11.6. Not surprisingly, the authors also conclude that higher pressures are needed to enhance reactivation rates as the volatility of the oligomeric coking compounds decrease.

In another test the authors deactivate the catalyst by introducing a small amount of a finely dispersed catalyst-fouling substance (MoS_2) into the reactor under liquid-phase reaction conditions ($T = 220°C$, $P = 493.3$ atm). In this instance the conversion-time curve is again characteristic of a reaction accompanied by catalyst deactivation (figure 11.7). If the reaction mixture is isobarically heated to 240°C, it becomes supercritical and eventually the catalyst activity is restored. Although it is not explicitly stated by the authors of this work, presumably the trace amounts of MoS_2 are solubilized by the reacting mixture.

In the final deactivation mode reported by the authors, the active acidic sites of the catalyst are poisoned ($T = 145°C$, $P = 49.3$ atm) by continuous addition of a very dilute solution of pyridine to the reacting mixture over a period of twelve hours (see figure 11.8). The catalyst can be reactivated by heating and compressing the reaction mixture to conditions well within the mixture critical region ($T = 250°C$, $P = 493.3$ atm). Tiltscher and co-workers report that the catalyst poison is precipitated from the product solution as

Figure 11.7 Effect of MoS_2 on the catalyst used for the isomerization of 1-hexene (Tiltscher, Wolf, and Schelchshorn, 1981).

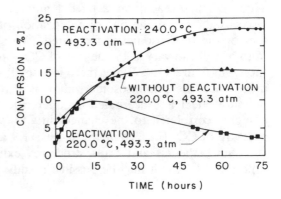

Figure 11.8 Effect of pyridine on the catalyst used for the isomerization of 1-hexene (Tiltscher, Wolf, and Schelchshorn, 1981).

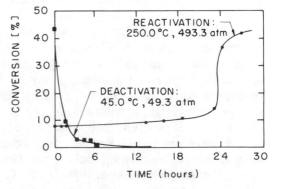

pyridinium chloride. Presumably only a very small amount of pyridinium chloride is needed to deactivate the catalyst since supercritical hexene probably would not be able to solubilize much of this salt. It is surprising however that supercritical hexene can overcome the acid-base interactions that are occurring on the catalyst surface and, hence, remove the pyridinium chloride.

VISCOSITY EFFECTS

It is well known that solvent viscosity can have an effect on the product distribution for certain reactions (Saltiel and Charlton, 1980). The effect of solvent viscosity can be studied with an SCF reaction medium since a wide range of viscosities can be studied with a single SCF solvent if the system is operated in the vicinity of the critical point of the solvent (see figure 1.6).

Squires, Venier, and Aida (1983) describe an experimental technique they use to study the effect of solvent viscosity on the cis/trans ratio of stilbene irradiated in supercritical CO_2. They use a dynamic-flow technique similar to that described in chapter 4. In their system trans-stilbene is coated onto glass beads, which are then packed into a high-pressure column. Supercritical CO_2 flows through the column and solubilizes some of the trans-stilbene. The CO_2-stilbene phase is continuously irradiated with ultraviolet light as it flows through a quartz photoreactor at a fixed temperature and pressure. As the solvent viscosity increases, the photoisomerization of the cis isomer is inhibited while that of the trans isomer is facilitated. We should expect to see the cis/trans ratio of stilbene vary as the density of CO_2 varies. This viscosity effect is clearly shown in figure 11.9. While there is a small effect of pressure on the cis/trans ratio when the photoisosomerization is run in near-critical liquid CO_2, the pressure effect is exacerbated in supercritical CO_2. This large pressure effect is highly correlated to the changes in CO_2 viscosity at 40°C near the critical pressure of CO_2 (i.e., compare figures 11.9 and 1.6).

Since the cis and trans structures exhibit different solubility levels in supercritical CO_2, it may be possible readily to separate the reaction mixture.

REACTION/SEPARATION SCHEMES

Supercritical fluid solvents can be employed as solvent media in chemically reacting mixtures, especially where it is difficult or prohibitively expensive to separate the desired species from a reaction-product mixture by conventional techniques such as distillation. It may be fruitful to consider using an SCF reaction medium in which the product can be more easily recovered from solution. For certain reactions using an SCF reaction medium can also improve the product selectivity without adversely affecting total conversion.

In a recent patent Kramer and Leder (1975) describe an SCF reaction scheme for isomerizing short-chain paraffinic hydrocarbons (4–12 carbon atoms). The reaction medium consists of CO_2, HBr, or HCl (as a promoter), a paraffinic hydrocarbon, and a Lewis acid catalyst (e.g, $AlBr_3$, $AlCl_3$, BF_3).

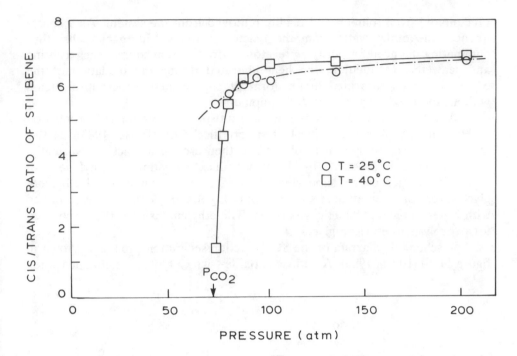

Figure 11.9 Transient-product distribution of the cis/trans isomer obtained when stilbene is irradiated in supercritical carbon dioxide at 40°C and 136 atm(Squires, Venier, and Aida, 1983).

An SCF reaction scheme offers several advantages as compared with a conventional subcritical-liquid CO_2 isomerization process. One obvious advantage is that hydrogen can be more easily dissolved in the SCF reaction phase as compared with a liquid reaction phase. The presence of hydrogen facilitates isomerization as opposed to cracking reactions and thus improves the selectivity of the reaction while not adversely affecting the conversion level.

As mentioned in chapter 10, SCF processing has been applied to the treatment of wastewater streams. In a very recent patent, Modell (1982) describes an efficient processing method for oxidizing the organic materials present in wastewater using supercritical water ($T_c = 374°C$, $P_c = 217.6$ atm). The reaction is performed in a single fluid phase at supercritical conditions. For the purpose of minimizing the energy requirements for the process, the heat generated in the reaction is efficiently transferred to the reactor feed stream. An important advantage of the SCF reaction scheme over conventional processing is that virtually total oxidation of the organics can be realized with higher reaction rates. Since the reaction mixture is completely miscible in the mixture critical region, stoichiometric amounts of oxygen are easily added to the system for total oxidation of the organics.

In this process inorganic salts, which are virtually insoluble in supercritical water (1 ppb to 100 ppm in the temperature range of 450–500°C), are easily precipitated from solution and readily removed from the system. As a consequence, the outlet water from the reactor is free of inorganic salts, thus eliminating the need for purifying reactor feedwater from sources such as brine and seawater. In addition, the heat liberated during the oxidation of the organics can be recovered in the form of superheated, supercritical steam without the need for heat-transfer equipment.

Another recent patent describes a multistep process for the production of ethylene glycol in near-critical or supercritical CO_2 (Bhise, 1983). In this instance CO_2 is first used as a solvent and then used as a reactant. Normally, ethylene oxide is produced by the vapor-phase oxidation of ethylene with molecular oxygen over a supported silver catalyst. In conventional ethylene-glycol processing, an effluent stream containing the ethylene oxide is scrubbed with water to recover the ethylene oxide. The ethylene oxide is then recovered for hydrolysis to ethylene glycol.

A schematic diagram of the SCF reaction/separation process is shown in figure 11.10 (Bhise, 1983). An ethylene oxide–rich CO_2 phase is obtained when

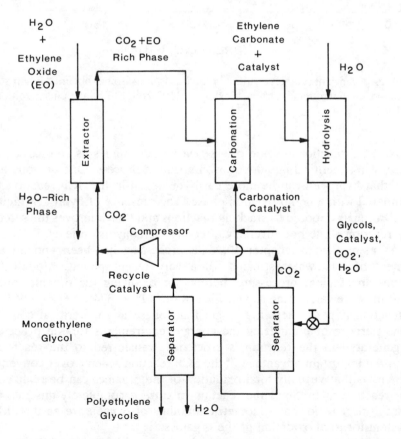

Figure 11.10   Proposed SCF reaction/separation process for producing ethylene glycol (Bhise, 1983).

the aqueous solution is mixed with near-critical or supercritical CO_2 at temperatures up to 100°C and pressures ranging to 300 atm. The ethylene oxide–CO_2 phase, which leaves from the top of the extractor (or from the bottom if the CO_2 is too dense), is then contacted with a carbonation catalyst (e.g., organic quaternary ammonium halides) and reacted to form a catalyst–ethylene carbonate–CO_2 stream. The catalyst–ethylene carbonate–CO_2 stream is then delivered to another reactor and hydrolyzed to form ethylene glycol and CO_2. In this process the carbonation catalyst also catalyzes the hydrolysis reaction. In the final steps of the process the CO_2 is flashed from the ethylene glycol stream and recycled to the extractor. The ethylene glycol and the catalyst are then recovered.

Direct hydrolysis of the ethylene oxide–water stream tends to produce more of the higher glycols, such as diethylene glycol, as compared with the SCF reaction/separation scheme.

ENHANCED REACTION RATES AND SELECTIVITIES

Certain chemical reactions, such as free-radical, vinyl-polymerization reactions, can exhibit enhanced reaction rates with different selectivities when the reaction occurs homogeneously in the mixture critical region as compared with heterogeneously in the subcritical gas-liquid region. Hence, it is possible to control the extent of reaction by isothermally adjusting the system pressure such that either the reaction proceeds rapidly when the reaction mixture exists as a single homogeneous supercritical mixture or the reaction slows considerably when the mixture exists as a heterogeneous gas-liquid mixture in the subcritical region.

In a very early study Patat (1945) investigated the hydrolysis of aniline to phenol in a water-based acidic solution in near-critical and supercritical water ($T_c = 374.2°C$, $P_c = 217.6$ atm). Phosphoric acid and its salts are used as the catalyst for this reaction. The reaction proceeds extremely slowly under normal conditions and reaches equilibrium at low conversion levels. For these reasons, Patat chooses to study the reaction in supercritical water to temperatures of 450°C and to pressures of 700 atm in a flow reactor. He finds that the reaction follows known, regular kinetics in the entire temperature and pressure space studied and the activation energy of the hydrolysis (approximately 40 kcal/g-mol) is the same in the supercritical as well as in the subcritical water. He suggests that the reaction is catalyzed by hydrogen ions formed from dissolution of phosphoric acid in supercritical steam. Very small amounts of phosphoric acid and the salts of the phosphoric acid are dissolved in the supercritical steam and are split into ions. Patat lists several dissolution constants for primary ammonium phosphates in supercritical steam. In this instance, the reaction performance is improved when the reaction is operated homogeneously in the mixture critical region and, thus, in intimate contact between the reactants and the catalyst.

Using a batch reactor Blyumberg, Maizus, and Emanuel (1965) studied the oxidation of *n*-butane at conditions near the critical point of butane (T_c = 152.1°C, P_c = 37.5 atm). Both liquid-phase and SCF-phase oxidations are studied. In this reaction butane hydroperoxide is first formed via a free-radical chain mechanism and then broken down into products.

With the liquid-phase oxidation a long induction period is observed, whereas the SCF-phase oxidation has much shorter induction times. Also, the liquid-phase oxidation products are predominantly acetic acid and methyl ethyl ketone, whereas the SCF-phase oxidation products are formaldehyde, acetaldehyde, methyl, ethyl, and propyl alcohols, and formic acid. The authors offer no explanation for the differences in product spectrum or induction periods for the reactions.

Subramaniam and McHugh (1986) suggest that the increased reaction rates in the SCF phase may be associated with the more efficient production of free-radical pairs. When initiator molecule AB dissociates to form a geminate radical pair ($A \cdot B \cdot$) it may either diffuse apart to form a free-radical pair or may recombine before it can diffuse apart in the so-called cage effect (Eckert, 1972):

$$AB \rightleftarrows (A \cdot B \cdot) \rightarrow A \cdot + B \cdot$$

Since the resistance to diffusion will be lower in the mixture critical region than that in the liquid phase it is expected that the ($A \cdot B \cdot$) radical pair should more readily diffuse apart in the critical region. Although applied hydrostatic pressure favors the recombination of ($A \cdot B \cdot$) to form AB, it seems reasonable to assume that the rate of diffusion dominates the pressure effect as long as the system pressure is maintained below approximately 1,000 atm. Therefore, the formation of free radicals should be facilitated in the SCF phase, as compared with the liquid phase, and shorter reaction times are to be expected.

The difference in product spectrum obtained from a system operating in the SCF phase as compared with the liquid phase is probably a function of the types of free radicals that are formed in each phase. In the SCF phase, the butane-derived free radicals have a higher probability of further decomposing into methyl radicals rather than terminating the reaction by recombining since the reaction temperature is greater in the SCF phase as compared to the liquid phase. If the methyl radicals undergo further oxidation, a broad spectrum of products will be obtained (Winkler and Hearne, 1961).

In a similar process Baumgartner (1983) describes a process for enhancing tertiary-butyl-hydroperoxide (TBHP) formation by reacting isobutane (T_c = 142°C, P_c = 37.0 atm) with oxygen in a dense-phase reaction mixture. In previous studies, Winkler and Hearne (1958, 1961) show that the catalytic oxidation of isobutane in the vapor phase produces significant amounts of tertiary butyl alcohol and minor amounts of other oxidation products such as acids, aldehydes, ketones, and other alcohols, in addition to the desired TBHP. They also demonstrate that reacting isobutane with molecular oxygen noncatalytically in the liquid phase of a two-phase liquid-gas mixture at 100–150°C and at 28.2 atm produces reaction products consisting of TBHP and tertiary alcohol. However, this liquid-gas phase reaction suffers from very low reaction rates and a low selectivity for TBHP. The occurrence of a broader spectrum of products in the gas-phase oxidation of isobutane, as compared with its liquid-phase oxidation, is consistent with the observations of Blyumberg, Maizus, and Emanuel (1965) in the case of the oxidation of *n*-butane.

In the work of Baumgartner, isobutane is oxidized at conditions significantly higher than the T_c and P_c of isobutane and also above the critical pressure of the reaction mixture. The reactor operating variables must be carefully optimized and controlled to attain enhanced TBHP selectivities. Also, as with the case of *n*-butane oxidation, enhanced TBHP formation is observed when the reaction is run homogeneously in the dense phase as compared with the corresponding formation obtained when the reaction is run in the liquid phase (Baumgartner, 1983).

Within the last two decades Ehrlich and co-workers have compiled a comprehensive picture of the free-radical polymerization of ethylene in supercritical fluid ethylene (T_c = 9.3°C, P_c = 49.7 atm) (Ehrlich and Mortimer, 1970; Takahashi and Ehrlich, 1982; Ehrlich and Pittilo, 1960; Ehrlich and Kurpen, 1963; Ehrlich, 1965; Takahashi, 1980).

As noted in chapter 6, early chromatography work showed that polymers, especially polystyrene, can be fractionated with a supercritical fluid mobile phase (Jentoft and Gouw, 1969, 1970). Ehrlich and Graham (1960) also found that polyethylene is soluble in supercritical propane when the pressure is increased above 500 atm. Knowledge of this solubility behavior is extremely important since it has a direct bearing on the interpretation of reaction-time data. Ehrlich has done a comprehensive study on the phase behavior of polyethylene-ethylene mixtures at high pressures. The results from his phase-behavior studies are shown in figure 11.11 as a schematic *P-T-x* diagram for

Figure 11.11 Schematic *P-T-x* diagram of the ethylene-polyethylene system (Ehrlich and Mortimer, 1970).

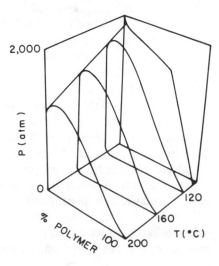

the polyethylene-ethylene system. Notice that the two-phase liquid-vapor region for polymer-solvent systems persists to very high pressures. Ehrlich and Mortimer (1970) conclude that kinetic studies reported in the literature on ethylene polymerization are often of little value since the authors of the studies are unaware of the phase behavior involved with SCF systems at moderate or high pressures. Many times polyethylene polymerization studies reported in the literature are performed on systems that are thermodynamically underdetermined because of the number of phases present and the number of constituents in the system.

In a 1946 patent Krase and Lawrence (1946) describe an SCF reaction process for making ethylene polymers. Ethylene is reacted in the presence of a catalyst at temperatures between 40°C and 400°C and at pressures from 800 to 4,000 atm. The polymer is then recovered using a stepwise reduction in pressure with the objective of reducing compression costs. The authors note in this very early patent that appreciable quantities of the polymer are still solubilized in the supercritical fluid phase at pressures as low as 150 atm. This solubility behavior suggests that the product polymer can be precipitated from solution essentially free of lower-molecular-weight oligomers, residual monomer, and catalyst.

In a patent entitled "Supercritical Polymerization of Olefins," Cottle (1966) describes a process for reacting and separating polymers made from olefins. In this case propylene is reacted to polypropylene in a process using a catalyst and operating at conditions above the critical temperature and pressure for propylene (T_c = 91.9°C, P_c = 45.6 atm). At the end of the reaction the system pressure is reduced to precipitate the crystalline polypropylene from solution while leaving the noncrystalline fraction solubilized in the propylene-rich phase. This fractionation behavior is another example of the effect of polymer tacticity on solubility level. In this process the supercritical fluid is used as both a reactant and a solvent, as in the ethylene polymerization processes previously described. Also, the example listed in this patent implies that the catalyst is soluble in the SCF phase, thus allowing for all the advantages of homogeneous reaction conditions.

It is clear from the several examples cited in this chapter that supercritical fluids can be advantageously used as reaction media. The field of reactions in supercritical fluids has, as yet, not been fully investigated. Isomerization reactions and free-radical oxidations of hydrocarbons are just two examples of the types of reactions that merit further study. There are still many unanswered questions in this area. How do near-critical or supercritical conditions affect the rates and paths of chemical reactions? How is the phase behavior of the initial reactants affected by product formation? Is it possible to exploit the above results to devise efficient reaction/separation schemes? These questions pose considerable experimental and theoretical challenges.

Most of the studies reported in this chapter fail to include the phase behavior of the reacting mixture. Since multiple phases can occur in the mixture critical region, reaction studies need to be complemented with phase-behavior studies so that we may gain an understanding of the fundamentals of the thermodynamics and kinetics of chemical reactions in solution. As described in chapter 5, a simple, cubic equation of state (EOS) can be used to extend and complement the phase-behavior studies. The location of phase-border curves in P-T space can be determined with an equation of state. Also, an EOS can be used with transition-state theory to correlate the pressure dependence of the reaction-rate constant when the pressure effect is large (i.e., at relatively high pressures).

The advantages of using a supercritical fluid reaction medium are that it may be possible to run the reaction in a single, homogeneous phase, thus eliminating interphase mass-transfer limitations, and labile reaction products may be more readily isolated from the reaction mixture by adjusting the pressure or temperature to induce a phase split, thus avoiding unwanted side-reactions. To a lesser degree, reaction rates may be advantageously enhanced by running the reaction in the dilute-mixture region at conditions close to the critical point of the pure supercritical fluid. However, the rate enhancement does not appear to be extremely large and it is restricted to the dilute-mixture region.

Special Applications

Three examples of the use of supercritical fluids, which have not been referenced in the literature, are described in this chapter. Discussion of these examples highlights properties of supercritical fluids that can be used advantageously.

NUCLEATION

As described in chapter 2 the first reports of solubility phenomena in supercritical fluids emphasize the pressure-dependent dissolution characteristics of high-pressure gases and liquids. However, the authors of those early papers point out the potential application of using SCF solvents as media from which to nucleate solid materials. For example, Hannay and Hogarth write in the closing statements of their 1879 publication, "We have, then, the phenomenon of a solid with no measurable gaseous pressure, dissolving in a gas. When the solid is precipitated by suddenly reducing the pressure, it is crystalline, and may be brought down as a 'snow' in the gas, or on the glass as a 'frost,' but it is always easily redissolved by the gas on increasing the pressure."

The "snow" and "frost" described are almost assuredly of different morphology, particle size, and size distribution than the starting material. Recall that Hannay and Hogarth studied salts such as cobalt chloride and potassium iodide. Incidentally, the reference to the precipitation of the solid is not an isolated report of nucleation from a supercritical fluid. For example, many other references to "snow," "fog," "fumes," and "crystals" formed during depressurization of a solution of a solute in a supercritical fluid have been made by researchers studying supercritical fluid solubility phenomena.

The particle size and size distribution of solid materials formed in industrial processes is frequently not the size that is desired for subsequent reaction or use of these materials. Crushing, grinding, ball milling, and precipitation from solution are examples of methods for particle-size redistribution applied to chemicals, pharmaceuticals, dyes, and polymers. Precipitation from solution is carried out on the basis of the temperature dependence of solubility in a liquid solvent, the reactivity of the desired component to form an insoluble component, or the application of an antisolvent to decrease the solubility of a material that is dissolved in solution. There are generally advantages and disadvantages with any particle-size-reduction process that must be evaluated for a specific material. Simple grinding is usually quite inexpensive, but it may not be applicable to certain polymers, for example, unless the grinding is carried out at cryogenic temperatures.

There are many other solids that are difficult to process by grinding or by solution techniques for one reason or another. For example, a few such difficult-to-comminute materials are certain dyes, explosives, biological compounds, and chemical intermediates that are subsequently used in solid-gas reaction schemes. Nucleation from supercritical fluid solutions containing such materials is an alternative comminution technique that can alter particle size and particle-size distribution at very mild temperatures, thus avoiding unwanted degradation of the material and, in some cases, unwanted reaction of the material. In this chapter the SCF nucleation of materials is described. Optical and scanning electron micrographs (SEM) are presented that show that the concept can be applied to a number of refractory materials. There are virtually no references in the literature on SCF comminution, and discussion of the concept derives from the work of Krukonis, who reported on this technique at the annual AIChE meeting in San Francisco, California, in November 1984 (Krukonis, 1984d). (For further information, see the discussion of U.S. patent 2,457,238 in appendix A.)

The compounds are dissolved in a supercritical fluid in a flow apparatus similar to the one described in chapter 4. For the most part, carbon dioxide at conditions of about 5,000 psia and 55°C is used as the solvent in the studies. The precipitated material is collected downstream of the pressure-reduction valve and is analyzed for particle size by optical microscopy. The optical microscopy is done at $150\times$ and $600\times$, and most of the SEM microscopy is carried out at about $2,000\times$. In some of the photographs that are presented the particles are so small that individual particles are barely discernible at $600\times$ magnification. However, the small particles that are formed attest to the potential of this technique. Although Krukonis presented results on numerous solid materials, only five of those solid materials are presented below.

Figures 12.1a and 12.1b compare "before" and "after" particles of β-estradiol. As figure 12.1a shows, particle sizes range from a few microns to hundreds of microns in the commercial β-estradiol. The material also appears to be crystalline, as suggested by the faceted particles. Although barely discernible, and almost a blur because the particles are at the limit of resolution at $600\times$, the nucleated particles shown in figure 12.1b are strikingly different in size from the parent particles. The magnification scale provides a measure for estimating the diameters of individual particles, which appear to be on the order of less than 1 micron.

Figures 12.2a and 12.2b show the photomicrographs of ferrocene (dicyclopentadienyl iron), as supplied and after supercritical fluid processing. The

Figure 12.1
Photomicrographs:
(a) virgin particles of β-estradiol; (b) particles of β-estradiol nucleated from an SCF solution.

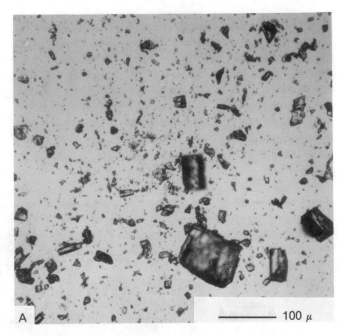

Figure 12.2
Photomicrographs:
(a) virgin particles of ferrocene; (b) particles of ferrocene nucleated from an SCF solution.

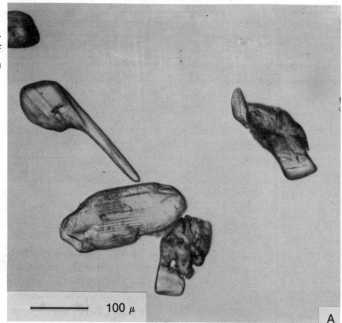

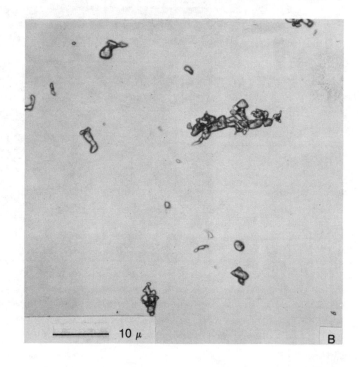

scales on the two figures allow the particle sizes to be readily compared, and again a size reduction is seen. It is quite interesting that ferrocene, a compound whose melting point is 178°C, exhibits a solubility level of the order of about 20 wt-% in carbon dioxide at 5,000 psia and 55°C.

Figures 12.3a and 12.3b, which are scanning electron micrographs, show the effects on the particle size and morphology of dissolving and subsequently nucleating a navy-blue dye. The structure of the dye is shown below.

$$O_2N \longrightarrow \overset{\displaystyle Br}{\underset{\displaystyle NO_2}{\bigcirc}} \longrightarrow N=N \longrightarrow \overset{\displaystyle OC_2H_3}{\underset{\displaystyle NHCOCH_3}{\bigcirc}} \longrightarrow N(CH_2CH_2OCOCH_3)_2$$

This dye is soluble in carbon dioxide at 5,000 psia to a level of a few tenths of a weight percent. The particle size of the commercial dye is about 50–150 microns as is seen from the low-magnification SEM. The particles formed during expansion of the SCF solution are much smaller in size, and in this case their size can be quantitatively estimated from figure 12.3b.

Figures 12.4a, 12.4b, and 12.4c are scanning electron micrographs of dodecanolactam (lauryl-lactam), the monomer that polymerizes to Nylon-12. The parent material, shown in figure 12.4a, is a powder composed of irregular particles of about 5–10 microns in size. Figure 12.4b, at a magnification of 2 mm per micron, shows what appear to be clumps of short fibers. Since the detail in figure 12.4b is relatively poor, the nucleated dodecanolactam was ultrasonically separated and subsequently inspected at a higher magnification, as shown in figure 12.4c. A quite large aspect (length-to-diameter) ratio is seen in this figure. The primary particles are needlelike in appearance with a length of 10–40 microns and with a diameter of less than 1 micron.

The final example of SCF comminution is a comparison of polypropylene particles "out of the bottle" and after supercritical fluid nucleation. In this case carbon dioxide was not used and instead supercritical propylene at 3,500 psia and 140°C is used to dissolve the sample of polypropylene. Figure 12.5a is a high-magnification SEM micrograph of a single parent particle. As shown in figure 12.5b, a very different particle size and shape results from the super-critical fluid process.

The optical and scanning electron micrographs presented in this chapter show that the particle size of solid materials such as polymers, monomers, and intermediate chemicals can be altered by precipitation from a supercritical fluid solution. The only requirement for carrying out the SCF particle-reduction process is that the compound must exhibit some solubility in a supercritical fluid. Because the pressure-reduction rates are so rapid during the expansion of the solution, supersaturation ratios can be achieved that are much, much

Figure 12.3 Scanning electron micrographs: (a) virgin particles of navy-blue dye; (b) particles of navy-blue dye nucleated from an SCF solution.

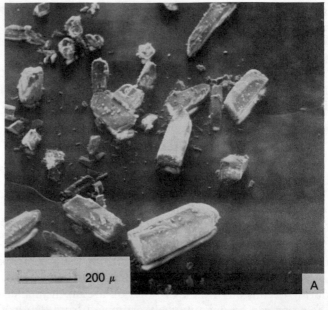

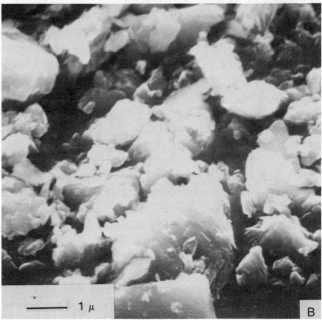

greater than can be achieved by thermal, chemical, or antisolvent precipitation processes. It is conjectured, furthermore, that such rapid nucleation rates can result in the particle formation of some materials with a size distribution or morphology that cannot now be achieved by any other process.

Figure 12.4 Scanning electron micrographs: (a) virgin particles of dodecanolactam; (b) particles of dodecanolactam nucleated from an SCF solution; (c) same as (b) except that the SCF-treated particles are sonically separated before being analyzed.

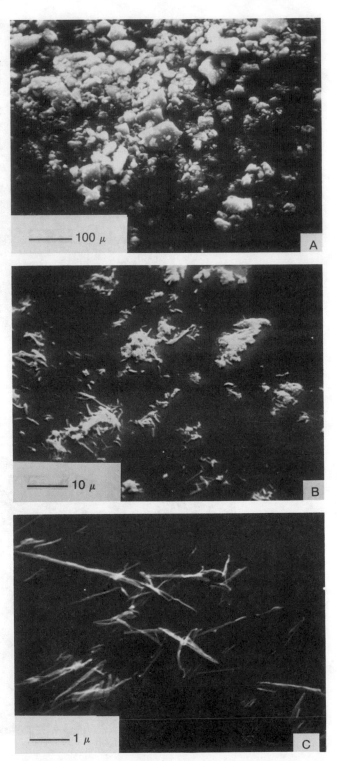

Figure 12.5 Scanning electron micrographs: (a) virgin particles of polypropylene; (b) particles of polypropylene nucleated from an SCF solution.

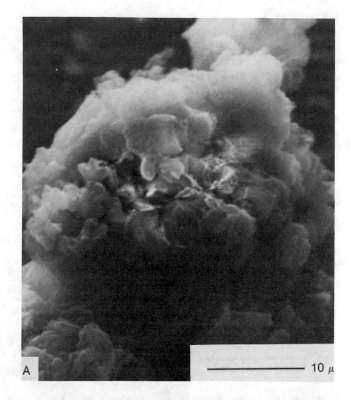

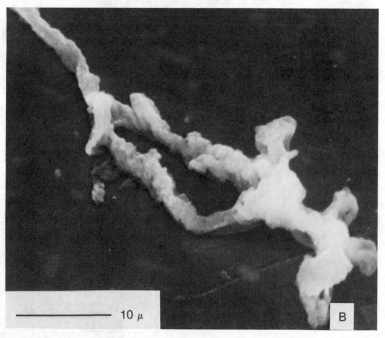

SWELLING OF POLYMERS

A different polymer-SCF application that does not fit readily into chapter 9 concerns the swelling of amorphous polymers in the presence of a supercritical fluid. As gas purification membranes are operated to higher and higher pressures, it will be very important to be able to predict and understand the changes in the dimensional integrity of the membrane. It may be possible to have an SCF-glass transition-point depression in a manner similar to the SCF melting-point depression of a solid described in chapter 3. The SCF–solid polymer information available in the literature is shown in table 12.1.

An example of SCF-solid, amorphous polymer behavior is described here

Table 12.1   Gas-Polymer Equilibrium Data for Molten Polymers

Polymer	Gas	Temperature (°C)	Weight Fraction of Gas Dissolved in Polymer ($\times 10^2$)	Pressure (atm)
Polyethylene (high density)	CH_4	140.03	0.36–4.1	51–238
		162.78	0.36–4.1	21–317
		188.31	0.36–3.3	24–253
Polyethylene (low density)	C_2H_4	124–300	0	>1
		143.2	0	69.4
		157.3	0	69.4
		200.5	0	69.4
		237.0	0	69.4
	CH_4	125.4	0.8–5.0	60–661
		227.0	1.0–6.4	69–661
	N_2	125.0	1.0–1.25	0.69
		155.4	0.6–3.9	62–540
		188.4	0.6–3.9	66–669
		226.1	0.9–4.5	64–547
Polyisobutylene	CH_4	101.86	0.4–2.4	23–341
		126.85	0.3–2.7	23–341
		155.41	0.4–3.0	23–341
		188.46	0.4–3.1	23–341
Polystyrene	CH_4	100.20	0.6–1.6	67–320
		125.42	0.5–2.0	50–668
		155.42	0.4–1.6	48–241
		188.40	0.5–2.2	67–312

Source: Bonner (1977).

for the polymethyl methacrylate (PMMA)–CO_2 system (Liau and McHugh, 1984). In this work the swelling of PMMA induced by carbon dioxide at temperatures ranging from 40°C to 70°C and over a pressure range of 0 to 4,000 psia is determined. Also, the sorption of carbon dioxide in PMMA over the same temperature and pressure ranges is determined. Shown in table 12.2 are the properties of PMMA. Note that the critical temperature of CO_2 is well below the glass transition temperature of PMMA.

The swelling of solid polymer in the presence of supercritical carbon dioxide is visually determined. Amorphous solid is chosen for the purpose of minimizing any irreversible morphology changes that can occur as it sorbs supercritical solvent. The techniques used to determine the swelling of PMMA are similar to those described in chapter 4 for the visual determination of the *P-T* trace of the freezing-point depression (SLV) curve of a crystalline solid. In this instance, though, the polymer sample is initially pretreated to remove any residual solvent and to relax any strain that may be present in the as-received sample (Ham, Bolen, and Hughes, 1962). The pretreatment consists of the following steps:

1. evacuating the polymer at an elevated temperature to remove any residual solvent or low-molecular-weight impurities;
2. soaking the polymer in liquid carbon dioxide to release any frozen-in strain that may be present in the solid sample; and
3. evacuating the polymer sample to remove any residual carbon dioxide.

Carbon dioxide is transferred from a holding tank to a high-pressure view cell, which is loaded with a PMMA sample molded into a cylindrical shape. The length of the sample is determined using a cathetometer. Equilibrium is reached when a constant pressure is obtained. Since it is assumed that the polymer swells isotropically (Ham, Bolen, and Hughes, 1962), the change in length of the sample is converted directly to a change in volume.

A simple static system similar to that described by Ozawa, Kusumi, and Ogino (1974) is used for these sorption studies. The PMMA sample in the view cell is pretreated as previously described in the swelling experiments. The total void space in the cell packed with PMMA is then determined. With valves 1, 2, and 4 open (see figure 12.6), helium is introduced into the holding tank while a vacuum is maintained inside the sample cell. Valve 1 is closed once the desired system pressure is obtained. The mass of helium in the holding tank is calculated from the volume of the holding tank and connecting lines,

Table 12.2   Properties of Polymethyl Methacrylate

Weight average molecular weight, M_w	60,600
Number average molecular weight, M_n	33,200
Weight/number average ratio, M_w/M_n	1.82
Glass transition temperature	105°C

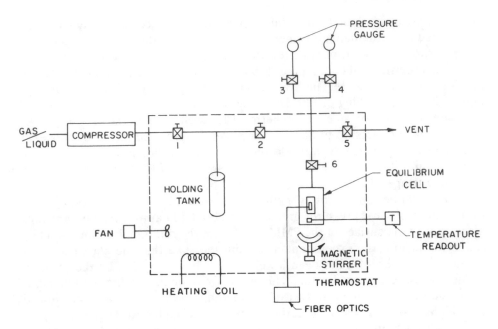

Figure 12.6 Schematic diagram of the experimental apparatus used to obtain sorption and swelling data (Liau and McHugh, 1984).

the helium pressure, and the temperature of the cell. After thermal equilibrium is reached, helium is then transferred into the view cell. At equilibrium, assuming no helium sorbs into PMMA, the void volume of the packed sample cell including the polymer void space is determined from the new equilibrium pressure, the volume of the holding tank and lines, the volume of the cell, and the temperature of the cell (Ozawa, Kusumi, and Ogino, 1974). The density of PMMA can also be calculated from the mass and the volume of the PMMA sample.

The system is then depressurized and evacuated at the elevated temperature to remove any residual helium. Initially the view cell is isolated from the system while the holding tank is pressurized with carbon dioxide by opening valves 1, 2, and 4. Valve 1 is closed once the desired pressure is obtained. Carbon dioxide is then transferred from the holding tank to the view cell. The pressure of the view cell eventually reaches an equilibrium pressure after approximately 50 minutes. The amount of carbon dioxide sorbed into PMMA is obtained from the difference between the initial and final mass of carbon dioxide in the void space in the cell, the holding tank, and the lines. The mass of carbon dioxide is determined from the volume of the vessel and the lines and the local carbon dioxide density. Initial and final temperature and pressure readings in each location are used to obtain the density of carbon dioxide using the equation of state described by Michels and Michels (1937). The void volume in the cell is reduced because of polymer swelling and is also incorporated into the sorption calculation. Isothermal sorption data at successive pressures are determined in a cumulative manner. After every few data points, the polymer is depressurized to atmospheric pressure to check for any irreversible swelling.

The experimental data on the carbon dioxide–induced swelling of PMMA obtained by Liau and McHugh at 41.8°C, 58.1°C, and 68.0°C are shown in figure 12.7. The swelling of PMMA in the presence of carbon dioxide exhibits very similar behavior at each isotherm. The swelling increases linearly with pressure for pressures up to about 50 atm. As the pressure increases above 50 atm, the swelling increases more slowly until it reaches a limiting value at very high pressures. As shown in figure 12.7, the swelling of PMMA decreases with increasing temperature.

It should be noted, however, that the surface of the PMMA rod appears to melt at 68.0°C for pressures greater than about 100 atm. This melting takes place only on the surface of the PMMA rod since the rod remains dimensionally stable throughout the experiment. It is quite possible that the glass transition temperature of PMMA has been lowered from 105°C to 68°C by the sorption of high-pressure carbon dioxide. This behavior is similar to the melting-point depression of crystalline solids such as naphthalene when they are pressurized by a high-pressure gas such as carbon dioxide (McHugh and Yogan, 1984).

As shown in figure 12.8, the sorption of carbon dioxide in PMMA increases linearly at low pressures for all the isotherms investigated in this study. This behavior is in agreement with the work done by Durrill and Griskey (1966).

The swelling of PMMA in the presence of CO_2 is different at low pressures than at high pressures. At low pressures, where CO_2 is gaslike, the amount of CO_2 sorbed into the polymer is a function of how easily CO_2 can fill the void spaces of the polymer. This void-space filling is a function of the characteristics of the penetrant molecule (i.e., the CO_2) and the rigidity of the PMMA.

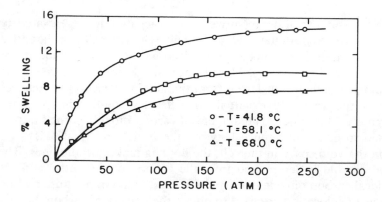

Figure 12.7   Swelling of PMMA in the presence of high-pressure carbon dioxide (Liau and McHugh, 1984).

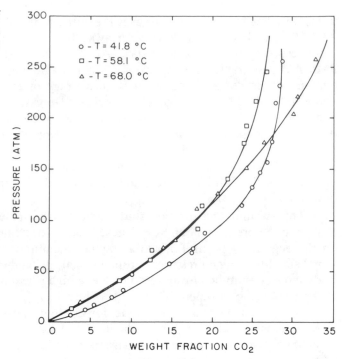

Figure 12.8 Sorption of carbon dioxide in PMMA at high pressures (Liau and McHugh, 1984).

The swelling of PMMA in the presence of carbon dioxide at 41.8°C is greater than the swelling at 58.1°C and 68.0°C. The sorption of carbon dioxide in PMMA at 41.8°C, which is shown in figure 12.8, is also greater than the sorption at 58.1°C and 68.0°C. At 41.8°C PMMA is very far removed from its glass transition temperature (T_g = 105°C). Below the glass transition temperature PMMA is a very rigid, solid polymer. At 41.8°C carbon dioxide is less expanded at low pressures than when it is at 58.1°C or 68.0°C. Hence, the low-pressure swelling of PMMA and the sorption of CO_2 in PMMA are greatest at 41.8°C.

At pressures greater than approximately 75 atm carbon dioxide at 41.8°C possesses a "liquidlike" density, which makes it more soluble in PMMA than at the higher temperatures of 58.1°C and 68.0°C. The solubility of CO_2 in PMMA at these high pressures can be modeled as the solubility of an SCF in a liquid (i.e., the amorphous, solid PMMA is treated as a liquid). The amount of CO_2 sorbed in PMMA at high pressures depends on how much PMMA "likes" CO_2.

A saturation loading of CO_2 in PMMA is reached at high pressures since increasing the pressure has very little effect on the properties of carbon dioxide. Therefore, both the swelling of PMMA in the presence of carbon dioxide and the sorption of carbon dioxide into PMMA reach limiting values at very high pressures at 41.8°C and 58.1°C.

Notice that at 68.0°C the sorption of carbon dioxide in PMMA appears to increase linearly with pressure over the entire range of pressure investigated. At 68.0°C, carbon dioxide is very far away from its critical temperature, thus it possesses "gaslike" characteristics. Also, the temperature is now closer to PMMA's glass transition temperature. For most polymers, the glass transition temperature is not a point, but it is an average of the transition interval of about 10°C or 20°C. At high carbon dioxide pressures, the glass transition temperature of PMMA may be lowered because of the high solubility of carbon dioxide in the polymer. At high pressures and 68.0°C PMMA loses some of the properties of the rigid, solid state and acquires some of the properties of a dense liquid. Because the experiment is designed to measure the sorption of CO_2 in solid PMMA the sorption results at this temperature are probably only valid up to 100 atm.

This swelling and sorption study indicates that polymer morphology can change in the presence of an SCF. These morphology changes pose a challenge for the engineer who must design a polymer membrane that retains its dimensional stability at high pressures. From a practical standpoint the results of this study indicate that the O-rings used to seal a high pressure apparatus may swell in the presence of a supercritical fluid. (They do.)

Also, it may be feasible to extract lower-molecular-weight impurities from solid, amorphous polymers. Since subcritical and supercritical CO_2 swells PMMA reversibly, one may envision an extraction process in which spent catalyst, entrapped solvent, or low-molecular-weight oligomers are extracted from swollen, solid polymers that retain their dimensional integrity. Caution must be exercised, however, to avoid melting the polymer at high loadings of solvent in the polymer at high operating pressures. In the case of PMMA, the glass transition temperature is decreased by as much as 35°C at CO_2 pressures in excess of 100 atm.

FORMATION OF POROUS POLYMERS

Polymers with wide molecular-weight distribution or with a specially constructed molecular-weight distribution can be extracted of low-molecular-weight oligomers to form a substrate with a different morphology. One example using isotactic polypropylene is described here in order to illustrate this concept.

The polymer discussed is composed of an artificially assembled distribution of oligomers obtained by admixing a certain amount of low-molecular-weight polypropylene with commercial polypropylene. The low-molecular-weight fraction is obtained by extracting commercial polypropylene with supercritical carbon dioxide at 6,500 psia and 155°C. At these conditions about 20% of the polypropylene is dissolved in a reasonable extraction period. The extract polypropylene is obtained in a powder or "fluff" form quite similar in appearance to the nucleated polypropylene particles whose structure is shown in figure 12.5b. The particles shown in that micrograph were obtained from a process using supercritical propylene as the extractant, but carbon dioxide was specifically used for extracting the low-molecular-weight fraction. It is reasoned that if the majority of the polymer is not dissolved by carbon dioxide at the conditions of 6,500 psia and 155°C, then the bulk of the substrate shape formed from a mixture of the original parent polymer and the carbon dioxide extract would not be altered "significantly" during extraction. As is subsequently seen, this reasoning resulted in a reasonable demonstration of the concept.

The synthetically prepared polypropylene mixture is composed of 50% parent polymer and 50% extract. The substrate "shape" that is tested to examine the feasibility of the concept is a thin sheet. To form the sheet a few grams of the synthetic mixture is pressed between heated platens maintained at 170°C. The thickness of the pressed preform is 4 mils. Depending upon the amount of polymer used, the sheets obtained were 3–5 inches in diameter.

The pieces for extraction were preforms cut into small sections; one was maintained for scanning electron microscopy (SEM) examination, and the others were extracted at a variety of conditions. The extraction system is a variation of that shown in figure 4.1, a flow-through system.

Figure 12.9 is an SEM of the pressed preform sheet. A scale marker, which is barely perceptible, is imprinted on the micrograph, and an additional scale marker is added for clarity. The magnification of the micrograph of the preform was made especially high in order to point out that the surface is quite

Figure 12.9 Scanning electron micrograph of pressed polypropylene.

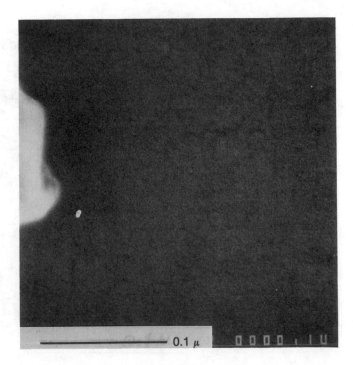

0.1 μ

smooth. (The white object at the left edge of the micrograph is a speck of dust used by the microscopist as an aid in focusing.)

A section of preform was extracted with supercritical carbon dioxide at a slightly lower pressure and temperature, 6,000 psia and 150°C, than was used in obtaining the low end from the parent polymer. Figure 12.10 is an SEM of the extracted sheet. A porous surface is formed and with the aid of the scale marker the "pores" can be determined to be a few tenths of a micron in size.

Another piece of the preform was extracted with carbon dioxide at 6,500 psia and 155°C (the same conditions used to obtain the fraction), and an SEM of the resultant membrane is shown in Figure 12.11. The surface appears to be "more fused" relative to the surface shown in figure 12.10. If we care to speculate, we can offer several explanations for the "more fused" surface appearance. For example, the higher pressure and temperature can influence the melting (softening) point of the polymer, causing the polymer preform to flow or rearrange during extraction of the low-molecular-weight polypropylene fraction, or the combination of conditions can be swelling the substrate more than in the previous test. A discussion of the latter phenomenon was presented previously in conjunction with the polymethyl methacrylate polymer-swelling experiments. Perhaps it is most reasonable not to speculate too much on the basis of differences observed in just two initial feasibility experiments.

A third piece of preform was extracted with supercritical propylene, at 3,000 psia and 135°C. In earlier experiments with the commercial powder it

Figure 12.10 Scanning electron micrograph of the pressed polypropylene sheet extracted with supercritical CO_2 at 6,000 psia and 150°C.

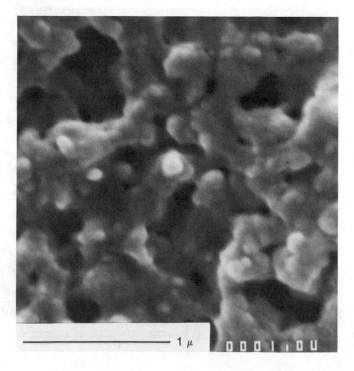

$1\ \mu$ 0001 00

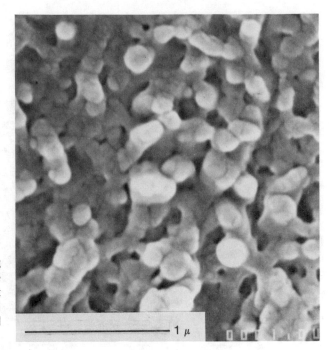

Figure 12.11 Scanning electron micrograph of the pressed polypropylene sheet extracted with supercritical CO_2 at 6,500 psia and 155°C.

was determined that at conditions of 3,500 psia and 140–150°C propylene dissolved significant amounts of the polypropylene polymer. Thus, a lower pressure and temperature, again somewhat arbitrarily chosen, was employed for the extraction. Figure 12.12 shows the surface of the membrane produced by treatment with supercritical propylene. The surface structure is similar to the surface structure seen in figure 12.10. As a final test, a section of pressed preform was extracted with supercritical propylene at higher pressure and temperature, 4,000 psia and 150°C, for 5 minutes. The surface that resulted is shown in the micrograph reproduced in figure 12.13, and it appears quite fused, although some small pores are visible.

The tests on porous polymer formation described in this section are quite rudimentary, and certainly more needs to be done before such factors as pore size and size distribution can be controlled or predicted. Examination of swelling, plasticization, and melting phenomena in a view cell, for example, as described in the previous section; determination of molecular-weight distributions of the extract and substrate (and of the parent polymer); and investigations of other thermoplastic polymers are just a few areas for study. However, in spite of the rudimentary nature of the experiments, the feasibility tests have established that the concept is reduced to practice, at least at the laboratory level. The formation of porous polymers by supercritical processing might show advantage in membrane or controlled-release applications.

In this chapter three quite different topics have been described where the combination of properties that supercritical fluids exhibit are advantageously

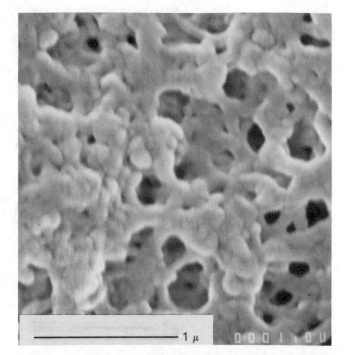

Figure 12.12 Scanning electron micrograph of the pressed polypropylene sheet extracted with supercritical propylene at 3,000 psia and 135°C.

Figure 12.13 Scanning electron micrograph of the pressed polypropylene sheet extracted with supercritical propylene at 4,000 psia and 150°C.

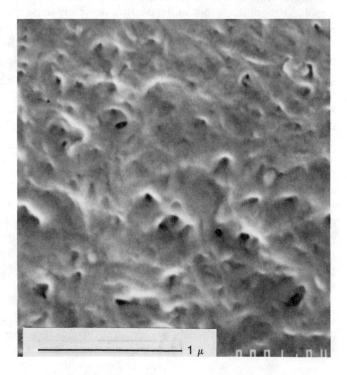

applied. There are scores of others that are either in still earlier investigation or only in the thinking stage. One example is the formation of aerogels, which are now receiving increasing attention. Aerogels are structures of ceramics or polymers with extremely small pores. If the liquid is removed, via evaporation, for example, the surface-tension forces active in small-diameter capillaries can collapse the structure. Critical-point drying was developed twenty years ago so that botanical and biological specimens to be examined by scanning electron microscopy could be dried quickly with preservation of structure. If, for example, the specimen were merely desiccated, surface-tension forces at the water vaporization interface can distort or collapse the structure, rendering it unfit for microscopy. In the critical-point drying process, the water is exchanged with a miscible organic liquid and the organic is exchanged with liquid carbon dioxide, which is subsequently raised to above its critical point and then removed under conditions in which the temperature never falls below 31°C. Because the pores are "filled" only with a gas during the pressure decrease, no collapse of the structure occurs.

A similar concept is applied to the removal of liquid from gels. Kistler (1932) studied the formation of transparent silica, alumina, stannic oxide, and other materials. More recently, Schmitt, Grieger-Block, and Chapman (1983)

Figure 12.14 Micrograph of a polyethylene aerogel produced by supercritical extraction.

presented a description of a process for forming transparent silica via this concept. They formed gels of silica in water, exchanged the water with methanol, then brought the system to above the critical point of methanol ($P_c = 79.9$ atm, $T_c = 239.4°C$) to remove the methanol while maintaining the methanol in the "gaseous" state.

The process is theoretically applicable to polymers, but, practically, most of the solvents that can support the formation of polymer gels of, say, polyethylene or polypropylene, have critical temperatures too high to permit polymer aerogels to be formed without melting. A variation of the critical-point drying method can be used, however; the solvent in which the polymer gel is formed can be exchanged with supercritical carbon dioxide (or some other low-critical-temperature gas such as ethylene, fluoroform, or chlorotrifluoromethane), and while the system is maintained above the critical temperature the solvent is removed. The carbon dioxide is then removed from the system while the system is maintained above the critical temperature of the gas. Figure 12.14 is a micrograph of a polyethylene aerogel produced by this technique (Krukonis, 1984a) from a polyethylene-xylene gel provided by Lawrence Livermore National Laboratories.

13

Epilogue

Having reached this chapter of the book the reader may be wondering how he might use SCF technology for a particular application. It is not our desire to espouse any "hard and fast" rules about SCF technology. In fact, the potential for this technology, in our opinion, is bounded only by the imagination of the researcher who speculates on its potential application. Certainly the literature should be reviewed to see whether SCF processing has either already been applied to the problem or whether the technology will a priori work for the application. It is important to remember that there are terminologies associated with any new technology. For instance, one needs to be aware of what some researchers define as "solubility" or "extractibility." As an example it is pertinent to consider further the work of Stahl and co-workers who present much of their data in terms of "threshold" pressures, that is, the pressure at which a compound is detected as being soluble in a supercritical fluid. The detection of a compound solubilized in an SCF is a function of the sensitivity of the detector and the measurement technique. For example in a flow system such as the type described in chapter 4 gravimetric analysis is usually used to identify the material collected. For this detection technique, levels of at least a few milligrams of collected material are required to establish the concentration of the compound with some reasonable accuracy. If, on the other hand, the same flow-through apparatus is used with a modified collection scheme consisting of a chromatographic valve-trap and the collected material measured by gas chromatography, as is also shown in chapter 4, substantially lower concentrations and absolute amounts of material can be determined quite accurately. As a third detection alternative, Stahl and co-workers (1980) use a flow-through system coupled with a thin-layer chromatograph (TLC). The expansion valve that is used in this system is an extremely small one with overall dimensions of a few tenths of an inch and with a short capillary tube of 0.002 inch inner diameter located downstream of the orifice. The compound that precipitates from the expanding stream impinges directly onto a TLC plate. The effect of system temperature and pressure on the extraction characteristics of the SCF is evaluated by allowing the stream leaving the expansion valve to impinge on different sections of the TLC plate, which is subsequently developed to determine the amount of material present. TLC analysis is an extremely sensitive analytical technique that will identify much smaller amounts of a compound at a given threshold pressure as compared with a gravimetric method.

Table 13.1 lists the detection limits (King, 1984) of a number of spectroscopic and chromatographic analytical methods employed in supercritical extraction studies. As related previously, a gravimetric method requires a few milligrams of material for analysis. TLC analysis can detect materials at solubility levels one billion (!) times lower. Thus, if one is measuring the threshold pressure at which the compound dissolves at a "detectable" level, an analytical method that can identify 10^{-12} gram will result in the identification of a lower threshold pressure than can be ascertained in the gravimetric method. The "threshold pressure" is therefore a function of the sensitivity of the analytical method.

A graph of data from one of Stahl's (Stahl et al., 1980) papers showing the solubility of a number of compounds in carbon dioxide is given in figure 13.1. This work is presented to highlight the relative order of progression of solubility of the compounds ranked on the basis of structure and functional groups. Although naphthalene is not shown in this graph, let us consider the solubility of naphthalene in CO_2 (see figure 2.2). Naphthalene is a simple aromatic hydrocarbon: it contains no dipole or hydrogen-bonding substituents that provide specific interactions between the solute molecules. Naphthalene is also of reasonably low molecular weight, so it would be expected to dissolve to some respectable concentration level. Benzoic acid, even though lower in molecular weight than naphthalene, can hydrogen-bond, thus increasing the difficulty for carbon dioxide to solubilize the compound. The solubility data for benzoic acid in this figure corroborate this fact. Progressing down the column of molecular structures, we find that increasing numbers of hydroxyl groups lower a compound's solubility quite dramatically. For example, frangulin exhibits a solubility level of only 0.0001 wt-%. The last, and least soluble, compound in the figure is glycine, the simplest amino acid. The values of solubility of glycine are obtained with TLC measurements. Strictly speaking, glycine is soluble in CO_2. However, a solubility level of approximately 0.00001 wt-% at a density of 1.0 g/ml (approximately 500 atm) is considered of little practical value.

Table 13.1 Detection Limits of Common Monitors

Detection Principle	Sensitivity (in grams)
Gravimetric	10^{-3}
Infrared spectroscopy	10^{-7}
Ultraviolet spectroscopy	10^{-9}
Mass spectrography	10^{-9}
Flame ionization	10^{-10}
TLC visualization	10^{-12}

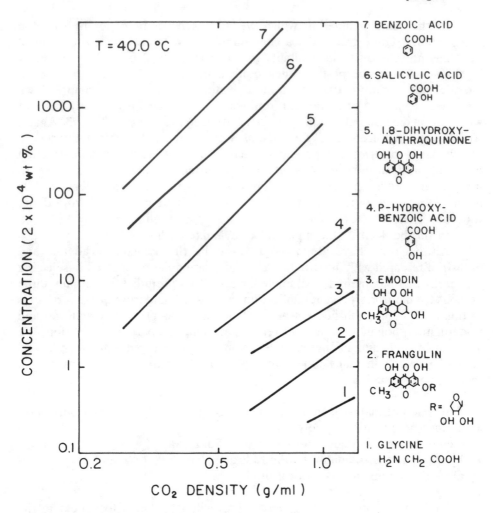

Figure 13.1 Solubility levels of various organic compounds in supercritical carbon dioxide.

There is also in the literature a reference to the solubility of carbohydrates in carbon dioxide. Specifically, Giddings, Myers, and King (1969) measured the migration of various compounds in ultrahigh-pressure carbon dioxide. At a pressure of 30,000 psi, for example, they "detected" sucrose through flame ionization detection. Note that table 13.1 indicates that the detection limit of flame ionization is 10^{-10} gram. For practical purposes, sugar is insoluble in carbon dioxide. Therefore, when one is referring to the literature for information on the solubility behavior of compounds in SCFs, it is important to evaluate as quantitatively as possible (or as realistically as possible) the rather qualitative question, "Is the compound soluble in carbon dioxide or any other SCF?"

In the same manner in which we discussed solubility let us examine extractability. Quite frequently a compound's extractability by a supercritical fluid has no relation to its solubility in that supercritical fluid. We saw early in chapter 8 that the pesticide diazinon dissolves to a high level in carbon dioxide, but it is not extractable from activated carbon. Later in chapter 8 we discussed separation of acetic acid from water. Acetic acid is infinitely miscible with carbon dioxide but it exhibits a distribution coefficient of only 0.03. Again, strictly speaking, acetic acid is extractable but we feel that extractability should be evaluated in terms of a potential practical process. Supercritical extraction of acetic acid would probably not be an attractive alternative relative to traditional distillation. On the other hand, a distribution coefficient of 0.03 might be satisfactory for the extraction of a heat-labile compound from dilute solution. Therefore, even though certain useful generalities have been developed in this book, it is still important to evaluate each case separately.

Although we have attempted to describe the available academic and industrial research with impartiality, both of us are quite prejudiced in selecting our areas of fundamental and applied work. This prejudice is perhaps quite obvious from our most recent publications and papers and from our descriptions in this book of unpublished research in such areas as polymer expansion and fractionation, polymer–organic solvent separation, and particle nucleation. We are individually, and in several cases, jointly, carrying out fundamental and applied research in many other areas of technology that are not covered in these chapters, such as

- deposition of materials in microporous substrates and nonporous polymers;
- surface modification of polymers;
- electro-organic synthesis in supercritical fluids; and
- hydrogenations, oxidations, free-radical polymerizations, and enzyme-catalyzed reactions in supercritical fluids.

Publications on several of these topics will soon begin to appear in the literature. However, even though we are working in these areas, our prejudices obviously cannot ensure that the applications will be economically viable. How does one evaluate the process viability of an SCF application? We have touched on economics several times in the preceding chapters, but only superficially. As there are no "hard and fast" answers to questions of viability with traditional processes, so are there none with supercritical fluid extraction. Nevertheless, both of us are asked quite frequently, How much will it cost? As an indication of why there is no single answer to this question, we list below just a few of the parameters that influence the cost of a supercritical fluid separation process:

- pressure level;
- pressure-reduction ratio;
- distribution coefficient;
- solubility level; and
- amount of material to be extracted.

All these items must be specified and they all affect capital and operating costs.

We have mentioned product cost several times in this book, but we do not mean to imply that product cost is the most important factor to be considered. As we related in chapter 7, there is a hop extraction plant in operation, and hop extract sells for $30 per pound; yet there are also many propane-desasphalting and residuum extraction plants in operation, and these petroleum products sell for only 10 cents per pound. These two products are on the opposite ends of the commodity spectrum, and their respective processes represent the potential breadth of application of supercritical fluid technology.

In the previous chapters we have attempted to give you an inclusive, in-depth analysis of an emerging technology. Our intent has been to teach you the fundamentals of this technology as much as to give you examples as to where it has been applied. In certain areas its application was successful and in some others it wasn't. However, in the analysis of these applications we have supplied you with guidelines and criteria which you can now apply when considering supercritical fluids for your particular needs. As the myth and mystery of supercritical fluids are removed, practicing scientists and engineers will become more comfortable with applying this technology to as yet undefined separation problems.

References

Abraham, K. P., and P. Ehrlich. 1975. Partial molar volume of a polymer in supercritical solution. *Macromolecules* 8:944.

Aida, T., and T. G. Squires. 1985. Organic chemistry in supercritical fluid solvents: photoisomerization of trans-stilbene. Paper presented at the ACS Meeting at Chicago, IL, September.

Alexander, G., and M. E. Paulaitis. 1984. Solvent effects on reaction kinetics in supercritical fluid solvents. Paper presented at the AIChE Annual Meeting at San Francisco, CA, November.

Allen, B., and C. H. Baker. 1965. Lower critical solution phenomena in polymer-solvent systems. *Polymer* 6:181.

Amagat, E. G. 1879. Researches on the compressibility of gases at elevated pressures. *Comptes Rendus des Séances de L'Academie des Sciences* 88(I):336.

Andrews, T. 1875–76. The Bakerian lecture—On the gaseous state of matter. *Proc. R. Soc. London* 24:455.

Anolick, C., and E. P. Goffinet. 1971. Separation of ethylene copolymer elastomers from their solvent solutions. U.S. Patent 3,553,156.

Anolick, C., and E. W. Slocum. 1973. Process for Isolating EPDM Elastomers From Their Solvent Solutions. U.S. Patent 3,726,843.

Anon. Krytox fluorinated lubricants. *duPont Tech. Bull.* G-6.

Anon. 1981a. Novel solvent recovery enhances residuum upgrading. *Chem. Eng.*, November 30, 69.

Anon. 1981b. Olefin polymers. In *Kirk-Othmer encyclopedia of chemical technology*, 3d ed., vol. 16. John Wiley and Sons.

Anon. 1982. Supercritical CO_2 cleans drill cuttings. *Chem. Eng. News*, February 8, p. 30.

Baker, C. H., C. S. Clemson, and G. Allen. 1966. Polymer fractionation at a lower critical solution temperature phase boundary. *Polymer* 1:525.

Balder, J. R., and J. M. Prausnitz. 1966. Thermodynamics of ternary liquid–supercritical gas systems with applications for high pressure vapor extraction. *Ind. Eng. Chem. Fundam.* 5:449.

Bangert, L. H., J. L. Lundberg, J. D. Muzzy, G. H. Hoyes, L. H. Olson, and W. D. Freeston, Jr. 1977. Advanced technology applications in garment processing. Report prepared for the National Science Foundation, National Technical Information Service Report PB 284,779, September.

Bardin, J. M., and D. Patterson. 1969. Lower critical solution temperatures of polyisobutylene plus isomeric alkanes. *Polymer* 10:9.

Barry, E. F., P. Ferioli, and J. A. Hubball. 1983. Purification of OV-17 by supercritical fluid fractionation for fused silica capillary gas chromatography. *J. High Resolut. Chromatogr. Chromatogr. Commun.* 6:172.

243

Baumgartner, H. J. 1983. Oxidation of isobutane in the dense phase and at low oxygen concentration. U.S. Patent 4,408,082.

Bhise, V. S. 1983. Process for preparing ethylene glycol. U.S. Patent 4,400,559.

Blyumberg, E. R., Z. K. Maizus, and N. M. Emanuel. 1965. The liquid-phase oxidation of *n*-butane at temperatures and pressures near to the critical. In *The oxidation of hydrocarbons in the liquid phase,* ed. N. M. Emanuel. New York: Macmillan.

Bonner, D. C. 1977. Solubility of supercritical gases in polymers—A review. *Polym. Eng. Sci.* 17:65.

Booth, H. S., and R. M. Bidwell. 1949. Solubility measurement in the critical region *Chem. Rev.* 44:477.

Brunner, G., and S. Peter. 1981. Zum Stand der Extraktion mit komprimierten Gasen. *Chem.-Ing.-Tech.* 53:529.

Büchner, E. G. 1906. "Die beschränkte Mischbarkeit von Flussigkeiten das System Diphenylamin und Kohlensäure." *Z. Phys. Chem.* 56:257.

Busche, R. M., E. J. Shimshick, and R. A. Yates. 1982. Recovery of Acetic Acid from Dilute Acetate Solution. Biotech. Bioeng. Symp. 12:249.

Cagniard de la Tour, C. 1822. Effect obtained by simultaneous application of heat and pressure on certain liquids. *Ann. chim.* 22:410.

Cailletet, L. 1891. Description of a manometer in open air of 300 meters, established at the Eiffel Tower. *Comptes Rendus des Séances de L'Academie des Sciences* 112:764.

Caywood, S. W. 1970. Crude EPDM copolymer stabilized with a Lewis base. U.S. Patent 3,496,135.

Chai, C. P. 1981. Phase equilibrium behavior for carbon dioxide and heavy hydrocarbons. Ph.D. diss., Univ. of Delaware.

Chang, H., and D. G. Morrell. 1985. Solubilities of methoxy-1-tetralone and methyl nitrobenzoate isomers and their mixtures in supercritical carbon dioxide. *J. Chem. Eng. Data* 30:74.

Chappelear, D. C. 1960. Phase equilibria in the critical region—Binary systems with chlorotrifluoromethane. Ph.D. diss., Princeton Univ.

Chappelear, D. C., and J. C. Elgin. 1961. Phase equilibria in the critical region: Binary systems with chlorotrifluoromethane. *J. Chem. Eng. Data* 6:415.

Christianson, D. D., J. P. Friedrich, G. R. List, K. Warner, E. B. Bagley, A. C. Stringfellow, and G. E. Inglett. 1984. Supercritical fluid extraction of dry-milled corn germ with carbon dioxide. *J. Food Sci.* 49:229.

Close, R. E. 1951. Vapor-liquid equilibrium in the critical region—Systems of aliphatic alcohols with propane and propylene. Ph.D. diss., Princeton Univ.

Copelin, H. B. 1981. Method for reducing oligomeric cyclic ether content of a polymerizate. U.S. Patent 4,306,058.

Cottle, J. E. 1966. Supercritical polymerization of olefins. U.S. Patent 3,294,772.

Cowie, J. M. G., and I. J. McEwen. 1974. Polymer-cosolvent systems. IV. Upper and lower critical solution temperatures in the systems methylcyclohexane–diethyl ether–polystyrene. *Macromolecules* 7:291.

Culberson, O. L., and J. J. McKetta. 1951. Phase equilibria in hydrocarbon-water systems. III. The solubility of methane in water at pressures to 10,000 psia. *Trans AIME, Petrol.* 192:223.

Dandge, D., J. P. Heller, and K. V. Wilson. 1985. Structure solubility correlations: Organic compounds and dense carbon dioxide binary systems. *Ind. Eng. Chem. Prod. Res. Dev.* 24:162.

de Fillipi, R. P., V. J. Krukonis, R. J. Robey, and M. Modell. 1980. Supercritical fluid regeneration of activated carbon for adsorption of pesticides. *Report* EPA-600/2-80-054, March.

de Fillipi, R. P., and J. E. Vivian. 1982. Process for separating liquid solutes from their solvent mixtures. U.S. Patent 4,349,415.

de Filippi, R. P., and M. E. Chung. 1985. Laboratory evaluation of critical fluid extraction for environmental applications. *Report* EPA-600/2-85-045. April.

Deiters, U., and G. M. Schneider. 1976. Fluid mixtures at high pressures: Computer calculations of the phase equilibria and the critical phenomena in fluid binary mixtures from the Redlich-Kwong equation of state. *Ber. Bunsenges. Phys. Chem.* 80:1316.

de Loos, T. W., W. Poot, and G. A. M. Diepen. 1983. Fluid phase equilibria in the system polyethylene + ethylene. I. Systems of linear polyethylene + ethylene at high pressure. *Macromolecules* 16:111.

de Swaan Arons, J., and G. A. M. Diepen. 1963. Thermodynamic study of melting equilibria under pressure of a supercritical gas. *Rec. Trav. Chim.* 82:249.

Diandreth, J., and M. E. Paulaitis. 1984. Three phase liquid-liquid-gas behavior in alcohol–water–supercritical fluid systems. Paper presented at the 1984 AIChE Annual Meeting, San Francisco, CA, November.

Dickinson, N. L., and J. M. Meyers. 1952. Solexol fractionation of menhaden oil. *J. Am. Oil Chem. Soc.,* June, 29:235–39.

Diepen, G. A. M., and F. E. C. Scheffer. 1948a. On critical phenomena of saturated solutions in binary systems. *J. Am. Chem. Soc.* 70:4081.

———. 1948b. The solubility of naphthalene in supercritical ethylene. *J. Am. Chem. Soc.* 70:4085.

———. 1953. The solubility of naphthalene in supercritical ethylene, II. *J. Phys. Chem.* 57:575.

Donnelly, H. G., and D. L. Katz. 1954. Phase equilibrium in the carbon dioxide–methane system. *Ind. Eng. Chem.* 46:511.

Durrill, P. L., and R. G. Griskey. 1966. Diffusion and solution of gases in thermally softened or molten polymers: Part I. Development of technique and determination of data. *AIChE J.* 12:1147.

Eckert, C. A. 1972. High pressure kinetics in solution. *Annu. Rev. Phys. Chem.* 23:239.

Eckert, C. A., D. H. Ziger, K. P. Johnston, and T. K. Ellison. 1983. The use of partial molal volume data to evaluate equations of state for supercritical fluid mixtures. *J. Fluid Phase Equilib.* 14:167.

Ehrlich, P. 1965. Phase equilibria of polymer-solvent systems at high pressures near their critical Loci. II. Polyethylene-ethylene. *J. Polym. Sci., Part A* 3:131.

———. 1971. Partial molal volume anomaly in supercritical mixtures and the free radical polymerization of ethylene. *J. Macromol. Sci. Chem.* A5:1259.

Ehrlich, P., and R. H. Fariss. 1969. Negative partial molar volumes in the critical region: Mixtures of ethylene and vinyl chloride. *J. Phys. Chem.* 73:1164.

Ehrlich, P., and E. B. Graham. 1960. Solubility of polymers in compressed gases. *J. Polym. Sci.* 45:246.

Ehrlich, P., and J. J. Kurpen. 1963. Phase equilibria of polymer-solvent systems at high pressures near their critical loci: Poly-ethylene with *n*-alkanes. *J. Polym. Sci., Part A* 1:3217.

Ehrlich, P., and G. A. Mortimer. 1970. Fundamentals of free-radical polymerization of ethylene. *Adv. Polym. Sci.* 7:386.

Ehrlich, P., and R. N. Pittilo. 1960. A kinetic study of the oxygen-initiated polymerization of ethylene. *J. Polym. Sci.* 43:389.

Ehrlich, P., and P. C. Wu. 1973. Volumetric properties of supercritical ethane–*n*-heptane mixtures: The isothermal compressibility in the critical region. *AIChE J.* 19:540.

Eisenbach, W. 1984. Supercritical fluid extraction: A film demonstration. *Ber. Bunsenges. Phys. Chem.* 88:882.

Elgin, J. C., and J. J. Weinstock. 1959. Phase equilibrium at elevated pressures in ternary systems of ethylene and water with organic liquids: Salting out with a supercritical gas. *J. Chem. Eng. Data* 4:3.

Ellis, S. R. M. 1971. Vapor phase extraction process. *Br. Chem. Eng.* 16:358.

Fall, D. J., J. L. Fall, and K. D. Luks. 1985. Liquid-liquid-vapor immiscibility limits in carbon dioxide + *n*-paraffin mixtures. *J. Chem. Eng. Data* 30:82.

Fall, D. J., and K. D. Luks. 1984. Phase equilibria behavior of the systems carbon dioxide + *n*-dotriacontane and carbon dioxide + *n*-docosane. *J. Chem. Eng. Data* 29:413.

Flory, P. J. 1984. Liquid-liquid phase separations in polymer systems from a molecular point of view. Paper presented at the Symposium on Application of Phase Diagrams in Polymer Science, at the National Bureau of Standards, Gaithersburg, MD, October.

Francis, A. W. 1954. Ternary systems of liquid carbon dioxide. *J. Phys. Chem.* 58:1099.

Freeman, P. I., and J. S. Rowlinson. 1960. Lower critical points in polymer solutions. *Polymer* 1:20.

Friedrich, J. P. 1984. Supercritical CO_2 extraction of lipids from lipid-containing materials. U.S. 4,466,923.

Friedrich, J. P., G. R. List, and A. J. Heaking. 1982. Petroleum-free extraction of oil from soybeans with supercritical CO_2. *J. Am. Oil Chem. Soc.* 59:288.

Friedrich, J. P., and E. H. Pryde. 1984. Supercritical CO_2 extraction of lipid-bearing materials and characterization of the products. *J. Am. Oil Chem. Soc.* 61:223.

Gangoli, N., and G. Thodos. 1977. Liquid fuels and chemical feedstocks from coal by supercritical gas extraction. *Ind. Eng. Chem. Process Des. Dev.* 16:208.

Gearhart, J. A., and L. Garwin. 1976. ROSE process improves resid feed. *Hydrocarbon Process.* May, 55:125–28.

Giddings, J. C., M. N. Myers, and J. W. King. 1969. Dense gas chromatography at pressures to 2000 atmospheres. *J. Chromatogr. Sci.* 7:276.

Gopal, J. S., J. D. Holder, I. Wender, and A. A. Bishop. 1983. Supercritical behavior in multicomponent systems. Paper presented at the AIChE Meeting, Houston, TX, March.

Gore, G. 1861. On the properties of liquid carbonic acid. *Philos. Trans. R. Soc. London, Ser. A* 151:83.

Ham, J. S., M. C. Bolen, and J. K. Hughes. 1962. The use of high pressure to study polymer-solvent interaction. *J. Polym. Sci.* 57:25.

Hannay, J. B. 1880. On the solubility of solids in gases, II. *Proc. R. Soc. London* 30:484.

Hannay, J. B., and J. Hogarth. 1879. On the solubility of solids in gases. *Proc. R. Soc. London* 29:324.

———. 1880. On the solubility of solids in gases. *Proc. R. Soc. London* 30:178.

Hannigan, K. J. 1981. Extraction process creates low fat potato chips. *Chiltons Food Eng.*, July, 53:77.

Hicks, C. P., and C. L. Young. 1975. The gas-liquid critical properties of binary mixtures. *Chem. Rev.* 75:119.

Hottovy, J. D., J. P. Kohn, and K. D. Luks. 1981. Partial miscibility behavior of the methane + ethane + n-octane system. *J. Chem. Eng. Data* 26:135.

———. 1982. Partial miscibility behavior of the ternary systems methane + propane + n-octane, methane + n-butane + n-octane, and methane + carbon dioxide + n-octane. *J. Chem. Eng. Data* 27:298.

Huie, N. C., K. D. Luks, and J. P. Kohn. 1973. Phase-equilibria behavior of systems carbon dioxide–n-eicosane and carbon dioxide–n-decane–n-eicosane. *J. Chem. Eng. Data* 18:311.

Hunter, E., and R. B. Richards. 1945. Polymeric fractionation. U.S. Patent 2,457,238.

Hyatt, J. A., 1984, "Liquid and Supercritical CO_2 as Organic Solvents," J. Org. Chem., 49:5097, 1984.

Igel, J. T. 1985. Model calculations of the phase behavior of mixtures at high pressures. M.S. thesis, Univ. of Notre Dame.

Irani, C. A., C. Cosewith, and S. S. Kasegrande. 1982. New method for high temperature phase separation of solutions containing copolymer elastomers. U.S. Patent 4,319,021.

Irani, C. A., and E. W. Funk. 1977. Separations using supercritical gases. In *CRC handbook: Recent developments in separation science,* vol. 3, Part A, 171. Boca Raton, FL: CRC Press.

Jacoby, R. H., and M. J. Rzasa. 1952. Equilibrium vaporization ratios for nitrogen, methane, carbon dioxide, ethane and hydrogen sulfide in absorber oil–natural gas and crude oil–natural gas systems. *Trans. AIME, Petrol.* 195:99.

Jentoft, R. E., and T. H. Gouw. 1969. Supercritical fluid chromatography of a "monodisperse" polystyrene. *J. Polym. Sci., Part B* 1:811.

———. 1970. Pressure-programmed supercritical fluid chromatography of wide molecular weight range mixtures. *J. Chromatogr. Sci.* 8:138.

Johnston, K. P. 1984. Supercritical fluids. In *Encyclopedia of Chemical Technology,* 3rd ed., Suppl. vol., p. 872. New York: John Wiley & Sons.

Johnston, K. P., and C. A. Eckert. 1981. An analytical Carnahan-Starling van der Waals model for solubility of hydrocarbon solids in supercritical fluids. *AIChE J.* 27:773.

Johnston, K. P., D. H. Ziger, and C. A. Eckert. 1982. Solubilities of hydrocarbon solids in supercritical fluids: The augmented van der Waals treatment. *Ind. Eng. Chem. Fundam.* 21:191.

Jonas, J. 1981. Critical fluid extraction of ethanol from water. Paper presented at the Central and South Jersey Section of the AIChE, September.

Kander, R. G., and M. E. Paulaitis. 1984. Alcohol-water separations using supercritical fluid solvents. Paper presented at the Annual AIChE Meeting, San Francisco, CA, November.

Kennedy, G. C. 1950. A portion of the system silica-water. *Econ. Geol.* 45:629.

Kim, Y. J., J. A. Carfagno, D. S. McCaffrey, and J. P. Kohn. 1967. Partial miscibility phenomena in the ternary system ethane + n-nonadecane + n-eicosane. *J. Chem. Eng. Data* 12:289.

King, A. D., Jr., and W. W. Robertson. 1962. Solubility of naphthalene in compressed gases. *J. Chem. Phys.* 37:1453.

King, J. W. 1984. Supercritical fluid chromatography measurements—Implications for critical fluid extraction. Paper presented at the 75th AOCS Meeting, Dallas, TX, April.

Kistler, S. S. 1932. Coherent expanded aerogels. *J. Phys. Chem.* 36:52.

Klesper, E., and W. Hartmann. 1977. Supercritical fluid chromatography of styrene oligomers. *Polym. Lett.* 15:9.

Kohn, J. P. 1967. Volumetric and phase equilibria of methane-hydrocarbon binary systems at low temperatures and high pressures. *Chem. Eng. Progr. Symp. Ser.* 63:57.

Kohn, J. P., E. S. Andrle, K. D. Luks, and J. D. Colmenares. 1980. Phase equilibria of ethylene and certain normal paraffins. *J. Chem. Eng. Data* 25:348.

Kohn, J. P., R. C. Merrill, Jr., and K. D. Luks. 1983. Liquid-liquid-vapor equilibria in cryogenic LNG mixtures. Phase III—Nitrogen rich systems. *Research Report* 67, Gas Processors Assoc., May.

Köll, P., and J. Metzger. 1978. Thermal degradation of cellulose and chitin in supercritical acetone. *Angew. Chem. Int. Ed. Engl.* 17:754.

Koningsveld, R., and G. A. M. Diepen. 1983. Supercritical phase behavior involving solids. *J. Fluid Phase Equilib.* 10:159.

Koningsveld, R., G. A. M. Diepen, and H. A. G. Chermin. 1966. Fluid phase equilibria in the system polyethylene-ethylene, II. Rec. Trav. Chim. 85:504.

Koningsveld, R., L. A. Kleintjens, and G. A. M. Diepen. 1984. Solubility of solids in supercritical solvents. I. General principles. *Ber. Bunsenges. Phys. Chem.* 88:848.

Kramer, G. M., and F. Leder. 1975. Paraffin isomerization in supercritical fluids. U.S. Patent 3,880,945.

Krase, N. W. 1945. Separating ethylene polymers. U.S. Patent 2,388,160.

Krase, N. W., and A. E. Lawrence. 1946. Process for the preparation of ethylene polymers. U.S. Patent 2,396,791.

Krukonis, V. J. 1977. A new process for activated carbon regeneration and for recovery of hazardous pesticide wastes. Report to the Environmental Protection Agency, Contract R804-554-010, September.

———. 1981a. Adsorption Isotherm for the caffeine–coffee–carbon dioxide system. Unpubl. data.

———. 1981b. Carbon dioxide extraction of low concentration formamide-water solutions. Unpubl. data.

———. 1981c. Distribution coefficients in the caffeine–water–carbon dioxide system. Unpubl. data.

———. 1981d. Purification of an acrylamide monomer. Unpubl. data.

———. 1981e. Solubility of atactic and isotactic polypropylene in carbon dioxide. Unpubl. data.

———. 1982a. Fractionation of chlorotrifluoroethylene oligomers. Unpubl. data.

———. 1982b. Fractionation of polyphenylmethylsiloxanes OV-17 and SC 2250. Unpubl. data.

———. 1982c. Supercritical fluid processing of dental monomers, silicone lens monomer, and coating monomer. Unpubl. data.

———. 1983a. Adsorption isotherm for the carbon dioxide–caffeine–activated carbon system. Unpubl. data.

———. 1983b. Fractionation of polystyrene. Unpubl. data.

———. 1983c. Supercritical fluid fractionation—An alternative to molecular distillation. Paper presented at AIChE Meeting, Houston, TX, March.

———. 1984a. Polyethylene gel production. Unpubl. data.

————. 1984b. Research on a new process to fractionate polymers. Report prepared for the National Science Foundation, contract CPE-8361087, September.

————. 1984c. Supercritical fluid fractionation of fish oils—Concentration of eicosapentaenoic acid. Paper presented at 75th Annual American Oil Chemists Society Meeting, Dallas, April.

————. 1984d. Supercritical fluid nucleation of difficult-to-comminute solids. Paper presented at the AIChE Annual Meeting, San Francisco, CA, November.

Krukonis, V. J., A. R. Branfman, and M. G. Broome. 1979. Supercritical fluid extraction of plant materials containing chemotherapeutic drugs. Paper presented at the AIChE Meeting, Boston, MA, August.

Krukonis, V. J., and R. T. Kurnik. 1985. Solubility of the solid aromatic isomers in carbon dioxide. *J. Chem. Eng. Data,* 30:247.

Krukonis, V. J., M. A. McHugh, and A. J. Seckner. 1984. Xenon as a supercritical solvent. *J. Phys. Chem.* 88:2687.

Kuenen, J. P., and W. G. Robson. 1899. On the mutual solubility of liquids—Vapour-pressure and critical points. *Philos. Mag.* 6th ser. 48:180.

Kuk, M. S., and J. C. Montagna. 1983. Solubility of oxygenated hydrocarbons in supercritical carbon dioxide. In *Chemical Engineering at supercritical fluid conditions,* ed. M. E. Paulaitis, J. M. L. Penninger, R. D. Gray, and P. Davidson, 101. Ann Arbor, MI: Ann Arbor Science.

Kurnik, R. T. 1981. Supercritical fluid extraction: A study of binary and multicomponent solid-fluid equilibria. Ph.D. diss., Massachusetts Institute of Technology, Cambridge, MA.

Kurnik, R. T., S. J. Holla, and R. C. Reid. 1981. Solubility of solids in supercritical carbon dioxide and ethylene. *J. Chem. Eng. Data* 26:47.

Kurnik, R. T., and R. C. Reid. 1982. Solubility of solid mixtures in supercritical fluids. *J. Fluid Phase Equilib.* 8:93.

Laidler, K. J. 1965. *Chemical Kinetics,* chap. 5. New York: McGraw-Hill Book Co.

Leder, F., G. M. Kramer, and H. J. Solomon. 1976. Hydrocarbon isomerization process. U.S. Patent 3,946,088.

Li, Y.-H., K. H. Dillard, and R. L. Robinson, Jr. 1981. Vapor-liquid phase equilibrium for carbon dioxide–*n*-hexane at 40, 80, and 120°C. *J. Chem. Eng. Data* 26:53.

Liau, I. S., and M. A. McHugh. 1984. High pressure solid polymer–supercritical fluid phase behavior. Paper presented at the AIChE Annual Meeting, San Francisco, CA.

Liphard, K. G., and G. M. Schneider. 1975. Phase equilibria and critical phenomena in fluid mixtures of carbon dioxide + 2,6,10,15,19,23-hexamethyltetracosane up to 423°K and 100 MPA. *J. Chem. Thermodyn.* 7:805.

List, G. R., J. P. Friedrich, and J. Pominski. 1984. Characterization and processing of cottonseed oil obtained by extraction with supercritical carbon dioxide. *J. Am. Oil Chem. Soc.* 61:1847.

Luks, K. D., and J. P. Kohn. 1984. The topography of multiphase equilibria behavior: What can it tell the design engineer. *Proc. 63rd Annu. Convention, Gas Processors Assoc.,* 181.

McCabe, W. L., and J. C. Smith. 1976. *Unit operations of chemical engineering.* New York: McGraw-Hill Book Co.

McClellan, A. K., E. G. Bauman, and M. A. McHugh. 1984. Polymer solution–supercritical fluid phase behavior, Paper presented at the AIChE Annual Meeting, San Francisco, CA.

McClellan, A. K., and M. A. McHugh, 1985. Separating polymer solutions using high pressure LCST phenomena. *J. Polymer Eng. Sci.* 25:1088.

McGrath, J. E., J. S. Riffle, A. K. Banthia, I. Yilgor, and G. L. Wilkes. 1982. An overview of the polymerization of cyclosiloxanes. *Am. Chem. Soc. Symp. Ser.* 212:145.

McHugh, M. A. 1981. An experimental investigation of the high pressure fluid phase equilibrium of highly asymmetric binary mixtures. Ph.D. diss., Univ. of Delaware.

―――. 1984. Calculated phase behavior for the supercritical xenon–naphthalene system. Unpubl. data.

―――. 1986. Extraction with supercritical fluids. In *Recent developments in separation science,* vol. IX, ed. N. N. Li and J. M. Calo., 75. Boca Raton, FL: CRC Press.

McHugh, M. A., and T. L. Guckes. 1985. Separating polymer solutions with supercritical fluids. *Macromolecules* 18:674.

McHugh, M. A., and V. J. Krukonis. 1984. Processing with supercritical fluids. Short course held at the AIChE Annual Meeting in San Francisco, CA, November.

McHugh, M. A., V. J. Krukonis, and P. Davidson. 1985. Extraction with supercritical fluids. Short course held at the University of Notre Dame, April 22–23.

McHugh, M. A., M. W. Mallett, and J. P. Kohn. 1983. High pressure fluid phase equilibria of alcohol–water–supercritical solvent mixtures. In *Chemical engineering at supercritical fluid conditions,* ed. M. E. Paulaitis, J. M. L. Penninger, R. D. Gray, and P. Davidson, 113. Ann Arbor, MI: Ann Arbor Science.

McHugh, M. A., and M. E. Paulaitis. 1980. Solid solubilities of naphthalene and biphenyl in supercritical carbon dioxide. *J. Chem. Eng. Data* 25:326.

McHugh, M. A., A. J. Seckner, and V. J. Krukonis. 1984. Supercritical xenon. Paper presented at the Annual AIChE Meeting, San Francisco, CA, November.

McHugh, M. A., A. J. Seckner, and T. J. Yogan. 1984. High pressure phase behavior of octacosane and carbon dioxide. *Ind. Eng. Chem. Fundam.* 23:493.

McHugh, M. A., and T. J. Yogan. 1984. A study of three-phase solid-liquid-gas equilibria for three carbon dioxide–solid hydrocarbon systems, two ethane–hydrocarbon solid systems, and two ethylene–hydrogen solid systems. *J. Chem. Eng. Data* 29:112.

Mackay, M. E., and M. E. Paulaitis. 1979. Solid solubilities of heavy hydrocarbons in supercritical solvents. *Ind. Eng. Chem. Fundam.* 18:149.

Mansoori, G. A., J. F. Ely, D. S. Hacker, and J. W. King. 1985. Supercritical fluid extraction/retrograde condensation with applications. AIChE Tutorial Symposium, held at the Gas Research Institute, Chicago, IL, May 25.

Merrill, R. C. 1983. Liquid-liquid-vapor phenomena in cryogenic liquefied natural gas systems. Ph.D. diss., Univ. of Notre Dame.

Merrill, R. C., K. D. Luks, and J. P. Kohn. 1983. Three phase liquid-liquid-vapor equilibria in the methane + *n*-pentane + *n*-octane, methane + *n*-hexane + *n*-octane, and methane + *n*-hexane + carbon dioxide systems. *J. Chem. Eng. Data* 28:210.

Metzger, J. O., J. Hartmans, D. Malwitz, and P. Köll. 1983. Thermal organic reactions in supercritical fluids. In *Chemical engineering at supercritical fluid conditions,* ed. M. E. Paulaitis, J. M. L. Penninger, R. D. Gray, and P. Davidson, 515. Ann Arbor, MI: Ann Arbor Science.

Michels and C. Michels. 1937. Series evaluation of the isotherm data of CO_2 between 0 and 150°C and up to 3000 atm. *Proc. R. Soc. London, Ser. A* 160:348.

Modell, M. 1982. Processing methods for the oxidation of organics in supercritical water. U.S. Patent 4,338,199.

Modell, M., R. D. de Fillipi, and V. J. Krukonis. 1978. Regeneration of activated carbon with supercritical carbon dioxide. Paper presented at the ACS Annual Meeting, Miami, FL.

Modell, M., R. J. Robey, V. J. Krukonis, R. D. de Fillipi, and D. Oestereich. 1979. Supercritical Fluid Regeneration of Activated Carbon. Paper presented at National AIChE Meeting, Boston, MA.

Morrison, R. T., and R. N. Boyd. 1983. *Organic chemistry*. Boston: Allyn and Bacon.

Moses, J. M., K. E. Goklen, and R. D. de Fillipi. 1982. Pilot plant critical fluid extraction of organics from water. Paper presented at the Annual AIChE Meeting, Los Angeles, November.

Najour, G. C., and A. D. King, Jr. 1966. Solubility of naphthalene in compressed methane, ethylene, and carbon dioxide: Evidence for a gas-phase complex between naphthalene and carbon dioxide. *J. Chem. Phys.* 45:1915.

Ng, H.-J., and D. B. Robinson. 1978. Equilibrium phase properties at the toluene–carbon dioxide system. *J. Chem. Eng. Data* 23:325.

Occhiogrosso, R. N. 1985. Phase behavior studies of organic hydrocarbon–supercritical carbon dioxide mixtures. M.S. thesis, Univ. of Notre Dame.

Occhiogrosso, R. N., J. T. Igel, and M. A. McHugh, 1986. The phase behavior of isopropyl benzene–CO_2 mixtures. *J. Fluid Phase Equilib.*, 26:165.

Ozawa, S., S. Kusumi, and Y. Ogino. 1974. High pressure adsorption of carbon dioxide on several activated carbons with different pore size distribution. *Proc. 4th Int. Conf. High Pressure, Kyoto, Japan.*

Passino, H. J. 1949. The solexol process. *Ind. Eng. Chem.* 41:280.

Patat, F. 1945. The hydrolysis of analine. *Monatsh. Chem.* 77:352.

Patterson, D. 1968. Role of free volume changes in polymer solution thermodynamics. *J. Polym. Sci., Part C* 16:3379.

———. 1969. Free volume and polymer solubility. A qualitative view. *Macromolecules* 2:672.

Paul, P. M. F., and W. S. Wise. 1971. *The principles of gas extraction*. London: Mills and Boon Ltd.

Paulaitis, M. E., M. L. Gilbert, and C. A. Nash. 1981. Separation of ethanol-water mixtures with supercritical fluids. Paper presented at the 2nd World Congress of Chemical Engineers, Montreal, Canada, October.

Paulaitis, M. E., R. G. Kander, and J. R. DiAndreth. 1984. Phase equilibria related to supercritical-fluid solvent extractions. *Ber. Bunsenges. Phys. Chem.* 88:869.

Paulaitis, M. E., V. J. Krukonis, R. T. Kurnik, and R. C. Reid. 1983a. Supercritical fluid extraction. *Rev. Chem. Eng.* 1:179.

Paulaitis, M. E., and M. A. McHugh. 1981. Practical application of high pressure phase equililbria near the critical region. Paper presented at the 17th State-of-the-Art Symposium, High Pressure as a Reagent and an Environment, American Chemical Society, Washington, DC, June 10.

Paulaitis, M. E., M. A. McHugh, and C. P. Chai. 1983. Solid solubilities in supercritical fluids at elevated pressures. In *Chemical engineering at supercritical fluid conditions*, ed. M. E. Paulaitis, J. M. L. Penninger, R. D. Gray, and P. Davidson, 139. Ann Arbor, MI: Ann Arbor Science.

Paulaitis, M. E., J. M. L. Penninger, R. D. Gray, and P. Davidson, eds. 1983b.

Chemical engineering at supercritical fluid conditions. Ann Arbor, MI: Ann Arbor Science.

Peng, D. Y., and D. B. Robinson. 1976. A new two constant equation of state. *Ind. Eng. Chem. Fundam.* 15:59.

Prasad, R., M. Gottesman, and R. A. Scarella. 1981. Decaffeination of aqueous extracts. U.S. Patent 4,246,291.

Prausnitz, J. M. 1969. *Molecular thermodynamics of fluid-phase equilibria,* chap. 5. Englewood Cliffs, NJ: Prentice-Hall Inc.

Prausnitz, J. M., and P. R. Benson. 1959. Solubility of liquids in compressed hydrogen, nitrogen, and carbon dioxide. *AIChE J.* 5:161.

Prins, A. 1915. On critical end-points and the system ethane-naphthalene. *Proc. Acad. Sci. Amsterdam* 17:1095.

Ramsay, W. 1880. On the critical state of gases. *Proc. R. Soc. London* 30:323.

Rance, R. W., and E. L. Cussler. 1974. Fast fluxes with supercritical solvents. *AIChE J.* 20:353.

Randall, L. G. 1982. The present status of dense (supercritical) gas extraction and dense gas chromatography: Impetus for DGC/MS development. *Sep. Sci. Tech.* 17:1.

Robey, R. J., and S. Sunder. 1984. Applications of supercritical fluid processing to the concentration of citrus oil fractions. Paper presented at the Annual AIChE Meeting, San Francisco, CA, November.

Rodrigues, A. B., and J. P. Kohn. 1967. Three phase equilibria in the binary systems ethane–*n*-docosane and ethane–*n*-octacosane. *J. Chem. Eng. Data* 12:191.

Rodrigues, A. B. J., D. S. McCaffrey, Jr., and J. P. Kohn. 1968. Heterogeneous phase and volumetric equilibrium in the ethane–*n*-octane system. *J. Chem. Eng. Data* 13:164.

Roselius, W., O. Vitzthum, and P. Hubert. 1974. Method for the production of caffeine-free coffee extract. U.S. Patent 3,843,824.

Rowlinson, J. S., and M. J. Richardson. 1958. The solubility of solids in compressed gases. *Adv. Chem. Phys.* 2:85.

Rowlinson, J. S., and F. L. Swinton. 1982. *Liquids and liquid mixtures,* 3rd ed., chap. 6. Boston: Butterworth and Co. Ltd.

Saeki, S., S. Konno, N. Kuwahara, M. Nakata, and M. Kaneko. 1974. Upper and lower critical solution temperatures in polystyrene solutions III. Temperature dependence of the X parameter. *Macromolecules* 7:521.

Saltiel, J., and J. L. Charlton. 1980. *Rearrangements in ground and excited states,* vol. 3, 25–89. New York: Academic Press.

Schmitt, W. J. 1984. The solubility of monofunctional organic compounds in chemically diverse supercritical fluids. Ph.D. diss., Massachusetts Institute of Technology.

Schmitt, W. J., R. A. Greiger-Block, and T. W. Chapman. 1983. The preparation of acid-catalyzed silica aerogel. In *Chemical engineering at supercritical fluid conditions,* ed. M. E. Paulaitis, J. M. L. Penninger, R. D. Gray, Jr., and P. Davidson. Ann Arbor, MI: Ann Arbor Science.

Schmitt, W. J., and R. C. Reid. 1984. The influence of the solvent gas on solubility and selectivity in supercritical extraction. Paper presented at the Annual AIChE Meeting, San Francisco, CA, November.

Schneider, G. M. 1970. Phase equilibria in fluid mixtures at high pressures. *Adv. Chem. Phys.* 17:1.

———. 1978. Physicochemical principles of extraction with supercritical gases. *Angew. Chem. Int. Ed. Engl.* 17:716.

Schneider, G. M., E. Stahl, and G. Wilke, eds. 1980. *Extraction with supercritical gases.* Weinheim, W. Germany: Verlag Chemie.

Scott, R. L. 1972. Thermodynamics of critical phenomena in fluid mixtures. *Ber. Bunsenges. Phys. Chem.* 76:296.

Scott, R. L., and P. B. van Konynenburg. 1970. Static Properties of Solutions—Van der Waals and related models for hydrocarbon mixtures. *Discuss. Faraday Soc.* 49:87.

Sherwood, R. T., R. L. Pigford, and C. K. Wilke. 1975. *Mass transfer.* New York: McGraw-Hill Book Co.

Shimshick, E. J. 1981. Removal of organic acids from dilute aqueous solutions of salts of organic acids by supercritical fluids. U.S. Patent 4,250,331.

Shreve, R. N., and J. A. Brink, Jr. 1977. Chemical process industries. In *Plastics industries.* New York: McGraw-Hill Book Co.

Simmons, G. M., and D. M. Mason. 1972. Pressure dependency of gas phase reaction rate coefficients. *Chem. Eng. Sci.* 27:89.

Simnick, J. J., C. C. Lawson, H. M. Lin, and K. C. Chao. 1977. Vapor-liquid equilibrium of hydrogen/tetralin system at elevated temperatures and pressures. *AIChE J.* 23:469.

Siow, K. S., G. Delmas, and D. Patterson. 1972. Cloud-point curves in polymer solutions with adjacent upper and lower critical solution temperatures. *Macromolecules* 5:29.

Smits, A. 1903. *Z. Electrochem.* 33:91.

Snyder, J. M., J. P. Friedrich, and D. D. Christianson. 1984. Effect of moisture and particle size on the extractability of oil from seeds with supercritical CO_2. *J. Am. Oil Chem. Soc.* 61:1851.

Soave, G. 1972. Equilibrium constants from a modified Redlich-Kwong equation of state. *Chem. Eng. Sci.* 27:1197.

Squires, T. G., C. G. Venier, and T. Aida. 1983. Supercritical fluid solvents in organic chemistry. *J. Fluid Phase Equilib.* 10:261.

Stahl, E., and K. W. Quirin. 1983. Dense gas extraction on a laboratory scale: A survey of some recent results. *J. Fluid Phase Equilib.* 10:269.

Stahl, E., and W. Schilz. 1979. Mikroanalytische Untersuchungen zur Losichkeit von Naturstoffen in überkritischem Kohlendioxid. *Talanta* 26:675.

Stahl, E., K. W. Quirin, A. Glatz, D. Gerard, and G. Rau, 1984. New developments in the field of high pressure extraction of natural products with dense gases. *Ber. Bunsenges. Phys. Chem.* 9:900.

Stahl, E., W. Schilz, E. Schutz, and E. Willing. 1980. A quick method for the microanalytical evaluation of the dissolving power of supercritical gases. In *Extraction with supercritical gases,* ed. G. M. Schneider, E. Stahl, and G. Wilke, 93. Deerfield Beach, FL: Verlag Chemie.

Streett, W. B. 1976. Phase equilibria in gas mixtures at high pressures. *Icarus* 29:173.

———. 1983. Phase equilibria in fluid and solid mixtures at high pressure. In *Chemical engineering at supercritical fluid conditions,* ed. M. E. Paulaitis, J. M. L. Penninger, R. D. Gray, and P. Davidson. Ann Arbor, MI: Ann Arbor Science.

Subramaniam, B., and M. A. McHugh. 1986. Reactions in supercritical fluids—A review. *Ind. Eng. Chem. Proc. Des. Dev.,* 25:1.

Swelheim, T., J. de Swaan Arons, and G. A. M. Diepen. 1965. Fluid phase equililbria in the system polyethene-ethene. *Rec. Trav. Chim.* 84:261.

Takahashi, T. 1980. Absolute rate constants for the free radical polymerization of ethylene in the supercritical phase. Ph.D. diss., State Univ. of New York at Buffalo.

Takahashi, T., and P. Ehrlich. 1982. Absolute rate constants for the free radical polymerization of ethylene in the supercritical phase. *Macromolecules* 15:714.

Tiffin, D. L., A. L. DeVera, K. D. Luks, and J. P. Kohn. 1978a. Phase-equilibria behavior of the binary systems carbon dioxide–*n*-butylbenzene and carbon dioxide–trans-decalin. *J. Chem. Eng. Data* 23:45.

Tiffin, D. L., G. Guzman, K. D. Luks, and J. P. Kohn. 1978b. Phase equilibria behavior of the ternary systems carbon dioxide–trans-decalin–*n*-eicosane and carbon dioxide–trans-decalin–2-methylnaphthalene. *J. Chem. Eng. Data* 23:203.

Tiltscher, H., H. Wolf, and J. Schelchshorn. 1981. A mild and effective method for the reactivation or maintenance of the activity of heterogeneous catalysts. *Angew. Chem. Int. Ed. Engl.* 20:892.

———. 1984. Utilization of supercritical fluid solvent-effects in heterogeneous catalysis. *Ber. Bunsenges. Phys. Chem.* 88:897.

Todd, D. B. 1952. Phase equilibria in systems with supercritical ethylene. Ph.D. diss., Princeton Univ.

Todd, D. B., and J. C. Elgin. 1955. Phase equilibria in systems with ethylene above its critical temperature. *AIChE J.* 1:20.

Treybal, R. E. 1968. *Mass-transfer operations,* 2nd ed., chap. 10. New York: McGraw-Hill Co.

Tsekhanskaya, Yu. V., M. B. Iomtev, and E. V. Mushkina. 1962. Solubility of diphenylamine and naphthalene in carbon dioxide under pressure. *Russ. J. Phys. Chem. (Engl. Transl.)* 36:1177.

———. 1964. Solubility of naphthalene in ethylene and carbon dioxide under pressure. *Russ. J. Phys. Chem. (Engl. Transl.)* 38:1173.

Vaidya, S. N., and G. C. Kennedy. 1971. Compressibility of 18 molecular organic solids to 45 kbar. *J. Chem. Phys.* 55:987.

Valteris, R. L. 1966. The solubility of materials in compressed hydrocarbon gases. *Birmingham Univ. Chem. Eng.* 17:38.

van Gunst, C. A. 1950. The solubility of mixtures of solids in supercritical gases. Ph.D. diss., Delft Univ., Netherlands.

van Gunst, C. A., F. E. C. Scheffer, and G. A. M. Diepen. 1953a. On critical phenomena of saturated solutions in binary systems—II. *J. Phys. Chem.* 57:578.

———. 1953b. On critical phenomena of saturated solutions in ternary systems. *J. Phys. Chem.* 57:581.

van Hest, J. A. M., and G. A. M. Diepen. 1963. Solubility of naphthalene in supercritical methane. *Symp. Soc. Chem. Ind., London* 10.

Van Leer, R. A., and M. E. Paulaitis. 1980. Solubilities of phenol and chlorinated phenols in supercritical carbon dioxide. *J. Chem. Eng. Data* 25:257.

van Welie, G. S. A., and G. A. M. Diepen. 1961a. The *P-T-x* space model of the system ethylene naphthalene (I). *Rec. Trav. Chim.* 80:659.

———. 1961b. The *P-T-x* space model of the system ethylene naphthalene (II). *Rec. Trav. Chim.* 80:666.

———. 1961c. The *P-T-x* space model of the system ethylene naphthalene (III). *Rec. Trav. Chim.* 80:673.

———. 1961d. The *V-T-x* space model of the system ethylene naphthalene (I). *Rec. Trav. Chim.* 80:683.

———. 1961e. The *V-T-x* space model of the system ethylene naphthalene (II). *Rec. Trav. Chim.* 80:693.

————. 1963. The solubility of naphthalene in supercritical ethane. *J. Phys. Chem.* 67:755.

Villard, P. 1896. Solubility of liquids and solids in gas. *J. Phys.* 5:455.

Villard, P. 1888. "On some new gas hydrates," *Comptes Rendus des Séances de L'Académie des Sciences,* 106:1602.

von Tapavicza, S., and J. M. Prausnitz. 1976. Thermodynamics of polymer solutions: An introduction. *Int. Eng. Chem.* 16:329.

Wagner, J. R., Jr., D. S. McCaffrey, Jr., and J. P. Kohn. 1968. Partial miscibility phenomena in the ternary system ethane–*n*-hexadecane–*n*-eicosane. *J. Chem. Eng. Data* 13:22.

Weinstock, J. J. 1952. Phase equilibrium at eleveted pressure in ternary systems of ethylene and water and organic liquids. Ph.D. diss., Princeton Univ.

Williams, D. F. 1981. Extraction with supercritical gases. *Chem. Eng. Sci.* 36:1769.

Wilson, R. E., P. C. Keith, and R. E. Haylett. 1936. Liquid propane—Use in dewaxing, deasphalting, and refining heavy oils. *Ind. Eng. Chem.* 28:1065.

Winkler, D. E., and G. W. Hearne. 1958. Tert-butyl hydroperoxide. U.S. Patent 2,845,461.

————. 1961. Liquid phase oxidation of isobutane. *Ind. Eng. Chem.* 53:655.

Wolf, B. A., J. W. Breitenbach, and H. Senftl. 1970. Upper and lower solubility gaps in the system butanone-acetone-polystyrene. *J. Polym. Sci., Part C* 31:345.

Wolkomir, R. 1984. Supercritical potato chips. *Omni,* 28. July.

Yang, H., K. D. Luks, and J. P. Kohn. 1976. Phase-equilibria behavior of the system carbon dioxide–*n*-butylbenzene–2-methylnapthalene. *J. Chem. Eng. Data* 21:330.

Yates, R. A. 1981. Removal and Concentration of Lower Molecular Weight Organic Acids from Dilute Solutions. U.S. 4, 282, 323.

Zarah, B. Y., K. D. Luks, and J. P. Kohn. 1974. Phase equilibria behavior of carbon dioxide in binary and ternary systems with several hydrocarbon components. *AIChE Symp. Ser.* 70, no. 140, 90.

Zeman, L., J. Biros, G. Delmas, and D. Patterson. 1972. Pressure effects in polymer solution phase equilibria. I. The lower critical solution temperature of polyisobutylene and poly-dimethylsiloxane. *J. Phys. Chem.* 76:1206.

Zeman, L., and D. Patterson. 1972. Pressure effects in polymer solution phase equilibria. II. Systems showing upper and lower critical solution temperatures. *J. Phys. Chem.* 76:1214.

Zosel, K. 1981. Process for the decaffeination of Coffee. U.S. Patent 4,260,639.

————. 1982. Process for the direct decaffeination of aqueous coffee extract solutions. U.S. Patent 4,348,422.

During the past fifty years or so at least two hundred patents have been issued on supercritical, near critical, or "para-critical" extraction and separation processes. Some were issued in the early '30's and are quite well known. We have searched the technical literature and the Official Gazette reasonably thoroughly to find the not yet widely referenced patents of the '70's to mid '80's. Inevitably, we missed some and space constraints prevented us from reviewing all the ones we found. However, we feel that the patents presented in this section are a good representation of the patent literature on supercritical fluids.

For a patent to be considered and included in this appendix the process described in the patent must utilize the separations advantage of operating in the critical region.

The ninety-five patents chosen describe quite diverse processes and represent many sectors of industry. We made our final selection for a variety of reasons; some of the patents are quite important and describe processes in use today, many have passed their seventeen year life but are interesting for historical or technical reasons, and some are chosen for their quite unusual application of super-critical fluids.

Patents usually follow a standard format. They contain a "Background" or "Prior Art" section that describes "old" processes noting their limitations and problems, an "Invention" section that describes the "new" process often including "Examples" of reduction to practice, and the "Claims" section that defines quantitatively the conditions and limits of the Invention. The information in a patent is reviewed by patent examiners, who frequently require that the limits of the claims be revised before the patent is issued. Even with this review process the limits of the claims are frequently much wider than covered in the Examples section. Not all patents have been reduced to practice, and we have included several of these which we refer to as "thought" patents. Some of the patents can work as described even though no data are presented; some cannot work even though "data" are presented.

Occasionally the Background section exaggerates the limitations of the "old" processes, and occasionally the Invention section makes liberal use of adjectives such as "surprising" and "unexpected" in presenting the results. Quite often the exclamations of surprise derive from an inappropriate comparison of "new" and "old" results. We present some commentary when we feel that "surprise" of the technical findings is unwarranted because of information that existed in the literature at the time of the filing, or when we can show that the "surprise" derives from comparing sets of data that have no relevance to each other. Patents are an excellent source of information, but each one must be read carefully and evaluated critically.

Now to the format of this Appendix. To provide the maximum amount of information (under a space constraint) we reproduce the face page of the patent, and on the facing page we explain the process usually with reference to a drawing that is on the patent face page. The patents are discussed in the following order:

1. "The Zosel patent," U.S. 3,969,196; we could make a separate appendix for this 30 page patent which includes 68 examples that describe all sorts of extractions and separations; we limit our discussion of this patent to three pages. It is must(!) reading for serious researchers and managers.
2. Petroleum and other fossil fuel separations.
3. Coffee decaffeination.
4. Extraction of vegetable and animal materials, e.g., spices, oil seeds, tobacco, wood, hops, animal fats, etc.
5. Polymer processing.
6. Separation of organic-water solutions.
7. Miscellaneous — the commonality in this section is the diversity of the patents. For example, patents describing a coal slurry combustion process, the dry cleaning of clothes with carbon dioxide, the separation of inorganic salts from water, and the growth of crystals from supercritical solution are grouped together.

Within each category of patents we generally follow the chronology of dates, but we deviate from chronology if material in a later patent helps explain an earlier one more easily. In discussing some of the patents we draw upon the literature for additional information. If a reference has been cited previously in this book, we refer to it in the normal manner, i.e., (author, year). If it is being cited for the first time in the patent discussion or if we present data that have not yet been published, we give the entire reference in the text. Finally, some of the patent face pages that are reproduced in this appendix are photographs of reproductions which themselves come from other reproductions. The detail on certain face pages may be lacking, but we think this will not detract from the discussion of the patent.

It is noted that this Appendix draws on information covered in many of the chapters of this book; therefore, the

critique and commentary of the patents will be more
meaningful if the material in the book is studied first.

Zosel, K., Process for the separation of mixtures of
substances, U.S. 3,969,196 (July 13, 1976).

United States Patent [19]

Zosel

[11]　**3,969,196**

[45]　**July 13, 1976**

[54]　**PROCESS FOR THE SEPARATION OF MIXTURES OF SUBSTANCES**

[75]　Inventor:　**Kurt Zosel,** Oberhausen-Rhineland, Germany

[73]　Assignee:　**Studiengesellschaft Kohle m.b.H.,** Mulheim (Ruhr), Germany

[22]　Filed:　**Dec. 9, 1969**

[21]　Appl. No.: **880,475**

Related U.S. Application Data

[63]　Continuation of Ser. No. 359,680, April 14, 1964, abandoned.

[30]　　**Foreign Application Priority Data**

Apr. 16, 1963	Austria	3085/63
July 26, 1963	Austria	6005/63
July 26, 1963	Austria	6006/63
Aug. 7, 1963	Austria	6366/63
Nov. 20, 1963	Austria	9310/63
Dec. 18, 1963	Austria	10203/63

[52]　U.S. Cl. 203/49; 208/308; 208/337

[51]　Int. Cl.² B01D 3/24; C10G 21/14

[58]　Field of Search 203/49; 62/16; 208/356

[56]　　　**References Cited**

UNITED STATES PATENTS

2,166,160	7/1939	King	208/313
2,242,173	5/1941	Buckley	62/16
2,391,576	12/1945	Katz et al	62/16
2,391,607	12/1945	Whaley	208/356
2,596,785	5/1952	Nelly, Jr. et al.	62/28 X
2,916,887	12/1959	Brooke	62/28 X

Primary Examiner—Norman Yudkoff
Assistant Examiner—J. Sofer
Attorney, Agent, or Firm—Burgess, Dinklage & Sprung

[57]　　　**ABSTRACT**

The process of separating a mixture which is in liquid state or solid state or liquid and solid state and contains at least one compound containing an organic group, which comprises

a. contacting said mixture with a gas maintained under supercritical conditions of temperature and pressure such that the gas will take up at least a portion of said mixture in a quantity varying inversely with said temperature, and effecting said contacting in a manner so that this occurs, and so that there is a substantial gas component that is identifiable as gas phase,

b. separating the gas in the form of said identifiable gas phase loaded with the compound taken up during said contacting from any of the mixture not taken up by the gas while still maintaining supercritical conditions as aforesaid,

c. thereafter separating the compound from the gas.

　　24 Claims, 6 Drawing Figures

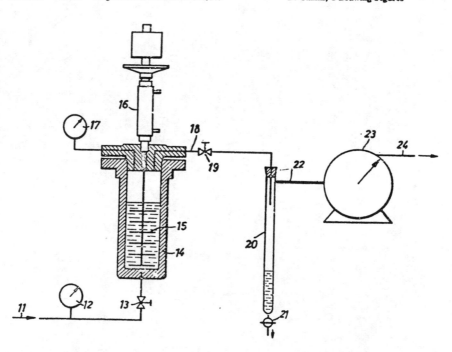

As we related in the introduction to Appendix A, this patent should be read by everyone involved in research and process development using supercritical fluids.

In his examples Zosel describes results on neat solubility, separations of liquids and solids, fractionation, etc. A wealth of information on the effects of various gases, e.g., ethylene, ammonia, ethane, carbon dioxide, in dissolving a variety of compounds is given. Several interesting experiments carried out in a plexiglass autoclave are described, and certain phase separations are noted. Some of the information can be found in other references, of course, but not in such succinct form.

It is of teaching value to reproduce one of the examples here.

Example 66

A stream of CF_3Cl is passed at $42^\circ C$ and 1000 psi through 20 ml of paraffin oil contained in a 50 ml. pressure vessel of plexiglass. The increase in volume of the paraffin oil occurring thereby is hardly noticeable. The supercritical gas withdrawn discharges paraffin oil, the amount of which is low, however, corresponding to the low degree of solvation. When increasing the pressure to about 1075 psi the density of the supercritical gas phase is higher than that of the paraffin oil. This has the result that the paraffin oil migrates to the top of the pressure vessel while the supercritical gaseous trifluorochloromethane is present below it at the bottom. Thus, continuous treatment of the paraffin oil with the supercritical gas requires reversal of the direction of flow of the supercritical gas stream. This example shows that even reversal of the relative densities between the inert gas phase and the mixture of substances to be separated can be achieved by selecting appropriate process conditions.

Many such observations and a quite detailed Invention section make this patent a valuable source of information. There are, however, a few examples which are not accurate, and we reproduce one below.

Example 61

Ethylene is passed through a mixture of 300 ml of water and 300 ml of ethanol contained in the apparatus shown in FIG. 1, the temperature being $20^\circ C$ and the pressure 2860 psi. The ethylene withdrawn did not take up ethanol which has been retained by the water wherein it is dissolved. The situation is the same if methanol is substituted for ethanol under

the same conditions and with the same relative
proportions.

If a mixture comprising water and propanol in
the same relative proportions is treated under
exactly the same operating conditions, 100 gms of
ethylene withdrawn discharge as much as 70 ml of 90%
propanol as determined by hydrometer. If a
corresponding mixture of water and butanol is treated
under the same conditions, 100 gm of ethylene
withdrawn discharge about 106 ml of butanol. The
significance of the hydroxyl group in proportion to
the hydrocarbon radical of the compound is clearly
obvious in this case. If the hydrocarbon radical
where solvation with the molecules of the
supercritical gas phase is initiated is not very
large, the linkage force of the hydroxyl group to
adjacent molecules predominates and the compound is
not taken up in the supercritical gas phase. However,
if the hydrocarbon radical becomes greater, this
solvation effect outweighs the additional hindrances
derived from the present hydroxyl group and the
compounds are taken up in the supercritical gas
phase.

This additional hindrance to being taken up in
the supercritical gas phase cannot only be attributed
to hydroxyl groups. A corresponding phenomenon is
also observed if a 1:1 mixture of acetone and water
is treated with supercritical ethylene at $20^{o}C$ and
2340 psi. Here again, acetone is not discharged by
the ethylene.

Zosel's explanation is generally accurate i.e.,
concerning the ratio of the hydrocarbon radical to the
hydroxyl group. However, ethanol can be extracted from
ethanol-water solutions by supercritical ethylene
(Paulaitis, Gilbert, and Nash, 1981) and so can acetone from
acetone-water solution (Elgin and Weinstock, 1959); a few
such inaccuracies still do not detract from the vast amount
of data that Zosel provides.

The first claim of the patent is also reproduced here
because of its teaching value.

What is claimed is:

1. The process of separating a mixture which is in
liquid state or solid state or liquid and solid state
composed of a plurality of compounds at least one of which
contains an organic group which comprises:

    a. contacting said mixture with a gas phase
        preferentially taking up said compound containing
        an organic group at the contacting conditions, said
        gas phase during said contacting being maintained

under supercritical conditions of temperature and
pressure such that the gas takes up at least a
portion of said compound containing an organic
group, the temperature being in a range in which
the quantity of said compound containing an organic
group taken up by said gas phase varies inversely
with said temperature, and effecting said contacting in a manner so that this occurs, and so
that there is a substantial gas component that is
identifiable as a gaseous component, the critical
temperature of said gas phase being in the range of
$0^{\circ}-200^{\circ}C$, the temperature of said gas phase during
said contacting being within about $100^{\circ}C$ above the
critical temperature.

b. separating the gas phase in the form of said
identifiable gaseous component loaded with said
portion of the compound containing an organic group
taken up during said contacting from any of the
mixture not taken up by the gas phase while still
maintaining supercritical conditions as aforesaid,

c. thereafter separating at least part of the compound
containing an organic group taken up, from the gas
phase.

Note that the claim covers only the retrograde region
of solubility behavior.

Auerbach, E.B., Process for treating, separating, and purifying oils, U.S. 1,805,751 (May 19, 1931).

Sullivan, F.W., Jr., Solvent fractionation, U.S. 2,034,495 (Mar, 17, 1936).

Lantz, V., Extraction process, U.S. 2,188,051 (Jan. 23, 1940).

Pilat, S. and M. Godlewicz, Method of separating high molecular weight mixtures, U.S. 2,188,013 (Jan. 23, 1940).

Lorenz, H.W.F., Apparatus for gaseous extraction, U.S. 2,194,708 (Mar. 26, 1940).

Van Dijck, W.J.D., Process for separating high molecular weight mixtures, U.S. 2,281,865 (May 5, 1942).

Lewis, W.K., Process for treating hydrocarbons with light hydrocarbons, U.S. 2,284,583 (May 26, 1942).

Katz, D.L. and T.H. Whaley, High pressure separation, U.S. 2,391,576 (Dec. 25, 1945).

Leonard, R.E., Energy efficient process for separating hydrocarbonaceous materials into various fractions, U.S. 4,305,814 (Dec. 15, 1981).

Gearhart, J.A., Solvent deasphalting, U.S. 4,239,616 (Dec. 16, 1980).

Leonard, R.E., Supercritical process for producing deasphalted demetallized and deresined oils, U.S. 4,290,880 (Sept. 22, 1981).

Roach, J.W., Fractionating coal liquefaction products with light organic solvents, U.S. 3,607,717 (Sept. 21, 1971).

Gearhart, J.A., Process for separating bituminous materials with solvent recovery, U.S. 4,278,529 (Jul. 14, 1981).

Roach, J.W., Process for separating bituminous materials, U.S. 4,279,739 (Jul. 21, 1981).

Audeh, C.A. and T.Y. Yan, Supercritical selective extraction of hydrocarbons from asphaltic petroleum oils, U.S. 4,354,928 (Oct. 19, 1982).

Poska, F.L., Supercritical tar sand extraction, U.S. 4,341,619 (Jul. 27, 1982).

Warzel, F.M., Discharge of solids, U.S. 4,397,731 (Aug. 9, 1983).

Kramer, G.M. and F. Leder, Paraffin isomerization in supercritical fluids, U.S. 3,880,945 (Apr. 29, 1975).

Zosel, K., Process for the production of aluminum alkyl compounds, U.S. 3,597,464 (Aug. 3, 1971).

Diaz, F. and J.H. Miller, Drying substantially supercritical CO_2 with glycerol, U.S. 4,478,612 (Oct. 23, 1984).

Weeter, R.F., Method for producing carbon dioxide from subterranean formations, U.S. 4,235,289 (Nov. 25, 1980).

Parrish, D.R., Method for enhanced oil recovery, U.S. 4,344,486 (Aug. 17, 1982).

Paspek, S.C., Jr., Oligomerization of olefins in supercritical water, U.S. 4,465,888 (Aug. 14, 1984).

Paspek, S.C., Jr., Upgrading heavy hydrocarbons with supercritical water and light olefins, U.S. 4,483,761 (Nov. 20, 1984).

Coenan, H., R. Hagen, and E. Kriegal, Supercritical extraction and simultaneous catalytic hydrogenation of coal, U.S. 4,485,003 (Nov. 27, 1984).

Zarchy, A.S., Process for producing high yield of gas turbine fuel from residual oil, U.S. 4,528,100 (Jul. 9, 1985).

Stearns, R.S. and E.J. Hollstein, Coal extraction process, U.S. 4,192,731 (Mar. 11, 1980).

Beggs, J.A., W.H. Corcoran, W.S. Fong, P. Pichaichanarong, P.C.F. Chen, and D.D. Lawson, Supercritical multicomponent solvent coal extraction, U.S. 4,388,171 (Jun. 14, 1983).

Francis, A.W., Solvent extraction, U.S. 2,698,277 (Dec. 28, 1954).

Roach, J.W., Recovery of organic solvents from liquid mixtures, U.S. 4,508,597 (Apr. 2, 1985).

Peter, S., Process for the catalytic gasification of solid fluids with steam, U.S. 4,508,543 (Apr. 2, 1985).

May 19, 1931.   E. B. AUERBACH   1,805,751

PROCESS FOR TREATING, SEPARATING, AND PURIFYING OILS

Filed Sept. 8, 1927

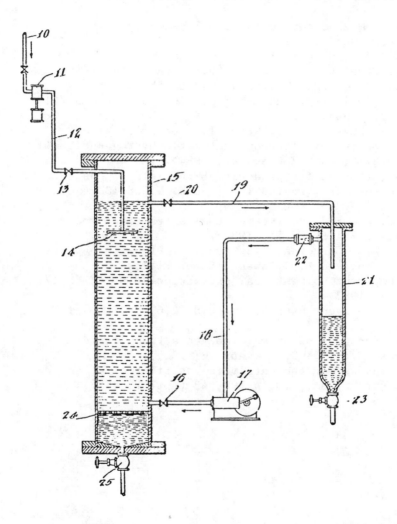

Inventor

Ernst B. Auerbach

By   Lyon & Lyon

Attorneys

This is the oldest patent discussed in this appendix, and it is quickly read that the patent was filed in 1927. When we covered the propane deasphalting process in Chapter 7, we selected some paragraphs from a literature reference that accurately described the technical facets of the process as well as the excitement of the researchers who reported the results (Wilson, Keith, and Haylett, 1936). We have selected a few paragraphs from this patent for the same purpose; the patentee writes,

"An object of this invention is to disclose a process by means of which oils may be treated and purified without the use of distillation or chemical decomposition. Another object is to disclose a novel method of separating oils substantially in the order of molecular weights of constituent parts thereof.

"I have discovered that the various constituents of oils show a very definite solubility in liquid carbon dioxide, and consequently I have invented a process of separating oils. I have found that my process enables me to separate different oils from each other not only ... in accordance with chemical composition ... but in proportion to the molecular weight."

Auerbach investigated fatty oils, terpenes, tar oil, resin oils, ester oils, etc., in the apparatus shown schematically on the patent face page. Operation is as follows: oil is supplied to the extractor 15 from line 10 and pressurized to extractor conditions by the pump 11 and distributed through the header 14. Carbon dioxide is pumped 17 to the lower section of the extractor. During the counter current extraction sequence, the carbon dioxide dissolves the soluble constituents of the oil, and the undissolved constituents travel downward and pass through the perforated plate 24. The extract leaves the vessel through line 19, is reduced in pressure through valve 20, and is discharged into the separator vessel 21, where the carbon dioxide is vaporized and recycled; the separated oil is removed via valve 23.

Many examples are given in the patent, and one is selected to show the separation of materials by molecular weight. 5 kgs of mineral lubricating oil which had an original viscosity of 5.2 cps was treated with 15 kgs of liquid carbon dioxide. 0.5 kg of oil with viscosity 2.2 cps was obtained from the carbon dioxide extract and the residual 4.5 kgs had a viscosity of 5.9 cps. (In a homologous series, increasing viscosity is a measure of increasing molecular weight.)

March 17, 1936.   F. W. SULLIVAN, JR   2,034,495

SOLVENT FRACTIONATION

Filed Aug. 31, 1933   2 Sheets—Sheet 1

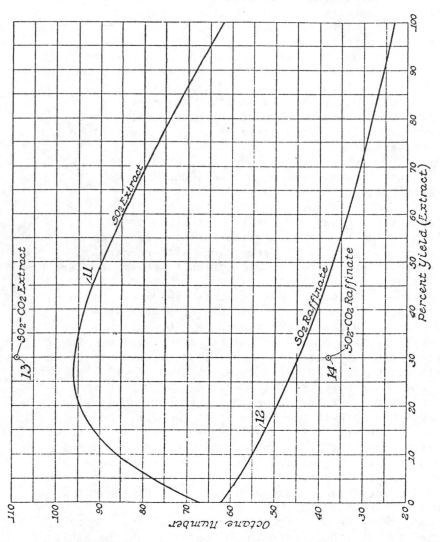

FIG. 1

INVENTOR
Frederick W. Sullivan, Jr.
BY
Bruce K. Brown
ATTORNEY

This patent describes results of extracting hydro-carbons with a mixture of two solvents, sulfur dioxide and carbon dioxide. Although the mixture is at conditions well below critical, the patent is included because it points out that liquid carbon dioxide was quite prevalently studied in the '30's.

Liquid sulfur dioxide has been used in refinery operations since the 1920's. The patentee describes that in the fractionation of motor fuel stocks only about 25% yield of a high (97) octane fuel can be obtained with sulfur dioxide at an extraction temperature of -65°C. The figure on the patent face page shows the yield-octane number curves for extraction of a motor fuel stock obtained from a cracking process using SO_2. Curve 11 is the extract yield curve and curve 12 is the corresponding raffinate octane number whose yield is equal to 100 minus the percent yield of extract. The patentee relates that -65°C is about the lowest temperature that can be reached with SO_2 alone, but he also relates that extraction at a lower temperature with SO_2 alone does not improve the yield or the octane number.

The invention is the use of a mixture of CO_2 and SO_2; with a mixture of CO_2 and SO_2 over a range of 1:1 to 1:5 CO_2/SO_2, higher yields and/or higher octane number are achieved than with SO_2 alone. Points 13 and 14 shown in the figure give the extract and raffinate yields and octane numbers when the separation is carried out with the mixture, and it is seen that a higher octane number in the extract is achieved.

Jan. 23, 1940.   V. LANTZ   2,188,051

EXTRACTION PROCESS

Original Filed Nov. 1, 1937   2 Sheets—Sheet 1

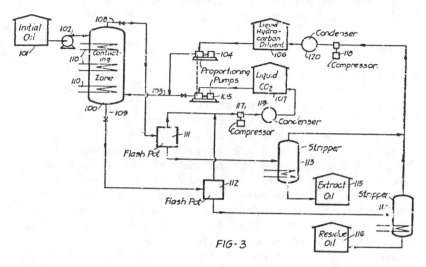

FIG-3

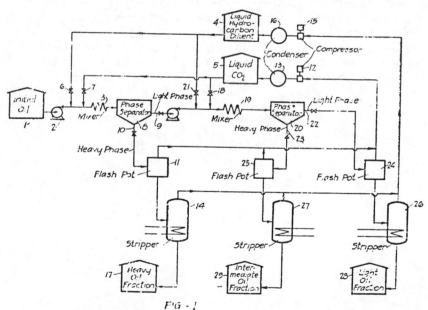

FIG - 1

Inventor:

Vernon Lantz

By his Attorney

This patent (like several others on hydrocarbon processing that we discuss) cites the Auerbach process in the prior art. The discussion in the patent relates that the Auerbach process suffers from the requirement of substantial carbon dioxide to separate the oil constituents. The new process utilizes a light liquid hydrocarbon plus carbon dioxide as the "extractant." The oil to be separated is dissolved in the hydrocarbon; the carbon dioxide is dissolved in the oil-hydrocarbon solution to lower the dissolving power of the hydrocarbon and, thus, to precipitate the oil.

Referring to Figure 1 (at the bottom of the page), oil from tank 1 is fed via pump 2 to a mixer 3 where it is mixed with liquid hydrocarbon from tank 4 (conveyed through valve 6) and with liquid carbon dioxide from tank 5 (conveyed through valve 7). The resulting mixture is conveyed to a phase separator where a light and heavy phase separate. The light phase consisting of carbon dioxide, hydrocarbon, and some light oil is withdrawn via valve 9 and pumped to another mixer where more hydrocarbon is added via valve 21 and carbon dioxide is added via valve 18. The mixture is sent to another phase separator 20 where another light phase and heavy phase form and are separated. The light phase consisting of carbon dioxide, hydrocarbon solvent, and lightest oil is sent to a flash pot 24 where carbon dioxide is separated and returned to the storage vessel, and the lightest oil-hydrocarbon stream sent to stripper 26 where solvent removal is effected and the oil is conveyed to vessel 28 for storage. The heavy phases leaving phase separators 8 and 20 are processed identically to the lightest phase as can be seen in the figure.

A number of examples give results, and the patentee shows that with isopentane plus carbon dioxide a separation into fractions can be made with much less carbon dioxide than for the pure carbon dioxide case.

Patented Jan. 23, 1940

2,188,013

UNITED STATES PATENT OFFICE

2,188,013

METHOD OF SEPARATING HIGH MOLECULAR MIXTURES

Stanislaw Pilat and Marian Godlewicz, Lwow, Poland, assignors to Shell Development Company, San Francisco, Calif., a corporation of Delaware

No Drawing. Application April 27, 1936, Serial No. 76,004. Renewed May 1, 1939. In Poland February 6, 1933

20 Claims.   (Cl. 196—13)

This invention pertains to a method of separating mixtures of high molecular substances into two or more fractions having different chemical and/or physical properties, and is a continuation-in-part of our application Serial No. 709,988 filed January 30, 1934.

Industrial materials which contain complex mixtures of organic or inorganic compounds may be separated into desirable fractions containing concentrates of one or more pure substances, or of one or more groups of substances which have similar physical properties and/or chemical compositions by many known methods, such as distillation, crystallization, treatment with selective solvents, adsorption, etc.

The known processes for effecting these separations have many limitations. For example, distillation methods often result in a decomposition of the materials being treated, and is, moreover, ineffective to separate substances having the same or almost the same vapor pressures; the degree of separation effected by crystallization methods and selective solvent extraction methods is such, that the products must often be further treated to obtain products of the desired purity; and considerable losses are often involved in the use of adsorption methods.

According to the present invention we provide a new and convenient method of separating high molecular mixtures into portions of different properties by means of gaseous carbon dioxide or a gas containing carbon dioxide and preferably of inert non-oxidizing character. Other objects of our invention will be apparent from a reading of the following specifications.

Our invention may, for example, be applied to the separation of liquid or meltable high molecular mixtures, or high molecular mixtures which may be brought into solution by the use of suitable solvents, such as crude mineral oils, their distillates or residues, mineral oil fractions obtained by extraction of petroleum oils, shale oils, and other hydrocarbon and non-hydrocarbon mixtures, like coal tar, coal tar oils, animal and vegetable oils, such as neat's foot oil, linseed oil, rapeseed oil, voltolized rapeseed oil and other mixtures of fatty acids, esters, phenols, alcohols, organic nitrogen-containing substances, chlor-derivatives, pharmaceutical preparations, preparations obtained from living organisms, such as, for example, hormones, and many other chemicals. The process may be applied to separate mixtures of different chemical classes of substances, or to free materials from impurities, or to separate mixtures of homologous or analogous

chemical groups. Thus, hydrocarbons may be separated from mixtures of hydrocarbons and the above non-hydrocarbons.

Our process is based upon our discovery that high molecular mixtures can be separated into portions containing substances of different molecular weights and/or chemical structure, by treating the mixture, while in the liquid state, under superatmospheric pressure with gaseous carbon dioxide under conditions which cause a lowering in the density of the mixture, thereby causing the mixture to "demix", i. e., to separate into two or more liquid phases of different densities, of which the lighter phase contains the greater part of carbon dioxide. Considerable advantages are inherent in our method of treatment, one of which is that relatively low pressures (far below liquefaction pressures of said gaseous substances) and ordinary or elevated temperatures (generally not exceeding 200° C.) may be employed in carrying out the process of our invention. No chemical changes are involved in separating mineral oils by the method of our invention, the treatment being a physical and not chemical type.

Briefly, the invention consists of introducing into a high molecular mixture gaseous carbon dioxide or a gas containing carbon under a superatmospheric pressure until a concentration is reached at which the mixture separates into two liquid phases of different specific gravities. Relative quantities and compositions of the components of the high molecular mixture in the phases are regulated by maintaining suitable treating temperatures and pressures, as well as by selecting or regulating the composition of the gaseous carbon dioxide.

The process can be modified by dissolving the mixture to be treated in a suitable solvent which may be of the type of known deasphalting agents, such as normally liquid or liquefied hydrocarbons, as propane, propylene, normal or iso-butanes, butylenes, normal or iso-pentanes, hexanes, or their mixture, light straight run naphthas, or other light aromatic-free fractions of mineral oil; or said solvent may be chosen from a group of what are known as selective or naphthenic solvents, such as liquid SO_2, furfural, nitrobenzene, chlorex, cresylic acid, phenol, aniline, and a large number of others, their mixtures, or solutions with diluents; we also found, that in practicing our invention auxiliary treating agents of the type of oil decolorizing agents, such as fuller's earth, naphthalene, phenacthrene, dinitrobenzene, and the like, may be ad-

Although the reproduction of the patent face page lacks clarity in some regions, it is readable; there is no drawing to show the operation of the invention but operation is described quite well in the first, second, and third paragraphs of the right hand column.

On page 3 of the patent, the patentees write,

"We are aware of the U.S. patent to Auerbach, No. 1,805,751 disclosing the extraction of oil with liquefied carbon dioxide. However, our invention, as described, is directed to the method of fractionating mineral oils under conditions at which the gaseous carbon dioxide is incapable of being liquefied. When higher pressures are necessary to effect the desired fractionation, our process may be operated at temperatures which are above $31^{\circ}C$, the critical temperature of carbon dioxide."

This is the earliest reference in the patent literature that we located on the use of supercritical (i.e., gaseous) carbon dioxide to separate hydrocarbons.

March 26, 1940.   H. W. F. LORENZ   2,194,708

APPARATUS FOR GASEOUS SOLVENT EXTRACTION

Filed Sept. 22, 1936

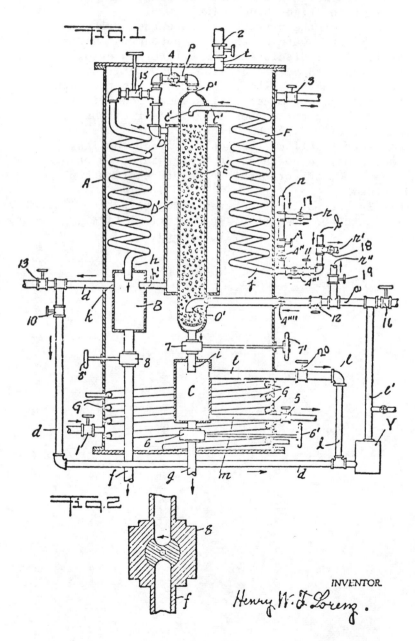

INVENTOR

Henry W. F. Lorenz.

This patent is one that we have chosen to include for its historical and teaching value. The apparatus on the face page is explained in much detail in the body of the patent. In brief summary, E' is the extractor which is fed with gaseous solvent at O' and with feed at C'; the extract leaves at P' and the raffinate through valve 7.

We think it is quite interesting to present several statements that Lorenz writes about the workings of his gaseous solvent; we have stated many times that solubility phenomena in supercritical fluids were not only known, but applied, many, many years ago. His statements,

"Before specifically describing my apparatus for continuous gaseous solvent extraction ... I desire to first elucidate the purposes of its use and to give a clear understanding of the subject and the principles involved ...

"Andrews proposed many years ago the use of the word 'gas' for a fluid at any temperature above its critical point ... For every 'gas' there is a certain temperature above which, no matter how high the pressure, it cannot be liquefied even under the greatest pressure ...

"'Gases' when under pressure, and especially high pressures, can possess a high solvent power ... even for bodies possessing little or no volatility the dissolving power may be considerable ..."

Lorenz goes on to relate the pressure dependent dissolving power, the ability to separate by molecular weight, the separation of phases, etc. He discussed the mixing of gases as a means of varying the solvent properties (in addition to changing temperature and pressure), and he relates "that it must also be kept in mind that the extract dissolved in the gaseous solvent has its effect markedly on the critical point of the gas mixture." He presents as two examples that by adding one drop of ethanol the critical temperature of a certain volume of chloroform is reduced $4^{\circ}C$ whereas its boiling point is reduced only $0.2^{\circ}C$, and that the addition of the drop of ethanol to a volume of ethyl chloride raises the critical temperature $7^{\circ}C$ whereas the boiling point is raised only $1^{\circ}C$.

Many researchers ignore this effect of dissolving a liquid in a supercritical fluid; although the solvent may enter an extractor at supercritical conditions, the solvent rich stream leaving the extractor is almost assuredly not supercritical.

May 5, 1942.   W. J. D. VAN DIJCK   2,281,865

PROCESS FOR SEPARATING HICH MOLECULAR MIXTURES

Filed March 20, 1936   2 Sheets—Sheet 1

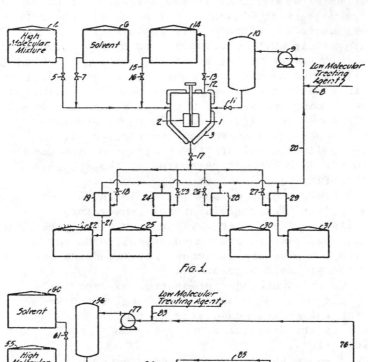

FIG. 1.

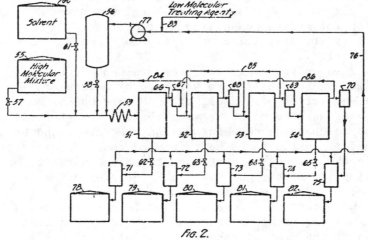

FIG. 2.

Inventor: Willem J.D. Van Dijck

By his Attorney:

The process described is somewhat similar to the propane deasphalting process. The first claim describes the use of a "low molecular weight treating agent in its paracritical state." Some of the patents have described paracritical to be slightly below the critical temperature; this one defines the state to be at a temperature above the critical temperature. The treating agent is used to dissolve a portion of a high molecular weight mixture and subsequently in another step the pressure is reduced to precipitate part of the extracted material.

The figure on the face page shows the process as operated with a solution of a high molecular weight material dissolved in a liquid hydrocarbon solvent. The examples, however, describe only the case of contacting the high molecular weight mixture with the low molecular weight treating agent without the liquid hydrocarbon solvent.

Examples of separating vegetable oils, stand oil, and lubricating oil residues are given; in each case, the first step in the process uses liquid propane (or some other low molecular weight treating agent) to dissolve part of the oils. The extract stream is raised in conditions to above the critical point before carrying out stage wise pressure reduction.

As we see again, the principles and applications of supercritical fluid solubility phenomena were quite well understood at the time of the filing of this patent, March 1936.

May 26, 1942.   W. K. LEWIS   2,284,583

PROCESS FOR TREATING HYDROCARBON OILS WITH LIGHT HYDROCARBONS

Filed Aug. 10, 1934

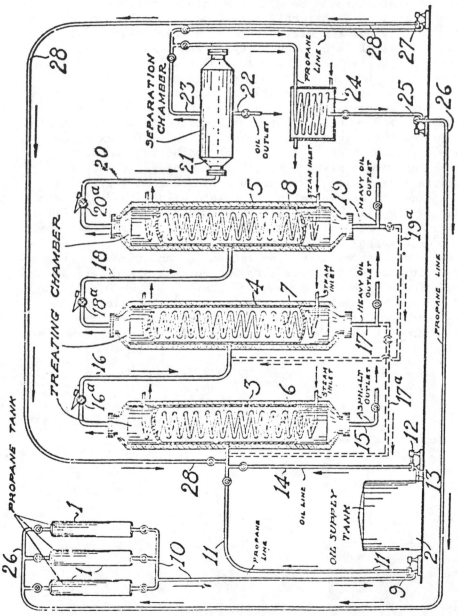

Warren K. Lewis Inventor

By *H. E. Currie* Attorney

Warren K. Lewis and J. M. Whitely in an earlier patent, U.S. 2,202,389, which is not reviewed in this appendix, described a method for changing the solvent power of a solvent in the near critical liquid region by varying the pressure on the liquid. In this patent, varying the solvent power by varying pressure of a solvent above its critical temperature is the invention, and specifically a process for the separation of hydrocarbon oils using 2 to 6 carbon aliphatic solvents is described.

The figure shows the operation of the process using propane as the solvent. Propane from tank 1 is pumped through line 11 and oil from tank 2 is pumped through line 14 and are contacted in chamber 3. The temperature is at or above the critical temperature of propane and the pressure is high enough to cause the desired oils, but not the asphalt, to dissolve; asphalt is withdrawn from the vessel through line 15.

The oil-propane solution is withdrawn from vessel 3, is expanded in pressure through valve 16a and is sent to vessel 4. Because of the reduction in pressure, the oil-propane solution loses its ability to dissolve the heavier fractions of the oil and part of the oil precipitates. The bottom layer (of precipitated oil) is removed through line 17, and the top phase is reduced in pressure again across valve 18a and sent to vessel 5 where another oil rich phase is removed from the bottom through line 19. The top phase is reduced in pressure to about the critical conditions of propane across valve 20a is sent to a separation chamber 21 where propane and remaining oil are separated.

Dec. 25, 1945.   D. L. KATZ ET AL   2,391,576
HIGH PRESSURE SEPARATION
Filed Sept. 5, 1942   3 Sheets-Sheet 1

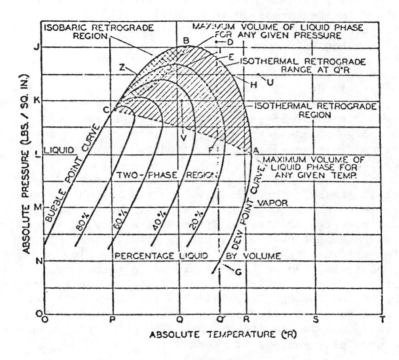

FIG. 1

INVENTORS
DONALD L. KATZ
THOMAS H. WHALEY, JR.
BY
Hudson, Young & Yniger
ATTORNEYS

Many of us have previously seen the drawing on the facing page and have studied it in distillation and thermo courses; retrograde condensation is the phenomenon depicted. We were surprised to find that the information presented in the drawing was the basis of a patent and thus we selected it for inclusion in this section.

It is, again, of historical and teaching value to present selected phrases and paragraphs of the invention.

"The present invention accomplishes separation of a complex hydrocarbon mixture into fractions by taking advantage of the remarkable change in some of the physical properties of hydrocarbons when the pressure to which the hydrocarbons are subjected is above 800 lbs. per sq. in.

"The present invention effects a separation of hydrocarbon mixtures into fractions by taking advantage of the effects sometimes referred to as 'retrograde vaporization' and 'retrograde condensation.' These concepts are useful in explaining the theoretical and scientific background upon which the invention is based and will be discussed in detail hereinafter."

Katz goes on to present a detailed account of the phenomenon, and he gives a number of examples of separating oil and gas mixtures by applying the phenomenon. This patent like the Zosel patent is must reading; in this case it is not for the many examples described but for the fundamentals that Katz develops.

United States Patent [19]

Leonard

[11]   **4,305,814**

[45]   **Dec. 15, 1981**

[54]   **ENERGY EFFICIENT PROCESS FOR SEPARATING HYDROCARBONACEOUS MATERIALS INTO VARIOUS FRACTIONS**

[75]   Inventor: Robert E. Leonard, Oklahoma City, Okla.

[73]   Assignee: Kerr-McGee Refining Corporation, Oklahoma City, Okla.

[21]   Appl. No.:   164,592

[22]   Filed: Jun. 30, 1980

[51]   Int. Cl.³ C10C 3/00
[52]   U.S. Cl. 208/309; 208/45
[58]   Field of Search 208/309, 312, 45

[56]   **References Cited**

U.S. PATENT DOCUMENTS

2,500,757	3/1950	Kiersted	208/45
2,940,920	6/1960	Garwin	208/309
3,775,292	11/1973	Watkins	208/309
3,830,732	8/1974	Gatsis	208/309
4,124,286	11/1978	Nolley	208/309
4,125,459	11/1978	Garwin	208/309
4,214,975	7/1980	Davis	208/309
4,239,616	12/1980	Gearhart	208/309

Primary Examiner—Brian E. Hearn
Attorney, Agent, or Firm—William G. Addison

[57]   **ABSTRACT**

An energy efficient process for separating a hydrocarbonaceous material into various fractions. The hydrocarbonaceous material is admixed with a solvent and the mixture is introduced into a first separation zone maintained at an elevated first temperature and pressure. The feed mixture separates into a first light phase comprising solvent and at least a portion of the lightest hydrocarbonaceous material and a first heavy phase comprising the remainder of the hydrocarbonaceous material and some solvent. The first heavy phase is introduced into a second separation zone maintained at a second temperature level above the first temperature level and at an elevated pressure. The first heavy phase separates into a second light phase comprising solvent and a second heavy phase comprising at least a portion of the hydrocarbonaceous material. The separated hydrocarbonaceous material fractions are recovered.

16 Claims, 1 Drawing Figure

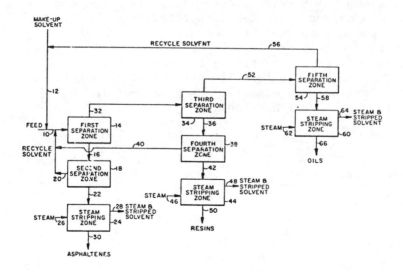

Leonard, Garwin, Gearhart, and Roach are names that appear liberally in the next few patents. They invented many variations of the basic ROSE process for Kerr–McGee Corporation. After having discussed the basic ROSE process operation in Chapter 7, we have selected other variations of the process to serve as additional teaching tools.

The drawing and discussion describe an energy efficient process for separating heavy hydrocarbons such as crude oil residuum, vacuum bottoms, etc. The operation in the block diagram is explained using as an example vacuum residuum consisting of asphaltenes, resins, and oils. The first separation zone 14 is supplied with a feed and a solvent, e.g., pentane, and is maintained at or above pentane's critical point. A heavy phase is withdrawn via line 16 and is introduced into another separation zone 18; the temperature in the second zone is maintained at a temperature higher than in the first zone and at about the same pressure. In the second zone, the heavy phase separates into a second light phase and a second heavy phase consisting of an asphaltene concentrate. The second light phase is withdrawn 20, recycled, and mixed with the feed. The second heavy asphaltene concentrate phase is withdrawn via line 22 and is steam stripped 24.

The first light phase (from the first separation zone 14) is introduced via line 32 to a third separation zone 34. The temperature is maintained at a temperature higher than in the first zone and a third light phase and a third heavy phase consisting of resins and some solvent are formed. The third heavy phase is withdrawn via line 36 and introduced to a fourth separation zone 38 (which is maintained at a still higher temperature and at about the same pressure) and the third heavy phase separates into a fourth heavy phase and a fourth light phase. The fourth light phase is recycled via line 40 and mixed with feed; the fourth heavy phase is steam stripped 44.

The third light phase is passed via line 52 from the third separation zone to a fifth separation zone 54; the temperature level is higher than in the third zone, and the phase separates into a fifth light phase and a fifth heavy phase. The fifth light phase is recycled via line 56 and mixed with the feed, and the fifth heavy phase is steam stripped; the fifth heavy phase is the desired oil fraction.

The example described shows that the method of operation of the invention results in an energy savings of 20% relative to the method of flashing the first and third heavy phases to recover the solvent.

United States Patent [19]

Gearhart

[11]   **4,239,616**

[45]   **Dec. 16, 1980**

[54] SOLVENT DEASPHALTING

[75] Inventor: Junior A. Gearhart, Oklahoma City, Okla.

[73] Assignee: Kerr-McGee Refining Corporation, Oklahoma City, Okla.

[21] Appl. No.: 59,719

[22] Filed: Jul. 23, 1979

[51] Int. Cl.³ C10G 21/00
[52] U.S. Cl. 208/309; 208/45
[58] Field of Search 208/45, 309

[56]   References Cited

U.S. PATENT DOCUMENTS

2,500,757	3/1950	Kiersted	208/309
2,527,404	10/1950	De Vault	208/309
2,729,589	1/1956	Waghorne et al.	208/309
2,783,188	2/1957	Agoston	208/309
2,940,920	6/1960	Garwin	208/45
2,980,602	4/1961	Garwin	208/45
3,003,945	10/1961	Garwin	208/45
3,003,946	10/1961	Garwin	208/45
3,003,947	10/1961	Garwin	208/45
3,005,769	10/1961	Garwin	208/45
3,053,751	9/1962	Garwin	208/45
3,364,138	1/1968	Campagne et al.	208/45
3,775,292	11/1973	Watkins	208/309
3,775,293	11/1973	Watkins	208/86
3,830,732	8/1974	Gatais	208/309
3,972,807	8/1976	Uitti et al.	208/309
4,101,415	7/1978	Crowley	208/45
4,125,459	11/1978	Garwin	208/309

Primary Examiner—Herbert Levine
Attorney, Agent, or Firm—William G. Addison

[57]   ABSTRACT

A process for effecting a deep cut in a heavy hydrocarbon material without a decrease in the quality of the extracted oil caused by the presence of undesirable entrained resinous bodies. The heavy hydrocarbon material is admixed with a solvent and introduced into a first separation zone maintained at an elevated temperature and pressure to effect a separation of the feed into a first light phase and a first heavy phase comprising asphaltenes and some solvent. The first light phase is introduced into a second separation zone maintained at an elevated temperature and pressure to effect a separation of the first light phase into a second light phase comprising oils and solvent and a second heavy phase comprising resins and some solvent. A portion of the first heavy phase is withdrawn and introduced into an upper portion of the second separation zone to contact the second light phase after which it separates therefrom. The contacting removes at least a portion of any entrained resinous bodies from the oil contained in the second light phase.

8 Claims, 2 Drawing Figures

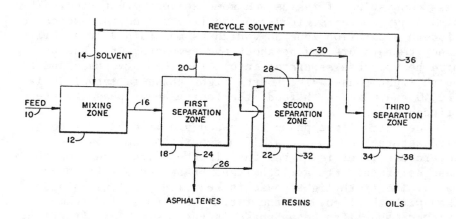

The background of this patent is quite extensive in describing variations of solvents and conditions which have been invented both by the assignee and others to produce separated fractions of a heavy hydrocarbon feed. The use of pentane, for example, results in a higher yield of desirable product than does the use of propane, but with pentane more undesired resinous bodies are present in the product.

One method to reduce the resins in the oil product is to employ some countercurrent extraction during the separations steps and the countercurrent contacting is the invention. In the particular embodiment described in this case, a portion of the asphaltenes from the first separation zone 18 is fed to the second separation zone 28 via line 26 in countercurrent extraction with the light oils (and resins) phase leaving the first separation zone. The countercurrent contact scrubs more of the resins from the oils in the second separation zone and results in a resin free oils fraction leaving the third separation zone.

United States Patent [19]

Leonard

[11]   **4,290,880**

[45]   **Sep. 22, 1981**

[54] **SUPERCRITICAL PROCESS FOR PRODUCING DEASPHALTED DEMETALLIZED AND DERESINED OILS**

[75] Inventor: Robert E. Leonard, Oklahoma City, Okla.

[73] Assignee: Kerr-McGee Refining Corporation, Oklahoma City, Okla.

[21] Appl. No.: 164,599

[22] Filed: Jun. 30, 1980

[51] Int. Cl.³ C10G 21/00
[52] U.S. Cl. 208/309
[58] Field of Search 208/45, 309, 311, 319

[56] **References Cited**

U.S. PATENT DOCUMENTS

2,940,920	6/1960	Garwin	208/45
2,943,050	6/1960	Beavon	208/309
3,507,777	4/1970	Hemminger	208/309
3,658,695	4/1972	Van Pool	208/309
3,775,293	11/1973	Watkins	208/86
3,972,807	8/1976	Uitti	208/309
3,981,797	9/1976	Kellar	208/309
3,998,726	12/1976	Bunas	208/309
4,239,616	12/1980	Gearhart	208/309

Primary Examiner—Brian E. Hearn
Attorney, Agent, or Firm—William G. Addison

[57]   **ABSTRACT**

A process for effecting a deep cut in a heavy hydrocarbon material without a decrease in the quality of the extracted oil caused by the presence of undesirable entrained resinous bodies and organometallic compounds. The heavy hydrocarbon material is contacted with a solvent in a first separation zone maintained at an elevated temperature and pressure to effect a separation of the feed into a first light phase and a first heavy phase comprising asphaltenes and some solvent. The first light phase is introduced into a second separation zone maintained at an elevated temperature and pressure to effect a separation of the first light phase into a second light phase comprising oils and solvent and a second heavy phase comprising resins and some solvent. A portion of the second heavy phase is withdrawn and introduced into an upper portion of the second separation zone to countercurrently contact the second light phase. The contacting removes at least a portion of any entrained resinous bodies and organometallic compounds from the oils contained in the second light phase.

14 Claims, 2 Drawing Figures

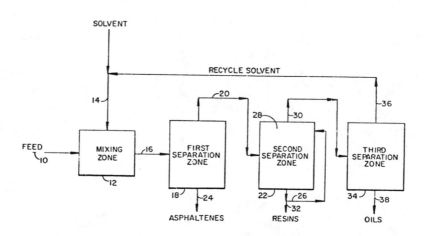

This patent is included to point out the similarity, yet difference, of this invention with the invention in the previous patent. The abstract on this patent face page and the drawing shown are variants of the previous ones.

The invention is as it was in the previous patent, the reduction of resins in the oils using a countercurrent contact in one of the separation zones. In this invention the reduction is accomplished slightly differently. Resins from the second separation zone 28 are recycled 26 and fed countercurrent to the oils stream. (Recall in the previous patent, the asphaltenes were fed countercurrent to the oils stream). In both cases, resins reduction in the oils leaving the second separation zone is effected (although the patent doesn't say which, if any, is the superior process).

United States Patent

[11] 3,607,717

[72]	Inventor	Jack W. Rosch
		Oklahoma City, Okla.
[21]	Appl. No.	1,818
[22]	Filed	Jan. 9, 1970
[45]	Patented	Sept. 21, 1971
[73]	Assignee	Kerr-McGee Corporation
		Oklahoma City, Okla.

[54] **FRACTIONATING COAL LIQUEFACTION
PRODUCTS WITH LIGHT ORGANIC SOLVENTS**
28 Claims, 2 Drawing Figs.

[52]	U.S. Cl.	208/8
[51]	Int. Cl.	C10g 1/00
[50]	Field of Search	208/10

[56]   **References Cited**
              UNITED STATES PATENTS

2,221,866	11/1940	Dreyfus	208/8
2,913,397	11/1959	Murray et al.	208/8
2,202,901	6/1940	Dreyfus	208/8
2,913,388	11/1959	Howell et al.	208/8

Primary Examiner—Delbert E. Gantz
Assistant Examiner—Veronica O'Keefe
Attorney—Shanley and O'Neil

ABSTRACT: Coal liquefaction products are separated into a plurality of fractions of varying softening points and molecular complexity by treatment with light organic solvents having critical temperatures below 800° F. under elevated temperature and pressure conditions. In one variant, coal is liquefied employing selected light organic solvents which are suitable for both liquefaction and fractionation, and thereafter the coal liquefaction products are separated into a plurality of fractions by treatment with the solvent contained in the resultant solution. Preferred solvents for liquefying coal include pyridine and benzene, and preferred fractionating solvents include pyridine, benzene and hexane. In a preferred variant, a solvent phase is recovered directly from the final fractionating stage and is passed in heat exchange relationship with solvent-rich streams to preceding fractionating stages to recover the heat content and provide cooled solvent for recycle. The invention further provides a method of separating finely divided insoluble material derived from coal during liquefaction thereof from an organic-solvent solution of coal liquefaction products.

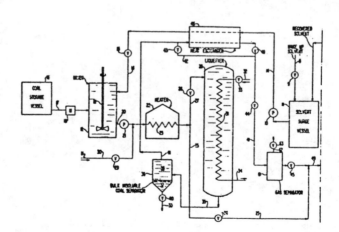

Three major objectives of the new coal liquefaction process are described, viz., to provide a novel method of separating coal liquefaction products into a plurality of products wherein the solvent may be recovered directly from the final fractionating stage . . ., to provide a novel process for liquefying coal employing selected light organic solvents . . ., to provide a novel method of separating finely divided insoluble materials derived from coal during liquefaction . . .

We have discussed the first two objectives, i.e., separation and fractionation of many chemicals, and, thus, the parts of this patent dealing with the first two objectives will not be elaborated upon here. The third objective, however, employs another of the properties of a near critical or supercritical solvent, viz., its low viscosity, to effect a sedimentation of particulates from what would, in the absence of the supercritical fluid, be a very viscous liquid.

Figure 1A is on the face page of the patent and describes the coal extraction process using liquid solvent at high pressure and subcritical temperature. There is another figure on the second page of that patent that describes de-ashing i.e., the separation of material matter in the coal, and a subsequent fractionation by successive pressure and temperature change. A heavy phase and a light phase form during a first pressure and temperature adjustment of the solvent and extract that results in the separation of ash particulates. It is theorized in the description of the invention that some of the coal liquefaction products coat the micron-sized ash particles causing them to agglomerate and settle in the low viscosity heavy phase. (The heavy phase viscosity is low because the supercritical fluid has dissolved in it.) The light phase leaving the de-asher is essentially ash-free and the ash containing heavy phase is removed. The light phase continues through the fractionation train where successive pressure and temperature change brings about successive fraction recovery.

United States Patent [19]

Gearhart

[11]   **4,278,529**

[45]   **Jul. 14, 1981**

[54] PROCESS FOR SEPARATING BITUMINOUS MATERIALS WITH SOLVENT RECOVERY

[75] Inventor: Junior A. Gearhart, Oklahoma City, Okla.

[73] Assignee: Kerr-McGee Refining Corporation, Oklahoma City, Okla.

[21] Appl. No.:   164,591

[22] Filed: Jun. 30, 1980

[51] Int. Cl.³ C10C 3/00; C10C 3/08
[52] U.S. Cl. 208/309; 208/321
[58] Field of Search 208/45, 309, 321

[56]   **References Cited**

U.S. PATENT DOCUMENTS

2,041,275	5/1936	Bray	208/309
2,940,920	6/1960	Garwin	208/45
3,403,093	9/1968	Mills	208/45
3,830,732	8/1974	Gatsis	208/309
3,847,751	11/1974	Godino	208/309
4,017,383	4/1977	Beavon	208/309
4,101,415	7/1978	Crowley	208/45
4,125,459	11/1978	Garwin	208/309

Primary Examiner—Brian E. Hearn
Attorney, Agent, or Firm—William G. Addison

[57]   **ABSTRACT**

A process for separating a solvent from a bituminous material by pressure reduction without carry-over of bituminous material. The fluid-like phase comprising bituminous material and solvent is reduced in pressure by passage through a pressure reduction valve and introduced into a steam stripper. The pressure reduction vaporizes part of the solvent and also disperses a mist of fine bituminous particles in the solvent. The solvent and mist are withdrawn from the steam stripper and introduced into a separation zone wherein they are caused to flow countercurrently to another stream of fluid-like bituminous material. The fluid-like bituminous material contacts the solvent and scrubs the fine bituminous material particles therefrom. The solvent is withdrawn and recovered. The fluid-like stream containing the bituminous particles can be recycled until the concentration is such that additional particles are not separated from the solvent after which a portion is bled off and fresh fluid-like material is added.

15 Claims, 5 Drawing Figures

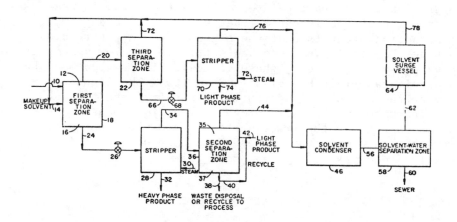

The prior art discussion presented in the patent describes a problem that is experienced in the operation of bituminous material extraction when the process is operated "normally," i.e., a supercritical extraction followed by pressure reduction. Pressure reduction through a pressure reduction valve 26 results in the formation of a fine mist that solidifies, emulsifies, and settles out in subsequent parts of the process eventually causing disruption of operation.

In the new process, other separation zones are added after the normal first separation zone. The heavy phase from the first zone is sent to a stripper 28. Vaporized solvent, steam, and fine mist particles are withdrawn via line 34 and are conveyed to the second separation zone 36. The heavy phase exits the stripper via 32. In the second separation zone, the stream consisting of solvent, steam, and mist particles are caused to flow through a circuitous path. In this zone the stream is contacted countercurrently with a stream of light oil 42 which scrubs the alphaltene and resin mist from the solvent. A portion of the light phase oil containing asphaltenes and resins is recycled to the second separation zone (or it can be recycled to the first separation zone). The solvent and steam mixture leaving the second zone is conveyed to a solvent condensor 46 and water separation zone 58. No emulsification problems are experienced because the mist particles have been removed in the first separation zone.

United States Patent [19]

Roach

[11]   **4,279,739**

[45]   **Jul. 21, 1981**

[54]   **PROCESS FOR SEPARATING BITUMINOUS MATERIALS**

[75]   Inventor: Jack W. Roach, Oklahoma City, Okla.

[73]   Assignee: Kerr-McGee Refining Corporation, Oklahoma City, Okla.

[21]   Appl. No.:   164,606

[22]   Filed: Jun. 30, 1980

[51]   Int. Cl.³ C10C 3/00; C10G 21/78; B01D 3/38

[52]   U.S. Cl. 208/309; 208/321; 208/363

[58]   Field of Search 208/45, 309, 363, 356, 208/321

[56]   **References Cited**

U.S. PATENT DOCUMENTS

2,041,275	5/1936	Bray	208/309
2,041,278	5/1936	Aldridge	208/309
2,940,920	6/1960	Garwin	208/309
3,403,093	9/1968	Mills	208/45
3,830,732	8/1974	Gatsis	208/309
4,101,415	7/1978	Crowley	208/45
4,125,459	11/1978	Garwin	208/309

Primary Examiner—Brian E. Hearn
Attorney, Agent, or Firm—William G. Addison

[57]   **ABSTRACT**

A process for separating a solvent from a bituminous material by pressure reduction and steam stripping without carry-over of entrained bituminous material. The fluid-like phase of bituminous material and solvent is reduced in pressure and introduced into a steam stripper. The solvent vaporizes upon pressure reduction and a mist of fine bituminous material particles forms and becomes dispersed in the vaporized solvent. The vaporized solvent and associated mist is separated from the bituminous material in the stripper and is withdrawn from the steam stripper and introduced into a condenser. The solvent and steam from the stripper condense, a substantial portion of the mist of entrained particles solidifies and an emulsion of water and fluid-like bituminous material from the mist forms. The liquid stream is withdrawn from the condenser and introduced into a separator. The liquid stream separates in the separator into an upper fraction comprising solvent, a middle fraction comprising emulsion and a lower fraction comprising water and the solidified particles of bituminous material. The liquid solvent is removed by passage over a weir in the separator and recovered. The emulsion, water and solids can be removed from the base of the separator for disposal.

23 Claims, 2 Drawing Figures

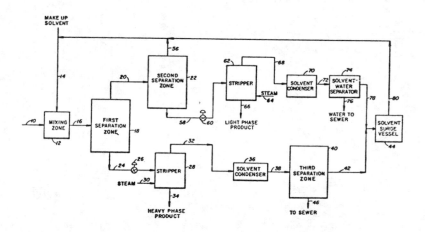

The prior art discussion in this patent also refers to the problem of mist formation when the heavy phase leaving the first separation zone is decreased in pressure, viz., in the "normal" operation a portion of the bituminous material introduced into the steam stripper 28 is carried out as a fine mist which solidifies and forms a water emulsion that subsequently settles within the process apparatus resulting in eventual plugging and disruption of the process.

This patent describes another method for removing the mist that is carried into the stripper. A third separation zone 40 is added downstream of the solvent condenser to eliminate the problem. The third separation zone 40 in this process variant is a conical vessel which allows the particulates to settle and be removed 46 from the solvent. This patent does not say which variant, this one or the previous one, is more efficient, but note that this patent and the previous one were both filed on the same day. Incidentally, there exists at least a score of other Kerr-McGee patents that we do not discuss in the appendix.

United States Patent [19]

Audeh et al.

[11]   **4,354,928**

[45]   **Oct. 19, 1982**

[54]   **SUPERCRITICAL SELECTIVE EXTRACTION OF HYDROCARBONS FROM ASPHALTIC PETROLEUM OILS**

[75]   Inventors: **Costandi A. Audeh**, Princeton, N.J.; **Tsoung Y. Yan**, Philadelphia, Pa.

[73]   Assignee: **Mobil Oil Corporation**, New York, N.Y.

[21]   Appl. No.:   **157,728**

[22]   Filed: **Jun. 9, 1980**

[51]   Int. Cl.³ C10C 3/00
[52]   U.S. Cl. 208/309; 208/311
[58]   Field of Search 208/45, 309, 311, 86, 208/3

[56]   **References Cited**

U.S. PATENT DOCUMENTS

2,940,920	6/1960	Garwin	208/45
2,980,602	4/1961	Garwin	208/309
3,321,394	5/1967	Mills	208/45
3,507,777	4/1970	Hemminger	208/309
3,511,774	5/1970	Long	208/86
3,607,716	9/1971	Roach	208/10
3,723,294	3/1973	Gatsis	208/309
3,798,157	3/1974	Manzanilla	208/309

4,082,695	4/1978	Rosinski	252/465
4,211,633	7/1980	Gleim	208/309
4,239,216	12/1980	Gearhart	208/45

Primary Examiner—Brian E. Hearn
Attorney, Agent, or Firm—Charles C. Huggett; Michael G. Gilman; Van D. Harrison, Jr.

[57]   **ABSTRACT**

An asphalt containing petroleum oil is deasphalted and extracted by contacting the oil with a solvent maintained at its critical temperature and pressure. With the solvent at its critical temperature and pressure, extraction of the valuable hydrocarbon oils present in the asphaltic feedstock is effected by way of vapor-liquid phase separation which serves to decompose the metal complexes present in the feedstock, thus reducing the metal content of the extracted hydrocarbon oil. Examples of solvents employed in the process of the invention include C₄-C₁₀ cuts of typical refinery streams, benzene, toluene, ethylene glycols and the like. In one process embodiment, promoters or catalyst are employed to further reduce the metal content of the extracted hydrocarbon oil.

3 Claims, 2 Drawing Figures

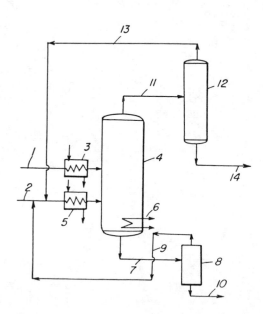

The process concept involves the extraction of light hydrocarbon oils from asphaltic petroleum supercritical solvents followed by a subsequent fractionation and separation of the oil from the solvent. It is stated that the metal compounds which are present in the asphaltic petroleum do not dissolve in the solvent under the conditions of operation. The primary difference claimed for this new process relative to the old processes is that the solvent is "at or above" the critical temperature rather than below the critical temperature as is described in prior art.

The operation is explained with the aid of Figure 1. Asphaltic feedstock is introduced into the extraction vessel 4 via conduit 1 and heat exchanger 3. The solvent is introduced via 2 and heat exchanger 5, and the two streams are mixed. The temperature is maintained at or above its critical. In the extractor, the non-solubles settle and are removed via 7 and sent to a stripper 8 to recover and recycle the solvent. Several examples give quantitative information when an asphaltic feedstock containing 28 ppm Ni, 220 ppm V is used. The oil yield and metal content results are given below for two cases where the solvent is catalytic cracker gasoline and propane, respectively.

	Example 1	**Example 2**
	Cat Cracker Gasoline	Propane
Solvent: Oil Ratio	2:1	6:1
Temperature, $^\circ$F	725	175
Pressure, psig	650	500
Deasphalted Oil		
Yield, wt%	75	68
Ni/V, w ppm	2/12	3/22
Asphalt		
Yield, wt%	26	31

Based upon the data in the table, the statement is made that the new invention using a solvent "at or above its critical point" provides improved yields and metal reduction relative to liquid propane extraction. It is not surprising that supercritical gasoline (at 725°F) gives different results than liquid propane (at 175°F) does; we've already seen the wide difference in results with two closely related solvents, such as liquid propane (for propane deasphalting) and liquid butane (in the Kear-McGee ROSE process) and we would expect even wider differences between supercritical gasoline and liquid propane which have huge differences in critical temperature. A more appropriate comparison to evaluate the advantage of the invention would have been to obtain results with liquid gasoline at the same reduced temperature (0.96) as the liquid propane in Example 2.

United States Patent [19]

Poska

[11]   **4,341,619**

[45]   **Jul. 27, 1982**

[54]   **SUPERCRITICAL TAR SAND EXTRACTION**

[75]   Inventor: Forrest L. Poska, Dallas, Tex.

[73]   Assignee: Phillips Petroleum Company, Bartlesville, Okla.

[21]   Appl. No.:   176,749

[22]   Filed: **Aug. 11, 1980**

[51]   Int. Cl.³ C10G 1/00
[52]   U.S. Cl. .... 208/11 LE
[58]   Field of Search .... 208/11 LE

[56]   **References Cited**

U.S. PATENT DOCUMENTS

700,489	4/1869	Long et al.	208/11 LE
3,208,930	9/1965	Androssy	208/11 LE
3,553,099	1/1971	Savage et al.	208/11 LE
3,558,468	1/1971	Wise	208/8
3,850,738	11/1974	Stewart et al.	208/3
3,970,541	7/1976	Williams et al.	208/8
4,108,760	8/1978	Williams et al.	208/11 LE
4,120,775	10/1978	Murray et al.	208/11 LE
4,189,376	2/1980	Mitchell	208/11 LE
4,197,183	4/1980	Audeh	208/11 LE

Primary Examiner—Delbert E. Gantz
Assistant Examiner—Joseph A. Boska

[57]   **ABSTRACT**

An integrated process for the recovery of carbonaceous material from tar sands by supercritical extraction involving countercurrent flow of the tar sand and the solvent is disclosed.

2 Claims, 1 Drawing Figure

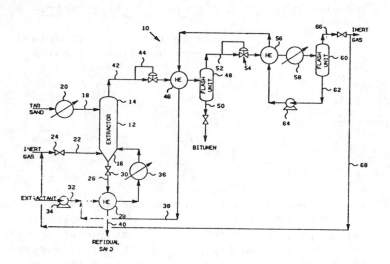

The invention described in this patent is the combination of using a supercritical fluid to dissolve the desired components from tar sands and to recover regeneratively heat from the tar free sand leaving the extractor.

Tar sands are fed to the extractor 12 where they are contacted countercurrently with supercritical aromatic solvents such as benzene, toluene, or other substituted benzenes, or with supercritical cycloaliphatic solvents such as cyclohexane, decalin, etc.; straight chain aliphatics can also be used. The extract phase leaving the extractor is reduced in pressure 44 and sent to a flash unit 48 for separation of the bitumin; the light phase leaving the extraction vessel is condensed and sent to another flash unit 60 for separation of light hydrocarbons from the solvent. Both the solvent and the light oil are returned via line 62 and the pump 64 of the extractor. The hot tar-free sand is passed through the recuperative heat exchanger 28 where the extractant is heated. The sand is discharged through valve 40 which as the patent states can be a star valve, a screw conveyer, or a "pressure drop channel." Such a "pressure drop channel" is described next.

United States Patent [19]

Warzel

[11]   **4,397,731**

[45]   **Aug. 9, 1983**

[54]   **DISCHARGE OF SOLIDS**

[75]   Inventor: F. Morgan Warzel, Bartlesville, Okla.

[73]   Assignee: Phillips Petroleum Company, Bartlesville, Okla.

[21]   Appl. No.:   282,770

[22]   Filed: Jul. 13, 1981

[51]   Int. Cl.³ C10G 1/04
[52]   U.S. Cl. .... 208/8 LE; 137/12; 340/626; 414/217
[58]   **Field of Search** .... 222/55, 56; 340/626; 414/221; 208/8 LE, 11 LE; 251/63.5; 137/12, 492

[56]   **References Cited**

U.S. PATENT DOCUMENTS

2,931,765	4/1960	Glinka	208/8 LE
3,173,852	3/1965	Smith	208/131
3,607,716	9/1971	Roach	208/8 LE
3,963,599	6/1976	Davitt	208/11 LE
3,977,423	8/1976	Clayton	137/12

OTHER PUBLICATIONS

T. C. Aude, N. T. Couper, T. L. Thomson and E. J.
Wasp; *"Slurry Piping Systems: Trends, Design Methods, Guidelines"*, Chemical Eng., vol. 78, pp. 74–90, Jun. 28, 1971.
Brodesell, *"Valve Selection"*, Chem. Eng./Deskbook issue, Oct. 11, 1971, pp. 119–121.

Primary Examiner—Delbert E. Gantz
Assistant Examiner—Glenn A. Caldarola

[57]   **ABSTRACT**

Finely divided particulate solids are discharged from a high pressure zone to a low pressure zone, e.g. to atmospheric pressure, by passing a dense bed of this particulate material through a long discharge channel and past a throttle element. The pressure drop across the throttle element is significantly reduced due to the fact that the moving dense bed in the discharge channel dissipates the pressure drop along this channel leaving only a small pressure drop to be achieved across the throttle element.

13 Claims, 3 Drawing Figures

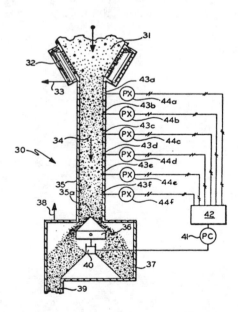

This patent describes the valve that was used in the previous patent to discharge the dry sand from the tar sands extractor. The flow of material in the channel is explained with reference to the drawing. A mixture of solids (the sand) and solvent (which is used to extract the hydrocarbon values from the tar sands) enters the discharge system 31. The composition at this point is about 50/50 solids/solvent. For the particular case discussed (and this is a calculated case), the solids flow is 140,000 lbs/hr, and the dimensions of the conduit 35 is 13.5 in I.D. and 150 ft long. Pressure at point 31 is about 1500 psi. The pressure measurement/transmitter devices 44a-f measure the pressure which is transmitted to the controller 42 which regulates the opening and closing of the solids throttle 36. The hydraulic system operating from the pressure signals actuates the throttle which can operate at a pressure drop of 1500 psi.

We wonder if this concept was ever tested experimentally in the laboratory.

United States Patent [19]

Kramer et al.

[11]   **3,880,945**

[45] **Apr. 29, 1975**

[54] **PARAFFIN ISOMERIZATION IN SUPERCRITICAL FLUIDS**

[75] Inventors: **George M. Kramer**, Berkeley Heights; **Frederic Leder**, Elizabeth, both of N.J.

[73] Assignee: **Exxon Research and Engineering Company**, Linden, N.J.

[22] Filed: **July 18, 1973**

[21] Appl. No.: **380,093**

Related U.S. Application Data

[63] Continuation-in-part of Ser. No. 207,603, Dec. 13, 1971, abandoned, which is a continuation-in-part of Ser. No. 23,002, March 26, 1970, abandoned.

[52] U.S. Cl. ... 260/683.75; 260/683.7; 260/683.68; 260/683.66

[51] Int. Cl. C07c 5/28

[58] Field of Search..... 260/683.65, 683.68, 683.66, 260/683.7, 683.75

[56]   **References Cited**

UNITED STATES PATENTS

2,249,366	7/1941	van Peski et al	260/683.7
2,265,548	12/1941	Schuit	260/683.75
2,271,043	1/1942	van Peski	260/683.66
2,318,226	5/1943	Ibatieff et al.	260/683.68
2,403,107	7/1946	McAllister et al.	260/683.75
3,674,681	7/1972	Lyon	260/683.65

Primary Examiner—Delbert E. Gantz
Assistant Examiner—G. J. Crasanakis
Attorney, Agent, or Firm—Marthe L. Gibbons

[57]   **ABSTRACT**

A paraffin of 4–12 carbon atoms is isomerized with a Lewis acid catalyst and solvent comprising, for example, carbon dioxide, hydrogen chloride or hydrogen bromide at a temperature above the critical temperature of the mixture of said hydrocarbon and solvent, under pressure sufficient to impart a density of at least about one-tenth that of pure solvent (liquid), saturated at 20°C. The pressure is in the range of 1,000 to 5,000 psig. In a preferred embodiment, normal paraffins containing from 4 to 12 carbons are isomerized with an aluminum bromide catalyst in the presence of carbon dioxide at a temperature above the critical temperature of the mixture and a pressure sufficient to impart a density of at least one-tenth that of pure CO_2 liquid saturated with vapor at 20°C.

16 Claims, No Drawings

The abstract is quite explanatory, and the invention of operating in the supercritical region is best shown by comparing operation at supercritical conditions vs. operation at liquid conditions. In one example hexane, a promoter (methyl tertiary amylether) and a catalyst (aluminum bromide) are reacted at $40^{\circ}C$ and 1 atm for 60 min. In another example the same ratio of hexane to promoter and catalyst is charged to an autoclave and carbon dioxide is added at a ratio of 500 g of CO_2 to 86 g hexane, to form a homogeneous phase. In both cases about 30-35% of the hexane cracked and isomerized to other products. However, in the case of the reaction with liquid hexane, the ratio of isomerization to cracking was 1:1. In the supercritical reaction isomerization was predominant at 5:1. In another example it was described that hydrogen was added to reduce cracking. Hydrogen was found to be miscible in the supercritical phase whereas it has only limited solubility in liquid hexane so that a higher concentration of hydrogen can be achieved in the supercritical reaction. The cracking reactions were virtually eliminated and conversion to isomerizates was 90% when the reaction was carried out with hydrogen added to the supercritical phase.

Aug. 3, 1971   K. ZOSEL   3,597,464

PROCESS FOR THE PRODUCTION OF ALUMINUM ALKYL COMPOUNDS

Original Filed March 1, 1965

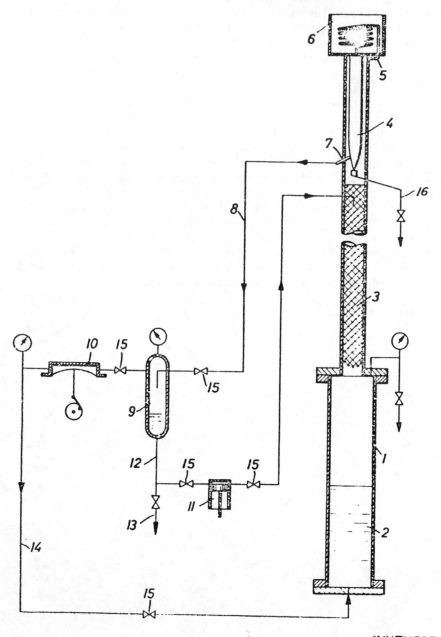

INVENTOR

KURT ZOSEL

BY

Burgess, Dinklage of Sprung

ATTORNEYS

   This patent predates, both in filing and in issue, the "big" Zosel patent described first in this appendix; there are many anecdotal stories, perhaps some apocryphal, that have circulated about the aluminum alkyl work carried out at the Max Planck Institut fur Kohlenforschung in Mulheim (Ruhr), West Germany. It was found during the aluminum alkyl synthesis studies that supercritical ethylene could separate aluminum trialkyls and olefins by carbon number.

   The Disclosure section gives an excellent summary of the invention and of the chemistry of the reactions which produce the alkyl aluminum mixtures. In brief review, a hydrogen dialkyl aluminum can react with alpha olefins to form long chain hydrocarbons in the range of C_{10} to C_{30}. (Ziegler catalysis mechanisms are in operation during the growth of the chain, and Ziegler, himself, was actively engaged in catalysis research at the Max Planck Institute during the period of Zosel's work.) The long chain hydrocarbon can subsequently be split from the aluminum alkyl compound to produce long chain length alpha olefins. It is also possible to oxidize the aluminum alkyl compounds to alkoxides and by hydrolysis to obtain long chain fatty alcohols. The process that is described in the patent employs supercritical fluids to separate the mixture of many trialkyl aluminum compounds that are formed during the process.

   The figure depicts one mode of operation.

   Vessel 1 is the batch extractor to which is charged the mixture to be separated. Gas is passed through the charge 2 via conduit 14. The extract phase passes overhead to a rectifying section 3. The process operates in the retrograde condensation region; thus, a "hot finger" 4 causes some of the (heavier) components to precipitate. Part of the condensate can be withdrawn at 16 and the remainder refluxed. The depleted gas stream is lowered in pressure and temperature to liquid conditions and passed into the separator 9. The liquefied gas is vaporized and recycled via compressor 10; the product is withdrawn 12, 13.

   Operating with supercritical ethane over an increasing pressure range from 75 to 100 atm, 50°C in the extractor and 98°C at the hot finger, a mixture consisting of 1.5 liters hexadecene, 1.5 liters octadecene, 5.2 liters eicosene and higher, and 1.55 liters tridodecyl were separated into 1 liter of pure hexadecene, 1 liter of an intermediate fraction, 1 liter of octadecene and 3 liters of a mixture up to C_{30} -ene; the olefins contained no aluminum alkyls. About 1 liter of a fraction containing some higher olefins and some tridodecyl aluminum, and 1.2 liters of pure aluminum tridodecyl were also separated.

United States Patent [19]

Diaz et al.

[54] **DRYING SUBSTANTIALLY SUPERCRITICAL CO₂ WITH GLYCEROL**

[75] Inventors: **Zaida Diaz,** Houston; **James H. Miller,** Katy, both of Tex.

[73] Assignee: **Shell Oil Company,** Houston, Tex.

[21] Appl. No.: **517,594**

[22] Filed: **Jul. 27, 1983**

[51] Int. Cl.³ B01D 53/14
[52] U.S. Cl. 55/29; 55/32
[58] Field of Search 55/29–32, 55/68

[11]   Patent Number: **4,478,612**

[45]   Date of Patent: **Oct. 23, 1984**

[56]   **References Cited**
            U.S. PATENT DOCUMENTS

2,235,322   3/1941 Martin 55/31
3,676,981   7/1972 Afdahl 55/30
4,005,997   2/1977 Fowler et al. 55/32
4,235,289 11/1980 Weeler 166/267

      FOREIGN PATENT DOCUMENTS

18268   8/1974 Japan 55/32

Primary Examiner—Charles Hart

[57]   **ABSTRACT**

In drying supercritical or nearcritical CO₂ for use at supercritical conditions, the loss of desiccant, contamination of product, compressor horsepower requirements, and heat requirements can be substantially minimized by using glycerol as the desiccant.

5 Claims, 4 Drawing Figures

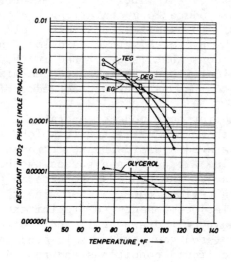

   Supercritical carbon dioxide is being used for enhanced
oil recovery. Carbon dioxide is quite plentifully available
in many subterranean formations, but these formations are
usually found far from oil fields, and thus, the carbon
dioxide must be conveyed to the fields by pipeline. Carbon
dioxide as it comes from the ground is usually wet, and is
thus quite corrosive to transmission lines. An ACS
monograph (Quinn, E.L. and C.L. Jones 1936. Carbon Dioxide,
Chap. 4, Reinhold Publishing Corp., New York.) gives data on
pH in a water solution as a function of pressure which is
partially reproduced below.

CO_2 Pressure — pH Relationship (20°C)	
Pressure of CO_2	**pH of water in equilibrium**
350 ppm (in laboratory air)	5.7
1 mm	5.4
10 mm	4.8
100 mm	4.3
1 atm	3.8
10 atm	3.3
100 atm	3.0

   We see the well-known value of 5.7 which results from
an equilibrium with laboratory air. We see further that at
high carbon dioxide pressure the pH levels out at about 3.0;
a pH of 3.0 is quite corrosive to carbon steel, and it is
desired to dry the CO_2 in order to reduce the corrosiveness.
   The background section of the patent gives a discussion
of various compounds that have been used to dry high pressure carbon dioxide. Triethylene glycol (TEG) has been used
primarily; TEG, however, exhibits appreciable solubility in
carbon dioxide at the conditions existing in pipelines con-
veying the carbon dioxide to enhanced oil recovery operations as the data in the graph on the patent face page show.
A high level of solubility can result in substantial loss of
the drying agent.
   Glycerol has a substantially lower solubility in carbon
dioxide and a graph of glycerol solubility is also given on
the facing page. The invention is the use of glycerol to
dry wet supercritical carbon dioxide.
   The examples given in this patent are quite interesting
because they are described in "dollars and cents" advantages. For instance, Example 2 states that the cost of the
dessicant lost in drying 400 million cubic feet/day of carbon dioxide at 1200 psi, 25°C, with TEG is $40,000,000/yr(!)
whereas when glycerol is used, the cost of dessicant lost is
only $300,000.

United States Patent [19]

Weeter

[11]   **4,235,289**

[45]   **Nov. 25, 1980**

[54]   METHOD FOR PRODUCING CARBON DIOXIDE FROM SUBTERRANEAN FORMATIONS

[75]   Inventor: Robert F. Weeter, Carrollton, Tex.

[73]   Assignee: Mobil Oil Corporation, New York, N.Y.

[21]   Appl. No.: 38,034

[22]   Filed: May 10, 1979

[51]   Int. Cl.^{2} E21B 43/16
[52]   U.S. Cl. 166/267; 166/68
[58]   Field of Search 166/314, 68, 68.1, 266, 166/267, 105, 106, 268

[56]   References Cited

U.S. PATENT DOCUMENTS

3,442,332	5/1969	Keith	166/266
3,887,008	6/1975	Canfield	166/68 X
4,007,787	2/1977	Cottle	166/267

OTHER PUBLICATIONS

Frick, *Petroleum Production Handbook*, vol. 1, *Mathematics and Production Equipment*, McGraw–Hill Book Co., Inc., N.Y., 1962, pp. 13–1 to 13–9.

Environmental Impact Assessment for the Wasson Field–Denver Unit CO_2 Project (Draft), Woodward–Clyde Consultants, Jul. 1978, pp. 1–1 to 1–29.

Renfro, "Sheep Mountain CO_2 Production Facilities–A Conceptual Design", SPE 7706, presented at 1979 Pro-

duction Operations Symposium of SPE of AIME, Oklahoma City, Okla., Feb. 25–27, 1979, 10 pages.

Primary Examiner—Stephen J. Novosad
Attorney, Agent, or Firm—C. A. Huggett; Drude Faulconer

[57]   ABSTRACT

A method for producing substantially pure carbon dioxide in a single phase at the surface from a subterranean formation. A pump means, e.g., electrically driven, submergible, centrifugal pump system, is positioned downhole in a carbon dioxide production well. The carbon dioxide flows from the formation to the inlet of the pump means wherein the carbon dioxide is compressed to raise the pressure to values greater than the critical pressure of the produced carbon dioxide plus the amount of pressure that the carbon dioxide will lose due to (a) the static fluid head above the pump means and (b) flow friction from the pump means to a central processing and compression station on the surface. By so boosting the pressure within the well, the carbon dioxide will be produced at the surface at a pressure greater than the critical pressure of the produced carbon dioxide, thereby insuring the carbon dioxide will be in a single phase, supercritical state.

8 Claims, 3 Drawing Figures

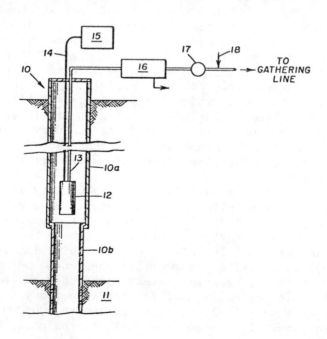

The previous patent was concerned with drying carbon dioxide before transmission to oil fields. This patent describes one method for pumping supercritical carbon dioxide from subterranean formations to the surface.

The background relates that carbon dioxide from a production well that reaches the surface under its own motive force arrives in a two-phase state, and that pumping such a mixture over long distances and varying elevations can create fluid "hammer" effects. These effects can cause serious damage to pipelines and related equipment and can result in considerable power loss.

It is the object of this invention to bring to the surface carbon dioxide in a single supercritical phase. This is accomplished by positioning a pump within a producing well; pressure is boosted to a value greater than the critical pressure plus the amount of pressure the carbon dioxide will lose due to static head and the pressure that will be lost due to friction in flowing the carbon dioxide to the surface.

The patentee describes a proposed field application and gives the conditions of the carbon dioxide at various positions in two situations, first, if the carbon dioxide flows to the surface under its subterranean formation pressure and, second, if the improved process is in operation. In the subterranean formation carbon dioxide is found at conditions of 2400 psig, 75°C. If it were to flow to the surface unaided, it would arrive there at 835 psig and 20°C. With reference to the figure, if a pump 12 is placed downhole at an appropriate distance, the carbon dioxide can be brought to the surface in a supercritical state. In the specific case discussed, "downhole" is at a depth of 6000 ft and the carbon dioxide is located at a depth of 6500 ft. Carbon dioxide reaches the pump at conditions of 1890 psig, 64°C, and it is boosted by 739 psig (but differing depending upon the amount of contaminants such as nitrogen) with concomitant temperature increase of 13°C. In its flow to the surface a static head of 1254 psig and flow losses of 75 psig are experienced, and the carbon dioxide arrives at the surface at approximately 1300 psig, 38°C, i.e., supercritical. This carbon dioxide is then sent to a central collection station and is pumped to an oil field. The next patent describes what is done with carbon dioxide containing contaminants.

United States Patent [19]

Parrish

[11]   **4,344,486**

[45]   **Aug. 17, 1982**

[54] **METHOD FOR ENHANCED OIL RECOVERY**

[75] Inventor: **David R. Parrish,** Tulsa, Okla.

[73] Assignee: **Standard Oil Company (Indiana),** Chicago, Ill.

[21] Appl. No.:   **238,874**

[22] Filed: **Feb. 27, 1981**

[51] Int. Cl.³ E21B 43/24; E21B 43/40

[52] U.S. Cl. 166/272; 166/266; 166/274

[58] Field of Search 166/256, 265, 266, 267, 166/268, 272, 274, 302, 303; 299/2

[56] **References Cited**

U.S. PATENT DOCUMENTS

2,623,596	12/1952	Whorton et al.	166/266 X
3,065,790	11/1962	Holm	166/274
3,075,918	1/1963	Holm	166/268 X
3,150,716	9/1964	Strelzoff et al.	166/266 X
3,193,006	7/1965	Lewis	166/266
3,228,467	1/'966	Schlinger et al.	166/266
3,480,082	11/1969	Gilliland	166/266
3,780,805	12/1973	Green	166/267 X
4,005,752	2/1977	Cha	299/2
4,114,688	9/1978	Terry	166/266 X
4,130,403	12/1978	Cooley et al.	55/16

Primary Examiner—Stephen J. Novosad
Assistant Examiner—George A. Suchfield
Attorney, Agent, or Firm—Scott H. Brown; Fred E. Hook

[57]   **ABSTRACT**

Disclosed is a method and apparatus for the enhanced recovery of liquid hydrocarbons from underground formations, said method comprising recovering a mixture comprising carbon dioxide and contaminants comprising hydrocarbon, hydrogen sulfide, or mixtures hereof, from an underground formation; combusting said mixture with an oxygen enriched gas to form a concentrated carbon dioxide stream; and injecting at least a portion of said concentrated carbon dioxide stream into an underground formation to enhance recovery of liquid hydrocarbon.

12 Claims, 1 Drawing Figure

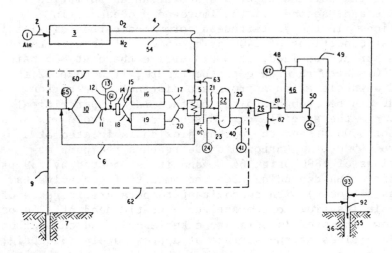

Although this patent on enhanced oil recovery immediately follows the one describing the production of supercritical carbon dioxide, the two processes are usually
carried out in locations separated by hundreds of miles
because the oil fields are usually not located next to
carbon dioxide "wells."

This patent relates that subterranean carbon dioxide is
often not pure and is found in conjunction with light
hydrocarbons and hydrogen sulfide. In order to take full
advantage in enhanced oil recovery operations the carbon
dioxide must be purified. Adsorption and cryogenic and
membrane separation have been used to carry out the purification. The new invention is the combustion of the hydrocarbon and hydrogen sulfide-containing carbon dioxide from
an underground formation with oxygen enriched gas to form a
concentrated carbon dioxide stream. This stream is then
used for enhanced oil recovery.

United States Patent [19]

Paspek, Jr.

[11]   Patent Number: **4,465,888**

[45]   Date of Patent: **Aug. 14, 1984**

[54]   **OLIGOMERIZATION OF OLEFINS IN SUPERCRITICAL WATER**

[75]   Inventor: **Stephen C. Paspek, Jr.,** North Royalton, Ohio

[73]   Assignee: **The Standard Oil Company,** Cleveland, Ohio

[21]   Appl. No.:   **485,094**

[22]   Filed: **Apr. 14, 1983**

[51]   Int. Cl.³ C07C 3/02

[52]   U.S. Cl. 585/520; 585/510; 585/732; 526/80; 526/84

[58]   Field of Search 585/510, 520, 732; 526/80, 84

[56]   **References Cited**

U.S. PATENT DOCUMENTS

2,214,463	9/1940	Ipatieff et al. .
2,422,692	6/1947	Mattox .
3,948,754	4/1976	McCollum et al. .
4,082,910	4/1978	Buechner et al. 585/510
4,087,602	5/1978	Mietzner et al. 585/510

FOREIGN PATENT DOCUMENTS

129807	12/1945	Australia	.... 585/520
612056	4/1947	United Kingdom	.... 585/520

Primary Examiner—Delbert E. Gantz
Assistant Examiner—A. Pal
Attorney, Agent, or Firm—Salvatore P. Pace; David J. Untener; Larry W. Evans

[57]   **ABSTRACT**

Fuel range liquid hydrocarbons are produced by the oligomerization of olefins in a process comprising contacting the olefins containing 5 or less carbon atoms with a water containing medium at a temperature sufficient to cause oligomerization and at a pressure sufficient to maintain the density of the medium at about 0.5 to about 1.0 grams per milliliter.

15 Claims, No Drawings

The patentee finds that olefins (of C5 or less) dissolved in near critical or supercritical water oligomerize;
no catalyst is required. The patentee proposes an explanation of the findings.

"...it is believed that the water-containing
medium functions as a catalyst, a reactant and as
a means to control the rate of reaction and rate
of heat transfer from the system. As a catalyst,
the water-containing medium moderates both free
radical and ionic mechanisms. As a reactant,
supercritical water is a donor of hydrogen for
saturating double bonds. This is evidenced by the
resulting liquid hydrocarbons being largely
paraffinic and the existence of carbon monoxide
and carbon dioxide in the gaseous effluent from
the reactor. Since water is a donor of hydrogen,
no externally supplied hydrogen is required for
the instant process.

"It is also theorized that in the instant
process, there are two competing reactions, the
oligomerization of olefins into liquids and the
thermal degradation of paraffinic liquids into
saturated gases. The water-containing medium
appears to suppress the thermal degradation-
reaction and there appears to be an upper limit on
the extent of oligomerization in the instant
process. The normally liquid hydrocarbons
produced by the instant process contain 4 to 20
carbon atoms and nearly all the saturated
hydrocarbons. These products are also highly
branched."

The patentee gives five examples where pressure, temperature, olefin, and water to olefin ratio, were varied.
For example, a 4:1 ratio of water to ethylene was reacted at
$427^{\circ}C$, 4960 psig, for 1 hr; a 72 per cent yield of light
liquids was obtained with no coke or oil formation.

United States Patent [19]

Paspek, Jr.

[11]   Patent Number: **4,483,761**

[45]   **Date of Patent:**   **Nov. 20, 1984**

[54] **UPGRADING HEAVY HYDROCARBONS WITH SUPERCRITICAL WATER AND LIGHT OLEFINS**

[75] Inventor: **Stephen C. Paspek, Jr.,** North Royalton, Ohio

[73] Assignee: **The Standard Oil Company,** Cleveland, Ohio

[21] Appl. No.: **510,524**

[22] Filed: **Jul. 5, 1983**

[51] Int. Cl.³ **C106 9/00**
[52] U.S. Cl. **208/106; 208/107; 208/125; 208/130**
[58] Field of Search 208/106, 130, 107, 125, 208/128

[56]   **References Cited**

U.S. PATENT DOCUMENTS

1,613,010	7/1923	Armstrong .
2,608,524	5/1948	Johnson et al. .
2,626,233	1/1953	Kimberlin et al. .
3,542,668	11/1970	Van Pool .
3,579,438	5/1971	Cruse .
3,617,497	11/1971	Bryson et al. .
3,758,400	9/1973	Hampton .
3,948,754	4/1976	McCollum et al. .
3,948,755	4/1976	McCollum et al. .
3,954,600	5/1976	Gladrow et al. .
3,960,708	6/1976	McCollum et al. .
3,989,618	11/1976	McCollum et al. 208/106
4,002,557	1/1977	Owen et al. .
4,005,005	1/1977	McCollum et al. .
4,146,465	3/1979	Blazek, Sr. et al. .
4,151,068	4/1979	McCollum et al. .
4,290,880	7/1981	Leonard .

Primary Examiner—Delbert E. Gantz
Assistant Examiner—Anthony McFarlane
Attorney, Agent, or Firm—Salvatore P. Pace; David J. Untener; Larry W. Evans

[57]   **ABSTRACT**

Heavy hydrocarbons are upgraded and cracked in a process comprising contacting the heavy hydrocarbons with olefins containing 5 or less carbon atoms and a solvent, at a temperature both sufficient for cracking and greater than or equal to the critical temperature of the solvent.

19 Claims, No Drawings

This invention by Paspek is the cracking of heavy hydrocarbons in a mixture of supercritical water and light olefins (up to C5), and it follows by a few months the previously discussed patent on the oligomerization of olefins in supercritical water. It is reported that the presence of olefins in the reaction mixture reduces gas formation during cracking because of equilibrium considerations; additionally, olefins increase the yield of light liquids by reacting and combining with thermally cracked fragments and by oligomerizing to liquid range products. It is found that the cracking reactions occur at highest yield in a solvent which can donate a hydrogen to a double bond; preferred solvents are water, alcohols, and their mixtures.

Three comparative examples taken from the patent verbatim delineate the yield improvement if the invention is practiced are given below.

Example A
Water and shale oil (W/O ratio = 2) were reacted in an autoclave at $425°C$, 4750 psig for 60 min. The product distribution was 75% (wt) distillate (the desired product), 5% gas, 2% coke. This example did not practice the invention.

Example B
Shale oil and ethylene (E/O ratio - 0.27) were loaded into the autoclave, and reacted at $425°C$, 990 psig for 60 min. The product distribution was 71% (wt) distillate, 10% wt gas, 31% coke. This example also does not practice the invention.

Example 1
Water and oil (W/O ratio = 2) was loaded into an autoclave, and ethylene was added to an E/O ratio = 0.2. Reaction was carried out at $425°C$, 4901 psig for sixty minutes. Product distribution was 83% distillate, 0% gas, 2 wt % coke. This example shows the benefits of cracking heaving hydrocarbons in the supercritical water-ethylene solvent.

Although it is not possible to close the material balance in all examples, the overall results show that the presence of olefins in the supercritical water enhances the yield of distillate.

United States Patent [19]

Coenen et al.

[11]   Patent Number: **4,485,003**

[45]   Date of Patent: **Nov. 27, 1984**

[54]   **SUPERCRITICAL EXTRACTION AND SIMULTANEOUS CATALYTIC HYDROGENATION OF COAL**

[75]   Inventors: Hubert Coenen; Rainer Hagen; Ernst Kriegel, all of Essen, Fed. Rep. of Germany

[73]   Assignee: Fried. Krupp Gesellschaft mit beschränkter Haftung, Essen, Fed. Rep. of Germany

[21]   Appl. No.:   402,933

[22]   Filed: Jul. 29, 1982

[30]   **Foreign Application Priority Data**

Aug. 25, 1981   [DE]   Fed. Rep. of Germany 3133562

[51]   Int. Cl.³ C10G 1/06
[52]   U.S. Cl. .... 208/10; 208/8 LE
[58]   Field of Search .... 208/8 R, 10, 8 LE

[56]   **References Cited**

U.S. PATENT DOCUMENTS

3,488,280	1/1970	Schulman	208/10
3,505,204	4/1970	Hoffman	208/10
3,660,269	5/1972	McCauley	208/8
3,745,108	7/1973	Schuman	208/10
3,850,738	11/1974	Stewart, Jr. et al.	208/8 R
4,019,975	4/1977	Uruqhart	208/10
4,056,460	11/1977	Malek	208/8 LE
4,222,849	9/1980	Shimizu	208/8 LE
4,237,101	12/1980	Willard, Sr.	208/8 LE
4,298,450	11/1981	Ross et al.	208/10
4,338,184	7/1982	Maa et al.	208/8 LE

Primary Examiner—Delbert E. Gantz
Assistant Examiner—Lance Johnson
Attorney, Agent, or Firm—Spencer & Frank

[57]   **ABSTRACT**

A process for producing liquid hydrocarbons from coal comprises treating comminuted coal at 380° to 600° C. and 260 to 450 bar with water in a high pressure reactor to form a charged supercritical gas phase and a coal residue. Simultaneously with the water treatment, hydrogenation with hydrogen takes place in the presence of a catalyst. The catalyst is selected from the group consisting of NaOH, KOH, Na₄SiO₄, NaBO₄, or KOB₂. Then, the gas phase is divided into several fractions by lowering its pressure and temperature. Energy and/or gas is generated from the coal residue.

15 Claims, 1 Drawing Figure

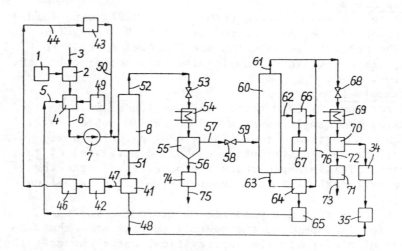

The patent face page shown is a corrected face page which is provided as of 28 May 1985.

With reference to the figure coal is comminuted 2, mixed with water 3, the slurry mixed with oil 5 in mixer 4 which is also supplied with catalyst 49. The coal–water–oil–catalyst mixture is conveyed to the extractor/reactor 8 where the pressure and temperature are maintained at about 350 bar, 500°C, for a reaction period of 40 min resulting in a supercritical water phase containing organic compounds and a coal residue. The rest of the flow sheet depicts condensation, rectification of oil fractions, separation of gases, gasification of coal residue, and recycle of some oil.

The description relates that it is desirable to use a concentration of 0.001 to 0.5 wt-% catalyst dissolved in the supercritical water; the catalysts are listed in the abstract.

United States Patent [19]

Zarchy

[11]   **Patent Number:**   **4,528,100**

[45]   **Date of Patent:**   **Jul. 9, 1985**

[54]   **PROCESS FOR PRODUCING HIGH YIELD OF GAS TURBINE FUEL FROM RESIDUAL OIL**

[75]   Inventor: **Andrew S. Zarchy,** Amawalk, N.Y.

[73]   Assignee: **General Electric Company,** Schenectady, N.Y.

[21]   Appl. No.:   **547,275**

[22]   Filed: **Oct. 31, 1983**

[51]   Int. Cl.^{3} **C10G 21/06**

[52]   U.S. Cl. **210/634;** 208/309

[58]   Field of Search .... 203/49; 208/208 R, 309; 210/511, 634

[56]   **References Cited**

U.S. PATENT DOCUMENTS

3,969,196	7/1976	Zosel	203/49
4,125,459	11/1978	Garwin	208/309
4,191,639	3/1980	Audeh et al.	208/309
4,349,415	9/1982	DeFilippi et al.	210/634
4,358,365	11/1982	Hutchings et al.	208/309
4,375,387	3/1983	DeFilippi et al.	210/511

Primary Examiner—Richard V. Fisher
Assistant Examiner—W. Gary Jones
Attorney, Agent, or Firm—Lawrence D. Cutter; James C. Davis, Jr.; Marvin Snyder

[57]   **ABSTRACT**

The acceptability of residual oil as a gas turbine fuel is greatly enhanced in a two step process which significantly decreases the vanadium content of the residual fuel. In the process, the residual oil is first broken down into an oil phase and asphaltene phase by either conventional or supercritical extraction. In this step, the majority of vanadium remains in the asphaltene phase. The vanadium is then removed from the asphaltenes by a supercritical solvent extraction process in which the vanadium free asphaltene phase is then re-dissolved in the oil for use as a gas turbine fuel. This fuel possesses significantly lower vanadium content, and thus permits gas turbine operation for greater periods of time without maintenance.

3 Claims, 1 Drawing Figure

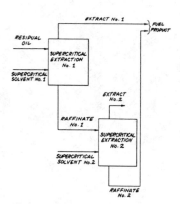

The process described employs two extraction steps (and two solvents) to produce a high yield of low metals oil which is then suitable for use as a gas turbine fuel.

The patentee relates that about 50% of the vanadium is present in residual fuel oil as a vanadyl porphyrin and the invention makes use of the relative solubilities of hydrocarbons and vanadyl porphyrin.

With reference to the drawing, residual oil and supercritical carbon dioxide (the preferred solvent, but hexane, propane, butane, etc., may be employed) are supplied to the first extraction vessel; 80–85 wt-% of the oil is extracted, and about 20–25% of the vanadium present in the residual oil appears in extract No. 1 leaving the extractor. The asphaltine phase (Raffinate No. 1) comprises 15–20 wt-% of fuel, and it contains 70–85% of the vanadium. The raffinate (No. 1) and supercritical carbon dioxide (the preferred solvent) are supplied to the second extractor and a second extract (No. 2) and a second raffinate (No. 2) are produced. The patentee relates that the extract (No. 2) contains 99% of the vanadium present in Raffinate No. 1, but he doesn't tell us the percentages of the two streams. He also doesn't tell us the conditions to carry out this separation.

United States Patent [19]

Corcoran et al.

[11]   **4,388,171**

[45]   **Jun. 14, 1983**

[54]   **SUPERCRITICAL MULTICOMPONENT SOLVENT COAL EXTRACTION**

[76]   Inventors: James M. Beggs, Administrator of the National Aeronautics and Space Administration, with respect to an invention of William H. Corcoran, San Gabriel, Calif.; William S. Fong, Cambridge, Mass.; Pavin Pichaichanarong; Paul C. F. Chan, both of Pasadena, Calif.; Daniel D. Lawson, Arcadia, Calif.

[21]   Appl. No.:   315,584

[22]   Filed: Oct. 30, 1981

[51]   Int. Cl.³ C10G 1/00; C10G 1/06
[52]   U.S. Cl. .... 208/8 LE; 208/10
[58]   Field of Search .... 208/8 LE, 10

[56]   **References Cited**

U.S. PATENT DOCUMENTS

3,558,468	1/1971	Wise	208/8 LE
3,607,716	9/1971	Roach	208/10 X
3,607,717	9/1971	Roach	208/8 LE
3,929,193	12/1975	Duke	208/8 LE X
3,970,541	7/1976	Williams et al.	208/8 LE
4,005,005	1/1977	McCallum et al.	208/11 LE
4,036,731	7/1977	Martin	208/8 LE
4,089,658	5/1978	Bay	208/8 LE X

Primary Examiner—Delbert E. Gantz
Assistant Examiner—William G. Wright
Attorney, Agent, or Firm—Paul F. McCaul; John R. Manning; Thomas H. Jones

[57]   **ABSTRACT**

The yield of organic extract from the supercritical extraction of coal with larger diameter organic solvents such as toluene is increased by use of a minor amount of from 0.1 to 10% by weight of a second solvent such as methanol having a molecular diameter significantly smaller than the average pore diameter of the coal.

14 Claims, 6 Drawing Figures

The relation of solvent molecule size and the ability to penetrate a coal structure on the yield of extract are described. It is related that a small molecule solvent may not be a good solvent but that it can penetrate the coal structure and a large molecule solvent may be a good solvent but that it might not be able to penetrate into small pores.

Data are presented which show that the use of a binary solvent extractant consisting of a minor amount of some solvent with a molecular diameter small relative to the average pore size of the coal in admixture with a good solvent with large diameter yield of material derived from coal. Furthermore, it is shown that there is an optimum ratio of the two solvents. Yield results for extracting an Illinois No. 6 high volatile bituminous coal with mixtures of methanol/toluene are given in the table below. Extraction conditions were 2000 psig, 360°C.

Table

Extraction with Methanol/Toluene Mixture

Volume Ratio, MeOH/Toluene	Weight Loss of Coal (Wt%)
0/100	16.4
2/98	17.4
5/95	19.0
10/90	16.6
16/84	14.4
20/80	10.5

United States Patent [19]

Stearns et al.

[11]   **4,192,731**

[45]   **Mar. 11, 1980**

[54]   COAL EXTRACTION PROCESS

[75]   Inventors: Richard S. Stearns, Malvern, Pa.;
Elmer J. Hollstein, Wilmington, Del.

[73]   Assignee: Suntech, Inc., Philadelphia, Pa.

[21]   Appl. No.: 918,216

[22]   Filed: Jun. 23, 1978

[51]   Int. Cl.^{2} C10G 1/00
[52]   U.S. Cl. .... 208/8 LE
[58]   Field of Search .... 208/8 LE

[56]   **References Cited**

U.S. PATENT DOCUMENTS

3,379,638	4/1968	Bloomer et al.	208/8 LE
3,558,468	1/1971	Wise	208/8 LE
3,966,585	6/1976	Gray et al.	208/8 LE
3,983,027	9/1976	McCollum et al.	208/8 LE
4,039,425	8/1977	Neavel	208/8 LE
4,077,866	3/1978	Owen et al.	208/8 LE X

FOREIGN PATENT DOCUMENTS

835217	1/1976	Belgium .	
835286	1/1976	Belgium .	
1261707	1/1972	United Kingdom	208/8 LE

Primary Examiner—Delbert E. Gantz
Assistant Examiner—William G. Wright
Attorney, Agent, or Firm—J. Edward Hess; Donald R. Johnson; Paul Lipsitz

[57]   **ABSTRACT**

Coal and other solid fossil fuels are subjected to supercritical gaseous extraction by heating a mixture of particulate coal and a solvent mixture of tetralin and xylene at supercritical temperature whereby high extractive yield is obtained and the residual solid material is easily separated from the liquid product.

5 Claims, No Drawings

The invention in this patent is the use of a supercritical fluid extractant consisting of a mixture of from 50
to 75 wt% tetralin and correspondingly from 50 to 25%
xylene. The examples give results of comparative coal
extraction tests using xylene, tetralin, and the xylene-
tetralin mixture. Extraction conditions in all tests were
$425°C$, 1250–1350 psi. With solely xylene as the extractant conversion of coal to useful products was found to be
low, viz., 24%. With solely tetralin the conversion was
high at 65%, but separation of undissolved particulates
(which were reduced to the form of powder) was difficult. A
50–50 xylene and tetralin mixture gave a high conversion,
about 40–60%, and, additionally, the separation of particulates was found to be quite easy.

One other example showed that the tetralin/xylene
mixture in the supercritical state was required. A test
carried out in the liquid region at $300°C$ and 250 psi gave a
conversion of only 9%. A temperature of $300°C$ is quite low
relative to the $425°C$ tests described above, and it would
have been of greater interest and information to carry out
the test at, say, about $10°C$ below T_c and at the vapor (or
higher) pressure; then we (and they) would have been able to
determine if there is any difference between yields with
strictly supercritical xylene-tetralin and a "very hot"
liquid xylene-tetralin mixture. As we have seen previously
and as we will see in other subsequent patents, quite often
certain specific and irrelevant tests are compared for the
purpose of showing that the invention is superior to other
methods of operation.

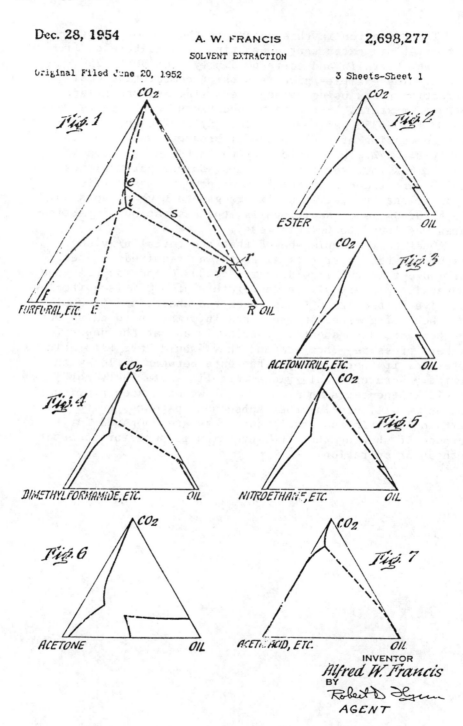

Dec. 28, 1954   A. W. FRANCIS   2,698,277
                            SOLVENT EXTRACTION

Original Filed June 20, 1952   3 Sheets-Sheet 1

Fig. 1

CO₂

e
i
s
r
p
f
FURFURAL, ETC.   E   R OIL

Fig. 2

CO₂

ESTER   OIL

Fig. 3

CO₂

ACETONITRILE, ETC.   OIL

Fig. 4

CO₂

DIMETHYLFORMAMIDE, ETC.   OIL

Fig. 5

CO₂

NITROETHANE, ETC.   OIL

Fig. 6

CO₂

ACETONE   OIL

Fig. 7

CO₂

ACETIC ACID, ETC.   OIL

INVENTOR
Alfred W. Francis
BY
Robert D. Lynn
AGENT

We would be remiss if we did not include at least one of Francis' many patents on the use of liquid carbon dioxide in separating hydrocarbons. Francis cites, among others, Lantz's patent (U.S. 2,188,051) in the prior art, and he states that the process described in that patent is not a simple extraction but a precipitation. Francis also makes use of carbon dioxide in conjunction with another solvent to separate oils, but in a different manner. Whereas in the Lantz process the solvent (a hydrocarbon) is completely miscible with the oil, Francis selects solvents that are not completely miscible with the oil, (but in both processes the solvent is miscible with carbon dioxide). Francis finds that carbon dioxide and the solvent in admixture exhibit a greater dissolving power for the oil than the solvent alone.

Figure 1 is a ternary diagram used to describe the results in one of the examples that Francis presents. Excerpting from his discussion,

"Figure 1 reveals that furfural and liquid carbon dioxide are completely miscible, that furfural has a low solvent power for the oil, and that liquid carbon dioxide has a low solvent power for the oil. The solubility of oil in furfural is 3% as indicated by point f of Figure 1. The solubility is increased to about 16% at i, by adding about 60% of liquid carbon dioxide in the solvent mixture. A system s is assembled with about 30% oil, 20% furfural and 50% carbon dioxide; this separates into two layers, e (upper) an extract layer, and r (lower) a raffinate layer.

"Following separation of layers e and r and release of carbon dioxide (to E and R, respectively), about 80% of the oil dissolved in the extract layer e is separated (at the top), leaving a dilute furfural solution f which is recycled without distillation. The only furfural which need be recovered by distillation or by other means is the relatively small amount dissolved in the raffinate R, and the small amount dissolved in the second oil layer (the extract-raffinate); about 2% of furfural is present in each of such layers. This represents a saving of about 90% in distillation requirements over conventional furfural extractions."

United States Patent [19]

Roach

[11] **Patent Number:**   **4,508,597**

[45] **Date of Patent:**   **Apr. 2, 1985**

[54] **RECOVERY OF ORGANIC SOLVENTS FROM LIQUID MIXTURES**

[75] Inventor: **Jack W. Roach,** Oklahoma City, Okla.

[73] Assignee: **Kerr-McGee Refining Corporation,** Oklahoma City, Okla.

[21] Appl. No.:   **366,040**

[22] Filed: **Apr. 5, 1982**

[51] Int. Cl.³ **B01D 3/38**
[52] U.S. Cl. **203/79; 203/85;**
203/95; 208/356; 208/361; 208/367; 585/835

[58] **Field of Search** 203/76, 79, 83, 85,
203/95–97, 42–46; 208/308, 347, 350, 356, 361,
362, 363, 367; 585/800, 833, 835, 867

[56]   **References Cited**

U.S. PATENT DOCUMENTS

2,166,160	4/1939	King	196/13
2,222,347	11/1940	Gard et al.	208/367
2,242,173	7/1941	Buckley	62/175.5
2,391,576	10/1945	Katz et al.	196/73
2,391,607	8/1945	Whaley	196/88
2,596,785	4/1952	Nelly et al.	48/190
2,886,610	5/1959	Georgian	203/83
2,940,920	12/1960	Garwin	208/45
3,607,716	5/1971	Roach	208/8

3,607,717	8/1971	Roach	208/8
3,969,196	5/1976	Zosel	203/49
4,273,644	6/1981	Harris et al.	208/309
4,305,814	12/1981	Leonard	208/321

OTHER PUBLICATIONS

Description in Prior Art Statement of Steam Stripping Conducted in Multi-Tray Vessel.

Primary Examiner—Frank Sever
Attorney, Agent, or Firm—William G. Addison

[57]   **ABSTRACT**

A method of recovering light organic solvent from a liquid mixture containing the solvent and a product material, such as asphaltenes or coal liquefaction products. The solvent-product material mixture is treated to separate a first vapor phase rich in solvent and a first liquid phase rich in product material. The first liquid phase is then intimately contacted with steam, under shearing conditions, in a static or dynamic mixer. The steam-liquid phase mixture is then treated to separate a second vapor phase, rich in steam and solvent, and a second liquid phase, rich in product material and substantially depleted of solvent. Solvent is recovered from the first and second vapor phases.

15 Claims, 2 Drawing Figures

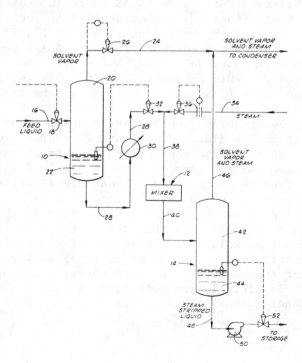

    This patent is the most recent one located that is
assigned to Kerr-McGee and is another variation of extraction of heavy hydrocarbons and coal liquids. The patent is
included for discussion here because it relates some
difficulties with the heavy hydrocarbon extraction-solvent
separation in other supercritical fluid extraction processes. Those of us who have carried out such extractions
are all too familiar with the problem described. For
example, when a heavy hydrocarbon is extracted with
supercritical pentane, for example, a light phase and a
heavy phase are formed. The heavy phase is usually subsequently freed of its solvent by a depressurization and
steam stripping step; during the process of steam stripping
and as the solvent is increasingly removed, the viscosity of
the asphalt-bituminous material (the heavy phase) increases,
and the high viscosity renders the mixture difficult to
strip of its solvent vestiges.

    The invention is a method to facilitate recovery of the
solvent from the asphalt or solvent refined coal. The heavy
phase 22 from the supercritical extraction in the extractor
10 is transferred 28, 30, and 38 to a high shear mixer 12
where it is admixed with steam 34, 36, and 38. The heat
exchanger 30 heats the heavy phase in order to achieve a low
viscosity for the mixing. The intimately-contacted mixture
is conveyed 40 to a solvent separation vessel 14. The
solvent-steam mixture 42 is withdrawn 46 from the separator
and sent to a condenser and solvent-water separator (not
shown). The second heavy liquid phase 44 from the second
vessel 14 is withdrawn 48, 50, and 52 and sent to storage.

United States Patent [19]

Peter

[11] Patent Number: **4,508,543**

[45] Date of Patent: **Apr. 2, 1985**

[54] **PROCESS FOR THE CATALYTIC GASIFICATION OF SOLID FLUIDS WITH STEAM**

[75] Inventor: **Siegfried Peter**, Erlangen, Fed. Rep. of Germany

[73] Assignee: **Kraftwerk Union Aktiengesellschaft,** Fed. Rep. of Germany

[21] Appl. No.: **29,719**

[22] Filed: **Apr. 13, 1979**

[30] **Foreign Application Priority Data**

Apr. 24, 1978 [DE] Fed. Rep. of Germany 2817835

[51] Int. Cl.^{3} **C10J 3/00**
[52] U.S. Cl. .... **48/197 R;** 48/202; 252/373
[58] Field of Search .... 48/202, 206, 210, 197 R, 48/214 A; 252/373; 423/650; 201/38

[56] **References Cited**

U.S. PATENT DOCUMENTS

2,543,795	3/1951	Mayer	48/202
2,694,624	11/1954	Sweetser	48/206

FOREIGN PATENT DOCUMENTS

2530600	1/1977	Fed. Rep. of Germany	48/202

Primary Examiner—Peter Kratz
Attorney, Agent, or Firm—Wyatt, Gerber, Shoup, Scobey and Badie

[57] **ABSTRACT**

Disclosed is a process for gasifying solid carbon fuels with steam. After forming a supersaturated solution of catalyst in steam the pressure is reduced to reaction pressure.

11 Claims, No Drawings

This process employs supercritical water to dissolve a catalyst such as alkali or alkaline earth salts and hydroxides, an expansion to a lower pressure level to nucleate the catalyst to a fine mist (or, if precipitation does not occur, to form an "oversaturated" solution), and a contact of this stream with a coal or coke bed at a temperature of about 850°C to convert the coal to gaseous compounds.

The results from one example best describe the invention. As a control pit coke (formed by heating pit coal to 700°) was reacted with steam at 140 bar, 850°C. The product gas was 2.4 standard liters per liter of coke; the gas analysis, 55% H_2, 11% methane, 4% CO, 30% CO_2. In a second series, pit coke was impregnated with potassium carbonate and reacted at the same conditions as given above. The product was 2.5 liters of gas with composition 56% H_2, 11% methane, 4% CO, 29% CO_2 i.e., the yield and analyses were about the same as for the previous test. In a third series, steam at 300 bar, 500°C was mixed with potassium carbonate solution, and was reduced in pressure to 140 bar, and this stream was reacted with pit coke at 850°C. The product was 5.8 liters of gas with composition 56% H_2, 11.5% methane, 2% CO, 30.5% CO_2. The results show that dissolving the potassium carbonate and subsequently nucleating it in the gas phase gives a higher yield of gas than either the control or the solution treated coal.

Zosel, K., Process for recovering caffeine, U.S. 3,806,619
    (Apr. 23, 1974).
Roselius, W., O. Vitzthum, and P. Hubert, Method for the
    production of caffeine-free coffee extract, U.S.
    3,843,824 (Oct. 22, 1974).
Vitzthum, O. and P. Hubert, Process for the decaffeination
    of raw coffee, U.S. 3,879,569 (Apr. 22, 1975).
Vitzthum, O. and P. Hubert, Process for the manufacture of
    caffeine-free black tea, U.S. 4,167,589 (Sep. 11,
    1979).
Roselius, L., H.A. Kurzhals, K.F. Sylla, and P. Hubert,
    Process of extracting stimulants from coffee, U.S.
    4,168,324 (Sep. 18, 1979).
Prasad, R., M. Gottesman, and R.A. Scarella, Decaffeination
    of aqueous extracts, U.S. 4,246,291 (Jan. 20, 1981).
Zosel, K., Process for the decaffeination of coffee, U.S.
    4,247,570 (Jan. 27, 1981).
Margolis, G. and J. Chiovini, Decaffeination process, U.S.
    4,251,559 (Feb. 17, 1981).
Roselius, L., H.A. Kurzhals, and P. Hubert, Method for the
    selective extraction of caffeine from vegetable
    materials, U.S. 4,255,458 (Mar. 10, 1981).
Jasovsky, G.A. and M. Gottesman, Preparation of a
    decaffeinated roasted coffee blend, U.S. 4,255,461
    (Mar. 10, 1981).
Zosel, K., Process for the decaffeination of coffee, U.S.
    4,260,639 (Apr. 7, 1981).
Roselius, W., O. Vitzthum, P. Hubert, Method of extracting
    coffee oil containing aroma constituents from roasted
    coffee, U.S. 4,328,255 (May 4, 1982).
Katz, S.N., Method for decaffeinating coffee, U.S. 4,276,315
    (Jun. 30, 1981).
Peter, S. and G. Brunner, Process for decaffeinating coffee,
    U.S. 4,322,445 (Mar. 30, 1982).
Zosel, K., Process for the direct decaffeination of aqueous
    coffee extract solutions, U.S. 4,348,422 (Sept. 7,
    1982).

United States Patent [19]

Zosel

[11]   **3,806,619**

[45]   **Apr. 23, 1974**

[54] PROCESS FOR RECOVERING CAFFEINE

[75] Inventor: **Kurt Zosel,** Oberhausen/Rheinland, Germany

[73] Assignee: **Studiengesellschaft Kohle m.b.H,** Mulheim/Ruhr, Germany

[22] Filed: **May 3, 1972**

[21] Appl. No.: **249,809**

[30]   **Foreign Application Priority Data**

May 7, 1971   Austria 4003/71

[52] U.S. Cl.............. **426/478, 426/427, 159/16 R,** 159/47, 203/49

[51] Int. Cl. **A23f 1/10**

[58] Field of Search .... 99/69, 70; 159/16 R, 47; 203/12, 24, 26, 49

[56]   **References Cited**

UNITED STATES PATENTS

1,640,648	8/1927	Cross	99/69
2,032,087	2/1936	Göth	159/16 R
2,042,488	6/1936	Theiler...........................	159/16 R X
2,342,419	2/1944	Martin	159/16 R X
2,619,453	11/1952	Andersen...........................	203/12 X

3,345,272	10/1967	Collins..............................	159/16 R

FOREIGN PATENTS OR APPLICATIONS

1,057,911	2/1967	Great Britain

Primary Examiner—Frank W. Lutter
Assistant Examiner—William L. Mentlik
Attorney, Agent, or Firm—Ralph D. Dinklage

[57]   **ABSTRACT**

A process for obtaining caffein from green coffee by withdrawing the caffein by means of recirculating moist carbon dioxide in supercritical state, which comprises removing the caffein from the caffein-loaded carbon dioxide by repeated treatment with water and recovering the caffein and the water from the resultant dilute aqueous caffein solution by recycling a stream of air or nitrogen under a superatmospheric pressure at about 1 to 5 atmospheres through the heated caffein solution and a heat exchanger, separating the caffein and the condensed water and recycling after admixture of cold caffein solution the gas through the heat exchanger in countercurrent flow relation and meeting the heat requirement by supplying heat to the hot caffein solution.

6 Claims, 1 Drawing Figure

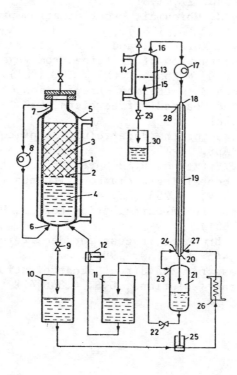

This patent is chronologically the first in the quite
long list of patents on supercritical fluid processing of
coffee. It describes along with supercritical extraction of
green coffee a means of obtaining crystallized caffeine,
from the carbon dioxide stream. In summary of the operation
of the process and with reference to the figure, carbon
dioxide leaving the compressor 12 is saturated with water 4
and is passed through the bed of moistened, green coffee
beans 3. The carbon dioxide stream that contains the
caffeine extracted from the beans leaves the coffee bean bed
at 7 and is recirculated to the water pool in the vessel at
6. The caffeine is extracted from the carbon dioxide by the
water. (Recall it was stated in Chapter 10 that the
distribution coefficient for extracting caffeine from water
with carbon dioxide is quite small ($\sim$0.03); thus, the
extraction from carbon dioxide using water is quite
favorable.) After about one-half the caffeine has been
extracted from the coffee beans, the water solution is
drained from the vessel into another vessel 10, fresh water
is added to the extractor, and the decaffeination is
continued until the caffeine content of the beans has again
dropped by one-half. This procedure is repeated two more
times, i.e., in all, four charges of water are added to the
vessel.

To start the separation of caffeine from the aqueous
solution, a small portion of the solution from vessel 10 is
pumped to vessel 13 and is heated to about 100°C. Air (or
N_2) at about 4 atm pressure is blown through the
caffeine-water solution in vessel 13. The moisture-laden
air leaving the vessel at 16 is cooled in the heat exchanger
19; the air and condensed water leaving the heat exchanger
at point 20 are separated in vessel 21. The water is
returned to vessel 11, and the cooled air is returned to the
outside shell of the heat exchanger at point 24. It is
mixed with cool caffeine-water solution that is pumped from
vessel 10 to point 27. The air-caffeine-water solution in
the shell side is heated by the hot air-water stream flowing
through the tube side; heat exchange causes the water to
vaporize into the air thus concentrating the caffeine in the
water solution 13. At the end of the stripping process,
after all the dilute caffeine-water solution has been pumped
through the heat exchanger and is then contained in vessel
13, the hot concentrated caffeine-containing solution is
cooled, most of the caffeine precipitates and is filtered
and the mother liquor is returned to vessel 10 for the next
coffee bean decaffeination sequence.

United States Patent [19]

Roselius et al.

[11]   **3,843,824**

[45]   **Oct. 22, 1974**

[54] METHOD FOR THE PRODUCTION OF
CAFFEINE-FREE COFFEE EXTRACT

[75] Inventors: Wilhelm Roselius, Bremen-St.
Magnus; Otto Vitzthum, Bremen;
Peter Hubert, Bremen-Lesum, all of
Germany

[73] Assignee: HAG Aktiengesellschaft, Bremen,
Germany

[22] Filed: **Apr. 19, 1972**

[21] Appl. No.: 245,501

[30]   **Foreign Application Priority Data**

Apr. 22, 1971   Germany.................... 2119678

[52] U.S. Cl.................. 426/386, 426/427, 426/478
[51] Int. Cl. A23f 1/10
[58] Field of Search 99/71, 70, 69; 426/386,
426/427, 478

[56]   **References Cited**
UNITED STATES PATENTS

1,640,648   8/1927   Cross 99/69

2,345,378	3/1944	Brandt	99/71
2,542,119	2/1951	Cole	99/71
2,563,233	8/1951	Gilmont	99/71
3,477,856	11/1969	Schultz	99/71 X

FOREIGN PATENTS OR APPLICATIONS

1,106,468	3/1968	Great Britain	99/71
1,057,911	2/1967	Great Britain	

Primary Examiner—Frank W. Lutter
Assistant Examiner—William L. Mentlik
Attorney, Agent, or Firm—Burgess, Dinklage &
Sprung

[57]   **ABSTRACT**

A method for the production of a caffein-free coffee
product which comprises separating coffee oil by extraction of roasted coffee with a dry supercritical
fluid, separating caffein from the roasted coffee by extraction with wet supercritical carbon dioxide, producing an extract from the decaffeinated roasted coffee
and recovering the extracted coffee oil and adding at
least a portion thereof to a coffee extract.

17 Claims, 3 Drawing Figures

One example from this patent was previously reproduced in Chapter 10, and one reason for the large carbon dioxide volume needed to decaffeinate coffee was developed. A three step process for producing a caffeine-free extract is described and additionally the examples contain information which points out that moist carbon dioxide is not selective for caffeine. The drawing is not given on the patent face page, but it is quite similar to the naphthalene extraction process depicted in Figure 6.1. In the first step, dry, coarse ground coffee is contacted with dry carbon dioxide to extract the aroma oils (which it is to be recalled are generated only during the roasting process). The aroma oil-carbon dioxide solution leaving the extractor is lowered in pressure and cooled to below the critical temperature of carbon dioxide which causes the oils to precipitate in a separator. Carbon dioxide is vaporized, is condensed, and is pumped to the extractor through a heat exchanger. This raises the carbon dioxide to above its critical temperature; the recycle process continues until all the aroma oils are extracted and collected in the separator.

The second step is the extraction of caffeine. Carbon dioxide is first humidified before being passed through the charge of ground coffee. As we have discussed, caffeine is extracted by the moist carbon dioxide. (Incidentally, one of the examples states that "residual oil," i.e., that which has not been extracted by dry carbon dioxide in the first step, is also extracted by the moist carbon dioxide, which further corroborates the information given in Chapter 10 on the "selectivity.)" The caffeine is separated from the carbon dioxide in another separator vessel. Aroma oil and carbon dioxide recycle continues until all the caffeine has been extracted.

Coffee extract is prepared by pumping water at $160^{\circ}C$ through the vessel containing the ground coffee; the solution is spray dried. The aroma oils that had been extracted from the ground coffee in step 1 are dissolved in a solvent, the solution added to the spray dried solids and the solvent is evaporated.

United States Patent [19]

Vitzthum et al.

[11]   **3,879,569**

[45] **Apr. 22, 1975**

[54] **PROCESS FOR THE DECAFFEINATION OF RAW COFFEE**

[75] Inventors: **Otto Vitzthum,** Bremen; **Peter Hubert,** Bremen-Lesum, both of Germany

[73] Assignee: **HAG Aktiengesellschaft,** Bremen, Germany

[22] Filed: **Mar. 12, 1973**

[21] Appl. No.: **340,187**

[30]   **Foreign Application Priority Data**

Mar. 14, 1972   Germany............................ 2212281

[52] **U.S. Cl.** 426/427; 260/256; 426/428
[51] **Int. Cl.** A23f 1/10
[58] **Field of Search** 426/427, 428

[56]   **References Cited**

FOREIGN PATENTS OR APPLICATIONS

2,005,293   11/1971   Germany 426/428

OTHER PUBLICATIONS

"Sugar, Cocoa, Coffee, Tea, Spice, Leaven" by Winton, Published by John Wiley and Sons 1939, pages 148–149.

Primary Examiner—Frank W. Lutter
Assistant Examiner—Neil F. Greenblum

[57]   **ABSTRACT**

Raw coffee moistened to a water content of about 10 to 60% by weight is extracted with aqueous liquid carbon dioxide at a pressure above the critical pressure to extract caffein values therefrom. The caffein may be separately recovered.

8 Claims, 2 Drawing Figures

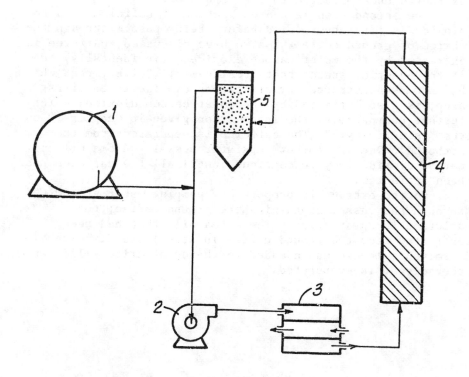

We stated in the introduction to this appendix that we would accent statements of "surprise" in patents when we felt information existed which would make the surprise statement unwarranted or confusing to a reader attempting to garner knowledge about supercritical fluid properties. In the prior art discussion the patentees present that previous coffee decaffeination processes including supercritical carbon dioxide extraction are deficient. We have no problem with that statement; they may very well be deficient. It is also related specifically that the temperature range of $40-80°C$ used in the supercritical carbon dioxide extraction process produces a coffee "not satisfactory as to taste"; although we have no experience in judging coffee flavor, we have no problem with that statement either. The patentees will show in their examples that liquid carbon dioxide will produce a decaffeinated coffee with improved flavor.

In the invention section, however, they compare results of tests that should not be compared for any relevance, and based upon the comparisons the patentees relate that they are "surprised" at the findings. For example, we read that liquid carbon dioxide has been reported to extract aroma oils from roasted coffee. Recall we stated that many aroma compounds are soluble in liquid or supercritical carbon dioxide, but recall also that we said that there are aroma oils only in roasted coffee because they are generated during the roasting process. Nevertheless, the invention is introduced by stating that "it has now surprisingly been discovered that raw coffee ... can be selectively extracted with liquid carbon dioxide at a pressure above the critical pressure to remove caffeine in a practically pure state without affecting the aroma content of the coffee."

The examples and claims cover the use of carbon dioxide with rather restrictive conditions, viz., a pressure above the critical pressure and a temperature below $31°C$, and they state that operating with these conditions produces a coffee with more satisfying taste. (Several other patents that we discuss subsequently will also claim the use of liquid carbon dioxide at pressures above the critical pressure; we shall refer to this state as "high pressure liquid carbon dioxide" in contradistinction to "liquid carbon dioxide" which is at or near its vapor pressure.)

United States Patent [19]

Vitzthum et al.

[11] **4,167,589**

[45] **Sep. 11, 1979**

[54] METHOD FOR THE MANUFACTURE OF CAFFEINE FREE BLACK TEA

[76] Inventors: Otto Vitzthurı, Bremen; Peter Hubert, Bremen-Lesum, both of Fed. Rep. oʃ Germany

[21] Appl. No.: 791,097

[22] Filed: Apr. 21, 1977

Related U.S. Application Data

[63] Continuation of Ser. No. 646,779, Jan. 6, 1976, abandoned, which is a continuation of Ser. No. 461,056, Apr. 15, 1974, abandoned, which is a continuation of Ser. No. 258,508, Jun. 1, 1972, abandoned.

[30] **Foreign Application Priority Data**

Jun. 1, 1972 [DE] Fed. Rep. of Germany 2127642

[51] Int. Cl.^{2} A23F 3/00

[52] U.S. Cl. 426/312; 426/318; 426/319; 426/386; 426/427; 426/428; 426/424; 426/478

[58] Field of Search 426/427, 428, 386, 424, 426/478, 312, 318, 319

[56] **References Cited**

U.S. PATENT DOCUMENTS

1,640,648	8/1927	Cross	426/354
3,477,856	11/1969	Schultz	426/424
3,532,506	10/1970	Rey et al.	426/435 X
3,806,619	4/1974	Zosel	426/427 X
3,823,241	7/1974	Patel et al.	426/386
3,843,824	10/1974	Roseluis et al.	426/386
3,879,569	4/1975	Vetzheem et al.	426/427

FOREIGN PATENT DOCUMENTS

82633	6/1971	German Democratic Rep.	426/427
2005293	10/1972	Fed. Rep. of Germany	426/428
43128	5/1938	Netherlands	426/386
1057911	2/1967	United Kingdom	426/386
1106468	3/1968	United Kingdom	426/386

Primary Examiner—Joseph M. Golian
Attorney, Agent, or Firm—Sprung, Felfe, Horn, Lynch & Kramer

[57]   **ABSTRACT**

A caffeine free black tea product is produced by an extraction procedure with a supercritical gas such as carbon dioxide in which first the aromatic content of the tea is extracted with dry gas, then the caffeine content is extracted with wet gas, and finally the decaffeinated tea is reimpregnated with the aromatic content.

19 Claims, 1 Drawing Figure

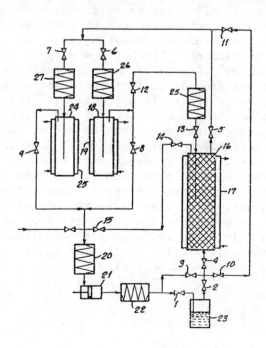

This patent on a three step tea decaffeination process is included in chronological order with the coffee patents because of its similarity to U.S. 3,843,824 which describes a three-step process for the decaffeination of roasted coffee. In the first step, tea aromas are removed from dry tea in vessel 17 and precipitated in vessel 18 using dry supercritical carbon dioxide. In a next step, the tea is moistened and moist carbon dioxide via 23 is passed through the tea to extract the caffeine. In a third step, the aromas (which have been collected in vessel 18) are transferred back to the tea. This is done, after the moist tea has been dried, by dissolving the aromas in vessel 18 in supercritical carbon dioxide, and passing the stream first through a heat exchanger 25 to liquify the carbon dioxide and then to vessel 17 containing the dried tea. When the vessel is filled with the solution of liquid carbon dioxide and the aromas, that were previously extracted, vapor carbon dioxide is withdrawn from the vessel 17 and the aromas precipitate into (and onto) the tea.

For some additional information here, we previously reviewed the patent that claimed the use of high pressure liquid carbon dioxide to decaffeinate coffee; there is no "sister" patent for using liquid carbon dioxide, either at high pressure or near its vapor pressure, to decaffeinate tea (at least not known to the authors), and there is probably a good reason for this, viz., it is quite difficult to decaffeinate tea with liquid carbon dioxide. Although the Vitzthum and Hubert patent gave only the elapsed time and not the volume of liquid carbon dioxide required to decaffeinate coffee, the ratio of liquid carbon dioxide required to decaffeinate coffee is about 150 lbs/lb coffee. However, the ratio of liquid carbon dioxide required to decaffeinate tea is 1200(!) (Krukonis 1981, unpublished data). Part of the reason for the higher ratio resides in the higher caffeine content of tea, typically 3% instead of the 1% level in most coffees; the other part of the reason is that it is "more difficult" to decaffeinate tea; the difficulty is associated with a quite-adverse caffeine equilibrium similar to that described for coffee in Chapter 10.

United States Patent [19]

Roselius et al.

[11]   **4,168,324**

[45]   **Sep. 18, 1979**

[54] **PROCESS OF EXTRACTING STIMULANTS FROM COFFEE**

[75] Inventors: Ludwig Roselius, Bremen; Hans-Albert Kurzhals, Heissenbüttel; Klaus F. Sylla, Bremen; Peter Hubert, Bremen-Lesum, all of Fed. Rep. of Germany

[73] Assignee: HAG Aktiengesellschaft, Fed. Rep. of Germany

[21] Appl. No.: 772,365

[22] Filed: Feb. 25, 1977

[30]   **Foreign Application Priority Data**

Aug. 30, 1976 [DE] Fed. Rep. of Germany 2639066

[51] Int. Cl.² A23F 1/04
[52] U.S. Cl. 426/312; 426/318; 426/319; 426/478; 426/481

[58] Field of Search 426/312, 318, 319, 478, 426/481

[56]   **References Cited**

U.S. PATENT DOCUMENTS

3,806,619 4/1974 Zosel 426/478
3,843,824 10/1974 Roselius .... 426/478 X

FOREIGN PATENT DOCUMENTS

1057911 2/1967 United Kingdom 426/478

Primary Examiner—Joseph M. Golian
Attorney, Agent, or Firm—Pollock, Vande Sande & Priddy

[57]   **ABSTRACT**

A method of producing coffee low in undesired stimulants by removing coffee wax from unroasted coffee by the use of a supercritical fluid and absorbing the coffee wax in an absorbent precharged with pure caffeine.

18 Claims, 2 Drawing Figures

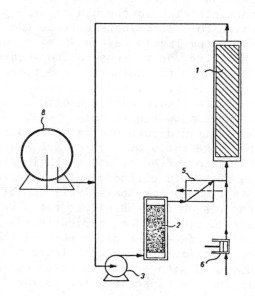

The background section of this patent explains that in addition to caffeine in coffee there are other ingredients that can have harmful physiological effects on the gastrointestinal system. These ingredients are lipophilic and are contained in the so-called coffee wax. The patent relates that when coffee wax is removed from coffee the digestibility of the coffee is improved. Carboxylic acid-5-hydroxy-tryptamides (C-5-HT) are compounds in the wax and serve as indicators in the removal of wax. The specific invention is the removal of coffee wax (and the C-5-HT) using a supercritical fluid extractant while maintaining caffeine content at its initial level in the coffee.

The water content of the raw coffee beans is adjusted to 20-35% and is contacted with supercritical carbon dioxide at 250 atm, 80°C. At these conditions, supercritical carbon dioxide will also extract caffeine. How, then, is the process operated so as to maintain the caffeine content of the coffee constant?

The figure on the patent face page is a flow chart of the process. Vessel 1 is originally charged with raw, moistened coffee beans. Vessel 2 contains activated carbon which has been contacted with saturated aqueous caffeine solution. The "first" portion of fresh supercritical carbon dioxide leaving vessel 1 contains "some" caffeine that is extracted from the coffee; it also contains C-5-HT and other coffee wax constituents. The stream leaving vessel 1 is circulated by pump 3 to the adsorber 2 containing activated carbon which has been saturated with caffeine; therefore, as the carbon dioxide stream that contains dissolved caffeine and C-5-HT is passed through the bed of activated carbon, caffeine is not removed from the carbon dioxide, but C-5-HT is. In the "next" pass of the carbon dioxide through the extractor no caffeine will be extracted (because the carbon dioxide and its dissolved caffeine are in equilibrium with the caffeine in the coffee substrate) but C-5-HT will continue to be extracted. In theory, it should be possible to adjust the caffeine loading on the activated carbon to match the equilibrium of the carbon dioxide-caffeine coffee system; in practice, however, this may be difficult to do and item 6 is a "dosing" pump used to inject a caffeine solution into the recirculated carbon dioxide to maintain the caffeine content of the coffee constant. The examples show that C-5-HT can be removed while maintaining the caffeine constant.

United States Patent [19]

Prasad et al.

[11] **4,246,291**

[45] **Jan. 20, 1981**

[54] **DECAFFEINATION OF AQUEOUS EXTRACTS**

[75] Inventors: Ravi Prasad, Middletown, N.Y.;
Martin Gottesman, Paramus, N.J.;
Robert A. Scarella, Hawthorne, N.Y.

[73] Assignee: General Foods Corporation, White
Plains, N.Y.

[21] Appl. No.: 23,878

[22] Filed: Mar. 26, 1979

[51] Int. Cl.³ A23F 5/18
[52] U.S. Cl. 426/387; 426/427
[58] Field of Search 426/387, 427

[56] **References Cited**

FOREIGN PATENT DOCUMENTS

2638383 3/1977 Fed. Rep. of Germany 426/427

Primary Examiner—Joseph M. Golian
Attorney, Agent, or Firm—Thomas R. Savoie; Daniel J. Donovan

[57]   **ABSTRACT**

Aqueous extracts of roasted coffee are stripped of aroma, concentrated and thereafter decaffeinated by means of contact with a decaffeinating fluid such as liquid or supercritical carbon dioxide. Aroma loss is minimized by using water to remove caffeine and aroma from the CO_2 stream, recovering aromatics from this caffeine-containing aqueous stream and adding-back these aromatics to the decaffeinated extract. Preferably equipment cost is minimized by use of a single pressure vessel to transfer the caffeine from the extract stream to the CO_2 and from the CO_2 to the water stream.

4 Claims, 1 Drawing Figure

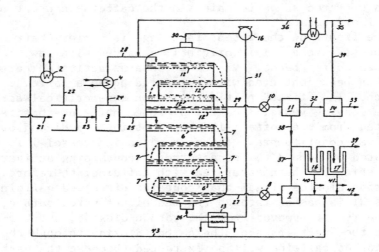

This is the first of the coffee decaffeination patents that describe that "chemical engineer's dream," i.e., a continuous, counter-current liquid-liquid extraction. A brief description of the process shown in the drawing on the facing page is provided here. A water extract of roasted coffee beans which contains aromas and caffeine (and other water soluble components such as carbohydrate and protein materials) is fed to the system at point 1, a vacuum strip-per. The extract (called coffee liquor) is concentrated to about 30-50% in the evaporator-condenser section 1 and 3, and the liquor is fed to a sieve tray tower via line 25. The liquor passes across the trays 6 in the tower downward through downspouts 7 countercurrent to supercritical carbon dioxide which enters the tower at 26 and passes upward through the holes in the sieve trays. Carbon dioxide extracts caffeine from the liquor, and the decaffeinated liquor leaves the tower via line 27. The condensate (water) from the vacuum evaporator section is fed to the sieve trays in the top section of the tower via line 28; the water washes the caffeine from the supercritical carbon dioxide passing upward. The caffeine-free carbon dioxide is recy-cled via pump 16 to the bottom of the column. (The sections to the right of the major tower represent other facets of the process. Although these sections are important for the total coffee preparation process, they are not relevant to this decaffeination discussion.)

An example described in the patent relates the extrac-tion conditions and the flow rates employed for a test. The flow rates reported are huge. The patent reports that cof-fee liquor containing 15% solids is fed at 11,000 lbs/hr to the evaporator and concentrated to 30% solids; 4950 lbs/hr of concentrate is fed to the extraction tower, and 5500 lbs/hr of condensate is sent to the top of the tower. Car-bon dioxide at 40°C and 300 atm and at a flow rate of 495,000 lbs/hr (!) is pumped to the bottom of the tower to strip caffeine from the coffee liquor passing downward through the tower.

It is informative to make some estimates about the size of the column used in this test. In normal liquid-liquid extraction, Treyball discusses that a typical "hole velocity," i.e., the velocity of the lighter liquid passing upward through the holes, is about 0.3 ft/sec, and that a typical hole area is about 10-20% of the plate area. If we use these values to estimate the diameter of the coffee de-caffeination tower, we calculate that the total hole area is about 8 ft^{2}; assuming an average 15% hole area the cross sectional area of the column is 54 ft^{2}, or a diameter of 8 ft. Like the 495,000 lb/hr flow rate related earlier, an 8 ft diameter column is quite a large column in which to carry out experimental decaffeination tests. Do the data that are reported in the example originate from the operation of a commercial facility somewhere or are the data made up?

United States Patent [19]

Zosel

[11]   **4,247,570**

[45]   **Jan. 27, 1981**

[54] **PROCESS FOR THE DECAFFEINATION OF COFFEE**

[75] Inventor: **Kurt Zosel**, Oberhausen, Feu. Rep. of Germany

[73] Assignee: **Studiengesellschaft Kohle mbH,** Kaiser-Wilhelm Platz, Fed. Rep. of Germany

[21] Appl. No.: **798,744**

[22] Filed: **May 19, 1977**

[30]   **Foreign Application Priority Data**

Aug. 4, 1976 [AT]	Austria	5769/76
Oct. 20, 1976 [AT]	Austria	7806/76
Dec. 14, 1976 [AT]	Austria	9248/76

[51] Int. Cl.^{3} A23F 5/20
[52] U.S. Cl. 426/481; 426/427
[58] Field of Search 426/427, 428, 481

[56]   **References Cited**

U.S. PATENT DOCUMENTS

1,930,257	10/1933	Stelkens	426/595 X
2,198,859	4/1940	Bürgin	426/427 X
2,375,550	5/1945	Grossman	426/427 X
3,418,134	12/1968	Rooker	426/386
3,806,619	4/1974	Zosel	426/427 X
3,843,824	10/1974	Roseluis et al.	426/427 X
3,879,569	4/1975	Vetzbium et al.	426/427

FOREIGN PATENT DOCUMENTS

553800	7/1932	Fed. Rep. of Germany	426/427
775227	7/1934	France	426/427

Primary Examiner—Joseph M. Golian
Attorney, Agent, or Firm—Sprung, Felfe, Horn, Lynch & Kramer

[57]   **ABSTRACT**

In the decaffeination of coffee by contacting the coffee with water-moist carbon dioxide above its critical temperature and critical pressure, during the contacting, the coffee is maintained in admixture with an adsorbent for the caffeine for takeup of caffeine from the carbon dioxide by the adsorbent.

18 Claims, No Drawings

A variant of the use of activated carbon to remove caffeine from carbon dioxide is described in this patent. A mixture of activated carbon and coffee beans is placed in a vessel, the vessel is pressurized with carbon dioxide to some supercritical condition, and the contents held statically at those conditions for a period of time. At the end of this period, the carbon dioxide is vented and the activated carbon is separated from the coffee bean by sieving.

One of the examples reports results obtained, viz., 22 lbs of moistened coffee is admixed with 15 lbs activated carbon and held at $80^{\circ}C$ under 190 atm pressure for 15 hours; during this contacting period the caffeine content of the coffee is reduced from 1% to 0.02%.

Conceptually, the operation of the process in this static mode eliminates the energy requirements of recycling the carbon dioxide. In brief explanation of the phenomena in operation in this process, caffeine from a source, the coffee, dissolves in carbon dioxide, diffuses through the supercritical phase to a sink, the activated carbon. In Chapter 1 we said that the high diffusion coefficients of materials in a supercritical fluid do not necessarily ensure that mass transfer will be rapid relative to mass transfer in a liquid; rate controlling steps must always be considered. However this process configuration may well be one where the higher diffusivity of a molecule in the supercritical phase can result in a higher "extraction" rate.

United States Patent [19]

Margolis et al.

[11]   **4,251,559**

[45]   **Feb. 17, 1981**

[54] DECAFFEINATION PROCESS

[75] Inventors: Geoffrey Margolis, Bussigny; Jacky Chiovini, Daillens, both of Switzerland

[73] Assignee: Societe d'Assistance Technique pour Produits Nestle S.A., Lausanne, Switzerland

[21] Appl. No.: 957,822

[22] Filed: Nov. 6, 1978

[51] Int. Cl.³ A23F 5/22
[52] U.S. Cl. 426/490; 426/427
[58] Field of Search 426/427, 428, 490

[56]   References Cited

FOREIGN PATENT DOCUMENTS

2005293 11/1972 Fed. Rep. of Germany 426/427
2638383 3/1977 Fed. Rep. of Germany 426/427

Primary Examiner—Joseph M. Golian
Attorney, Agent, or Firm—Watson, Leavenworth, Kelton & Taggart

[57]   **ABSTRACT**

Caffeine is extracted from solutions thereof with supercritical carbon dioxide having a density of at least 0.85 g/ml.

8 Claims, No Drawings

This patent is another one on extraction of caffeine from aqueous solution. The examples cover extraction of caffeine from solutions of tea, coffee, and neat caffeine. Various experimental modes of operation, e.g., batch autoclave extraction, batch-continuous extraction, and continuous counter current extraction are described. The patent gives a large table of decaffeination results, and some of the results are reproduced below. Distribution coefficients given in the last column are calculated from batch-continuous extraction mathematics using the relation $DC \times R = \ln C_i/C_f$.

Decaffeination Results

Solution	CO_2 Ratio	Temp. $^\circ C$	Press. Bars	% Decaf.	Dist.Coef.
Green	50	70	250	79	0.031
Coffee,	20	70	250	42	0.026
10% Solids	10	70	250	18	0.017
	50	80	450	98a	0.078a
	20	80	450	85a	0.095a
Tea,	40	91	450	83	0.044
11.8% solids	30	91	450	72	0.042
	8	91	450	24	0.034
	40	80	450	96a	0.080a
	30	70	600	98a	0.130a
	8	70	650	97a	0.44a
Caffeine,	50	70	175	71	0.024
0.4%	30	70	300	80	0.053
	20	70	300	64	0.051
	50	92	500	96a	0.064a
	30	92	500	89a	0.070a
	20	70	500	90a	0.115a

The decaffeination values accented (with an a) are achieved with a CO_2 density of 0.85 or greater. The invention is the use of carbon dioxide of density 0.85 or greater; the table shows if the density is less, the decaffeination values and distribution coefficients calculated are lower with values ranging from 0.017-0.053.

United States Patent [19]

Roselius et al.

[11]   **4,255,458**

[45]   **Mar. 10, 1981**

[54]   **METHOD FOR THE SELECTIVE EXTRACTION OF CAFFEINE FROM VEGETABLE MATERIALS**

[75]   Inventors: Ludwig Roselius, Bremen; Hans-Albert Kurzhals, Heibenbüttel; Peter Hubert, Bremen, all of Fed. Rep. of Germany

[73]   Assignee: Hag Aktiengesellschaft, Bremen, Fed. Rep. of Germany

[21]   Appl. No.: **914,811**

[22]   Filed·   **Jun. 12, 1978**

[30]   **Foreign Application Priority Data**

Jun. 16, 1977 [DE] Fed. Rep. of Germany 2727191

[51]   Int. Cl.³ A23F 3/20; A23F 3/38; A23F 5/20; A23F 5/22

[52]   U.S. Cl. 426/424; 426/427; 426/428

[58]   Field of Search 426/427, 428, 424

[56]   **References Cited**

U.S. PATENT DOCUMENTS

1,957,358	5/1934	Scheele	426/428
3,769,033	10/1973	Panzer et al.	426/428
3,806,619	4/1974	Zosel	426/427 X
3,843,824	10/1974	Roselius et al.	426/427 X
3,879,569	4/1975	Vitzhum et al.	426/427
4,081,561	3/1978	Meyer et al.	426/427 X

Primary Examiner—Joseph M. Golian
Attorney, Agent, or Firm—Pollock, Vande Sande & Priddy

[57]   **ABSTRACT**

Method of removing caffeine from vegetable materials using a solvent containing two components:

(a) a first component which is inherently gaseous under operational conditions, and (b) a second component which, by itself, has physical properties such that a mixture of (a) and (b) is liquid at the operating temperature.

20 Claims, 2 Drawing Figures

This patent discusses the decaffeination of coffee using a co-solvent (entrainer) admixed with a supercritical fluid. The wording of the first claim describes the state of the mixture, i.e., "a two component mixture a) whose first component is inherently gaseous under operating conditions of temperature and pressure and b) whose second component is an organic solvent which, by itself has physical properties such that a mixture of a) and b) is liquid at the operating temperature." Use of this mixture is the invention.

One of the examples discusses results of decaffeinating coffee with a carbon dioxide-acetone mixture. Raw coffee with a moisture content of 36% is extracted with 92% carbon dioxide, 8% acetone at 90 atm, $40°C$ for 8 hours. The caffeine content of the coffee, originally 1.15%, was reduced to 0.07%.

Incidentally, it is not stated in the discussion of the invention whether the phase behavior of an 8% acetone solution at 90 atm, $40°C$ was determined, i.e., is it truly liquid as the claim requires, or is it supercritical.

United States Patent [19]

Jasovsky et al.

[11]   **4,255,461**

[45]   **Mar. 10, 1981**

[54] **PREPARATION OF A DECAFFEINATED ROASTED COFFEE BLEND**

[75] Inventors: George A. Jasovsky, Bayonne; Martin Gottesman, Paramus, both of N.J.

[73] Assignee: General Foods Corporation, White Plains, N.Y.

[21] Appl. No.: 93,787

[22] Filed: Nov. 13, 1979

[51] Int. Cl.^{3} A23F 5/20
[52] U.S. Cl. 426/595; 426/427; 426/388
[58] Field of Search 426/388, 427, 595

[56] **References Cited**

U.S. PATENT DOCUMENTS

3,640,726	2/1972	Bolt et al.	426/595
3,767,418	10/1973	Ponzoni	426/461
3,840,684	10/1974	Fazzina et al.	426/427 X

3,843,824	10/1974	Roselius et al.	426/427 X

FOREIGN PATENT DOCUMENTS

926693   5/1973   Canada

Primary Examiner—Joseph M. Golian
Attorney, Agent, or Firm—Thomas R. Savoie; Daniel J. Donovan

[57]   **ABSTRACT**

A lower-grade green coffee bean fraction is moisturized to above 37% by weight and then decaffeinated by extraction with a moist supercritical fluid having a temperature of at least 100° C. This decaffeinated coffee is then combined, either before or after roasting, with a higher-grade coffee fraction. Typically the higher-grade fraction will be coffee which has been decaffeinated by extraction with a moist supercritical fluid at a temperature below about 85° C.

5 Claims, No Drawings

This patent teaches that lower grade (i.e., poor flavor) coffee beans can be extracted with carbon dioxide at specific conditions to yield a preferred characteristic. The background relates that most high grade coffees are best decaffeinated at a moisture content of between 26 and 33% using supercritical carbon dioxide at a temperature between 60 and 85°C and a pressure of at least 200 atm. If low grade coffee is decaffeinated at the same temperature conditions, the flavor of the low grade coffee (when blended with high grade coffee) is not satisfactory. However, when the low grade coffee is moistened to higher moisture content between 37 and 50% and is extracted at between 100 to 160°C, the flavor characteristic of the low grade coffee (when blended with high grade coffee) is better. Example 1 from the patent is reproduced in its entirety to explain the results.

Example 1

Two separately decaffeinated roasted and ground coffees were obtained for taste comparison with a water-decaffeinated, roasted and ground coffee product produced in accordance with the aforementioned Berry et al, patent. (The Berry et al patent referred to is U.S. 2,309,092.) Using comparable equipment and procedures, batches of Colombian, Brazilian and Robusta (the lower grade coffee) green coffee beans were separately decaffeinated by first moisturizing green coffee beans to 30% weight and then contacting the moisturized coffee with a stream of supercritical CO_2 at conditions of 80°C and 250 atmospheres until about 97% of the caffein was removed. The thus decaffeinated coffees were then dried to between 10 and 14% moistures and subsequently were separately roasted with the Colombian coffees being split into two fractions and with each fraction being roasted to comparable but discernably different roast colors. A portion of the green Robusta coffee beans employed above was separately moisturized to 45% water by weight and then contacted with a stream of supercritical CO_2 at conditions of 100°C and 250 atmospheres. These decaffeinated Robusta beans were then roasted to color comparable to above roasted Robusta beans. Two separate roasted coffee blends were formulated each consisting on a weight basis of 30%, Colombians (15% each roast color) 15% Brazilian and 55% Robusta with Blend A containing the Robustas decaffeinated at 80°C and Blend B containing the Robustas decaffeinated at 100°C. Blends A and B were ground and brewed and the resulting beverage was compared to a control beverage prepared from a decaffeinated roasted and ground coffee decaffeinated in accordance with the aforementioned Berry et al, patent and containing 55% Colombian coffees and 45% Robusta coffees. In consumer taste tests Blend A lost to the control (46.5% to 53.5%) while Blend B was preferred to the control (52% to 48%).

United States Patent [19]

Zosel

[11]   **4,260,639**

[45]   **Apr. 7, 1981**

[54]   **PROCESS FOR THE DECAFFEINATION OF COFFEE**

[75]   Inventor: Kurt Zosel, Oberhausen, Fed. Rep. of Germany

[73]   Assignee: Studiengesellschaft Kohle MBH, Mulheim, Fed. Rep. of Germany

[21]   Appl. No.:   364,190

[22]   Filed: **May 25, 1973**

Related U.S. Application Data

[63]   Continuation-in-part of Ser. No. 110,428, Jan. 28, 1971, abandoned.

[30]   **Foreign Application Priority Data**

Feb. 5, 1970 [DE]   Fed. Rep. of Germany 20052931
Feb. 12, 1970 [AT]   Austria 61298/70

[51]   Int. Cl.² A23P 1/00
[52]   U.S. Cl. 426/478; 426/427
[58]   Field of Search 426/481, 427, 428; 260/256

[56]   **References Cited**

U.S. PATENT DOCUMENTS

1,640,648   8/1927   Cross .... 426/377 X

3,418,134   12/1968   Rooker 426/386
3,806,619   4/1974   Zosel 426/427
3,842,824   10/1974   Roselius et al. 426/386

FOREIGN PATENT DOCUMENTS

553800   6/1932   Fed. Rep. of Germany 426/427
37854   4/1931   France 426/427
779451   4/1935   France 426/427
287352   7/1931   Italy 426/427
1057911   2/1967   United Kingdom 426/427
1290117   9/1972   United Kingdom 426/427

Primary Examiner—Frank Sever
Attorney, Agent, or Firm—Sprung, Felfe, Horn, Lynch & Kramer

[57]   **ABSTRACT**

A process for the decaffeination of coffee which comprises contacting the coffee with moist carbon dioxide in the supercritical state to effect removal of caffeine therefrom and recovering a substantially decaffeinated coffee. Preferred conditions for contact of the moist carbon dioxide are a temperature within the range of 40°–80° C., a pressure within the range of 120–180 atmospheres and a contact time of from 5 to 30 hours.

14 Claims, 2 Drawing Figures

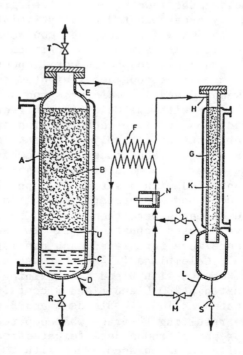

The difference between this patent for decaffeinating raw coffee and the previous Vitzthum and Hubert patent for decaffeinating raw coffee resides in the moisture content of the coffee. Examples in this patent show that raw coffee need not be pre-treated with water; moist carbon dioxide by itself is sufficient to extract the caffeine. (One of the authors (VJK) has tested moist carbon dioxide on dry coffee and tea; it works, but a higher recycle ratio of carbon dioxide is required if the materials are not also moistened.)

It is of further value to discuss some incorrect statements made in this patent.

Let us start with the "surprising" results, viz., "...the observation that caffeine could be removed relatively easily from moist raw coffee by subjecting it to a supercritical gas phase, for the following reason." The patentees then go on to relate that "The German Democratic Republic Pat. No. 41,362 and also the corresponding British Pat. No. 1,057,911 are concerned with processes for separating mixtures of substances by means of gases in the supercritical state. It is shown in Examples 61 and 62 that substances which are dissolved in water or which are present in an aqueous emulsion can only be taken up, with very great difficulty, in a supercritical gas. However, caffeine, dissolved in water, can be taken up relatively easily in gaseous carbon dioxide in the supercritical state, whereas dry caffeine is not."

We have already seen in Chapter 10, Figure 10.1 that dry caffeine does dissolve in dry carbon dioxide; Stahl (1979) and Krukonis (1981) show this. Therefore, the statement that dry caffeine is not taken up by (dry) carbon dioxide is wrong. Now let's see if we can determine what is meant by the statement, "substances dissolved in water can only be taken up with great difficulty in a supercritical gas, but caffeine dissolved in water, is taken up relatively easily." Example 61 from the British patent, (which is not reproduced here because of space considerations) describes the extraction of several alcohols from water solution with supercritical ethylene; the example states that no ethanol is extracted from solution by ethylene. We know that carbon dioxide, on the other hand, can extract ethanol from solution, and, therefore, it is of no relevance to compare the inability of ethylene to extract ethanol with the ability of carbon dioxide to extract ethanol (or caffeine).

If the reader checks each example and each reference cited for specifics, he will find these quite frequent inconsistent comparisons. Incidentally, he will also find that ethylene can in fact extract ethanol (Paulaitis, Gilbert, and Nash, 1981).

United States Patent [19]

Roselius et al.

[11]   **4,328,255**

[45]   * **May 4, 1982**

[54]   METHOD OF EXTRACTING COFFEE OIL
CONTAINING AROMA CONSTITUENTS
FROM ROASTED COFFEE

[75]   Inventors: Wilhelm Roselius, Bremen St.
Magnus; Otto Vitzthum, Bremen;
Peter Hubert, Bremen-Lesum, all of
Fed. Rep. of Germany

[73]   Assignee: Studiengesellschaft Kohle m.b.H.,
Mulheim, Fed. Rep. of Germany

[*]   Notice: The portion of the term of this patent
subsequent to Oct. 22, 1991, has been
disclaimed.

[21]   Appl. No.: 804,830

[22]   Filed: Jun. 8, 1977

Related U.S. Application Data

[63]   Continuation of Ser. No. 222,625, Feb. 1, 1972, abandoned, and a continuation of Ser. No. 499,944, Aug. 23,
1974, abandoned, and a continuation of Ser. No.
641,214, Dec. 16, 1975, abandoned.

[30]   Foreign Application Priority Data

Feb. 10, 1971 [DE] Fed. Rep. of Germany 2106133

[51]   Int. Cl.^{3} A23F 5/48
[52]   U.S. Cl. 426/417; 426/312;
426/386; 426/481; 426/425

[58]   Field of Search 426/312, 386, 425–434,
426/481, 417

[56]   References Cited

U.S. PATENT DOCUMENTS

3,477,856	11/1969	Schultz	426/424
3,806,619	4/1974	Zosel	426/427
3,843,824	10/1974	Roselius et al.	426/386
3,939,281	2/1976	Schwengers	426/429 X

FOREIGN PATENT DOCUMENTS

1057911	2/1967	United Kingdom	426/429
1106468	3/1968	United Kingdom	426/429

OTHER PUBLICATIONS

Chem. Abstracts 54:17744c, The Antioxygenic Proper-
ties of Coffee, 1958.
Coffee Processing Technology, Switz, vol. 2, 1963, Avi
Publ Co., Westport, Conn., pp. 22–23.

Primary Examiner—Joseph M. Golian
Attorney, Agent, or Firm—Sprung, Felfe, Horn, Lynch
& Kramer

[57]   ABSTRACT

A method of extracting coffee oil containing aromatic
constituents in high yield and in stable form by extracting solid, roasted coffee with dry carbon dioxide under
super-critical conditions of temperature and pressure.

3 Claims, 1 Drawing Figure

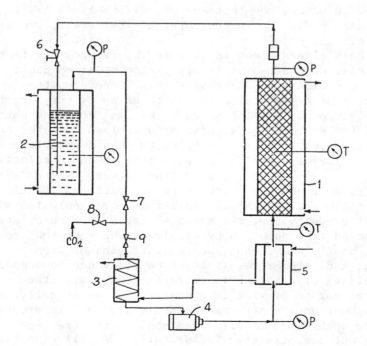

This invention is concerned with a process to remove the aroma constituents from roasted coffee. The prior art discussion brings out that although liquid carbon dioxide can also extract the aroma substances, it does not extract the natural antioxidants that are present in roasted coffee; the extracted oils, therefore, are not stable. Supercritical carbon can extract the natural anti-oxidants along with the oils.

As we have seen in other patents discussed, there are some "surprise" statements in this patent. For example, the patentees state "From (the) literature it is known that the ability of gaseous CO_2 to absorb oils increases with rising pressure and attains its maximum in the case of liquid CO_2; it is also known that supercritical CO_2 has increasing solvent power with rising pressure, and that this is so only up to a maximum value which corresponds to that of liquid CO_2."

We wonder what literature they have been reading that leads them to conclude that supercritical CO_2 cannot dissolve substances to a greater level than liquid CO_2 can. Based upon this conclusion, in any event, they now make their surprise statement, "It is therefore extremely surprising that in the method of the invention the ability of the supercritical CO_2 phase to absorb aroma constituents, coffee oils, and antioxidants is considerably greater than the solvent power of liquid CO_2." We certainly have no problem with the finding that supercritical CO_2 can "absorb" coffee oils and anti-oxidants to a greater level than liquid CO_2 can, but the finding is not "extremely surprising."

United States Patent [19]

Katz et al.

[11]   **4,276,315**

[45]   **Jun. 30, 1981**

[54]   **METHOD FOR DECAFFEINATING COFFEE**

[75]   Inventors: **Saul N. Katz,** Monsey, N.Y.; **Martin Gottesman,** Paramus, N.J.

[73]   Assignee: **General Foods Corporation,** White Plains, N.Y.

[21]   Appl. No.:   **11,263**

[22]   Filed: **Feb. 12, 1979**

[51]   **Int. Cl.³** **A23F 5/20**
[52]   **U.S. Cl.** **426/428; 426/427**
[58]   **Field of Search** 426/427, 428

[56]   **References Cited**

U.S. PATENT DOCUMENTS

3,769,033	10/1973	Panzer et al.	426/428
3,806,619	4/1974	Zosel	426/427 X
3,843,824	10/1974	Roselius et al.	426/427 X
3,879,569	4/1975	Vitzhum et al.	426/427
4,081,563	3/1978	Hudak et al.	426/427 X

FOREIGN PATENT DOCUMENTS

2005293	11/1972	Fed. Rep. of Germany	.... 426/427
2357590	5/1975	Fed. Rep. of Germany	
2638383	3/1977	Fed. Rep. of Germany	
7207534	12/1972	Netherlands	.... 426/427
206145	9/1924	United Kingdom	
1057911	2/1967	United Kingdom	.... 426/427

Primary Examiner—Joseph M. Golian
Attorney, Agent, or Firm—Thomas R. Savoie; Daniel J. Donovan

[57]   **ABSTRACT**

Liquid propane, liquid butane or mixtures thereof at a temperature of from 30° C. to 95° C. is employed to selectively remove caffeine from moistened green coffee. The resulting decaffeinated coffee is then roasted and processed to ground or soluble coffee products which will possess the flavor and aroma of comparable non-decaffeinated coffee products.

7 Claims, No Drawings

The abstract on the patent face page describes the invention, viz., the use of liquid propane or butane as a decaffeinating solvent. (Note again the use of the phrase "selectively remove caffeine from moistened green coffee.")

To describe how effective liquid propane is as a decaffeinating solvent, it is most informative to reproduce Example 3 from the patent.

Example 3

As shown in the following Table, the use of liquid propane at low pressures is equally effective to decaffeinate green coffee beans. In this set of experiments, two kilograms of green Colombian coffee beans were moisturized, placed in a pressure vessel (10 mm internal dia., 91.4 cm in height) and decaffeinated by means of recirculating stream of liquid propane flowing at a rate of 60 kgs/kg beans/hour and a velocity through the bean vessel of about 1.25 cm/sec. The propane was freed of caffeine by passage through a vessel (10 mm internal dia., 45.7 cm high) containing 625 grams of activated charcoal.

TABLE

Pressure (atm)	Temp. (^{o}C)	% Moisture (by wt)	Time (hrs)	% Decaffeination (by wt)
200	80	50	10	80
200	80	35	14	82
40	80	35	10	80
40	70	35	10	73

The decaffeinated beans from Example 3 were roasted and brewed and the flavor of the beverage was considered to be of good quality and comparable to a control beverage prepared from beans which had been decaffeinated by means of supercritical CO_2 at 80°C and 200 atmospheres.

A quick multiplication provides information on the recycle ratio; 60 kgs/kg beans/hr x 10 hours = 600 kgs/kg. As the table shows, that ratio achieves only 80% decaffeination, and we suggest that a ratio of at least 1200-1500 kgs/kg(!) coffee is required to achieve 97+% decaffeination.

United States Patent [19]

Peter et al.

[11]   **4,322,445**

[45]   **Mar. 30, 1982**

[54]   **PROCESS FOR DECAFFEINATING COFFEE**

[76]   Inventors: Siegfried Peter, Lange Zeile 138½, 8520 Erlangen; Gerd Brunner, Weinweg 10, 8541 Eckersmülilen, both of Fed. Rep. of Germany

[21]   Appl. No.: **933,482**

[22]   Filed: **Aug. 14, 1978**

[51]   Int. Cl.³ A23F 5/20
[52]   U.S. Cl. 426/312; 426/318; 426/319; 426/427; 426/428; 426/481
[58]   Field of Search 426/427, 428, 312, 318, 426/319, 481

[56]   **References Cited**

U.S. PATENT DOCUMENTS

3,806,619 4/1974 Zosel .... 426/427 X
3,843,824 10/1974 Roselius et al. .... 426/427 X
3,879,569 4/1975 Vitzlium et al. 426/427

FOREIGN PATENT DOCUMENTS

2005293 11/1972 Fed. Rep. of Germany 426/427
1057911 2/1967 United Kingdom 426/427

Primary Examiner—Joseph M. Golian
Attorney, Agent, or Firm—Thomas V. Michaelis

[57]   **ABSTRACT**

The invention involves a process for the decaffeination of coffee, wherein—usually moistened—coffee is exposed to a circulating medium essentially composed of a compressed gas and an entrainer; this medium is subjected to partial condensation of the caffeine containing entrainer, in the absence of decompression; the caffeine is recovered from the condensate by evaporation of the entrainer portion thereof, and the medium is recycled to the coffee for continued extraction of caffeine therefrom.

4 Claims, 1 Drawing Figure

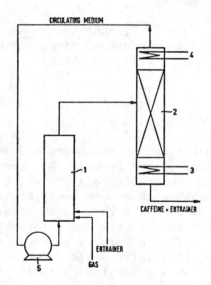

Before describing the invention, it is of value to discuss the background section of this patent, since it is noteworthy for its confusing statements.

The invention in this patent is the use of compressed gases and co-solvents (entrainers) and operating so that the co-solvent and caffeine are subsequently separated from the gas. One example describes that nitrogen at conditions of 200 atm, 40°C containing 3% formaldehyde dimethylacetal can decaffeinate raw coffee.

In a discussion of prior art, Peter and Brunner refer to an article (Sivetz, M. 1963. Coffee Processing Technology, Vol. 2, 21, Avi Publishing, Westport, CT) which describes the use of liquid carbon dioxide to produce aroma oil from coffee; however, they do not explain in the prior art section that the article describes aroma extraction from coffee which has been roasted. They then refer to a second article on the use of liquid carbon dioxide to produce aroma concentrates, Food Technol, No. 23, 11, 50 (1969) (which we could not locate in Vol. 23) and they write, "Thus, in the extraction of raw coffee with liquid carbon dioxide removal of caffeine is accompanied by the simultaneous removal of other substances."

Peter and Brunner then refer to the data of Vitzthum and Hubert in U.S. 3,879,569 on the high pressure liquid carbon dioxide extraction of raw coffee, and they state "an increase of pressure on the extractor, greatly increases the selectivity of liquid carbon dioxide for caffeine."

What Peter and Brunner apparently want to leave the reader with here is that near-critical liquid carbon dioxide (at 850 psi and 25°C) will extract both aromas and caffeine from raw coffee whereas high pressure liquid carbon dioxide (at 2000 psi and 25°C) will extract only the caffeine. We must comment here that increasing the pressure certainly will not increase the selectivity of carbon dioxide for caffeine in raw coffee. However, any conclusion can be drawn in comparisons of raw and roasted coffee extraction results or in comparisons of the extraction of aromas and extraction of caffeine. Incidentally, this background discussion which serves to confuse the reader has no relevance to the use of a mixture of high pressure nitrogen and formaldehyde dimethylacetal for extracting caffeine from coffee.

United States Patent [19]

Zosel

[11]   **4,348,422**

[45]   **Sep. 7, 1982**

[54]   PROCESS FOR THE DIRECT DECAFFEINATION OF AQUEOUS COFFEE EXTRACT SOLUTIONS

[75]   Inventor: Kurt Zosel, Oberhausen, Fed. Rep. of Germany

[73]   Assignee: Studiengesellschaft Kohle m.b.H., Kaiser-Wilhelm-Platz, Fed. Rep. of Germany

[21]   Appl. No.:   906,882

[22]   Filed: May 17, 1978

Related U.S. Application Data

[63]   Continuation-in-part of Ser. No. 877,535, Feb. 13, 1978, abandoned.

[51]   Int. Cl.^{3} A23F 5/22
[52]   U.S. Cl. 426/475; 426/427; 426/478
[58]   Field of Search 426/427, 475, 478, 481

[56]   **References Cited**

U.S. PATENT DOCUMENTS

3,806,619	4/1974	Zosel	426/427 X
3,843,824	10/1974	Roselius et al.	426/427 X
3,879,569	4/1975	Vetzhum	426/427
3,969,196	7/1976	Zosel	203/49

FOREIGN PATENT DOCUMENTS

2005293   11/1972   Fed. Rep. of Germany .
1057911   2/1967   United Kingdom .

OTHER PUBLICATIONS

Swetz, Coffee Processing Technology, 1963, vol. II, The Avi Publ. Co.; Westport, Conn., p. 214.

Primary Examiner—Joseph M. Golian
Attorney, Agent, or Firm—Sprung, Horn, Kramer & Woods

[57]   **ABSTRACT**

A process for the direct decaffeination of aqueous coffee extract solutions by contacting the surface of a thin film of an aqueous coffee extract solution with carbon dioxide under supercritical conditions of temperature and pressure to thereby remove the caffeine into the CO_2 and directly recover the aqueous coffee extract solution substantially free from caffeine. The contacting of the aqueous coffee extract solution and the CO_2 is preferably effected by passing the aqueous coffee extract solution downwardly through a packed column, while passing the CO_2 upwardly in countercurrent contact therewith.

16 Claims, 1 Drawing Figure

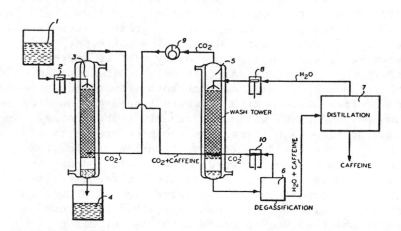

Zosel explains in the prior art section that foam formation during supercritical carbon dioxide extraction of coffee liquor is a problem; the invention eliminates the foaming problem. The improvement in a countercurrent contacting of coffee liquor is to form a thin film of the liquor in the extractor rather than to contact coffee liquor on a sieve tray. The film can be formed in a number of ways, e.g., on packing or in a thin film evaporator.

The stream designations on the figure are quite explanatory of the overall process. Coffee extract solution from reservoir 1 is pumped to a packed column 3 (filled with, for example, Rashig rings, stainless steel spirals, etc.). The coffee liquor flows downward over the packing and is contacted by upward flowing supercritical carbon dioxide. Caffeine is extracted from the coffee liquor which exits at the bottom of the column, and the caffeine-laden carbon dioxide stream leaves the extraction column and enters the water wash tower (which is also a packed column) where the carbon dioxide is stripped of its caffeine. The caffeine-free carbon dioxide is recirculated to the coffee liquor extraction tower, and the caffeine-water solution is evaporated and the caffeine recovered.

An example gives quantitative data. Coffee liquor is pumped to the column at 17 g/min, and carbon dioxide at 200 atm and $50^{\circ}C$ is fed at 800 g/min (a solvent to feed ratio of about 50). More than 98% of the caffeine is extracted.

Roselius, W., O. Vitzthum, and P. Hubert, Method of
    producing cocoa butter, U.S. 3,923,847 (Dec. 2, 1975).
Zosel, K., Process for the simultaneous hydrogenation and
    deodorization of fats and/or oils, U.S. 3,969,382
    (July 13, 1976).
Zosel, K., Process for deodorizing fats and oils, U.S.
    4,156,688 (May 29, 1979).
Zosel, K., Production of fats and oils from vegetable and
    animal products, U.S. 4,331,695 (May 25, 1982).
Schwengers, D., Extraction of fat from starch-containing
    vegetable matter, U.S. 3,939,281 (Feb. 17, 1976).
Vitzthum, O. and P. Hubert, Process for the production of
    spice extracts, U.S. 4,123,559 (Oct. 31, 1978).
Roselius, W. and O. Hubert, Process for the extraction of
    nicotine from tobacco, U.S. 4,153,063 (May 8, 1979).
Schultz, W.G., Process for extraction of flavors, U.S.
    3,477,856 (Nov. 11, 1969).
Schultz, W.G., Process for removing residual solvents, U.S.
    3,966,981 (June 29, 1976).
Laws, D.R.J., N.A. Bath, C.S. Ennis, and A.G. Wheldon, Hop
    extraction with carbon dioxide, U.S. 4,218,491
    (Aug. 19, 1980).
Sims, M., Liquid carbon dioxide extraction of pyrethrins,
    U.S. 4,281,171 (Jul. 28, 1981).
Friedrich, J.P., Supercritical CO_2 extraction of lipids
    from lipid-containing materials, U.S. 4,466,923
    (Aug. 21, 1984).
Friedrich, J.P. and A.C. Eldridge, Production of defatted
    soybean products by supercritical fluid extraction,
    U.S. 4,493,854 (Jan. 15, 1985).
Christianson, D.D. and J.P. Friedrich, Production of
    food-grade germ product by supercritical fluid
    extraction, U.S. 4,495,207 (Jan. 22, 1985).
Heigel, W., Process for the production of pure lecithin
    directly usable for physiological purposes, U.S.
    4,367,178 (Jan. 4, 1983).
Schutz, E., H.R. Vollbrecht, K. Sandner, T. Sand, and P.
    Muhlnickel, Method of extracting the flavoring
    substances from the vanilla capsule, U.S. 4,470,927
    (Sept. 11, 1984).
Makin, E.C. Purification of vanillin, U.S. 4,474,994
    (Oct. 2, 1984).

Coenen, H., R. Hagen, and M. Knuth, Method for obtaining aromatics and dyestuffs from bell peppers, U.S. 4,400,398 (Aug. 23, 1983).

Heine, C. and R. Wust, Method for the production of food additives with improved taste, U.S. 4,427,707 (Jan. 24, 1984).

Behr, N., H. van der Mei, W. Sirtl, H. Schnegelberger, and O. von Ettingshausen, Process for the preparation of spice extracts, U.S. 4,490,398 (Dec. 25, 1984).

Biernoth, G. and W. Merk, Fractionation of butterfat using a liquefied gas or a gas in the supercritical state, U.S. 4,504,503 (Mar. 12, 1985).

Amer, G.I., Separation of neutrals from tall oil soaps, U.S. 4,422,966 (Dec. 27, 1983).

Lawson, N.E. and G.I. Amer, Acidulation and recovery of crude tall oil from tall oil soaps, U.S. 4,495,095 (Jan. 22, 1985).

Fremont, H.A., Extraction of Coniferous woods with fluid carbon dioxide and other supercritical fluids, U.S. 4,308,200 (Dec. 29, 1981).

United States Patent [19]

Roselius et al.

[11]   **3,923,847**

[45]   **Dec. 2, 1975**

[54]   **METHODS OF PRODUCING COCOA BUTTER**

[75]   Inventors: **Wilheim Roselius, Bremen-St. Magnus; Otto Vitzthum, Bremen; Peter Hubert, Bremen-Lesum,** all of Germany

[73]   Assignee: **Studiengesellschaft Kohle m.b.H., Mulheim (Ruhr), Germany**

[22]   Filed: **May 23, 1973**

[21]   Appl. No.: **363,098**

[52]   U.S. Cl............................ **260/412.8;** 260/412.8
[51]   Int. Cl.²... **C11B 1/10**
[58]   Field of Search.................................. 260/412.8

[56]   **References Cited**
            UNITED STATES PATENTS

2,735,624   2/1956   Beck.................................. 260/412.8

3,064,018   11/1962   Bruera............................. 260/412.8
3,093,480   6/1963   Arnold............................. 260/412.8

FOREIGN PATENTS OR APPLICATIONS

1,057,911   2/1967   United Kingdom.............. 260/412.8

Primary Examiner—Elbert L. Roberts
Attorney, Agent, or Firm—Burgess, Dinklage & Sprung

[57]   **ABSTRACT**

Process of extracting cocoa butter from sources thereof by use of supercritical gases which are solvents therefor, especially carbon dioxide.

9 Claims, 1 Drawing Figure

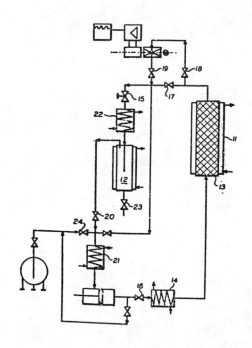

Cocoa butter is the triglyceride which derives from cocoa beans; it is composed of a large amount of palmitic acid on the glyceral backbone. Because of the high saturation, cocoa butter is a solid and exhibits a rather sharp melting point at about body temperature which incidentially, is partially responsible for the pleasant mouth feel of high quality chocolates.

The invention concerns the use of supercritical solvents to extract the cocoa butter from cocoa nibs (comminuted cocoa beans) and cocoa mass (finely crushed beans). The description of other processes in the prior art section of the patent points out that organic solvent extraction results in the presence of residual solvents; additionally, some of the newer pressing methods, via expellors, for example, introduce waste bean contaminants into the butter which must be removed with economic and taste penalties.

Examples of the application of supercritical carbon dioxide at typically, 200–400 atm, 40–60°C to extract both finely crushed cocoa mass and cocoa nibs are presented. It is related that cocoa mass can be extracted of 99% of its cocoa butter and that cocoa nibs, whether roasted or not or whether treated with caustic or not, can be extracted of 74% of their cocoa butter. One of the authors (VJK) has verified the results with cocoa mass, but finds that less than 5% of the cocoa butter can be extracted from raw, untreated cocoa nibs, even if the extraction is carried out at 7000 psi, 40–60°C for a period of 8 hours! On the other hand theobromine and caffeine can be extracted from the nibs almost quantitatively at much less severe conditions resulting in a cocoa product containing almost all its original cocoa butter and flavor but no adverse stimulants (Krukonis unpublished data, 1982).

United States Patent [19]

Zosel

[11]   **3,969,382**

[45]   **July 13, 1976**

[54]   **PROCESS FOR THE SIMULTANEOUS HYDROGENATION AND DEODORISATION OF FATS AND/OR OILS**

[75]   Inventor: Kurt Zosel, Oberhausen, Germany

[73]   Assignee: Studiengesellschaft Kohle m.b.H., Mulheim, Germany

[22]   Filed: **Aug. 29, 1974**

[21]   Appl. No.: **501,733**

[30]   **Foreign Application Priority Data**

Aug. 30, 1973   Austria 7525/73

[52]   U.S. Cl 260/409; 260/420; 260/428

[51]   Int. Cl.² C11C 3/12

[58]   Field of Search 260/409, 420, 428

[56]   **References Cited**

UNITED STATES PATENTS

2,282,791	5/1942	Murher	260/428
2,292,027	8/1942	Glenn	260/409
2,359,404	10/1944	Colgate	260/409
2,521,602	9/1950	Potts et al	260/409
2,773,081	12/1956	Brown	260/409
3,758,532	9/1973	Gibble	260/420

FOREIGN PATENTS OR APPLICATIONS

1,057,911   4/1964   United Kingdom 409/

Primary Examiner—Patrick P. Garvin
Assistant Examiner—John F. Niebling
Attorney, Agent, or Firm—Burgess, Dinklage & Sprung

[57]   **ABSTRACT**

Process for the simultaneous hydrogenation and deodorisation of at least one product from the group consisting of fats and oils, wherein said product is treated with carbon dioxide at a temperature of from 100° to 250°C and a pressure of from 150 to 300 atmospheres in the presence of a hydrogenation catalyst, and hydrogen.

The fats and oils hydrogenated and deodorised in this process are used in the manufacture of margarine.

22 Claims, 3 Drawing Figures

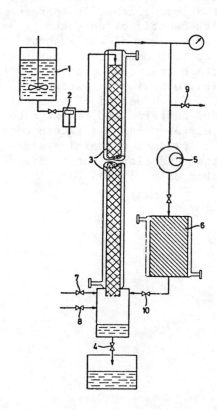

Seed oils such as soy bean and corn germ consist largely of triglycerides of oleic acids and are liquid at room temperature. Industrially, they are partially hydrogenated to produce higher melting point triglycerides that are used as commercial shortenings. The hydrogenation ("hardening" as it is called in the trade) is normally carried out by suspending a catalyst, typically nickel, in the oil and contacting the oil with 1 to 10 atm H_2 partial pressure; no supercritical processing of any kind is involved in current practice.

In this patent a simultaneous deodorization and hardening are described in which the gas phase consisting of carbon dioxide containing about 1% hydrogen counter-currently contacts a film of oil in a packed column at conditions of 220 atm, 200°C. The carbon dioxide extracts the fatty acids (they are largely responsible for the odor and off flavors), and the hydrogen dissolves into the oil and reacts with the unsaturated bonds of the triglycerides.

In the figure shown the packed column 3 contains glass beads. Oil from the reservoir 1 is pumped 2 to the column. Carbon dioxide is recycled via 10. The extract phase containing the fatty acids (and containing also, although not stated in the examples, a small amount of triglyceride) exits at the top of the column and is recycled to the column by the compressor 5 after first having passed through an activated carbon adsorber for removal of fatty acids from the carbon dioxide. Valve 9 allows the recycle gas to be sampled so that the hydrogen make up can be determined.

Several examples are given. Free fatty acids present in the feed oil are reduced by 95+%, and the iodine number (a measure of unsaturation) is reduced from 191 to 66. Furthermore the melting point of the triglyceride is increased from -2°C to 34°C pointing out that substantial hydrogenation occurred.

United States Patent [19]

Zosel

[11]   **4,156,688**

[45]   **May 29, 1979**

[54]   **PROCESS FOR DEODORIZING FATS AND OILS**

[75]   Inventor: Kurt Zosel, Oberhausen, Fed. Rep. of Germany

[73]   Assignee: Studiengesellschaft Kohle mbH, Mülheim an der Ruhr, Fed. Rep. of Germany

[21]   Appl. No.: **814,614**

[22]   Filed: **Jul. 11, 1977**

Related U.S. Application Data

[63]   Continuation of Ser. No. 630,827, Nov. 11, 1975, abandoned, which is a continuation of Ser. No. 369,689, Jun. 13, 1973, abandoned.

[30]   **Foreign Application Priority Data**

Jun. 26, 1972 [AT]   Austria 5469/72

[51]   Int. Cl.^{2} C11B 3/00

[52]   U.S. Cl. .... 260/420; 252/411 R; 260/428; 426/417

[58]   Field of Search 260/420, 428, 428.5; 426/417, 429, 430

[56]   **References Cited**

U.S. PATENT DOCUMENTS

1,805,751	5/1931	Averbach	260/428.5
3,558,468	1/1971	Wise	208/8
3,843,824	10/1974	Roselius et al.	426/386

FOREIGN PATENT DOCUMENTS

1057911   2/1967   United Kingdom.

Primary Examiner—Patrick Garvin
Assistant Examiner—P. E. Konopka
Attorney, Agent, or Firm—Sprung, Felfe, Horn, Lynch & Kramer

[57]   **ABSTRACT**

Process for deodorizing fat or oil containing odoriferous material by contacting the same with carbon dioxide at a temperature of 150° to 250° C. and a pressure of 100 to 250 atmospheres for the selective take-up by the carbon dioxide of the odoriferous material, thereby separating odoriferous material from the fat or oil.

8 Claims, 1 Drawing Figure

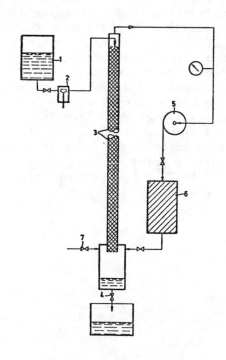

This patent is similar to the previous one except that the simultaneous hydrogenation is not carried out. Note that the figure does not show the values 8 and 9 of the previous figure (since no sample need be taken and no hydrogen is introduced).

The examples show that 95+% of the odoriferous material is removed by treating seed oil with carbon dioxide at 200 atm, 250-200°C. It is noteworthy that the major claim is quite restrictive, viz., "Process of deodorizing fat or oil characterized by the presence of odoriferous material, comprising contacting the fat or oil with carbon dioxide at a temperature of 150-250°C, and a pressure of 100 to 250 atm. . . . ." The reason for using such a high temperature is not given. One of us (VJK) has carried out similar free fatty acid removal from seed oils at a much lower temperature of 80°C also with 95+% removal (Krukonis unpublished research 1981). Other data on deodorizing spent cooking oils with supercritical carbon dioxide at equivalent low temperature have also been reported. (Caragay, A. B. and V. J. Krukonis, 1981. "Supercritical Fluid Extraction of Triglycerides" at 72nd AOCS Meeting, New Orleans, May.)

United States Patent [19]

Zosel

[11]   **4,331,695**

[45]   **May 25, 1982**

[54] PRODUCTION OF FATS AND OILS FROM VEGETABLE AND ANIMAL PRODUCTS

[75] Inventor: Kurt Zosel, Oberhausen, Fed. Rep. of Germany

[73] Assignee: Studiengesellschaft Kohle mbH, Mülheim, Fed. Rep. of Germany

[21] Appl. No.:   769,326

[22] Filed: Feb. 16, 1977

Related U.S. Application Data

[63]   Continuation of Ser. No. 658,658, Feb. 17, 1976, abandoned, which is a continuation of Ser. No. 452,485, Mar. 18, 1974, abandoned, which is a continuation-in-part of Ser. No. 424,241, Dec. 12, 1973, abandoned.

[30]   Foreign Application Priority Data

Dec. 22, 1972 [AT]   Austria 10999/72

[51]   Int. Cl.^{3} A23L 1/20; C09F 5/02; C11B 1/10
[52]   U.S. Cl. 426/430; 426/417; 426/429; 260/412.4; 260/412.8
[58]   Field of Search 426/427, 429, 430, 417; 260/412.4, 412.8

[56]   **References Cited**

U.S. PATENT DOCUMENTS

2,548,434	4/1951	Leaders	260/412.4
2,560,935	7/1951	Dickinson	260/412.4
2,682,551	6/1954	Miller	260/412.8
3,843,824	10/1974	Roselins et al.	426/427 X
3,939,281	2/1976	Schwengers	426/429 X

Primary Examiner—David M. Naff
Attorney, Agent, or Firm—McAulay, Fields, Fisher, Goldstein & Nissen

[57]   **ABSTRACT**

Fats or oils are extracted from animal or vegetable products by a process of contacting the product with a solvent in the liquid phase and at a temperature below the critical temperature of the solvent to extract fat or oil from the product, separating the solvent containing extracted fat or oil from the residue of the product, and precipitating the extracted fat or oil from the solvent by heating the solvent to above the critical temperature of the solvent without taking up heat of vaporization. The resultant precipitated fat or oil contains no more than 3 ppm of solvent which makes the fat or oil suitable for use in foodstuffs without further processing to remove solvent. The temperatures of the solvent may be 0°-100° C. during extraction and 50°-200° C. during precipitation, and the pressure may be the same during extraction and precipitation.

21 Claims, 1 Drawing Figure

Zosel was a prolific experimenter and inventor, and it is instructive to include many of his patents. The abstract on the face page summarizes this invention well. Near critical liquids are employed to extract triglycerides from a variety of animal and vegetable materials. Seven examples present data; liquid propane at 42 atm, $80^{\circ}C$ and $20^{\circ}C$; liquid ethane at 48 atm, $20^{\circ}C$; liquid carbon dioxide at 73 atm, $18^{\circ}C$, liquid N_2O at 72 atm, $20^{\circ}C$; and liquid isobutane, 37 atm, $120^{\circ}C$ were tested on a variety of vegetable and animal fats and oils. Residual fat contents in extracted seeds, flake, germ, and ground bones was of the order of 1% or less.

By now we assume that the general similarities among many of the patents are becoming obvious, but we see also that the inventions are different in some slight way; so, of course, are the specific limits in the claims. For example, a near critical liquid at its vapor pressure is different from a high pressure liquid above the critical pressure (but still below its critical temperature) which in turn is different from a supercritical fluid. We continue to read that the prior art in many of the patents describe the "limitations" of all the other processes and point out the advantages of the instant process.

United States Patent [19]

Schwengers

[11]   **3,939,281**

[45]   **Feb. 17, 1976**

[54]   **EXTRACTION OF FAT FROM STARCH-CONTAINING VEGETABLE MATTER**

[75]   Inventor: **Dieter Schwengers, Dormagen, Germany**

[73]   Assignee: **Pfeifer & Langen, Cologne, Germany**

[22]   Filed: **Nov. 9, 1973**

[21]   Appl. No.: **414,495**

[30]   **Foreign Application Priority Data**

Nov. 14, 1972   Germany............................ 2255666
Nov. 14, 1972   Germany............................ 2255667

[52]   U.S. Cl.................... 426/11; 195/31 R; 426/16; 426/417; 426/425; 426/429; 426/430
[51]   Int. Cl.² .. C11B 1/04; C11B 1/10; C12C 11/00
[58]   Field of Search .... 426/429, 430, 425, 436, 426/16, 11, 417; 195/31 R

[56]   **References Cited**

UNITED STATES PATENTS

2,107,529   2/1938   Fetzer .... 426/436 X
2,286,334   6/1942   Brandt 426/430
3,155,523   11/1964 Reich 426/430

3,337,414   8/1967   Wilson .... 195/31 R
3,519,431   7/1970   Wayne .... 426/430 X
3,795,750   3/1974   Levine .... 426/429 X

Primary Examiner—David M. Naff
Attorney, Agent, or Firm—Burgess, Dinklage & Sprung

[57]   **ABSTRACT**

Fat is removed from starch-containing vegetable material such as cereal grains, potatoes or tapioca by a process involving crushing the vegetable material, contacting the crushed material with a normally gaseous inert solvent under supercritical condition at a temperature of about 20° to 100°C and a pressure of about 30 to 1000 atmospheres to dissolve fat from the vegetable material into the solvent, separating the fat-containing solvent from the resultant substantially fat-free vegetable residue, and separating the dissolved fat from the solvent by raising the temperature and/or lowering the pressure to separate vaporized solvent from the fat. The vaporized solvent may be liquefied and recycled. The fat-free residue may be treated to dissolve away gluten, to form glucose by enzymatic hydrolysis and/or subjected to alcoholic fermentation.

9 Claims, 3 Drawing Figures

The abstract gives what appears at first glance to be the range of coverage. It also gives the motivation for extracting fat from the materials, i.e., the residual de-fatted material will be used in other operations.

In the discussion of the invention the patentee states that high pressure liquid (again that combination of temperature less than the critical temperature and pressure much higher than the critical pressure) is "more advantageous." Although he uses the term "supercritical" in the abstract, the claim is restrictive to high pressure liquid, i.e., "a normally gaseous inert solvent in liquid state at a temperature of about 20°-100°C and below the critical temperature and a pressure of about 30 to 1000 atm and above the critical pressure of the inert solvent which solvent has a critical temperature below about 200°C."

In this patent we see that the term "supercritical" is used a second way. We have used the term "supercritical" to refer to the state where pressure and temperature are both above their critical values. We shall see when we discuss a vanillin purification patent, U.S. 4,474,994, that the patentee defines supercritical to be a temperature higher than critical temperature but a pressure not higher than critical pressure. As we have said a number of times concerning such terms as solubility and extractability, we recommend that the reader examine how supercritical is defined.

United States Patent [19]

Vitzthum et al.

[11]   **4,123,559**

[45]   **Oct. 31, 1978**

[54] PROCESS FOR THE PRODUCTION OF SPICE EXTRACTS

[75] Inventors: Otto Vitzthum; Peter Hubert, both of Bremen, Fed. Rep. of Germany

[73] Assignee: Studiengesellschaft Kohle mbH, Mulheim, Ruhr, Fed. Rep. of Germany

[21] Appl. No.: 754,803

[22] Filed: Dec. 27, 1976

Related U.S. Application Data

[63] Continuation of Ser. No. 560,432, Mar. 20, 1975, abandoned, which is a continuation of Ser. No. 258,586, Jun. 1, 1972, abandoned.

[30] **Foreign Application Priority Data**

Jun. 3, 1971 [DE] Fed. Rep. of Germany 2127611

[51] Int. Cl.^{2} A23L 1/22; A23L 1/221

[52] U.S. Cl. 426/312; 426/318; 426/319; 426/431; 426/478; 426/655

[58] Field of Search 426/312, 318, 319, 386, 426/425, 431, 478, 489, 387, 424, 427, 428, 655

[56]   **References Cited**

U.S. PATENT DOCUMENTS

3,477,856 11/1969 Schultz 426/424

FOREIGN PATENT DOCUMENTS

1,057,911 4/1963 United Kingdom 426/312
1,106,468 3/1968 United Kingdom 99/140

Primary Examiner—Kenneth M. Schor
Attorney, Agent, or Firm—Burgess, Dinklage & Sprung

[57]   **ABSTRACT**

Process for the preparation of spice extracts by extraction of the natural spice with a supercritical gas such as carbon dioxide in which the aroma contents are first extracted with a dry gas; the flavor contents are then extracted with a moist gas and the extracted materials recovered and mixed.

9 Claims, 1 Drawing Figure

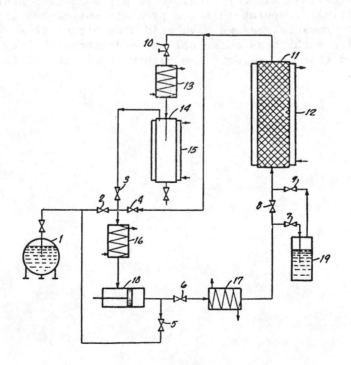

This patent describes a process that is similar to the supercritical extraction of roasted coffee beans using dry, then, moist carbon dioxide. Spices are also extracted in a two step process, the first a dry carbon dioxide extraction to dissolve the essential oils which represent the aroma constituents, and the second, a moist carbon dioxide extraction to obtain the flavor components.

With reference to the figure carbon dioxide (dry) from vessel 1 is pumped via 18 through a heat exchanger 17 and valve 8 into vessel 11 containing crushed spice mass. The extract solution leaving the vessel is expanded to a lower pressure through valve 10, and the temperature is adjusted in heat exchanger 13. The components precipitated from the carbon dioxide are separated in vessel 14, and the carbon dioxide is recycled to the extractor. When the desired level of aroma extraction has been accomplished, the carbon dioxide is then diverted to the humidifier 19 before being passed through the spice mass; moist carbon dioxide extracts the desired flavor component(s). The extract solution is separated into its components either in the same vessel 14 or in another vessel not shown in the figure depending upon the intended use of the extract.

A number of examples describe the extraction of crushed black pepper, ground cloves, crushed cinnamon sticks and crushed vanilla pods. For the case of black pepper, part of the flavor component, piperine, can be extracted with dry carbon dioxide and part is extracted with the moist carbon dioxide.

United States Patent [19]

Roselius et al.

[11]   **4,153,063**

[45]   **May 8, 1979**

[54] PROCESS FOR THE EXTRACTION OF NICOTINE FROM TOBACCO

[75] Inventors: Wilhelm Roselius, Magnus; Otto Vitzthum, Bremen; Peter Hubert, Bremen-Lesum, all of Fed. Rep. of Germany

[73] Assignee: Studiengesellschaft Kohle mbH, Mülheim, Ruhr, Fed. Rep. of Germany

[21] Appl. No.: 390,967

[22] Filed: **Aug. 23, 1973**

Related U.S. Application Data

[63] Continuation of Ser. No. 177,220, Sep. 2, 1971, abandoned.

[30]   **Foreign Application Priority Data**

Sep. 2, 1970 [DE] Fed. Rep. of Germany 2043537
Aug. 23, 1971 [DE] Fed. Rep. of Germany 2142205

[51] Int. Cl.^{2} A24B 3/14
[52] U.S. Cl. .... 131/143; 131/17 R; 131/144
[58] Field of Search .... 131/17, 143, 144, 135, 131/140 C; 260/291

[56]   **References Cited**

U.S. PATENT DOCUMENTS

3,424,171   1/1969   Rooker 131/143

FOREIGN PATENT DOCUMENTS

1512060 12/1967   France 131/143
1111422 7/1965   United Kingdom 131/143
1057911 2/1967   United Kingdom 131/135

OTHER PUBLICATIONS

"Dangerous Properties of Industrial Materials," Sax, 3rd edition, 1968, Reinhold Publishing Co., N.Y., pp. 962, 968, 780, 1129.
Luganskaja, L. N. et al., "On the Aromatization of Tobacco" and "Use of Tobacco Dust Extract for Aromatizing Purposes", pub.—from "Tobacco Abstracts", vol. 12, #6, Jun. 1968, pp. 394 and 395, abstracts 1258 and 1259.

Primary Examiner—Robert W. Michell
Assistant Examiner—V. Millin
Attorney, Agent, or Firm—Sprung, Felfe, Horn, Lynch & Kramer

[57]   **ABSTRACT**

Process for extracting nicotine is disclosed in which tobacco is exposed to an extracting solvent in either liquid or gaseous state at temperatures below about 100° C. and at high pressures. The aroma generating substances can be removed by conducting the extraction with the tobacco in dry condition. Thereafter the tobacco can be moistened, and on further contacting nicotine is removed. The aroma generating substances can then be recombined with nicotine free tobacco.

32 Claims, 6 Drawing Figures

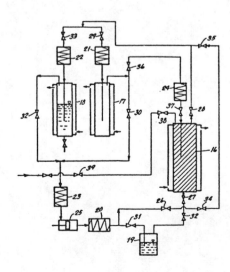

Extraction of nicotine from tobacco using supercritical fluid is carried out in a manner quite similar to the decaffeination of roasted coffee described in U.S. 3,843,824. With reference to the figure, tobacco in vessel 16 is first contacted with dry supercritical carbon dioxide entering at point 27. Aroma constituents are dissolved by the dry carbon dioxide; the stream leaving the extraction vessel is expanded to subcritical via valve 29 and is passed into separator vessel 17, where carbon dioxide is vaporized, resulting in the precipitation of aromas. The vapor is recompressed, is adjusted in temperature to supercritical conditions via heat exchangers 23 and 20, and is recycled to the extractor via the compressor 25; the aromas extraction step continues until the aroma constituents are removed from the tobacco.

In the second step of the process, the supercritical carbon dioxide is humidified (in vessel 19) before being passed through the tobacco; nicotine is extracted by the wet carbon dioxide. Nicotine is removed from the carbon dioxide by passing the stream through vessel 18 containing a sulfuric acid solution that reacts with the nicotine to form a salt insoluble in carbon dioxide. The nicotine-free carbon dioxide leaving the vessel is adjusted in temperature and moisture and is recycled until a satisfactory level of nicotine removal has been achieved. At the end of the nicotine extraction cycle, the tobacco in vessel 16 is dried. The aroma constituents contained in vessel 17 are dissolved in a liquid solvent and the solution introduced into the extractor containing the tobacco. The solvent is vaporized resulting in the precipitation of aromas in the tobacco.

As a variation of the three step procedure described above, the patent also relates that if tobacco is first moistened, solely nicotine can be extracted with supercritical carbon dioxide. For example, carbon dioxide at 70°C, 300 atm passed through moistened tobacco reduced the nicotine content from 1.36 to 0.08% (dry basis) while leaving the aromas untouched. One of the authors (VJK) has not been able to reproduce this finding in tests with moistened tobacco from commercial cigarettes; aromas were found to be extracted along with the nicotine. Another example in the patent contains some other curious information, viz., it is related that 5 wt-% ammonia is added to supercritical carbon dioxide at 70°C, 250 atm and the mixture used to extract nicotine. One of the authors (VJK) has tested this mixture and finds that carbon dioxide and ammonia react to form a compound, probably ammonium carbamate, which is insoluble in supercritical carbon dioxide, at 70°C, 250 atm.

Nov. 11, 1969   W. G. SCHULTZ   3,477,856
PROCESS FOR EXTRACTION OF FLAVORS
Filed Nov. 10, 1965

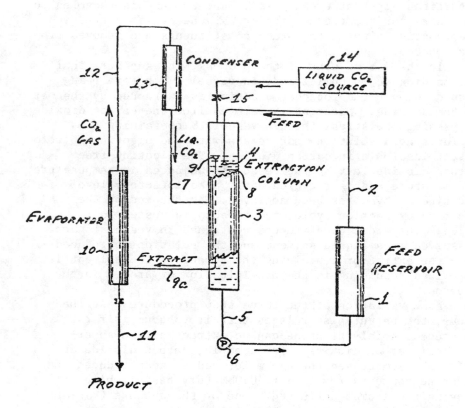

W.G. SCHULTZ
INVENTOR.

BY R. Hoffman
ATTORNEY

Although this patent is also not a supercritical one it is included in this section for its historical value and because of the renown of the patentee. William Schultz of the USDA's Western Regional Research Center published extensively during the 60's on flavors, aromas, and essences extraction from fruits, and the information he describes for liquid carbon dioxide is applicable to supercritical carbon dioxide. He was not referenced previously in this book, but two of his quite well known, often-cited publications on flavors and aromas are listed below.

The figure is a flow sheet showing the carbon dioxide extraction of flavor components from a fruit juice. Vessel 1 is a reservoir which holds the fruit juice; the juice is conveyed to the top of the extraction column 3. A spray nozzle in the column disperses the juice which contacts liquid carbon dioxide which is introduced at the mid section of the column via line 7. The liquid carbon dioxide (with density of about 0.7 g/cc) rises in the extractor extracting the flavor components which are esters, aldehydes, ketones and similar compounds. The extract leaves the column via the adjustable intake 9 in the column and flows via line 9a to the evaporator 10 where the liquid carbon dioxide is vaporized. The gaseous carbon dioxide is conveyed to the condenser 13 and a concentrated flavors stream leaves the evaporator by line 11. Make up carbon dioxide is added from the CO_2 reservoir 14 via valve 15 when required.

Two of the Schultz papers are:

Schultz, W. G., T. H. Schultz, R. A. Carlson, and J. S. Hudson, 1974. Pilot plant extraction with liquid carbon dioxide, Food Technol., 28, 32.

Schultz, W. G., J. M. Randall, 1970. Liquid carbon dioxide for selective aroma extraction, Food Technol., 24, 94.

United States Patent [19]

Schultz

[11]   **3,966,981**

[45]   **June 29, 1976**

[54] **PROCESS FOR REMOVING RESIDUAL SOLVENTS**

[75] Inventor: William G. Schultz, El Cerrito, Calif.

[73] Assignee: The United States of America as represented by the Secretary of Agriculture, Washington, D.C.

[22] Filed: Nov. 26, 1974

[21] Appl. No.: 527,402

[52] U.S. Cl. .... 426/425; 134/25 R; 134/42; 426/430

[51] Int. Cl.^{2} B01D 11/02

[58] Field of Search .... 426/425, 429, 430, 478, 426/489; 260/412.4, 417; 134/25 R, 40, 42

[56]   **References Cited**

UNITED STATES PATENTS

| 3,252,807 | 5/1966 | Kuramoto | 426/430 |
| 3,477,856 | 11/1969 | Schultz | 426/424 |

FOREIGN PATENTS OR APPLICATIONS

| 1,057,911 | 2/1967 | United Kingdom | 426/430 |
| 1,106,468 | 3/1968 | United Kingdom | 426/430 |

OTHER PUBLICATIONS

Abstract, "Solubility of CO_2 and H_2S in Liquid Hydrocarbons at Cryogenic Temperatures," 70:413125, 1968.

Abstract, "Low Temperature Absorption of CO_2 by Acetone," 68:99188f, 1967.

"Bland Undenatured Soybean Flakes . . . ." by Mustakas et al., found in The Journal of the Am. Oil Chemists Society, Sept. 1961. Issue vol. 38, No. 9, pp. 473–478.

"Determination of Residual Solvent in Oilseed Meals and flours . . . ." found in The Journal of the Am. Oil Chemists Society, vol. 47, No. 1, pp. 17–18.

Primary Examiner—Frank W. Lutter
Assistant Examiner—N. Greenblum
Attorney, Agent, or Firm—M. Howard Silverstein; David G. McConnell; William Takacs

[57]   **ABSTRACT**

Process for removing residual solvent from materials containing the same which involves extracting the material with liquid CO_2, separating the phases, and evaporating CO_2 from the treated material. For example, residual hexane can be removed from de-fatted soybeans by this procedure.

1 Claim, No Drawings

This patent on liquid carbon dioxide is also included in this section because the same technique of solvent removal can be carried out with supercritical carbon dioxide. This patent addresses another area of application, the removal of residual (organic) solvents from solvent extracted residues such as soy bean flake; the background relates that it is difficult to free the flake of its hexane residuals.

One example gives quantitative data. 450 g of hexane extracted soy bean flake with a residual hexane content of 228 ppm was contacted with 4250 ml liquid carbon dioxide for 72 hrs at $22^{o}C$ and 65-75 atm in a batch extractor. The flakes were separated, air dried, and the residual hexane content measured as 44 ppm. (The background section of the patent stated that 60 ppm is the maximum allowed by FDA and thus the single extraction was satisfactory to produce a within specifications material.) Subsequent extractions lowered the hexane content to 0.7 ppm.

As an aside here, the process could have been carried out in a batch-continuous mode, with carbon dioxide, either liquid or supercritical flowing through the charge; a thorough extraction could have been achieved in a much shorter time than 72 hours.

United States Patent [19]

Laws et al.

[11] **4,218,491**

[45] **Aug. 19, 1980**

[54] **HOP EXTRACTION WITH CARBON DIOXIDE**

[75] Inventors: **Derek R. J. Laws**, Bexleyheath; **Nigel A. Bath**, London; **Colin S. Ennis**, Chislehurst; **Alfred G. Wheldon**, Galley Wood, all of England

[73] Assignee: **The Brewing Research Foundation**, England

[21] Appl. No.: **870,084**

[22] Filed: **Jan. 17, 1978**

[30] **Foreign Application Priority Data**

Jan. 18, 1977 [GB] United Kingdom 1944/77

[51] Int. Cl.^{2} C12C 3/00; C12C 9/02
[52] U.S. Cl. 426/600; 426/655; 426/429
[58] Field of Search 426/429, 600, 16, 11, 426/655

[56] **References Cited**

U.S. PATENT DOCUMENTS

3,979,527　9/1976　Laws et al. 426/592

FOREIGN PATENT DOCUMENTS

4844864　12/1970　Japan .
1388581　3/1975　United Kingdom

Primary Examiner—David M. Naff
Attorney, Agent, or Firm—Wenderoth, Lind & Ponack

[57] **ABSTRACT**

A method of preparing a hop extract is described in which liquid carbon dioxide is passed at a temperature of from $-5°$ C. to $+15°$ C. through a column of hop material to extract α-acids contained therein. The method gives a primary extract which is of much higher purity than has been previously described particularly in comparison to presently commercially available solvent extracts.

9 Claims, 4 Drawing Figures

This patent covers a liquid carbon dioxide extraction process, and it is included here because of the large amount of interesting information about hops. In the background section of this patent current hop extraction procedures are described. Organic solvents such as methylene chloride and methanol are used to extract hops, and the crude extract that is obtained must be purified extensively before it yields the alpha-acid resins suitable for isomerization. The iso-alpha-acids are the main bittering components of beer. In traditional beer making the hops are added directly. When hops are added directly, only about 25% of the alpha-acids are utilized. With an organic solvent extraction of hops about 60-80% of the alpha-acids present in the hops is utilized. However, there are solvent residues present in the purified organic solvent extract, and although the extract meets current public health requirements, it may not in the future because of increasing attention that is being directed to the presence of residual solvents in food and beverage products. Carbon dioxide extraction is proposed as the new method.

In the preferred embodiment liquid carbon dioxide at conditions of between -5°C and 15°C is used. The temperature range of -5°C to 15°C is preferred. At conditions below -5°C, waxes in the hops dissolve preferentially resulting in an impure alpha-acids product. At conditions above 15°C the solubility of alpha-acids is low requiring long extraction times and, thus, -5°C to 15°C is optimum. The solution leaving the extractor vessel is conveyed to a separator vessel where the carbon dioxide is separated from the extract by evaporation. The carbon dioxide is condensed and is recycled to the extractor.

A later patent assigned to the Brewing Patents Limited, Laws, D. R. J., N. A. Bath, C. S. Ennis, J. A. Pickett, and A. G. Wheldon, Production of an Iso-Alpha-Acid Preparation from Hops, U.S. 4,298,626, Nov. 3, 1981, describes the isomerization of the alpha-acids obtained by carbon dioxide extraction; it describes the advantages of using a supercritical carbon dioxide extract in the subsequent isomerization process.

United States Patent [19]

Sims

[11]   **4,281,171**

[45]   **Jul. 28, 1981**

[54] **LIQUID CARBON DIOXIDE EXTRACTION OF PYRETHRINS**

[76] Inventor: Marc Sims, 5835 Colton Blvd., Oakland, Calif. 94611

[21] Appl. No.:   60,886

[22] Filed: Jul. 26, 1979

[51] Int. Cl.³ C07C 67/48
[52] U.S. Cl. 560/124
[58] Field of Search 560/124

[56]   **References Cited**

U.S. PATENT DOCUMENTS

1,595,538	8/1926	Yamamoto	560/124
1,786,967	12/1930	Trevillian	560/124
1,915,662	6/1933	Gnadinger	560/124
2,050,974	8/1936	La Forge	560/124
2,056,438	10/1936	Ward	167/24
2,372,183	3/1945	Barthel	560/124
2,376,702	5/1945	Komeda	560/124
2,413,107	12/1946	Kuhn	560/124
2,449,671	9/1948	Rhodes	560/124
2,467,859	4/1949	Sankowsky	560/124
3,042,706	7/1962	Haus	560/124
3,083,136	3/1963	Levy	424/305
3,333,962	8/1967	Prebluda	99/2
3,835,776	9/1974	Mutsuo	560/124
3,862,174	1/1975	Mizutani	560/124
3,894,073	7/1975	Alexander	560/124
3,973,036	8/1976	Hirano	424/304
4,012,194	3/1977	Maffei	8/742
4,024,163	5/1977	Elliott	260/347.4

FOREIGN PATENT DOCUMENTS

702886	1/1954	United Kingdom	560/124

OTHER PUBLICATIONS

Sax, "Dangerous Properties of Industrial Materials," 5th Ed., pp. 756 & 863 (1979).
Casida, "Pyrethrum the Natural Insecticide," pp. 25–53 (1973).
Schultz, Food Technology, 24, pp. 94–98 (1970).

Primary Examiner—Natalie Trousof
Assistant Examiner—Michael Shippen
Attorney, Agent, or Firm—Cushman, Darby & Cushman

[57]   **ABSTRACT**

Pyrethrum flowers are extracted with liquid carbon dioxide in suitable equipment to yield a pale, transparent, concentrated extract of pyrethrins. The extract is useful as the active material in safe insecticidal formulations. Alternatively, crude oleoresin produced by extraction of pyrethrum with organic solvents can also be purified by treatment with liquid carbon dioxide.

4 Claims, 1 Drawing Figure

The extraction of pyrethrin from pyrethrum flowers has received a reasonable amount of mention in the technical and trade press during the past few years. One article on the liquid carbon dioxide extraction of these materials has appeared recently. (Sims, M. 1982. Process uses liquid CO_2 for botanical extractions, Chem. Eng. Jan. 25, 50.) Thus this patent is included for brief discussion.

Pyrethrins are natural insecticides. They have low mammalian toxicity and do not accumulate in the environment. The lack of persistence has prevented insects from adapting a resistance to the pyrethrins and thus they are environmentally attractive insecticides. Pyrethrins are low molecular weight ester compounds with additional ether, aldehyde, and ketone functionality. These compounds are very soluble in liquid carbon dioxide. Other materials that are present in the pyrethrum flower such as long chain fatty acids, sterols, and higher alkanes are only sparingly soluble in liquid carbon dioxide. Because of the differential solubilities of the pyrethrins and the other compounds present in the flowers an extract with quite high content of pyrethrin can be obtained using liquid carbon dioxide. Liquid organic solvents cannot differentiate between the active and inactive compounds as finely.

United States Patent [19]

Friedrich

[11]   Patent Number: 4,466,923

[45]   Date of Patent: Aug. 21, 1984

[54] SUPERCRITICAL CO₂ EXTRACTION OF LIPIDS FROM LIPID-CONTAINING MATERIALS

[75] Inventor: John P. Friedrich, Green Valley, Ill.

[73] Assignee: The United States of America as represented by the Secretary of Agriculture, Washington, D.C.

[21] Appl. No.: 364,290

[22] Filed: Apr. 1, 1982

[51] Int. Cl.³ C11B 11/00
[52] U.S. Cl. 260/412.4; 260/410.7; 260/412.8; 260/428.5
[58] Field of Search 260/410.7, 412.4, 412.8, 260/428.5

[56]   References Cited

U.S. PATENT DOCUMENTS

3,843,824	10/1974	Roselius et al.	426/386
3,939,281	2/1976	Schwengers	426/11
4,168,324	9/1979	Roselius et al.	426/312
4,280,961	7/1981	Schneider et al.	260/412.8
4,331,695	5/1982	Zosel	260/412.8 X
4,367,178	1/1983	Heigel et al.	260/412.4 X

FOREIGN PATENT DOCUMENTS

2709033	9/1978	Fed. Rep. of Germany .	
1356749	6/1974	United Kingdom .	
1356750	6/1974	United Kingdom .	
2091292	7/1982	United Kingdom	260/412.4

OTHER PUBLICATIONS

Stahl et al., "Extraktion von Lupinenöl mit überkritischem Kohlendioxid," Fette, Seifen, Anstrichmittel 83(12): 472–474, (1981).
Stahl et al., "Extraction of Seed Oils with Liquid and Supercritical Carbon Dioxide," J. Agr. Food Chem. 28(6): 1153–1157, (1980).
Caragay et al., "Supercritical Fluid Extraction for Purification and Fractionation of Fats and Oils," presented at 72nd Annual Meeting of American Oil Chemists Society, New Orleans, LA, May 18, 1981, pp. 11, 18–24, & 27–32.
Brunner et al., "The State of the Art of Extraction with Compressed Gases," Lecture presented at Annual Meeting of Process Engineers, Strassburg, Oct. 1–3, 1980, pp. 1, 8–12, 14, 34, & 35.
Johnston et al., "An Analytical Carnahan–Starling–van der Walls Model for Solubility of Hydrocarbon Solids in Supercritical Fluids," AIChE Journal 27(5): 773–779, (Sep. 1981).
Hubert et al., "Extraction with Supercritical Gases," G. M. Schneider/E. Stahl/G. Wilke, eds., Verlag Chemie, Deerfield Beach, FL, 1980, pp. 27–28.
Stahl et al., "A Quick Method for the Microanalytical Evaluation of the Dissolving Power of Supercritical Gases," Angew, Chem. Int. Ed. Engl. 17: 731–738, (1978).

Primary Examiner—Thomas A. Waltz
Attorney, Agent, or Firm—M. Howard Silverstein; David G. McConnell; Curtis P. Ribando

[57]   ABSTRACT

In the extraction of lipid-containing substances with supercritical CO₂, triglyceride solubilities of up to 20% or more are obtainable by the simultaneous application of temperatures in excess of about 60° C. and pressures of at least 550 bar.

7 Claims, 2 Drawing Figures

Some of the solubility data given in this patent have already been discussed in Chapter 10. Friedrich has found that at conditions above 60°C and 550 atm the solubility of triglycerides in carbon dioxide rises dramatically, and he shows that soy bean triglycerides become infinitely miscible above about 800 atm and 70°C. Based upon these findings he proposes a process for extracting soy beans, cotton seed, and similar oil seeds, with a minimum of carbon dioxide recycle using carbon dioxide at very high pressure. For example solubility levels of 20–40% are reported at conditions of 600 atm and 70°C.

One might extrapolate that such levels of solubility could lead to a process that might not employ the recycle of gas in its operation (Friedrich, private communication 1983). In the case of soy beans, which have an oil content of about 16%, a solubility level of 40% wt-% oil in carbon dioxide calculates to a carbon dioxide requirement only 0.24 lbs/lb soy beans. At a carbon dioxide usage of only 0.24 lbs, the capital and operating cost of recycling the gas could well be more than the 1 cent cost of the carbon dioxide.

United States Patent [19]

Friedrich et al.

[11]   Patent Number: 4,493,854

[45]   Date of Patent: Jan. 15, 1985

[54]   **PRODUCTION OF DEFATTED SOYBEAN PRODUCTS BY SUPERCRITICAL FLUID EXTRACTION**

[75]   Inventors: **John P. Friedrich**, Green Valley; **Arthur C. Eldridge**, Morton, both of Ill.

[73]   Assignee: **The United States of America as represented by the Secretary of Agriculture**, Washington, D.C.

[21]   Appl. No.:   **534,015**

[22]   Filed: **Sep. 20, 1983**

[51]   Int. Cl.^{3} A23L 1/20; C11B 1/10
[52]   U.S. Cl. **426/629**; 426/417; 426/425
[58]   Field of Search 426/425, 424, 629, 656, 426/489, 417

[56]   **References Cited**

U.S. PATENT DOCUMENTS

3,939,281   2/1976   Schwengers 426/11
4,123,559   10/1978   Vitzthum et al. 426/312
4,255,346   3/1981   Kock 260/412.4

FOREIGN PATENT DOCUMENTS

2748885   5/1979   Fed. Rep. of Germany 426/425

OTHER PUBLICATIONS

J. P. Friedrich et al., "Petroleum–Free Extraction of Oil from Soybeans with Supercritical CO_2," JAOCS 59(7): 288–292, (Jul. 1982).
Von Egon Stahl, "Komprimierte Gase zur Gewinnung von Naturstoffen," Fette. Seifen. Anstrichmittel 84(11): 444–451, (1982).
K. Warner et al., "Relationships of Sensory Characteristics and Gas Chromatographic Profiles of Soybean Protein Products," Cereal Chem. 60(2): 102–106, (1983).

Primary Examiner—George Yeung
Attorney, Agent, or Firm—M. Howard Silverstein; David G. McConnell; Curtis P. Ribando

[57]   **ABSTRACT**

The raw grassy and bitter principles in soybeans are reduced to acceptable levels for purposes of human consumption without significant degradation of the nutritional properties. This result is achieved by a lipid extraction process in which raw soybean material is treated with carbon dioxide under carefully controlled supercritical conditions. Of particular importance are the moisture content of the bean material as well as the pressure, temperature, and contact time of the carbon dioxide extractant.

12 Claims, No Drawings

The prior art section in the patent explains that
conventional hexane extraction of soy beans leaves
constituents in the extracted meal that give raw, grassy,
and bitter flavors that are detrimental to the meal's
organoleplic quality. Emphasis has been directed to replace
the hexane used in the traditional process, and work is
ongoing on the development of a supercritical carbon dioxide
extraction process; most of the research effort has been
directed to achieving a high quality of oil. When soy bean
flakes are extracted with carbon dioxide, the color,
quality, metals content etc., of the oil are excellent, but
the residual flake still retains some of the grassy and
bitter off flavors.

The invention that is described concerns the finding
that if the moisture content of flake is first adjusted to
about 6.5-15% and then extracted with carbon dioxide, a meal
with high organoleptic and protein solubility character is
produced. Twenty separate examples are presented in the
patent which present a panel evaluation of the protein
solubles and flavor scores of the carbon dioxide de-oiled
soy bean meal. When the moisture content is maintained in
the range of 6.5-15% during carbon dioxide extraction, the
quality of the soy bean flour is acceptable; if the moisture
content lies outside that range during extraction, the
flavor is not acceptable.

United States Patent [19]

Christianson et al.

[11]   **Patent Number:**   **4,495,207**

[45]   **Date of Patent:**   **Jan. 22, 1985**

[54]   **PRODUCTION OF FOOD-GRADE CORN GERM PRODUCT BY SUPERCRITICAL FLUID EXTRACTION**

[75]   Inventors: **Donald D. Christianson**, Peoria; **John P. Friedrich**, Green Valley, both of Ill.

[73]   Assignee: **The United States of America as represented by the Secretary of Agriculture**, Washington, D.C.

[21]   Appl. No.:   **436,541**

[22]   Filed: **Oct. 25, 1982**

[51]   Int. Cl.³ A23L 1/172
[52]   U.S. Cl. 426/312; 426/622; 426/627; 426/417
[58]   Field of Search 426/622, 627, 417, 425, 426/312, 481

[56]   **References Cited**

U.S. PATENT DOCUMENTS

3,939,281   2/1976   Schwengers 426/11
4,331,695   5/1982   Zosel 426/417
4,427,707   1/1984   Heine et al. 426/425

FOREIGN PATENT DOCUMENTS

1356749   6/1974   United Kingdom .

OTHER PUBLICATIONS

Stahl et al., "Extraction of Seed Oils with Liquid and Supercritical Carbon Dioxide," J. Agric. Food Chem. 28(6): 1153–1157 (1980).

Friedrich et al., "Petroleum–Free Extraction of Oil from Soybeans with Supercritical CO_2," JAOCS 59(7): 288–292, (Jul. 1982).

Christianson et al., "Super Critical CO_2 Extraction of Oil and Water from Wet Milled Corn Germ and Quality Evaluation of Extracted Flour," Abstract presented at 66th Annual AACC Meeting, Denver, CO (Oct. 25–29, 1981).

Blessin et al., "From a Commercial Dry-Milled Corn Fraction," Cereal Sci. 19(6): 224–225, (Jun. 1974).

Canolty et al., "Relative Protein Value of Defatted Corn Germ Flour," J. Food Sci. 42: 269–270 (1977).

Primary Examiner—Raymond Jones
Assistant Examiner—Elizabeth C. Weimar
Attorney, Agent, or Firm—M. Howard Silverstein; David G. McConnell; Curtis P. Ribando

[57]   **ABSTRACT**

A high-protein, food-grade product is prepared by de-fatting dry-milled corn germ fractions with carbon dioxide under supercritical conditions. The residual lipid and peroxidase activity responsible for development of off-flavors during storage are reduced to a fraction of the levels obtainable by conventional hexane extraction methods.

16 Claims, No Drawings

   The background and prior art section relates that the
corn germ flour produced by hexane extraction of corn germ
suffers from long term stability problems. The residual
lipids left in the germ during normal hexane extraction
auto- or enzymatically oxidize and the oxidized products
reduce the organoleptic and nutritional qualities of the
flour. Inactivation of the oxidative enzymes by toasting
has been found to be unsatisfactory from effectiveness and
economic considerations.
   The results of tests with corn germ flour which has
been extracted with carbon dioxide show that the product
contains one-half the residual oil of hexane-extracted
flour. Furthermore, the enzymatic activity of carbon
dioxide extracted corn germ flour is reduced seven fold and
results in an extended shelf life product with acceptable
flavor.

United States Patent [19]

Heigel et al.

[11]   **4,367,178**

[45]   **Jan. 4, 1983**

[54]   **PROCESS FOR THE PRODUCTION OF PURE LECITHIN DIRECTLY USABLE FOR PHYSIOLOGICAL PURPOSES**

[75]   Inventors: Walter Heigel, Ludwigshafen; Rolf Hueschens, Laatzen, both of Fed. Rep. of Germany

[73]   Assignee: Kali-Chemie Pharma GmbH, Hanover, Fed. Rep. of Germany

[21]   Appl. No.:   238,704

[22]   Filed: Feb. 27, 1981

[30]   **Foreign Application Priority Data**

Mar. 22, 1980 [DE]   Fed. Rep. of Germany 3011185

[51]   Int. Cl.³ C11B 1/10

[52]   U.S. Cl. 260/403; 260/412.4; 260/412.8

[58]   Field of Search 260/403, 412.4, 412.8

[56]   **References Cited**

U.S. PATENT DOCUMENTS

3,923,847 12/1975 Roselius et al. 260/412.4

FOREIGN PATENT DOCUMENTS

7207441 12/1972 Netherlands 260/412.4

Primary Examiner—John F. Niebling
Attorney, Agent, or Firm—Schwartz, Jeffery, Schwaab, Mack, Blumenthal & Koch

[57]   **ABSTRACT**

Disclosed is a process for the production from raw lecithin of pure lecithin directly usable for physiological purposes, comprising the steps of contacting raw lecithin with gas as the extraction medium under supercritical conditions with respect to pressure and temperature in an extraction stage to produce a gas containing an extract; passing the gas containing the extract from the extraction stage into a separation stage; varying at least one of the pressure and the temperature of the gas in the separation stage to separate the extract-containing gas into the gas and the extract; recycling the gas after the step of varying the pressure and/or temperature; and removing pure lecithin from the extraction stage.

18 Claims, 1 Drawing Figure

Lecithin, a mixture of phosphatidyl choline, phosphatidyl ethanolamine, and phosphatidyl inositol, is used as a surfactant in many food, pharmaceutical, and cosmetic products. Lecithin is a product of soy bean oil degumming operations. It is obtained from the hexane extract of flaked soy beans which contains the seed oil and a portion of the phosphatides that are initially present in the soy bean membrane. The extract is treated with water at $80^{\circ}C$, and the phosphatides are hydrated rendering them oil insoluble; they separate from the oil and are filtered. This oil insoluble fraction is termed crude lecithin and consists of about 70% phosphatides, 30% oil. De-oiled lecithin is obtained by treating the crude lecithin with acetone. Lecithin is insoluble in acetone and the oil is, and a separation into a 90–95% phosphatides fraction can be achieved quite readily. The prior art discussion in the patent describes the disadvantages of the hexane extraction process, viz., residual solvents, energy requirements to evaporate the solvents, and the like.

The new process involves the production of de-oiled lecithin by subjecting crude lecithin (which contains 30% oil) to supercritical carbon dioxide extraction; the soy bean oil dissolves in carbon dioxide and lecithin does not. One of the examples relates that 1000 g of crude lecithin is extracted with carbon dioxide at $60^{\circ}C$, 400 atm for 4 hours. The carbon dioxide extracts 380 g of a yellow, clear oil 30 g of water, and the residual material, 580 g of a solid, light yellow substance, which is the de-oiled lecithin, is removed from the extraction vessel at the end of the cycle.

United States Patent [19]

Schütz et al.

[11]   Patent Number: **4,470,927**

[45]   Date of Patent: **Sep. 11, 1984**

[54]   **METHOD OF EXTRACTING THE FLAVORING SUBSTANCES FROM THE VANILLA CAPSULE**

[75]   Inventors: **Erwin Schütz, Palling; Heinz-Rüdiger Vollbrecht, Stein; Klaus Sandner, Trostberg; Theodor Sand; Peter Mühlnickel, both of Holzminden, all of Fed. Rep. of Germany**

[73]   Assignees: **SKW Trostberg Aktiengesellschaft, Trostberg; Haarmann & Reiner, Holzminden, both of Fed. Rep. of Germany**

[21]   Appl. No.:   **416,732**

[22]   Filed: **Sep. 10, 1982**

[30]   **Foreign Application Priority Data**

Sep. 18, 1981   [DE]   Fed. Rep. of Germany 3137230

[51]   Int. Cl.³ C07G 11/00
[52]   U.S. Cl. 260/236.5
[58]   Field of Search 260/236.5

[56]   **References Cited**
           FOREIGN PATENT DOCUMENTS

2127611 12/1942 Fed. Rep. of Germany 426/312
1336511 11/1973 United Kingdom 426/312

Primary Examiner—Albert T. Meyers
Assistant Examiner—John Rollins, Jr.
Attorney, Agent, or Firm—Felfe & Lynch

[57]   **ABSTRACT**

A process for recovering flavoring substances from the vanilla capsule with carbon dioxide under fluid conditions is described, which consists in performing the extraction at temperatures between 10° and 30° C. and pressures of 80 to 350 bar, and producing the separation of the extract at temperatures of 0° to 30° C. and pressures of 30 to 60 bar. In this manner it is possible by a one-step process to extract all of the flavoring substances of the vanilla capsule with the recovery of a highly concentrated vanilla flavoring, and to obtain a material which is considerably superior to the products obtained by conventional extraction with organic solvents.

5 Claims, No Drawings

The patentees describe a process for extracting the aromatic flavoring from vanilla beans. The beans are finely ground at a temperature of -40°C, and the ground mass subjected to high pressure liquid carbon dioxide extraction. We again use the term "high pressure liquid" because the invention claims the use of carbon dioxide at a pressure substantially above the vapor pressure and a temperature below the critical temperature.

In one example the ground material was extracted with carbon dioxide at 160 atm and 25°C; a 98.5% yield of aromatics was obtained. THe carbon dioxide extract and an alcohol extract of another sample of ground vanilla beans were used in comparative tests to flavor ice cream mixtures. In an evaluation test by a panel of 14 persons, the carbon dioxide extract flavored ice cream was preferred unanimously. Gas chromatographic analyses of the carbon dioxide and alcohol extracted materials showed that the carbon dioxide extract contained 20–30% more of the components responsible for vanilla flavor, and additionally, the carbon dioxide extract was found to contain some high volatile flavor components which were not detected in the alcohol extract.

United States Patent [19]

Makin

[54] **PURIFICATION OF VANILLIN**

[75] Inventor: Earle C. Makin, Dickinson, Tex.

[73] Assignee: Monsanto Company, St. Louis, Mo.

[21] Appl. No.: 417,314

[22] Filed: Sep. 13, 1982

[51] Int. Cl.³ C07C 45/78
[52] U.S. Cl. 568/438; 203/39
[58] Field of Search 568/438; 210/767

[56] **References Cited**

U.S. PATENT DOCUMENTS

3,477,856 11/1969 Schultz 99/105
4,075,248 2/1978 Marshall et al. .... 568/438 X

[11] **Patent Number:** **4,474,994**

[45] **Date of Patent:** **Oct. 2, 1984**

4,198,432 4/1980 Vitzthum et al. 426/312

FOREIGN PATENT DOCUMENTS

318939 9/1929 United Kingdom 568/438

Primary Examiner—Bernard Helfin
Attorney, Agent, or Firm—Jon H. Beusen; James C. Logomasini; Arnold H. Cole

[57] **ABSTRACT**

Crude vanillin is purified by supercritical extraction of impurities. The process is especially useful in purifying crude vanillin obtained from paper mill waste liquors. Preferred supercritical extraction fluid is CO_2.

10 Claims, No Drawings

The patent describes a new supercritical fluid process
for purifying crude vanillin which derives from eugenol,
safrole, or preferably from wood products, e.g., lignins,
lignosulfonates, or spent sulfite cooking liquor. Currently,
crude vanillin is obtained from wood products as a result of
some fairly lengthy processing. In summary of the current
process, waste sulfite liquor is reacted with air, and NaOH
and some of the lignosulfonate in the liquor is oxidized.
The reacted mass is extracted with 1-butanol, and this
extract is reacted with aqueous $NaHSO_3$. The aqueous phase
from this extraction is subsequently reacted with H_2SO_4 and
air to produce SO_2 and crude vanillin. A vacuum distillation
of the organic phase increases the purity of the crude
vanillin to 50-70%.   Purified vanillin can be obtained from
the crude material by a multiple crystallization process
which is related in the background to be expensive. In the
reaction scheme to convert lignin to vanillin co-products
such as p-hydroxybenzaldehyde, acetovanillone, 5-formyl
vanillin, and others are produced with the vanillin and
their presence increases the complexity of the total
purification process.

In one of the examples, it is described that
"supercritical" carbon dioxide at conditions of 53 atm, $40^{o}C$
in a static reactor increased the purity of vanillin from
82% to 93% in a single stage. Compounds such as guaiacol,
"light ends and tar," and acetovanillone were taken up by
the carbon dioxide preferentially. For additional
experimental results, the patentee related that he repeated
all the tests described in the examples with liquid carbon
dioxide at $25^{o}C$ (no pressure was stated) and that no purity
improvement was seen. At the end of the invention section
the patentee states that he considers the term
"supercritical" in his claims to consist of a temperature
higher than the critical temperature but not necessarily a
pressure higher than the critical pressure.

United States Patent [19]

Coenen et al.

[11]   **4,400,398**

[45]   **Aug. 23, 1983**

[54] **METHOD FOR OBTAINING AROMATICS AND DYESTUFFS FROM BELL PEPPERS**

[75] Inventors: Hubert Coenen; Rainer Hagen, both of Essen; Manfred Knuth, Hamburg, all of Fed. Rep. of Germany

[73] Assignee: **Fried. Krupp Gesellschaft mit beschränkter Haftung, Essen, Fed. Rep. of Germany**

[21] Appl. No.: **365,473**

[22] Filed: **Apr. 5, 1982**

[30]   **Foreign Application Priority Data**

Apr. 10, 1981 [DE] Fed. Rep. of Germany 3114593

[51] Int. Cl.³ A23L 1/277; A23L 1/28; A23L 1/221

[52] U.S. Cl. 426/429; 426/430; 426/475; 426/478; 426/651; 426/655; 426/540

[58] Field of Search 426/429, 430, 475, 478, 426/655, 250, 540; 260/412.4

[56]   **References Cited**

U.S. PATENT DOCUMENTS

3,526,509	9/1970	Yamada	426/429
3,939,281	2/1976	Schwengers	426/429
4,104,409	8/1978	Vitzthum et al.	426/655
4,123,559	10/1978	Vitzthum et al.	426/655
4,233,210	11/1980	Koch	426/429
4,331,695	5/1982	Zosel	426/429

Primary Examiner—Jeanette M. Hunter
Attorney, Agent, or Firm—Spencer & Kaye

[57]   **ABSTRACT**

Method for obtaining aromatics and/or dyestuffs from bell peppers wherein red pepper is extracted with a solvent which is in a supercritical state and is gaseous under normal conditions. The extraction takes place at a pressure of $> P_k$ to 350 bar and a temperature of $> T_k$ to 70° C. The extracted aromatics and/or dyestuffs are separated from the separated supercritical gas phase by lowering the density of the gas phase.

25 Claims, 1 Drawing Figure

A process for extracting the aromatics and dyestuffs from sweet and hot red peppers is described. Depending upon the method of operation the aromatics and dyestuffs can be individually concentrated. Hot red peppers contain an aromatic fraction consisting of a variety of organic compounds, the most pungent of which is the alkaloid, capsaicin, and a carotinoid fraction, the largest component of which is capsanthin. It is possible to extract the aromatics "preferentially" (i.e., they are much more soluble than are the carotinoids) by operating at two sequential and increasing pressure levels. First, extraction is carried out at a low pressure to extract the aromatic fraction and when the aromatics are dissolved and separated from the gas, a much higher pressure is used to extract the capsanthin.

One of the examples describes the results. 930 g of dried, ground, very hot red pepper is extracted with 120 kg of carbon dioxide at 120 atm, 40°C. The extract is 140 g of extremely pungent, orange-yellow paste. The extraction pressure is increased to 320 atm and 50 kg of carbon dioxide is passed through the charge to extract 22.7 g of dark red liquid concentrate. The dyestuff (the dark red liquid) is free of flavor and fragrance and can be used as a food dye.

United States Patent [19]

Heine et al.

[11]   **4,427,707**

[45]   **Jan. 24, 1984**

[54]   **METHOD FOR THE PRODUCTION OF FOOD ADDITIVES WITH IMPROVED TASTE**

[75]   Inventors: **Christian Heine,** Monheim; **Reinhold Wüst,** Kaarst, both of Fed. Rep. of Germany

[73]   Assignee: **Henkel KGaA,** Fed. Rep. of Germany

[21]   Appl. No.:   **361,781**

[22]   Filed: **Mar. 25, 1982**

[30]   **Foreign Application Priority Data**

Apr. 11, 1981 [DE]   Fed. Rep. of Germany 3114783

[51]   **Int. Cl.³** A23L 1/20; A23G 1/00
[52]   **U.S. Cl.** 426/312; 426/573; 426/425; 426/430; 426/486; 426/488; 426/629
[58]   **Field of Search** 426/573, 312, 425, 430, 426/486, 488, 615, 629, 472, 467, 468, 469

[56]   **References Cited**

U.S. PATENT DOCUMENTS

479,512	7/1892	Jacobs	426/469
3,939,281	2/1976	Schwengers	426/429
4,123,559	10/1978	Vitzthum et al.	426/312
4,168,324	9/1979	Roselius	426/312
4,198,432	4/1980	Vitzthum et al.	426/312
4,200,656	4/1980	Cohen et al.	426/312
4,328,255	5/1982	Roselius et al.	426/425

Primary Examiner—Jeanette M. Hunter
Attorney, Agent, or Firm—Hammond, Littell, Weissenberger and Muserlian

[57]   **ABSTRACT**

Locust Bean Pod Powder, Locust Bean Gum Powder and Guar Gum Powder originally having odor and taste characteristics making them unsuitable as food additives, can be made suitable therefor by extraction with gases at supercritical temperatures.

2 Claims, No Drawings

The background section relates that the beans of the locust bean tree yield a gum powder that is a swelling substance and that the pods which house the beans yield a product which, because of its brown color, is suitable for extending or substituting for cocoa powder. Sometimes the locust pod powder has an unpleasant odor and tastes like burned fat so that it cannot be used to produce a high quality substitute for cocoa powder. The locust bean gum powder often has an unpleasant taste and odor. The discussion also relates that other gums such as quar gum powder also have similar sensory problems. The gums, incidentally, are used in the manufacture of such products as ice cream, sauces, and puddings.

Several examples gave results of the extraction of locust bean pod powder (the cocoa substitute) and of locust bean and quar gum powder with carbon dioxide at 350 atm, 45°C. The extraction with carbon dioxide produced powders with pleasant odor and agreeable taste.

United States Patent [19]

Behr et al.

[11]   Patent Number: **4,490,398**

[45]   Date of Patent: **Dec. 25, 1984**

[54]   **PROCESS FOR THE PREPARATION OF SPICE EXTRACTS**

[75]   Inventors: **Norbert Behr,** Haan; **Henk van der Mei,** Rinteln, both of Fed. Rep. of Germany; **Wolfgang Sirtl,** Zurich, Switzerland; **Harald Schnegelberger,** Leichlingen; **Othmar von Ettingshausen,** Düsseldorf-Unterbach, both of Fed. Rep. of Germany

[73]   Assignee: **Henkel Kommanditgesellschaft auf Aktien,** Düsseldorf-Holthausen, Fed. Rep. of Germany

[21]   Appl. No.:   **337,388**

[22]   Filed: **Jan. 6, 1982**

Related U.S. Application Data

[63]   Continuation of Ser. No. 173,403, Jul. 29, 1980, abandoned.

[30]   **Foreign Application Priority Data**

Aug. 2, 1979 [DE]   Fed. Rep. of Germany 2931393

[51]   Int. Cl.^{3} **A23L 1/221**
[52]   U.S. Cl. **426/312;** 426/318; 426/319; 426/650; 426/638
[58]   Field of Search 426/638, 655, 312, 318, 426/319, 429, 431, 425, 442, 478, 506, 650

[56]   **References Cited**

U.S. PATENT DOCUMENTS

2,571,948	10/1951	Sair et al.	426/655
4,104,409	8/1978	Vitzthum et al.	426/318
4,123,559	10/1978	Vitzthum et al.	426/655
4,167,589	9/1979	Vitzthum et al.	426/312
4,198,432	4/1980	Vitzthum et al.	426/638

FOREIGN PATENT DOCUMENTS

2127611 12/1971 Fed. Rep. of Germany .

Primary Examiner—Hiram H. Bernstein
Attorney, Agent, or Firm—Hammond & Littell, Weissenberger & Dippert

[57]   **ABSTRACT**

This invention is directed to a process for the production of extracts from spices in two stages by extraction with a non-toxic gas as solvent, the improvement which comprises in a first stage extracting from the spices essential oils functioning as aroma components by contacting the spices with liquid solvent, at a pressure in the supercritical range and a temperature in the subcritical range, separating the solvent from the spice, evaporating the solvent and separating essential oils, and in a second stage extracting from the spices the portions acting as flavor carriers by contacting the spices from the first stage with gaseous solvent, at a pressure and a temperature both in the supercritical range, separating the gaseous solvent from the spice, reducing the pressure and temperature, and separating the flavor carriers from the gaseous solvent.

4 Claims, 2 Drawing Figures

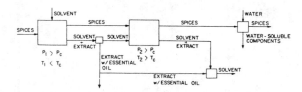

We previously reviewed a spice extraction patent, U.S. 4,123,559, that described a two step process, first the use of dry carbon dioxide to extract aromas and then, moist carbon dioxide to extract the flavor components. The two step process in this patent is different and is summarized in the abstract. Subcritical carbon dioxide is first used to extract the aroma components, typically ester, aldehyde, and ketone compounds, but it is not of sufficient dissolving power to extract the alkaloid (flavor) components.

The patentees carry out carbon dioxide extraction of black pepper "Madagascar" operating according to the instant invention and according to the invention of the other spice extraction patent, U.S. 4,123,559. The table below taken from the patent compares the results of extracting pepper using both processes.

Comparison of Extract Yields and Analysis

Process	CO_2 Conditions	Yield and Analysis
This patent		
Step 1	liquid, 300 bar, 29°C	4.5% (2.1% essential oil, 0.9% piperine)
Step 2	supercritical, 350 bar, 55°C	6.4% (0.1% essential oil, 6.3% piperine)
U.S. 4,123,559		
Step 1	dry supercritical, 350 bar, 57°C	10.4% (1.1% essential oil, 8.2% piperine)
Step 2	moist supercritical, 350 bar, 58°C	1% (1% piperine)

The patentees state that the total yields in both cases are about the same but that the new process results in the fractionation of piperine from the oils. However, we bring out here that the patentees of U.S. 4,123,559, Vitzthum and Hubert, stated specifically that for the case of black pepper dry supercritical CO_2 extracted some of the alkaloid flavor component, whereas for some of the other spices they tested dry CO_2 does not extract the alkaloid flavors. It would have been a better evaluation of the effectiveness of the current patent if Behr et al had performed comparative experiments on a spice that Vitzthum and Hubert found to require water in the second step. (Incidentally, it can be determined from the data in the table that the liquid CO_2 that Behr et al employ in the first step is "high pressure liquid" and not near critical liquid. In the abstract they refer to it as "pressure in the supercritical range and temperature in the subcritical range.")

United States Patent [19]

Biernoth et al.

[11]   **Patent Number: 4,504,503**

[45]   **Date of Patent: Mar. 12, 1985**

[54]   **FRACTIONATION OF BUTTERFAT USING A LIQUEFIED GAS OR A GAS IN THE SUPERCRITICAL STATE**

[75]   Inventors: **Gerhard Biernoth,** Quickborn; **Werner Merk,** Buchholz, both of Fed. Rep. of Germany

[73]   Assignee: **Lever Brothers Company,** New York, N.Y.

[21]   Appl. No.:   **413,937**

[22]   Filed: **Sep. 1, 1982**

[30]   **Foreign Application Priority Data**

Sep. 9, 1981 [GB]   United Kingdom 8127261

[51]   Int. Cl.³ **A23D 5/02**
[52]   U.S. Cl. **426/312;** 426/318; 426/319; 426/607; 426/417; 426/425; 260/428.5
[58]   Field of Search 426/312, 317, 318, 319, 426/417, 425, 603, 607; 260/428, 428.5

[56]   **References Cited**

U.S. PATENT DOCUMENTS

1,805,751	5/1931	Auerbach	260/428
2,247,496	7/1941	Hixson et al.	260/428.5
2,467,906	4/1949	Passino et al.	260/428.5
2,613,215	10/1952	Mattil	426/313 X
3,519,435	7/1970	MacCollom	426/417 X
3,939,281	2/1976	Schwengers	426/429 X
4,005,228	1/1977	Norris	426/429 X
4,109,409	8/1978	Vitzthum et al.	426/319 X
4,280,961	7/1981	Schneider et al.	260/428.5 X
4,400,398	8/1983	Coenen et al.	426/478 X

Primary Examiner—Robert Yoncoskie
Attorney, Agent, or Firm—James J. Farrell

[57]   **ABSTRACT**

A process for producing a mixture of triglycerides displaying butter-like properties by fractionating fats with a liquefied gas or a gas under supercritical conditions. Said mixture of triglycerides predominantly consists of triglycerides with a carbon number ranging from 24 to 42 and can be used as one of the fat components of a margarine fat blend in order to improve its butter-like properties.

6 Claims, 5 Drawing Figures

Butterfat is a complex mixture of triglycerides composed of fatty acids that range from butyric acid (C4) to stearic acid (C18). The major components (in decreasing order of concentration) are lauric (C12), oleic (C18:1), stearic (C18), myristic (C14), caproic (C6) and caprylic (C8). For comparison most vegetable oils such as corn, cottonseed, soybean, and sunflower are made up essentially exclusively of C16 and C18 fatty acids of varied unsaturation. Because of the closeness of molecular weight and especially because of varying unsaturation within a carbon number seed oil triglycerides cannot be readily fractionated by supercritical fluid extraction; however, because butterfat is composed of a much wider range of molecular weight, it can be fractionated.

An example provides quantitative information on the use of supercritical carbon dioxide to separate a butter oil into two fractions. Conditions of 200 bar 80°C were used in the extractor and 30 bar, 30°C in the separator. The feed was 700 g; an extract of 135 g and a residue of 560 g were obtained. The extract consisted primarily of triglycerides composed of C4–C12 fatty acids with only a small amount of C18's; the residue consisted of primarily C18 fatty acid triglycerides. The extract was used in formulating a margarine blend, and the residual is useful in fat blends used for making (puff) pastry.

United States Patent [19]

Amer

[11]   **4,422,966**

[45]   **Dec. 27, 1983**

[54]   **SEPARATION OF NEUTRALS FROM TALL OIL SOAPS**

[75]   Inventor: **Gamal I. Amer,** Lawrenceville, N.J.

[73]   Assignee: **Union Camp Corporation,** Wayne, N.J.

[21]   Appl. No.:   **476,599**

[22]   Filed: **Mar. 18, 1983**

[51]   Int. Cl.³ C09F 1/00
[52]   U.S. Cl. 260/97.6; 260/97.7
[58]   Field of Search 260/97.7, 97.6

[56]   **References Cited**

U.S. PATENT DOCUMENTS

3,965,085   6/1976   Holmbom et al. 260/97.7
3,969,196   7/1976   Zosel 203/49
4,308,200 12/1981   Fremont 260/97.7

4,349,415   9/1982   De Filippi et al. 203/14

FOREIGN PATENT DOCUMENTS

2032789   5/1980   United Kingdom .

OTHER PUBLICATIONS

Francis, Physical Chem. 58, (1954), pp. 1099-1114.
Francis, Ind. & Eng. Chem. 47 (1975) pp. 231-233.

Primary Examiner—H. S. Cockeram
Attorney, Agent, or Firm—Kane, Dalsimer, Kane, Sullivan & Kurucz

[57]   **ABSTRACT**

The disclousre is of a process for separating neutrals from salts of fatty/resin acids by extraction of tall oil soaps with supercritical fluid solvents.

7 Claims, 1 Drawing Figure

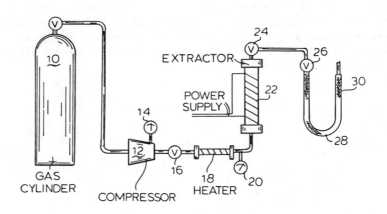

Crude tall oil is a mixture of fatty acids, resin acids, and neutrals (i.e., no carboxylic acid functionality). The background section relates that neutrals interfere with the separation of the fatty acids from the resin acids and in industrial practice the neutrals are removed by molecular distillation; however, it is difficult to separate the neutrals from the other components because of vapor pressure similarity considerations. Tall oil soap, the precursor to crude tall oil, is a pasty emulsion of the neutrals and the sodium salts of the fatty and resin acids. The patent states that is is possible to extract neutrals from the soap with a liquid hydrocarbon solvent, but the prior art discussion relates that subsequent liquid hydrocarbon solvent recovery steps are relatively difficult. The neutrals can be separated from the soaps by a hydrocarbon solvent, incidentally, because the neutrals are lipophiles whereas the soaps are ionic and do not dissolve in the hydrocarbon. Similarly the neutrals will dissolve in a supercritical fluid like ethylene, or propane, or the chlorofluorocarbons, and the use of these gases in the supercritical state is the invention. Like the case of liquid hydrocarbon solvents, the ionic soap compounds will not dissolve in the supercritical gases. (Carbon dioxide is specifically not listed among the gases, and we shall discuss the case of carbon dioxide extraction of the emulsion later which is the subject of the next patent.)

The figure shown on the patent face page is a flow chart of the laboratory apparatus which was used to carry out the test. A sample of 15 g tall oil soap was charged to the extractor 22; the charge contained 4.9% neutral oil. The sample was extracted with ethylene at 4000 psi, 70°C. An extract sample weighing 0.54 g was analyzed and was found to contain 64% neutrals which represented almost one-half the neutrals present in the charge. The identity of the other 36% fraction of the extract was not reported but probably consisted of free resin and fatty acids.

United States Patent [19]

Lawson et al.

[11]   Patent Number: **4,495,095**

[45]   Date of Patent: **Jan. 22, 1985**

[54]   **ACIDULATION AND RECOVERY OF CRUDE TALL OIL FROM TALL OIL SOAPS**

[75]   Inventors: **Nelson E. Lawson**, Trenton; **Gamal I. Amer**, Lawrenceville, both of N.J.

[73]   Assignee: **Union Camp Corporation**, Wayne, N.J.

[21]   Appl. No.:   **481,811**

[22]   Filed: **Apr. 4, 1983**

[51]   Int. Cl.³ C09F 93/00; C11D 15/00
[52]   U.S. Cl. 260/97.7; 260/97.6
[58]   Field of Search 260/97.6, 97.7

[56]   **References Cited**

U.S. PATENT DOCUMENTS

2,232,331	2/1941	Leithe et al.	260/419
3,965,085	6/1976	Holmbom et al.	260/97.7
3,969,196	7/1976	Zosel	203/49
4,075,188	2/1978	Vardell	260/97.7
4,250,331	2/1981	Shimshick	562/485
4,308,200	12/1981	Fremont	260/97.7
4,349,415	9/1982	De Filippi et al.	203/14
4,422,966	12/1983	Amer	260/97.7

Primary Examiner—Herbert S. Cockeram
Attorney, Agent, or Firm—Kane, Dalsimer, Kane, Sullivan and Kurucz

[57]   **ABSTRACT**

In the present invention, tall oil acids are prepared by acidulating tall oil soap with supercritical fluid carbon dioxide. The method of preparation is carried out at a temperature of from about 31° to 400° C. and the supercritical carbon dioxide is under a pressure of from about 1075 to about 50,000 psi. The acidulate is extracted into the fluid phase of the supercritical carbon dioxide. The resultant tall oil acids are then recovered from the carbon dioxide fluid phase.

4 Claims, 1 Drawing Figure

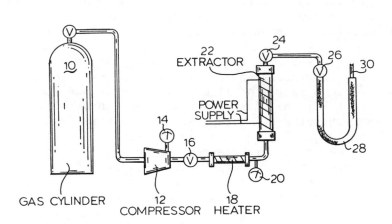

We presented some data on pH of carbon dioxide solutions when we discussed glycerol drying of carbon dioxide (U.S. 4,478,612), and we also discussed the (partial) conversion of acetate salts to acetic acid using carbon dioxide as an extractant of acetate solutions. This patent makes use of the ability of wet carbon dioxide to convert soaps (sodium salts of fatty acids) to fatty acids which are soluble in carbon dioxide.

The pK's of long chain fatty acids are about 5; thus, if a soap is "in solution," treating the solution with carbon dioxide will convert some of the salt to free acid and will result in an extraction of the acid into the carbon dioxide. Strictly speaking, the salts of, say, C18 acids are not soluble in water; however, all that is required is that the carbon dioxide be moist; dry salts will be converted to free fatty acid by the action of moist carbon dioxide. (Krukonis 1981. Unpublished data, fatty and aromatic acids extraction from salts).

Returning now to the patent, the invention taught is the contacting of crude tall oil soaps (a moist mixture of neutrals and sodium salts of fatty and resin acids) with carbon dioxide; the carbon dioxide converts the salts to free fatty and resin acids which then dissolve in the carbon dioxide (but probably so are some of the neutrals). One example describes a laboratory test, viz., from a charge of 9.65 gm tall oil soap five fractions were extracted with supercritical carbon dioxide. The first fraction analyzed 88% resin + fatty acids, and the fifth analyzed 72%.

United States Patent [19]

Fremont

[11]   **4,308,200**

[45]   **Dec. 29, 1981**

[54] EXTRACTION OF CONIFEROUS WOODS WITH FLUID CARBON DIOXIDE AND OTHER SUPERCRITICAL FLUIDS

[75] Inventor: Henry A. Fremont, Wyoming, Ohio

[73] Assignee: Champion International Corporation, Stamford, Conn.

[21] Appl. No.:   168,443

[22] Filed: Jul. 10, 1980

[51] Int. Cl.³ C09F 3/00; C09F 1/00
[52] U.S. Cl. 260/110; 260/97.7
[58] Field of Search 260/110, 97.7

[56]   **References Cited**

U.S. PATENT DOCUMENTS

1,762,785 6/1930 Little 260/110
2,388,412 11/1945 Hixson et al. 260/97.6
3,969,196 7/1976 Zosel 203/49

Primary Examiner—H. S. Cockeram
Attorney, Agent, or Firm—Evelyn M. Sommer

[57]   **ABSTRACT**

Disclosed is a process for extraction of coniferous woods, such as pine, with supercritical fluids to recover tall oil and turpentine, or components thereof. Gases such as carbon dioxide, nitrous oxide, nitrogen, and lower alkanes or lower alkenes at temperatures above critical and pressures of about 100 psi above critical; i.e., supercritical fluids, are contacted with subdivided wood. The extracted wood is suitable for pulping and subsequent papermaking. The extract-bearing fluid is preferably stripped of the extracts by reducing the pressure in stages, each pressure reduction effecting removal of extracts of a narrowly-defined molecular weight range. The fluid is recompressed and recycled.

9 Claims, 1 Drawing Figure

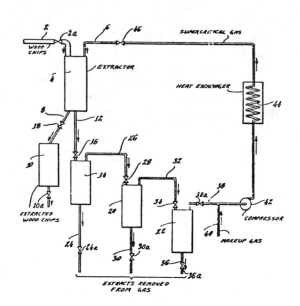

The process to extract chemical components from wood is shown in the figure. Wood chips are charged (batchwise) to the extractor 4. Carbon dioxide at conditions of about 1175 psi and 40°C is fed to the extractor via line 6. The extract stream consisting of organics such as tall oil and turpentine which dissolve in carbon dioxide exits the extractor via line 12, and the stream is reduced stagewise in pressure in vessels 14, 20, and 22. Depending upon the particular conditions of pressure and expansion, it is related that two fractions, tall oil and turpentine, or a plurality of fractions, individual terpenes, individual fatty acids, and individual resin acids, can be separated.

We discussed two tall oil extraction patents earlier, and we related that tall oil is the material that derives from wood pulping and that it consists of a mixture of resin acids, fatty acids, and neutrals. Fatty acids are present in trees in primarily triglyceride form, and the triglycerides are saponified to fatty acids during pulping, so we wonder if the patentee means triglycerides are extracted instead of fatty acids. As we develop later, we wonder about many other things that he relates.

An example describes a specific test. Twenty lbs of pine chips (and we assume they contain their normal moisture of about 50+%) are extracted with 29 lbs of carbon dioxide at 1175 psi and 40°C. At the end of one minute of contact the carbon dioxide solution is drawn from the vessel and decreased in pressure stagewise, first to 1145 psi and 40°C where 0.24 lb of resin acid precipitates from solution, second to 1115 psi and 38°C where 0.11 lb fatty acids precipitates and last to a vessel at 34°C and 1085 psi where 0.037 lb of turpentine collects.

We are very surprised that a pressure decrease of only 30 psi and a simultaneous temperature decrease of only 2°C can result in the separation of resin acids from fatty acids, and we bring up the subject of fatty acids again. We don't believe there is 0.11 lb fatty acid in 20 lbs of moist pine chips (and this has been verified in discussions with technical personnel in the pulp and paper industry). Again, we wonder if the patentee means 0.11 lb triglycerides. From the data given in the above example, we can calculate a minimum solubility of the "fatty acids" in CO_2 at 1145 psi, 40°C; it is 0.20 wt-%. Even though we wonder if the patentee means triglycerides instead of fatty acids, we now state that the 0.11 lb of "fatty acid" recovered in the second pressure reduction step cannot be triglycerides either; the solubility of triglycerides in carbon dioxide at 1145 psi, 40°C is only 0.02 wt-%. We wonder what the patentee has extracted. Additionally, he could not have precipitated turpentine at 34°C, 1085 psi because the absolute solubility of turpentine is much higher than the 0.07% we calculate from his values. (Krukonis 1984. Unpublished data).

Krase, N.W. and A.E. Lawrence, Process for the preparation of ethylene polymers, U.S. 2,396,791 (Mar. 19, 1946).

Krase, N.W., Process of separating ethylene polymers, U.S. 2,388,160 (Oct. 30, 1945).

Hunter, E. and R.B. Richards, Fractionation of polymeric ethylene, U.S. 2,457,238 (Dec. 28, 1948).

Cottle, J.E., Supercritical polymerization, U.S. 3,294,772 (Dec. 27, 1966).

Copelin, H.B., Method for reducing oligomeric cyclic ether content of a polymerizate, U.S. 4,306,058 (Dec. 15, 1981).

March 19, 1946.   N. W. KRASE ET AL   2,396,791

PROCESS FOR THE PREPARATION OF ETHYLENE POLYMERS

Filed Dec. 19, 1942

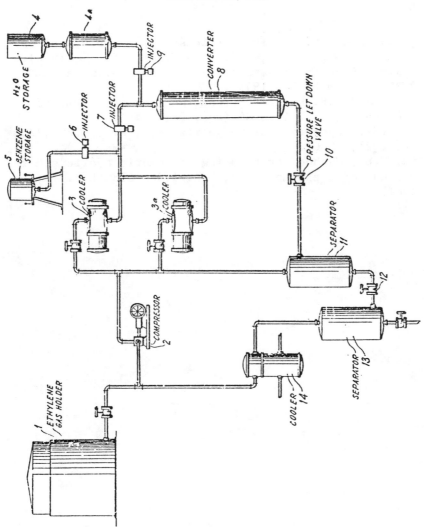

Norman W. Krase
Allen E. Lawrence INVENTORS

BY
ATTORNEY

This patent is concerned primarily with the polymerization of ethylene at conditions high above its critical
temperature and pressure. The Krase and Lawrence patent
covers polymerization but it also describes the separation
of various oligomers by stagewise pressure reduction. The
multi-step sequence results in a lower energy recycle-
separation process which produces discreet fractions of
polyethylene of different molecular weight.

A portion of the example and process operation is
excerpted from the patent to point out once more that
supercritical fluid extraction and separation have been
known and understood for 40-50 years, viz.,

> "....the reaction mixture is passed from the
> reactor (the converter 8 shown in the figure) to a
> pressure let-down valve 10 wherein the pressure is
> reduced from 4000 atm to below 500 atm. The
> stream passes from this valve to a separator 11 in
> which the liquid and solid constituents separate
> from the gas...."

Operation of the total process with the multiple
pressure reduction steps results in a lowest energy
consumption process.

Patented Oct. 30, 1945

2,388,160

UNITED STATES PATENT OFFICE

2,388,160

PROCESS OF SEPARATING ETHYLENE POLYMERS

Norman William Krase, Swarthmore, Pa., assignor to E. I. du Pont de Nemours & Company, Wilmington, Del., a corporation of Delaware

No Drawing.   Application December 9, 1942,
Serial No. 468,419

6 Claims.   (Cl. 260—94)

This invention relates to the separation of high molecular weight products and more particularly to the separation of products from a mixture of high molecular weight compounds obtained by the treatment of ethylene in the presence of oxygen 5 type and similar catalysts.

It is known that monoolefinic hydrocarbons and more particularly ethylene can be converted into products having a linear polymeric structure and, likewise, that solid and semi-solid products of 10 high molecular weight can be produced by subjecting these hydrocarbons to polymerization pressures ranging between 500 and 3000 atmospheres and at temperatures between 40° and 400° C. in the presence of molecular oxygen or com- 15 pounds which give up oxygen, or the process may be conducted at the higher pressures in the substantial absence of added catalyst. When the polymerization is conducted in the presence of molecular oxygen, or under conditions that 20 give similar results, products are obtained which constitute a mixture of many individual compounds. These individual compounds have widely different chemical and physical properties, and are herein referred to as high pressure peroxygen- 25 catalyzed olefine or ethylene products.

An object of the present invention is to provide an improved process for the separation of the high pressure oxygen catalyzed olefine products into products having uniform properties. 30 Another object of the invention is to provide a means of separating such products into fractions in which the molecular weights of the constituents present are relatively of the same order of magnitude. Yet another object of the invention 35 is to provide a process for the precipitation of such products and especially the high pressure peroxygen-catalyzed ethylene products from solution in hydrocarbon vapors or in ethylene by differential pressure or differential temperature 40 fractionation. Still another object is to provide a means of separation by a combination of differential pressure and differential temperature stages. Other objects and advantages of the invention will hereinafter appear. 45

In the preparation of high molecular products from the monoolefinic hydrocarbons and especially ethylene the reaction is, as has been stated, generally catalyzed by peroxygen-type catalysts at extremely elevated pressures and at these pres- 50 sures a large amount of the products is dissolved in the vapors. In accord with this invention, it has been found that products having different physical and chemical properties can be obtained by lowering the pressure under substantially con- 55 stant temperatures by a series of stages and collecting the products which precipitate from each stage. By this method it is possible to obtain high molecular weight products from ethylene, that vary in physical characteristics from hard horny 60

solid masses to waxy semi-solid masses, while intermediate products between the extreme limiting products are obtainable varying in properties in accord with the number of pressure stages used in separating them.

Similarly, it has been found that, in lieu of dropping the pressure in stages, effective fractionation can be realized by dropping the temperature in stages while maintaining the pressure substantially constant, and it has been found that each one of the individual fractions has physical and chemical properties different from the properties of the fractions obtained at higher or lower temperatures. A modification of the aforesaid procedures may also be effected by changing both temperature and pressure at each stage. By these expedients, which involve utilizing differential pressure, differential temperature, or a combination of both differential temperature and pressure, it is possible, in accord with the invention, to separate a valuable series of products from the high pressure polymerized olefine products.

The invention is adapted to the treatment of the polymers, interpolymers or other high molecular weight products of whatever nature prepared from ethylene per se, or from ethylene or other polymerizable monoolefinic hydrocarbons, under high pressure and catalyzed by peroxygen-type catalysts or catalyzed by no catalysts under very high pressures. Such olefines may be reacted under such conditions with the following compounds, such as for example, the other olefines, propylene, butylene, isobutylene; dichlorethylene, 2 - chloro-propene - 1, tetrafluorethylene; vinyl ethers, ketones, esters and other vinyl compounds such as methyl, ethyl and propyl vinyl ethers, vinyl chloracetate, vinyl chloride, vinyl acetate, vinyl propionate, N-vinylphthalimide, vinyl thioacetate, methyl vinyl thioether, methyl vinyl sulphone, N-vinylcarbazole, vinyl sulphonic esters; styrene; stilbene; acrylic and methacrylic amides, nitriles, esters and other acrylic and methacrylic compounds, e. g. methylene diacrylate and dimethacrylate, ethyl, propyl, butyl and amyl acrylates and methacrylates; alpha-haloacrylic acids and their esters, e. g., methyl alpha-chloroacrylate; esters of crotonic and itaconic acids, e. g., methyl crotonate and diethyl itaconate; butadiene, isoprene, chloro-2-butadiene-1,3; terpenes, e. g., limonene and camphene. The high molecular weight polymers obtained from ethylene with saturated organic acids, esters, anhydrides, aldehydes, alcohols, ethers, halogenated aliphatic hydrocarbons, etc., vinyl halides, sulphonyl halides, sulfur halides, etc. alkyl sulfates may likewise be fractionated in accord with the process of the invention.

The peroxygen-type catalyst which may be employed in the aforesaid reactions includes molec-

This patent was filed earlier and issued earlier than the previous Krase and Lawrence patent just discussed. The previous one described a two (or more) step pressure reduction as part of the overall polymerization process. This one describes the use of isobaric temperature change in some regions of operating space and simultaneous adjustment of pressure and temperature in others.

In a discussion of the invention we learn that

"...it has been found that, in lieu of dropping the pressure in stages, effective fractionation can be realized by dropping the temperature in stages while maintaining the pressure substantially constant, and it has been found that each one of the individual fractions has physical and chemical properties different from the fractions obtained at higher or lower temperature."

A question to the reader here: In what regime of polyethylene solubility must the polymerization process be operating in order to be able to carry out the separation by isobaric temperature decrease? Refer to the naphthalene solubility diagram, Figure 6.2, and recall our statement that many solids and liquids (as long as they are not infinitely miscible) behave as depicted in that diagram.

Patented Dec. 28, 1948   **2,457,238**

UNITED STATES PATENT OFFICE

2,457,238

**FRACTIONATION OF POLYMERIC
ETHYLENE**

Edward Hunter and Raymond B. Richards,
Northwich England, assignors to Imperial
Chemical Industries Limited, a corporation of
Great Britain

No Drawing. Application October 25, 1944, Serial
No. 560,352. In Great Britain November 29,
1943

2 Claims. (Cl. 260—94)

This invention relates to a new and improved process for fractionating mixtures of solid polymers, and for comminuting those solid polymers which are normally difficult to obtain in the form of fine granules or powders.

It is known that certain liquids and a few solids dissolve in certain compressed gases, and that with some gases it is not necessary to use very great pressures to show that the solubility in a gas may be as great as in a liquid solvent. For example, camphor and paraffin can be dissolved in very noticeable quantities even in only 1 cc. of compressed methane, i. e., less than a decigram. On removing the pressure these bodies are deposited; the camphor crystallises on the walls, and paraffin as brilliant flakes. Above 150 atmospheres, ethylene dissolves paraffin abundantly, and on removing the pressure the latter becomes solid again. So far, however, all the results which were known to be obtainable by distillation in gases at these pressures could more readily be obtained by conventional methods, and there has been no purpose in trying to overcome the practical difficulties involved in any industrial application of this laboratory phenomenon.

Many solid polymers of high molecular weight have recently become available, generally in the form of mixtures of solids of a wide range of molecular weights. When molten, they are themselves known to dissolve gases under high pressures. These polymers are difficult to fractionate into solids of a narrower range of molecular weights by conventional fractional crystallisation or dissolution, and they are generally difficult to prepare in powdered or granular forms. We have now found that solid polymers obtained from compounds having monoolefinic unsaturation can be dissolved in high pressure organic gases, and that fractions of progressively lower molecular weight can then be deposited as granular or powdered solids.

According to the present invention we provide a process which comprises dissolving solid polymers of compounds which have monoolefinic unsaturation, in an organic gas at a high pressure preferably exceeding 500 atmospheres, and a raised temperature preferably between 50° and 350° C., by providing intimate contact between them, and thereafter at least partially reducing the pressure and/or temperature of the gaseous phase.

The solid polymers of compounds which have monoolefinic unsaturation to which this invention is applicable are the essentially straight or branched chain polymers of mean molecular

weight exceeding 5000, generally 10,000–40,000 and even higher, and virtually free from cross-linkages. They contain homologues of much lower molecular weight and also of higher molecular weight than the mean; the lower molecular weight fractions have been found to lead to undesirable properties such as low softening point and low tensile strength. The aim in polymerisation is frequently to obtain products of high mean molecular weight with only a narrow range of molecular weights. These polymers may be obtained from one or more compounds having monoolefinic unsaturation, i. e. compounds having one carbon-carbon double bond, alone or together with compounds with which they can interpolymerise, by the methods known for polymerising such compounds. The principal polymers to which the invention is applicable are polythene, polyisobutene, polyvinyl chloride, polystyrene and polymethyl-acrylate. All the polymers to which the invention is applicable are soluble in some organic liquid solvent, such as aliphatic or aromatic hydrocarbon liquids, ethers, alcohols, carbon tetrachloride and chloroform, generally at a raised temperature such as 60°–120° C.

Dissolution in a compressed gas is effected at a raised temperature preferably between 50° and 350° C., by bringing the polymer into intimate contact with the gas while the gas is in motion, e. g. stirred or circulating. The solubility of polymers in compressed gases is due to a small extent to the raising of the partial pressure of polymers of high molecular weight by the high total pressure; and also in the case of solvent gases to the much greater solvent effect of these substances at high densities and high pressures. Thus we prefer to employ solvent gases, by which we mean one of the following classes: (a) gases which in the liquid state have a solvent action on the polymer, (b) gases which belong to the same homologous series as liquids which have a solvent action on the polymer, (c) gases whose simple substituted liquid derivatives have a solvent action on the polymer. For example, for polythene which is soluble in most liquid hydrocarbons at 70°–120° C., and polyisobutene and polystyrene which are soluble in some liquid hydrocarbons at 20° C. and above, we prefer to use a paraffin or olefine of 1–4 carbon atoms. For polymethylmethacrylate which is soluble in liquid chloroform or acetone we prefer to use methyl chloride or gaseous acetone. For halogen-containing polymers such as polyvinyl chloride which are soluble in ethylene dichloride at 80° C. we generally use halogen-containing solvents such as methyl

Reference to parts of this patent was made in Chapter 9; as a quick reading of the first paragraph of the patent points out, there are actually two processes described that are carried out with supercritical fluids, viz., fractionation of solid polymers and comminution of solid polymers that are normally difficult to obtain in the form of fine granules or powders. In the examples given, a number of polymers, operating conditions, and observations are presented. One of the examples is presented here for its informational value.

Example 3

A stirred vertical cylindrical vessel contains a mixture of 12 parts polyethylene of mean molecular weight 21,500 and 100 parts of ethylene at 1400 atm, 90°C. The vessel is then cooled by a blast of cold compressed air to 30°C, the pressure falling to 450 atm. The vessel is blown down to atmospheric pressure and opened. The upper part of the vessel is found to contain 1.2 parts of powdered polyethylene composed of loose aggregates of approximately spherical particles of average diameter below 0.01 mm. of molecular weight 9000, while the bottom of the vessel contains a fused mass of 10.8 parts of polyethylene of molecular weight 23,000.

In brief explanation of the findings, the information tells us that 21,500 MW polymer does not dissolve completely in ethylene, and a "top" phase and a "bottom" phase are formed. When the vessel is cooled (by the blast of cold air), both the phases are, of course, cooled. The example does not say if during the subsequent ethylene blowdown step any polyethylene escapes; however, at the cooled conditions polyethylene solubility in ethylene is virtually nil, and therefore we suggest that the aggregates of polyethylene are formed during the cooling step. The description of the polyethylene at the bottom of the vessel, "a fused mass," indicates that most of the ethylene had left the polyethylene before it solidified.

Dec. 27, 1966   J. E. COTTLE   3,294,772

SUPERCRITICAL POLYMERIZATION

Filed June 17, 1963

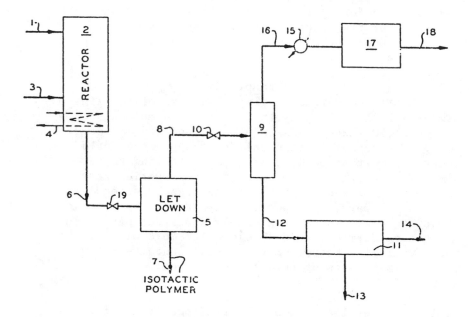

INVENTOR.
J. E. COTTLE

BY   *Young* & *Quigg*

ATTORNEYS

The prior art discussion in the patent tells us that during the reaction to form polypropylene (and other 1-olefin polymers) both crystalline and non-crystalline polymers are produced in the process. For many purposes only the crystalline form is desired, and the non-crystalline polypropylene must be removed in some additional processing steps which add capital and operating costs to the overall process.

The improved polymerization process described in this patent operates at supercritical propylene conditions. The crystalline polymer that is formed (and that is dissolved in the propylene) is separated from the non-crystalline form by pressure reduction. A separation between the two forms is effected because the crystalline polymer precipitates while the non-crystalline polymer remains dissolved. The non-crystalline polymer is separated from the propylene solvent in another pressure reduction stage, and the propylene (both as reactant and solvent) is recycled.

The flow chart of the process is presented in the figure. The monomer (propylene) is introduced via line 1 into the reactor 2; a catalyst is introduced via line 3. After the desired conversion is achieved, the reactor effluent is reduced in pressure across valve 19 and is passed to vessel 5. Conditions are adjusted by valves 19 and 10 so that the crystalline polypropylene (which is much less soluble than non-crystalline polypropylene) precipitates as a powder and is removed from the vessel via line 7. The remaining solution of non-crystalline polypropylene catalyst and propylene is conveyed to the fractionator 9 where the solvent/monomer is separated from the remaining polypropylene and recycled. An example gives quantitative information, viz.; the reaction is carried out at 750 psig, 210°F, and after sufficient polymerization the reactor effluent is expanded to 130 psig and 60°F. The crystalline polypropylene precipitates, and the non-crystalline material remains dissolved and can thus be separated.

The molecular weight of the crystalline polypropylene formed is not given in the example, but we find it surprising that crystalline polypropylene of any significant molecular weight can be dissolved in supercritical propylene at conditions just barely above its critical point. Recall that in Chapter 9 we reported that propylene at much higher conditions of 6500 psi and 155°C dissolved only about 20% of a commercial isotactic (crystalline) polypropylene; furthermore, that fraction of dissolved polypropylene probably consisted only of the lower oligomers (Krukonis 1981e).

United States Patent [19]

Copelin

[11]   **4,306,058**

[45]   **Dec. 15, 1981**

[54] **METHOD FOR REDUCING OLIGOMERIC CYCLIC ETHER CONTENT OF A POLYMERIZATE**

[75] Inventor: Harry B. Copelin, Wilmington, Del.

[73] Assignee: E. I. Du Pont de Nemours and Company, Wilmington, Del.

[21] Appl. No.: 208,422

[22] Filed: Nov. 19, 1980

[51] Int. Cl.³ B01D 3/24; C10G 21/14
[52] U.S. Cl. 528/498; 203/49
[58] Field of Search 528/417, 481, 483, 497, 528/498, 501, 502; 568/579; 203/49

[56]   **References Cited**

U.S. PATENT DOCUMENTS

3,202,605	7/1965	Redcay	208/309
3,806,619	4/1974	Zosel	426/478
3,969,196	7/1976	Zosel	203/49
4,202,964	5/1980	Pruckmayr et al.	528/482

FOREIGN PATENT DOCUMENTS

1474207 5/1977 United Kingdom .

Primary Examiner—Frank Sever

[57]   **ABSTRACT**

The oligomeric cyclic ether content of a tetrahydrofuran-, an alkylene oxide- or a tetrahydrofuran/alkylene oxide polymerizate can be reduced by bringing the polymerizate into contact with a gas in the supercritical state.

10 Claims, No Drawings

Homo and copolymers of tetrahydrofuran (THF) and alkylene oxides (AO) are used as "soft segment" glycols in the preparation of polyurethanes. In the process of producing the THF-AO homo and copolymers certain oligomeric cyclic ethers are also produced and can comprise 7-15% of the polymer; these cyclic ethers are undesirable because when the polymers are used to prepare polyurethane the cyclic ethers tend to degrade the polyurethane's properties.

The use of supercritical fluids to extract the cyclic ethers from the polymerizate is described. In one example it is related that a charge of THF/EO (ethylene oxide) polymerizate containing 8% cyclic ethers is contacted in batch continuous mode with propylene at 100°C, 83 atm. The residual polymerizate was measured to contain 2% cyclic ether content. No gas volume is given in this example or in the three other examples with other polymers and copolymers using supercritical ethylene and propylene; thus, no distribution coefficients can be calculated to determine the potential industrial value of this patent.

deFilippi, R.P. and J.E. Vivian, Process for separating
    organic liquid solutes from their solvent mixtures,
    U.S. 4,349,415 (Sept. 14, 1982).
Hagen, R. and J. Hartwig, Method for separating ethanol from
    an ethanol containing solution, U.S. 4,492,808 (Jan. 8,
    1985).
Victor, J.G., Ethanol extraction process, U.S. 4,508,928
    (Apr. 2, 1985).
Bhise, V.S. and R. Hock, Process for recovering ethylene
    oxide from aqueous solutions, U.S. 4,437,938 (Mar. 20,
    1984).
Bhise, V.S., Process for preparing ethylene glycol, U.S.
    4,400,559 (Aug. 23, 1983).
Hardman, H.F., Dehydration of water soluble monomers with
    liquid carbon dioxide, U.S. 4,253,948 (Mar. 3, 1981).
Shimshick, E.J., Removal of organic acids from dilute
    aqueous solutions of salts of organic acids by
    supercritical fluids, U.S. 4,250,331 (Feb. 10, 1981).

United States Patent [19]

DeFilippi et al.

[11]   **4,349,415**

[45]   **Sep. 14, 1982**

[54]   PROCESS FOR SEPARATING ORGANIC
LIQUID SOLUTES FROM THEIR SOLVENT
MIXTURES

[75]   Inventors: Richard P. DeFilippi, Cambridge; J.
Edward Vivian, Arlington, both of
Mass.

[73]   Assignee: Critical Fluid Systems, Inc.,
Cambridge, Mass.

[21]   Appl. No.:   79,935

[22]   Filed: Sep. 28, 1979

[51]   Int. Cl.³ B01D 3/34; B01D 11/04
[52]   U.S. Cl. 203/14; 203/16;
203/17; 203/18; 203/19; 203/26; 203/43;
203/49; 203/73; 203/88; 208/339; 208/353;
208/361; 210/634; 560/261; 562/608; 568/410;
568/749; 568/869; 568/916
[58]   Field of Search 203/14–19,
203/26, 49, 24, 73, 78, 80, DIG. 20, 88, 98,
43–46, 39; 202/180; 210/634; 196/14, 52;
208/339, 352, 353, 361; 422/256–260; 560/261;
562/608; 568/410, 749, 869, 916

[56]   References Cited

U.S. PATENT DOCUMENTS

2,130,147	9/1938	Milmore	208/319
2,281,865	5/1942	Van Dijck	260/428
2,282,982	5/1942	Jewett	203/24
3,098,107	7/1963	Becker	203/26
3,349,007	10/1967	Ciborowski et al.	203/26
3,423,295	1/1969	Holden	203/26
3,477,856	11/1969	Schultz	426/424
3,568,457	3/1971	Briggs et al.	203/26
3,806,619	4/1974	Zosel	203/49
3,966,981	6/1976	Schultz	426/425
3,969,196	7/1976	Zosel	203/49
4,035,243	7/1977	Katz et al.	203/DIG. 14
4,161,249	7/1979	Baiel et al.	203/26
4,177,137	12/1979	Kruse	203/26

Primary Examiner—Wilbur L. Bascomb, Jr.
Attorney, Agent, or Firm—Schiller & Pandiscio

[57]   **ABSTRACT**

Process and apparatus for extracting an organic liquid
from an organic liquid solute/solvent mixture. The
mixture is contacted with a fluid extractant which is at
a temperature and pressure to render the extractant a
solvent for the solute but not for the solvent. The resulting fluid extract of the solute is then depressurized to
give a still feed which is distilled to form still overhead
vapors and liquid still bottoms. The enthalpy required
to effect this distillation is provided by compressing the
still overhead vapors to heat them and indirectly to heat
the still feed. The process is particularly suitable for
separating mixtures which form azeotropes, e.g., oxygenated hydrocarbon/water mixtures. The energy required in this process is much less than that required to
separate such mixtures by conventional distillation techniques.

32 Claims, 5 Drawing Figures

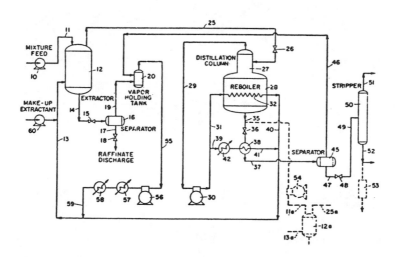

The use of this process concept for the separation of ethanol from water was discussed in detail in Chapter 8. The invention is the combination of an extractor using near critical liquid or supercritical fluid, a high pressure distillation column to separate ethanol from the extractant, and a vapor recompressor for raising the temperature of the recycled extractant. This stream provides the energy source to the reboiler to carry out the distillation.

One other figure in the patent is worthy of discussion, viz., Figure 2 which is reproduced below and which gives the distribution coefficients for various alcohols and esters in equilibrium with carbon dioxide-water. Note that the units of the ordinate are not given; throughout this book we have been giving all distribution coefficients in weight units; recall from the discussion in Chapter 9 that for ethanol the value is about 0.09. We see in Figure 2 that the value for ethanol (C2 on the abscissa) is about 0.24; therefore, these values must have been calculated on a mol basis but the units are not given in the figure. They are different from the weight basis values by a factor of 2.4, the ratio of molecular weights of CO_2 and water. This fact by itself is not important, since any consistent units for calculating the distribution coefficient are satisfactory as long as they are specified; not specifying them can lead to confusion. For example, an evaluation of the economic viability of the ethanol separation process has recently been carried out. (Fong, W. S., 1982. Process Economics Program Report 149, Ethanol for Gasohol, SRI International, Inc.). For fixing the solvent to feed ratio in the economic analysis a value of 0.24 for the distribution coefficient was taken from Figure 2; however, it was assumed that Figure 2 gives weight basis coefficients (which it does not). With a distribution coefficient that is too high, the extraction is predicted to be too easy, and the economics are projected to be optimistic.

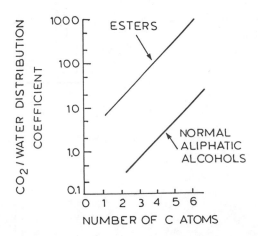

United States Patent [19]

Hagen et al.

[11] Patent Number: **4,492,808**

[45] Date of Patent: **Jan. 8, 1985**

[54] **METHOD FOR SEPARATING ETHANOL FROM AN ETHANOL CONTAINING SOLUTION**

[75] Inventors: Rainer Hagen; Jürgen Hartwig, both of Essen, Fed. Rep. of Germany

[73] Assignee: Fried. Krupp Gesellschaft mit beschränkter Haftung, Essen, Fed. Rep. of Germany

[21] Appl. No.: 600,301

[22] Filed: **Apr. 13, 1984**

[30] **Foreign Application Priority Data**

Apr. 14, 1983 [DE] Fed. Rep. of Germany 3313530

[51] Int. Cl.³ C07C 29/76; C07C 28/86; C07C 29/78; C07C 31/08

[52] U.S. Cl. 568/916; 568/913; 568/917; 568/918; 435/161; 435/311

[58] Field of Search 568/917, 918, 916, 913; 435/161, 311

[56] **References Cited**

U.S. PATENT DOCUMENTS

4,124,528	11/1978	Modell	252/411
4,260,836	4/1981	Levy	568/916
4,349,415	9/1982	DeFilippi et al.	568/918
4,358,536	11/1982	Thorsson et al.	435/161
4,359,593	11/1982	Feldman	568/916

4,376,163	3/1983	Ehnstrom	435/161
4,383,040	5/1983	Fricker	435/161

FOREIGN PATENT DOCUMENTS

2840440 3/1980 Fed. Rep. of Germany 568/913

OTHER PUBLICATIONS

Kittur et al., "Proc. Indian Academy of Science", vol. IV A, p. 569 (1936).

Groszek, "Chemistry and Industry", pp. 1754–1756, (Oct. 15, 1966).

Primary Examiner—J. E. Evans
Attorney, Agent, or Firm—Spencer & Frank

[57]   **ABSTRACT**

A process is disclosed for the separation of ethanol from an ethanol containing water solution, wherein the ethanol containing solution is extracted by means of a solvent which is in the liquid or supercritical state, the ethanol containing solvent phase is separated into its components by being conducted over an adsorption medium without changing the pressure or temperature, and the ethanol is recovered by treating the ethanol containing adsorption medium with the solvent used for the extraction at a pressure from 1 to 30 bar and at a temperature from 150° to 300° C.

11 Claims, 1 Drawing Figure

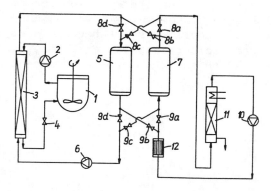

In this invention ethanol is extracted from solution with supercritical carbon dioxide. The carbon dioxide rich phase leaving the extractor is passed over activated carbon which adsorbs the ethanol isobarically. The ethanol-free carbon dioxide is then recycled to the extractor. When the activated carbon is loaded with ethanol, it is regenerated using gaseous carbon dioxide.

A flow chart of the process is shown in the figure. The stream from the fermenter 1 containing 5.6 wt % ethanol is heated to 75°C and pumped via 2 to the column 3 where it is contacted with carbon dioxide at 80 atm (and 75°C). The raffinate leaving the column contains 2.2% ethanol and is returned to the fermenter through valve 4. (Note that with recycle of the raffinate to the fermenter, it is not necessary to achieve a high recovery of ethanol.) The carbon dioxide-ethanol stream (which also contains some dissolved water) leaving the top of the extractor is conveyed to vessel 5 which is filled with activated carbon. The ethanol is adsorbed by the activated carbon, and the carbon dioxide is recycled by compressor 6 to the extractor.

When the activated carbon becomes saturated with ethanol, it is regenerated by passing carbon dioxide at 200°C, 10 atm through the bed. The hot gas stream is cooled to 75°C in column 11 which causes the ethanol to condense. Ethanol of 98.5% concentration is recovered from the condenser. The carbon dioxide/feed ratio in the extractor is 7 lbs/lb, and the regeneration of activated carbon requires 7 lbs carbon dioxide/lb activated carbon.

Although it is not given in the example, the ethanol concentration (CO_2-free) of the extract at the conditions of extraction is about 40-50 wt %. This value can be calculated from the distribution coefficient data given in Figure 8.12 and from the solubility of water in carbon dioxide at 75°C which is about 0.6% at conditions in the example. Thus we learn from the patent that the activated carbon acts as a concentration stage, i.e., the activated carbon apparently adsorbs the alcohol preferentially.

United States Patent [19]

Victor

[11]   **Patent Number:**   **4,508,928**

[45]   **Date of Patent:**   **Apr. 2, 1985**

[54]   **ETHANOL EXTRACTION PROCESS**

[75]   Inventor: **John G. Victor,** Indian Head Park, Ill.

[73]   Assignee: **Institute of Gas Technology,** Chicago, Ill.

[21]   Appl. No.:   **374,402**

[22]   Filed: **May 3, 1982**

[51]   Int. Cl.³ C07C 29/86
[52]   U.S. Cl. 568/916; 568/918
[58]   Field of Search 568/916, 918

[56]   **References Cited**

U.S. PATENT DOCUMENTS

1,524,192	1/1925	Mann	568/916
2,048,178	1/1936	Carney	202/41
2,080,064	5/1937	Roelfsma	202/39
2,081,721	5/1937	Van Dijck et al.	260/122
2,100,437	11/1937	Engs et al.	260/156
2,140,694	12/1938	Evans	202/42
2,196,177	4/1940	Burk et al.	260/639
2,510,806	6/1950	Egberts et al.	260/643
2,582,214	1/1952	Twigg	202/60
2,591,672	4/1952	Catterall	202/39.5
2,597,009	5/1952	Lobo et al.	260/450
3,455,664	7/1969	Rosscup et al.	568/918
4,261,702	4/1981	Sweeney et al.	568/916
4,306,884	12/1981	Roth	568/918
4,308,106	12/1981	Mannfeld	203/DIG. 4
4,349,415	9/1982	DeFilippi et al.	203/14

OTHER PUBLICATIONS

Othmer and Wentworth, "Absolute Alcohol—An Economical Method for Its Manufacture", Industrial & Engineering Chemistry, Dec. 1940, pp. 1588-1593.
Sherwood and Pigford, "Absorption and Extraction", 1952, pp. 391-392, 465.
Elgin and Weinstock, "Phase Equilibrium at Elevated Pressures in Ternary Systems of Ethylene and Water with Organic Liquids", J. Chem. and Engr. Data, vol. 4, No. 1, Jan. 1952, pp. 3-12.

Primary Examiner—J. E. Evans
Attorney, Agent, or Firm—Allegretti, Newitt, Witcoff & McAndrews, Ltd.

[57]   **ABSTRACT**

A process for the separation of ethanol from water using solvent extraction at elevated pressures is disclosed. Separation is effected by contacting aqueous ethanol with either propylene (propene), allene (propadiene), methyl acetylene (propyne), or methyl allene (1,2-butadiene). This produces two liquid phases which separate because of the difference in their densities, and are easily drawn off as separate streams. The solvent is recovered by distillation and condensation using a heat pump to transfer heat. The ethanol and water remain in a liquid state and are substantially recovered.

7 Claims, 2 Drawing Figures

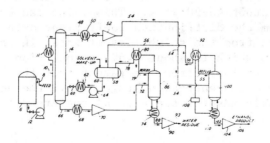

   In some respects this patent is like the deFilippi and
Vivian patent, U.S. 4,349,415 (although the deFilippi patent
claims all near-critical liquids and supercritical fluids
for extracting all organics while this one claims propylene
as the extractant for ethanol). Both patents describe that
the solvent and the extracted organic are separated by
distillation. The major difference is in the supply of
energy to the reboiler in the solvent distillation column;
U.S. 4,349,415 utilized vapor recompression while this one
uses a heat pump.
   The figure on the patent face page, although quite
small in size, shows the flow sheet for the process. The
left hand side of the flow chart shows the extraction
sequence, and the right hand side, specifically, column 100
and associated pumps and heat exchangers, the solvent-
organic separation; by now the extraction side should be
quite familiar.
   The heat pump philosophy is the new twist here. Item
110 is a heat exchanger which supplies energy to vaporize
propylene from the alcohol. The vaporized propylene exits
at the top of the column and is condensed in heat exchanger
92. Item 108 is a heat pump which "works" on the heat of
condensation of propylene to supply the energy to the
reboiler 110.
   It would have been informative if the patentee had
compared the heat pump and vapor recompression processes.

United States Patent [19]

Bhise et al.

[11]   **4,437,938**

[45]   **Mar. 20, 1984**

[54] **PROCESS FOR RECOVERING ETHYLENE OXIDE FROM AQUEOUS SOLUTIONS**

[75] Inventors: **Vijay S. Bhise,** Bloomfield, N.J.; **Robert Hoch,** Ridgewood, N.Y.

[73] Assignee: **The Halcon SD Group, Inc.,** New York, N.Y.

[21] Appl. No.: **284,153**

[22] Filed: **Jul. 17, 1981**

[51] Int. Cl.^{3} B01D 3/34; C07D 301/32
[52] U.S. Cl. 203/14; 203/42; 203/43; 203/47; 203/49; 203/70; 549/541
[58] Field of Search 260/348.37; 203/43, 203/68, 70, 67, 14, 49, 42, 91; 422/256–260; 196/14.52; 210/634, 511; 202/169; 549/541

[56]   **References Cited**

U.S. PATENT DOCUMENTS

1,805,751	5/1931	Auerbach .	
2,771,473	11/1956	Courter	260/348.37
3,265,593	8/1966	Leis et al.	203/63
3,418,338	12/1968	Gilman et al.	260/348.37
3,806,619	4/1974	Zosel	426/478
3,964,980	6/1976	Ozero	203/42
3,969,196	7/1976	Zosel	203/49
4,134,797	1/1979	Ozero	203/75

4,250,331	2/1981	Shimshick	562/485
4,253,948	3/1981	Hardman et al.	210/634
4,349,415	9/1982	De Flippi et al.	203/14

FOREIGN PATENT DOCUMENTS

1290117	9/1972	United Kingdom .	
1388581	3/1975	United Kingdom .	
2032789	5/1980	United Kingdom	203/49
2059787	4/1981	United Kingdom .	

OTHER PUBLICATIONS

Stahl et al., Angew. Chem. Int. Ed. Engl. 17, pp. 731–738, (1978).
J. Am. Chem. Soc., 58, 1099, (1954), Francis, A. W.

Primary Examiner—Wilbur L. Bascomb, Jr.
Attorney, Agent, or Firm—William C. Long; Riggs T. Stewart; Harold N. Wells

[57]   **ABSTRACT**

Ethylene oxide is recovered from aqueous solutions by extracting with carbon dioxide in the near-critical or super-critical state, thereby selectively removing the ethylene oxide from water, and thereafter recovering ethylene oxide from the carbon dioxide by distillation or other suitable means.

6 Claims, 2 Drawing Figures

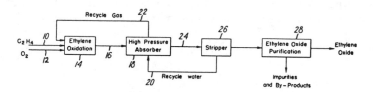

In the current process for producing ethylene oxide from ethylene and oxygen, large amounts of water are used to extract the product from the reacted gas stream containing the ethylene oxide. The quite dilute ethylene oxide-water stream from this gas-liquid absorption process is then subjected to a distillation in a subsequent step which the patent says is costly.

The improved process utilizes carbon dioxide to extract ethylene oxide from water in a flow scheme which is similar to the other liquid extractions described previously. The block diagram depicts operation of the process. Ethylene oxidation 14 and adsorption of the ethylene oxide in the absorber 18 are carried out in the traditional manner, but the water stream is then sent to a stripper 26 where carbon dioxide strip extracts the ethylene oxide from the water solution. The carbon dioxide stream containing the ethylene oxide is lowered in pressure and sent to a (high pressure) distillation column called the ethylene oxide purifier 28. Carbon dioxide is vaporized, and we know from previous discussions that vapor carbon dioxide exhibits little dissolving power so that almost pure carbon dioxide vapor is distilled and condensed, and a concentrated ethylene oxide stream (containing some carbon dioxide) is obtained.

The example relates that an aqueous solution containing 0.24 wt % ethylene oxide is extracted with carbon dioxide at 1250 psi, 32°C to remove all the product. (In the example concentrations are given in mol % and they have been converted to wt % for this discussion.) Based upon the CO_2 and product data given in the example we calculate that the solvent to feed ratio is 0.084 lbs CO_2/lb feed, which is a very small (and very attractive) value. From this value we can also scope out the level of the distribution coefficient. If we assume that the extraction of ethylene oxide from water by the carbon dioxide was at "near equilibrium" conditions inverse of the solvent to feed ratio of 0.084 is the distribution coefficient and is about 12.

Other data in this ethylene oxide extraction patent provide an independent method to calculate the distribution coefficient. Examples state that the carbon dioxide stream leaving the extractor contains 2.9 wt % ethylene oxide which is in equilibrium with a liquid solution containing 0.24 wt % ethylene oxide. The y/x ratio is 12, a very good independent corroboration of the value calculated from the inverse of the solvent to feed ratio (and the assumption that the extraction was an equilibrium one).

United States Patent [19]

Bhise

[11]   **4,400,559**

[45]   **Aug. 23, 1983**

[54]   ꟼROCESS FOR PREPARING ETHYLENE GLYCOL

[75]   Inventor: Vijay S. Bhise, Bloomfield, N.J.

[73]   Assignee: The Halcon SD Group, Inc., New York, N.Y.

[21]   Appl. No.:   388,395

[22]   Filed: Jun. 14, 1982

[51]   Int. Cl.³ C07C 31/20
[52]   U.S. Cl. 568/858; 549/230; 549/513; 203/49; 260/463
[58]   Field of Search 568/858

[56]   References Cited

U.S. PATENT DOCUMENTS

4,117,250	9/1978	Foster et al.	568/858
4,237,324	12/1980	Rainer et al.	568/858
4,283,580	8/1981	Odanaka et al.	568/858

FOREIGN PATENT DOCUMENTS

267618   7/1970   U.S.S.R. 568/858

OTHER PUBLICATIONS

Peppel, "Industrial and Engineering Chemistry", vol. 50, No. 5 (May 1958), pp. 767-770.
U.S. Ser. No. 284,153, filed 7/17/81, Bhise, et al.
U.S. Ser. No. 321,966, filed 11/16/81, Bhise, et al.
U.S. Ser. No. 326,447, filed 12/2/81, Harvey

Primary Examiner—J. E. Evans
Attorney, Agent, or Firm—William C. Long; Riggs T. Stewart; Harold N. Wells

[57]   ABSTRACT

Ethylene glycol is prepared by a process in which ethylene oxide is extracted from an aqueous solution with near-critical or super-critical carbon dioxide. Thereafter an ethylene oxide—carbon dioxide—water mixture is contacted with a catalyst to form ethylene carbonate, which is then hydrolyzed to ethylene glycol in the presence of the same catalyst. The ethylene glycol is separated as product and the carbon dioxide and the catalyst are recycled.

9 Claims, 2 Drawing Figures.

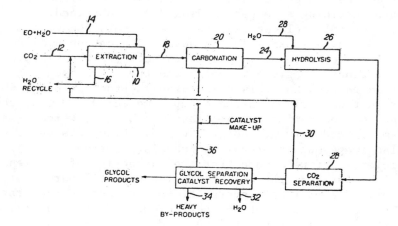

As an extension of the patent describing the use of supercritical carbon dioxide to extract ethylene oxide from water solution, this patent describes a process which employs a subsequent chemical reaction in the carbon dioxide-ethylene oxide stream to form ethylene glycol.

The extraction/reaction process concept is explained with reference to the block diagram. As we saw in the previous patent, aqueous ethylene oxide solution and supercritical carbon dioxide are fed to a contactor 10 where carbon dioxide extracts the ethylene oxide. The carbon dioxide-ethylene oxide stream leaving the extractor enters the carbonation tower 20. A suitable catalyst such as quaternary ammonium or phosphonium halide is supplied to the carbonation tower via conduit 22; ethylene oxide and carbon dioxide react to form ethylene carbonate. The reacted stream 24 still containing the catalyst is conveyed to another reactor 26 to which water is added 28. Hydrolysis of the ethylene carbonate takes place at about $90-200^{\circ}C$ to form monoethylene glycol and some higher homologues. Carbon dioxide is separated 28 from the water-ethylene glycol mixture and is recycled to the ethylene oxide extractor. The ethylene glycol is separated from by-products and catalyst.

United States Patent [19]

Hardman et al.

[11]   **4,253,948**

[45]   **Mar. 3, 1981**

[54] **DEHYDRATION OF WATER SOLUBLE MONOMERS WITH LIQUID CARBON DIOXIDE**

[75] Inventors: Harley F. Hardman, Lyndhurst; Albert P. Schwerko, Solon, both of Ohio

[73] Assignee: Standard Oil Company, Cleveland, Ohio

[21] Appl. No.: 38,744

[22] Filed: May 14, 1979

[51] Int. Cl.³ B01D 11/04; C07C 121/30; C07C 51/42

[52] U.S. Cl. 210/634; 210/642; 260/465.9; 562/660; 203/DIG. 21

[58] Field of Search .... 210/21, 59, 65; 260/705, 601 R, 465.9; 562/600; 560/218; 203/88, DIG. 21; 208/188, 321

[56] **References Cited**

U.S. PATENT DOCUMENTS

2,029,120	1/1936	Schilling et al.	55/65
2,744,855	5/1956	Arnold	208/188
2,922,815	1/1960	Faerber	203/62
3,133,018	5/1964	Watanabe	210/21
3,414,485	12/1968	Speed	203/DIG. 21
3,692,829	9/1972	Sennewald et al.	203/62
3,781,193	12/1973	Sennewald et al.	203/62

OTHER PUBLICATIONS

"Ternary Systems of Liquid Carbon Dioxide", Alfred W. Francis, *Journal of Physical Chemistry* 58, 1099 (1954).

Primary Examiner—Ivars C. Cintins
Assistant Examiner—E. Rollins Cross
Attorney, Agent, or Firm—David J. Untener; Herbert D. Knudsen; Larry W. Evans

[57]   **ABSTRACT**

Separation of certain water soluble organic monomers such as acrylic acid from an aqueous solution can be accomplished by extraction with carbon dioxide, crystallizing the extract to remove carbon dioxide hydrate, and flashing off the remaining carbon dioxide solvent from the extract.

12 Claims, No Drawings

As we related in Chapter 2, Historical Perspective, Villard reported on phase equilibria of gas hydrates in the late 1800's. Relative to this patent, hydrates form in the liquid carbon dioxide-water system at a temperature of 5°C. The stoichiometry of the hydrate has been determined by a number of workers, the formula of the hydrate is $CO_2 \cdot 6H_2O$ (Milton, D. J., 1974. Carbon Dioxide Hydrates and the Floods on Mars, Science, 183, 654.)

This patent makes use of the phenomenon of forming carbon dioxide hydrates to concentrate and separate organics from water (or, more accurately stated, to separate water from organics). In the specific way the process is described it is applied to aqueous solutions containing quite high concentrations of acrylic acid.

In one of the examples a 31% solution of acrylic acid in water is contacted (in a static vessel) with a liquid CO_2 at 25°C, 850 psi; at a ratio of 1.97:1 CO_2 to solution. After equilibration the lower aqueous phase was withdrawn (the concentration of residual acrylic acid in the withdrawn aqueous phase was not stated in the example). The top CO_2-rich phase which contained a high concentration of acrylic acid and "some" water was then cooled to 0°C, and it is related that white crystals were formed; the crystals are the hydrate. The crystals were separated from the liquid phase and the CO_2 evaporated. The resultant acrylic acid contained only 0.9% water.

In another example and in a countercurrent column composed of six theoretical stages, an aqueous solution of 34 wt % acrylic acid was contacted at 25°C, 850 psi with carbon dioxide at a solvent to feed ratio of 3. Recovery of acrylic acid was 95.3% in the extraction, and the composition of the extract phase on a carbon dioxide-free basis was 92.5% acrylic acid-7.5% water. To remove the water the extract phase (including the carbon dioxide) was cooled to 0°C, crystals were formed and were filtered. The resultant acrylic acid product contained only 1% water.

United States Patent [19]

Shimshick

[11]   **4,250,331**

[45]   **Feb. 10, 1981**

[54] **REMOVAL OF ORGANIC ACIDS FROM DILUTE AQUEOUS SOLUTIONS OF SALTS OF ORGANIC ACIDS BY SUPERCRITICAL FLUIDS**

[75] Inventor: **Edward J. Shimshick,** Wilmington, Del.

[73] Assignee: **E. I. Du Pont de Nemours and Company,** Wilmington, Del.

[21] Appl. No.:   **83,147**

[22] Filed: **Oct. 9, 1979**

[51] Int. Cl.^{3} C07C 51/42; C07C 53/00
[52] U.S. Cl. 562/485; 562/494; 562/580; 562/593; 562/600; 562/606; 562/608
[58] Field of Search 562/600, 606, 608, 485, 562/486, 494, 580, 593

[56]   **References Cited**

U.S. PATENT DOCUMENTS

3,969,196   7/1976   Zosel 203/49
4,061,566   12/1977   Modell 210/32

FOREIGN PATENT DOCUMENTS

521202   5/1940   United Kingdom .
1057911   2/1967   United Kingdom .

Primary Examiner—Alan Siegel

[57]   **ABSTRACT**

Process for recovering carboxylic acids from dilute aqueous solutions of alkali metal salts of such carboxylic acids by mixing such solutions with from 10 to 1000% of a supercritical solution comprising at least 10 mole % carbon dioxide at a pressure from 80 to 500 atm and preferably 100 to 350 atm and at a temperature of from 35° to 200° C. and preferably from 35° to 100° C. whereby the salt reacts with the carbon dioxide to form the carboxylic acid which dissolves in the supercritical fluid. The aqueous phase is allowed to separate from the supercritical fluid phase. The pressure of the supercritical phase is lowered which lowers the solubility of the carboxylic acid in the supercritical fluid so that an acid phase is formed separate from the supercritical fluid phase whereby recovery of the acid is effected.

8 Claims, 2 Drawing Figures

A specific example from this patent was discussed in Chapter 8; it was offered that extraction of carboxylic acids (which have pK's of about 4-5) from solutions of pH greater than pK was not a very attractive process because all the anion is not converted to the acid form by action of the carbonic acid equilibrium. The abstract of the patent states that carbon dioxide will react with the salt to form the (free) carboxylic acid which can dissolve in carbon dioxide; that is strictly correct, but we always suggest that the absolute values be examined to determine such factors as yield and distribution coefficient.

Table 1 below summarizes the results obtained. The last column gives an estimate of the distribution coefficient calculated from the material balance and concentration data given in the patent under the assumption that the extraction occurred via extraction into a fixed volume of carbon dioxide from a fixed volume of liquid containing the carboxylic acid (as the sodium salt).

Distribution Coefficients for Extraction of Carboxylic Acids

Example	Acid	Dist. Coef. (Wt. Basis)
1	butyric	0.083
6	acetic	0.004
9	methacrylic	0.083
10	benzoic, terephthalic	0.042, 0.058

As the table shows, the distribution coefficients are higher for the higher carboxylic acids. We chose acetic acid for the discussion in Chapter 8, incidentally, because it is a large volume chemical that was considered to be a potential application for supercritical fluid extraction. We know a number of companies evaluated the carbon dioxide process for recovering acetic acid from water.

Hess, H.V., Recovery of fresh water from brine, U.S. 3,318,805 (May 9, 1967).

Maffei, R.L., Extraction and cleaning process, U.S. 4,012,194 (Mar. 15, 1977).

Modell, M., Process using a supercritical fluid for regenerating synthetic organic polymer adsorbents and wastewater treatment embodying the same, U.S. 4,061,566 (Dec. 6, 1977).

Modell, M., R.C. Reid, and S.I. Amin, Gasification process, U.S. 4,113,446 (Sept. 12, 1978).

Modell, M., Processing method for the oxidation of organics in supercritical water, U.S. 4,338,199 (Jul. 6, 1982).

Jennings, W.G., R.H. Wohleb, and N.W. Wohlers, High pressure soxhlet extractor, U.S. 4,265,860 (May 5, 1981).

Dickenson, N.L., Pollutant-free low temperature slurry combustion process utilizing the super-critical state, U.S. 4,292,953 (Oct. 6, 1981).

Perrut, M., Fractionation process for mixtures by elution chromatography with liquid in supercritical state and installation for its operation, U.S. 4,478,720 (Oct. 23, 1984).

Eppig, C.P., B.M. Putnam, and R.P. deFilippi, Apparatus for removing organic contaminants from inorganic-rich mineral solids, U.S. 4,434,028 (Feb. 28, 1984).

Avedesian, M.M., Apparatus and method involving supercritical fluid extraction, U.S. 4,493,797 (Jan. 15, 1985).

Sumner, W.C., Jr., G.G. Hoyer, and W.G. Kozak, Method of removing water from alkali metal hydroxide solutions, U.S. 4,505,885 (Mar. 19, 1985).

Schlichta, P.J., Method for growth of crystals by pressure reduction of supercritical or subcritical solution, U.S. 4,512,846 (Apr. 23, 1985).

May 9, 1967

H. V. HESS ETAL   3,318,805
RECOVERY OF FRESH WATER FROM BRINE
Filed Nov. 16, 1964

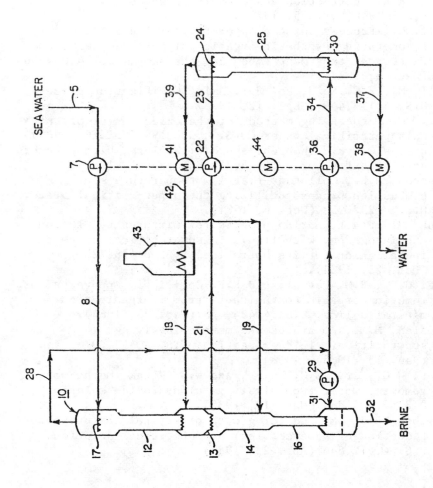

This patent describes an invention for separating fresh water from brine. The patentees utilize two pieces of information, the very low solubility of inorganic salts in organic hydrocarbons and the high-pressure phase behavior of organic hydrocarbon-water mixtures, to develop a novel process for recovering salt-free water and for concentrating water soluble salts. The key to the success of the process is the formation of a miscible water-organic hydrocarbon mixture.

As noted in Chapter 3 of this book, the mutual solubility of water-organic mixtures at ambient temperature is very low regardless of the system pressure. The patentees correctly note that the mutual solubility increases as the temperature of the system is increased to near the critical temperature of water. In fact, there is a range of temperatures and pressures in which water and an organic hydrocarbon are completely miscible. This type of phase behavior is not surprising since it was reported in 1959 by Rebert and Kay (AIChE J., 5, 285, 1959) for the benzene-water system. The phase diagram for this system is shown in Chapter 3 of this book and the principles of the high-pressure phase behavior of water-organic hydrocarbon systems are described in detail as a Type IV system.

The first step of the process for recovering fresh water is the removal of inorganic salt, and it is accomplished by forming a water-hydrocarbon phase and an inorganic salt-water phase. The inorganic salt-water phase is then removed from the system. The next step, the recovery of water from the water-hydrocarbon mixture, is accomplished by isothermally increasing the system pressure until the mixture splits into two phases, viz., water-rich phase and a hydrocarbon-rich phase. The degree of separation of water from the hydrocarbon increases with increasing pressure. As we showed in Chapter 3 it is also possible to form two phases by an isobaric temperature change; the patentees relate that the separation of water from the hydrocarbon is more efficient when using an isothermal pressure increase rather than a large isobaric temperature decrease.

United States Patent [19]

Maffei

[11]   **4,012,194**

[45]   **Mar. 15, 1977**

[54]   **EXTRACTION AND CLEANING PROCESSES**

[76]   Inventor: **Raymond L. Maffei**, 639 Front St., San Francisco, Calif. 94111

[22]   Filed: **Aug. 2, 1973**

[21]   Appl. No.: **384,908**

Related U.S. Application Data

[63]   Continuation of Ser. No. 186,089, Oct. 4, 1971, abandoned.

[52]   U.S. Cl. 8/142
[51]   Int. Cl.^{2} D06L 1/02
[58]   Field of Search .... 8/137, 137.5, 138, 139, 8/139.1, 142; 68/18 L; 252/364

[56]   **References Cited**

UNITED STATES PATENTS

1,197,495	9/1916	Jefferson	8/139.1
1,805,751	5/1931	Auerbach	208/177

Primary Examiner—Stephen C. Bentley
Attorney, Agent, or Firm—Naylor, Neal & Uilkema

[57]   **ABSTRACT**

Extraction and cleaning processes characterized by the use of liquid carbon dioxide as the extraction and cleaning solvent. This solvent is disclosed as being applied to plant material for the extraction of essential oils and as being used in place of the conventional solvents in the dry cleaning of garments.

1 Claim, 2 Drawing Figures

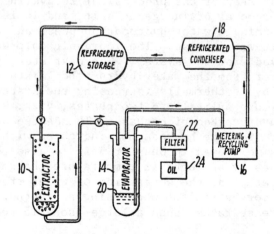

Another thought patent and probably not thought out very thoroughly.

In the operation of the invention, soiled garments are placed batchwise in the extractor 10, flushed with liquid carbon dioxide, and a solution of "garment oil" and carbon dioxide is separated in the evaporator 14. The carbon dioxide is recycled, the process continuing until all the garment oil has been extracted.

The process could work (at least technically) for garments soiled with, say, salad oil or light hydrocarbon lubricants; however, garments soiled with, for example, milk, spaghetti sauce, beet juice, various desserts; and the like, exemplifying protein, carbohydrate, and anthocyanin dye stains would not be cleaned by this process.

United States Patent [19]

Modell

[11]   **4,061,566**

[45]   **Dec. 6, 1977**

[54] **PROCESS USING A SUPERCRITICAL FLUID FOR REGENERATING SYNTHETIC ORGANIC POLYMERIC ADSORBENTS AND WASTEWATER TREATMENT EMBODYING THE SAME**

[75] Inventor: **Michael Modell, Cambridge, Mass.**

[73] Assignee: **Arthur D. Little, Inc., Cambridge, Mass.**

[21] Appl. No.: **677,387**

[22] Filed: **Apr. 15, 1976**

Related U.S. Application Data

[63] Continuation-in-part of Ser. No. 512,124, Oct. 4, 1974.

[51] Int. Cl.^{2} **B01D 15/06; B01J 1/09; B01J 31/40**
[52] U.S. Cl. .... **210/32; 210/34; 210/40; 252/411 R; 210/186; 210/269**
[58] Field of Search .... **252/411 R, 412, 414, 252/415; 210/24, 30, 32, 39, 40; 260/627 R; 208/263; 55/74, 75**

[56]   **References Cited**

U.S. PATENT DOCUMENTS

3,325,971	6/1967	Rosman	55/62
3,492,223	1/1970	Walles	210/24 R
3,843,824	10/1974	Roselius et al.	426/386
3,923,847	12/1975	Roselius et al.	260/412.8
3,939,281	2/1976	Schwengers	426/430
3,969,196	7/1976	Zosel	203/49
3,979,287	9/1976	Vulliez-Serment et al.	208/263

Primary Examiner—Winston A. Douglas
Assistant Examiner—P. E. Konopka
Attorney, Agent, or Firm—Bessie A. Lepper

[57]   **ABSTRACT**

An adsorbate is removed from a polymeric adsorbent by contacting the adsorbent with a supercritical fluid which is a solvent for the adsorbate. The supercritical fluid containing the dissolved adsorbate is then subjected to a physical treatment which renders the supercritical fluid a nonsolvent for the adsorbate and makes it possible to remove the adsorbate from the supercritical fluid. The supercritical fluid is then subjected to another physical treatment to restore it to a state wherein it is a solvent for the adsorbate so that it may be reused. The process is particularly suitable for adsorbent regeneration in the treatment of wastewaters.

24 Claims, 6 Drawing Figures

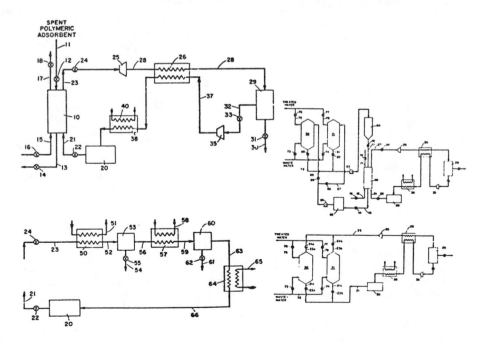

Three closely related patents on adsorbent regeneration
were published between 1977-79, with Modell as the patentee
and Arthur D. Little, as the assignee. One of the activated
carbon regeneration patents was discussed in Chapter 8.

The first in this series of three patents is the
application of supercritical fluids to the regeneration of
polymeric resin adsorbents. Four flow diagrams of the
operation of the process are shown on the face page of the
patent, and they depict various operating modes. A
polymeric adsorbent spent with organics (from a wastewater
treating process, for example,) is regenerated by a supercritical fluid which dissolves the adsorbed organic. The
supercritical fluid solution is freed of its dissolved
organics by changing pressure and/or temperature of the
solution leaving the desorber. In one operating mode shown
in the drawing the supercritical fluid exiting the desorber
is passed through a turbo-expander to recover energy. In
another mode a reactant is added to the supercritical fluid
to bring about a chemical reaction with the adsorbate.

The other two regeneration patents by Modell are:

U.S. 4,124,528   Process for regenerating adsorbents
with supercritical fluids, Nov. 7, 1978.

U.S. 4,147,624   Wastewater treatment with desorbing of
an adsorbate from an adsorbent with a solvent in a near
critical state, Apr. 3, 1979.

United States Patent [19]

Modell et al.

[11]   **4,113,446**

[45]   **Sep. 12, 1978**

[54] **GASIFICATION PROCESS**

[75] Inventors: Michael Modell, Cambridge; Robert C. Reid, Lexington, both of Mass.; Sanjay I. Amin, Kalamazoo, Mich.

[73] Assignee: Massachusetts Institute of Technology, Cambridge, Mass.

[21] Appl. No.: 742,712

[22] Filed: Nov. 17, 1976

Related U.S. Application Data

[63] Continuation-in-part of Ser. No. 598,102, Jul. 22, 1975, abandoned.

[51] Int. Cl.² C10J 3/16
[52] U.S. Cl. 48/202; 48/206; 48/209; 252/373
[58] Field of Search .... 48/202, 206, 214 A, 48/214 R, 209, 204, 197 R, DIG. 7; 252/373; 423/650

[56]   **References Cited**
                    U.S. PATENT DOCUMENTS

3,148,227	9/1964	Hearon et al.	48/209
3,715,195	2/1973	Tassoney et al.	48/197 R
3,890,113	6/1975	Child et al.	48/214 R
3,919,114	11/1975	Reynolds	252/373
3,926,583	12/1975	Rostrup-Nielsen	48/214 A
3,929,431	12/1975	Koh et al.	48/214 A

Primary Examiner—Robert L. Lindsay, Jr.
Assistant Examiner—George C. Yeung
Attorney, Agent, or Firm—Arthur A. Smith, Jr.; Paul J. Cook

[57]   **ABSTRACT**

Solid or liquid organic materials are converted to high BTU gas with little or no undesirable char formation by reaction with water at or above the critical temperature of water and at or above the critical pressure of water to achieve the critical density of water. The reaction can be conducted either in the presence or in the absence of a catalyst.

10 Claims, No Drawings

The better known process which utilizes oxygen or air dissolved in supercritical water to oxidize wastes has been described in Chapter 10 (and it is the next patent covered in this appendix). The present patent was issued three years earlier, and it discusses the gasification (and liquification) of liquid and solid (or dissolved solid) organic materials in supercritical water.

Examples relate that the gasification tests carried out at conditions above the critical point of water result in little or no char formation whereas tests with the same materials at conditions below the critical point result in substantial and undesirable char yield. For example, at a reaction temperature $350^{\circ}C$, 165 atm about 10% of the carbon in glucose was found as a solid char. If the reaction is carried out at a temperature of $374^{\circ}C$, 218 atm, no char is formed.

United States Patent [19]

Modell

[11] **4,338,199**

[45] **Jul. 6, 1982**

[54] **PROCESSING METHODS FOR THE OXIDATION OF ORGANICS IN SUPERCRITICAL WATER**

[75] Inventor: **Michael Modell, Cambridge, Mass.**

[73] Assignee: **Modar, Inc., Natick, Mass.**

[21] Appl. No.: **147,946**

[22] Filed: **May 8, 1980**

[51] Int. Cl.³ C02F 1/72
[52] U.S. Cl. 210/721; 210/761
[58] Field of Search 210/761, 762, 721, 722, 210/774, 766; 48/209, 202, 210

[56] **References Cited**

U.S. PATENT DOCUMENTS

3,207,572	9/1965	Saul	210/761 X
3,876,497	4/1975	Hoffman	210/761 X
3,920,506	11/1975	Morgan	210/761 X
4,000,068	12/1976	Nelson et al.	210/762 X
4,013,560	3/1977	Pradt	210/761 X
4,141,829	2/1979	Thiel et al.	210/762

OTHER PUBLICATIONS

Wightman, "Studies in Supercritical Wet Air Oxidation", Master's Thesis, University of California, Berkeley, Mar. 1981.

Primary Examiner—Thomas G. Wyse

[57] **ABSTRACT**

Organic materials are oxidized in supercritical water to obtain useful energy and/or resultant materials. In one embodiment, conventional fuels are oxidized with high efficiency to obtain useful energy for power generation and/or process heat. In another embodiment toxic or waste materials are converted to useful energy for power and heat and/or to non-toxic resultant materials. The method is also useful to permit use of a wide range of organic materials as a fuel in the desalination of seawater and brine or the removal of certain inorganic salts from water.

29 Claims, 5 Drawing Figures

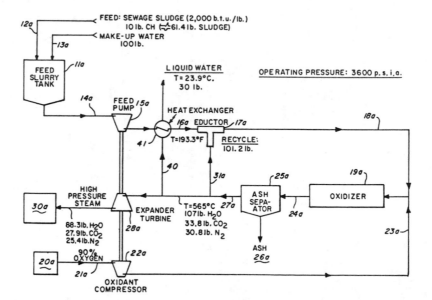

This supercritical water patent has been discussed
briefly in Chapters 10 and 11, but it is reviewed here
briefly in conjunction with the figure on the patent face
page. The figure gives the operating conditions for one of
the examples.

A mixture of sewage sludge and water in the feed slurry
tank 11a is pumped through a heat exchanger, to an eductor
17a where the sludge is mixed with recycle water (in the
supercritical state). This hot mixture is mixed with oxygen
(or air) and is passed into the oxidizer where reaction of
the organics takes place. The heat of reaction raises the
temperature of the stream to well above the supercritical
temperature of water (374°C). At these conditions any
inorganic materials present in the sludge or the feed water
precipitate from solution (because supercritical water is
not a good solvent for salts). The precipitated inorganic
matter is removed in the ash separator. Part of the
supercritical water which contains carbon dioxide formed
from the oxidation reactions is sent to a turbine 28a for
power generation, and the other part is recycled to the heat
exchanger and eductor as described earlier.

United States Patent [19]

Jennings et al.

[11]   **4,265,860**

[45]   **May 5, 1981**

[54]   **HIGH PRESSURE SOXHLET EXTRACTOR**

[75]   Inventors: Walter G. Jennings, Davis; Robert H. Wohleb, Orangevale; Norman W. Wohlers, Davis, all of Calif.

[73]   Assignee: J & W Scientific, Incorporated, Rancho Cordova, Calif.

[21]   Appl. No.:   134,625

[22]   Filed: Mar. 27, 1980

[51]   Int. Cl.³ B01D 11/02
[52]   U.S. Cl. 422/280; 202/169; 422/101
[58]   Field of Search .... 422/101, 280, 281, 285, 422/288, 290; 202/168, 169, 170, 170 D; 156/DIG. 90

[56]   **References Cited**

U.S. PATENT DOCUMENTS

2,006,513	7/1935	Rascher et al.	422/101
2,095,056	10/1937	Clough	202/168 X
2,478,619	8/1949	Arnold	422/101 X
3,107,205	10/1963	Moran et al.	422/101 X
4,006,062	2/1977	Bhuchar et al.	422/101 X

FOREIGN PATENT DOCUMENTS

844363	9/1952	Fed. Rep. of Germany	202/168
547772	9/1942	United Kingdom	422/280

Primary Examiner—Joseph Scovronek
Attorney, Agent, or Firm—Lothrop & West

[57]   **ABSTRACT**

The numerous advantages of a Soxhlet apparatus are combined with the nice pressure and temperature controls afforded by a pressure vessel to enlarge the scope and efficacy of both pieces of equipment. A judicious selection of solvent, such as CO_2, provides a solvent-free extract which is ideal for gas chromatographic studies and can advantageously be used in an ever-widening spectrum of analyses including research, food and flavor, pheromone analysis and essence extraction. The extraction of oil from coal and oil shale, in comminuted form, is also facilitated by the use of the apparatus operated under reflux conditions, controlled pressure-temperature relations and appropriate choice of extractant.

6 Claims, 1 Drawing Figure

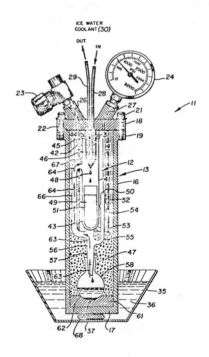

This patent is also, like some others we've discussed, not strictly supercritical extraction; however, it is a very clever invention. The device has been used by many groups in their preliminary research programs evaluating supercritical (or liquid) carbon dioxide extraction.

The drawing which shows what is literally a Soxhlet extractor inside a pressure vessel virtually explains itself. In operation an amount of "dry ice" is placed in the vessel. A solid material 49 which is to be extracted, for example, a botanical of some kind, is placed in the thimble 51, and the vessel is assembled. Heat is applied to the bath 35 and 36 which vaporizes the carbon dioxide. Cooling water in the condenser 31 condenses the vapor carbon dioxide (shown as drops 48) which trickles downward through the bed of solid material in the thimble. The extract (consisting of liquid carbon dioxide and dissolved organics) continues downward to collect in the flask 58 where the carbon dioxide is vaporized by the action of the heating bath. The gaseous carbon dioxide rises through the annular spaces and is recondensed by the condenser 31 to continue its extraction path. When extraction is complete, the system is depressurized slowly. The extract is collected in the flask 58 and the residue in the thimble 51.

In repetition, a quite clever device.

United States Patent [19]

Dickinson

[11]   **4,292,953**

[45]   **Oct. 6, 1981**

[54] **POLLUTANT-FREE LOW TEMPERATURE SLURRY COMBUSTION PROCESS UTILIZING THE SUPER-CRITICAL STATE**

[76] Inventor: Norman L. Dickinson, Box 211, Lavallette, N.J. 08735

[21] Appl. No.: 948,682

[22] Filed: **Oct. 5, 1978**

[51] Int. Cl.³ F24J 3/00
[52] U.S. Cl. .... 126/263; 110/106; 110/204; 110/216; 110/266; 110/345; 122/4 R
[58] Field of Search .... 110/347, 266, 265, 342–345, 110/204, 216, 232, 106; 431/4 R, 190; 122/4 R

[56]   **References Cited**

U.S. PATENT DOCUMENTS

772,704	10/1904	Detweiler	122/4 R
955,977	4/1910	Mirick	122/4 R
1,027,815	5/1912	Bynoe	122/4 R
1,970,109	8/1934	Stratton	110/266
2,547,135	4/1951	Mercier	122/4 R
2,601,667	6/1952	Permann	110/205 X
3,089,539	5/1963	Vermillion et al.	431/4 R
3,207,102	9/1965	Seibold	110/265
3,313,251	4/1967	Jonakin	110/265
3,818,869	6/1974	Blaskowski	110/345
3,941,552	3/1976	Cottell	431/4
4,013,428	3/1977	Babbitt	110/347 X

4,052,138	10/1977	Gieck	431/4
4,057,021	11/1977	Schoppe	110/347 X
4,147,134	4/1979	Vogt et al.	110/205 X

Primary Examiner—Stephen P. Garbe

[57]   **ABSTRACT**

A continuous process for the combustion of solid fuels in the presence of an aqueous liquid phase under conditions such that oxides of nitrogen are not formed and oxides of sulfur and particles of ash are effectively prevented from contaminating the gaseous products released to the atmosphere. Fuel is charged as a slurry in alkaline aqueous solution and contacted with combustion air so that the catalytic properties of both water and alkali operate to permit rapid and complete combustion at comparatively low temperatures. Temperatures in the adiabatic reactor are, however, permitted to exceed the critical temperature of the liquid phase. Under the conditions of the process, formation of nitrogen oxides is negligible, sulfur in the fuel goes to sulfur trioxide which dissolves completely in the alkaline liquid phase which also retains particles of ash and unburned fuel. The resulting flue gas is essentially free from objectionable pollutants. Heat is made available at a temperature high enough to generate and superheat steam.

16 Claims, 2 Drawing Figures

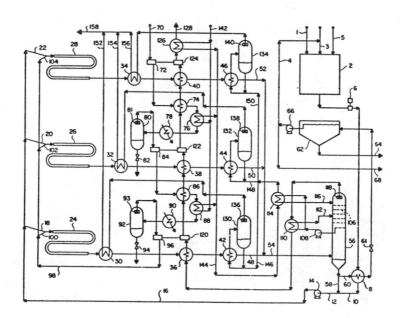

The figure showing the process which operates according to the invention is quite detailed, and the complete description of the operation is quite lengthy and involved. There are no data given so we conclude that this is a thought patent, but it is presented to show the breadth of supercritical fluid applications (in this case not because of solubility and separations considerations).

In overview of the invention a combustion process is described using a slurry of pulverized coal in a mixture of water and air. (The mixture also contains some alkali which is stated to serve as a combustion catalyst.) Combustion of the coal raises the temperature to above the critical temperature of water, and the ash that is present in the coal remains suspended in the supercritical medium. This supercritical fluid combustion stream is used to boil water and superheat steam in a countercurrent superheater-boiler train; the steam that is formed in the boiler is used to generate power.

We wonder what the power generation industry thinks about the potential for the invention.

United States Patent [19]

Perrut

[11]   Patent Number: **4,478,720**

[45]   **Date of Patent:**   **Oct. 23, 1984**

[54]   **FRACTIONATION PROCESS FOR MIXTURES BY ELUTION CHROMATOGRAPHY WITH LIQUID IN SUPERCRITICAL STATE AND INSTALLATION FOR ITS OPERATION**

[75]   Inventor: **Michel Perrut**, St Nicolas de Port, France

[73]   Assignee: **Societe Nationale Elf Aquitaine**, Courbevoie, France

[21]   Appl. No.:   **499,597**

[22]   Filed: **May 31, 1983**

[30]   **Foreign Application Priority Data**

Jun. 3, 1982 [FR]   France 82 09649

[51]   Int. Cl.³ **B01D 15/08**
[52]   U.S. Cl. **210/659; 55/67;**
                                                   55/197; 210/198.2
[58]   Field of Search 55/67, 197, 386;
                                                   210/656, 659, 198.2

[56]   **References Cited**

       FOREIGN PATENT DOCUMENTS

       1673089 1/1971 Fed. Rep. of Germany .
       2729462 1/1979 Fed. Rep. of Germany .
       1350580 4/1974 United Kingdom .

OTHER PUBLICATIONS

Hardware Adaptations to HPLC Apparatus to Enable Operation as a Supercritical Fluid Chromatograph by McManigill et al. in Hewlett Packard Bulletin 43–59-53–1647, pp. 21–23, 5/1983.
Introduction to Modern Liquid Chromatography by Snyder et al. (Second Edition) pp. 519–522, 1979.
Angewandte Chemie, vol. 19, No. 8, Aug. 1980, pp. 575–587.
Analytical Chemistry, vol. 44, No. 4, Apr. 1972, pp. 681–686.

Primary Examiner—John Adee
Attorney, Agent, or Firm—Schwartz, Jeffery, Schwaab, Mack, Blumenthal & Koch

[57]   **ABSTRACT**

The present invention concerns a fractionation process of a mixture by elution chromatography.

It is characterized in that the collected eluent is purified, restored to supercritical state and recycled in the head of the column.

It concerns a cracking process of mixtures by elution chromatography with liquid in the supercritical state and an installation for its operation.

14 Claims, 2 Drawing Figures

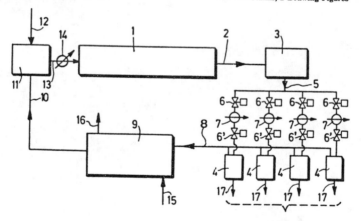

This is the first reference to supercritical fluid chromatography located in the patent literature (although we referenced several supercritical fluid chromatography articles from the technical literature in Chapter 9). The prior art discussion in the patent describes the use of supercritical fluid chromatography for analytical purposes. As described in the patent and in other supercritical fluid chromatography references, gas chromatography cannot be used for separating compounds with high molecular weight if the vapor pressure of these compounds is very low. The patentee relates that liquid chromatography has been effective, but liquid chromatographic separations quite frequently require a quite lengthy analysis time.

The invention is the extension of supercritical fluid chromatography to a scale suitable for the industrial processing of chemicals. The overall process concept and some detailed operation are shown in the flow scheme. The supercritical fluid flows continuously through the chromatographic column 1. Periodically a sample which is to be separated 12 is injected into the mixing station 11 where it is dissolved by the supercritical fluid which first passes through the heat exchanger 14 before entering the column 1. The column is typically a cylindrical tube filled with a suitable granular porous adsorbent. The components in the mixture are displaced at different rates during travel through the column because of their differential affinities for the adsorbent and thus are separated. The separated components are monitored by the detector 3 which actuates the valves 6, 7, 6' sequentially so that the separate components can be isolated in the traps 4. Separation of the components from the fluid by temperature and pressure change occurs in the traps, and the fluid is recycled to the mixer. (Element 9 is a dryer for treating the fluid and is used for those cases where water can interfere with the separation.)

Examples presented describe the separation and purification of naphthalene from its associated impurities, alkylated mono- and dicyclic aromatics. Supercritical pentane at 42 atm, 215°C and a chromatography adsorbent of baked brick impregnated with polyethylene glycol (6000 MW) are used to separate a 95% naphthalene -5% alkylated aromatics mixture into a 99.5% naphthalene fraction of 70% yield and a concentrated impurities fraction of 10% of the feed; 20% of the product is recycled.

United States Patent [19]

Eppig et al.

[11]   **4,434,028**

[45]   **Feb. 28, 1984**

[54] **APPARATUS FOR REMOVING ORGANIC CONTAMINANTS FROM INORGANIC-RICH MINERAL SOLIDS**

[75] Inventors: **Christopher P. Eppig**, Arlington; **Bruce M. Putnam**, Wayland; **Richard P. de Filippi**, Cambridge, all of Mass.

[73] Assignee: **Critical Fluid Systems, Inc.,** Cambridge, Mass.

[21] Appl. No.: **255,037**

[22] Filed: **Apr. 17, 1981**

[51] Int. Cl.³ **B01D 11/00**
[52] U.S. Cl. **196/14.52; 202/168**
[58] Field of Search 202/168-170; 422/261, 284, 281; 196/14.52; 134/40, 31; 175/206, 207, 212; 23/306, 307; 423/658.5; 208/311, 314, 320-324; 585/808, 861

[56]   **References Cited**

U.S. PATENT DOCUMENTS

2,152,665 4/1939 Rosenthal 202/168
3,177,263 4/1965 Francis 208/321

Primary Examiner—Frank Sever

Attorney, Agent, or Firm—Schiller & Pandiscio

[57]   **ABSTRACT**

Method and apparatus for removing oil and other organic constituents from particulate, inorganic-rich mineral solids. The method and apparatus are particularly suitable for removing oil from oil-contaminated drill cuttings. The solids to be treated are transferred into pressure vessel means wherein they are contacted with an extractant which is normally a gas but is under conditions of pressure and temperature to provide the extractant in a fluidic solvent state for the constituents to be removed, whereby the constituents are transferred to the extractant. The extractant containing the constituents is withdrawn from the pressure vessel and depressurized to render it a nonsolvent for the constituents and to form a two-phase system which can then be separated into extractant for repressurizing and recycling with proper handling of the constituents removed. In the case of removing oil from drill cuttings, the essentially oil-free cuttings can be disposed of in any suitable manner including dumping overboard from an offshore drilling rig.

17 Claims, 4 Drawing Figures

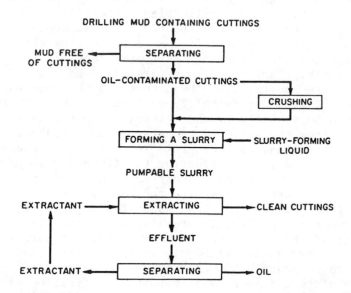

The motivation for applying supercritical fluids to the problem of cleaning contaminated solids deriving from platform drilling operations was described in Chapter 10.   A block diagram of the process is given in the figure and depicts the operation; the system would be located on a drilling platform.

In the patent many examples of extracting such materials as drilling mud, cuttings, and sand contaminated with fuel oil are given; carbon dioxide, halocarbons, and hydrocarbons were tested as the extraction solvents.   For example, 48.6 g of drilling mud and cuttings were extracted with 36.4 g of carbon dioxide at $30^{\circ}C$, 1500 psi to yield 1.56 g of clear oil and a non-oily solids product.   In another example 32.3 g of oil and cuttings were extracted with 89 g of propane at $60^{\circ}C$, 500-1200 psi to yield 3.5 g clear oil and a gray, dry, non-oily substrate.

United States Patent [19]

Avedesian

[11]   **Patent Number:**   **4,493,797**

[45]   **Date of Patent:**   **Jan. 15, 1985**

[54]   **APPARATUS AND METHOD INVOLVING SUPERCRITICAL FLUID EXTRACTION**

[76]   Inventor: **Michael M. Avedesian**, 128 Beacon Hill Rd., Beaconsfield, Quebec, Canada, H9W 1S9

[21]   Appl. No.:   **564,500**

[22]   Filed: **Dec. 22, 1983**

[51]   Int. Cl.³ C07G 1/00
[52]   U.S. Cl. 530/507
[58]   Field of Search 260/124

[56]   **References Cited**

PUBLICATIONS

Chem. Abstr., vol. 66, (1967), 56775m.

Chem. Abstr., vol. 84, (1976), 123660g.

Primary Examiner—Delbert R. Phillips

[57]   **ABSTRACT**

An autoclave extraction apparatus using supercritical fluid is used for supercritical fluid extraction of one or several compounds. The supercritical fluid containing the compound(s) may then be processed in a pressurized bed reactor under supercritical conditions. The bed being a fluidizable catalytic bed to carry out a catalytic reaction of the compound(s).

The method is particularly applicable to recover valuable lignin and other extractable components from kraft black liquor.

10 Claims, 2 Drawing Figures

Although the patentee describes four "examples," we conclude that the examples are made up and that this has to be another thought patent.

It is of interest to reproduce the first two paragraphs of the patentee's Prior Art section. He writes, "An extensive literature search conducted by the inventor has revealed that no one has published any information which may have bearing on applicant's invention:

"The search has revealed that no one has thought of extracting lignin and other components from black liquor using supercritical gases, nor of reacting lignin dissolved in supercritical gaseous product in a fluid bed catalytic reactor."

There is one very important reason why the patentee found no published information which "may have bearing on the invention": supercritical carbon dioxide cannot dissolve lignin, let alone extract it from a black liquor solution. The patentee describes his four "examples," and we excerpt from one of them.

"Weak black liquor (14% solids) is fed to the autoclave. Carbon dioxide is heated to 60°C and compressed to 150 bar. The supercritical CO_2 containing the liquor derived organic compounds leaves the autoclave."

And Claim 1 of the patent states:

"A method to extract lignin from a black liquor containing lignin comprising (a) dissolving a black liquor containing lignin in a supercritical fluid, at about or above critical temperature and pressure, (b) separating the black liquor depleted from said lignin from the supercritical fluid containing lignin."

He describes the many advantages of using carbon dioxide as the extractant in this application, e.g., low cost, ease of separation from the extract, nonflammability, etc.; these advantageous features, however, aren't going to make the concept of extracting lignin from black liquor using carbon dioxide work.

United States Patent [19]

Sumner, Jr. et al.

[11]   **Patent Number: 4,505,885**

[45]   **Date of Patent: Mar. 19, 1985**

[54]   **METHOD OF REMOVING WATER FROM ALKALI METAL HYDROXIDE SOLUTIONS**

[75]   Inventors: **William C. Sumner, Jr.; Gale G. Hoyer,** both of Midland, Mich.; **William G. Kozak,** Decatur, Ill.

[73]   Assignee: **The Dow Chemical Company,** Midland, Mich.

[21]   Appl. No.:   **505,639**

[22]   Filed: **Jun. 20, 1983**

[51]   Int. Cl.³ **C01D 1/00**
[52]   U.S. Cl. **423/592; 423/641**
[58]   Field of Search 423/583, 641, 592; 210/21

[56]   **References Cited**

U.S. PATENT DOCUMENTS

1,961,590	6/1934	MacMullin	423/643
2,196,593	4/1940	Muskat	423/643
2,196,594	4/1940	Muskat	423/643
2,285,300	6/1942	Muskat	23/302 R
2,373,257	4/1945	Muskat	23/302 R
3,308,063	3/1967	Hess et al.	210/59
3,316,172	4/1967	Hess	210/59
3,318,805	5/1967	Hess et al.	210/21
3,325,400	6/1967	Hess et al.	210/21
3,350,299	10/1967	Hess et al.	210/22
3,350,300	10/1967	Hess et al.	210/22
3,373,105	3/1968	Quptill, Jr. et al.	210/642
3,395,098	7/1968	Hess et al.	423/157
3,706,659	12/1972	Davis	210/21
3,983,032	9/1976	Hess et al.	210/21

OTHER PUBLICATIONS

G. P. Golysheva et al., Russian Journal of Physical Chemistry, 50(4), p. 635, 1976.

Primary Examiner—Veronica O'Keefe
Attorney, Agent, or Firm—Joe R. Prieto

[57]   **ABSTRACT**

A method removing water from aqueous alkali metal hydroxide solutions by contacting the solution with an organic liquid at elevated temperatures and pressures to form an organic liquid-water phase and a hydroxide solution phase and thereafter separating the organic water phase from the hydroxide solution phase.

26 Claims, 1 Drawing Figure

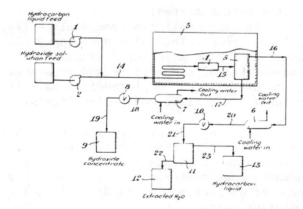

This patent utilizes the same principles that the Hess patent, U.S. 3,308,063, that we discussed previously does, viz., the ability of an organic compound at high pressure and temperature to dissolve water. The objective of the Hess patent is the dissolution of water from sea water for subsequent recovery of salt-free water and the salt water is discarded; the objective of the Sumner et al patent is the dissolution of water from sodium hydroxide solution for the purpose of concentrating the sodium hydroxide and the extracted water is discarded.

With reference to the drawing the sodium hydroxide solution to be concentrated and a hydrocarbon (e.g., ethyl benzene or t-butyl benzene) are pumped to a pressure of 2000 psig and passed to a static mixer 4 kept at 330°C. From the mixer the stream is conveyed to a phase separator 5 also kept at 335°C, where the heavier sodium hydroxide phase settles to the bottom. The hydrocarbon-water phase is withdrawn from the top of the separator through conduit 16, is cooled in heat exchanger 6, depressurized to ambient across valve 10. The hydrocarbon and liquid water separate in vessel 11 and are withdrawn separately. (The formation of distinct water and hydrocarbon phases actually occurs during the cooling step in heat exchanger 6.)

A number of examples are given. Example 3 shows that a 10.9 wt-% NaOH solution is concentrated to 21.6% using an apparatus schematically shown in the drawing. The solution feed rate was 360 g/hr, the hydrocarbon (t-butyl/benzene) was 236 g/hr, and the extraction was carried out at a pressure of 2000 psig and a temperature of 330°C.

United States Patent [19]

Shlichta

[11]   **Patent Number:**   **4,512,846**

[45]   **Date of Patent:**   **Apr. 23, 1985**

[54]   **METHOD FOR GROWTH OF CRYSTALS BY PRESSURE REDUCTION OF SUPERCRITICAL OR SUBCRITICAL SOLUTION**

[75]   Inventor: **Paul J. Shlichta,** San Pedro, Calif.

[73]   Assignee: **The United States of America as represented by the Administrator of the National Aeronautics and Space Administration,** Washington, D.C.

[21]   Appl. No.:   **342,944**

[22]   Filed: **Jan. 26, 1982**

[51]   Int. Cl.³ C30B 7/10
[52]   U.S. Cl. .... 156/623 Q; 23/295 R
[58]   Field of Search .... 423/339, DIG. 11; 156/621, 623 R, 623 Q, DIG. 89; 23/295 R

[56]   **References Cited**

FOREIGN PATENT DOCUMENTS

28272   3/1979   Japan .... 23/295 R

OTHER PUBLICATIONS

Phase Diagrams, vol. 3, 1970, Academic Press, Nielsen et al., pp. 36, 37, 40.
P. J. Shlichta and R. E. Knox, *J. Crystal Growth*, 3, 4 (1968), 808–813.
H. S. Booth and R. M. Bidwell, *Chem. Rev.*, 44 (1949), 447–513.
V. J. Krukonis et al., "Supercritical Fluid Extraction of Plant Materials Containing Chemotherapeutic Drugs," manuscript paper presented at AIChE 87th National Meeting, Boston, MA, 1979.

R. J. Janssen–van Rosmalen and P. Bennema, *J. Crystal Growth*, 42 (1977), 224–227.
P. S. Chen, P. J. Shlichta, W. R. Wilcox and R. A. Lefever, *J. Crystal Growth*, 47 (1979), 43–60.
Abstract of Thesis, P. S. Chen, Ph.D., Chem. Eng. Dept., Univ. of Southern California (1977).
P. J. Shlichta, "Crystal Growth in a Spaceflight Environment," MPS Experiment #770100, Third Semi–Annual Report (Oct. 1979–Mar. 1980), Jet Propulsion Laboratory.
P. J. Shlichta, "Minimization of Convection during Crystal Growth from Solution," paper presented at the AACG Meeting, San Diego, CA, 7/25/81.
J. F. Kramer and W. A. Tiller, *J. Chem. Phys.*, 37 (1962), 841.
R. F. Sekerta, ibid, 46 (1967), 2341–2351.
E. D. Kolb, J. C. Grenier and R. A. Laudise, "Solubility and Growth of AlPO₄ in a Hydrothermal Solvent:HCl," *J. Crystal Growth*, 51 (1981), 178–182.

Primary Examiner—Hiram H. Bernstein
Attorney, Agent, or Firm—Paul F. McCaul; John R. Manning; Thomas H. Jones

[57]   **ABSTRACT**

Crystals (51) of high morphological quality are grown by dissolution of a substance (28) to be grown into the crystal (51) in a suitable solvent (30) under high pressure, and by subsequent slow, time-controlled reduction of the pressure of the resulting solution (36). During the reduction of the pressure interchange of heat between the solution (36) and the environment is minimized by performing the pressure reduction either under isothermal or adiabatic conditions.

15 Claims, 10 Drawing Figures

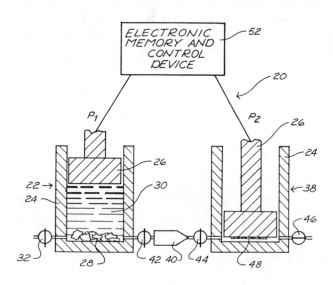

This patent describes a different application of the
properties of supercritical fluids, i.e., using the
supercritical fluid as a medium from which to grow crystals
and the abstract and the drawing on the face page present
the invention. Whereas the nucleation process discussed in
Chapter 12 involved homogeneous nucleation during the
pressure reduction, (Krukonis, 1984d.) this invention
involves heterogeneous deposition from an expanding gas
solution.

The prior art discussion relates that current crystal
growing techniques suffer from some limitations in their
operation, specifically that the "temperature driven
crystallization" method requires precise time-temperature
regulation and that the earth's gravity field causes
convection currents that can interfere in crystal growth.

The patentee employs a "pressure driven crystallization" to form crystals from material dissolved in a
supercritical fluid. A seed crystal acts as the hetero-
genous nucleation site for the precipitating material when
the pressure is reduced, and the drawings on the face page
illustrate this. We don't know, however, how the patentee
intends to prevent homogeneous nucleation during the
"pressure driven crystallization."

APPENDIX B. Computer Programs
for Calculating Phase Behavior

Three programs are included in this Appendix: one for calculating binary vapor-liquid or liquid-liquid equilibria, one for calculating both the pressure-temperature trace of the solid-liquid-vapor line and solid-vapor equilibria, and one for calculating the phase behavior of ternary mixtures. The three programs are similar in that they all use the Peng-Robinson equation-of-state (PR-EOS). These programs require normally readily available (or calculable) physical property data such as critical temperature, critical pressure, molecular weight, vapor pressure data, solid molar volume, and accentric factor. Two equation of state parameters, an interaction parameter and a size parameter, are needed for each binary pair of the components of the mixture. The program which calculates the phase behavior for ternary mixtures prompts the user for the feed composition in weight fractions and returns the calculated tie-line in terms of weight fractions. The other programs input and output exclusively in mole fractions.

```
C-------------------------------------------------------------------
C     THIS PROGRAM IS USED TO CALCULATE BINARY VAPOR-LIQUID EQUILIBRIA
C     (VLE) OR LIQUID-LIQUID EQUILIBRIA (LLE).  THE PROGRAM USES THE
C     PENG-ROBINSON EQUATION OF STATE (PR-EOS) WITH TWO ADJUSTABLE
C     PARAMETERS, RK12 AND ETA.  RK12 IS A MEASURE OF THE INTERACTIONS
C     BETWEEN THE TWO COMPONENTS PRESENT.  ETA IS A MEASURE OF THE SIZE
C     DIFFERENCE BETWEEN THE TWO COMPONENTS.  A TEMPERATURE OF INTEREST
C     AND AN INITIAL STARTING PRESSURE ARE INPUTTED INTO THE PROGRAM.
C     A PARTICULAR RK12 AND ETA ARE INPUTTED FOR THIS TEMPERATURE AND
C     PRESSURE.  THE PROGRAM THEN GENERATES THE P-x PHASE ENVELOPE BY
C     CALCULATING TIE LINES.  TO ASSIST IN THE SUCCESSFUL GENERATION OF
C     A PARTICULAR TIE LINE THE METHOD OF SUCCESSIVE SUBSTITUTION IS
C     USED TO UPDATE THE EQUILIBRIUM K (DISTRIBUTION COEFFICIENT) VALUES
C     BETWEEN ITERATIONS TO HELP CONVERGE TO THE EXACT K VALUE.  THE
C     NEXT TIE LINE IS GENERATED BY INCREMENTING THE PRESSURE BY A VALUE
C     DP AND CONVERGING AGAIN TO THE PROPER K VALUE AT THE PRESSURE,
C     P+DP.
C     FINALLY, A LEAST SQUARES ANALYSIS IS ALSO PERFORMED.  THIS IS DONE
C     BY COMPARING EXPERIMENTAL DATA WITH THE DATA CALCULATED BY THIS
C     PROGRAM.  SPECIFICALLY, THE PRESSURES OF THE EXPERIMENTAL AND
C     CALCULATED DATA AT A PARTICULAR MOLE FRACTION ARE SUBTRACTED AND
C     THE DIFFERENCE IS SQUARED.  THIS IS PERFORMED FOR ALL EXPERIMENTAL
C     VLE OR LLE DATA POINTS AND THE TOTAL SUM OF ALL THE SQUARES IS
C     MINIMIZED BY VARYING RK12 AND/OR ETA FOR THE SAME TEMPERATURE AND
C     INITIAL PRESSURE.
C     NOTE :
C        IN ACTUALITY, THE MOLE FRACTIONS OF THE EXPERIMENTAL AND
C     CALCULATED DATA DIFFER BY <0.01 FOR THE LIQUID MOLE
C     FRACTIONS AND BY <0.001 FOR THE VAPOR (OR 2ND LIQUID
C     PHASE IN LLE) MOLE FRACTIONS.
C     -------------------------------------------------------------
C     THE FOLLOWING IS A LIST OF ALL PERTINENT VARIABLES USED IN THE
C     MAIN PROGRAM & THEIR MEANING.  SOME OF THESE VARIABLES WILL BE
C     DESIGNATED BY DIFFERENT "LETTERS" IN THE SUBROUTINE, PHI.
C            H = THE DISTRIBUTION COEFFICIENT (USUALLY DESIGNATED BY
C                THE LETTER K).  H=Y/X OF A COMPONENT IN VLE OR
C                X1/X2 IN LLE.
C            X = THE MOLE FRACTION OF A COMPONENT IN THE LIQUID.
C            Y = THE MOLE FRACTION OF A COMPONENT IN THE VAPOR FOR VLE
C                OR FOR THE 2ND LIQUID PHASE IN LLE.
C            TCRIT = THE CRITICAL TEMPERATURE
C            PCRIT = THE CRITICAL PRESSURE
C            OMEGA = THE ACENTRIC FACTOR
C            FUGL = THE FUGACITY IN THE LIQUID PHASE
C            FUGV = THE FUGACITY IN THE VAPOR FOR VLE OR IN THE 2ND
C                   LIQUID PHASE IF LLE.
C            FPL = THE FUGACITY COEFFICIENT IN THE LIQUID
C            FPV = THE FUGACITY COEFFICIENT OF THE VAPOR FOR VLE OR 2ND
C                  LIQUID PHASE IF LLE
C            JFLAG = THE COUNTER WHICH INDICATES THE # OF ITERATIONS
C                    NEEDED FOR GENERATION OF A SINGLE TIE-LINE.
C            Z = THE COMPRESSIBILITY FACTOR
C            VM = THE MOLAR VOLUME OF EITHER THE LIQUID OR VAPOR FOR
C                 VLE OR OF EITHER OF THE TWO LIQUID PHASES FOR LLE.
C     SEVERAL OTHER VARIABLES USED STRICTLY IN THE SUBROUTINE, PHI, :
C            a = A TEMPERATURE DEPENDENT VARIABLE USED IN THE PR-EOS.
C                IT IS A MEASURE OF THE INTERMOLECULAR ATTRACTION FORCE
```

```
C                      BETWEEN THE TWO COMPONENTS.
C               b = A CONSTANT USED IN THE PR-EOS.  IT IS A MEASURE OF THE
C                   SIZE OF THE HARD SPHERES.
C               G = A DIMENSIONLESS FUNCTION OF REDUCED TEMPERATURE AND
C                   THE ACENTRIC FACTOR.
C         SEVERAL OTHER VARIABLES USED IN THE LEAST SQUARES ANALYSIS :
C               ISQ = THE VARIABLE WHICH DESIGNATES THE # OF EXPTL. DATA
C                     POINTS USED IN COMPARISON WITH THE CALCULATED DATA
C                     POINTS. ** NOTE ** IDEALLY, THIS #, ISQ, SHOULD =
C                     THE # OF EXPTL. DATA POINTS READ INTO THE PROGRAM.
C                     HOWEVER, IT CAN BE LESS THAN OR POSSIBLY EVEN
C                     GREATER THAN THIS # OF EXPTL. DATA POINTS!!
C               PPP = THE ABSOLUTE VALUE DIFFERENCE BETWEEN THE
C                     CALCULATED AND EXPTL. DATA POINTS' PRESSURES.
C               XXX = THE ABSOLUTE VALUE DIFFERENCE BETWEEN THE CALCULATED
C                     AND EXPTL. DATA POINTS' MOLE FRACTIONS.
C-----------------------------------------------------------------------
C      DIMENSIONALIZE ALL NECESSARY ARRAYS
       COMMON/PROPS/TCRIT(2),PCRIT(2),OMEGA(2)
       DIMENSION H(2,1000),Q(2,1000),FUGL(2),FUGV(2),TEST(2),VV(2)
       DIMENSION X(2),Y(2),XC(2),YC(2),FPV(2),FPL(2),U(2),V(2),S(2),T1(2)
       DIMENSION KAPPA(2),XD(1000),PD(1000)
       INTEGER LFLAG,L
       REAL LSV
C -----------------------------------------------------------------------
C      VARIABLES SUBSCRIPTED WITH A #1 DESIGNATE THE HEAVY COMPONENT
C      VARIABLES SUBSCRIPTED WITH A #2 DESIGNATE THE LIGHT COMPONENT
C      THE SECOND SUBSCRIPT IN DOUBLE SUBSCRIPTED VARIABLES IS FOR THE
C      ITERATION NUMBER.  HENCE, H(2,1) = THE EQUILIBRIUM Y/X VALUE
C      FOR COMPONENT #2 FOR THE FIRST ITERATION.
C-----------------------------------------------------------------------
C      READ IN THE CRITICAL TEMPERATURE. CRITICAL PRESSURE, AND ACENTRIC
C      FACTOR FOR THE TWO COMPONENTS.
       DO 1 II=1,2
          READ(10,*) TCRIT(II),PCRIT(II),OMEGA(II)
     1 CONTINUE
C -----------------------------------------------------------------------
       PRINT 5
     5 FORMAT(//,3X,'PLEASE TYPE IN THE FOLLOWING : (1) # OF COMBIN',
     x 'ATIONS'/1X,'OF RK12 & ETA FOR THIS TEMPERATURE?'/
     x'(2) TEMP(C), & (3) # OF EXPTL. DATA POINTS')
       READ(5,*)ICSE,T,NUM
       DO 10 ID=1,NUM
          READ(15,*) XD(ID),PD(ID)
          WRITE(6,8) XD(ID),PD(ID)
     8    FORMAT(1X,2F12.5/)
    10 CONTINUE
C-----------------------------------------------------------------------
C      START THE MAJOR LOOP OF THE PROGRAM FOR CALCULATING BINARY EQUIL.
       DO 110 J=1,ICSE
       ISQ=0
       LSV=0.0
C-----------------------------------------------------------------------
C      INPUT INTERACTION AND SIZE PARAMETERS
       ICRIT=0
       PRINT 15
    15 FORMAT(//,'  RK12')
       READ(5,*) RK12
```

```
        PRINT 20
   20   FORMAT(//' ETA')
        READ(5,*)ETA
        PRINT 25
   25   FORMAT(//,' INITP, DP, FINP: IN PSIA')
        READ(5,*) P,DP,FINP
        P=P/14.7
        DP=DP/14.7
        FINP=FINP/14.7
C  -----------------------------------------------------------------
C       INPUT TEMPERATURE AND ECHO-PRINT RK12 AND ETA
        PRINT 30,T
        WRITE(11,30)T
   30   FORMAT(///,10X,'TEMPERATURE=',F7.3,3X,'DEG.C')
        PRINT 35,RK12
        WRITE(11,35)RK12
   35   FORMAT(10X,'RK12=',8X,F8.5)
        PRINT 40,ETA
        WRITE(11,40)ETA
   40   FORMAT(10X,'ETA=',9X,F8.5)
        PRINT 45
   45   FORMAT(///1X,'X-HEAVY',3X,'Y-HEAVY',6X,'PRESSURE',6X,'VOL-L',5X,
        x 'VOL-FL',2X,'# ITNS.')
        PRINT 50
   50   FORMAT(24X,'(PSIA)',5X,'(CC/GMOL)',2X,'(CC/GMOL)')
        PRINT 55
   55   FORMAT(3X,'**********************************************************
        X**********************',/)
        WRITE(11,45)
C  -----------------------------------------------------------------
C       INPUT GAS CONSTANT, INITIAL ESTIMATED K VALUE, & INITIAL COUNTERS
        R2=82.06
        H(1,1)=0.05
        H(2,1)=4.0
        JFLAG=0
        XJ=1.00
        YJ=0.0
        ICOUNT=0
        LFLAG=1
C-------------------------------------------------------------------
C       INCREMENT PRESSURE FOR NEXT TIE LINE
   60   P=P+DP
        ICOUNT=ICOUNT+1
   65   JFLAG=JFLAG+1
C-------------------------------------------------------------------
C       CALCULATE MOLE FRACTIONS FROM K (DISTRIBUTION COEFF.) VALUES
        X(1)=(1.-H(2,JFLAG))/(H(1,JFLAG)-H(2,JFLAG))
        X(2)=1.0-X(1)
        Y(1)=H(1,JFLAG)*X(1)
        Y(2)=1.0-Y(1)
        T=T+273.15
        IF(JFLAG.GE.1000) GO TO 70
C-------------------------------------------------------------------
C       CALL THE SUBROUTINE TO CALCULATE THE FUGACITY COEFFICIENTS
C       OF BOTH COMPONENTS IN BOTH PHASES AND THE MOLAR VOLUMES OF
C       BOTH PHASES.
        NNN=0
        CALL PHI(T,P,Y,RK12,ETA,FPV,VM,NNN)
```

```
            VMV=VM
            NNN=1
            CALL PHI(T,P,X,RK12,ETA,FPL,VM,NNN)
            VML=VM
            T=T-273.15
C-------------------------------------------------------------------------
C       CALCULATE THE FUGACITIES OF BOTH COMPONENTS IN BOTH PHASES
            FUGL(1)=X(1)*P*EXP(FPL(1))
            FUGL(2)=X(2)*P*EXP(FPL(2))
            FUGV(1)=Y(1)*P*EXP(FPV(1))
            FUGV(2)=Y(2)*P*EXP(FPV(2))
C-------------------------------------------------------------------------
C       TEST TO DETERMINE IF THE FUGACITY OF EACH, INDIVIDUAL COMPONENT
C       IS EQUAL IN BOTH PHASES
            Q(1,JFLAG)=FUGL(1)/FUGV(1)
            Q(2,JFLAG)=FUGL(2)/FUGV(2)
            TEST(1)=ABS(Q(1,JFLAG)-1.0)
            TEST(2)=ABS(Q(2,JFLAG)-1.0)
            IF(TEST(1).LE..0001.AND.TEST(2).LE..0001) GO TO 70
            H(1,JFLAG+1)=H(1,JFLAG)*Q(1,JFLAG)
            H(2,JFLAG+1)=H(2,JFLAG)*Q(2,JFLAG)
            GO TO 65
C -------------------------------------------------------------------------
C       EQUILIBRIUM BETWEEN BOTH PHASES HAS BEEN REACHED.   NOW
C       OBTAIN A GUESS OF X AND Y FOR BOTH COMPONENTS IN BOTH
C       PHASES FOR THE NEXT PRESSURE P + DP.
     70     P1=P-DP
            P2=P+DP
            S(1)=(P2-P1+((P-P1)/(X(1)-U(1)))*U(1))/((P-P1)/(X(1)-U(1)))
            IF(ICOUNT .EQ. 1)S(1)=X(1)
            S(2)=1.-S(1)
            T1(1)=H(1,JFLAG)*S(1)
            T1(2)=1.-T1(1)
            H(1,1)=T1(1)/S(1)
            H(2,1)=T1(2)/S(2)
            L=JFLAG+1
            U(1)=X(1)
            U(2)=X(2)
            V(1)=Y(1)
            V(2)=Y(2)
C-------------------------------------------------------------------------
C       DETERMINE THE DIFFERENCE IN THE PRESSURE BETWEEN THE EXPERIMENTAL
C       AND CALCULATED DATA POINT, SQUARE THIS DIFFERENCE, AND ADD IT TO
C       THE PREVIOUS SUM OF THE SQUARES.  ** NOTE ** THIS STEP IS PER-
C       FORMED, AT MOST, ACCORDING TO THE # OF EXPERIMENTAL DATA POINTS.
            P=P*14.7
            DO 72 ILS=1,NUM
                XXX=ABS(X(1)-XD(ILS))
                PPP=ABS(P-PD(ILS))
                IF((XXX.LE.0.01).AND.(PPP.LE.(DP*14.7))) THEN
                    ISQ=ISQ+1
                    LSV=((PPP/PD(ILS))**2.0)+LSV
                    WRITE(6,71) XD(ILS)
                    WRITE(11,71) XD(ILS)
     71             FORMAT(/1X,'THE EXPTL. MOLE FRACTION ',F12.5,' HAS MAT',
         x              'CHED A'/1X,'COMPUTER CALCULATED MOLE FRACTION VALUE.'/1X,
         x              'IF THIS EXPTL. VALUE IS USED AGAIN IN COMPARISON WITH'/
         x              1x,'A SLIGHTLY DIFFERENT CALCULATED VALUE THEN THE TOT',
```

```
     x          'AL'/1X,'# OF EXPTL. DATA POINTS USED FOR COMPARISON,ISQ,'
     x          /'SHOULD BE GREATER THAN THE ACTUAL TOTAL # OF EXPTL.',
     x          ' DATA'/1X'POINTS BY THE AMOUNT OF EXTRA TIMES THIS PAR',
     x          'TICULAR EXPTL. DATA POINT IS USED.')
        ENDIF
           YYY=ABS(Y(1)-XD(ILS))
           IF((YYY.LE.0.001).AND.(PPP.LE.(DP*14.7))) THEN
              ISQ=ISQ+1
              LSV=((PPP/PD(ILS))**2.0)+LSV
              WRITE(6,71) XD(ILS)
              WRITE(11,71) XD(ILS)
           ENDIF
   72  CONTINUE
C-----------------------------------------------------------------
C      DETERMINE IF THE MIXTURE CRITICAL POINT IS REACHED.
C      IF NOT, THE PROGRAM AUTOMATICALLY BEGINS TO DETERMINE
C      THE NEXT TIE LINE.
       IF(((XJ.LE.X(1)).OR.(Y(1).LE.YJ)).AND.(ICRIT.LE.1)) THEN
              GO TO 80
           ELSE
              ICRIT=ICRIT+1
       ENDIF
       IF ((XJ-X(1)).LE.-5E-3) WRITE(6,75)
       IF ((Y(1)-YJ).LE.-5E-3) WRITE(6,75)
       IF ((Y(1).LE.0.0).OR.(X(1).LE.0.0)) WRITE(6,75)
       IF (X(1).LE.Y(1)) WRITE(6,75)
   75  FORMAT(' NEAR THE  MIXTURE CRITICAL POINT')
       IF((XJ-X(1)).LE.-5E-3) GO TO 95
       IF((Y(1)-YJ).LE.-5E-3) GO TO 95
       IF ((Y(1).LE.0.0).OR.(X(1).LE.0.0)) GO TO 95
       IF (X(1).LE.Y(1)) GO TO 95
       IF(R.GT.0.100) XJ=X(1)
   80  YJ=Y(1)
       WRITE(6,85) X(1),Y(1),P,VML,VMV,JFLAG
   85  FORMAT(/,1X,F8.6,2X,F8.6,4X,F8.2,4X,F9.3,2X,F9.3,1X,I4)
       WRITE(11,85)X(1),Y(1),P,VML,VMV,JFLAG
       P=P/14.7
       JFLAG=0
       IF (ICOUNT.EQ.1) THEN
           HORIZ1=0.0
       ELSE
           HORIZ1=HORIZ2
       ENDIF
       HORIZ2=X(1)-Y(1)
       IF (((HORIZ1-HORIZ2).GE.1D-3).OR.(HORIZ2.LE.0.3)) LFLAG=0
       IF (LFLAG.EQ.1) GO TO 90
       R=Y(1)/X(1)
       IF(R.GT.0.250) DP=1.0/14.7
       IF(R.GT.0.550) DP=0.5/14.7
       IF(R.GT.0.700) DP=0.1/14.7
   90  IF(P.LT.FINP) GO TO 60
   95  CONTINUE
C      PRINT OUT THE LEAST SQUARE VALUE OBTAINED AT THIS TEMPERATURE
C      FOR THE RK12 AND ETA CHOSEN.  ALSO PRINT THE # OF EXPERIMENTAL
C      DATA POINTS USED IN ARRIVING AT THIS LEAST SQUARE VALUE.  IF
C      ALL THE EXPT'L DATA WAS NOT USED THEN THE RK12 AND ETA
C      CHOSEN WERE NOT THE OPTIMAL VALUES FOR THIS TEMPERATURE.
       IF(ISQ.LT.NUM) THEN
```

```
          WRITE(6,100) NUM,ISQ,ISQ,LSV
          WRITE(11,100) NUM,ISQ,ISQ,LSV
100       FORMAT(///1X,'THE # OF EXPTL. DATA POINTS IS = ',I3/1X,
      x      'HOWEVER, EACH OF THESE DATA POINTS ARE',
      x      ' NOT'/1X,'ACCOUNTED FOR IN THE LEAST SQUARES OPTIMIZATION',
      x      ' PROCEDURE.'/1X,' THE # OF DATA POINTS ACCOUNTED FOR IS ',I3,
      x      /1X,'THE LEAST SQUARE VALUE, LSV, OBTAINED FROM THE ',I3/1X,
      x      ' EXPTL. DATA POINTS IS = ',F15.8)
       ELSE
          WRITE(6,105) NUM,NUM,LSV
          WRITE(11,105) NUM,NUM,LSV
105       FORMAT(///1X,'ALL',I3,' EXPTL. DATA POINTS ARE ACCOUNTED FOR'/
      x      ' IN THE LEAST SQUARES OPTIMIZATION PROCEDURE.  THE LEAST'/1X,
      x      'SQUARE VALUE, LSV, OBTAINED FROM THESE',I3,' EXPTL. DATA'/1X,
      x      'POINTS IS = ',F15.8/1X,'THIS VALUE CAN NOW BE COMPARED TO',
      x      'OTHER LSV VALUES'/1X,'OBTAINED BY VARYING RK12 &-OR ETA ',
      x      'RESULTING ULTIMATELY'/1X,'IN THE OPTIMAL VALUES FOR RK12',
      x      ' & ETA.')
       ENDIF
110    CONTINUE
C-------------------------------------------------------------------
C      THE PROGRAM HAS COMPLETED THE # OF COMBINATIONS OF RK12
C      AND ETA FOR THIS TEMPERATURE.
       PRINT 115
115    FORMAT(////,8X,'THE PROGRAM IS COMPLETED')
       END
C*******************************************************************
C*******************************************************************
C      THIS SUBROUTINE, PHI, IS USED TO CALCULATE THE FUGACITY COEFFICI-
C      ENTS FOR THE TWO COMPONENTS IN ONE PHASE.  ** NOTE ** EACH TIME
C      THIS SUBROUTINE IS CALLED IT IS WORKING ON ONE PHASE ONLY!!!
       SUBROUTINE PHI(T,P,Y,RK,ETA,FP,VM,NNN)
       COMMON/PROPS/TCRIT(2),PCRIT(2),OMEGA(2)
       DIMENSION Y(2),FP(2),W(2),B(2,2),A(2,2),TC(2),PC(2)
       DIMENSION TERM1(2),TERM2(2),TERM3(2),G(2),TR(2)
       DIMENSION ROOT(3),RA(4),Z(3),KAPPA(2)
       COMPLEX Z
       BM=0.0
       AM=0.0
       R2=82.06
       SQ2=2.0**0.5
       Q1=1.0+SQ2
       Q2=SQ2-1.0
       Q3=2.0*SQ2
C-------------------------------------------------------------------
C      LOAD IN THE PURE COMPONENTS' a,b,CRITICAL PROPERTIES, & G
       DO 120 I=1,2
       B(I,I)=0.0778*R2*TCRIT(I)/PCRIT(I)
       TERM3(I)=0.0
       W(I)=OMEGA(I)
       TC(I)=TCRIT(I)
       PC(I)=PCRIT(I)
       TR(I)=T/TC(I)
       G(I)=(1.+(0.37464+1.54226*W(I)-0.26992*W(I)
      x**2)*(1.-TR(I)**0.5))**2
       A(I,I)=0.45724*R2**2*TC(I)**2/PC(I)*G(I)
120    Continue
C-------------------------------------------------------------------
```

```
C       APPLY THE MIXING RULES TO CALCULATE a & b OF THE MIXTURE.
        A(1,2)=(A(1,1)*A(2,2))**0.5*(1.0-RK)
        A(2,1)=A(1,2)
        B(1,2)=((B(1,1)+B(2,2))/2.0) * (1.-ETA)
        B(2,1)=B(1,2)
        DO 125 I=1,2
        DO 125 J=1,2
           AM=AM+Y(I)*Y(J)*A(I,J)
           BM=BM+Y(I)*Y(J)*B(I,J)
 125    CONTINUE
        AA=AM*P/R2**2/T**2
        BB=BM*P/R2/T
C---------------------------------------------------------------------
C       THE PR-EOS CAN BE REWRITTEN IN TERMS OF A CUBIC IN Z RESULTING IN
C       3 ROOTS.
C                                                          THE 3
C       ROOTS OF Z ARE CALCULATED HERE; HOWEVER, ONLY ONE IS ACTUALLY USED
C       IN THE REST OF THIS IMPLIMENTATION OF THE SUBROUTINE.
        RA(1)=1.0
        RA(2)=BB-1.0
        RA(3)=AA-2.0*BB-3.0*BB**2
        RA(4)=BB**3+BB**2-AA*BB
        CALL ZPOLR(RA,3,Z,IER)
C---------------------------------------------------------------------
C
C
C
C
C
        DO 140 J=1,3
           IF(AIMAG(Z(J))) 130,135,130
 130       ROOT(J)=-1.0E+9
           GOTO 140
 135       ROOT(J)=Z(J)
 140    CONTINUE
        DO 145 J=1,3
           IF(ROOT(J).LT.0.AND.NNN.EQ.1) ROOT(J)=1.0E+10
 145    CONTINUE
        IF(NNN.EQ.0) ZM=AMAX1(ROOT(1),ROOT(2),ROOT(3))
        IF(NNN.EQ.1) ZM=AMIN1(ROOT(1),ROOT(2),ROOT(3))
        VM=ZM*R2*T/P
C---------------------------------------------------------------------
C       THE ACTUAL FUGACITY COEFFICIENT FOR EACH COMPONENT IS
C       NOW CALCULATED.
        DO 155 I=1,2
        IF(I.EQ.1)BJJ=B(2,2)
        IF(I.EQ.2)BJJ=B(1,1)
        BPRIME=Y(I)*B(I,I)*(2.-Y(I))+((1.-Y(I))**2)*(2*B(1,2)-BJJ)
        TERM1(I)=BPRIME*(ZM-1.0)/BM-ALOG(ZM-BB)
        TERM2(I)=BPRIME*AA*ALOG((ZM+Q1*BB)/(ZM-Q2*BB))/BM/BB/Q3
        DO 150 J=1,2
 150    TERM3(I)=TERM3(I)+2.0*Y(J)*A(I,J)
        TERM3(I)=AA*ALOG((ZM+Q1*BB)/(ZM-Q2*BB))*TERM3(I)/BB/AM/Q3
        FP(I)=TERM1(I)+TERM2(I)-TERM3(I)
 155    CONTINUE
        RETURN
        END
```

```
C*****************************************************************************
C       PROGRAM TO SOLVE SOLID - VAPOR (SV) OR SOLID - LIQUID - VAPOR (SLV)
C       EQUILIBRIUM.
C*****************************************************************************
C
C       ....... DECLARE ARRAYS  .....................
C
        COMMON/PROPS/TC(2),PC(2),W(2)
        DIMENSION TS(20),PS(20),XS(20)
        DIMENSION X(2),Y(2),XC(2),YC(2),FPV(2),FPL(2),U(2),V(2),S(2),T1(2)
        REAL LASDEV
C
C       ....... COMPONENT 1 IS XENON
C               COMPONENT 2 IS NAPHTHALENE  ...................
C
C       ....... INPUT COMPONENT PHYSICAL PROPERTIES  .............
C
        TC(1) = 289.81
        TC(2) = 748.4
        PC(1) = 58.0
        PC(2) = 40.0
        W(1) = 0.002
        W(2) = 0.302
        R2 = 82.06
        V2S = 111.94
        X(1) = 0.005
        X(2) = 1.- X(1)
   10   IFIRST = 1
C
C       ....... INPUT SYSTEM TEMPERATURE AND INTERACTION AND SIZE PARAMETRES  ..
C
        WRITE(6,*) ' TEMPERATURE (C),  K12,  ETA'
        READ(5,*) T,RK,ETA
C
C       ....... SPECIFY TYPE OF CALCULATION TO BE PERFORMED  .............
C
C       ....... IF SOLID-VAPOR EQUILIBRIUM TO BE SOLVED, THEN SPECIFY THE
C               FINAL PRESSURE AT WHICH THE CALCULATIONS ARE TO BE TERMINATED  ..
C
        WRITE(6,*) ' TYPE OF CALCULATIONS? 1 = SV; 2 = SLV'
        READ(5,*) ITYPE
        IF(ITYPE.EQ.1) THEN
        WRITE(6,*) ' INPUT FINAL PRESSURE'
        READ(5,*) FINP
        ENDIF
C
C       ....... SOLID-VAPOR CALCULATIONS -- COMMON FOR S-V AND S-L-V
C               EQUILIBRIUM CALCULATIONS  ..............
C
        P = 0.0
        XJ=1.0
        YJ=0.0
        DP = 10.0
   20   P = P+DP
        DT = 1.5
        LASDEV =0.0
```

```
    30  P2S = 10.**(10.0896-2926.61/(T+237.332))/760.
        IF(IFIRST.EQ.1) THEN
        Y(2) = P2S
        Y(1) = 1.-Y(2)
        P = 1.0
        IF(ITYPE.EQ.1) P=60.0
        ENDIF
        T = T+273.15
        ALPHA = ALOG(P2S/P)+V2S*(P-P2S)/(R2*T)
        JFLAG = 0
C
C   ...... CALL SUBROUTINE PHI TO CALCULATE COMPONENT FUGACITIES IN PHASES  ..
C
    40  CALL PHI(T,P,Y,RK,ETA,FPV,VM,0)
        YC(2) = EXP(ALPHA-FPV(2))
        DELY = ABS(YC(2)-Y(2))/Y(2)
        JFLAG=JFLAG+1
        IF(JFLAG.GT.500) GO TO 50
        Y(2) = YC(2)
        Y(1) = 1.-Y(2)
C
C   ...... TEST TO TERMINATE S-V CALCULATIONS AT ONE PRESSURE  ........
C
        IF(DELY.GE.0.001) GO TO 40
        IF(ITYPE.EQ.1) GO TO 60
C
C   ...... LIQUID-VAPOR PART OF S-L-V EQUILIBRIUM CALCULATIONS  ........
C
        IFLAG = 0
        FCTRX1 = Y(1)*EXP(FPV(1))
        FCTRX2 = Y(2)*EXP(FPV(2))
C
C   ...... CALL SUBROUTINE PHI TO CALCULATE COMPONENT FUGACITIES IN PHASES  ..
C
    70  CALL PHI(T,P,X,RK,ETA,FPL,VM,1)
        XC(1) = EXP(-FPL(1))*FCTRX1
        XC(2) = EXP(-FPL(2))*FCTRX2
        DELX = (ABS(XC(1)-X(1)))/X(1)
        IFLAG = IFLAG+1
        IF(IFLAG.GT.500) GO TO 80
        X(1) = XC(1)
        X(2) = 1.-X(1)
C
C   ...... TEST TO TERMINATE CALCULATIONS  ...............
C
        IF(DELX.GE.0.00025) GO TO 70
        SUMX = XC(1)+XC(2)
        DEV = 1.-SUMX
        SEX = ABS(DEV)
C
C   ...... AT CONSTANT PRESSURE AN APPROPRIATE INCREMENT IS INTRODUCED
C           IN TEMPERATURE SUCH THAT THE PROGRAM EVENTUALLY COMPUTES
C           THE S-L-V EQUILIBRIUM POINT  ............
C
        IF(SEX.GT.0.0001) THEN
        IF((DEV*LASDEV).LT.0.0) THEN
```

```
          DT=0.5*DT
          ENDIF
          T = T+SIGN(DT,DEV)-273.15
          LASDEV=DEV
          ENDIF
          IF(SEX.GE.0.0001) GO TO 30
     60   T=T-273.15
C
C   ....... PRINTS OUT RESULTS AT ONE TEMPERATURE AND PRESSURE  .........
C
          IF(ITYPE.EQ.1) WRITE(6,*)'  VAPOR=',Y(2),P,T
          IF(ITYPE.EQ.2) WRITE(6,*)'  LIQUID=',X(2),' VAPOR=',Y(2),P,T
C
C   ....... FOR S-V CASE, CALCULATIONS ARE TERMINATED IF PRESSURE
C           EXCEEDS SPECIFIED FINAL PRESSURE  ..................
C
          IF((ITYPE.EQ.1).AND.(P.GE.FINP)) GO TO 100
C
C   ....... METHOD TO DECREASE INCREMENT IN PRESSURE AS MIXTURE CRITICAL
C           POINT IS APPROACHED  .............
C
          R = Y(2)/X(2)
          IF(R.GT.0.05)  DP = 5.0
          IF(R.GT.0.090) DP = 2.5
          IF(R.GT.0.130) DP = 0.5
          IF(R.GT.0.200) DP = 0.25
          IF(R.GT.0.300) DP = 0.10
          IF(R.GT.0.350) DP = 0.05
          IF((IFIRST.EQ.1).AND.(ITYPE.EQ.2)) P=P-1
C
C   ....... TESTS TO TERMINATE CALCULATIONS NEAR MIXTURE CRITICAL POINT  ..
C
          IF((ITYPE.EQ.2).AND.(DP.LE.0.25)) THEN
          IF((XJ-X(1)).LE.-5.E-03.OR.(Y(1)-YJ).LE.-5.E-03) WRITE(6,110)
          IF((Y(1).LE.0.).OR.(X(1).LE.0.).OR.(X(1).LE.Y(1)))WRITE(6,110)
          IF((XJ-X(1)).LE.-5.E-03.OR.(Y(1)-YJ).LE.-5.E-03) GO TO 100
          IF((Y(1).LE.0.0).OR.(X(1).LE.0.0).OR.(X(1).LE.Y(1))) GO TO 100
          XJ=X(1)
          YJ=Y(1)
          ENDIF
          IFIRST = 2
C
C   ....... AFTER SOLVING EITHER CASE FOR A CERTAIN PRESSURE, ITERATE AGAIN
C           TO SOLVE FOR NEW PRESSURE  ...................
C
          GO TO 20
     80   WRITE(6,*)'  WARNING : ITERATIONS EXCEEDED (VLE)'
          WRITE(6,*)P,X(1),XC(1)
          GO TO 90
     50   WRITE(6,*)'  WARNING : ITERATIONS EXCEEDED (SVE)'
          WRITE(6,*)P,Y(1),YC(1)
    110   FORMAT(5X,'NEAR MIXTURE CRITICAL POINT')
    100   CONTINUE
```

```
C
C  .......  IF THE PROGRAMMER WISHES TO SOLVE FOR ANOTHER CASE, HE MAY
C           DO SO  ........................
C
  90   WRITE(6,*)'  ANOTHER CASE? 1 = YES, 2 = NO'
       READ(5,*) NEXT
       P=1.0
       IF(NEXT.EQ.1) GO TO 10
       STOP
       END


C*****************************************************************************
C    SUBROUTINE PHI TO CALCULATE THE COMPONENT FUGACITIES IN PHASES
C    USING PENG - ROBINSON EQUATION OF STATE ( P - R EOS)
C*****************************************************************************
C
C  .......  DECLARE ARRAYS  ...........................
C
       SUBROUTINE PHI(T,P,Y,RK,ETA,FP,VM,NNN)
       COMMON/PROPS/TC(2),PC(2),W(2)
       DIMENSION Y(2),FP(2),B(2,2),A(2,2)
       DIMENSION TERM1(2),TERM2(2),TERM3(2),G(2),TR(2)
       DIMENSION ROOT(3),RA(4),Z(3),KAPPA(2)
       COMPLEX Z
C
       BM=0.0
       AM=0.0
       R2=82.06
       SQ2=2.0**0.5
       Q1=1.0+SQ2
       Q2=SQ2-1.0
       Q3=2.0*SQ2

       DO 210 I=1,2
       B(I,I)=0.0778*R2*TC(I)/PC(I)
       IF(I.EQ.2) B(I,I)=0.9945*B(I,I)
       TERM3(I)=0.0
       TR(I)=T/TC(I)
       G(I)=(1.+(0.37464+1.54226*W(I)-0.26992*W(I)
      x**2)*(1.-TR(I)**0.5))**2
       A(I,I)=0.45724*R2**2*TC(I)**2/PC(I)*G(I)
  210  CONTINUE

       A(1,2)=(A(1,1)*A(2,2))**0.5*(1.0-RK)
       A(2,1)=A(1,2)
       B(1,2)=((B(1,1)+B(2,2))/2.0) * (1.-ETA)
       B(2,1)=B(1,2)

       DO 220 I=1,2
       DO 220 J=1,2
       AM=AM+Y(I)*Y(J)*A(I,J)
       BM=BM+Y(I)*Y(J)*B(I,J)
  220  CONTINUE
```

```
C
C   ....... RE-WRITTEN P-R  EOS  ..............
C
      AA=AM*P/R2**2/T**2
      BB=BM*P/R2/T
      RA(1)=1.0
      RA(2)=BB-1.0
      RA(3)=AA-2.0*BB-3.0*BB**2
      RA(4)=BB**3+BB**2-AA*BB
C
C   ....... CALLS CANNED SUBROUTINE ZPOLR FROM IMSL LIBRARY
C           TO FIND ROOTS OF A CUBIC EQUATION (P-R EOS)  ..............
C
      CALL ZPOLR(RA,3,Z,IER)
      DO 230 J=1,3
      IF(AIMAG(Z(J))) 240,250,240
  240 ROOT(J)=-1.0E+9
      GO TO 230
  250 ROOT(J)=Z(J)
  230 CONTINUE
      DO 260 J=1,3
      IF(ROOT(J).LT.0.AND.NNN.EQ.1) ROOT(J)=1.0E+10
  260 CONTINUE
C
C   ....... DEPENDING UPON PHASE, PROGRAM PICKS UP PROPER ROOT FOR THE
C           CUBIC EQUATION -- (LARGEST IF VAPOR, SMALLEST IF LIQUID)  ....
C
      IF(NNN.EQ.0) ZM=AMAX1(ROOT(1),ROOT(2),ROOT(3))
      IF(NNN.EQ.1) ZM=AMIN1(ROOT(1),ROOT(2),ROOT(3))
      VM=ZM*R2*T/P

      DO 270 I=1,2
      IF(I.EQ.1)BJJ=B(2,2)
      IF(I.EQ.2)BJJ=B(1,1)
      BPRIME=Y(I)*B(I,I)*(2.-Y(I))+((1.-Y(I))**2)*(2*B(1,2)-BJJ)
      TERM1(I)=BPRIME*(ZM-1.0)/BM-ALOG(ZM-BB)
      TERM2(I)=BPRIME*AA*ALOG((ZM+Q1*BB)/(ZM-Q2*BB))/BM/BB/Q3
      DO 280 J=1,2
  280 TERM3(I)=TERM3(I)+2.0*Y(J)*A(I,J)
      TERM3(I)=AA*ALOG((ZM+Q1*BB)/(ZM-Q2*BB))*TERM3(I)/BB/AM/Q3
      FP(I)=TERM1(I)+TERM2(I)-TERM3(I)
  270 CONTINUE
      RETURN
      END
```

```
C*******************************************************************
C      PROGRAM TO SOLVE TERNARY SYSTEMS
C      ----   MAIN PROGRAM  ------
C      ....... RUNS IN SINGLE PRECISION .......
C*******************************************************************

      PROGRAM MULTI3

C ...... FIRST TRY 2-PHASE CALCULATIONS FOR VARIOUS LOADING POINTS.
C        TRY FOR TIE LINES GOING IN DIFFERENT DIRECTIONS FOR EACH
C        OF THESE LOADINGS. IF THE PROGRAM RETURNS ONLY ONE TIE LINE
C        THEN THAT POINT IS IN 2-PHASE REGION. IF THE PROGRAM RETURNS
C        MORE THAN ONE TIE TINES GOING THROUGH THE SAME LOADING, THEN
C        THAT POINT IS PROBABLY IN 3-PHASE REGION. AND IF THE PROGRAM
C        FAILS REPEATEDLY, TO PERFORM 2-PHASE CALCULATIONS AND RETURNS
C        ONE PHASE RESULTS, THEN THAT POINT IS PROBABLY IN ONE PHASE
C        REGION.
C        ALSO, SINCE THE 3-PHASE CALCULATIONS ARE SENSITIVE TO INITIAL
C        PHASE COMPOSITION GUESSES, CARE SHOULD BE TAKEN WHILE SUPPLYING
C        THE GUESSES. ................
      WRITE(6,10)
 10   FORMAT(3X,'HOW MANY COMPONENTS EXIST IN THE SYSTEM?')
      READ(5,*) NCOMP
C
C ...... CALLS MAIN SUBROUTINE TERN ............
C
      CALL TERN(NCOMP)
      END

C*******************************************************************
C      MAIN SUBROUTINE TERN
C ...... USES SUBROUTINES NPHI2,NPHI,FLASH2,FLASH,AFIND,BFIND,PHI
C        AND CANNED SUBROUTINE ZPOLR FROM IMSL LIBRARY ........
C*******************************************************************
C
C ...... DECLARE ARRAYS ..........
C
      SUBROUTINE TERN(N)
      DIMENSION TC(3),PC(3),W(3),ETA(3,3),RK(3,3),PR(3),TR(3)
      DIMENSION ZC(3),R(3),TESTA1(3),TESTB1(3),TEST1(3),TEST2(3),Q(3)
      DIMENSION TESTA2(3),TESTB2(3),XB(3),FPL2(3),FPL22(3)
      DIMENSION XA(3),FPV2(3),FPL12(3),ZZ(3),Y(3),FPV(3),FPL1(3)
      DIMENSION NAME(3)
      REAL KA(3),KA2(3),KA3(3),KAP(3),MW(3),LA,LAK(3),LBK(3),YK(3)
      REAL KBP(3),KB(3),LB,KB2(3),KB3(3)
      INTEGER NPHASE,FINAL,EQUIL,FLAG
C
C ......  INPUT COMPONENT PHYSICAL PROPERTIES ......
C
```

```
       DO 101 I=1,N
          NAME(I) = I
          WRITE(6,*) ' INPUT PROPERTIES OF COMPONENT ',NAME(I)
          WRITE(6,*) ' MOLECULAR WEIGHT?'
          READ(5,*) MW(I)
          WRITE(6,*) ' CRITICAL TEMPERATURE(DEGREES KELVIN)?'
          READ(5,*) TC(I)
          WRITE(6,*) ' CRITICAL PRESSURE(ATMOSPHERES)?'
          READ(5,*) PC(I)
          WRITE(6,*) ' ACENTRIC FACTOR?'
          READ(5,*) W(I)
          RK(I,I)=0.0
          ETA(I,I)=0.0
  101 CONTINUE
C
C  ......  INPUT SYSTEM TEMPERATURE AND PRESSURE  ........
C
       WRITE(6,*) ' ENTER SYSTEM TEMP(CELSIUS) AND PRESSURE (ATM)'
       READ (5,*) T,P
  102 J=N-1
C
C  ......  INPUT SIZE AND INTERACTION PARAMETERS  ........
C
       DO 103 I=1,J
          DO 104 K=I,J
             WRITE(6,*) ' INPUT INTERACTION PARAMETER BETWEEN COMPONENT'
             WRITE(6,105) NAME(I),NAME(K+1)
             READ(5,*) RK(I,K+1)
             RK(K+1,I)=RK(I,K+1)
  105        FORMAT(I12,2X,'AND',2X,I12)
             WRITE(6,*) ' INPUT SIZE PARAMETER BETWEEN COMPONENT'
             WRITE(6,105) NAME(I),NAME(K+1)
             READ(5,*) ETA(I,K+1)
             ETA(K+1,I)=ETA(I,K+1)
  104     CONTINUE
  103  CONTINUE
C
C  ......  PRINTS OUT DATA SUPPLIED SO FAR  ......
C
       DO 106 I=1,N
          WRITE(6,107) NAME(I)
  107     FORMAT(5X,'COMPONENT',I4)
          WRITE(6,*) ' MW=', MW(I), ' TC=', TC(I)
          WRITE(6,*) ' PC=',PC(I),' W=',W(I)
  106  CONTINUE
       WRITE(6,*) ' INTERACTION PARAMETERS RK'
       DO 108 I=1,N
          WRITE(6,*) (RK(I,J), J=1,N)
  108  CONTINUE
       WRITE(6,*) ' SIZE PARAMETERS ETA'
       DO 109 I=1,N
          WRITE(6,*) (ETA(I,J), J=1,N)
  109  CONTINUE
C
  110 ZZZ=0.0
       NUMIT=0
C
C  ......  INPUT WT. FRACTION OF EACH COMPONENT IN FEED  .......
C
       DO 111 I=1,N
```

```
          WRITE(6,112) NAME(I)
 112      FORMAT(' INPUT WEIGHT FRACTION OF COMPONENT ',I4)
          READ(5,*) ZC(I)
C
C  ......  PARAMETERS Q,R USED IN WEGSTEIN METHOD TO CALCULATE
C          DISTRIBUTION COEFFICIENTS, K  ......
C
          Q(I)=0.9
          R(I)=0.9
          TEST2(I)=1000.0
          TESTA2(I)=1000.0
          TESTB2(I)=1000.0
          ZZZ=ZZZ+ZC(I)
 111   CONTINUE
       IF (ABS(ZZZ-1.0).GE.1E-5) THEN
          WRITE(6,*) ' FEED COMPOSITIONS DON''T SUM TO 1.0. RE-ENTER.'
          GO TO 110
       ENDIF
C
C  ......  PROGRAM CONVERTS WT. FRACTIONS TO MOLE FRACTIONS  ......
C
       ZZZ=0.0
       DO 113 I=1,N
          WRITE(6,*) ' WT. FRACTION OF COMPONENT ',I,' = ',ZC(I)
          ZZZ=ZC(I)/MW(I)+ZZZ
 113   CONTINUE
       DO 114 I=1,N
          ZZ(I)=(ZC(I)/MW(I))/ZZZ
          PR(I)=P/PC(I)
          TR(I)=(T+273.15)/TC(I)
 114   CONTINUE
C
C       ----------  3 PHASE CALCULATIONS  --------------------------
C
C  ......  INPUT GUESSED COMPOSITION OF EACH PHASE  .......
C
       WRITE(6,*) ' INPUT TYPE OF EQUILIBRIUM CALCULATION.'
       WRITE(6,*) ' 1 = LL,   2 = LV,   3 = LLV'
       READ(5,*) EQUIL
       IF (EQUIL.LE.2) GO TO 125
C
       FLAG = 0
 115   NPHASE = 2
       WRITE(6,*) ' FIRST LIQUID PHASE COMPOSITION.'
       DO 116 I=1,N
          WRITE(6,117) NAME(I)
 117      FORMAT(' INPUT GUESSED WT. FRACTION OF COMPONENT',2X,I4)
          READ(5,*) LAK(I)
 116   CONTINUE
       WRITE(6,*) ' SECOND LIQUID PHASE COMPOSITION.'
       DO 118 I=1,N
          WRITE(6,119) NAME(I)
 119      FORMAT(' INPUT GUESSED WT. FRACTION OF COMPONENT',2X,I4)
          READ(5,*) LBK(I)
 118   CONTINUE
       WRITE(6,*) ' VAPOR PHASE COMPOSITION.'
       DO 120 I=1,N
          WRITE(6,121) NAME(I)
 121      FORMAT(' INPUT GUESSED WT. FRACTION OF COMPONENT',2X,I4)
          READ(5,*) YK(I)
```

```
 120  CONTINUE
C
C  ......  PROGRAM CONVERTS WT. FRACTIONS  TO MOLE FRACTIONS  ......
C
      ZZA=0.0
      ZZB=0.0
      ZZY=0.0
      DO 122 I=1,N
         ZZA=LAK(I)/MW(I)+ZZA
         ZZB=LBK(I)/MW(I)+ZZB
         ZZY=YK(I)/MW(I)+ZZY
 122  CONTINUE
      DO 123 I=1,N
         LAK(I)=(LAK(I)/MW(I))/ZZA
         LBK(I)=(LBK(I)/MW(I))/ZZB
         YK(I)=(YK(I)/MW(I))/ZZY
         KA2(I)=YK(I)/LAK(I)
         KB2(I)=YK(I)/LBK(I)
 123  CONTINUE
C
C  ......  CALLS SUBROUTINE NPHI2 TO CALCULATE FUGACITY COEFFICIENTS
C          FOR THREE PHASES  ......
C
 124  CALL NPHI2(T,P,XA,XB,Y,FPV2,FPL12,FPL22,VM,N,KA2,LA,KB2,
     1 LB,NUMIT,ZZ,NAME,NPHASE,FLAG,EQUIL,PC,W,RK,ETA,TC,TR,PR)
      IF (NPHASE.EQ.5) GO TO 115
C
C  ......  IF MASS BALANCE IS NOT SATISFIED IN THREE ATTEMPTS, GO TO
C          2 PHASE CALCULATIONS  ........
C
      IF (NPHASE.EQ.2) THEN
         NUMIT=0
         GO TO 125
      ENDIF
C
C  ......  WEGSTEIN METHOD  ........
C
      DO 126 I=1,N
         KA3(I)=(1.0-Q(I))*FPL12(I)/FPV2(I)+Q(I)*KA2(I)
         KB3(I)=(1.0-R(I))*FPL22(I)/FPV2(I)+R(I)*KB2(I)
 126  CONTINUE
      TEST=0.0
C
C  ......  TESTS TO ADJUST Q AND R PARAMETERS  .......
C
      DO 127 I=1,N
         TESTA1(I)=ABS((KA3(I)-KA2(I))/KA3(I))
         TESTB1(I)=ABS((KB3(I)-KB2(I))/KB3(I))
         TEST=TESTA1(I)+TESTB1(I)+TEST
         IF (TESTA1(I).GE.TESTA2(I)) THEN
            Q(I)=0.5*Q(I)
            IF (Q(I).GE.-1E-3) Q(I)=0.9
         ELSE
            TESTA2(I)=TESTA1(I)
         ENDIF
         IF (TESTB1(I).GE.TESTB2(I)) THEN
            R(I)=0.5*R(I)
            IF (R(I).GE.-1E-3) R(I)=0.9
         ELSE
            TESTB2(I)=TESTB1(I)
```

```
          ENDIF
 127  CONTINUE
C
C  ......  IF CONVERGENCE NOT ACHIEVED FOR K VALUES, ITERATE AGAIN  ......
C
      IF (TEST.GE.1E-2) THEN
          DO 128 I=1,N
             KA(I)=KA2(I)
             KA2(I)=KA3(I)
             KB(I)=KB2(I)
             KB2(I)=KB3(I)
             FPV(I)=FPV2(I)
             FPL1(I)=FPL12(I)
             FPL2(I)=FPL22(I)
 128      CONTINUE
          GO TO 124
      ENDIF
      GO TO 129
C
C  -------------- 2 PHASE ( L-L OR L-V ) CALCULATIONS -----------------
C
 125  IF (EQUIL.EQ.3) EQUIL=2
      WRITE(6,*) ' TWO PHASE CALCULATION.'
C
C  ......  INPUT GUESSED COMPOSITION OF EACH PHASE  .......
C
      FLAG = 0
 130  NPHASE = 1
      WRITE(6,*) ' FIRST LIQUID PHASE COMPOSITION.'
      DO 131 I=1,N
          WRITE(6,132) NAME(I)
 132      FORMAT(' INPUT GUESSED WT. FRACTION OF COMPONENT',2X,I4)
          READ(5,*) LAK(I)
 131  CONTINUE
      IF (EQUIL.EQ.1) THEN
          WRITE(6,*) ' SECOND LIQUID PHASE COMPOSITION.'
          DO 133 I=1,N
             WRITE(6,134) NAME(I)
 134         FORMAT(' INPUT GUESSED WT FRACTION OF COMPONENT',2X,I4)
             READ(5,*) LBK(I)
 133      CONTINUE
      ELSE
          WRITE(6,*) ' VAPOR PHASE COMPOSITION.'
          DO 135 I=1,N
             WRITE(6,136) NAME(I)
 136         FORMAT(' INPUT GUESSED WT FRACTION OF COMPONENT',2X,I4)
             READ(5,*) YK(I)
 135      CONTINUE
      ENDIF
C
C  ......  CONVERTS WT. FRACTIONS TO MOLE FRACTIONS  .......
C
      ZZA=0.0
      ZZB=0.0
      ZZY=0.0
      DO 137 I=1,N
          ZZA=LAK(I)/MW(I)+ZZA
          IF (EQUIL.EQ.1) THEN
             ZZB=LBK(I)/MW(I)+ZZB
          ELSE
```

```
                    ZZY=YE(I)/MW(I)+ZZY
              ENDIF
137   CONTINUE
      DO 138 I=1,N
          LAK(I)=(LAK(I)/MW(I))/ZZA
          IF (EQUIL.EQ.1) THEN
              LBK(I)=(LBK(I)/MW(I))/ZZB
              KA(I)=LAK(I)/LBK(I)
          ELSE
              YK(I)=(YK(I)/MW(I))/ZZY
              KA(I)=YK(I)/LAK(I)
          ENDIF
          KA2(I) = KA(I)
138   CONTINUE
      WRITE(6,*) ' DO YOU WANT DAMPED CONVERGENCE? (1=YES, 2=NO)'
      READ(5,*) IDAMP
      DO 139 I=1,N
          IF (IDAMP.EQ.1) THEN
              Q(I)=0.5
          ELSE
              Q(I)=-1.0
          ENDIF
139   CONTINUE
C
C     ...... CALLS SUBROUTINE NPHI TO CALCULATE FUGACITY COEFFICIENTS
C            FOR TWO PHASES .......
C
140   CALL NPHI(T,P,XA,Y,FPV2,FPL12,VM,N,KA,LA,NUMIT,
     1 ZZ,NAME,NPHASE,EQUIL,FLAG,PC,W,RK,ETA,TC,PR,TR)
      IF (NPHASE.EQ.5) GO TO 130
C
C     ...... IF TWO PHASE CALCULATION FAILS, ONLY ONE PHASE EXISTS .......
C
      IF (NPHASE.EQ.1) GO TO 141
C
C     ...... WEGSTEIN METHOD .......
C
      DO 142 I=1,N
          KA3(I)=(1.0-Q(I))*FPL12(I)/FPV2(I)+Q(I)*KA2(I)
          IF (KA3(I).LT.0.0) KA3(I)=0.001
142   CONTINUE
      TEST=0.0
C
C     ...... TESTS TO ADJUST Q PARAMETER ........
C
      DO 143 I=1,N
          TEST=TEST+ABS((KA3(I)-KA2(I))/KA3(I))
          TEST1(I)=ABS((KA3(I)-KA2(I))/KA3(I))
          IF (TEST1(I).GE.TEST2(I)) THEN
              Q(I)=0.5*Q(I)
              IF(Q(I).GE.-1E-3) Q(I)=0.5
          ELSE
              TEST2(I)=TEST1(I)
          ENDIF
143   CONTINUE
C
C     ...... IF CONVERGENCE IS NOT ACHIEVED FOR K VALUES, ITERATE AGAIN ....
C
      IF (TEST.GE.1E-5) THEN
          DO 144 I=1,N
```

```
            KA(I)=KA3(I)
            KA2(I) = KA3(I)
  144     CONTINUE
          GO TO 140
        ENDIF
C
C     ....................................................................
C
  129 XXA=0.0
      YYY=0.0
      XXB=0.0
C
C ......   PROGRAM CONVERGED FOR THESE CONDITIONS
C          PRINTS OUT MOLE FRACTIONS OF COMPONENTS IN PHASES  .......
C
      DO 145 I=1,N
        Y(I)=Y(I)*MW(I)
        YYY=YYY+Y(I)
        XA(I)=XA(I)*MW(I)
        XXA=XXA+XA(I)
        IF (NPHASE.EQ.3) THEN
            XB(I)=XB(I)*MW(I)
            XXB=XXB+XB(I)
        ENDIF
  145 CONTINUE
      DO 146 I=1,N
        XA(I)=XA(I)/XXA
        Y(I)=Y(I)/YYY
        IF (NPHASE.EQ.3) XB(I)=XB(I)/XXB
  146 CONTINUE
      WRITE(6,*) ' PRESSURE = ',P,' ATMOSPHERES'
      WRITE(6,*) ' TEMPERATURE = ',T,' DEG. C.'
      IF (NPHASE.EQ.2) THEN
          VAPOR=(ZC(1)-XA(1))/(Y(1)-XA(1))
          LA=1.0-VAPOR
      ELSE
          DO 147 I=1,N
            KA(I)=Y(I)/XA(I)
            KB(I)=Y(I)/XB(I)
  147     CONTINUE
          NUMIT = 0
          FINAL=0
C
C ......   MASS BALANCE ( SUBROUTINE FLASH2 ) MUST BE EXECUTED ONE MORE
C          TIME TO DETERMINE (V/F, L1/F AND L2/F) VALUES FOR
C          3 PHASE CALCULATIONS ............
C
          CALL FLASH2(LA,LB,KA,XA,KB,XB,ZC,Y,FINAL,N,NUMIT)
          VAPOR=1.0-LA-LB
      ENDIF
C
C ......   PRINTS RESULTS AS WT. FRACTIONS OF COMPONENTS IN PHASES  .......
C
  141 DO 148 I=1,N
        WRITE(6,149) NAME(I)
  149   FORMAT(5X,'COMPONENT',I4)
        WRITE(6,*) '  OVERALL COMP: ',100.*ZC(I),' WEIGHT %'
        IF ((NPHASE.GT.1).AND.(EQUIL.GE.2)) THEN
            WRITE(6,*) ' VAPOR COMP: ',100.*Y(I),' WEIGHT %'
            WRITE(6,*) ' LIQUID COMP: ',100.*XA(I),' WEIGHT %'
```

```
            IF (NPHASE.EQ.3) WRITE(6,*) ' SECOND LIQUID COMP:
    1       100*XB(I),' WEIGHT %'
          ENDIF
          IF((NPHASE.GT.1).AND.(EQUIL.EQ.1)) THEN
            WRITE(6,*) ' FIRST LIQUID COMP: ',100.*Y(I),' WEIGHT %'
            WRITE(6,*) ' SECOND LIQUID COPM:  ',100.*XA(I),' WEIGHT %'
          ENDIF
  148   CONTINUE
        IF (NPHASE.GT.1) THEN
          WRITE(6,150) VAPOR,LA
  150     FORMAT(3X,'VAPOR=',F12.5,2X,'LIQUID=',F12.5)
          IF (NPHASE.EQ.3) WRITE(6,*) 'SECOND LIQUID=',LB
        ENDIF
C
C  ...... IF THE USER WISHES TO DO ANOTHER CALCULATION, HE MAY DO SO  ....
C
        WRITE(6,*) ' MORE CASES WITH THESE COMPONENTS? (1=YES  0=NO)'
        READ(5,*) KEY
        IF (KEY.EQ.1) GO TO 102
        WRITE(6,*) ' THE PROGRAM IS COMPLETED.'
        RETURN
        END

C*****************************************************************
C       SUBROUTINE NPHI2
C       ------ GIVEN DISTRIBUTION COEFFICIENTS (K), IT CALCULATES
C              FUGACITY COEFFICIENTS FOR 3 PHASE CALCULATIONS  ------
C*****************************************************************
C
C  ...... DECLARE ARRAYS ........
C
        SUBROUTINE NPHI2(T,P,XAN,XBN,YN,FPVN,FPL1N,FPL2N,VM,N,KAN,LA,
    1   KBN,LB,NUMIT,ZZ,NAME,NPHASE,FLAG,EQUIL,PC,W,RK,ETA,TC,TR,PR)
        DIMENSION XAN(3),NAME(3),XBN(8),YN(3),FPVN(3)
        DIMENSION FPL1N(3),FPL2N(3),ZZ(3)
        REAL KAN(3),KAP(3),KBN(3),KBP(3),LA,LB
        INTEGER FLAG,NPHASE,NUMIT
C
C  ...... CALL MASS BALANCE SUBROUTINE FLASH2 TO CALCULATE PHASE
C         COMPOSITIONS ................
C
        CALL FLASH2(LA,LB,KAN,XAN,KBN,XBN,ZZ,YN,FLAG,N,NUMIT)
C
C
C  ...... IF MASS BALANCE FAILS, RETURN TO SUBROUTINE TERN AND
C         INPUT NEW GUESSES FOR COMPONENT WT. FRACTIONS ........
C
        IF (((FLAG.GE.1).AND.(FLAG.LE.3)).AND.(NUMIT.EQ.0)) THEN
          WRITE(6,*) ' MASS BALANCE DID NOT CONVERGE FOR GUESSED'
          WRITE(6,*) ' K VALUES IN ',FLAG,' ATTEMPT.'
          WRITE(6,*) ' TRY AGAIN WITH NEW GUESSES FOR WT. FRACTIONS'
          WRITE(6,*) ' OF COMPONENTS IN DIFFERENT PHASES.'
          NPHASE = 5
          GO TO 201
        ELSE
          IF (FLAG.GE.3) THEN
            WRITE(6,*) ' 3-PHASE CALCULATIONS FAILED. TRY 2-PHASE'
            WRITE(6,*) ' CALCULATIONS.'
            NPHASE=2
            GO TO 201
```

```
          ENDIF
       ENDIF
C
       T=T+273.15
       NUMIT=NUMIT+1
C
C   ......  MASS BALANCE CONVERGED, CALCULATE FUGACITY COEFFICIENTS  .......
C
C   ......  CALCULATE PHI FOR THE VAPOR PHASE  ..........
C
       CALL PHI(T,P,YN,FPVN,VM,0,N,TC,PC,TR,PR,W,RK,ETA)
C
C   ......  CALCULATE PHI FOR THE FIRST LIQUID PHASE  ........
C
       CALL PHI(T,P,XAN,FPL1N,VM,1,N,TC,PC,TR,PR,W,RK,ETA)
C
C   ......  CALCULATE PHI FOR THE SECOND LIQUID PHASE  .......
C
       CALL PHI(T,P,XBN,FPL2N,VM,1,N,TC,PC,TR,PR,W,RK,ETA)
       T=T-273.15
       NPHASE = 3
  201  RETURN
       END

C*****************************************************************
C     3 PHASE MASS BALANCE SUBROUTINE FLASH2
C     ------  GIVEN DISTRIBUTION COEFFICIENTS (K), SUBROUTINE NPHI2
C                CALCULATES COMPOSITIONS OF THREE PHASES  ---------
C*****************************************************************
C
C   ......  DECLARE ARRAYS  ........
C
       SUBROUTINE FLASH2(LA,LB,KAF,XAF,KBF,XBF,ZZ,YYF,FLAG,N,NUMIT)
       DIMENSION XAF(3),XBF(3),YYF(3),ZZ(3)
       REAL KAF(3),KBF(3)
       REAL LA,LB
       INTEGER FLAG,NUMIT
C
       A=0.0
C
C   ......  CALLS SUBROUTINE BFIND TO CALCULATE BETA (B)  .......
C
  301  CALL BFIND(A,B,KAF,KBF,ZZ,N)
       IF ((B.GT.0.0).AND.(B.LT.1.0)) GO TO 302
  303  A=A+0.05
C
C   ......  MASS BALANCE NOT SATISFIED EVEN FOR ONE ITERATION  ......
C
       IF (A.GT.0.96) THEN
          GO TO 304
       ELSE
          GO TO 301
       ENDIF
  302  A1=A
C
C   ......  AFTER B IS CALCULATED ,CALCULATE ALPHA (A) USING
C              SUBROUTINE AFIND  ........
C
       CALL AFIND(A1,B,KAF,KBF,ZZ,N)
       IF ((A1.LE.0.0).OR.(A1.GE.1.0)) GO TO 303
```

```
        A=A1
        TESTA=0.0
  305   AO=A
        BO=B
        TESTAO=TESTA
        CALL BFIND(A,B,KAF,KBF,ZZ,N)
        CALL AFIND(A,B,KAF,KBF,ZZ,N)
C
C  ......  CRITERIA FOR CONVERGENCE FOR MASS BALANCE CALCULATIONS  .......
C
        IF ((ABS((AO-A)/AO).LE.1E-4).AND.(ABS((BO-B)/BO).LE.1E-4))
      1    GO TO 306
        IF (((A.LE.0.0).OR.(A.GE.1.0)).OR.((B.LE.0.0).OR.(B.GE.1.0)))
      1    GO TO 304
        TESTA=AO+A
        IF (ABS(TESTAO-TESTA).LE.1E-5) A=(A+AO)/2.0
        GO TO 305
C
C  ......  AFTER TWO MORE ITERATIONS MASS BALANCE DIVERGES  .......
C
  304   IF (NUMIT.EQ.0) FLAG = FLAG+1
        IF (NUMIT.GT.0) FLAG = 3
        GO TO 307
  306   SUMXA=0.0
        SUMXB=0.0
        SUMY=0.0
C
C  ......  ONCE MASS BALANCE IS CONVERGED, CALCULATE COMPOSITION OF
C          EACH PHASE  .........
C
        DO 308 I=1,N
        XAF(I)=ZZ(I)/(B*(1.0-A)+(1.0-A)*(1.0-B)*KAF(I)/KBF(I)
      1     +A*KAF(I))
        YYF(I)=KAF(I)*XAF(I)
        XBF(I)=YYF(I)/KBF(I)
        SUMXA=SUMXA+XAF(I)
        SUMXB=SUMXB+XBF(I)
        SUMY=SUMY+YYF(I)
  308   CONTINUE
        DO 309 I=1,N
        XAF(I)=XAF(I)/SUMXA
        XBF(I)=XBF(I)/SUMXB
        YYF(I)=YYF(I)/SUMY
  309   CONTINUE
        LA=B*(1.0-A)
        LB=(1.0-A)*(1.0-B)
        FLAG=0
  307   RETURN
        END

C*******************************************************************
C       SUBROUTINE BFIND
C       ------  GIVEN ALPHA (A = L/F), IT CALCULATES BETA (B = L1/(L1+L2))
C               USING BISECTION METHOD  --------------
C*******************************************************************
C
C  ......  DECLARE ARRAYS  .......
C
        SUBROUTINE BFIND(AN,BN,KAN,KBN,ZZ,N)
        DIMENSION ZZ(3)
```

```
      REAL KAN(3),KBN(3)
C
      BL=0.0
      BH=1.0
      F2A=0.0
      F2B=0.0
C
C   ...... FIRST SEE IF BETA LIES BETWEEN 0 AND 1 FOR GIVEN A VALUE ......
C
      DO 401 I=1,N
          DENOM=BL*(1.0-AN)+(1.0-AN)*(1.0-BL)*KAN(I)/KBN(I)+AN*KAN(I)
          F2A=F2A+ZZ(I)*(1.0-KAN(I)/KBN(I))/DENOM
          DENOM=BH*(1.0-AN)+(1.0-AN)*(1.0-BH)*KAN(I)/KBN(I)+AN*KAN(I)
          F2B=F2B+ZZ(I)*(1.0-KAN(I)/KBN(I))/DENOM
  401 CONTINUE
      IF ((F2A*F2B).LT.0.0) THEN
          GO TO 402
      ELSE
          IF (F2A.GT.0.0) THEN
             BN=1.0
          ELSE
             BN=0.0
          ENDIF
          GO TO 403
      ENDIF
  402 B=(BL+BH)/2.0
      F2=0.0
C
C   ...... BISECTION METHOD ............
C
      DO 404 I=1,N
          DENOM=B*(1.0-AN)+(1.0-AN)*(1.0-B)*KAN(I)/KBN(I)+AN*KAN(I)
          F2=F2+ZZ(I)*(1.0-KAN(I)/KBN(I))/DENOM
  404 CONTINUE
C
C   ...... CRITERIA FOR CONVERGENCE FOR BISECTION METHOD .......
C
      IF (ABS(F2).LE.1E-6) GO TO 405
      IF (((F2A.GT.F2B).AND.(F2.GT.0.0)).OR.((F2A.LT.F2B).AND.
     1    (F2.LT.0.0))) THEN
          BL=B
      ELSE
          BH=B
      ENDIF
      GO TO 402
  405 BN=B
  403 RETURN
      END

C*********************************************************************
C     SUBROUTINE AFIND
C     ------ GIVEN BETA, IT CALCULATES ALPHA (A) USING
C            BISECTION METHOD -----------
C*********************************************************************
C
C   ...... DECLARE ARRAYS ........
C
      SUBROUTINE AFIND(AN,BN,KAN,KBN,ZZ,N)
      DIMENSION ZZ(3)
      REAL KAN(3),KBN(3)
```

```
C
      AL=0.0
      AH=1.0
      F1A=0.0
      F1B=0.0
C
C   ......  SEE IF A LIES BETWEEN 0 AND 1 FOR GIVEN B VALUE  .......
C
      DO 501 I=1,N
         DENOM=BN*(1.0-AL)+(1.0-AL)*(1.0-BN)*KAN(I)/KBN(I)+AL*KAN(I)
         F1A=F1A+ZZ(I)*(1.0-KAN(I))/DENOM
         DENOM=BN*(1.0-AH)+(1.0-AH)*(1.0-BN)*KAN(I)/KBN(I)+AH*KAN(I)
         F1B=F1B+ZZ(I)*(1.0-KAN(I))/DENOM
  501 CONTINUE
      IF ((F1A*F1B).LT.0.0) THEN
         GO TO 502
      ELSE
         IF (F1A.GT.0.0) THEN
            AN=0.0
         ELSE
            AN=1.0
         ENDIF
         GO TO 503
      ENDIF
  502 A=(AL+AH)/2.0
      F1=0.0
C
C   ......  BISECTION METHOD  ..........
C
      DO 504 I=1,N
         DENOM=BN*(1.0-A)+(1.0-A)*(1.0-BN)*KAN(I)/KBN(I)+A*KAN(I)
         F1=F1+ZZ(I)*(1.0-KAN(I))/DENOM
  504 CONTINUE
C
C   ......  CRITERIA FOR CONVERGENCE FOR BISECTION METHOD  .......
C
      IF (ABS(F1).LE.1E-6) GO TO 505
      IF (((F1A.GT.F1B).AND.(F1.GT.0.0)).OR.((F1A.LE.F1B).AND.
     1   (F1.LT.0.0))) THEN
         AL=A
      ELSE
         AH=A
      ENDIF
      GO TO 502
  505 AN=A
  503 RETURN
      END

C*****************************************************************************
C     SUBROUTINE NPHI
C     ------  GIVEN DISTRIBUTION COEFFICIENTS (K), IT CALCULATES
C             FUGACITY COEFFICIENTS FOR TWO PHASE CALCULATIONS  --------
C*****************************************************************************
C
C   ......  DECLARE ARRAYS  .......
C
      SUBROUTINE NPHI(T,P,XN,YN,FPVN,FPLN,VM,N,KAN,LA,NUMIT,
     1   ZZ,NAME,NPHASE,EQUIL,FLAG,PC,W,RK,ETA,TC,PR,TR)
      DIMENSION XN(3),NAME(3),YN(3),FPVN(3),FPLN(3),ZZ(3)
      DIMENSION PC(3),TC(3),W(3),PR(3),TR(3),ETA(3,3),RK(3,3)
```

```
        REAL KAN(3),KAP(3),LA
        INTEGER FLAG,EQUIL
        NFLAG = 1
C
C    ......   CALL MASS BALANCE SUBROUTINE FLASH TO CALCULATE
C             PHASE COMPOSITIONS  ........
C
        CALL FLASH(LA,KAN,XN,ZZ,YN,FLAG,N,NUMIT,NFLAG)
C
C    ......   IF MASS BALANCE FAILS, RETURN TO SUBROUTINE TERN AND
C             INPUT NEW GUESSES FOR COMPONENT WT. FRACTIONS  ........
C
        IF ((FLAG.GE.1).AND.(NUMIT.EQ.0)) THEN
            WRITE(6,*) ' MASS BALANCE DID NOT CONVERGE FOR GUESSED
      1     K VALUES IN ',FLAG,' ATTEMPT. TRY AGAIN WITH NEW GUESSES.'
            NPHASE = 5
            GO TO 601
        ENDIF
        IF (NFLAG.EQ.3) THEN
            WRITE(6,*) ' 2-PHASE CALCULATIONS FAILED. EITHER ONLY ONE '
            WRITE(6,*) ' PHASE EXISTS OR THE SUGGESTED DIRECTION OF THE'
            WRITE(6,*) ' TIE LINE IS INCORRECT.'
            NPHASE=1
            GO TO 601
        ENDIF
C
        T=T+273.15
        NUMIT=NUMIT+1
C
C    ......   MASS BALANCE CONVERGED, CALCULATE FUGACITY COEFFICIENTS  ......
C
        IF (EQUIL.EQ.2) THEN
C
C    ......   CALCULATE PHI FOR THE VAPOR PHASE  .......
C
            CALL PHI(T,P,YN,FPVN,VM,0,N,TC,PC,TR,PR,W,RK,ETA)
        ELSE
C
C    ......   CALCULATE PHI FOR THE FIRST LIQUID PHASE  .......
C
            CALL PHI(T,P,YN,FPVN,VM,1,N,TC,PC,TR,PR,W,RK,ETA)
        ENDIF
C
C    ......   CALCULATE PHI FOR EITHER THE SECOND OR ONLY LIQUID PHASE  ......
C
        CALL PHI(T,P,XN,FPLN,VM,1,N,TC,PC,TR,PR,W,RK,ETA)
        T=T-273.15
        NPHASE = 2
  601   RETURN
        END

C******************************************************************************
C    2 PHASE MASS BALANCE SUBROUTINE FLASH
C    ------   GIVEN DISTRIBUTION COEFFICIENTS (K), IT CALCULATES
C             COMPOSITIONS OF TWO PHASES USING BISECTION METHOD  -------
C******************************************************************************
C
C    ......   DECLARE ARRAYS  ........
C
        SUBROUTINE FLASH(LA,KAF,XAF,ZZ,YYF,FLAG,N,NUMIT,NFLAG)
```

```
      DIMENSION XAF(3),YYF(3),ZZ(3)
      REAL KAF(3)
      REAL LA
      INTEGER FLAG,NUMIT
C
      AL=0.0
      AH=1.0
      FA=0.0
      FB=0.0
      DO 701 I=1,N
         FA=FA+ZZ(I)*(KAF(I)-1.0)/((KAF(I)-1.0)*AL+1.0)
         FB=FB+ZZ(I)*(KAF(I)-1.0)/((KAF(I)-1.0)*AH+1.0)
  701 CONTINUE
C
      IF (NUMIT.EQ.0) FLAG = FLAG+1
      IF (NUMIT.GT.0) NFLAG = 3
      IF ((FA*FB).GT.0.0) GO TO 700
C
      NFLAG=1
  702 A=(AL+AH)/2.0
      F=0.0
C
C ...... BISECTION METHOD ........
C
      DO 703 I=1,N
         F=F+ZZ(I)*(KAF(I)-1.0)/((KAF(I)-1.0)*A+1.0)
  703 CONTINUE
C
C ...... CRITERIA FOR CONVERGENCE FOR BISECTION METHOD .........
C
      IF (ABS(F).LE.1.E-6) GO TO 704
      IF (((FA.LT.0.0).AND.(F.LT.0.0)).OR.((FA.GT.0.0).AND.
     1   (F.GT.0.0))) THEN
         AL=A
      ELSE
         AH=A
      ENDIF
      GO TO 702
C
  704 SUMX=0.0
      SUMY=0.0
C
C ...... CALCULATE PHASE COMPOSITIONS .........
C
      DO 705 I=1,N
         XAF(I)=ZZ(I)/((KAF(I)-1.0)*A+1.0)
         YYF(I)=KAF(I)*XAF(I)
         SUMX=SUMX+XAF(I)
         SUMY=SUMY+YYF(I)
  705 CONTINUE
      DO 706 I=1,N
         XAF(I)=XAF(I)/SUMX
         YYF(I)=YYF(I)/SUMY
  706 CONTINUE
      LA=1.0-A
      FLAG=0
  700 CONTINUE
      RETURN
      END
```

```
C********************************************************************
C      SUBROUTINE PHI  -----  GIVEN THE COMPOSITION OF A PHASE, IT
C      CALCULATES FUGACITY COEFFICIENTS FOR THAT PHASE USING
C      PENG - ROBINSON EQUATION OF STATE  ------
C********************************************************************
C
C  ......  DECLARE ARRAYS  .......
C
       SUBROUTINE PHI(T,P,YF,FP,VM,NNN,N,TC,PC,TR,PR,W,RK,ETA)
       DIMENSION TC(3),PC(3),W(3),ETA(3,3),RK(3,3),PR(3),TR(3)
       DIMENSION YF(3),FP(3),B(3,3),A(3,3)
       DIMENSION TERM1(3),TERM2(3),TERM3(3),F1(3),ROOT(4)
       DIMENSION RA(4),POL(4)
       COMPLEX Z(3)
C
       BM=0.0
       AM=0.0
       R2=82.06
       SQ2=2.0**0.5
       Q1=1.0+SQ2
       Q2=SQ2-1.0
       Q3=2.0*SQ2
       DO 801 I=1,N
         B(I,I)=0.0778*R2*TC(I)/PC(I)
         TERM3(I)=0.0
         F1(I)=(1.0+(0.37464+1.54226*W(I)-0.26992*W(I)**2)*
      1    (1.0-TR(I)**0.5))**2
         A(I,I)=0.45724*(R2**2)*(TC(I)**2)/PC(I)*F1(I)
  801  CONTINUE
       J=N-1
C
C  ......  INTERACTION AND SIZE PARAMETERS A AND B  .......
C
       DO 802 I=1,J
           DO 803 K=I,J
             L=K+1
             A(I,L)=(A(I,I)*A(L,L))**0.5*(1.0-RK(I,L))
             A(L,I)=A(I,L)
             B(I,L)=(B(I,I)+B(L,L))/2.0*(1.0-ETA(I,L))
             B(L,I)=B(I,L)
  803      CONTINUE
  802  CONTINUE
       DO 804 I=1,N
           DO 805 J=1,N
             BM=BM+YF(I)*YF(J)*B(I,J)
             AM=AM+YF(I)*YF(J)*A(I,J)
  805      CONTINUE
  804  CONTINUE
C
C  ......  RE-WRITTEN P-R EQ. OF STATE, RA'S ARE COEFFICIENTS OF CUBIC
C          EQUATION .............
C
       AA=AM*P/((R2**2)*(T**2))
       BB=BM*P/(R2*T)
       RA(1)=1.0
       RA(2)=BB-1.0
       RA(3)=AA-2.0*BB-3.0*(BB**2)
       RA(4)=BB**3+BB**2-AA*BB
C
C  ......  CALL THE CANNED SUBROUTINE ZPOLR TO CALCULATE THE THREE
```

```
C             ROOTS OF THE EQUATION OF STATE  ........
C
      CALL ZPOLR(RA,3,Z,IER)
C
      DO 806 I=1,3
      IF (AIMAG(Z(I))) 807,808,807
 807  ROOT(I) = -1.0 E9
      GOTO 806
 808  ROOT(I) = Z(I)
 806  CONTINUE
C
C .....  IF PHASE IS VAPOR, TAKE THE LARGEST POSITIVE REAL ROOT.
C          IF PHASE IS LIQUID, TAKE THE SMALLEST POSITIVE REAL ROOT  .......
C
      DO 809 I=1,3
         IF ((ROOT(I).LT.0.0).AND.(NNN.EQ.1)) ROOT(I)=1.0E9
 809  CONTINUE
      IF(NNN.EQ.0) ZM=AMAX1(ROOT(1),ROOT(2),ROOT(3))
      IF(NNN.EQ.1) ZM=AMIN1(ROOT(1),ROOT(2),ROOT(3))
C     WRITE(6,*) 'Z=',ROOT(1),ROOT(2),ROOT(3)
C     WRITE(6,*) 'ZM=',ZM
      BPRIME=0.0
      DO 810 J=1,N-1
      DO 811 I=J+1,N
         BPRIME=-2.0*YF(I)*YF(I-J)*B(I,I-J) + BPRIME
 811  CONTINUE
 810  CONTINUE
      BP1=0.0
      DO 812 IN=1,N
         BP1=-1.0*(YF(IN)**2.0)*B(IN,IN)+BP1
 812  CONTINUE
      BPRIME=BPRIME+BP1
C
C ......  CALCULATE FUGACITY COEFFICIENTS  ........
      DO 813 I=1,N
         BP2=0.0
         DO 814 INN=1,N
            BP2=2.0*YF(INN)*B(I,INN)+BP2
 814     CONTINUE
         BPRIME=BPRIME+BP2
         TERM1(I)=BPRIME*(ZM-1.0)/BM-ALOG(ZM-BB)
         TERM2(I)=BPRIME*AA*ALOG((ZM+Q1*BB)/(ZM-Q2*BB))
     1      /(BM*BB*Q3)
         DO 815 J=1,N
            TERM3(I)=TERM3(I)+2.0*YF(J)*A(J,I)
 815     CONTINUE
         TERM3(I)=AA*ALOG((ZM+Q1*BB)/(ZM-Q2*BB))*TERM3(I)
     1      /(BB*AM*Q3)
         FP(I)=EXP(TERM1(I)+TERM2(I)-TERM3(I))
         BPRIME=BPRIME-BP2
 813  CONTINUE
      RETURN
      END
```

Index